# ASHE Reader on Finance in Higher Education

Edited by
David W. Breneman,
University of Virginia

Larry L. Leslie and Richard E. Anderson

Series Editor
Bruce Anthony Jones

**ASHE READER SERIES**

SIMON & SCHUSTER
CUSTOM PUBLISHING

Printed in the United States of America

10 9 8 7 6 5

ISBN 0–536–58352–8
BA 97502

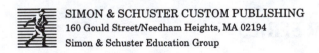

**SIMON & SCHUSTER CUSTOM PUBLISHING**
160 Gould Street/Needham Heights, MA 02194
Simon & Schuster Education Group

# COPYRIGHT ACKNOWLEDGMENTS

# Contents

# Introduction

When the First Edition of this *Reader* was organized in the mid-1980s, American higher education was enjoying a period of relative prosperity. The funding "recession" that had occurred in the early 1980s largely had been forgotten, and the hard times at the beginning of the decade were little more than a distant memory. As the 1990s unfold, however, financial conditions facing America's colleges and universities are once again uncertain at best, and extremely difficult at worst. Students and families are facing growing problems in financing a college education, often having to go heavily into debt to achieve educational goals. As in all such periods of financial stress, optimism about the future seems in short supply.

But how should the future be viewed? Are the prospects for higher education, like the economy, merely cyclical? Is prosperity, once again, just around the corner? Or are we, in fact, entering a new era in the financing of higher education?

Two decades ago, Leslie and Miller (1974) observed that there is a strong tendency during periods of fiscal duress to view the future merely as an extension of the past. They demonstrated that, historically, higher education has indeed been a "cyclical industry." Taking the longer view, they argued that colleges and universities, as key components of "essential social systems," promise to expand over the long term so long as society itself is not in permanent decline.

While this view would forecast a return in the mid-1990s to the relative prosperity of the recent past, an alternative view suggests that higher education may not again experience the gains in public financial support that have marked the Post-WW II era. Significant changes in the economy, in demography, and in public policy point toward a possible new future in which higher education must make do with less.

## Higher Education at a Climacteric

It is surely noteworthy when Robert Atwell, President of the American Council on Education and the leading national spokesman for higher education, writes that, ". . . higher education is in its most dire financial condition since World War II. . . ." and "I do not think things will get better until sometime after the year 2010 . . ." (1992). Apart from the audacity required to forecast 17 years ahead, one is most struck by the political significance of such a statement; public pronouncements from leaders in higher education are usually either optimistic and upbeat, or filled with dire forecasts coupled with barely plausible claims of associated educational and social disaster. By contrast, Atwell's argument is sober, well-reasoned, and not apocalyptic, a refreshing change from the recent level of much public discourse on the fate of higher education.

Atwell's essay is also significant because his outlook is increasingly shared by a number of close observers of the economics and financing of higher education. Although only time will tell whether this view is correct—and the track-record of past forecasts is not impressive—it will be helpful to lay out the elements of this evolving perspective, for it undergirds much of the current policy discussion at state, federal, and institutional levels. In doing so, we are specifying elements of a belief system, albeit one grounded in extensions of current realities.

The first element is the belief that higher education is entering a fundamentally new era, sharply different from the breathtaking growth in enrollments and resources that typified the last four decades. While annual changes were not smooth or steady in the post-WW II era, the overall pattern was one of explosive growth, as higher education underwent a remarkably rapid transformation from an elite to a mass phenomenon. This era is ending now, as enrollment prospects in most states stabilize, and public and private resources become increasingly scarce.

The wellsprings of this remarkable period of expansion were two-fold; demographic trends, and a sharp increase in the share of educational expense underwritten by state and federal governments. Both of these engines of growth are diminished now. With the exception of a handful of states, population pressure no longer fuels expansion, and the capacity of state or federal governments to absorb more of the cost of higher education is severely limited. Indeed, the latter fact may be of overriding importance, for even in such states as California, where relevant population growth continues, the ability of the state to pay for it is in doubt. The immediate response has been enrollment caps, reduced access, and a shifting burden of educational expense from the state to those families that can afford it.

A second element in the belief system is that federal and state budgetary problems are not exclusively short-run and cyclical, caused by the recent recession, but rather have become long-run and structural in nature, and are likely to continue even when the economy resumes "normal" growth. As far ahead as anyone can see, there appears to be little discretionary revenue available for increased public spending on higher education. In large measure, this situation is attributable to the destructive fiscal policies of the Reagan and Bush administrations, coupled with the increased responsibilities shifted to state governments for spending on health care, schools, highways, prisons, and welfare. As a consequence, at the state level, higher education has increasingly become a residual claimant for shrinking discretionary dollars, a situation unlikely to change in the foreseeable future. While the political power of the phrase *"No New Taxes"* may be waning, along with the political paralysis that it induced, no reasonable observer thinks that the federal budget deficit will be eliminated in this decade, nor are most state budgets likely to experience discretionary surpluses for higher education.

Without elaboration, we simply state that additional elements in the belief system under discussion include equally bearish views regarding the expansion of private revenue sources, whether in the form of sharply increased tuitions or growth in endowments and annual gifts. The one exception is the belief that tuition in the public sector could be substantially increased *without curtailing access* if a portion of the new tuition revenue could be recycled as increased need-based student aid. In short, the one revenue source that could grow substantially is public sector tuition, for many students enrolled in public colleges and universities come from families wealthy enough to pay a greater share of the education bill. While this policy is broadly supported by most economists and others who have studied the matter carefully—this topic is discussed thoroughly in many of the articles in this volume—until now it has had little political marketability. We may be at a point where economic policy arguments coincide with a practical need for increased revenue, resulting in both more efficient and more equitable financing of higher education.

The above themes capture the beliefs about the future that may have in mind when thinking and writing about public policy for higher education in the 1990s and beyond. Rarely are such fundamental judgments articulated fully, and it is one of the merits of Atwell's essay that he is so explicit about these views. Although events may prove these judgements wrong, we cannot know that now—and yet college and university administrators must decide where they stand on these fundamental issues. If one agrees with this general view, then one would not simply hunker down and spread budget cuts evenly across all units. In the forlorn hope that a resumption of economic growth will allow the college to get back on its prior budget track. Instead, options at the institutional level become sharper and more dramatic including:

(1) Promotion of the high-tuition, high-aid policy at the state level;

(2) Doing less with less, by striking to maintain expenditures per student at a constant level, even if the result is reduced access to some potential students;

(3) Doing the same with less, which is essentially a short-run response that gambles on a rapid return of financial support;

(4) Changing the educational delivery system, by restructuring the curriculum, programs offered, and faculty incentives;

(5) Sharpening and differentiating institutional mission, by deliberate decisions to emphasize certain programs and eliminate others.

Our purpose in mentioning the above options is not to suggest that they are comprehensive or even the best ones to pursue; that would require a separate article. Instead, we use them illustratively to show how much rides on the attitude one takes to the vision sketched out by Atwell and others. Few educational decisions in the 1990s will prove so important, and it is our hope that this volume contributes to that essential debate.

## Organization of this Volume

In preparing this revised edition, we began by surveying professors of higher education finance to seek their advice and comments for ways to improve the volume. The many helpful responses we received confirmed the continuing need for a book of readings that encompasses two different aspects of the broad topic—public finance and financial management. As a consequence, Section I covers fundamental issues in the financing of higher education, addressing such questions as who benefits?, who pays?, and who should pay? These issues are generally explored in this section through the analytical framework of public finance, a branch of applied economics.* Breneman and Leslie selected and organized the articles in Section I.

The second dimension of the topic, financial management, is the subject of Section II, which focuses on how financial resources are allocated within colleges and universities. One way to distinguish between the two dimensions of the subject is to note that public finance is concerned with external resource *acquisition*, while financial management is concerned with internal resource *allocation*. Included in financial management are such issues as fund accounting, budgeting, financial control, and strategic planning. Anderson selected and organized the articles in Section II.

## Overview of Section I

The articles in Section I are subdivided chronologically into a group of older, classic articles, dating from the late-1960s through 1981, and a second, more current group covering the 1980s and early 1990s. While the financial data in the older articles are clearly outdated, the fundamental arguments and positions presented are still relevant, and in several cases, have not been presented better or more forcefully since the original publication. In fact, one could well argue that the late-1960s and 1970s were years of extraordinary productivity in this field, as judged by both the quantity and quality of thought devoted to the economics and financing of higher education.

The articles by economists Armen Alchian and Lee Hansen and Burton Weisbrod raised early questions about both the equity and efficiency of low (or no) tuition in public higher education, exemplified most strikingly in the three-tiered system of California public higher education. The issues raised in those two seminal articles continue to reverberate down through the decades of debate about financing policies. Howard Bowen, an economist and former college president, was among those who responded most vigorously to the challenges raised by his more skeptical colleagues, and his 1971 article attests. The chapter by Neil Singer is taken from his 1972 public finance textbook, and shows that the economist's tendency to question the value of broad state subsidy for institutions of higher education as well established over 20 years ago.

The 1970s witnessed numerous national commissions devoted to recommending public policy toward higher education. Foremost among them was the Carnegie Commission on Higher Education, chaired by Clark Kerr, former president of the University of California. One of the Commission's finest reports was *Higher Education: Who Pays? Who Benefits? Who Should Pay?*, published in 1973. Indeed, a good case can be made that this is the last comprehensive report published in this country that advances an overall vision and set of proposals for the financing of higher education. Although 20 years old, its recommendations still merit consideration, and continue to guide the thinking of many in the policy arena. The Committee on Economic Development's 1973 report also contributed to the debate with its controversial proposal for a sharp increase in public-sector tuition.

By 1974, analysts were becoming wary of the attempt to apply market models to higher education, and the article by Leslie and Johnson questioned many of the assumptions undergirding the new thinking. Kern Alexander's paper also takes a broad view of the social and non-market benefits associated with higher education, and makes a strong case for additional public investment in higher education. Each of these early articles grapples well with issues that continue to be central to contemporary discussion—the balance between private and public benefits, the best way to encourage equal educational opportunity, and the optimal amount of higher education for our society.

The last three articles in this first part look at specific aspects of institutional finance. Bowen examines the forces that determine educational costs, and puts forward his simple, but insightful, "revenue theory of costs." Breneman and Nelson explore the intricacies of community colleges and their financing, while Herzlinger and Jones discuss the growing tuition gap in the 1970s among public and private colleges and universities, with special reference to the state of Massachusetts.

The second set of articles in the first section of the volume are of more recent origin, and are organized around five topics: (1) Financial Trends for Institutions of Higher Education, (2) Financing Students: Access and Choice, (3) State Budgeting and Policy, (4) Federal Programs and Policies, and (5) Changing Public Attitudes. Within each of these basic categories we have presented representative samples of recent work, touching on such diverse issues as economic trends, capital costs, tuition discounting, student aid, state formula budgets, student loans, and federal policy. The reader will quickly see that most of the issues raised in the classic articles are still with us today, although changing times add new dimensions to the discussion. As the work in this section attests, however, scholars continue to strive for understanding that gives practical meaning of the twin objectives of public finance—equity and efficiency.

## Overview of Section II

The purpose of the second part of the Reader is to provide a review of the business operation of colleges and universities. Everyone with a responsible position in higher education should have a working knowledge of these functions and the decision making process of the business office. Effective business practices are critical to both the short-term effectiveness and the long-term survival of higher education and they should be understood and supported by the institution's various constituents. Too often, the business function has not been given the attention and support that it deserves. Less thoughtful faculty may even take a certain pride in their disdain for financial matters. On the other hand, some financial decision makers can be equally narrow minded, viewing their institution as a revenue machine. To them, education and research is simply the "business" in which they are engaged. It is with concern for the latter error that we open the section with the late Kenneth Boulding's "In Praise of Inefficiency." Boulding, an economist, certainly did not support institutional waste. But, as an insightful academic, he understood the complexity of the institutional enterprise and urged its managers to expect and accept ambiguity.

Having acknowledged the legitimacy of the claim that colleges are not businesses and should not be run like businesses (but can be managed more "business-like"), we argue that the current economic situation facing American higher education is entirely different from that faced in the recent past. The imbalances between revenues and expenditures in the post-WWII environment resulted in part from rapid expansion and increased demands on higher education services. In the 1990s, the constraints are exacerbated by larger macroeconomic imbalances. Put simply, the American economy is not growing rapidly enough to support all the promises, explicit and implicit, that have been made to citizens. The article by Anderson, published in 1988, is dated, but the imbalances he described persist and continue to threaten future prosperity. After a short period of progress, U.S. budget and trade deficits are again growing, and net national savings is approaching zero. Politicians seem unable to take sufficient action. As of this writing, the economy is recovering from a recession but the rebound is weak. The employment picture is discouraging and state budgets remain under stress. In 1992, for the first time since records have been kept, state spending for higher education declined. The consequence of slow economic growth is that most institutions, higher education included, will have difficulty in generating the resources they require.

The third article, by William Bowen (including comments by various chief financial officers), describes in broad terms the role of the business officer. It is over twenty years old but that is not a severe handicap as these general functions have not changed. The age of the article serves a secondary purpose of reminding the reader that the issues of insufficient revenues are not new. The next piece by Ford is a chapter from the 1992 edition of *College and University Business Administration*. The entire three volume set, edited by Deidre Green, is an important resource for college and university financial administrators. The Ford chapter offers a more detailed and functional review of the activities of the business office and places those activities in a large institutional context.

Before embarking on a more detailed review of institutional financial activities it is important that the reader have some acquaintance with financial definitions and institutional accounting. For example, in considering institutional well-being it is important to understand that, under certain circumstances, a college can grow wealthy while consistently showing deficits—or become impoverished while showing surpluses, year-in and year-out. Anderson offers a brief introduction to current accounting issues while Meisinger and Dubeck provide a more substantive guide to higher education and accounting practices. Finally an article by Gordon Winston, an economist and former Provost of Williams College, advances a provocative thesis for a revolution in financial accounting, that would concentrate on gains and losses in wealth, as opposed to the partial view provided by the operating budget.

The meat and potatoes of institutional financial management is budgeting, raising revenue and controlling expenditures. If one believes the media and legislators, higher education has not been particularly effective in these activities. Although the press and politicians are naturally inclined toward hyperbole, higher education is not blameless. The February 1991 issue of *Policy Perspectives* argues that institutional financial and academic leaders must provide a strategic vision and be willing to make difficult choices.

Once again we turn to *College and University Business Administration* for a functional, but necessary and insightful, review of institutional planning and budgeting. The first chapter by Dunn gives a comprehensive review of institutional financial planning. Dickmeyer, in the second chapter, offers a detailed look at both operational and capital budgeting.

As we began the section with Boulding's plea that institutional managers accept ambiguity, we end with an ambiguous research finding. Anyone familiar with higher education is aware of apparent continuing financial crisis. Budgets are being cut and programs terminated. Yet after systematically reviewing the evidence, Skolnik cannot objectively document the damage. The message is not that the cuts aren't hurtful—certainly they are. But colleges and universities are complex organizations and they will survive these hard times. For those of us engaged in managing and working in higher education this is a hopeful conclusion.

## A Final Word

We began this Introduction by suggesting that the financing of higher education faces fundamental—and new—challenges in the years ahead. That discussion was necessarily speculative, however, and unforeseen developments will, no doubt, alter the actual course of events. Nonetheless, we hope that the articles in this volume provide the reader with the necessary background to form his or her own judgment about the best way to pay for this form of investment in human capital, and to manage effectively the scarce resources of the nation's colleges and universities.

| David W. Breneman | Larry L. Leslie | Richard E. Anderson |
|---|---|---|
| Harvard University | Univ. of Arizona | Washington University |

## Notes

*Some professors may find it helpful to supplement this Reader with a brief introductory text on public finance.

## References

Robert H. Atwell, "Financial Prospects for Higher Education," *Policy Perspectives*, The Pew Higher Education Research Program, Sept. 1992, Vol. 4, No. 3, Sec. B, p. 5B.

Larry L. Leslie and Howard F. Miller, Jr., *Higher Education and the Steady State* (Washington, D.C.: The American Association for Higher Education, 1974).

# SECTION I
## *FINANCING HIGHER EDUCATION*

# PART A
## *Classic Articles*

*This section presents classic articles from the late 1960s through the early 1980s covering the central financing issues of those years—and of today. While the financial data are out-of-date, the policy issues discussed in these articles are still relevant.*

# The Economic and Social Impact
# of Free Tuition (1968)

## Armen A. Alchian

Rarely do educational issues provoke as much passion as the proposal to raise tuition fees in California colleges. Unfortunately, the passion has not been matched by reason—it is hard to find a clear statement of the consequences of or reasons for a zero tuition or a high tuition fee. It is hard to determine from the public comments whether the antagonists differ about what the consequences of alternative tuition arrangements would be or have different preferences with respect to well perceived consequences. Some defenders of zero tuition have asserted that zero tuition is necessary for aid to poorer students, for the maintenance of our great system of higher education, for the preservation of free and prosperous society, for achievement of great social benefits, for educational opportunity for all, is a hallowed century-old tradition, and that tuition is a tax on education. Some proponents of tuition fees have argued, for example, that the university and colleges are harboring delinquents who would not be there with full tuition, the poor are aiding the rich, students should pay tuition in order to appreciate their education, taxes are excessive, and low tuition requires exploitation of an underpaid faculty, to cite a few. Most of these arguments are so patently fallacious or nonsensical or irrelevant that they do disservice to the more intelligent arguments. But there are some propositions that merit closer examination. To evaluate them it is first necessary to identify at some length the issues that are involved in analyzing and thereby choosing among the alternatives—and in the process make clear my own preferences. If I overlook significant objectives or consequences, perhaps others will be stimulated to fill the gaps.

The issues represent a classic topic for applied economics—the effects of different means of allocating scarce resources among competing claimants. A rational analysis of the consequences of tuition systems requires separation of two questions: (1) Who should bear the costs of education? (2) If someone other than the student should pay for his education, in what form should the aid be given?

Unless the distinction between these two issues is grasped, confusion is inevitable. The case for zero tuition is *not* established by demonstrating that aid to students is desirable. Full tuition may still be desirable, with the desired aid taking the form of explicit grants-in-aid or scholarships from which the student pays the tuition fee of his chosen school.

The issue of the most desirable form of aid should be separated from still another closely related question: What is the desired method of financing and controlling *colleges*—as distinct from financing *students*? For example, aid to students in the form of zero tuition means also that the state finances the colleges' activities directly by legislative appropriations with the students and their parents having less influence on financing and controlling the activities of colleges. Where student aid is in the form of grants-in-aid or scholarships, students and parents paying full tuition to their chosen colleges have a greater role in determining which colleges shall be financed and rewarded for superior performances. Recognition of these differences in effect explains why some people have asserted the administrators and members of state universities and colleges, which are currently financed by direct legislative appropriation, have sought from self-interest, rather than educational interest, to maintain the impression that zero tuition is the only feasible or sensible means of aid to students—in order to repress student influence and control over the colleges while retaining the influence of politicians.

Advocates of subsidization of college students (regardless of the method) assume that if each student bore the full cost there would be too little college education as well as a decrease of educational opportunity. What makes it desirable to have more education than if students pay full costs? Several arguments are advanced. Let us discuss these in ascending order of sophistication.

(1) "Although the costs of education are less than the gains to the students themselves, some are unable to finance their education now. A subsidy would provide educational opportunity to the poor." (2) "Cultural education, though not profitable in market earnings, and hence not capable of being paid for out of enhanced earnings, is nevertheless desirable." (3) "Even if every student acquires as much education as is worthwhile to him, he would take too little, because the individual ignores the beneficial social gains indirectly conferred on other members of society—giving what some people call 'external social effects.' Therefore, society at large should induce students to take more education than indicated by their private interests."

The argument that the poor cannot afford to pay for a profitable college education is deceptive. What is meant by a "poor" person. Is he a college-caliber student? All college-caliber students are rich in both a monetary and nonmonetary sense. Their inherited superior mental talent—human capital—*is* great wealth. For example, the college-caliber student is worth on the average about $200,000, and on the average, approximately $20,000-$50,000 of that has been estimated as the enhanced value derived from college training, depending upon his major field and profession.

Failure to perceive this inherent wealth of college-caliber students reflects ignorance of two economic facts. One is the enormous human wealth in our society. Every good educator recognizes that inanimate capital goods are not the only forms of wealth. The second fact is the difference between current earnings and wealth. For example, a man with a million dollars' worth of growing trees, or untapped oil is a rich man—though he is not *now* marketing any of his wealth or services. So it is with the college-caliber student. Though his *current* market earnings are small, his wealth—the present wealth value of his future earnings—is larger than for the average person. This is true no matter what the current earnings or wealth of his parents. It is *wealth*, not current earnings nor parent's wealth, that is the measure of a student's richness. College-caliber students with low current earnings are not poor. Subsidized higher education, whether by zero tuition, scholarships, or zero-interest loans, grants the college student a second windfall—a subsidy to exploit his initial windfall inheritance of talent. This is equivalent to subsidizing drilling costs for owners of oil-bearing lands in Texas.

There remains an even more seriously deceptive ambiguity—that between the subsidization of college education and provision of educational *opportunity*. Educational *opportunity* is provided if any person who can benefit from attending college is enabled to do so despite smallness of *current* earnings. Nothing in the provision of full educational *opportunity* implies that students who are financed during college should not later repay out of their enhanced earnings those who financed that education. Not to ask for repayment is to grant students a gift of wealth at the expense of those who do not attend college or who attend tuition colleges and pay for themselves. This is true because, for one reason, our tax bills do not distinguish between those directly benefited by having obtained a zero-tuition educational subsidy and those not so benefited. Alumni with higher incomes pay more taxes, but they do not pay more than people with equal incomes who financed their own education or never went to college.

Many discussions about educational opportunity refer to proportions of students from poorer and richer families at tuition-free colleges. However strong the emotional appeal, the proportion of rich and poor family students is relevant only to the separate issue of wealth redistribution, per se, consequent to state-operated zero-tuition education. It has nothing to do with the extent of educational opportunity. Though data for California colleges and taxes suggest that lower-income groups provide a smaller proportion of students than of taxes to support education, such comparisons are irrelevant, so far as provision of educational *opportunity* is concerned. These data tell how much wealth redistribution there is among the less educated, the poor, the educated, and the rich. That wealth redistribution is good or bad depending upon whether one believes the educational system should be used as a device to redistribute wealth as well as to enhance wealth, knowledge, and educational opportunity. No matter how zero tuition in tax-supported schools may redistribute wealth, the provision of full educational opportunity does *not* require redistributions of wealth. Yet, it seems to me, many people confuse these two entirely separate issues or think the latter is necessary for the former. To think that college-caliber students should be given zero tuition is to think that smart people should be given wealth at the expense of the less smart.

When some zero-tuition university alumni say that without zero tuition they could not have attended college, they should have a modest concern for the implications of that statement. One poor, "uneducated" resident of Watts, upon hearing Ralph Bunche say that he could not have had a college education unless tuition were free, opined, "Perhaps it's time he repay out of his higher income for that privilege granted him by taxes on us Negroes who never went to college." That reply spots the difference between educational opportunity and a redistribution of wealth.

Full educational *opportunity* would be provided if college-caliber students could borrow against their future enhanced earnings. Students could repay out of their enhanced future earnings. Although, currently, loans are available from private lenders and also from publicly supported loans, a subsidy could provide a state guarantee of repayment of educational loans exactly as housing loans are guaranteed for veterans. Students could select among optional repayment methods. Some could contract to repay in full with interest; others could opt for a sort of insurance system, whereby the amount repaid was related to their income, with upper and lower limits to amounts repaid being specified. A host of possibilities are available. In fact today with income taxes, the college alumni are repaying part of the educational costs via taxes (but so are others who did not attend college).

Some people are impressed by the size of the debt that a college graduate would have to repay, but they should be impressed with the fact that the debt is *less* than the enhanced earnings he has thereby obtained and is an indication of the wealth bonanza given the student who is subsidized by society.

There remains one more facet of the educational opportunity argument. Even if a college education may be a very profitable investment for some person, he may, because of inexperience or lack of confidence, not appreciate his situation or be willing to borrow at available rates of interest. This presumably is an argument for subsidizing those students who lack confidence or understanding of their possibilities, and it may be a meaningful argument on its own ground, but it is not an argument for subsidizing "poor" students.

Pleas are made for subsidizing *cultural* education which, though it may add nothing to the student's future market earnings, will enhance his general welfare. But a person's welfare is increased if he gets more food, housing, recreation, beer drinking, and fancier cars. It would seem therefore that the relevant argument for helping students is one of helping them regardless of whether they wish their welfare increased via cultural education or better food. A grant of money to be spent  as the recipient deems appropriate is an efficient form of aid—as judged by the recipient. Subsidized cultural education rather than money gifts could be justified if the giver knows better than the recipient what is good for the recipient. I cannot make that leap of faith for the collegiate student, although other people do it easily and confidently.

A case can be made for subsidizing the poor *and* the rich to take more education—more than a person would take when motivated by his own interests alone. It is often said there are privately unheeded, net social benefits, so each person will underinvest in education from the social point of view, regardless of whether he is rich or poor; but we must separate the illusory from the real external available gains.

Education makes a person more productive, as a doctor, lawyer, merchant, or engineer. Other people benefit from his greater productivity, because more engineers enable lower costs of engineering services for the rest of society. Engineers, looking only to their private gain would, it is said, undervalue the total benefit of having more engineers; too few people would seek sufficient engineering education. If this sounds persuasive, economics can teach you something. The increased supply of engineers reduces the prices of engineering services—even if by only a trivial amount—and thereby reduces the income of *other* engineers. Their income loss is the gain to the rest of society. This is a *transfer* of income from existing engineers to nonengineers; it is *not* a net social gain. The benefited parties gain at the expense of existing members of the engineering profession, who lose some of their scarcity value as more educated people are created. This is a transfer from the more educated to the less educated. A striking awareness of this effect is evident in the advocacy by labor groups of immigration restriction. Restricting the inflow of laborers of particular skills prevents reductions in wages of incumbent workers with similar skills and prevents a transfer of wealth from them to the rest of American society. An immigrant or a more educated person would have provided an increased product and he would have obtained that value by the sale of his services, but the lower wages to that *type* of services would have transferred some of the incomes of similar workers to the rest of society. This external *transfer* effect is not a net contribution to social output. It is not a reason for subsidizing education.

For external effects to serve as a valid basis for more education two conditions must be satisfied: (1) There must be a net social *gain* (not transfer) unheeded by the student. The ability to read reduces dangers and inconvenience to other people; ability to be sanitary enhances health of other people, or economic education may—but probably will not—prevent passage of socially detrimental, special-interest legislation. These are examples of education with external social gains, which we shall assume are not heeded by the student in his private actions because they do not affect the marketable value of his services. Professional education of doctors, engineers, lawyers, economists, mathematicians, etc.; has not been shown to fit in that category. Perhaps education at the undergraduate collegiate level in the elements of law, psychology, political science, mathematics, economics may make for better *nonmarket* decisions or actions.

I confess to a strong suspicion that such education is most significant at the grade school level, diminishes at higher levels, and disappears for professional or cultural, artistic, personal satisfaction courses, and is possibly *reversed* at graduate levels (by overtraining and insistence on excessively high standards of training for granting of licenses to practice in some professions—though this is a point the validity of which is not crucial to the main issue here).

(2) The second condition is that there must be *further* external gains unheeded by students at the college level. The fact of having *achieved* net external gains is not sufficient to warrant subsidization. The crucial condition is the failure to achieve still further available *incremental* net social gain from *further* education. Before concluding that they exist because of a tendency for people to ignore them, we should note that people attend college for reasons other than financial marketable gain. College attendance for personal reasons includes cultural, artistic education, and attendance to find mates. All these tend to extend education beyond maximizing one's market wealth and possibly even beyond that yielding unheeded social gains. But the facts are not conclusive in *either* direction.

Incidentally, an especially common but erroneous contention, presumably relying on the external effect, is that the growth, prosperity, and unusual position of California depend upon the free-tuition, higher education system. What does this mean? If this means that free tuition has contributed to higher wealth for the educated then this is no argument for either free tuition or more education. If it means the prosperity and growth of aircraft, electronics, motion picture, or agricultural industries in California are dependent upon free tuition, the contention remains unsupported by any analytic or factual evidence, and in fact can be falsified by comparisons with other states. Even if it could be demonstrated that *subsidized* higher education was responsible, the issue of *free* tuition would still not be touched. If this means that free tuition did attract some people to seek their education in California, they proceeded to reap the gain in their own higher income. If they provided a real net social benefit, it should have exceeded the extent of their subsidization to be justifiable. The same proposition holds for residents of California. If this argument is accepted, it is difficult to justify charging newcomers a full tuition while permitting existing residents a "free tuition." Yet, we have seen no proponent of zero tuition advocate zero tuition for all newcomers from all other states. If this means that the higher incomes for more people increase tax receipts, then the relevance of that completely escapes me. If this means California has a larger population, then this means higher land prices. But in so far as benefits to "California" have any relevance, I believe they should be viewed as benefits to people in California rather than as benefits to owners of a geographically identified piece of land, unless by "California" one means "landowners or politicians," who indeed do prefer larger populations as a source of political power and higher land values.

To induce students to take more education than is privately worth their while—in order to obtain the otherwise unheeded external gains—does call for payments to students. If a student were paid for doing what he would have done anyway, or if his education were subsidized to increase *his* wealth, he would be receiving a gift. But a payment (whether as zero tuition or a money payment) to the student to *extend* his education, for the sake of achieving *real*, external benefits that he otherwise would have not produced, is a payment for services, much as if he were to build houses, for the benefit of the rest of society. Such payments may well be independent of the income or future income of the student as well as of his parents. Though there is nothing that says the rich would provide less real external effects from more education, my conjecture is that the rich would in any event take more education than the poor for cultural reasons and would therefore require a smaller inducement to take the "optimal" extra amount of education for external social benefits. This can form a basis for advocating more educational inducements to the poor than to the rich, but not necessarily by a zero-tuition inducement to rich and poor alike.

It should be noted however that there is already subsidization of higher education by private philanthropy on a scale that staggers the imagination. The endowment funds of colleges and philanthropic foundations aiding education run into the scores of billions. Even if only half that were used to subsidize education (and the rest for research), the amount can not be regarded as minor, on any standard.

No matter what your beliefs about the validity or relevance of the preceding consideration, let us accept them, for the sake of analysis of alternative *means* of providing aid, for full educational opportunity, cultural aid, or extra inducements to education. (Of course, those who think the preceding arguments are too weak to warrant taxpayers' giving aid to college students can ignore all that follows, for to them there is no case for any state action, nor of zero tuition.) The rest will want to ask, "What is the best form of aid or inducement?"

We can enable or induce students to take more education with the following offer: "On the condition that you take certain kinds of education, we shall bear enough of the costs to induce you to do so." The costs he would have borne are the income forsaken and the tuition costs. (Food and living costs can be ignored for he would be incurring them no matter what he did.) Which of the following is the preferred way of extending that aid to potential students? (1) We pay directly the costs of extra education by operating the school to provide the extra education; this is the zero-tuition system. (2) We pay him an equal amount on the condition he take the additional, specified type of education, but he decides which school to attend and he pays the tuition to the school. This is an educational voucher or G.I.-type educational bill-of-rights (used after World War II for veterans).

The first requires *also* that the state directly finance and operate the school providing the education; the second permits the student to choose from competing schools and direct payment to the school he chooses. These two alternatives are sufficient to illustrate the major implications of zero versus high tuition modes of subsidy. The wealth effect for the student is superficially the same in either case, and the financial cost to the subscriber can be the same in each case, once it is decided how much education to subsidize for whom. The costs to the subscriber may be the same, but the results are not.

In the California state system of higher education, the tuition fee is zero for *all* state schools and for *all* kinds of training, regardless of whether it contributes to a net social gain or not, and regardless of how rich the student is.

Zero tuition implies that the appropriate aid or subsidy for every student of a state school is exactly equal to the tuition cost no matter what subject he takes. No basis for zero tuitions as being the proper amount has ever been presented; maybe the aid should be even larger, to compensate for forsaken earnings.

Because low- or zero-tuition schools are believed to have a larger proportion of less wealthy students than high-tuition colleges, zero-tuition schools are believed to do a better job of providing educational opportunity for less wealthy students. But this entails the earlier confusion between provision of *opportunity* and provision of a wealth *bonanza*; zero-tuition schools give bigger wealth gifts to the mentally able students than do the high-tuition schools.

Of course, higher tuition will, *other things left unchanged*, reduce the number of financially insecure students attending tuition colleges. The case for raising tuition is not that aid should be denied but instead that "zero-tuition" is a less desirable means of providing aid to students; it entails undesirable controls and political interference with education and lowers the quality of education. Yet there is another method of providing full educational opportunity *and* at the same time improving the quality and quantity of education and reducing political controls. The alternative is a system of full tuition supplemented by grants-in-aid to those who qualify as financially insecure and deserving students.

It is important to note that the financing of *colleges* to provide education is different from subsidizing *students*. The zero tuition is a subsidy to the *college* as well as to the student. Subsidies to *students* alone can be provided with a full-tuition system: in fact they are now being so provided by many private schools that do charge full tuition.

The alternative to the zero-tuition method of providing educational opportunity or giving aid is tuition, *with* loans or with grants of money. The critical difference, in my opinion, between no tuition and tuition, under these circumstances, is that the former lets the state politician and college administrator and faculty directly exert more control over education whereas the latter enables the student to exercise more power by his choice of college.

Subsidies to whatever extent desired could be provided by a system of grants-in-aid via scholarships. That would appear to be more expensive *administratively* (but only administratively) than zero tuition, precisely because an effort is made to eliminate the haphazard bonanzas in the zero-tuition system. The presumption is that the cost of selecting the students to be subsidized is less than the savings from the avoidance of subsidies to all students.

Tuition with grants-in-aid to students is not visionary. It is proven, practical, economical and currently used. New York State already has a large system of Regents scholarships. California has a smaller scale system with about 2,000 scholarships. After World War II, the federal government granted millions of veterans educational vouchers for tuition, books, and incidental expenses under an enormously successful act known as the G.I. Bill. All these granted aid regardless of the student's current financial status. In California the university and state colleges now receive about $500 million annually directly from the legislature. That would finance 250,000 scholarships of $2,000 each. The university's budget would finance 125,000 students, more than the number now attending.

At present many arrangements exist whereby private colleges take into account the financial status of students in deciding how much tuition to charge each student. Even more efficient would be a system of loans with interest to be repaid after graduation out of the student's enhanced earnings. Under a loan system, the problem of filtering rich students from the financially distressed would be reduced to trivial dimensions, since the rich would have little, if anything, to gain by borrowing. This would provide full educational opportunity with little need for a means test.

Full tuition does not in any way restrict the achievability of full education opportunity. That can be achieved explicitly and openly by the scope of grants and subsidized loans. Just as social security and welfare payments are made in money with the recipient choosing his purchases from competing producers, so a full-tuition system with grants-in-aid or loans would enable separation of the issue of the amount, if any, of the subsidy from that of the best means of providing and controlling education.

Under a system of full-tuition fees, with whatever loans and scholarship voucher grants are deemed desirable, students could choose their education from the whole world. Any accredited college or educational institution whether it be for barbers, television technicians, beauty operators, mechanics, butchers, doctors, lawyers, or historians could serve. Ours would then really be the best educational system in the world; no longer would Californians be confined to California state-operated schools. Whatever one's beliefs about the desirable degree of subsidy for more education, and whatever his beliefs about who should get it, the full tuition voucher coupled with scholarships and loans would magically open a new, larger world of choice.

An alternative form of aid to students is a tax-credit allowance whereby parents, or students, could later receive a tax offset to their payments for tuition. This would put private college students on a more equal basis with low tuition public colleges. In my opinion, this would be equality at the wrong level of equality. Rather than give tax credits as a means of maintaining zero tuition, I would prefer placing a tax *liability* on students attending public colleges with low or zero tuition. Whereas the tax credit provides subsidies and aid to all students at the expense of nonstudents, the tax-liability assessment places the costs of providing the education more squarely on those who benefit from the education. A tax credit gives *equal* treatment to private and public college students—at the expense of nonstudents. A tax liability gives equality to private and public college students and to college and noncollege people, with each bearing only the costs of service provided for their benefit. If tax-liability assessments are out of the question politically, the tax credit would be the next best, but it would not achieve one of the major purposes of a full tuition system.

With full-cost tuition, competition among California colleges, and even among academic departments would change. Instead of competition for funds being negotiated among university committees, deans, regents, state college boards, and legislators, competition would rely more on classroom behavior of instructors who would be more dependent on student attendance *vis-à-vis* other departments and other colleges. This would enormously enhance the power of the student in the former zero-tuition colleges. Giving students more attention and influence in the university would indeed occur, exactly as the customer exercises more power at the grocery—by his purchases and choice among competing products and stores, but not by leaping over the counter and insisting on power to run the store, as occurs with current protest. Currently at the grade school level many parents are turning to private schools precisely because the parents can choose more fully the kind of education given their children—via the power of the purse. The poorer people do not have that option—but they would with a tuition-grant system.

Since the producer usually knows more about what he is producing than does the consumer, the producer illogically tends to conclude that he is a better judge about the appropriate quality and quantity for the consumer. This tendency is especially rewarding if the producer can thereby obtain a sheltered competitive position in the production of the good. He would tend to produce a quality and quantity in a style related more to that which enhances his welfare and less to what students and parents prefer.

It is easy to see that with zero tuition the university faculty benefits from research and graduate activity that builds an impressive publication record and research status, with the currently less rewarding teaching of undergraduates being relegated to the less "distinguished," lower-ranking faculty or graduate students. The "publish or perish" rule would be less powerful under full tuition, because teaching would become a more important source of student directed funds. Survival of the better teachers who are weak in publication would be enhanced. It is interesting and amusing to note, incidentally, that students at the University of California are now attempting to protect some members of the faculty from being dropped because of inadequate research and publication. The protection comes by the students "donating" funds to hire the man to give classes; this *is* a voluntary, spontaneous full-tuition system. If allowed to expand, students would determine who was on the staff and who got the bigger incomes, just as they now decide which restaurants shall survive and prosper.

This is a simple application of the old, powerful, fundamental principle of behavior. The lower the price at which goods are distributed, relative to the market value, the greater the degree of discrimination and arbitrary criteria that the "seller" will display. Its corollary is that the lower the seller's right to the monetary proceeds, the greater his gain from underpricing the goods. The gains to the university administration and faculty from low tuition are classic examples, first expounded in Adam Smith's *The Wealth of Nations.* The greater the portion of a college's funds coming from tuition fees, the greater the power of the students and the greater the role teaching will play in the survival and prosperity of the members of the faculty. The less will the faculty choose which students shall attend, how they shall behave, etc. The lower is the ratio of tuition payments, the greater the power of the faculty over the students because the students are less able to exert significant effects on the financing of schools or departments as a reward for "good" performance—as they can with restaurants. The faculty says "education is different" and students are poor judges of good education; students are swayed by popular, theatrical teachers and do not appreciate the more valuable scholarly teachers. One wonders how students happen to go to the better and possibly tougher schools in the first place. The faculty of any college prefers lower tuition—until the budget expenditures can not be met from nontuition sources. And even then there is conflict of interest within the college between those who are threatened by the budget cut and those with tenure who are not. If the cut, or loss of income, would mean merely fewer undergraduates and fewer *new* teachers, clearly the least difficult resolution from the current faculty's interest is the reduction in new students, rather than an increase in tuition.

With zero tuition the state schools have expanded relative to higher-tuition private colleges, and the state university with its higher-salaried teachers and more expensive education is more attractive to students than the state colleges and junior colleges. The ex-president and the administrators of zero-tuition institutions correctly insist that *zero* tuition is the great principle underlying the *growth* of the university; but it is not a source of better education for California students. We should not confuse the *amount* of money with the *way* the money is obtained. More and better education, as judged by students, could be obtained at the same, or less, cost with the full tuition in control of colleges coupled to loans and whatever grants-in-aid are desirable.

With full-cost tuition, the less expensive junior colleges would attract students and income from the university and colleges. Predictably, the few administrative voices heard in favor of higher tuition seem, from my observation, to come from junior college administrators—who believe they would outperform the university if put on a quality-cost basis of competition for students.

A counter argument to the preceding propositions is that junior college education is "inferior" to university education. Although the quality of the university as a research institution is high, not as much can be established for its quality as a teaching institution to educate college students. The move to junior colleges with full tuition would occur if the more expensive university education were not matched by the higher quality as judged by students and parents. The university would have to improve its teaching to hold students at its higher costs. If it could not, the results would constitute evidence that the high-cost and high-quality combination was not a superior combination of quality, cost, and quantity. A Rolls-Royce gives higher-quality transportation than a Ford, but it does not follow that more Rolls should be produced than Fords. *Education* must be judged by the quality, quantity, and costs, rather than in terms of only those who are educated at the highest, most expensive levels.

Yet, despite this patent fact of life, when faced with a budget cut the administrators of the state university plump four square for "quality at all costs"—for maintenance of quality education for a selected few regardless of how many must be turned away and given instead an "inferior" education. On what criterion is it established that it is better to maintain the level of quality of education for fewer students at the cost of sacrificing education for others? Would one argue that in the event of a social security reduction, we should reduce the *number* of recipients in order to maintain the quality of those lucky enough to keep getting social security payments? But analogies aside, the elite, authoritarian arguments by university administrators and faculty for a given level of quality, regardless of the sacrifices imposed on excluded students or on taxpayers, are sobering evidence of the seductiveness of self-interest pleading.

The faculty and administration of higher education in California have evolved in the zero-tuition environment, with appropriately adapted behavioral traits. They have learned to use that political structure; they have learned how to appeal to the political processes and to legislators and governors for more financing. They have been almost exclusively reliant on the political process. They praise politicians for statesmanlike, responsible behavior when the university budget is increased; but if it is decreased, they cry of political interference. Having accepted almost exclusive dependence on financing directly from the political and legislative processes, they should not complain of "political interference" when that same political process examines more intently the budget and the operations of the university. Are they really surprised that the venerable law "He who pays, controls" still is effective?

Legislators generally tend to favor direct state legislative financing of education coupled with no tuition, rather than full tuition with grants-in-aid. The closer the tuition approaches full cost, the less the power of the legislators over the educational institutions. It is not entirely accidental that Congress used a grant-in-aid system for veterans; there was no federal college system.

We must constantly remember the difference between paternalism and independence. Independence from the competition of political processes and politicians' interests can be enhanced by full tuition, but it will bring greater dependence on competition among educators in satisfying students' whims and interest Either the students pay and control, or the political processes and politicians do. Yet some of the faculty seem to think they can avoid both. For educators there is no free lunch nor "free" tuition.

The situation reminds one of the Russian plight. Dissatisfaction with the quality of goods produced by Russian firms is sparking attempts to restore market prices as reflections of consumers' interests. While the Russian economists and consumers advocate more control via the market, producers and politicians show far less interest in weakening their power by moving away from socialism.

There remains a subtle, but effective means whereby full tuition would lead to *more* education than if directly provided by government at zero tuition. As matters stand now, an education at a tuition school may be worth $2,000, or say, $500 *more* than the education at zero-tuition state schools. For that superior education worth $500 *more*, the student would have to pay the full-tuition cost of $2,000. He gets no relief for not using state schools. If education were on a full-tuition basis, this obstacle to more and higher quality education would be removed. We should not assume that spending more by government for *direct* provision of education necessarily yields more education. This phenomenon, I conjecture, is powerful at all levels of education.

A preference for full tuition implies nothing whatsoever about the desirable extent of aid or subsidy to students. Unfortunately much of the debate has erroneously assumed that zero tuition is a necessary or a preferred method of aid while full tuition is a device to avoid aid to students. No matter how much aid, if any, should be given to students, the case for full tuition does not rest on a denial of aid. It rests on the premise that, whether or not aid is given to students, the financing of schools should be controlled more directly by students and their parents because the kind of education thereby made available is deemed to be better—by those who advocate full tuition.

Full tuition, plus grants-in-aid to whatever extent one believes is justified, directs educational activities more to the interest of students and less to that of the university staff. And after all, is it not the students whose interests are fundamental rather than the university's as an institution? Is it the students' interests as reckoned by students and parents rather than the convenience to the educators that is a better guide? My choice of answers is obvious. I suspect that these are the crucial issues on which advocates of zero tuition will differ with me.

My opposition to zero tuition arises because I do not like the way it redistributes wealth, nor do I like the totality of the effects of the kinds of competition it induces relative to that which would prevail under full tuition, supplemented by grants and loans. The latter yields more variety of educational opportunities and just as much educational opportunity and presumptively, greater detectability and survival of superior education. It reduces the producers' control over the products that the customers can have. The influence of selecting their colleges and controlling payments is a trait with high survival in the world outside of academia and which should be cultivated. The decreased role of the state and political activity in administering education is also a consequence I find congenial. Higher tuition would improve the quality of education rather than reduce it. The quantity would be affected not by either a zero or a high tuition, but by how much is spent for education. Zero tuition does not mean more is spent for education, nor that more poor people can attend. To believe it does is to think zero tuition is the only or best way to subsidize or aid students—and that contention begs the fundamental question of what is the best way.

All these consequences seem to work against my interests as a member of a zero-tuition college. If I thought this one exposition of economic analysis and one man's preferences really were capable of converting our system of educational subsidies from the zero-tuition to a full-tuition system with scholarships, loans, and vouchers, I might be less willing to expose it, for the price may be high enough to make me join with those who, whatever may be their reason, prefer the Holy Zero (excuse me, the *free*) *tuition system.*

Acknowledgment is made to the Lilly Endowment, Inc., for a research grant to UCLA during which the present article was written. The opinions expressed here in no way reflect any conditions of that research grant.

# An Optimal Policy for Financing Higher Education—Some Guidelines (1969)

W. LEE HANSEN AND BURTON A. WEISBROD

The preceding chapters have dealt with means for assessing the costs and benefits of public higher education—from the point of view of any particular state. Now we leave this subject to consider some broader issues in the financing of public higher education. These two subjects are closely related, however, in that the main reason for interest in the magnitudes and distributions of the costs and benefits of public higher education stems from the search by individuals and legislators for a desirable system of educational finance. Thus, although this epilogue—which does stand somewhat independently—could have been omitted from this volume, its inclusion seemed appropriate.

It is not our purpose here to examine the varied educational finance plans that have been put forth, such as income tax credits for college expenses, the Educational Opportunity Bank, or substantial general Federal support for education. These plans have already been explored by others. Nor is it our objective to propose a "best" financing plan. In fact, we do not propose any specific plans. Not that one is not needed, but the state of knowledge simply prevents us from making a precise set of recommendations as to the level or levels of tuition, the appropriate percentage distribution of governmental support (federal, state, and local), and the terms under which loan funds should be available. Making such recommendations requires first identifying and defining—at the *conceptual* level—a desirable finance plan, and second, devising *operational* measures of those concepts. We cannot deal with the second task because of the formidable problems of quantifying the magnitudes of such variables as the external benefits of public higher education, value added by education, and so on. This chapter deals with and indeed is restricted to the first task—the clarification and sharpening of the conceptual issues.

To discover the characteristics of a "best" system for financing public higher education is to find answers to the questions of *who* should bear the costs of public higher education and *how* the portion of costs that is borne by students should be paid. More precisely, the main question of *who* should pay involves determining the share of costs to be paid by students versus taxpayers. (There is, of course, the question of how the taxpayers' portion of the costs is to be shared among various groups, but we do not deal with this matter.)

The question of *how* students should pay relates directly to the tuition issue, but the term tuition is not a simple one. Should tuition be the same for all students? Whatever the level or levels of tuition, should it be paid at the time the education is received or later? Should the level of tuition be determined at the time the education is received, or should the amount be contingent on future benefits? The nature of these choices will be described more fully below. Throughout our analysis we rely heavily on the search for efficient and equitable solutions to these educational finance questions. Indeed, this chapter is divided into two sections, the first focusing on efficiency in the pricing of higher education and the second focusing on equity.

As with this entire study, we continue to direct our attention to decision-making in the public sector. This is somewhat artificial; the fact that there exists a private as well as a public sector in higher education means that success in devising an efficient and equitable finance system for the public sector does not assure either efficiency or equity for the higher education system as a whole. The question of what separate and distinct roles ought to be fulfilled by the public and private sectors in higher education is, in our view, an important one, but scant attention has been given to it. And to deal with the question here would have further complicated an already knotty set of issues.

## Efficient Pricing

In this section we discuss efficient pricing from the individual and the social points of view since both are relevant in evaluating alternative methods of financing public higher education.

The cost of a college education to a student and his family—apart from the income foregone—can be analyzed in two parts. One is what can be termed the price of the education—the tuition charge, the books and supplies, and so forth. The second is the ease of financing that price—that is, the availability and terms of loan funds and scholarships.

The level of the price of college education and the ease of financing it are jointly relevant to individuals' decisions. An apparently high tuition rate may be quite manageable if grants or scholarships are widely available or if loans can be obtained at sufficiently low interest rates. Similarly, even a total failure of scholarship programs and capital markets to provide financing assistance can turn out to be inconsequential if the *total* price of education (including foregone income) is sufficiently low. Thus, there would seem to be trade-off possibilities between the price of education and the means of financing it—combinations among which any particular individual would be indifferent.

But considerations of public policy dictate that we go beyond an analysis of any individual's preferences to take account of the resources used up in the process of satisfying those preferences. This involves recognition of a socially efficient price as well as of a socially efficient set of finance terms, including an interest rate.

Efficiency may be said to exist in a market when the price of the good or service is equated with the marginal opportunity cost (value of the best alternative use) of the resources used to produce it, and both are equated with the benefits from an additional unit of the good. Thus, given the distribution of income, the preferences of all individuals in society, and the technological production possibilities, the efficient price for any given unit of production (e.g., year) of higher education is the price which is equal to the marginal *net* social cost of providing that education and to the marginal benefit received by the student. By *net* cost we mean the marginal cost of production *minus* the marginal external benefits (if any), the latter being the externalities noted in Chapter II.[1] These externalities, it may be recalled, consist of the benefits that are not captured by the individuals whose education produced them.

To the extent that such uncaptured external benefits occur, the efficient price of education—to be charged of students—would be below the marginal cost of producing the education services. (It is difficult to estimate marginal costs, but it might reasonably be assumed that long run marginal costs can be approximated by average instructional plus capital costs.) Thus, the likelihood of *under*-investment in education is reduced (though the probability of *over*-investment is increased) as the price confronted by the student and his family is cut via a public subsidy which, at least in principle, is a reflection of the external social benefits from an incremental unit of education.

This view of pricing clearly implies that society (taxpayers in general) should subsidize higher education as a matter of efficiency. Since some external benefits may be realized within local areas while others may be distributed more broadly, all levels of government—federal, state, and local—would presumably share in the costs. Insofar as the bulk of externalities accrue at the national level—in part because of population migration—this would argue for a reallocation of public financing of higher education away from state and local governments and to the federal government.

These subsidies could take any of a variety of forms. One is the obvious and currently prominent low (presumably below-cost) tuition rates. Others include income tax credits or deductions to parents and outright cash grants to students—all of which can be equivalent to a tuition reduction. Any of these forms, and no doubt others as well, could be used to produce the desired public subsidy and, in turn, result in an efficient price. The choice among them rests largely on equity considerations—that is, the extent to which persons not in need would benefit. For example, income tax credits would have a negligible effect on low income groups inasmuch as they had little or no income tax liability anyway. Later in this chapter we do discuss broad equity issues, although we regard it as beyond our objective to examine in detail the case for each possible form of subsidy.

## Educational Capital Markets—Pay Now or Pay Later

Just as there is a socially efficient price for higher education, there is also a socially efficient borrowing rate for those who cannot or prefer not to finance their education from past savings, current income, or family gifts and transfers. The capital market constitutes a device for financing education in a series of installments rather than fully at the time of purchase. But insofar as the capital market for higher education finance reflects a divergence between the private borrowing rate and the social opportunity cost, there will be smaller expenditures for higher education than are optimal.

There is a discrepancy between these two rates because the private risk (to lenders) on loans for education exceeds the social risk—a point which we shall elaborate momentarily. As a result, education loans will tend, in the private market, to be excessively difficult to obtain. For persons whose income and/or asset position is strong, high private borrowing rates will not be a significant barrier to borrowing, for they can utilize collateral other than the prospect of financial gain from education. For the less affluent, however, the difficulty of borrowing to finance the costs of higher education can prove serious. Both equity and efficiency suffer when the market interest rate exceeds the optimal rate. We shall return to equity matters later. Let us now consider efficiency in the loan market in more detail.

Why has there been such a limited development of an organized private capital market to finance student loans for higher education? Several major reasons emerge. Higher education, unlike ordinary commodities, is intangible. A refrigerator, an automobile, or a factory can be repossessed by the mortgage holder in the event of default on a loan. Since education is embodied in the individual, such repossession is impossible in a free society. Thus, given the difficulty of assessing individual integrity and of gaining access to a claim on the borrower's income, the lender's risk in making loans to finance higher education is raised. Higher education is also embodied in a highly mobile form. Because people—especially the better educated—are highly mobile geographically, a private lender finds it risky to finance higher education; subsequent collection is difficult (costly) if the individual moves and especially if he is hard to locate. This situation is in marked contrast with the case of many categories of physical capital which are usually more difficult to move.

There is, in addition, lack of certainty that higher education actually will bring financial benefits for any particular individual. The individual may die prematurely, become disabled, or fail to find regular employment for his skills. These contingencies are analogous to the possibility that a factory will not be profitable because it is destroyed by fire or storm, or because the demand for the product is insufficient. Since some of these events are insurable, it would seem possible to develop an insurance arrangement with respect to the variety of contingencies that might prevent higher education from producing financial benefits for the individual.

However, some reasons for loss may not be easily insurable, inasmuch as a moral hazard may exist. For example, an individual may *choose* a low-paying job over a high-paying one or, particularly in the case of women, may not choose to work for pay at all. Or education may have been acquired solely for consumption purposes or to provide the option of a more attractive, though not necessarily more financially rewarding, job. Again, insurance against these possibilities might be developed but the problem of adverse selection—heavy borrowing by persons who are particularly likely to default—could be serious. This might help to explain the lack of development of private insurance in this area.

Were it not for these special characteristics of the private capital market for higher education loans, there would be no particular reason for concern about whether the price of higher education was paid at the time the education was received or whether it was paid subsequently—just as there is no particular concern about whether business firms finance their investments in plant and equipment in cash or through borrowed funds, or about whether automobile-buying consumers pay in cash or in installments.

An efficient capital market—just as an efficient price—can be achieved in several ways. These include, for example, loan guarantees, interest rate subsidies, and assistance to private lenders in the collection of loans, e.g., through the federal income tax system. (We shall discuss such possibilities in more detail below.) The effect of these subsidies would be two-fold: First, by reducing the cost of capital to students, some students would be permitted to attend college who otherwise would not; and second, some shift in the method of student financing of college costs would occur, with more of the individuals' costs being shifted to later time periods. It should be pointed out, however, that *any* device that encourages people to go to college by making available to them low cost loans—as distinguished from reduced tuition, increased grants and scholarships, and so forth—will cause more of them to go into debt. This does raise an equity point that we note in passing. Indebtedness in low income families is especially likely to grow. Borrowing by higher income students (or their parents) may grow up too, simply because of the attractive interest rates, but these students (or their families) have less basis for concern about their ability to repay. One expected result of interest rate subsidization is, thus, to increase the availability of higher education to low income students, but it does so at the price of burdening them with debts with which their more fortunate colleagues need not be concerned.

It is also important to point out that these subsidies logically would be paid for by the federal government. Efforts by local governments or even states to establish a socially efficient interest rate will not work effectively, particularly in view of national mobility patterns.

We now recapitulate. Assuming the presence of external benefits and the special characteristics of the capital market for college loans, there will exist divergencies between marginal private production costs (to the schools) and net social costs. Prices based on the marginal net social costs of education and interest rates based on the marginal social cost of borrowing to finance such education are requisites for an efficient pricing system in both the higher education and the capital markets. Determination of the appropriate magnitudes for these prices and interest rates remains a matter for further study.

With respect to the interest rate, efficiency in the allocation of resources between higher education and other public and private uses suggests that the appropriate concept for determining the interest rate is the opportunity cost of the funds—that is, the rate of return available on alternative investments. There has been considerable literature dealing with the appropriate rate of interest (or discount) for use in evaluating government expenditure programs, but there is little professional consensus. Recently, however, the Joint Economic Committee of the United States Congress has favored using the private opportunity cost of capital in evaluating all government programs. While no specific figure was recommended, there were references to magnitudes of perhaps 10 percent—a figure which is a rough estimate of the average pretax rate of return on manufacturing capital in the United States. This is not the appropriate place for a discussion of conceptual issues involved in evaluating government expenditure programs. Suffice it to say that discount rates considerably lower than 10 percent are being used in the evaluation of many government expenditure programs—rates as low as 2 percent not being unheard of. Thus, since the opportunity cost of foregoing some projects is 2 percent, while for others it is 10 percent or more, it seems reasonable to settle on a discount rate which falls somewhere in the middle of the range.

If, for example, an interest rate of 5 percent were charged on loans for higher education, it is quite likely that there would be an extremely high demand for such funds, simply because this rate is below that of most market rates confronting individual borrowers today. Thus, such a program would call for setting an upper limit on the amount of the loans so that unlimited borrowing for a wide variety of other purposes could not take place under the guise of financing higher education.

The notion that low interest rate loans are desirable for the financing of higher education is hardly novel, and, in fact, there are already a number of such programs in existence financed by the federal government, state and local governments, and by private groups. It is worth pointing out, though, that one's support for low interest rate loans can be based on considerations of economic efficiency alone, independent of considerations of equity, such as the desire for equality of access to higher education.

Whatever may be the attractiveness of low interest loans, it is not a matter of indifference to state legislators whether the student's share (price) of higher education is paid now or later. There frequently are political and legal constraints on the degree to which the state can borrow in order to finance expenditures, even though repayment (in this case by students) is expected in the future.

A well developed capital market for higher education would provide a means of coping with this situation. Students and their families could choose between paying the price of higher education out of their own funds or borrowing and repaying in installments; and in either case the state could receive immediate payment. An analogy is the case of an individual buying a new automobile: The automobile dealer (state government) receives cash for the sale either directly from the buyer (student) or indirectly, from the finance company, in the event that the buyer prefers to pay on an installment basis.

## Contingent or Fixed Payment

The opportunity for students to pay for higher education in installments rather than fully at the time the education is received suggests the possibility of making the amount of the payment contingent on some subsequent events, such as the realization of financial benefits from that higher education. Our earlier discussion of the price of education had assumed a *fixed* price, but we now interpret it as an average, expected price—some persons paying more, others less.

A pricing system in which the price is contingent on events occurring subsequent to the date of purchase (transaction) is not new. It is found generally in the insurance field. The total price that an individual pays for a $10,000 ordinary life insurance policy, for example, depends on how long he lives, and the total price that one pays for disability insurance depends on the actual occurrence or lack of occurrence of a disability. Pursuing the life insurance analogy a bit further, it is worth noting that everyone who has such a life insurance policy will eventually collect $10,000, although some individuals will have paid much more than that, and others will have paid much less. The *average* price paid for that $10,000 policy will be approximately $10,000, but the price paid by particular individuals will vary substantially around that average. As with all analogies, that between life insurance and higher education is less than perfect, but our point here is simply to note the practical possibilities for development a system in which the price actually paid for higher education by a specific individual is not the same *ex post facto* for all individuals and is a function of developments occurring subsequent to the time of purchase of the education.

The above discussion implies that if the pay-now option is selected, the fixed sum would be paid, whereas, if the pay-later option is chosen, either the fixed-sum or variable-sum alternative is available. We judge that as a practical matter this is the case. It is logically possible, however, to utilize the variable-sum alternative regardless of whether the pay-now or pay-later option is selected; the latter would probably require, however, an awkward arrangement of periodic rebates and/or additional payments.

If a variable-sum repayment plan were adopted, the need to define the nature of the variable sum to be repaid would have to be faced. We would argue, on efficiency grounds, for repayment to be based upon the value added by higher education. While value added cannot be comprehensively measured to include both money and non-money returns, money benefits may serve as a reasonable proxy for total benefits. In any case, it is the *additional* benefits (increase in income) directly attributable to a unit of education that are relevant—rather than simply the level of benefits (level of income).

If students and parents are risk averters, a requirement that the price of higher education be fixed independently of the financial benefits actually received will depress purchases of higher education to a level that is suboptimal in terms of expected income gains. Adoption of a pricing system based on incremental income, by contrast, would be more congenial to risk averters, for it would amount to a profit-sharing plan in which taxpayers as a whole shared in the additional productivity (earnings) resulting from higher education. When the additional productivity is small, the bulk of the higher education cost would be borne by taxpayers generally; only when the additional productivity is large would the individual be expected to pay a large fraction of the cost of his education.

One point to note with respect to any plan which bases payments (price) on money income—either on the value added by education or on the absolute level of income—is that higher education provides people with options to choose either higher paying jobs or more pleasant and enjoyable but not so high paying jobs. Thus, a pricing system based only on money income would still have some incentive (efficiency) effects insofar as people were encouraged to reorient their work effort toward jobs producing less money income but more non-money benefits.

Suggestions have been made recently—e.g., the Educational Opportunity Bank proposal—to base charges for higher education on the absolute level of one's subsequent income. This would make the price of education a variable one, but would not relate the price of education to its value-added. Many variables other than schooling also affect incomes; consequently, a pricing system for higher education that makes price simply a function of income level would overprice education relative to its financial benefits for some persons and underprice it for others.

Both the equity and the allocative efficiency of such a pricing system are questionable. While little is known about the quantitative nature of individuals' responses to a pricing system based on one's actual income level rather than on the expected value added, we can analyze the types and directions of the responses.

It would be useful, albeit rather arbitrary, to divide all potential students into two groups: Group A, consisting of those for whom education is an investment in increased earnings, and Group B, consisting of those for whom education is essentially a consumer good. Members of group B—who do not expect a college education to increase their incomes significantly—may be subdivided into group $B_1$, those (including many women, but also including the lazy and unambitious) who expect relatively low incomes whether they go to college or not; and group $B_2$, those (including some women) who expect *high* incomes whether they go to college or not—simply because they are very able, energetic, hard-working people.

If repayment is to be based upon value added, Groups $B_1$ and $B_2$ pay no tax because their education produces no incremental income. But if repayment is based upon *levels* of income, the impact is quite different. Members of Group $B_1$, whose incomes would be low, would still pay little or nothing. But members of Group $B_2$, whose incomes would be high—though not as a consequence of their education—would pay much more in taxes. Thus, the consumer-good benefits of higher education would be a bargain for persons in Group $B_1$, compared with those in Group $B_2$.

Since the price confronting members of Group $B_1$ would be lower than under the presently existing pricing system, we could expect an increased amount of higher education to be demanded by them. At the same, because Group $B_1$ members would not be paying their own way, members of Group $B_2$ and A would be faced with prices (tax payments) greater than under the existing system. Although we do not know the precise nature of the demand function for higher education for each of these three groups, we can be reasonably certain that they are downward sloping (the lower the price, the greater will be the quantity of education demanded). Thus, we can predict an increase in the number of people from Group $B_1$ taking advantage of the bargain rate and a reduction in the numbers from Groups $B_2$ and A. We would expect further that some persons from these latter groups would opt for alternatives to college. These alternatives might include on-the-job training, schooling that is the equivalent of college but which goes by some other name, or still other forms of activity which are designed to do essentially what colleges now do; presumably, these could accomplish everything now done by colleges except providing "college" degrees.

We need not dwell on these and other possibilities. Our principal objective has been to examine some consequence of a pricing system that disregards the value added by education. Lest we appear to be advocating a pricing system based only on value added, we hasten to add that the value-added basis for pricing college education also poses serious problems. One is the empirical problem of estimating value added, a matter which was noted above. A second problem is the conceptual issue of whether actual or potential value added should be measured. Actual and potential value added may deviate substantially, especially if only money income is considered; this is particularly true for women not in the labor force and for others who accept lower paying but otherwise more attractive jobs.

A third problem with the value-added approach is that a *market* income measure of either actual or potential value added is incomplete. The value of education as a consumer good is not reflected by money income data.

## Equity in Higher Education Finance

While the subsidization of the price of education and of the interest rate for college loans can provide an efficient solution to college financing questions, equity considerations must still be treated. Many people who desire to go to college and who would profit from it may still be unable to attend even under socially efficient pricing arrangements. And so we explore methods by which equity objectives can be achieved in order to move closer to the goal of equality of educational opportunity for all.

There are some individuals who may be qualified for college but who will not attend college because the combinations of available price and interest charges are excessive relative to their financial situation and the strength of their desire to attend. The unwillingness to incur these costs is conditioned, however, by various factors including family income and wealth, family size, parental health, etc. At the same time there may be a social determination that these factors ought not to bar college attendance so that needy individuals with the ability and motivation to benefit from college should go.

If compulsion is to be avoided, these barriers to college attendance could be offset in three general ways: Incomes of such students and their families might be supplemented; the price of college education for them could be reduced; the interest rate applicable to their borrowing for college could be lowered.

It might be argued that the judgment that a student should go to college even though family circumstances would lead him not to go represents an implicit social decision that his family's income is too low. Thus, an increase in family income would seem called for. If the objective, however, is to make it possible for this student to attend college at a minimum cost to others, the approach of giving needy students cash transfers which are not restricted as to use is likely to be inefficient; very substantial transfers might be required before any of the additional money would be used for this student's higher education. A possible variant is to restrict the use of cash grants to higher education. But this alternative may be difficult to implement, since as a practical matter there is no means for preventing some of the grant money from going to families—even some of them with very low incomes—whose children would have gone to college anyway, and who now, having received the grant, will be able to increase their expenditures on other goods and services. Grants to such families are not necessarily undesirable. The point is that the grants are not required to achieve educational objectives, however justified they may be from the point of view of a more general anti-poverty effort.

Consider now the alternatives of reducing the price or interest rate for the needy. If, to begin with, the price and interest rate were set at socially efficient levels, as discussed above, then further reductions would involve distorting the structure of prices. Thus, further reductions would some-what sacrifice allocative efficiency in order to bring about effects that were deemed more equitable. Such a trade-off of efficiency for equity is by no means unique to higher education, nor is it necessarily undesirable.

In practice each of the three alternatives is bound to fall short of fully realizing equity objectives. Cash subsidies, tuition rate reductions, or reductions in interest rates are all certain to go to some persons other than those whom society specifically wishes to assist, since the needy and deserving are frequently difficult to discern. The result is that subsidies, in any of the three forms discussed, would go to some extent to the wrong people, with taxpayers, some of whom are themselves worthy of help, paying the cost.

Some perspectives on the dimensions of need can be obtained by dividing the population into several different groups. Group I includes those students (and their families) who are willing and able to pay the full long-run marginal cost (which we suggested above might be approximated by average instructional plus capital cost) and the full market interest rate. There is clearly no need to assist this group. Group II includes those who are willing and able to pay the *optimal* (efficient) price and interest rate (not of external benefits), but not the full price or interest rate; a portion of Group II, while willing to pay these costs, can do so only by incurring some hardship. Group III includes those who are willing and able to pay some positive price and interest rate, though less than the optimal levels; some fraction of this group could pay these amounts but only with some hardship. Finally, Group IV includes those people who would need cash grants to cause them to attend college, being unwilling to attend at any combination of a positive price and interest rate. All four groups are defined to include only those deemed "eligible" in terms of aptitude and motivation to attend college.

One of the implications of the structuring of these four groups is that the amount of subsidy required to cause an individual to attend college is a continuous variable with a wide range. Some students will require very substantial subsidies and others none at all in order to provide full equality of opportunity in higher education.

Identifying those who are deserving of additional subsidies to enable them to go to college is a most difficult task. If we assume, however, that the need for higher education subsidies can be estimated in a satisfactory, if rough, manner (perhaps applying the well-defined standards used in student financial aid analysis), then the perplexing question is who should pay for these equity-based subsidies? Taxpayers? Utilization of this source, while having merit, implies that any sum of money that students and their families cannot afford to pay *can* be paid by, and *should* be paid by, taxpayers in general. But when it is borne in mind that taxpayers in general include many quite low income taxpayers, it becomes clear that a shifting of the financial burden from students and their families to taxpayers involves, to some extent, a shift of the burden to families whose incomes and ability to pay may be less than the ability to pay on the part of students and their parents.

This raises a more fundamental issue of the meaning of "ability to pay." Just as standards have been established for determining how much a family can afford to pay for *higher education*, so might standards be established to determine how much a family could afford to pay in *taxes*. If such a study were done, it might well conclude that families of given size, given needs, and with incomes below some specified amount could not afford to pay any taxes at all; nevertheless, we know that many such families are, in fact, actually paying taxes—and that they would be required to pay even more taxes if state support for higher education were increased.

Another source of subsidy funds for the needy is college students and their parents. We noted above that there are some families, particularly in Group I, who are able and willing to pay more than the efficient price of education. If they were charged a higher price, the subsidies required could be obtained outside the tax system. That is, higher income families would pay more tuition, with the extra funds being made available to permit lower payments for low income students. This would amount to the use of classic price discrimination, to charge what the traffic will bear. One might think of the resulting schedule of charges as reflecting a sliding-scale college payment plan, with the possibility of negative charges for the most needy.

There is still a larger issue, touched on in an earlier chapter, concerning the propriety of limiting subsidies to those who choose college rather than some other means of enhancing individual and social well-being. For the many young people not qualified for college or not interested in attending college under any reasonable pricing conditions, there are a variety of other methods by which they can enhance their incomes and future satisfaction and otherwise become effective citizens. Job training and investments in small businesses are only two substitutes to college-going. Whether from the standpoint of achieving equity or efficiency in resource allocation, it would be highly desirable to make these and perhaps other alternatives available to those young people not opting for college. A broadened subsidy program might well be more costly. But, it would at the same time do much to provide greater equality of opportunity for *all* young people, not merely for college students.

The concepts of efficiency in the allocation of resources and equity in the distribution of access to higher education provide useful starting points in the search for a set of operational norms to be used in the pricing and financing of higher education.

Even after the conceptual issues have been fully explored, the thorny problems of measurement still remain. Once agreement is reached on the kinds of information that are needed, however, it should be possible to develop ways to obtain this information. Although the tasks of quantifying such variables as external benefits and value added in education are *substantial,* we are optimistic that progress can be made. Just as over the past decade a real breakthrough has been made in measuring the direct impact of education on earnings and economic growth, we judge that these remaining measurement problems will also yield to a concentrated measurement effort.

We have noted that efficient pricing of higher education involves a number of dimensions, all of which are subject to conscious choice—for example: whether the price (cost) of higher education must be paid at the time the education is received, or whether it can be financed through time; whether the price should be fixed, independent of subsequent income and other factors, or contingent on post-education events; and whether, if the latter approach is adopted, payment should depend on the level of one's income or the increase in that level (the value added by education).

We have pointed out, further, that subsidies of interest rates to facilitate student borrowing can be substituted for lower tuition rates; and that whereas both interest rates and tuition charges can be varied so as to influence who attends college and how much they are burdened financially in the process, neither interest nor tuition charges can be altered without producing side effects on the allocation of resources.

An effort was also made to spell out the alternative means for achieving greater equity in educational finance through cash grants, reduced tuition rates, or reduced interest rates on college loans for the needy. The question of who should pay for these subsidies was also raised. Should it be taxpayers or should it be other students and their families? Finally, the possibility of extending subsidies for college age people to activities other than college attendance was briefly noted.

We embarked on this chapter to see what we, as economists, could say about how public higher education should be financed. Our own assessment is that although we have been able to point out the relevance of a number of concepts—e.g., marginal cost pricing, value-added pricing, external benefits (to persons other than students)—we have been unable to show how those concepts can be made operational. Our frustration in this respect is matched, however, by the firmness of our view that educational finance decisions cannot be made on a more rational basis until economists and other social scientists and educators turn their attention to quantifying these cost and benefit concepts.

## Note

1.  At the conceptual level, the possibility of external costs as well as benefits should be considered. It is not generally argued, however, that such costs are notable in higher education.

# Society, Students and Parents— A Joint Responsibility:
## Finance and the Aims of American Higher Education (1971)

HOWARD R. BOWEN

The American plan of financing higher education has long included low tuitions, unrestricted appropriations and gifts to institutions, and the use of grants (or scholarships) in the finance of students. The purpose of these financial arrangements have been to extend higher education even more widely and to create independent colleges and universities where ideas could flourish. The result has been a system of higher education which, despite shortcomings, is the envy of the entire world. It has contributed enormously to social and economic progress, and is today the principle hope for solving the great social problems of this country.

But now we hear from all sides, including Washington, proposals to raise tuitions drastically and to finance students by putting them heavily into debt. These proposals are attractive to hard-pressed public officials who would like to remove educational costs from the public budget and are attractive also to some educators who think they might banish financial worries by shifting the costs to students. These proposals are deceptively simple and plausible. But the trouble is that they are based on a gross misconception of the nature of higher education.

It is anomalous, even tragic, that America would seriously consider abandoning its historic system of educational finance at the very time when it must extend opportunity to millions of hitherto excluded young people and when the country depends on independent colleges and universities as the principle source of values, ideas, and techniques needed to regenerate American society.

The present system of financing higher education is admittedly complex. It is financed by local, state, and federal taxes; by earnings on endowments; by voluntary gifts of individuals, companies and foundations; by tax exemptions; by contributions of parents, spouses, and relatives of students; by student earnings; by tuitions; by receipts from the sale of products and services; and by various forms of loans to institutions and to students.

This diversity of finance is due partly to the complexity of the higher educational system—to the many kinds of institutions and the varied sponsorship. It is due partly to the historic fact that colleges and universities have been free, and pressed by financial need, to obtain money wherever it could be found. They have been ingenious in discovering sources. The result is a variegated, perhaps a bit tattered, crazy-quilt of financial devices and practices. It is hard to explain this financial system in terms of *principles*. It has grown up over many years of incremental decisions to meet various needs and problems. But merely because it is complex, it cannot be dismissed as wrong or bad. It may be that improvement should come through further incremental adjustment rather than through radical change as is so often suggested today.

The policy problem before the nation at this time is to modify these complex financial devices in ways that will help attain the several broad objectives we hold for higher education. The problem is urgent because of the vast increases in funds that will be needed in the next decade.[1] Our conclusions about finance should flow logically from our view of the aims of higher education. Much of the controversy over finance is due to lack of agreement of these aims or to differences in the weight attached to different aims.

# The Aims of Higher Education

Let me try to state some of the aims of American higher education which seem to have gained considerable public assent and point out some of their financial implications.[2]

## 1. Opportunity

Young people, regardless of circumstances, should have access to as much higher education as they can handle. This aim is based on the idea that to widen opportunity will not only benefit individuals but will also enrich the culture by adding to the number of educated persons and foster economic growth by adding to the supply of professional and skilled workers. This goal calls for very large enrollments. Recent evidence suggests that the innate ability to do intellectual work at the college level is much more widely distributed among the population than has previously been believed. This is so because intellectual ability is deeply affected by family income and family background.[3] Another reason for extending enrollments is that the system of higher education is an efficient device for discovering talent and sorting people according to their interests and abilities. It helps young people find the careers in which they can be most productive and happy.[4] The goal of extending opportunity has had a profound effect on the system of finance. It explains the traditional emphasis on low tuitions and student financial aid. This goal also has much political steam behind it. Surveys show that families of all income classes are counting on, or at least hoping for, a college education for their children.

## 2. Varied Programs

Institutions and instructional programs should be varied to suit persons of different abilities and interests. Only if varied experiences are offered will genuine educational opportunity be available and academic standards in each type of education be upheld. The system should include many kinds of vocational training, academic programs, and opportunities for adults and for former dropouts or flunkouts. The system as a whole should be fitted to the students rather than the students to the system. The meteoric rise of community colleges[5] with their combined academic, vocational, and adult programs and the enormous scope of proprietary education are evidences of the reality of this goal.

## 3. Student Freedom

Students should be free to choose institutions according to their abilities and their tastes. Financial aid to students, therefore, should come at least in part from sources other than the institutions, and the aid should be designed so that genuine choice exists. Students should also have reasonable geographic mobility—which may call for the eventual end of nonresident tuitions in state institutions.[6] And they should have free choice of major fields according to their abilities. For example, the choice between chemistry and economics, or medicine and law, should not be influenced by relative fees charged or aid granted but only by student interests and aptitudes. Also, programs such as medicine, which are unable to accept all qualified applicants, should be expanded. To carry freedom even further, students in postsecondary education should, on the whole, be treated as adults and should be free of unnecessary control, by parents and institutions, over their personal lives. This is, of course, a new and controversial item in the list of freedoms but one that is being increasingly realized among graduate students and older undergraduates. It suggests, in the long run, diminishing financial responsibility of parents and institutions and increasing financial support of students by government. The ultimate in student freedom is, of course, far from realization, and financial realities, as well as conflict of opinion, will prevent its achievement in the near future. Yet the system of higher education appears to be headed toward widening the freedoms of choice for students.

## 4. Academic Freedom

Colleges and universities should enjoy freedom of thought and expression, and also substantial freedom to choose what shall be taught, what shall be studied, and what research and scholarship to undertake, and what public services to offer with only the most general outside influence.[7] The goal of academic freedom calls for substantial amounts of unrestricted funds and diversity in sources of support. Academic freedom is also advanced when the patterns of support and control vary among institutions, so that not all are subject to the same kind of authority or influence. Parenthetically, the question of academic freedom also raises timely issues about the efficacy of local initiative as compared with central planning in higher education.

## 5. Efficiency

Efficiency is an elusive goal in higher education. The activities of each institution are an amalgam of instruction, research, and public service, all jointly produced. It is extraordinarily hard to calculate the cost assignable to any one program. And the product of these efforts is virtually impossible to measure, except intuitively. Brushing aside the problem of measurement, the argument is sometimes advanced, on the analogy of the private economy, that efficiency would be promoted if each user of a service paid a price equal to the cost of that service. Under this system, students would pay tuition equal to the cost of instruction, government agencies and business would pay for research at cost on a contract basis, and users of consulting and other public services would pay a fee to cover cost. Under this system, no one would be tempted to accept instruction or other services unless they were deemed to be worth what they cost, and the college or university would no longer be tempted to offer services except when someone on the outside judged them worth the cost. The college or university would then become a self-supporting enterprise catering for a market.

   The difficulty with this theory is that the customers, whether they be young men and women, business men, or public officials, are not in a strong position to decide the complex issues of what should be taught and what should be studied.[8] Moreover, there are vast social benefits from higher education, and it is undoubtedly in the social interest to provide more instruction, research, and public service than individuals or agencies would demand if they were required to pay the full cost. There must be in society at least one agency which has substantial freedom to pursue knowledge in an exploratory way without concern for the immediate results, without knowing what the results may be, and with only the confidence that knowledge is good for its own sake and often has manifold unforeseen consequences. True efficiency from the long-range point of view probably requires that institutions have substantial unrestricted funds with which to advance instruction, learning, and public service in ways different from those which would be dictated by the market with its relatively short perspective. For efficiency, we must rely largely on the intuitive judgments of scholars, and they must be given the financial freedom to make choices independently of the market. This freedom carries with it heavy responsibility for colleges and universities to be responsive to the deeper and longer-range interests of society. But there is no alternative to granting this freedom.

Another aspect of efficiency relates to the allocation of resources among institutions and among regions of the country. These resources include bright students, competent faculty, and good facilities. If institutions must compete for these resources in the open market, some institutions and some regions will be left with dregs. The free working of the market will not necessarily achieve a socially desirable distribution of resources. A system of financing may be needed to give each institution and each region a chance for a diverse student body including a reasonable number of bright students, some capable faculty members, and some decent facilities. Statewide or nation-wide grants to institutions may be needed, as well as the traditional scholarship system by which institutions can attract superior students.

## 6. Equity

A goal of increasing public concern is fairness among persons and classes in allocating the costs of higher education, particularly as between taxpayers and donors who represent "society" and the students and their families who are the principal individual beneficiaries. Some economists have been arguing that, with tuition below cost of instruction, low income taxpayers are put in the position of subsidizing upper income students.

This argument is weak. It suffers from the fallacy of singling out one public service, higher education, and focuses on its effects while ignoring other public services (e.g., social welfare) which have quite different and possibly offsetting effects. This argument also belittles the social benefits of higher education.

The cost of higher education is divided into three parts: The first is the income of the student that is foregone because he chooses to be in college. This is by far the biggest part of the cost. The second is the cost of the student incidental to his education; for example, books. The third is the institutional cost of instruction. If we concentrate only on instructional costs, as many people do, then it can be shown that, on the average, students and their families are paying less than one-fifth of the bill which, it is argued, is too small for those who benefit most.

However, when incidental expenses and foregone income are included, students are contributing about three-quarters of the cost of their education (including tuition).[9] Three-quarters seems an adequate contribution in view of the substantial social benefits derived from higher education.[10]

## 7. Balanced Budgets

A pragmatic, but nonetheless influential goal is to help balance public budgets by keeping the costs of higher education out of public accounts. Governments, both federal and state, are tempted to finance students aid and academic buildings by means of loans which are shifted to the private capital market. This device is of course a subterfuge. It does not eliminate or reduce the social costs of higher education. It only shifts them to another account where they do not affect the public budget. Nevertheless, the goal of technical budget balancing strongly favors credit as a method of financing both students and institutions.

## 8. Advancement of the Civilization

I conclude my recital of the aims of higher education with the most important goal of all—namely, that higher education should preserve and enrich the civilization it serves. For generations, this aim was taken for granted. But recently it is being challenged by those who say that social benefits, aside from advantage to the individual, do not exist or are too nebulous to be seriously considered. Writers on finance often implicitly assume that the system of higher education is a mere factory grinding out credit-hours of instruction which will be converted by students into personal income. The truth is that even higher education's instructional activities, narrowly defined, yield substantial social benefits which are not necessarily harvested by alumni as additional income. The mere presence of large numbers of educated men and women improves society by providing social, political, civic, and intellectual leadership that is enlightened and humane. The home, the church, the government, the community are all enhanced by the efforts and influence of the college educated. The presence of educated men and women increases the productivity of all labor and capital and has a favorable effect on national economic growth in ways that are not reflected fully in the personal incomes of the educated.[11] For example, the presence of educated men and women results in the discovery and diffusion of new ideas, new technology, and new ways of doing things. Moreover, college graduates man many professions in which the returns are below earnings in comparable occupations. These include teaching, the ministry, social work, and public service. The point is that the instructional activities of higher education contribute toward a better society in many ways that do not necessarily add to the incomes of their alumni.

But institutions of higher education are not merely engaged in instruction, as important and as socially beneficial as that function may be. They also serve as centers of *learning* with many cultural, political, and economic influences that radiate out to society. Colleges and universities are the foundations of our civilization. They are the repository and guardian of accumulated knowledge and wisdom; they are centers for the advancement of fresh ideas and new interpretations of old values; they are the main source of new science and technology; they are centers of aesthetic, moral, and social criticism; they are major patrons of the arts and literature; they are of critical importance in advancing the health and safety of the nation; and they provide a great pool of talent that engages in study and evaluation on a multitude of social problems.

All of these things are accomplished jointly with instruction. To be successful in instruction, an institution cannot avoid being a center of learning. The services to students are invariably linked with the services to society. This is true not only of the great national universities with their vast research and service activities but also of small colleges and perhaps especially of community colleges. Each institution serves in its own way as a center of learning and a pool of talent with influence radiating to the outside community. It is a narrow and demanding misconception to regard institutions of higher education as merely places of instruction, or to assume that the role of instruction can be separated from the role of center of learning. In a sense, instruction is a by-product of a center of learning rather than the center of learning a by-product of instruction.[12]

I have dwelt at perhaps excessive length on the matter of social benefits, because of the rampant misconceptions about the social role of higher education—misconceptions that seem to be especially prevalent among economists and budget officers and which are being used to justify the shifting of an excessive part of higher educational costs to students.

## Financial Implications of the Several Goals

So much for the recital of the aims of higher education. Clearly, these eight aims are not all mutually consistent. They certainly do not all lead to the same system of finance. For example, if emphasis is placed on extending enrollment and providing varied instructions to accommodate the widest possible range of persons, and if the social benefits of higher education are highly valued, the required plan of finance is low tuition, primary use of grants in the finance of students, and solid general support of institutions by government and private donors. Or if emphasis is placed on the private benefits from higher education, and on the goals of efficiency (in terms of market criteria), equity, and "balanced" public budgets, then the recommended plan of finance will be high tuitions, heavy use of loans in the finance of students, and limited general support of institutions by government and donors. If the emphasis is put on freedom of choice and adult status for students, public support to higher education will be funneled to institutions via grants or loans to students, and tuitions will become a major source of income to institutions. If emphasis is placed on institutional autonomy and academic freedom, there will be large unrestricted funds available to institutions and diverse sources of support without any one source dominating the higher educational system.

The complexity of financing higher education is due to the fact that there are many goals, not all consistent, and that there are differences of opinion on the relative weights to be assigned the various goals. No simplistic solution will reconcile all the conflicting aims. That is why the system's financing is complex and probably must remain so. And that is why changes in the system should be made incrementally and not by drastic overhaul. My remarks in no sense suggest that there should be no change.

## Alternative Financial Patterns

There are three basic patterns for the finance of higher education. I shall call them full cost pricing, free public education, and a conglomerate.

With *full cost pricing*, each student would be charged a tuition to cover the cost of instruction in his particular program and he would also be charged prices for the use of auxiliary enterprises. Also, if the logic were followed, activities such as research and public service would be financed by user charges—sometimes in the form of contracts with government or business. The institutions would then be self-supporting and would operate as any private business would do. Under this system, students who could not afford to pay the entire cost, including living expenses and incidentals as well as tuition, would receive grants or loans from public or private sources to cover their deficits. Many advocates of this plan believe that student aid should be in the form of loans to be repaid over a lifetime with the amount of repayment contingent upon income.[13]

Under the *free public education* model, instruction would be provided without cost to students (though auxiliary enterprises would be charged for as at present). Presumably, also research and public service would be provided largely without cost to users as at present. The institutions would be financed mainly from public appropriations and private gifts. The finance and operation of colleges and universities would then be like that of public secondary education. Student aid, when needed to meet living costs, would be provided either through grants, loans, or a combination. Many proponents of the free public education model favor emphasis on grants.

The third or *conglomerate* model is of course what we now have. The cost is covered partly by tuitions and partly by public appropriations and private gifts, and student aid is a mixture of loans and grants—some of the latter tied to work programs. The underlying issue is whether the conglomerate system should veer toward the full cost model or toward the free public education model, and, in either case, whether student financial aid should be mainly in the form of grants or loans.

## Conclusion

I shall conclude with a brief sketch of my own views on financial policy. I rate highly the goals of wide-open opportunity, freedom of student choice, academic freedom, and the college or university as a center of learning yielding important social benefits. These aims lead me to the following recommendations which are conceived as incremental changes to be implemented over time.

1.  Colleges and universities should charge relatively low tuitions and much of their research and other services should be financed in large part with public appropriations and private

gifts. I would argue that the system of finance should veer toward the free public education model rather than toward the full cost model.[14]

2.    Over a period of time, the age at which students are emancipated from their families should be lowered to perhaps 20 or 21. At this age, the responsibility of parents for the finance of students should cease and the means test in connection with student aid should be abolished. This proposal merely suggests extending the precedent set by the GI Bill and by many graduate fellowships. This of course would not deny the right of parents to assist their emancipated children if they wished.

3.    Student financial aid should be basically in the form of grants rather than loans. Grants should not be lavish.[15] Grants should be designed to get students to, and through, whatever higher education they wish to pursue from the freshman year to the PhD or MD, but without frills. Loans should be supplemental to provide flexibility, to ease budgets, to meet emergencies, and to open opportunity. But no student who is willing to work a reasonable amount and to live modestly should have to go deeply into debt to secure an education. Heavy use of loans is an impediment to opportunity; it results in serious inequities between upper and lower income groups, and it serves no social purpose because the economic costs of higher education cannot be shifted to the future anyway. Such loans as are made—I think the total amount would be sizable—should allow repayments over long periods, possibly with the amount repaid to be contingent on earnings. Some form of public or quasi-public bank for the finance of student loans should be created, and it should charge an interest rate that would cover both operating and capital costs.

4.    The basic program of student aid should be administered outside the institutions to remove an element of institutional paternalism, to reduce financial influences in choice of institutions, and to relieve institutions of an onerous financial burden.[16]

5.    In the interest of academic freedom, the income of institutions should be derived from varied sources and should include substantial unrestricted income. The full cost model is weak in that institutional income would come predominantly from students and other users of services who would then be able to wield enormous power. A system that was toward the free public education model, on the other hand, would provide substantial unrestricted funds and diversity of sources and make possible institutional self-direction. A conglomerate arrangement—with income deriving from many sources—has virtues even if it may seem untidy.[17]

6.    Private institutions should receive public funds to assist them in holding down tuitions and in carrying out research and other services having social benefits. These funds might come from the states, the federal government, or both. The funds might take a number of forms. I would favor a combination of grants to students to help offset high tuitions in private colleges and grants to private institutions based on increases in enrollment and in cost per student. Useful precedents have been set in New York, Pennsylvania, Iowa, and other states. Proposals are being considered in many other states, including California.

My final word is one of vigorous opposition to the idea, so widely bandied about these days, that colleges and universities should be operated like commercial enterprises—selling their instruction to students, their research on contract to government and business, their public services in the market. The result would be institutions without autonomy and without the inner direction of a community of scholars. Colleges and universities would be subservient to every whim of the customers. If young students were among the customers, the power they would exercise would be awesome. Society has plenty of proprietary schools, and consulting, and R & D organizations. But it has only one inner-directed center of learning, namely, the nonprofit college or university. The first step in the destruction of higher education would be to put it into the arena of commerce. Moreover, at a time when we are trying to bring millions of minority and poor people into the mainstream of American society, it would seem perverse to raise the price of higher education and to offer it only to those willing to go heavily into debt.

# Appendix on the Social Benefits of Higher Education

The following outline is provided to define specifically some of the benefits from higher education which accrue to society beyond those which are enjoyed exclusively by individual alumni in the form of personal income or personal satisfaction.

It is perhaps immodest for one who is a product of the higher educational system to extol the virtues of his own group. However, at a time when the social benefits from higher education are being doubted or denied, it seems necessary to spell out these benefits. There is no intention of claiming perfection for college-educated people. They are human. Some are narrow, some selfish, some ignorant, some dishonest, some immoral. Moreover, some of their alleged good works are undertaken for selfish reasons or for personal gratification. Nevertheless, it cannot be denied that as a group they contribute to society enormously in ways that do not result in personal compensation.

# I. Social benefits from instruction

1. Improving the allocation of labor by helping students to find careers that match their aptitudes and interests—the sorting function.

2. Improving citizenship. Educated people are better informed, more conscientious, and more active than uneducated people.

3. Reducing crime. Crime rates among the educated are low.

4. Providing volunteer social, political, civic, and intellectual leadership for a myriad of organizations such as Boy Scouts, PTA, churches, lodges, artistic organizations, school boards, hospital boards and auxiliaries, cooperatives, labor unions, professional societies, public commissions, etc. An enormous amount of volunteer or minimally compensated work is done by educated people.

5. Providing millions of persons who enter professions having compensations below rates in comparable occupations, e.g., teachers, ministers, social workers, nurses, and public officials. Many professional occupations pay lower wages than occupations requiring no college education.

6. Improving the home care and training of children.

7. Providing a large corps of persons who can bring humane values and broad social outlook to government, business, and other practical affairs.

8. Enhancing manners and refinement of conduct and beauty of surroundings and thus adding to the graciousness and reducing the tensions of social intercourse.

9. Providing the leadership in charting new courses for society. For example, the current drive to improve the environment originated among the educated group and is now spreading to the whole population and is thus becoming politically feasible.

10. Speeding the acceptance and diffusion of new technology, and new ideas, and new ways of doing things.

11.  Contributing many new ideas which improve business or governmental efficiency but which are not patentable, or the advantages of which are quickly eroded by imitation.

12.  Providing a great reservoir of technical skill and versatile leadership which is the base of national military power.

## II.  Social benefits as a center of research, scholarship, and criticism

It would seem unnecessary to belabor the social benefits from these activities. Through research, the colleges and universities provide knowledge which is regarded as a good in itself, and they build the foundation of our technology (broadly defined); through scholarship, they preserve the cultural heritage and interpret it to the present, discover values and meanings, and distill wisdom out of past human experiences; through criticism, they present ideas of use in shaping the future. Through these activities, which are complementary to instruction, colleges and universities contribute to society far more than their cost.

Who knows the value of keeping Shakespeare alive, or Veblen's critiques of American society, of developing the scientific knowledge underlying hybrid seed corn, of discovering DNA, or of inventing the electronic computer?

## III. Social benefits as a versatile pool of talent

Colleges and universities provide a pool of talent available to society for a wide variety of problems as they emerge, and which are available in emergencies. The standby value of this pool of talent must be enormous.

## IV. Social benefits as patron of the arts

Colleges and universities are the principle patrons and promoters of the arts, both by employing artists, staging the performing arts, and by educating oncoming generations to appreciate the arts. Most of the artistic activity of the society occurs on campuses or radiates out from them.

## V.  Social benefits from the Community College

The Community College is often thought of as strictly an institutional center having no function but to educate and train young people. As such it has important social benefits. But it too provides—or should provide—benefits that flow from its position as a center of learning. It is a cultural center for its community, it is a patron of the arts, a center of discussion, a place for individual consultation and guidance, a humane influence, and a pool of talent to help with community problems. A community college is of great value to a community aside from the credit hours of instruction it generates.

## Notes

1.  In another paper, I have estimated that, at a minimum and with the assumption of constant price levels, the expenditures for educational and general expenses will increase from $13.4 billions in 1968-69 to $32.8 billions in 1980-81, and that as percent of GNP these expenditures will increase from 1.5 percent in 1968-69 to 2.4 percent in 1980-81. See "The Financial Need of Higher Education in the 1970s: A Realistic Appraisal," *Proceedings of the Academy of Political Science*, forthcoming issue.

When I use the term higher education, I refer to all branches of postsecondary education including community colleges, vocational schools, four-year colleges, and universities. And I include the functions of research, scholarship, publication, and public service as well as general, vocational, and professional instruction. I view higher education in this country as a unified and coherent *system*. The functions of the various types of institutions are overlapping, and almost all of them are engaged in producing socially valuable outcomes beyond mere instruction as measured by credit hours. One of the fallacies in much current discussion of educational finance is that it focuses on the costs of undergraduate instruction narrowly conceived and fails to recognize higher education as a system in which many socially important "products" are produced jointly along with undergraduate instruction.

2. Cf. "The Rivlin Report," *Toward a Long-Range Plan for Federal Financial Support for Higher Education*, U.S. Department of Health, Education, and Welfare, January 1969, pp. 3-4.

3. For a thorough discussion of these matters, see Robert H. Berls, "Higher Education Opportunity and Achievement in the United States," in *The Economics and Financing of Higher Education in the United States* (Washington, D.C.: U.S. Government Printing Office, 1969), pp. 145-204.

4. Cf. T. W. Schultz, "Resources for Higher Education: An Economists's View," *Journal of Political Economy*, May/June 1968, 327-347.

5. The number of students in community colleges has doubled in the past five years, and the influence of these institutions is gaining rapidly. See: K. Patricia Cross, "The Quiet Revolution," *The Research Reporter*, The Center for Research and Development in Higher Education. Berkeley, Vol. IV, No. 3, 1969, 1-4; and *The Two-Year College and Its Students*, The American College Testing Program, Iowa City, Ia., 1969.

6. Because geographic mobility is expensive, there should be no areas without higher education or with grossly inferior education. To overcome regional variations in accessibility and quality probably calls for differential federal aid to various sections of the country.

7. Also, these freedoms should not be abridged from within the university by the actions of administrators, students, or faculty members.

8. The system of reviewing research proposals by peers, followed by many federal agencies as a basis for research grants, is one useful way to bridge the gap between the outside customers and the universities.

9. See my paper "Tuitions and Student Loans in the Finance of Higher Education," Joint Economic Committee, U.S. Congress, 91st Congress, 2nd Session, U.S. Government Printing Office, 1969, pp. 619-621.

10. It has been argued that the individual benefits to students are sufficient that they should bear the whole cost, and that the social benefits should become a kind of social dividend financed by the students.

11. Edward F. Denison, *The Source of Economic Growth in the United States*, Committee for Economic Development, New York, 1962, pp. 251-253.

12. There are of course differences among institutions in relative social and individual benefits. I suspect that those institutions which rate low on the scale of social benefits also rate low on the scale of individual benefits. An institution cannot succeed as a place of instruction unless it is also a center of learning. If it is a center of learning it will inevitably confer great benefits on society aside from the enhanced earning power of its students.

13. For a discussion of this plan, see Milton Friedman, "The Higher Schooling in America," *The Public Interest*, Spring 1968, 108-112. One variant would be to finance instruction by full cost pricing but to finance other activities from public appropriations or gifts.

14. I have developed the arguments for this position in greater detail elsewhere. See "Tuition and Loans in the Finance of Higher Education," op. cit.: "The Financing of Higher Education: Issues and Prospects," in *The Future Academic Community*, American Council on Education, Washington, 1969, pp. 69-83; *The Finance of Higher Education*, Carnegie Commission on Higher Education, Berkeley, 1968. Those who oppose the free public education concept and lean to the full cost concept are chiefly concerned about the fact that this system involves a public subsidy to upper income groups. Most college students either are, or will be, in the upper income brackets while taxes are paid by all income classes. I believe this view underrates the broad social consequences of higher education for all classes, the substantial contributions of students in the form of foregone income, and the importance of encouraging open opportunity. Most significant, in considering the equity problem, it is inappropriate to single out higher education from among all public

goods and focus on its redistributional effects. One must consider the distributional consequences of all public goods (elementary education, social welfare, health, conservation, labor programs, national defense, etc.) and all taxes (federal, state, and local) to determine the redistributional consequences of the body politic. To select and analyze the distributional consequences of any one item of expenditure or any one sector of the tax system does not prove anything. It is sometimes argued that in the interest of equity young people who do not attend colleges should receive a subsidy for personal advancement equal to that received by college students. This proposal has some merit. The subsidy could be used for training, to help start a business, or for other self-developmental activities.

15. Grants can often be associated with work as in the current work-study program. Work should not be excessive so as to interfere unduly with studies and student participation in college activities. It should so far as possible be of a type that will contribute to the student's education.

16. A modest scholarship program might be useful, however, to assure an equitable distribution of talent.

17. One serious danger of varied sources of institutional income is that no source will feel ultimate responsibility for the advancement of the institutions. When states were the principal source of support for public colleges and universities, and tuition and private donors the principal source for private institutions, clear responsibility existed. As many federal agencies, foundations, and corporations entered the finance of higher education, responsibility tended to be diffused. Today there is danger that increases in effort of any one source will tend to reduce the effort of other sources. The problem of responsibility is a serious one. In my judgment, the federal government is best fitted to be the ultimately responsible agency, and will need to design its aid so that incentives are provided for increasing support from other sources. I incline to the view, however, that the states are well qualified to administer public higher education and aid to private institutions. Some federal aid might be in the form of grants to the states, some unrestricted and some perhaps earmarked for higher education.

# Financing Education (1972)

## NEIL M. SINGER

Education is the largest category of expenditures for state and local governments and recently has begun to attract some federal funds as well. Although private education is also a big business, public funding accounts for about 80 percent of all expenditures on education, over $43 billion in 1968. The predominantly public nature of educational expenditures is partly a historical accident, stemming from the communal responsibility that early Americans felt for their children's education. But public funding must also represent a social consensus, for not only the United States but virtually every other developed country treats education as a governmental function.

Our interest is in whether education constitutes an efficient use of public funds. First we must investigate the nature of the benefits of education to determine whether they can be provided efficiently by the private sector or whether some government intervention is required. Then we shall compare the existing pattern of funding with that justified by economic analysis to discover the extent and direction of the implicit transfer payments that now are present in public funding.

## The Benefits of Education

Before discussing the private and public benefits derived from education, we should distinguish between general and vocational training. General education may be thought of as the process of learning common skills such as reading and acquiring a body of general information unrelated to the student's future occupation or income. The information (such as an understanding of the legislative process) may help the student function as a member of society, or it may be a kind of consumer good (such as a taste for fifteenth-century music and an understanding of Darwin's theory of evolution) of value to the student only in his private activities. Vocational education, in contrast, is defined broadly as any training that increases the student's productivity and marketability as a member of the labor force. Although both types of education yield private and public benefits, the benefits differ in how well we can evaluate them.

### Private Benefits

Education traditionally has been thought of as a civilizing, acculturating process whose output is an improvement in the "quality of life." The great English economist Alfred Marshall considered the value of education to be that it "stimulates mental activity," "fosters . . . a habit of wise inquisitiveness," and "raises the tone of . . . life"; "regarded as an end in itself, it is inferior to none of those which the production of material wealth can be made to subserve."[1] This view clearly considered education to be a substitute for other forms of consumption and took as its value the utility that the individual derives from the educational process. Well-educated people were thought to be happier and capable of greater self-fulfillment than those with little education. There is some evidence that these benefits still provide some rationale for people to acquire education (for example, through adult extension courses or college-level and high school-level electives), but most education today appears to be more of a vocational than of a general nature.

Vocational education can be thought of as an item of capital equipment that the student obtains because he expects to receive net benefits whose present value is positive. This criterion applies whether the education yields an elementary or high school diploma that certifies the student as an employable member of the labor force or whether it leads through an intensive course of study and practice to a lucrative career in neurosurgery. Whatever the type of vocational education, the gross benefit it confers is the present value of the increase in future income that can be attributed to the additional education. Its cost is the present value of the resource cost incurred by the student during the educational process plus the opportunity cost of the income that he could have earned instead of staying out of the labor market and receiving vocational education.

These net benefits of vocational education can be summarized in a fairly simple equation. Suppose that an eighteen-year-old must choose between entering college or taking a full-time job. (He will retire at age sixty-five in either case.) As we saw in Chapter 13, the criterion that he should adopt is to invest in the education if its net present value is positive. Let $E_1$ be the income that the student expects to receive in year $i$ if he is educated, and $U_1$ be the income that he will earn otherwise ($E_1$ is zero until year 5 because the student is in school). We assume that the discount rate is 10 percent and that the student's income during the four years of college is zero. Finally, we denote the annual cost of college by $C_1$. Under these assumptions, the student can calculate the net present value (NPV) of a four-year college education as

$$NPV = \sum_{t=5}^{47} \frac{E_1 - U_1}{(1.10)^1} - \sum_{t=1}^{4} \frac{U_1 + C_1}{(1.10)^1}$$

Alternatively, the student can calculate the internal rate of return, the discount rate that makes the net present value zero. If the internal rate of return is higher than the market interest rate, then it must also be true that the net present value at the market rate is positive. Thus, the student can compare the market and internal rates of return and choose the college education if the internal rate is higher than the market rate.

Many problems arise in estimating the internal rate of return from vocational education. One obvious problem is that the income attributable to education will vary according to the student's ability. It may also vary for reasons beyond his control, such as changes in the prices of labor and capital and cyclical recessions that cause unemployment. The return to education also will vary with the student's occupation, sex, race, place of residence (urban or rural), and geographic location. Nonetheless, the internal rate of return is conceptually the correct measure of the productivity of vocational education compared to other investments, and the net present value is the correct measure of the dollar benefits to the student.

Attempts have been made to estimate both rates of return and net present values for broad classes of students and different levels of education. The general conclusion reached is that investment in "human capital" offers rather high rates of return and large net present values at most levels of education. Some of the estimates include a 29 percent rate of return for an elementary diploma, a 15 to 20 percent return for a high school education, and 12 to 15 percent returns for a college degree.[2] The rates of return to graduate-level education are somewhat lower. These results should be interpreted skeptically because of the difficulties already noted, but they indicate that the private benefits from vocational education continue to be substantial up to high levels of educational achievement.

These private benefits are high compared to the returns likely to be available from alternative investments. Nonetheless, there are some reasons to believe that students will not invest in human capital up to the point where the expected return is equal to the market interest rate. For the individual student, self-investment is risky, for he cannot be sure of his own future productivity. The same risk will deter lenders from offering funds to prospective students, even though the average yield may be well above the market interest rate. And students' ignorance of the returns from education may prevent them from investing up to the efficient point. We will examine the appropriate governmental response to these imperfections in the next section of this chapter. For now, it is enough to note that the very high rates of return that have been estimated as the private benefits of vocational education may be consistent with rational investment behavior by both students and lenders.

## Public Benefits

General education confers benefits on society at large in a variety of ways. It is generally accepted that minimal levels of education are necessary to permit the functioning of a developed economy and a democratic society. Literacy, familiarity with elementary mathematics, and an acquaintance with cultural and political institutions are essential for minimal participation in economic and political affairs. Although these minimal skills also convey private benefits, society historically has ignored the private benefits in decreeing that these skills should be provided to all its members and that the costs should be financed out of public revenues. We cannot place a value upon these public benefits of general education, but this social policy is a clear assertion that the social value of the benefits is well in excess of the cost of the general education that provides them. Moreover, this public policy removes from the individual's control the decision of whether to acquire general education.

The level of education involved, however, is quite low. The literacy tests that admit an adult to full participation in the political process usually test a reading standard well below the eighth-grade level. Basic arithmetic, fractions, and decimals all are learned by the time a child enters high school. The process of learning those facts about society that society deems essential may take longer, but the current consensus is that this process does *not have* to extend through high school. (Compulsory attendance usually ends at either fourteen or sixteen years of age.) Thus, the public benefits of general education are limited to primary and some secondary schooling.

Vocational education confers many kinds of public benefits, although perhaps none as socially vital as those of general education. First, let us consider the different kinds of externalities. One externality arises when education increases the productivity and income of a worker who was formerly supported by redistributional transfer payments. In this case, taxpayers at large receive the external benefit in the form of a reduction in their tax liabilities. The amount of the externality, however, is equal to the reduction in transfer payments, which typically is smaller than the full amount of the increase in productivity. Only if we hold the newly educated worker's income constant does the entire benefit of education accrue as an externality. Conversely, if the worker's income rises by the full amount of his productivity increase, then he and not other taxpayers receives all the benefit of vocational education. The public benefit is nil, since other members of society are not affected in any way.

Another externality that may arise because of the high correlation between education and income is a reduction in crime. By increasing labor productivity, education raises the opportunity cost of crime, the losses that the criminal suffers if he is caught and the income that he might have earned as a member of the labor force. Since the criminal imposes substantial costs on the rest of society whether or not he is caught, a reduction in crime must lead to a decrease in these external costs.

An externality frequently mentioned in discussions of education and training programs is the increase in taxes paid by students or trainees as a result of the higher income they earn because of their training. These taxes constitute an external benefit to the rest of society if they lead to a reduction in others' tax burden. In imputing this external benefit to education, however, we are assuming implicitly that the additional education does not lead to a greater demand for government services, so that society's total tax liability remains constant. This is not a good assumption as long as the income-elasticity of demand for public services is greater than zero. Before we accept increased taxes as an external benefit, therefore, we should net out the increase in the size of the budget that constitutes a claim on these additional revenues.

Inter-regional externalities may arise from educational expenditures since local and state governments, not the federal government, are the principal sources of funding. When a student who has been educated at the expense of New York taxpayers moves to California, the social benefits that California derives from his presence are an externality conferred by New York. Out-migration may be a significant deterrent to local expenditures on education, since local residents will be unwilling to subsidize residents of other areas. Although these externalities obviously cancel out for the United States as a whole (neglecting international flows, which on balance have favored the United States), they do not cancel out for each locality or state.

In addition to the externalities that are conferred on specific recipients (such as particular taxpayers or residents of states that attract in-migrants), education offers some benefits that are best thought of as public goods. One public good is the advance of knowledge produced by people who are highly educated. Basic research, for example, may shift the economy's overall production possibility curve outward, making new levels of output attainable without any increase in resource inputs. But the discoveries that lead to this shift are not usually appropriable by the researchers who make them; instead, the value of the discoveries can be thought of as a public good and the researchers' incomes as its cost of supply.

As well as increasing the level of aggregate income, education may contribute to an increase in the growth rate. The overall efficiency of resource use apparently is higher in economies with high general levels of education than in those with lower average educational attainment. Education seems to increase the productivity of factors of production in a multiplicative way, so that the increase in productivity that can be attributed to the training of each worker is amplified by the increased productivity of everyone else.

Another public benefit often claimed for education is that it enables society to provide for its future manpower needs by training students in the specialties and skills that will be essential for tomorrow's or the next decade's economic growth. Usually underlying this argument is the claim that we will experience a shortage of engineers, physicists, doctors, or even economists, unless our government takes action (such as subsidizing certain types of education) to insure that the needed future supply is forthcoming. There are two problems with this argument. One is technical, that we are not able to specify accurately what the occupational distribution of the demand for labor will be ten or twenty years from now. Thus, a policy of publicly providing for future manpower needs is as likely to yield future costs as it is to yield future benefits.

The other problem is that a shortage can exist only if markets are not functioning or if the implicit distribution of income is unacceptable to society. Suppose that we foresee the prospect of a severe shortage of doctors twenty years from now (based on current ratios of doctors to total population). If markets work properly, two things may happen: (1) more students will enter the medical profession in the expectation of higher future incomes that will result from an increase in the demand for medical care relative to its supply; and (2) there may be a substitution of capital-intensive medical techniques for the traditional labor-intensive methods. The "shortage" will only cause an increase in the price of medical services (and even then, perhaps, only for a short time while supply adjusts to the increase in demand).

This market adjustment will not be acceptable if we have some commitment to supply medical care at a fixed price, perhaps in order to make it available to low-income families. But such a policy simply amounts to subsidizing low-income families (or, more generally, consumers of medical care) *inefficiently*, through a transfer payment to future doctors.[3] For society in general, medical care is no more a "free good" than water is and is no more suitable a subject for supply at a price below marginal cost. Since this argument also applies to other kinds of education (in addition to medical training), providing for future manpower "needs" through subsidies to certain types of education does not confer a benefit upon society but only constitutes a redistribution of income in favor of certain groups of consumers.

## Summary

The private benefit of general education is the utility that the student derives from developing basic skills and from broadening his horizons in a way not related to his occupation or income. The public benefits of general education are the value to society of the individual's possession of basic skills, cultural values, and information about political and economic institutions. These public benefits are sufficient to justify public insistence upon a minimum level of educational attainment. Compulsory attendance laws, however, suggest that the minimum level is something less than a high school education.

Vocational education yields private benefits in the form of increased future income for the student. In obtaining vocational education, the individual must make an investment decision in which he compares the rate of return he can expect from investing in himself with the return he could earn from a non-educational allocation of resources. Despite difficulties in estimating the rates of return from education, many studies have concluded that education is an attractive investment compared to physical assets.

The public benefits of vocational education include reduced levels of crime, lower tax costs of supporting untrained indigents, and perhaps the increased future taxes that trained workers will pay. Other benefits are a more efficient use of resources and the nonappropriable research discoveries made by highly trained personnel. Inter-regional and international externalities may also arise from the migration of productive workers. The provision of skilled manpower to meet future demands is not a benefit of education but constitutes only an inefficient transfer to particular consumer groups.

## Efficient Supply of Education

The existence of public benefits (public goods and externalities) from education offers a reason for governments to intervene in the private sector's allocation of resources for education. The first question to answer is whether the conditions of production are such that the private sector is unable to supply the efficient amount of education even if there is a public expression of demand. As we saw in Chapter 5, public supply may be justified if a good is produced under conditions of decreasing cost, so that market demand is large enough to support only one producer.

Although indivisibilities characterize the supply of education when the only schooling is provided by the local municipal school district, there is no conclusive evidence that the average (per-pupil) cost of education falls as the size of a school rises. A particular school or district may exhibit decreasing costs temporarily because its physical plant is fixed in supply in the short run, but school facilities are not usually overbuilt to take advantage of decreasing costs. Hirsch has concluded that the average cost of schooling is constant over wide variations in school enrollment.[4] The successful operation of many private and parochial schools of different sizes is a corroborating bit of evidence, attesting to the fact that the basic unit of schooling is the classroom and that factor proportions cannot vary widely within its walls. On economic grounds, public supply of education does not appear to be preferable to private supply.

Public demand for education and public supply have not been separated in the past either because of a confusion between general and vocational education or because of a desire to redistribute income through education or to achieve non-economic goals. The most dramatic example of non-economic objectives is the use of schools to promote social and racial integration, objectives the schools have attained less than perfectly. Nonetheless, the existence of social objectives like these is a constraint on any proposal to separate public supply from public demand for education. Society's demand that particular skills and attitudes be taught in the early years of the educational process also constitutes a restriction on the private supply of education.

An interesting proposal for separating public demand for education from private supply was initially presented by Friedman and has since received some attention within the federal government.[5] Friedman suggests that virtually all the public benefits from education, whether general or vocational, accrue at the primary and secondary levels of education. For the sake of economic efficiency, accordingly, the public sector should confine its activities to ensuring that all members of society receive these minimum levels of education and to imposing upon the private suppliers of education whatever non-economic objectives society may specify.[6] Parents and children would then be left to obtain whatever schooling they wanted in excess of the social minimum, subject to these public constraints.

Friedman envisioned his system as working around a government voucher for schooling that would be distributed to parents. The voucher would enable a school to collect from the government an annual sum representing the value that society places on minimal levels of education. In practice, the value of the voucher would have to be roughly equal to the current cost of a year of primary or secondary public education, for (1) there is no other way to specify the quality of education that society demands and (2) it can be argued that the cost of public education provides an indication of the value that society places upon it. Private schools, however, would not be prevented from charging parents more than the value of the voucher, and parents presumably would accept prices in excess of the voucher if the quality of schooling and their demand for it were both sufficiently high.

The chief advantage that Friedman claims for his proposal is that it would permit students and parents to express their demand for different qualities of education. Through such an expression of demand, schools would be forced to compete for students and for good teachers, and the overall quality of education (including that provided by schools that accepted vouchers without any surcharge) would rise. Wealthy parents probably would buy more and better schooling for their children than poor parents, just as they do now. But it would be easier for poor families who place a high value on education to obtain good schooling than is the case under current public school operation.

Friedman's proposal separates not only the supply and demand for education but also efficiency and equity considerations. The social objective of economic integration, equality of opportunity, dictates that all children must have access to equally good schooling. In practice, however, this objective is never attained, even within those school districts that encompass neighborhoods with wide variations in income and racial composition. Public supply of education amounts to a form of transfer to low-income families, but the transfer is never as great in fact as in theory. Thus, even if we agree with the goal of equal educational opportunity, we may agree with Friedman that public supply of education is not a good way to achieve it.

In criticizing Friedman's simple voucher scheme, Levin has claimed that its effects on the poor would be very different from what Friedman predicts.[7] One problem is that private schools might refuse to locate in poor neighborhoods, preferring instead to compete for wealthier students. Thus, economic and social segregation might be increased by the voucher system. Another difficulty is that vouchers would perpetuate inequities in the distribution of income, since wealthy parents would have a stronger incentive to invest in more education and higher future incomes for their children.

Levin accepts Friedman's basic premise, that public supply of education is unsatisfactory and that some way must be found to encourage competition. One way is to combine vouchers with direct income redistribution, either through offering vouchers only to the poor or by making the size of the voucher vary with income. Or local communities might contract out the educational function to private companies. This step has been taken by some school systems for particular activities such as remedial reading. Modifications of this kind in Friedman's voucher proposal may be more acceptable to the electorate than the analytically correct measure, direct income transfers to poor families.

Friedman denies that there is any reason for governments to be concerned with vocational education, for he believes that the full value of vocational training can be captured by the student. In the preceding section, however, we mentioned several sources of external and public-good benefits in vocational education. Adopting Friedman's argument, we may conclude that even if students were to invest in the privately efficient amount of vocational education (that is, the amount that makes the internal rate of return equal to the market interest rate), there would be some basis for public subsidization of vocational training, although not for public provision of it.

Most of the external benefits mentioned are derived from rather low levels of vocational training (primary and secondary schooling). In addition, training programs that supplement formal schooling for dropouts and workers whose skills have become technologically obsolete frequently provide these externalities. Friedman's argument, therefore, justifies some public support for these kinds of vocational education. If efficiency is our objective, the amount of public support should be limited to the value of the externalities that society as a whole derives from the programs (net of the value that the trainee derives). Otherwise, the government voucher would include a transfer element and the efficient amount of vocational education would not be supplied.

This approach suggests that there should be no governmental support of higher education, since the externalities cited earlier are generally received from low levels of education and training. Some of the benefits from higher education may be public goods in the form of new research discoveries and overall productivity increases. The latter, however, cannot be attributed solely or even primarily to higher education, since most members of the labor force are not formally educated beyond high school. (Although on-the-job training is a major source of education, it does not receive much governmental support.) Basic research should be supported directly, rather than implicitly in the form of subsidies to higher education, if our goal is to undertake the efficient amount of research investment. Public support for higher education, therefore, cannot seriously be justified on the grounds that higher education confers extensive public benefits.

Nonetheless, the studies cited earlier indicated that society probably underinvests in education (including higher education) compared to its investment in physical capital goods. The market imperfections that give rise to this underinvestment provide a basis for particular kinds of public support for higher education as well as for vocational training at lower levels. Three of these market imperfections are risk, lack of information, and differences in rates of time-preference.

## Risk and Educational Investment

There are several sources of risk in educational investment. A student (borrower) cannot be sure of his own ability to repay a loan. Lenders will view student loans as risky because of variations in students' abilities and motivation. The high levels of investment needed for some kinds of professional education necessitate lengthy repayment periods, in turn increasing lenders' uncertainty about borrowers' abilities to repay. Moreover, students may develop a distaste for the process of education itself, leading them to curtail their self-investment before they had planned to do so.

The proper governmental policy in these cases, as in other instances of capital-market imperfections, is to bring the private (risky) rate of return into equilibrium with the social (risk-free) rate. One way to do this is for the government to insure loans to students as it insures home mortgages, in effect reducing the lender's risk to zero. Students would then be on a par with other borrowers of investible funds and would not invest in higher education unless they believed that the increase in their future incomes warranted such self-investment. Since there is no reason to believe that students' risk aversion is any more intense than that of other borrowers, the bias against educational investment should be eliminated by this policy.

## Information About the Returns to Education

There is no question that most students do not have accurate information about the value of different levels of education. In large part, this shortcoming arises because accurate information is scarce and poorly disseminated. As risk averters, accordingly, students will underinvest in education compared to what their level of investment would be if the rate of return were known.

In this case, the appropriate public policy is to provide information about the returns that students can expect from different amounts of education. To offer a complete guide to efficient investment, such information should be very detailed, including breakdowns by age, sex, race, residence, region, occupation, and "ability" (measured, perhaps, by standardized tests). Econometric studies of the value of education have not yet provided such detailed estimates of rates of return. Public policy should be concentrated on improving the quality of information of this type, rather than on offering blanket support for all types of higher education.

## Differences in Rates of Time-Preference

Some economists have argued that too little educational investment is undertaken because students' rates of time-preference are higher than those of the population at large. This argument is often applied to poor students and blacks in an attempt to explain high dropout rates. Rather than a high rate of time-preference, however, it seems likely that these groups have low expectations of their future incomes and that in many cases these expectations are well founded in past experience. Active governmental policies designed to increase the equality of opportunity, especially for blacks and residents of depressed regions such as Appalachia, probably would be effective in increasing the demand for higher levels of educational achievement. There is no evidence that rates of time-preference differ systematically among population groups, although they certainly may differ widely among individuals.

Some of the federal government's policies toward higher education are consistent with our conclusion that efficient public policies should be aimed at removing market imperfections. For example, the federal government increases the supply of loans to students directly, through extensions of capital to colleges and universities, and indirectly, by underwriting private loans through the Office of Education. Some studies of the private returns to education are supported by federal funds, although there is no broad program of financing such studies. But the bulk of the public funds used to finance education comes from state and local governments, whose expenditures all too often do not satisfy the criterion of allocational efficiency or of distributional equity.

# Patterns of Funding Education

Most expenditures on primary and secondary education are financed by the real property taxes levied by local governments. As we saw in Chapter 10, the incidence of this tax is probably close to proportional with respect to total income. The vocational training component of formal education can be assumed to lead to a proportional increase in all students' incomes, so that the net redistribution of income from the tax and vocational training "package" is nil. (At a more detailed level of analysis, we would have to note the slightly higher returns to low levels of education and the probable slight regressivity of the property tax, leading on balance to the same negligible redistribution of income.) The incidence of taxes used to fund the general education component of primary and secondary schooling can be thought of as representing a social judgment about the equitable means of financing these benefits, which are impossible to evaluate. In sum, there may be no significant redistribution from rich to poor (or vice versa) in the funding of lower-level education.

The principal transfer that arises in funding primary and secondary education is an intergenerational one. Especially with respect to the benefits of vocational education, the beneficiaries of lower-level schooling are primarily the students themselves. The costs of their schooling, however, are financed by taxes on their parents, who may eventually receive secondary benefits in either a monetary or a non-monetary form, and on other members of society who receive at most some benefits from the general education component of schooling. Although the size distribution of income may not be altered by this transfer, the age distribution of income and wealth certainly is affected. The cost of schooling through high school is at least $10,000 per child in most parts of the United States and is frequently considerably more. Since the rate of return to primary and secondary schooling is high, the value of this transfer to the student is well above this amount. Thus, the funding of lower-level education out of tax revenues creates a large transfer of income and wealth from older generations to younger ones.

The same intergenerational transfer applies when we shift our attention to higher education and supplemental training for dropouts and workers whose skills have become technologically obsolete. Public funding of higher education causes a number of transfers and allocational inefficiencies. First, by lowering the price of higher education to the student, public higher education induces overinvestment in education, especially by encouraging college attendance by some students who cannot profit from it. Second, public funding of particular institutions (state universities, colleges, and junior colleges) discriminates against private institutions offering education of equal caliber. Third is the intergenerational transfer that arises because students' vocational education is financed by older taxpayers at large. Fourth, the income size distribution of the beneficiaries of public support of higher education differs substantially from that of taxpayers at large.

This last point is a new one and needs some elaboration. Hansen and Weisbrod examined the subsidies that students in various California state institutions of higher education received in the form of the difference between the resource costs of their education and prices that they actually paid.[8] As we might expect, the subsidy was smallest ($720 per year) for junior college students, larger ($1400) for students in the state college systems, and highest ($1700) for those enrolled in the University of California system. Hansen and Weisbrod found a high correlation between family income and the institution in which a student was enrolled; thus, in 1964 the median family income of junior college students was $8800, that of state college attendees was $10,000, and that of enrollees in the University of California was $12,000. Since the tax structure of California (state and local taxes) was regressive or proportional up to the $25,000 level of family income, the distribution of tax payments was not as progressive as the distribution of subsidies. In particular, the annual net subsidy (the difference between the gross subsidy and average *total* state and local taxes) for families with a child in junior colleges was $40. Families with a child enrolled in state colleges received a $630 annual net subsidy, and those with a University of California student received an annual net subsidy of $790. In contrast, families without children enrolled in the state system of higher education paid a net transfer of $650 per year out of their median income of only $7900.

It is difficult to justify this redistribution of income. It is not efficient, for the external benefits from higher education are unlikely to be very valuable. It cannot be equitable if society's concept of equity is that embodied in either the personal income tax or the (nearly proportional) overall federal, state, and local tax structure. It does not promote equality of educational opportunity, for it does not make higher education *relatively* more available to students from poor families than to those from rich ones. On the basis of this redistribution and the misallocations mentioned earlier, we can only conclude that current methods for funding public higher education in California and probably in other states as well are inferior from the standpoints of equity and efficiency to a system of charging students for the full resource cost of their education, as long as the latter system includes some distributional transfers and public policies to eliminate market imperfections.

Redistributional aspects also dominate the benefits of remedial and retraining programs such as the Job Corps and the Manpower Development and Training Act. These programs are usually defended as efficient investments in human resources, a claim that becomes embarrassing when studies of the increase in labor productivity conclude that the net benefits of the programs are close to zero and in many cases are probably negative. This approach to evaluating such programs ignores their two most important characteristics: (1) they confer sizable externalities in the way that any other program of lower-level vocational education confers external benefits; (2) they are a means for transferring income from rich to poor. Public funding of such programs may be justified, regardless of their net benefits (or benefit-cost ratio), if the combination of the externalities they confer and the amount and direction of redistribution they provide makes them attractive to the electorate.

## Summary

Both vocational and general education confer private and public benefits. Lower-level (primary and secondary) education has a strong general component, which perhaps confers more public benefits than private ones. Some secondary and nearly all higher education is vocational, with some public benefits but, especially in the case of higher education, primarily private ones in the form of increased labor productivity.

Because of its public benefits, primary and secondary education should be supported publicly. There is no evidence, however, that the supply conditions of education necessitate public supply. Just such a separation of public demand and private supply is at the heart of Friedman's voucher scheme, which would enable the public sector to express the benefits that it receives from education while letting individual students and parents express the strength of their own demands. Although this approach would justify supporting some (lower-level and remedial) vocational education, it suggests that governments should not support higher education.

Nonetheless, a basis for public action can be found in the existence of market imperfections that make the allocation of resources to higher education inefficient. The presence of risk aversion justifies public insurance programs that would make the private discount rate for "human capital" investments equal to the social rate of return on other investments. Students' lack of information about the returns to education provide an incentive for the public sector to make this information available in a sufficiently detailed manner to be useful inputs to students' investment decisions. These policies should eliminate whatever bias exists in investment markets against making investments in human capital.

Actual patterns of public funding for education are extensively redistributional. Even though state and local funding of primary and secondary education probably is close to neutral with respect to total income, it creates a large intergenerational transfer in favor of the young. When we consider higher education, however, we find that usual methods of funding public institutions lead to a large net subsidy in favor of high-income families at the expense of the poor. This subsidy arises because students do not pay the full resource cost of their education and because enrollees in institutions of higher learning come predominantly from high-income families while taxes fall more heavily on low-income families. Redistributional effects also arise with remedial education and retraining programs, but in these cases the redistribution is in favor of the poor. Even if these programs lead to negative net benefits, they may be justified by the externalities that they confer and the redistribution that they accomplish.

# Notes

1. Alfred Marshall, *Principles of Economics*, 8th ed. (New York: Macmillan, 1959), pp. 176-77.

2. W. Lee Hansen, "Total and Private Rates of Return to Investment in Schooling," *Journal of Political Economy* 71 (April 1963): 128-40; and Gary Becker, *Human Capital* (New York: National Bureau of Economic Research, 1964).

3. An efficient subsidy would be simply a grant of either income or medical services to give low-income families access to medical care. For some evidence that the market for medical services is inefficient and that direct subsidies are ineffective, see Martin Feldstein, "The Rising Price of Physicians' Services," *Review of Economics and Statistics* 52 (May 1970): 121-33.

4. Werner Z. Hirsch, *The Economics of State and Local Government* (New York: McGraw-Hill, 1970), pp. 176-82 and Table 8-1.

5. Milton Friedman, *Capitalism and Freedom* (Chicago: University of Chicago Press, 1962), ch. 6.

6. Although such objectives can be introduced compatibly with Friedman's proposal, his own preference is for none at all to be imposed.

7. Henry M. Levin, "The Failure of the Public Schools and the Free Market Remedy," *Urban Review* 2 (June 1968): 32-37.

8. W. Lee Hansen and Burton A. Weisbrod, "The Search for Equity in the Provision and Finance of Higher Education," in Joint Economic Committee, *The Economics and Financing of Higher Education in the United States* (1969), pp. 107-23.

# Major Themes (1973)

## CARNEGIE COMMISSION

**1.** From the point of view of individual and national welfare, higher education is one of the most important qualitative services in the United States. Quantitatively, colleges and universities account for expenditures totaling about one-fortieth of our national production of goods and services—2.5 percent. How higher education is financed is of substantial significance to millions of individuals and to society as a whole.

**2.** Higher education in the United States now costs 1970-71 data) about $22 billion in *monetary outlays* for the educational and living expenses of students. Counting also the net loss of potential income to students, the *economic costs* are about $39 billion. . . .

Monetary outlays are borne about one-third by students and their parents, and about two-thirds by public sources and philanthropy.[1] In terms of economic costs, however, the figures are reversed—students and their parents bear about two-thirds of the burden and public sources and philanthropy about one-third. (See Chart 1.)

From the point of view of social justice, the distribution of economic costs is more important than the distribution of monetary outlays alone. Thus a basic question is: are economic costs assessed in some rough proportion to benefits?

**Chart 1**
**Costs of higher education**

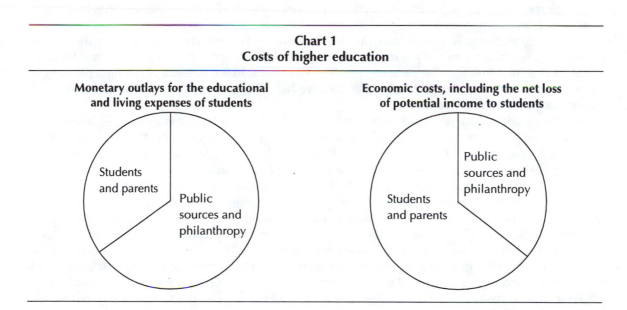

Monetary outlays for the educational and living expenses of students

Students and parents

Public sources and philanthropy

Economic costs, including the net loss of potential income to students

Public sources and philanthropy

Students and parents

An alternative method of looking at economic costs is to count only the subsistence costs of students and not the part also of forgone earnings that exceeds subsistence costs. Such an approach gives rise to a different balance between private and public total costs. We strongly favor the forgone earnings approach, however. There is a clear cost in output to the economy of college attendance as compared with the employment of students in gainful occupations. And, while it is true that the alternative to education for some students would be consumption (travel or leisure) and not work production, for most students it would be employment. And this is increasingly the situation as more students enroll from low-income families, as the average age of students rises, and as more young persons are "independent" at age 18. The economy forgoes current output and most individuals involved forgo current income.

**3.** Benefits take many forms. Some are individual and accrue to the direct recipients of education; among other advantages are a higher income, a more satisfying job, greater effectiveness as a consumer, greater ability in allocating time as well as money, direct enjoyment of the educational process and its related activities, and lifetime enhancement of cultural and other experiences. Some benefits are social and accrue to nonrecipients as well as to direct recipients of education; among the gains are greater economic growth based on the general advancement of knowledge and elevation of skills and on the higher proportion of the population in the labor force and the enhanced mobility of members of the labor force; greater political effectiveness of a democratic society based on the more adequate knowledge and more active participation of citizens; greater social effectiveness of society through the resultant better understanding and mutual tolerance among individuals and groups; the more effective preservation and extension of the cultural heritage; the greater ability of individuals and groups to accept and adjust to rapid change; and the greater potential contribution of educated parents to the welfare of their children.

**4.** No precise—or even imprecise—methods exist to assess the individual and societal benefits as against the private and the public costs. It is our judgment, however, that the proportion of total economic costs now borne privately (about two-thirds) as against the proportion of total economic costs now borne publicly (about one-third) is generally reasonable.[2] We note that for one item—additional earned income by college graduates—about two-thirds is kept privately and about one-third is taken publicly in the form of taxes. We also note that this two-thirds to one-third distribution of total economic costs has been a relatively stable relationship for a substantial period of time (although the internal components of each share have changed—for example, the private share is now more heavily composed of forgone income and less of tuition charges). . . .

We see no strong reason to change this distribution in any revolutionary fashion either in the direction of full costs privately borne or full costs publicly borne, although there are forceful advocates for fundamental change in each of these directions. In the absence of stronger proof than we have seen or stronger arguments than we have heard, we accept the current distribution of burden as generally reasonable.

We recognize, of course, that there are some negative results of higher education—for example, the individual frustrations resulting from the current surplus of Ph.D.'s and the public unhappiness with past outbreaks of campus disruption—and we have sought to take them into account in reaching our judgment. We also recognize that, without any public subsidy, some of the social benefits of higher education would come as *side effects* of privately financed education in any case. Whether this would be entirely fair is another question. But some benefits would not come at all or at least not to the same extent, such as greater equality of opportunity through higher education and much basic research, and each of these is of great social importance.

In the absence of better knowledge about the relationships between specific subsidies and the specific social benefits that may in part or in whole be dependent upon the subsidies, it is our view that historical arrangements should not now be suddenly rearranged; that we should be cautious in what we do, and that, in any event, public opinion would need to be better prepared than it now is for any drastic changes such as full-cost pricing to the student or full-cost pricing to the public. We believe that history and myriad public and private decisions have given us, for the present time at least, a generally acceptable balance in the distribution of overall costs between the private and the public sectors as compared with the distribution of benefits.

**5.** We do see, nevertheless, several specific adjustments that should be made and that, if made, would yield greater justice. In their totality—and they should be viewed as a totality—these changes are both substantial and important to improved national welfare:

(1) *A temporary reduction in the comparative charge of monetary outlays to private individuals and an equivalent increase in public funding* in order to make possible the attendance of more students from low-income families dependent upon public support. We say *temporary* because the rising level of incomes will reduce over time the need for this additional public support. The current private share of monetary outlays thus might drop somewhat and then gradually rise again. We define as *temporary* at least the next decade.

(2) *A redistribution in total governmental costs from the states and localities to the federal government.* The federal government has a larger and more expansible income than do the states and localities, and it is collected on the basis of more progressive taxes. Also the federal government has a special interest in and responsibility for equality of opportunity—this is a national promise, and the states, given their varied economic situations, cannot provide equivalent opportunities in any event. The federal government, additionally, bears responsibilities for basic research; for training of high-level and highly mobile skilled persons such as medical doctors and Ph.D.'s; for invention and innovation in the structures and processes of higher education; and for providing a nationwide student loan program. The states (and local governments) now bear the total governmental costs of higher education on a ratio of about 57.5 to 42.5 percent (see *Table 1*) in comparison with federal support, and we suggest that this become more nearly 50 to 50. About 20 percent of the federal 42.5 percent now takes the form of veterans' benefits; as these benefits are reduced drastically over time, the opportunity is created for the federal government to increase its funds for equality of opportunity more generally without raising the expenditures in total—about $1 billion a year is potentially available. Thus we suggest that the federal share rise to 50 percent and remain there even as veterans' benefits are reduced.

Federal interests in equality of opportunity, in basic research and in high-level professional skills, in particular, have risen over the past two decades, and the federal government, given its tax structure, also obtains most of the tax benefits from the added incomes of the more highly educated. The states now make most of the governmental investment in higher education and the federal government reaps most of the gain through tax receipts.

This is not to suggest that state effort should decline—quite the contrary; more students will be in public institutions, costs per student will rise, more state support will go to private institutions, more state tuition grants will go to students at both public and private institutions—but rather to suggest that federal effort should increase faster than state effort, particularly in the area of supporting equality of opportunity. The federal share, as we calculate it, is less than the federal government currently calculates it to be. We do not count the unsubsidized portions of federal loan programs as a federal contribution, since they are subject to repayment by the borrowers. Loans can be very helpful, but they are not gifts.

(3) *A redistribution of student subsidies in favor of those from low-income families.* Students are now subsidized indirectly through tuitions that are less than the costs of education and directly through student aid. Total subsidies may now be nearly adequate in amount, but they require some major redistribution to accomplish equity goals. Perhaps as much as two-thirds or more of all subsidies,[3] and certainly at least one-half, take the place of private expenditures, since the private expenditures would be made if the subsidies did not exist—the students would go to college in any event. These subsidies are "replacements" for private funds that would otherwise be forthcoming.

We favor a gradual redistribution of subsidies (a) by charging higher tuition to those who can afford to pay it—rising over a period of years; and (b) by providing more aid to students from lower-income families, particularly through the full funding of the Basic Opportunity Grants program provided by the Education Amendments of 1972,[4] and through liberalization, for lower-division students, of the limitation on the proportion of student costs that can be covered.

We believe that the President and the Congress made an historic step toward greater equality of opportunity through higher education in the Higher Education Act of 1972. It is of great importance that it be fully funded and that the 50-percent limitation be raised at least for lower-division students.

We believe that it is reasonable to move toward a redistribution of subsidies so that more like one-third rather than two-thirds would replace private funds. We do not believe that it is reasonable at this time to suggest that more subsidies than this be replaced by private funds that otherwise could and would be paid. The tradition of history is too strong in favor of broader subsidies; the politics of a democracy with a strong middle class run against it; and there are some adjustment problems, in any event, in phasing one level of subsidy into the next and then into none at all. But net subsidies (and subsidies adjusted for taxes paid) are as great for families in middle-income groups as they are for those from the lowest-income group. This "middle class" generally, considering the relatively high percentage of college-age youth from this income group that goes to college, does quite well in the proportions of public subsidies that it receives. Greater equity can be achieved through a reasonable redistribution of subsidies. A policy of low tuition by itself does no good for a student who cannot afford to go to college even at low tuition.[5]

The basic responsibility for equalizing opportunity should be carried as a public cost, and particularly at the federal level, and not as a cost assessed against individual institutions of higher education or against other students. Greater responsibility for these costs by the federal government (and by the states) would do much to ease the financial problems of many private institutions that tend to run their heaviest deficits in the student-aid area. We believe that these costs, in all equity, should be borne by the public at large and not by private institutions or by fellow students.

The general effort, however accomplished, should be to do less for those who now benefit most and to do more for those who now benefit least.

(4) *An increase in subsidies to institutions in the private sector* without injuring the public sector. Graduates from private colleges and universities make the same contributions to social benefits as do those from public colleges and universities. Private colleges and universities also provide a substantial proportion of the diversity that marks American higher education. They are now, however, threatened by the growing tuition gap between public and private institutions. Many of them have reached a peril point in their financing. This should be a source of great public concern.

We believe that the states should increasingly support private institutions in ways that best preserve institutional independence, and that also make possible, in particular, the attendance of more students from low-income families. We especially favor aid through students in order to help preserve the independence of the private institutions and to increase the options open to students. We favor comparatively greater aid to low-income students so that they may have a better chance to attend private colleges if they so desire and so that the private colleges may have a student body more balanced among income classes—they should not be forced into becoming "class-status" schools nor should low-income students be impelled to go only to public institutions. Clear class-stratification between private and public institutions would be quite unwise.

Thus we prefer that states make tuition grants to students in accordance with their ability to pay. Federal funding of the State Incentive Grants program in the Higher Education Act of 1972 would encourage the states to embark upon or expand such programs. As such programs are introduced or extended, low-income students can be given a better chance to attend college and can have more options between public and private institutions open to them. At the same time, private institutions can be assisted in obtaining larger enrollments, meeting their costs, and getting a more balanced student body.

Only the states can gear together tuition policies at public institutions and tuition grants to students attending both public and private institutions. The states, and only the states can construct effective programs in these areas. Also, the states, and not the federal government, should take basic responsibility for *institutional* welfare within higher education.

Situations vary greatly from state to state in the proportion of students in private and in public institutions, and in other ways. There are, also, a number of alternative means of aiding private institutions. While we believe that tuition grants to lower-income students are a preferred device both for aiding such students and for the institutions they choose to attend, we also believe that there should be considerable diversity and experimentation among the states.

Private institutions must recognize that the more public funds they receive, the more accountable they will be held by public authorities. It is not likely to be possible to get subsidies on an "arbitrary amount" basis with no formulas for the amount and no reporting on its use. Private institutions must be prepared to consider methods of accountability along with methods of public funding.

Private institutions do, of course, now receive some indirect public subsidies, as well as some direct help from the federal government and from some of the states. Tuition on the average covers about three-fifths of educational costs, gifts and endowments about one-fourth, and direct public contributions about one-sixth. All of the direct public contributions and about half of gifts and endowments (because of forgone taxes) are a burden on public sources. Also, private institutions of higher education, along with public ones, do not pay property taxes and usually do not pay local assessments for public services, and parents of dependent students receive a personal income tax deduction. Thus, perhaps, the direct and indirect public subsidy is already 25 to 30 percent of the educational costs in private institutions. The public subsidy of public institutions is, however, more than 80 percent, since tuition covers less than 20 percent of educational costs.

The suggestions we make would greatly aid private institutions by (a) public assumption of more of the costs of student aid, (b) narrowing the gap between private and public tuition levels, and (c) providing tuition grants to lower-income students or in other ways assisting private colleges.

**6.** We make these additional suggestions:

(1) Tuition in private colleges and universities is likely to continue to rise, as it has historically, at about the rate of the rise in per capita disposable personal income[6] (a rough measure of rising ability to pay) or preferably at a somewhat slower rate; that it should rise faster than this in public colleges and universities until it reaches the level of about one-third of the educational costs of institutions as compared with the current one-sixth, in order (among other reasons) to narrow the tuition gap; and total student aid should rise sufficiently so that no one now going to college will be denied the opportunity because of rising tuition and so that others who cannot now go for financial reasons be able to attend. *We are opposed to any increase in tuition at public institutions except as such increases are offset by the availability of adequate student aid for lower-income students.*

We do not suggest that tuition at public colleges rise, even in the very long run, to the full amount of the educational costs of institution, but rather that it might rise to about one-third of institutional educational costs, roughly in keeping with a division of total economic costs, two-thirds to students and parents and one-third to public sources and philanthropy as discussed above. This calculation assumes that all forgone earnings are included in total economic costs.

If public tuition were to rise to around one-third of educational costs, this would considerably narrow the gap with private tuition, which now offsets about three-fifths of the educational costs at private institutions. This does not imply that private tuition would then be less than twice as high as public tuition. (It is now on the average about four times as high at the undergraduate level.) The ratio would be more like 2-1/2 to 1, since educational costs at private institutions are higher by about 15 percent than at public institutions. This proposed adjustment, however, would substantially reduce the ratio that now exists. We believe the resulting gap in tuition would be both reasonable and viable. The historic ratio has been about 3 to 1, but the dollar gap in absolute terms is, of course, greater as costs rise and the absolute differences in tuition are important as well as the ratio.

We suggest that public tuition be set at about one-third of educational costs as a *general* rule, subject to adjustments for a low-tuition policy in public community colleges, for possible special consideration to Ph.D. candidates, and for other particular situations.

We regret the necessity of recommending any rise in public tuition, but (a) public tuition has been lagging behind private tuition very considerably in recent times, (b) greater equity in treatment between high- and low-income students requires some rise in tuition for those who can pay as well as more subsidies for those who cannot, and (c) public tuition is less of a burden on many families than it once was as the general level of incomes has risen. Also, many private institutions now have an excess capacity that will only be used as they appear more attractive to students on a comparative basis, including tuition costs. Additionally, the competition between public and private institutions is now too heavily based on price considerations alone. Both systems would benefit if the competition were based more on quality of effort.

It will take some time for public tuition to rise to one-third of educational costs without departing too greatly from recent developments. Public tuition has risen over the past five years at a rate 20 percent faster than the rate of increase in per capita disposable income during the period 1960 to 1972. If this faster rate of increase of tuition were to continue, and if educational costs were to rise at the same rate as per capita disposable income (which is the long term tendency), it would take a very long time (well into the twenty-first century!) for public tuition to reach one-third of educational costs. To reach the one-third in one decade (1983) would take a rise of up to twice the rate of increase in per capita disposable income (or an increase of about 10 to 12 percent per year in tuition if per capita disposable income were to rise 5.8 percent per year as it did from 1960 to 1972).

Our views about tuition take into account the fact, set forth later, that the "real" cost of tuition (adjusted for general inflation) has remained stable for 40 years, while the "real" cost of public subsidies has tripled during this same period of time.

(2) Tuition should vary by level of education and thus by level of costs—less at the lower division than at the upper division and less at the upper division than at the graduate level. Costs at these levels now run on the ratio of about 1 to 1-1/2 to 3 or more, but tuition is more nearly 1 to 1 to 1 in many institutions. We do not mean to suggest—quite the contrary—that lower-division education *should* cost less than upper-division education. We only note this as a current fact. We strongly favor, instead, a major redistribution of resources into lower-division teaching. Currently, however, lower-division students pay a higher proportion of their total educational costs than do upper-division or graduate students. They are, in some situations, actually subsidizing the more advanced students. We especially favor low tuition at the lower-division level so that students may be given a better chance to get at least this much higher education and to try out their interests in academic life—they are often quite undecided at this stage. We do not favor a comparatively high tuition barrier against getting started in higher education as compared with continuing in it; such a barrier is more likely to discourage low-income than high -income students.

We particularly favor raising comparative tuition at the graduate level because of (a) the higher costs at this level, (b) the growing surplus of Ph.D.'s, (c) the greater opportunities of graduate students to support themselves as teaching assistants, as research assistants, and in other ways, (d) the comparatively high incomes for those who enter professional fields, and (e) the reality that many of the "externalities" or social benefits from higher education in political and social behavior will have been developed at the undergraduate level, if they are developed at all, and will not be increased much by graduate study. We recognize, however, that graduate schools are in great competition for the best students, and that this tends to drive down the price charged to graduate students as compared with the price charged to undergraduate students. Also, faculty members in universities with graduate students tend to prefer graduate to undergraduate students. The setting of policies for graduate tuition is an exceedingly complex matter. Situations vary greatly as among the M.A. level, the Ph.D. level, the several professional fields, and in other ways.

Overall, we believe that tuition should be more nearly proportional to costs, rather than regressive as against students at the lower levels. Thus we favor separately determined tuition levels for:

> The associate in arts degree
>
> The B.A. and M.A. degrees
>
> The Ph.D. degree
>
> Other advanced professional degrees.

(3) A much improved national loan program should be developed. Students will increasingly assume more financial responsibility for themselves at earlier ages for several reasons, including reaching their majority at age 18. With more "stop-outs" for young persons and more "recurrent" education for older persons, the average age of students may rise (it is now 25 in the California community college system), and students will have higher costs because of greater family responsibilities. Public subsidies are likely to decrease in the long run as incomes rise, as less comparative educational deprivation must be overcome among segments of the American population, and as all remnants of deficits of highly trained manpower tend to disappear. Thus, other sources of income will need to be found. If both parents and the public come to feel less financial responsibility, the students will need to assume more responsibility, and an effective loan program will be necessary to make this possible. In any event, some greater charge to the users as compared with nonusers seems both equitable and inevitable in the long run—currently about one-third of adults are or have been users of subsidized higher education, and two-thirds are not and have not been.

The current national loan program has at least four major disadvantages—it does not provide for major or even for catastrophic risks, it is subject to a heavy default rate, it forgives rather than postpones interest while the student is in college, which can encourage undue short-term borrowing, and it makes no special allowance for the nonworking wife in a lower-income family. A better loan program is an urgent necessity.

7. We suggest funding in terms of major accounts as follows:

- Basic research by government, mostly federal, and by philanthropy on the merit of individual projects.

- Auxiliary enterprises by charges to the users.

- Service activity by charges to the users, where possible, and by the appropriate level of government, where not possible.

- Student aid basically by government—primarily the federal government—primarily the federal government—and by philanthropy.

- Teaching by a combination of tuition, adjusted through state tuition grants for ability to pay; of philanthropy; and of government support, primarily state and local. We do not consider it to be either wise or necessary for the federal government to assume responsibility for basic institutional support for teaching in its totality.

- Net forgone earnings by the users, with subsistence costs met through student aid on the basis of need.

- Loan programs provided basically by the federal government with provision for full repayment, over variable periods of time as related to income, by the individual borrowers except in very special personal circumstances.

**8.** We cannot answer the very basic question of whether total economic costs of higher education are matched or more than matched by the total benefits. Institutional costs of higher education now account for about 2.5 percent of the GNP. If recent trends continue, this percentage will run to 3.3 percent in 1980. We have suggested elsewhere (*The More Effective Use of Resources,* 1972) that this percentage can be held to 2.7 percent without loss of quality while increasing equality of opportunity. There is no known way to prove whether more or less than this percentage of the GNP should be spent on higher education as compared with each and all of the other ways the GNP might be spent. The suggested figure of 2.7 percent for 1980, however, appears reasonable in our general judgment about the allocation of resources.

Were it possible to determine scientifically what percentage of the GNP should be spent on higher education, however, it would not be possible within the American system to do much about it. Our economy is not totally planned with a central budget that is disaggregated. Instead, expenditure patterns are aggregated from myriad individual and group decisions. Parents and students decide how much tuition they are willing to pay and how much money they are otherwise willing to spend for educational purposes. Federal agencies decide how much research they want. Donors decide how much money they want to give. States decide on what subsidies they wish to provide. A very large number of decisions are made by a very large number of people, and they add up to a certain percentage of the GNP. The real question is, then, whether the decision-making processes are generally good ones—do the right people have good enough information to make the right decisions under the right circumstances for the right reasons? We generally accept the decision-making processes now in effect, with the one major exception that we favor gradually more reliance on the market choices of students.

**9.** No "equal and exact justice" is possible, however desirable, in the distribution of the costs of and benefits from higher education. Among other reasons, the problems are too complex and the available data too inadequate. We are concerned, however, that a greater approximation to justice could be achieved if the changes we recommend were put into effect, and we believe they should be given a high order of priority. The directions, as we see them, are:

- A short-term increase in the public share of monetary costs for education to be followed by a long-term increase in the private share until it again reaches about current proportions

- A redistribution of the governmental burden from the states and localities toward the federal government

- A redistribution of student subsidies from higher- to lower-income groups

- A greater amount of support for private colleges and universities

- A comparative, although modest and gradual, rise in public as against private tuition

- A reevaluation of tuition policy to gear it more to the actual costs of education by level of the training

- Greater reliance on better loan programs in the longer-run future and on charges to users

- Careful conservation in the use of resources to minimize the rising impact on the GNP.

We also are concerned that the totality of funds available to higher education be adequate.

The recommendations we make in this report are aimed at these results. (For a schematic outline of most of these recommendations see Table 1.) These recommendations should be considered all at once, and no one recommendation should be taken out of the context of this total additive approach to financing—for example, the raising of tuition without an increase in student aid.

This series of recommendations reflects some hard choices in the contest among groups of people and institutions for comparative preferment. We have favored in our proposals:

- A larger public and a smaller private share of monetary outlays for education on a temporary basis in order to make possible greater equality of educational opportunity

- A greater comparative burden on the federal government as compared with the states and localities

- A greater advantage to lower-income and a lesser advantage to higher-income students

- A more competitive tuition situation for private as compared with public institutions

- A greater consideration for lower-division as compared with upper-division and graduate students in tuition policy.

### Table 1
### Suggested directions of movement in financing higher education, 1973 to 1983

| | Actual 1973 | Proposed 1983 |
|---|---|---|
| Percentage of the GNP expended on institutional costs of higher education | 2.5 | 2.7 |
| Private share of monetary outlays on education, in percentages | 37.0 | 34.0 |
| Governmental and philanthropic share of total monetary outlays on education, in percentages | 63.0 | 66.0 |
| Federal share of total governmental costs for higher education, in percentages | 42.5 | 50.0 |
| State and local share of total governmental costs for higher education, in percentages | 57.5 | 50.0 |
| Percentage of student subsidies that are "replacements" of private funds | 66.0 | 33.0 |
| State support of private institutions, or for students attending them | 35 states | 50 states |
| Percentage of educational costs at private institutions met by tuition | 60.0 | 60.0 |
| Percentage of educational costs at public institutions met by tuition | 17.0 | 33.0 |
| Ratio of private to public tuition at the undergraduate level* | 4.0 to 1** | 2.5 to 1 |
| Tuition policy as related to cost by level of instruction | Generally equal tuition regardless of level of costs | Tuition geared more to costs by level of instruction |
| Loan programs | Moderate emphasis | Greater emphasis and substantial improvement in terms |

*Costs at private institutions now average 15 percent higher than at public institutions. This percentage will rise somewhat as the mix of students in public institutions shifts in the direction of community and comprehensive colleges.

**The ratio is 4.9:1 when comparing charges for typical in-state undergraduates in public institutions and comparable charges at private colleges and universities; based on total FTE enrollment in the public and private sectors, however, the ratio is 4.3:1.

Not everybody can be comparatively better off in every way at the same time. The issues at stake are very substantial. We are considering here the means of financing one of the most important series of services in American society.

**10.** We recognize that, at some point in the future, the United States may need a more drastic overhaul of the financing of postsecondary education than we suggest here. However, the steps we do suggest are essential and, we believe, they can and should be undertaken now.

History has given us a very complex system of financing postsecondary education and one that is also deeply embedded in legislation and in expectations; thus it is not easy to change. Concern about this system of financing, however, has greatly increased in recent years and we expect that the level of this concern will be maintained and perhaps even heightened in the future. Factors at work include:

- The increase by nearly 2-1/2 times in a single decade in the percentage of the GNP being spent on institutional costs of higher education—from 1960 to 1970.

- The greater concern for equality of opportunity to attend college, and also for current inequities in subsidies between those who do and those who do not go to college. As more and more young people do go to college, these imbalances in subsidies will become both more serious and more publicly evident.

- The battle among the federal, state, and local governments over the responsibility for financing programs in the area of human welfare.

- The higher proportion of enrollments in institutions under public control. The system of higher education was once largely private, and financed more by philanthropy and less out of the public purse. It is now largely public and becoming more so.

- The perilous financial condition of some private colleges.

- The rising standard of family income that creates greater general ability to pay. Also, the demand for higher education is income elastic—it rises faster than incomes rise, and incomes keep on rising.

- The emancipation of youth with its reduced sense of dependence on family guidance and support, and a concomitant potentially reduced sense of responsibility by parents and other adults. Achievement of legal majority at age 18 is a social factor of very great potential significance. Among other things, it can change the definition of who is a resident of a particular state, with great implications for in-state and out-of-state tuition levels.

- The changing labor market that finds fewer deficits and more surpluses of academically trained persons, and thus creates less national need for constantly increasing enrollments.

- The continuing tensions between the "adversary culture" followed by some persons on campus and large elements of the public.

- The increasing element of *consumption* in a college education—(1) more current attention to personal enjoyment on campus through a more responsive environment and (2) more preparation for an interesting life, as through training in the creative arts. *Consumption functions* are inherently more of a private concern than are *production functions*.

- Economists who once neglected this area of financing are now studying it with more and more depth and perception. More highly trained analysts are at work within federal and state agencies dealing with the financing of higher education.

Thus we have a complicated and embedded system of financing of postsecondary education, but one that is now subject to major and continuing pressures. It is highly unlikely that these pressures will not result in some major changes. Consequently, the financing of higher education will and should remain on the agenda for continuing examination for the foreseeable future. Any report on it, as a consequence, must be *interim* in nature, as is this one. Basic questions will be under discussion for a long time, not only about where we would like to be but also about how we get from here to there. We set forth in this report our current views of where we are, of where we think we should be, and of how we should manage the transition between the two.

# Notes

1.  Inclusion of calculated capital costs with operating costs adds about 12 to 15 percent to monetary outlays, and shifts the burden somewhat more heavily toward public sources and philanthropy, which bear a heavier share of capital costs than of operating costs.

2.  Bowen and Servelle (1972, Sec. 9) have recently reached much the same conclusion: that it is reasonable to have about a two-thirds private and one-third public sharing of the total economic costs.

    We define *private* costs for these purposes as those borne by the family unit (parents and students), and *public* costs as those borne by government agencies and philanthropy. The former might alternatively be called *personal* and the latter *nonpersonal* costs. Philanthropy, of course, is a different phenomenon than direct governmental support, although about one-half of philanthropy consists of taxes forgone by public bodies. *Governmental costs* are those borne by federal, state, and local governments.

3.  See Peltzman (1973).

4.  Hereafter, these amendments will be referred to as the Higher Education Act of 1972, a designation commonly used.

5.  See Hoenack (1971).

6.  See O'Neill (1973). Over the past few years, it has risen faster than this historic rate. It is unlikely this will happen in the future, however, because of the increasing competition for students.

# A Strategy for Better-Targeted and Increased Financial Support (1973)

## Committee for Economic Development

The funding gap facing the colleges can be attacked not only by better management of resources (as set forth in previous chapters) but also by securing more income from public and private sources. Earlier in this statement, we expressed our judgment that increased government support might be expected to match increased enrollment and increases in the cost of living and that such support per student in real terms would be maintained. If the cost of instruction per student continues to rise considerably faster than the cost of living, a funding gap will remain that can be met only from private sources. In this chapter, we review the pattern of financing for colleges and outline a strategy that can be expected to increase the resources available to the colleges and at the same time improve educational opportunity for students from lower-income families.

In order to understand how the funding pattern can be improved, it is necessary to know what that pattern is. Funding for undergraduate education flows through various channels from four sources: students and their families, state and local governments, the federal government, and gifts and endowments. These flows are traced in the Annex, which describes the financing system for the academic year 1969-70.

Families and students pay for nearly 60 per cent of all the costs associated with undergraduate education in the United States. By far the greater part of this expenditure is for food, housing, clothing, books, and other living expenses. These noninstructional costs constitute about 46 per cent of total expenditures for undergraduate education.

In developing a strategy for increasing financial support, we concentrate in this chapter on the instructional costs that account for the other 54 per cent of total expenditures for undergraduate education. These expenditures are funded largely (nearly 70 per cent) by government. State and local governments contribute nearly one-half of the monies used for undergraduate instructional purposes, and the federal government contributes about one-fifth. Parents and students finance about one-fifth of the expenditure. (However, on a gross basis, including government subsidies and allowances on behalf of students, parents and students pay two-fifths of the instructional bill through tuition and fees.) Gifts and endowment income fund approximately one-tenth of these costs. Although we believe that corporate and private giving should, and will, increase, the major source of increased support other than government is students and their parents.

This raises a central question. How should the costs of higher education be shared by society and individuals?

As we pointed out in discussing the basic purposes of higher education . . ., the benefits to society and the individual derived from undergraduate education are not mutually exclusive. It is clear that each gains both culturally and economically from higher education, with the benefits

61

appearing to accrue chiefly to society in some instances and to individuals in others. The education of individuals should benefit society by the extension of knowledge and skill, the cultivation of greater social intelligence and cultural vitality, and increased economic productivity. At the same time, an individual may generally be expected to benefit by increased income and an improved quality of life.[1]

The problem of funding colleges and universities would be simple if it were possible to assign some values of higher education exclusively to the individual and the remainder to society. The student and his family would pay the cost for the individual benefits realized, while society would pay for the balance through government and corporate appropriations and gifts. But a precise division of values and costs in this regard is quite impossible.

Because higher education produces extensive social values, we do not recommend that all or even most students be required to pay the full costs of their schooling through tuition and fees. On the contrary, we advocate government subvention of both institutions and individuals. Nevertheless, because of the benefits of education to the individual, we consider it appropriate for students and their families to pay as large a part of the cost as they can afford.

## Equalizing Opportunity by Grants to Students

We have raised the question of whether government support is effectively directed toward the goal of equalizing educational opportunity. We have found that to a marked degree those who stand in greatest need of assistance as college students because of disparities in family income are receiving a disproportionately small share of the support.

Analysis of how much government support is received by students from families with various income levels . . . shows that although government support has been greatest for low-income students, it has also been extensive for students from higher-income families. Moreover, support has been as great for students from higher-income families as for those from moderate-income families. With government support so distributed, it is not surprising to find that a college-age person from a family with annual income of $15,000 or more was almost five times more likely to be in college than one from a family with income of $3,000 or less. In our opinion, the present distribution of state and federal funding cannot bring about substantial improvement in the equality of opportunity in undergraduate education because aid is not concentrated on those who need it most. Moreover, as we shall show, correcting this faulty distribution of government aid by targeting it primarily to those who need it most can become a key factor in obtaining more resources for higher education.

We believe that the equalization of educational opportunity should be a major social goal and therefore a basic responsibility of government. State governments bear a large measure of the responsibility for in-state equalization, but general equalization extending beyond state systems is appropriately a task for federal government.

Equality of educational opportunity can conceivably be achieved in several ways. College costs for students who could not otherwise enroll can be reduced through (1) general grants to institutions, whether based on enrollment or on some other criterion; (2) grants to institutions based specifically on enrollment of lower-income students; or (3) direct grants to lower-income students. Which funding mode will most efficiently support the goal of equalizing opportunity?

General grants to institutions, the most common form of aid, can result in any of the following: an increase in institutional quality without an increase in tuition, a general reduction in tuition for all students, or an institutionally administered selective reduction in tuition for lower-income students. Only if the latter result occurred would the advantage of public support be equitably distributed in terms of need. For this reason we prefer the method of direct aid to low-income students. It ensures that public resources will in fact lower the personal cost of college attendance for the grant recipients. A program of grants to lower-income students can effectively concentrate public resources on the goal of equality of educational opportunity and at the same time provide additional support for the colleges.

We wish to make it entirely clear that although we favor the use of public money to equalize educational opportunity, we are not advocating that college and universities lower or abandon their academic standards. On the contrary, an individual's eligibility for a grant should be tied to his or her admission to a qualified institution. Public funds should be made available only to those who can profit from postsecondary education, whether in a college, university, or vocational; technical school. Every institution should guard against the temptation to permit the pursuit of equal opportunity to endanger the quality of education.

Although federal funding practices should be more or less constant throughout the country, state practices may be expected to vary. In some states, for instance, the tradition of private education is stronger than it is in others. In these states, individual student grants from public money may be more acceptable to the taxpayer than they would be in states where most higher education takes place in state-owned and state-operated institutions. State-funded student grants may be more acceptable in the East and Middle West than in areas where there are comparatively few private college and universities, notably the Southwestern, Rocky Mountain, and Pacific regions.

We recommend that federal funding of undergraduate education be primarily through grants and loans to individual students in accordance with their ability to pay. We also recommend that funding patterns of state governments place more emphasis on grants and loans to students according to the same criterion. We further urge that wherever possible the federal government employ its undergraduate financial assistance in a manner which will contribute to more equal educational opportunity among the states. The unequal financial status of these states places this responsibility on the federal government.

Because tuition typically does not cover the full cost of education, we believe that direct student grants should be accompanied by institutional grants to cover a part of the additional cost incurred by the enrollment of students receiving grants. We recognize that the present and recent practice of the federal government in joining institutional grants to graduate fellowships and traineeships has proved its value, and we believe it should be extended to future undergraduate student-grant programs.

Coupling institutional grants with student grants has particular importance not only for technical colleges but also for community colleges, which train large numbers of paraprofessionals and technicians. Such technical and occupational training is more costly, often considerably so, than traditional undergraduate education. At present, these low-tuition technical and community colleges are a major force in the equalization of educational opportunity. It is therefore vitally important to assure their continuance by covering at least part of the added costs that result from both remedial and technical training. This by no means gainsays the urgent need to provide much greater opportunities for those who are economically disadvantaged to attend liberal arts colleges and universities.

Because of the increased cost of educating the economically disadvantaged, we recommend that institutions enrolling such persons holding government-supported grants and loans receive appropriate institutional grants.

Although government student grants should be made directly to the individual recipients (perhaps on the pattern of GI payments), thus leaving them free to select their schools, we believe that it would be advisable for the government to contract with colleges and universities to provide services in support of the grants program. Otherwise it may be necessary to create a large and expensive bureaucracy to administer the grants. The determining factors here should be effectiveness in achieving the goal of equality of educational opportunity and efficiency in administering the funds.

# Enlarging the Student-Loan Program

As part of a more efficient use of government funds to support higher education, ample resources should be provided for loans to students to meet financial deficiencies from grants and from family resources. The student-loan market must ensure that youths from low- and moderate-income families, whose parents cannot contribute extensively (if at all) to their college education, will have access to capital. It may be detrimental to the academic success of these students to demand that they work extensively to finance a major share of their college expenses unless cooperative school–work programs operate at their institutions. Moreover, access to supplemental financial resources is also necessary to many middle- and upper-income families if they are to finance a greater share of college costs.

We recommend an expanded federally operated student-loan system to provide students and their families guaranteed access to supplemental funds. Past experience justifies continuing studies of loan programs and experimentation with structure and administration.

Although we are confident that middle- and upper-income groups can and will pay larger shares of college costs, it is unrealistic to require that all college expenses be paid out of current income and assets. Moreover, as college costs rise, the income level at which grants and loans are made available must also rise.

We recognize that both annual repayment levels and the risk involved in incurring large-scale, long-term debt may be important detriments to student borrowing. Furthermore, although loans are not unattractive alternatives to persons of typical middle-class economic experience, they may in other cases be formidable barriers to an education. This problem can probably be best handled by a loan program that permits (1) income-contingent repayments for low-income persons and (2) constant repayments for middle- and upper-income borrowers. Of course, there must be a limit on income-contingent loans to prevent overcommitment. Moreover, extended repayment terms should be possible, together with certain kinds of forgiveness features.

Government-sponsored loan programs to supplement student grants put market restraints on both students and institutions that may in the long run benefit the quality of individual education by strengthening institutional management. Another important aspect of extensive loan programs is the implicit recognition of the increasing maturity and independence of college-age students.

# Raising Low Tuition and Fees

The shift to increased federal funding through direct student grants and loans and increased emphasis on direct state aid to students, as opposed to institutional or institutionally administered programs, would alter considerably the support patterns and the tuition requirements of individual institutions. To the extent that this change achieves its objective, there would be an increase in the number of students from low-income families attending college. Because tuition income generally represents only a fraction of instructional cost, most colleges may not recapture (at present tuition levels) the whole of the institutional support they may have lost by the shift to funding through student grants and loans. Moreover, many of the disadvantaged students who would enroll under an expanded grant and loan program may require special instruction to remedy academic deficiencies, which would raise the cost of instruction. These adverse effects on colleges can be avoided by revising tuition charges. It should be emphasized that the shift from institutional to student grants and the increase in tuition are inseparable parts of the program.

The second part of our proposed strategy for increasing financial support for the colleges therefore calls for an increase in tuition charges where these are relatively low. They are, of course, generally low in public institutions. An increase in tuitions and fees would enable these colleges to recapture government aid from students receiving grants and, more importantly, to increase their income from students whose families are able to pay. The increase in tuition charges should be large enough to increase the total volume of resources available to the colleges.

We believe that tuition charges at many colleges and universities are unjustifiably low. We recommend an increase in tuitions and fees, as needed, until they approximate 50 per cent of instructional costs (defined to include a reasonable allowance for replacement of facilities) within the next five years. For two-year community colleges and technical colleges, we recommend that the increase be phased over ten years. Most of this increase may be expected to occur in the public sector.

The recommendation that the suggested increase in the case of community and technical colleges be phased over ten years gives recognition to the special problems of this group of institutions. As previously noted, instruction at community colleges tends to be high cost because of the technical or professional nature of the training and also because of the large numbers of disadvantaged students enrolled. Time should be allowed for these institutions to create long-range plans for the effective use of resources, to develop special funding for needed programs, to reduce duplication and redundant courses and facilities, to make consortia arrangements, and to make similar managerial and organizational improvements suggested elsewhere in this statement.

The dollar amount of the increase suggested (averaging $540 a student in universities and four-year colleges) is in line with increases actually realized by private colleges in the decade of the 1960s. Moreover, even after the increase, the level of tuition at public four-year colleges would be only about one-half that of private four-year colleges.

## Effects of Increasing Support Through Student Grants and Higher Education

If a policy of pricing tuition and fees at one-half of instructional costs had existed in the last decade, we estimate that the revenues of public undergraduate institutions in 1969-70 would have been increased by nearly $1.7 billion. (This assumes that the program was five years old and that two-year community colleges and technical colleges had raised tuition by only one-half the difference between current tuition and 50 per cent of cost.) Not all of this increase would have been a net increment to the resources available to support colleges. Some of the increased tuition revenues would have been provided as student grants or loans to low- and moderate-income students to enable them to meet higher tuition costs. We estimate that approximately $600 million of $1.7 billion would have been utilized to meet tuition increases. As a result of the increase in direct support by the colleges for low- and moderate-income students, few, if any, of these students would have faced higher college costs as a result of the tuition increases. We estimate that government grants to low-income students would have exceeded the tuition increase for all students whose family income (in 1969-70) was less than $8,600. The government grant program would therefore have stimulated attendance by students from lower-income families (see Annex).

The effect of the proposed changes in government support could greatly reduce the proportion of institutional support received by the colleges from government (from 77.7 to 38 per cent) and greatly increase the proportion of government support received through student grants. Most important, of course, would be a net increase in annual college income of $1.1 billion, or 18 per cent, from private sources.

It is important to recognize that under our proposal the increases in tuition are intended not to preceded but to follow or coincide with the availability of funds to the prospective students to pay that tuition. We are not proposing that institutions raise tuition under circumstances where the funds for that tuition will not be forthcoming.

The Committee is fully aware of the controversial nature, particularly within the academic community, of any recommendation to raise the tuitions of public institutions to approximately 50 per cent of instructional costs. We are aware also that to the extent that our recommendations produce shifts away from institutional funding they will incur considerable opposition. Several of the Subcommittee's nontrustee members and advisors and the project director have expressed their disagreement with these recommendations. We would like to note here their dissent from the position on these matters taken by the trustees.

# Relating Institutional Support to Social Goals

We have stated our conviction that funding should be related to goals and that the goals of education can best be achieved by a combination of institutional and student support from government. The large task of extending equality of educational opportunity can best be achieved by increased student grants and loans as we have recommended. The other basic goals of education can best be achieved by institutional grants and appropriations because these require direct institutional action in establishing and maintaining instructional programs.

In considering patterns of funding, we are conscious of the economic, social, and political realities of the present institutional structure. We are concerned not with some ideal society but with this country and its institutions over the foreseeable future. Qualified institutions now in existence must be adequately funded if individual students are to receive the educational opportunities we believe they should have and if the needed social gains from higher education are to be realized. Although important changes in methods can be made, the nation's educational establishment or social and political conventions cannot be simply abolished or completely reconstructed.

There are important differences between public and private institutions, and funding by public money should respect those differences. Public institutions are subject to governmental control and are expected to respond to public interests in a number of ways, in such matters as admission and retention and through such programs as continuing education and certain kinds of public service. The land-grant colleges are an excellent example of tax-supported institutions that have traditionally served broad, publicly conceived social goals. A private liberal arts college, on the other hand, may prefer to concentrate its energies on a specialty with limited social interests.

It is appropriate that public colleges and universities receive a larger percentage of their income from tax monies than private institutions. Moreover, governments grants to private institutions should take account of the income available to those institutions from private sources. Otherwise, those grants would generate disproportionate funding of private institutions that already have large incomes from nongovernmental funds. Private colleges and universities may be expected to continue to receive larger sums from private gifts than public institutions. In matters pertaining to religion, of course, funding with public money is subject to the law and court decisions.

We distinguish three major categories of funding that effectively relate the social goals of education to institutional support.

## General-purpose grants

The acquisition of knowledge and the stimulation of learning occur throughout the college years in all types of programs and in all types of institutions. This is the basic purpose of every educational institution. Therefore, a funding program designed to achieve this goal should not be restricted to specific institutions or types of institutions or to specific academic fields; rather, it should provide resources on an equitable basis to those colleges and universities that are capable of producing quality education.

We believe that the most equitable basis for the distribution of such funds is the total student enrollment at all undergraduate levels because that enrollment is an index of institutional costs. We recognize that different types of institutions have differing patterns of nongovernmental support, that they incur different levels of cost (e.g., technical colleges as compared with liberal arts colleges), and that therefore differential institutional grants based on institutional type are warranted. We believe that since the education of an informed citizenry should be a basic function of every postsecondary institution (a function that we expect of every college and university), this goal should also be supported by general institutional grants.

We recommend the continuation of general-purpose grants and appropriations to institutions as the primary form of funding by state and local governments. The amount of these grants and appropriations should be based on undergraduate enrollment and type of undergraduate institution. They should be available to all types of public or tax-supported institutions.

## Categorical Grants

We assume that it is advisable at various times for both federal and state legislatures to fund educational programs for achieving specific social objectives. Educational programs intended to satisfy professional and paraprofessional or other manpower demands are best served by categorical institutional grants designed to increase institutional quality and capacity in specific fields. Programs established in the past for such purposes as advancing science or improving space technology have been obviously successful. Now there are new needs—for example, in environmental management and other domestic areas affecting the quality of human life—where infusions of new resources are desirable. Today, few institutions can move into new educational programs, however valuable to society, without the new money that depends largely on categorical grants from federal and state or private sources.

We recommend a system of federal and state categorical grants to both public and private institutions to fund special educational programs designed to meet particular social objectives where those programs cannot be financed from regular budgets or private grants. We are especially conscious of the fact that some special programs (e.g., in advanced language and area studies) are of value to the nation as a whole, not simply to a single state or region, and that they therefore justify federal support.

## Contractual Arrangements

While some public institutions are overburdened with undergraduate students for whom they cannot provide adequate facilities and faculty, many private schools have space for additional students and in fact need more students to maintain their quality and meet their financial obligations. There are other situations in which considerations of economy indicate that private universities with long-established graduate and professional programs should make contractual arrangements with the state to expand their capacity and productivity rather than have the state duplicate them with new programs in public institutions.

It is clearly in the public interest in such instances to negotiate contracts that would supply public funds to private schools to enable them to enroll additional students and to carry on specified educational functions. Such arrangements can provide needed education at a financial saving to the public and at the same time contribute to the strength of private higher education.

We recommend that state and local governments contract with private colleges and universities to provide undergraduate, professional, and graduate education where public facilities are not adequate. In this way, underutilized private resources will be put to use instead of being duplicated at additional cost.

# Strengthening Voluntary Support of Higher Education

Finally, in recognition of the importance of private gifts and grants as a source of institutional income, we believe that public policies aimed at encouraging private financial support of colleges and universities (both public and private) should be maintained and strengthened.

Prior to the establishment of the land-grant colleges and state universities, private funds of this character constituted the most important single source of income to higher education. As a result of the growth of governmental support in the last hundred years, private giving has declined in relative importance as a component of total income, and today it accounts for less than 10 per cent of all funds received by all undergraduate institutions. . . . For a majority of the institutions, however, gift income continues to be a vital element in the financing of undergraduate education.

We believe that the importance of voluntary support of higher education transcends its relative magnitude as a component of institutional funding. For many institutions, these funds provide a vital margin for educational quality. They have made possible buildings, grounds, equipment, and other facilities that are indispensable parts of the physical plants of colleges and universities and have financed the appointment of first-rank scholars and teachers. They have made possible scholarships, grants, and other forms of student aid that otherwise would not have been available. New instructional programs and techniques and curricular changes of critical importance to education would have been impossible without them. Moreover, they have supported special efforts in connection with the particular educational requirements of certain groups, such as women, racial minorities, rural communities, and those gifted in the arts, sciences, and humanities. Finally, for many private colleges and universities, these funds often make the difference between survival and extinction.

We have concluded that the flow of private support is essential to the diversity, strength, and vitality of the nation's colleges and universities. It provides a means of achieving the high degree of independence and freedom indispensable to the attainment and preservation of superior quality in education. We therefore conclude that the encouragement of private support is very much in the national interest.

It is clear that public policy in general and tax policy in particular influence the extent to which individuals, corporations, foundations, and other donors are willing and able to support higher education. We urge that this influence be explicitly recognized in the formulation and implementation of public policy so that it will have a maximum favorable impact on educational philanthropy.

Changes in tax policy and other matters related to philanthropic giving may be proposed for reasons not related to the problems of higher education, and these changes, if enacted, could well have an adverse impact on the levels of private support of higher education. Such a development would seriously compound the existing and prospective problems of college and university funding. Specifically, it would add greatly to the needs of both private and public colleges and universities for additional public funds, and this requirement could gravely complicate our recommendations for governmental programs of educational support.

In view of these considerations, we urge that the existing tax incentives for voluntary support of higher education be maintained and, to the extent not incompatible with other objectives, expanded in order to strengthen the base of financial support of all colleges and universities.

## Note

1. We are aware, of course, that the relationship between education and increased personal income is a matter of controversy.

# The Market Model and Higher Education (1974)

### Larry L. Leslie and Gary P. Johnson

## Introduction

This paper deals with the increasing tendency of government to finance higher education through students, a trend having important policy implications for higher education. This trend and numerous related governmental decisions have been based almost exclusively upon economic rationale. The rationale itself has largely been developed and couched in terms of one particular concept—the perfectly competitive market, or more generally, the market model. This is clearly evidenced in Federal policy statements and various position papers concerned with changing patterns of governmental financing of higher education.[1] These documents indicate, in part, the extent to which the market concept is presently being used to support and justify Federal policy decisions regarding higher education, and how the market concept is tied to funding higher education through students.

Nowhere is this fact more clearly evidenced than in one of the MEGA documents entitled, "Students Assistance," passed on by Secretary Elliot Richardson to Secretary Casper Weinberger when the former moved from HEW to Defense:

> The fundamental premise of this paper is that a freer play of market forces will best achieve Federal objectives in post-secondary education. . . . Accordingly, this paper describes what we should do to give individuals the general power of choice in the education market place, and proposes levels and types of student support which will make most institutional aid programs unnecessary.[2]

It is the contention of this paper that the market model is tenuous as a rationale for financing higher education, a contention we base on two major observations: First, many policy-makers have misinterpreted the perfectly competitive market model. These misinterpretations have resulted in numerous fallacies and incorrect inferences. Secondly, certain institutional characteristics indigenous to higher education have been either overlooked or ignored in the application of the model; and these institutional characteristics act as structural and functional constraints; severely limiting the applicability of the market model to higher education.

The implication of this contention is that if policy bases are invalid, then that policy itself is subject to serious question. More specifically, if the policy trend toward financing higher education through students is based on the market model and the market model is determined to be inapplicable or inappropriate to higher education, then the policy of financing higher education through students must be reexamined.

The remainder of this paper is divided into five major sections. Section one confirms the trend toward financing higher education through students. Section two sets out the market model and discusses its various components. Section three examines certain methodological limitations which have important implications for continued use of the market model as a policy basis for higher education. Section four discusses the extent to which higher education can be conceptualized within the market context, and indicates the inappropriateness of the concept to government finance policy. Section five presents the conclusions.

## The Trend Toward Financing Higher Education Through Students

There appear to be two clear indications that a trend toward financing higher education through students[3] exists: (1) the passage of the federal education amendments of 1972 and subsequent related events, and (2) certain changes in state funding patterns.

Under the education amendments of 1972, federal funding of higher education was to take the following form: for direct grants to students, there was to be an extension of the present, supplemental educational opportunity grant program for four more years with the maximum amount per year raised from $1,000 to $1,500. In addition, there were to be basic educational opportunity grants (BOGs) in the amount of $1,400 minus family contributions.[4] Direct grants to institutions were also to be tied to student grants in the following way: 45 percent of such grants were to be awarded on the basis of dollars received by the institution for Education Opportunity (EOGs), work-study grants, and National Defense Student Loans; 45 percent were to be awarded on the basis of the *number* of entitlement awards at the institution; and 10 percent were to be awarded on the basis of the number of graduate students enrolled. Thus, 90 percent of the allocation was to be tied strictly to student awards, whether loans or grants. The other features of the amendments involved relatively minor amounts.

The Administration, however, made it clear that the amendments did not go far enough in the grant direction. Although the President signed the supplementary appropriation bill which contained only $122.1 million for BOGs, the President's accompanying message made clear his position vis-à-vis BOGs. It is widely assumed that BOGs will soon becomes the major vehicle for Federal support in undergraduate education. The amendments and the supplementary appropriation have been viewed as establishing the machinery for a greatly expanded BOG program.

Patterns of state funding are also changing. Contained within the amendments is a clause worthy of special note. This regulation would require federal matching of increased state appropriations for student need-based grants. The implications of this clause are considerable. Traditionally, state agencies have regulated in a general way the expenditure of state appropriations for higher education, but institutions have had wide latitude in the internal allocation of resources. Under the amendments, however, states would be induced to increase support for student grants, most surly at the expense of general institutional grants. Although the initial appropriation for this program was to be only $50 million per year, "such sums as may be necessary" were authorized by the amendments for continuation grants. While grants are presumed by many to lessen the likelihood of federal interference in state funding patterns and to reduce the possibility of a single federal system of higher education, this clause calls this presumption into question.

The magnitude of federal support is small in comparison to the size of state support for higher education. Nevertheless, it appears clear that under these amendments the federal government would play an important role in determining the nature of state government funding. Further, federal inducements come at a time when the portion of state monies already being channeled through student grants in quit sizable and in increasing rapidly.

In 1967-68, six states had state scholarship or grant programs; in 1971-72, the number was 22. Since 1969, the average percentage increase if state funds for these programs has been 18 percent per year. Although the average award rose only gradually during the past three years, the number of separate awards rose greatly, increasing 14 percent in 1970-71 and 19 percent in 1971-72.[5]

In sum it seems an inescapable conclusion that a trend toward government financing of higher education through students exists, both at the Federal and at the state level. The trend appears to be a major one only now on its beginning phases.

Why has the trend occurred? What do the causes of the trend portend for higher education?

Although there is a host of listed purposes to be served by student grants, all may be collected under two general headings. The first is the purpose of equalizing educational opportunity, and the second is the perceived need to respond to the current financial crisis in higher education. The two purposes are closely related; both are basically economic motives. The perceived need for equalizing educational opportunity, which is aimed at equalizing economic opportunity, occurs in a period of financial retrenchment. Because of the presumed efficiencies suggested by the market model, the student grant has appeal in that it is broadly perceived as exemplifying an important condition of the market place—casting students in the roles of consumers. Concomitantly, the perceived needs generated by the financial crisis gain attention not only because of the efficiency to be gained, but also because of the equality of educational opportunity that is expected to result.

It is not necessary to detail here either the existence of a financial crisis of the present inequality of higher educational opportunity. The Carnegie Commission, the Association of American Colleges, and the National Association of State Universities and Land-Grant Colleges have conducted studies demonstrating that such crisis exists [4, 7, 8]. As to the second point, the reader need only be reminded that at all ability levels, the percentage of individuals attending college from higher socioeconomic backgrounds is two or three times greater than the percentage of those from lower socioeconomic backgrounds {2, 15].

## The Market Model

As a theoretical construct, the term "market" is not only complex but is also subject to varying interpretations and definitions. Stigler suggests a market be defined as an "area within which the price of a commodity tends to uniformity, allowance being made for transportation costs" [14:85]. Elsewhere a market defined as "an area over which buyers and sellers negotiate the exchange of a well-defined commodity" [11:74]. Elaborating on this second definition, the authors suggest that "from the point of view of a consumer, the market consists of those firms from which the consumer can buy a well-defined product; from the point of view of the producer, the market consists of those buyers to whom he can sell a single well-defined product (if the conditions of sale are sufficiently favorable)" [11:272].

From the above generally accepted definitions there emerge certain aspects of a market which should be noted and made explicit for purposes of subsequent analysis. First, to the economist, market does not refer to a fixed structure in which exchange or trading takes place. Rather, a market as defined above incorporates all individuals or institutions that remain in contact concerning any good or service. Second, there are two distinct parts or sides to any market: the producer's side and the consumer's side. Thus, in discussing a market for a particular commodity both sides of the market must be discussed. Third, the only criteria for inclusion in a market are the desire and ability to participate. Therefore, markets do not necessarily have fixed boundaries. Instead, they are delimited by distance; time; and psychological, personal and financial factors which operate essentially as constraints. Fourth, a particular market must be defined and discussed with references to or in terms of a specific commodity or service. Last, it should be noted that while it is a relatively simple matter to describe a potential market it is considerably more difficult and often impossible to specify exactly who is and who is not a part of that market. Economists, in attempting theoretically to explain and predict various market phenomena, have developed several analytically distinct market types or structures.[6] The market type which provides the rationale or basis for the present trend toward financing higher education through student grants is the perfectly competitive type of model.

There are four fundamental conditions which define perfect competition. Taken together, these conditions guarantee a free impersonal market in which the forces of demand and supply—or of revenue and cost—determine the allocation of resources [5]. First, perfect competition requires every economic agent in the market to be so small, relative to the total market, that it cannot influence the market price in any way. From the standpoint of buyers this implies that each consumer, taken individually, must be so unimportant that he is unable to obtain special consideration from the sellers. From the seller's standpoint a perfectly competitive market requires each producer to be so small that he is unable to affect the market price by changes in his output.

A second and closely related requirement of the perfectly competitive market is that the product of any one seller must be identical to the product of any other seller. This ensures that buyers in the market are indifferent or have no preference regarding the particular firm from which they purchase the product. It is worth restating here that the product or commodity must be identical in every respect. If it is not, the producer who has a slightly differentiated product has a degree of control over the market and , therefore, over the price of his slightly different product. The producer under these conditions could affect market price by changes in his output which, as indicated, is incompatible with perfect competition.

A third condition necessary for a perfectly competitive market is that all resources be perfectly mobile. This requirement is sometimes referred to as the "freedom of entry and exit" assumption [1]. This assumption means that in response to monetary signals each resource can move in and out of the market without hindrances. Any firm or individual that has the funds and desire to enter a particular industry characterized as perfectly competitive can do so without barriers, artificial or real.

The fourth requirement of perfect competition is that producers, consumers, and resource owners must posses perfect knowledge. If perfect knowledge does not exist about alternatives, prices, and relevant market data, there sill be a broad array of prices at which transactions will take place. This could lead, among other things, to a situation termed bilateral monopoly which violates the perfectly competitive model.

The discussion to this point can be summarized as follows: In a perfectly competitive market each economic agent is so small relative to the market that it can exert no perceptible influence on price; the product is homogeneous; there is free mobility of all resources including free and easy entry and exit of firms into and out of an industry; and all economic agents in the market possess complete and perfect knowledge [5]. These characteristics, it should be noted, yield what is called price-taking behavior.

Price-taking behavior and freedom or entry and exit are the two conditions sufficient to result in a perfectly competitive market. That is, the conditions set out above are sufficient conditions to yield price-taking behavior. However, there are other sets of conditions that may also lead to price taking, and the conditions listed above may be modified or changed considerably while still resulting in price-taking behavior.

In other words, the theory of perfect competition is actually built on two fundamental assumptions that can be met in numerous ways and under differing conditions:[7] one is about the behavior of the individual firm and the other is about the nature of the industry in which it operates. First, the firm operating in a perfectly competitive market is assumed to behave or act as if it can change its rate of production and output within any feasible range without having any significant effect on the price of the product it sells. This assumption suggests a firm can double or triple its output or stop producing entirely without effecting the market price; thus, the firm has no influence over price and must passively accept whatever price happens to be ruling in the market. Here it is said that the firm is a price taker, or it behaves as if it were a price taker.[8] The second fundamental assumption, as noted above, requires the industry to be such that any new firm is free to begin production if it wishes and any existing firm is free to shut down production and leave the industry if it so desires. This implies that existing firms cannot prohibit the entry of new firms and that there are no legal; limitations on entry or exit.

# Methodological Aspects Of The Perfectly Competitive Market Model

It was suggested earlier that much of the rationale for student grants in higher education has been based on incorrect or incomplete methodologically related knowledge about the market model. Having set out the basic tenets of the perfectly competitive market model, it is now possible to discuss certain of the methodological aspects of the model which have either been misunderstood, misinterpreted or ignored by various policy-makers in their development of federal financing policy for higher education.

First, it must be clearly understood that the perfectly competitive market is an "ideal type" or "pure" concept. No market exists that is perfectly competitive.[9] Theoretically and conceptually the economic concept of perfectly competitive market is analogous to the sociological concept of bureaucracy developed by Weber. Each concept was developed as an analytical tool to increase the clarity and efficiency in the analysis of particular phenomena, with the recognition that the ideal or pure type, as specified, was non-existent and essentially unattainable in the real world. In the case of the pure, perfectly competitive market concept, the distinguishing feature of the model is the fact that when its assumptions or conditions are strictly construed, they are applicable to nothing actual. This kind of theoretical construct results in conceptual "cleanness," clarity and relatively high degree of generality in the analysis of given phenomena.

What is or should be the primary function of such a model? And more specifically, to what extent must the real world approximate the assumptions or conditions specified in the perfectly competitive market model for it so have any significant degree of explanatory or predictive power? Regarding the first of these questions it is suggested that the fundamental function of a "pure" model is to serve as a point of analytical departure for subsequent theoretical analysis. Earnest Nagel has suggested with reference to such ideal types [12]:

> a law [theory] so formulated states how phenomena are related when they are unaffected by numerous factors whose influence may never be completely eliminated but whose effects generally vary in magnitude with differences in the attendant circumstances under which the phenomena actually recur. Accordingly, discrepancies between what is asserted for the pure case and what actually happens can be attributed to the influence of factors not mentioned in the law [theory]. Moreover, since these factors and their effects can often be ascertained, the influence of the factors can be systematically classified into general types; and in consequence, the law can be viewed as the limiting case of a set of other laws corresponding to these various types, where each further law states a modified relation of dependence between the phenomena because of the influence of factors that are absent in the pure case. In short, unrealistic theoretical statements. . . serve as a powerful means for analyzing, representing, and codifying relations of dependence between actual phenomena.

Nagel has limited his discussion to explanatory theory while neglecting to discuss the possible role and utility of pure model types in predictive theory.

The perfectly competitive market model is presently being used by higher education policy-makers in the predictive context. Specifically, perfectly competitive markets (i.e., those which meet the conditions outlined in the previous section) lead to a productive optimum in that costs are kept to a minimum, output is maximized and resources are allocated in the most efficient way possible.[10] Thus, those policy-makers who support student grants hope to make the system more competitive, with the ultimate goal of increasing efficiency and rationality in the internal allocation of resources, of increasing educational productivity and of reducing costs. Implicit in this policy recommendation, however, is explicit quantitative knowledge about the *actual* effect of student grants on both inputs and outputs in higher education. Even more importantly, it suggests the existence of theoretical knowledge indicating: (1) at what point a particular system or market moves from a noncompetitive or imperfectly competitive market to one characterized as competitive or perfectly competitive; (2) what kinds of phenomena will move a particular system from a noncompetitive state to a competitive state; and (3) at what point on the continuum labeled "competitive system" does the degree of competition present lead to the production optimum discussed above.

It is suggested here that we have neither the actual nor the theoretical knowledge outlined above. Regarding the lack of theoretical knowledge in particular, Stigler [14:89] has commented: "The reason for not stating the weakest assumptions (necessary conditioned) for competition is that they are difficult to formulate, and in fact are not known precisely."

This is the first methodological aspect of the perfectly competitive market model we wish to emphasis: specifically, the theoretical knowledge about the minimum conditions necessary to generate a competitive market is not presently known.[11] Also, nothing is known theoretically or otherwise about items two and three above. Given this lack of knowledge, it seems absolutely necessary and indeed appropriate that the real world (i.e., higher education) to a very great extent be congruent with the conditions specified in the perfectly competitive market model if we are to have any faith in the predictive power of the theory for higher education, or if we are to feel comfortable about using it in its predictive context as a policy basis.[12]

The only market theory which might conceivably be used to discuss certain phenomena in higher education is the theory of imperfect or monopolistic competition developed by Chamberlin and Robinson [3, 13]. Unfortunately, this market theory suffers from an even greater lack of theoretical development, refinement and sophistication than the theory of perfect competition. As the theory of imperfect competition is presently formulated it represents little more than an interesting intellectual device with extremely limited implications for either explaining or predicting a class of substantive market phenomena. Friedman has stated regarding the market theory of monopolistic competition [6]:

> It possesses none of the attributes that would make it useful general theory. . . . The deficiencies of the theory are revealed most clearly in its treatment of, or inability to treat, problems involving groups of firms—Marshallian "industries.". . . The theory of monopolistic competition offers no tools for the analysis of an industry and so no stopping place between the firm at one extreme and general equilibrium at the other. It is therefore incompetent to contribute to the analysis of a host of important problems; the one extreme is too narrow to be of great interest; the other, too broad to permit meaningful generalizations.

Thus, both the imperfectly competitive and the perfectly competitive market models have conceptual and analytical inadequacies stemming from limited theoretical development and refinement. These inadequacies not only prevent the models from dealing effectively with various substantive questions, but they also limit considerably their explanatory and predicative power.

A second methodological aspect of the perfectly competitive market model which bears on the question of the model's appropriateness and validity as a policy basis for higher education concerns the productive optimum outcome. As suggested, perfect competition leads, in equilibrium, to the "best" possible use of resources in the sense that it results in the most efficient allocation of resources possible. The essence of the argument consists of two propositions: first, in a perfectly competitive market, marginal cost[13] equals price; and secondly, in equilibrium, the level of cost is the lowest level attainable given the technology of the society.

The significance of having outputs produced at their lowest possible costs is obvious. Less obvious is the significance of the proposition that marginal cost equals price. Given such a situation and the existence of other strict conditions, an optimum situation results in the sense that it is impossible to make some customers better off without simultaneously making others worse off. A second suboptimal situation occurs when marginal cost equals price in some but not all industries.

Under these circumstances, it is possible to make some consumers better off without making any consumers worse off by changing certain prices and outputs in the economy.

This latter proposition, which comes from theoretical welfare economics, has had a strong effect on the attitudes of many economists and policy-makers alike, and in some instances (e.g., higher education) has led to the uncritical application and support of the perfectly competitive market model. However, there are certain hazards in applying the model uncritically, and where this has occurred certain facts have been either overlooked or not fully understood. Perhaps most important of these is that optimal resources allocation requires the simultaneous fulfillment of at least four conditions which are seldom, if ever, met in reality.[14]

Two of these conditions, in particular, serve to indicate further the theoretical limitations of the market model, and more specifically its general analytical inappropriateness as a viable model for higher education. First, the conditions necessary to generate an optimum allocation of resources must exist everywhere simultaneously in the economy. That is, there cannot be any monopolies or oligopolies. Unless this is the case it becomes impossible to determine the effect of prices equaling marginal costs in some industry or part of society. That is, if we take some industry out of an economy of mixed market structures and make it competitive, we have no presumption (even in a theoretical model) about the probability of this moving us closer to or further away from an optimum position or solutions.[15] The second condition dictates there be no divergence between private and social costs and between private and social benefits anywhere in the economy.[16]

That either of these conditions is even approximated in higher education need not be debated or elaborated. The price of higher education, as measured by tuition and fees, is fixed at a level almost always below marginal cost which indirectly and eventually results in resource allocation distortions of various magnitudes. The regional nature[17] of the higher educational market, consisting as it does of many smaller submarkets, makes homogeneity and simultaneity of markets and conditions highly unlikely. Lastly, while little quantitative knowledge exists about the divergence of private and social costs and private and social benefits in higher education, there are numerous valid theoretical arguments and considerations which suggest some divergence between the two in both costs and benefits. Thus, the perfectly competitive market model yields a much publicized and well-known production optimum, but does so only under certain strict conditions which are seldom met in reality and oar often overlooked.

A third methodological aspect of the market model relevant to our discussion concerns the concept of efficiency and it interpretation. Much of the support for financing higher education through students and making the system more competitive has been the projected gains in efficiency. It is argued that significant gains in efficiency will manifest themselves in lowered per-student costs and much needed savings if the perfectly competitive market model and conditions consistent with it are invoked in higher education. What makes this statement erroneous is a misunderstanding or misinterpretation of efficiency in the perfectly competitive market. Efficiency in the perfectly competitive market refers to allocative efficiency which centers in *resource* allocation and utilization. It is not synonymous, as is often thought, with costs or cost reductions. That is, the perfectly competitive market model, when used to examine and analyze the allocative efficiency of a particular organization, assumes constant costs over some relevant range of output. More specifically, by making an industry and its firms competitive (i.e., moving it from a monopoly situation to a competitive one) the allocative efficiency of both the industry and the firms will be increased and a better utilization of resources results. This manifests itself in a lower unit price and increased output levels, with no implications for production costs while remain constant.

Further, and perhaps most important, considerable evidence presently exists to suggest the welfare gain in allocative efficiency achieved by moving to a competitive situation is so significant as to render it inconsequential. Emerging research suggests that allocative inefficiency is frequently of small magnitude involving no more than one tenth of one percent [10].

In summary of this section, certain methodological aspects of the perfectly competitive market model were discussed which appear to have been misunderstood or ignored by policy-makers who use the market model to support the present governmental trend toward financing higher education thorough students. These methodological aspects tend to limit rather severely the applicability of the market model to higher education in addition to raising certain questions concerning the validity and appropriateness of the model as a justifiable basis for the present student grant policy.

# The Market Model And Higher Education

In this section two issues are discussed: (1) the extent to which higher education corresponds to certain conditions of the perfectly competitive market model; and (2) the probability that financing higher education through student grants will result in the projected changes i.e., increased institutional responsiveness, greater efficiency and reduced costs. Regarding the importance of the first issue, if higher education does not, in fact, approximate the various conditions necessary for competition, it becomes extremely doubtful that any single alternation in the market, such as the introduction of student grants, will result in significant changes in the competitive nature of the market. As for the second issue, student grants have been chosen as a specific operational means for increasing institutional responsiveness, efficiency and student choice. Thus, it is necessary to examine carefully the various market and institutional factors that either facilitate or impede the effectiveness of the student grant in achieving these desired policy objectives.

## The Market For Higher Education

The market for higher education can, on the whole, be characterized as many submarkets which are to a large extent coterminous with regional or state boundaries.[18] That is, by far the majority of colleges students attend institutions proximate to their homes or at least within their home states. Perhaps the only notable exception is the case of certain distinctive institutions. Specifically, geography has been found to be the primary predictor of whether a student will go to college and more importantly which college he will attend.[19] Perhaps one of the most important factors delimiting the higher education market is the differential between in-state and out-of-state tuitions and fees.[20] Other limiting factors are transportation costs, family disposable income, close family relationships and geographic limits of student knowledge. Thus, institutions view the higher education market as consisting largely of local or at best in-state students, while students view the institutional market in reciprocal fashion.[21]

A second aspect of the higher education market concerns the nature of the commodity itself. The commodity which students and institutions "negotiate" the exchange of is, in fact, enrollment space. Universities and colleges sell enrollments, not products; and enrollments and products are not interchangeable. An enrollment can be considered a space to be filled; and from consumer or student perspective, the space may be either a desirable or an undesirable one. From the seller's or institutional perspective, a space is often conceived of as a station to be filled with a desirable or less than desirable student.

It should be noted that this enrollment space is differentiated by students and institutions alike. Within any state, there exists a variety of institutions selling qualitatively different types of enrollment space. This space is differentiated by the various factors affecting it. These factors include such things as institutional mission, student needs, faculty quality, and a varying entrance requirements.[22] While the quantitative differences in enrollment space may, in fact, be more imagined than real, it is apparent that both institutions and students often behave in a manner consistent with these perceptions.[23]

The final aspect of the higher education market to be noted concerns the kind of competition found in higher education. Competition is of the non-price variety. That is, institutions in the market set their own price (tuition and fees) dependent upon operating cost, endowments, and income from governments and other sources. Specifically, each institution, system of institutions, or institutions having a common governing structure fix their particular price independent of other institutions and in this sense act a monopolists.[24] Competition, however, occurs in terms of the perceived differences in the enrollment space and certain process inputs—namely, students and faculty.

It was suggested earlier that certain market-related aspects of higher education should approximate the various conditions of the perfectly competitive market model if the market model is to have any significant degree of predictive power and be justified as a policy base for higher education. Upon considering collectively the above major aspects of the higher education market, it becomes evident that while higher education can be generally and broadly discussed within the context of certain market terminology, the various market-related characteristics of higher education in no way approximate the sufficient conditions of the perfectly competitive market model.

To begin with, individual institutions and systems of institutions, in having complete discretion over tuition and fees, can neither be labeled price takers nor can they be assumed to behave as if they were price takers.[25] Instead, they are at the other end of the "effect-price "continuum, and consequently might be more accurately described as price setters. That is, there exists within any single state higher education market a range of enrollment space prices which are in a one-to-one correspondence with those set by institutions within that market. That is, there is no one uniform market price.

Secondly, that state higher education market is characterized by formidable barriers to both entry and exit, such as various legal, financial and political factors. Regarding specifically the entrance of new institutions into a given market, perhaps the single most significant barrier is the size of the market itself, which is limited largely by the number of in-state college age students and by existing statewide institutional capacity.

Thirdly, it was noted above that enrollment space in higher education is differentiated qualitatively by students and institutions alike. This leads to certain market behavior inconsistent with the perfectly competitive market model. Enrollment space is not homogeneous; nor can it be said that either students or institutions behave as if it were homogeneous.

Thus, the market-related characteristics of higher education neither correspond to, nor are consistent with, the sufficient conditions or assumptions describing the leading to a perfectly competitive market. Nor do they approximate the requirements of the model. Instead, higher education can be characterized as a situation where: (1) non-price limited competition for students and faculty exists; (2) prices are individually determined by institutions and statewide systems of institutions without significant attention to market conditions; (3) the consumption and distribution of enrollment space is determined unilaterally by institutions; and (4) the internal allocation of institutional resources takes place largely independent of market forces. Not only does this incongruence between higher education and the model suggest that the perfectly competitive market model is inappropriate and inadequate as a descriptor of higher education, but it also calls into question the potential and probable effect of any single new mode for financing higher education (i.e., the student grant).

## Student Grant Effectiveness: Institutional and Market Constraints

The introduction of student grants in higher education represents an attempt to operationalize certain policy recommendations that are based upon and couched in terms of the market model. It has been shown that the perfectly competitive market model is inappropriate as a descriptor of market-related conditions and characteristics of higher education. If, as has been suggested, higher education does not approximate a competitive situation, what is the probability that student grants will significantly alter the competitive nature of the system and thereby affect substantively the desired and predicted outcomes (which are based on the perfectly competitive market model)? The answer, in part, can be obtained by examining those market and institutional characteristics inconsistent with the conditions and assumptions of the model.

Let us first consider the predicted policy outcome of increased student choice. It has been suggested by their proponents that student grants will widen the number of possible educational alternatives presently available to students. Yet a number of factor appear to severely limit student grants as a means of increasing available alternatives. When one considers out-of-state tuition and fees,[26] transportation costs, the regional nature of the higher education market in general[27] and the relatively small absolute dollar amount of even the largest student grant plan,[28] it is soon realized that student grants in and of themselves do little to effectively increase student alternatives.[29] Other factors such as institutional academic standards and entrance requirements are seen to further limit student choice and render student grants ineffectual in this context.

It has also been suggested that student grants will increase institutional responsiveness generally. Here also several institutional and market factors act to minimize the grants' predicted effects. They are: (1) faculty tenure; (2) non-price competition; (3) academic freedom; (4) the relatively small number of students in any one institution expected to hold grants at any one time; (5) the structurally "loose" authority relationship between faculty and administration; and (6) the wide dispersion of grant holders throughout the various departments of any one institution. Finally, it should be noted that the G.I. Bill, which is essentially a grant or voucher plan, has done little to cause changes in institutional programs, save some hucksterism among a few proprietary schools.

Lastly, it has been suggested that student grants, by increasing competition between institutions, will increase institutional operating efficiency.[30] There is little evidence to support this contention, particularly in light of the various market characteristics of higher education discussed earlier. Many of the factors constraining the effects of student grants on institutional responsiveness also operate to constrain grant effectiveness in increasing institutional efficiency.

In sum, certain market factors and institutional characteristics, acting as structural and functional constraints, operate to severely limit the effectiveness of student grants in achieving predicated and desired outcomes. It appears that introduction of student grants will result in, at best, only marginal changes in the competitive nature of higher education.

## Conclusions

The preceding analysis suggests that the perfectly competitive market model is inadequate and inappropriate as a policy basis for higher education. It further suggests that financing higher education through students has a low probability of achieving the desired outcomes.

The model is inadequate because it does not provide specific theoretical knowledge indicating the necessary conditions leading to the establishment of a competitive situation. Without such information it is difficult, if not impossible, to determine the effect of a specific market change on the competitive nature of the market. In the case of higher education, it has been argued that financing through students is a step in the "right direction." Yet, we presently have no way of knowing what the qualitative or quantitative effect of such policy would be in terms of outcomes. Thus, while it might be a step in the "right direction," it might also be a totally ineffectual one.

The model was determined to be inappropriate for higher education because certain characteristics inherent in higher education were found to be inconsistent with the various conditions of the perfectly competitive market. Specifically, higher education was in no way found to approximate the sufficient conditions which characterize and result in a perfectly competitive market. In this situation policy that is based on the market model and is applied to higher education may or may not be "good" policy. But it becomes impossible to evaluate such policy on the basis of the model and its predicted outcomes because the predicted outcomes themselves are no longer probable or valid.

Finally, it was suggested that, because of certain functional and structural characteristics existing in higher education, the present governmental policy of financing higher education through students has a low probability of success in achieving the desired outcomes. These various characteristics, operating as constraints, are so limiting to the application of the market model that massive and radical changes in them appear to be the only possible means of making the market model appropriate and valid as a viable policy base in higher education.

Many individuals argue that this is precisely what is needed in higher education today—massive and radical change resulting in a responsive and efficient system. These same individuals maintain that this is precisely why financing higher education through students is appropriate and sound.

Yet, those who would argue in this way seem not only to be preoccupied with higher education means (efficiency) at the possible expense of ends (goals), but also to have ignored the possibility that the various organizational characteristics (viewed as *constraints* within the context of the perfectly competitive market model) indigenous to higher education may have evolved legitimately in the natural process of achieving various institutional objectives. It is entirely possible that the various goals of higher education and their achievement are partially or completely inconsistent with the economic values inherent in the perfectly competitive market model.

The Carnegie Commission, in a recent report, stated that the main purposes of higher education for the present and future were:

1.  the provision of opportunities for the intellectual, aesthetic, ethical, and skill development of individual students, and the provision of campus environments which can constructively assist students in their more general development growth;

2.  the advancement of human capability in society at large;

3.  the enlargement of educational justice for the post-secondary age group;

4.  the transmission and advancement of learning and wisdom;

5.  the critical evaluation of society—through individual thought and persuasion—for the sake of society's self-renewal.[31]

That the accomplishment of these objectives requires a system of organization which is inconsistent with the perfectly competitive market model neither implies that the present system is necessarily inefficient nor that it is in need of radical change. This is particularly true if we consider the possible existence of conflict between economics values and the process of achieving certain institutional and social objectives.

It is possible that radical and massive change in higher education consistent with the perfectly competitive market model may eliminate various "constraints," reduce costs and increase allocative efficiency; but it may also reduce considerably or eliminate altogether institutional ability to achieve some or all of the goals listed above.

In light of the foregoing considerations one important question remains—why does the market model and policy based on it continue to be so strongly advocated by economists and policymakers alike? The answer, we think, is partly suggested by Carl Kaysen, Director of the Institute for advanced Study at Princeton [9]:

Typically, in these cases [argument such as monopoly vs. competition] economists offer advice within a partial rather than a general equilibrium framework, and, on the whole, much more in qualitative than in quantitative terms. These characteristics are not all logically inevitable; they reflect in part historical and present limitations on conceptual tools in relation to the difficulty of the problems and data available. To some extent these are underdeveloped areas of analysis to which the newer conceptual and statistical technology of economics is just beginning to be applied. However, many of the intellectual intractabilities involved lie very deep indeed, and may simply prove to be insoluble in the terms in which they are usually posed. . . . The striking fact, however, is that these limitations have done little or nothing to inhibit economists from giving policy advice on this range of problems. In fact, the opposite is the case. The absence of all the difficulties and obvious limitations of models involving checkable quantitative forecasts appears to lead to vigorous and confident policy prescriptions and, indeed, to a wide degree of professional agreement on the prescriptions. All, or nearly all, respectable economists are for . . . more competition, though few or none are prepared to estimate the . . . value of increasing the degree of competition in some sectors of the economy while accepting as inevitable a high degree of market power in other sectors.

In both cases, the confidence of economists' policy recommendations is essentially ideological: it rests on their commitment to the competitive market as an ideal, and on the consequent belief that any step in the direction of the ideal is a desirable one. While this, in my judgment, is the main ingredient of economists' policy recommendations on these points, it is clearly not the only one. There are, in addition, more directly and self-consciously political grounds for preferring more to less competitive domestic markets; i.e., arguments articulated in terms of political liberty rather than economic efficiency. Typically, however, these are not the arguments of the majority of the profession.

# Notes

1. Generally, this evidence is implicitly stated; occasionally it is stated explicitly. See, for example, *The Economics and Financing of Higher Education in the United States,* a compendium of papers submitted to The Joint Economic Committee of Congress, Washington, USGPO, 1969; *Financing Higher Education: Alternatives for the Federal Government,* edited by M.D. Orwig, Iowa City. The American College Testing Program, 1971: *Universal Higher Education: Costs and Benefits.* Washington. The American Council on Education. 1971: *Investment in Education: The Equity Efficiency Quandry,* edited by Theodore W. Schultz, *The Journal of Political Economy.* Volume 80. Number 3. Part II, May/June 1972; *The Management and Finance of Colleges.* New York: The Committee for Economic Development, 1973.

2. The MEGA documents were a series of papers prepared by the HEW staff which were used in the formulation of basic HEW policies.

3. Before proceeding, let us substitute the term "student grant" or substitute "basic opportunity grant" (BOGs) for the more cumbersome phrase, funding higher education through students. Excluded are traditional student scholarships. This paper speaks strictly to the present trend toward governmental provision of funds to students on the basis of need. These funds are commonly called need-based grants or basic opportunity grants. Loans are another form these disbursements may take. Students may take them to or "activate them" at almost any post-secondary institution of their choice.

4. Public Law 92-318, the education amendments of 1972. Note: In all these programs there were to be varying fundable thresholds so that the amount available to any given program would depend in some way upon the amount available for other programs. See the specific wording for elaboration.

5. In five states awards are not based solely on need, but are generally competitive. Further, in only nine of the remaining seventeen states are all or virtually all awards purely need-based. These data are taken from "Inventory of Student Financial Aid Programs, Phase I Report," ED0589939. (Washington: ERIC, 1971 and 1971-72, pp. 6-16); and Joseph Boyd, "Comprehensive State Scholarship Grant Program-Third Annual Survey," (Deerfield, Illinois: Illinois State Scholarship Commission, 1972).

6. See, for example, William J. Baumol, *Economic Theory and Operations Analysis,* Second Edition (New Jersey: Prentice Hall), pp. 311-34, who discusses and differentiates eight major market structures including perfect or pure competition, pure monopoly, monopolistic competition, monopsony, discriminating monopoly, bilateral monopoly, duopoly and oligopoly.

7. The conditions set out above which define a perfectly competitive model are the "ideal" set which, in fact, *guarantee* a perfectly competitive market.

8. Price taking can be explained in terms of the firm's elasticity of demand. Specifically, every firm in a perfectly competitive market is assumed to have a *firm* elasticity of demand so high that it may ignore the influence that may change in its output might have on market price. Alternatively stated, the firm acts as if the elasticity of demand for its product is infinite.

9. While no market for a particular commodity can be labeled perfectly competitive, there are several markets that provide a reasonably good approximation: certain grain markets and the stock market are often cited as examples.

10. For a detailed analysis and discussion confirming this statement see Lloyd G. Reynolds, *Economics*, Third Edition (Homewood, Illinois, Illinois: Richard D. Irwin. Incorporated, 1969), Chapters 17-19.

11. Whether or not the student grant system can increase the competitive nature of higher education, so as to result in some kind of productive optimum, is discussed in the next section.

12. The extent to which higher education is congruent with conditions and characteristics specified in the model is taken up in the nest section.

13. Marginal cost refers to the cost of producing the last unit of output.

14. For a more detailed discussion of these conditions, see Richard Lipsey and Peter O. Steiner, *Economics*, Second Edition, (New York: Harper & Row, 1969), Chapters 17 and 21.

15. This proposition is often called the "theory of second best" and refers to the fact that if it may be possible to identify the best of all possible worlds (from the limited point of view of the optimum under consideration) but it may be impossible to order two states of the very imperfect world in which we live.

16. Here private cost and social cost should be taken to mean the value of the best alternative uses of the resources available to the firm, as evaluated by the firm and the value of the best alternative uses of resources that are available to the whole society, as evaluated by society, respectively. Private benefits and social benefits refer to gains which accrue to producers of goods or services (usually the revenue from the sale of his product) and the value of the gains that everyone together obtains from the production of a good, respectively.

17. The regional nature of higher education is discussed in the nest section.

18. It is recognized that the higher education market could be conceptualized as national and even worldwide in scope, in that every institution faces the possibility of receiving application and admission requests from students everywhere in the U.S. and throughout the world. However, we are restricting our analysis to the major attendance patterns that characterize higher education.

19. There seems to be no exception to this conclusion in the literature. See, for example, Elizabeth Douvan and Carol Kay, "Motivational Factors in College Entrance," in Nevitt Sanford, ed., *The American College*, (New York John Wiley and Sons, Inc. 1962), pp. 193-223: and the citation of the works of Holland on National Merit Scholars, ibid., p. 219.

20. That tuition and fees may influence the demand for higher education is suggested by an empirical study conducted by R. Campbell and B. Siegel in which they found both price (as measured by an index of tuition deflated by the consumer price index) and disposable income were important determinants of the demand for higher education in the U.S. See R. Campbell and B. Siegel, "The Demand for Higher Education in the United States, 1919-1964," *American Economic Review*, 57 (1967), 482-94.

21. As out-[of-state and in-state differentials are eliminated and as disposable family income continues to rise, some present major trends in the higher education market will become increasingly difficult to identify and label, and the market itself may someday escape even broad or general description.

22. For a detailed discussion of institutional differentiation by students, see Larry L. Leslie, "The Trend Toward Government Financing of Higher Education Through Students," University Part, Pa.: Center for the Study of Higher Education, 1973.

23. In terms of market effects or outcomes, it is only necessary that either group in the market conduct their affairs *as if* enrollment space were qualitatively dissimilar. The perception need not be accurate; the outcome will be the same regardless.

24. In other words few, if any, institutions or system of institutions which constitute a market attempt to compete for students and sell enrollment space on the basis of price.

25. Further, it is difficult to conceive of a situation in which a major university might close its doors without there being an upward pressure on prices for enrollment space at other institutions throughout the state, unless institutions responded to increases in demand for enrollment space by raising entrance requirements and academic standards.

26. Litigation presently pending before the courts, suggests of course, that interstate tuition barriers will eventually yield.

27. For instance, in Pennsylvania, the only state that allows significant "export" of grants, the ratio of state scholarship recipients electing to attend out-of-state colleges and universities has been diminishing each of the past four years from 14.8 percent in 1969-70 to 12.6 percent in 1972-73.

28. Proposed  federally financed student grants would reach $1,400 or one-half the cost of attendance, whichever is less. However, present funding levels afford a maximum grant of only $600 and an average of $240 for freshman only.

29. This need not be the case if student grants were to cover out-of-state tuition and transportation costs. However, other non-monetary constraints determining student choice of institutions might outweigh the effects of even full-cost grants.

30. It should be noted that considerable controversy presently exists as to whether or not higher education is operating efficiently. Some individuals argue that institutional values, outcomes, and the process leading to those outcomes are such that higher education should not be compared to private business. Individuals taking this position suggest it is entirely possible that higher education is, in fact, quite efficient, that there is not simple way to achieve institutional goals while significantly reducing cost.

31. The Carnegie Commission of Higher Education, *The Purposes and Performance of Higher Education in the United States: Approaching the Year 2000*, (New York: McGraw-Hill, 1973).

# Literature Cited

1. Baumol. W.J. *Economic Theory and Operations Research* (2nd ed.). Englewood Cliffs, New Jersey: Prentice Hall, 1970. p. 313.

2. The Carnegie Commission on Higher Education. *New Students and New Places*. New York: McGraw-Hill. 1971. pp. 26-29.

3. Chamberlin, E.H. *The Theory of Monopolistic Competition* (6th ed.). Cambridge Massachusetts: Harvard University Press, 1950.

4. Cheit, E. F. *The New Depression in Higher Education*. New York: McGraw-Hill, 1971.

5. Ferguson, C.E. *Microeconomic Theory*. Homewood, Illinois: Richard D. Irwin, Inc., 1966. pp. 192-95.

6. Friedman, M.J., "The Methodology of Positive Economics," *Readings in Microeconomics*, W. Breit and H. Hochman, eds. New York: Holt Rinehart & Winston. 1968. pp. 44-45.

7. Hudgins, G., and I. Phillips. *Public Colleges in Trouble: A Financial Profile of the Nation's State Universities and Land Grant Colleges*. Washington D.C.: NASULGC, 1971.

8. Jellema, W. W. "The Red and the Black," and "Redder and Much Redder." Washington, D.C.: The Association of American Colleges, 1971.

9. Kaysen, C., "Model-Makers and Decision-Makers: Economists and the Policy Process," *Economic Means and Social Ends*. Englewood Cliffs, New Jersey: Prentice Hall, 1969. pp. 139-40.

10. Leibenstein, H. "Allocative Efficiency vs. X Efficiency," *American Economic Review* (June, 1966).

11. Lipsey, R., and P. Steiner. *Economics* (2nd ed.). New York: Harper and Row, 1969.

12. Nagel, E. "Assumptions in Economic Theory" *Readings in Microeconomic Theory*, W. Breit and H. Hochman, eds. New York: Holt, Rinehart & Winston, 1968. pp. 64-65.

13. Robinson, J. *The Economics of Imperfect Competition*. London, England: Macmillan and Company, 1933.

14. Stigler, G. J. *The Theory of Price* (3rd ed.). New York: Macmillan and Company, 1966.

15. U.S. Bureau of the Census, "Characteristics of American Youth: 1972," Series P-23, No. 44.

# The Value of an Education (1976)

## Kern Alexander

In the early 1960s, economists advanced the idea that education was a significant economic investment increasing both the financial well-being of the state and the individual. During the sixties many studies were conducted quantifying the benefits accruing from enhancement of the nation's human capital through education, and educational proponents utilized this concept to justify greater governmental appropriations. More recently, though, the concept has faded somewhat from the forefront of the educational funding debate and has been used only sparingly by education advocates.

This paper reviews the development of the investment concept, analyzes some of its strengths and weaknesses, and cites recent data bearing directly on the desirability of further educational investment. A substantial portion of the paper is devoted to identifying educational benefits which are not commonly recognized and because they are difficult to quantify are not usually included in economic analyses assessing the value of an education.

The economics of education first came into focus as a legitimate source of economic enquiry in T. W. Schultz's presidential address to the American Economic Association in 1960 in which he observed that human capital formation is an important aspect of economic development and that the economic advancement of any country depends to a great extent on its storehouse of human resources. Until this time the concept of "human capital" was looked upon with disdain by economists and represented little more than a "metaphor without substantive economic meaning."[1] The more perceptive observed that some countries recovered much more rapidly than others from the devastation of war which left physical capital in the form of railroads, factories, bridges, machinery, and structures generally in a mass of rubble. But standard economic thought failed to identify and attribute the recovery and growth of the various national economies to human capital.[2] Some economists had observed that increases in national output far exceeded the investment increases in physical capital, and had even theorized that human capital might be an element of the total economic capital by which a country advances,[3] but none had synthesized the concept to produce a workable definition until Schultz's presentation in 1960.

An obvious implication of the earlier view was that human resources were merely "labor oriented" and did not require knowledge or skill. As Johns has observed, society itself was "labor-intensive" rather than "brain intensive," and the production required more muscle and bone than brains.[4] As society advanced, the concept of human capital was a natural development. Laborers' human capital increases not from some minor diffusion of investment in stock of companies but by the acquisition of valuable knowledge and skills.

Today human resources—not capital, nor income, nor material resources—are looked upon by some as the true basis for the wealth of nations. Physical capital and natural resources of a country are passive factors contributing to production while human beings are the catalytic agents in producing capital, building social, economic, and political organizations, and promoting natural development. Human resources are the energies, talents, skills, and knowledge which can be applied to inert physical factors to produce goods and services, and to produce additional human resources. As Harbison observes, human resources "connotes man in relationship to the world of work, and such work involves producing things and providing services of all kinds in the social, political, cultural, and economic development of nations."[5] Modern theorists have thus accused traditional economists of having "tunnel vision"[6] where the wealth of nations is concerned. The standard of wealth probably should not be income maximization, as measured by Gross National Product or Gross Domestic Product, but more realistically the wealth of nations should be measured by some quantification of human resources using indices reflecting minimization of population growth and improvement of the environment. These standards are at least as important as income maximization.

Investing in people makes it possible to create and adapt to technological progress. Health and formal education constitute the two major ways investment in human capital can be made. Advancements in health extend the productivity of the individual and make any investment in education more rewarding. While the contribution of education to earning capacity is significant, the external benefits which form an educated citizenry may constitute the more important aspect of human capital development.[7] Benefits of schooling to persons other than the student himself are not difficult to identify. Obvious benefits accrue to the student's children who will derive educational advantage from an enlightened parent, to neighbors who may be affected by the development of social values which enhance interpersonal relationships, to employers seeking a trained labor force or at least one which has the necessary knowledge beyond literacy to benefit from on-the-job training, and in no small degree to society generally by developing an informed electorate.

The benefits of education may be broadly categorized as anything which (a) increases production through income in the capacity of the labor force, (b) increases efficiency by reducing unnecessary costs, thereby reserving resources for the enhancement of human productivity—for example, the release of public resources from law enforcement to more productive pursuits—and (c) increases the social consciousness of the community so that living conditions are enhanced.[8]

To theorize that human capital plays a major role in the production and welfare of a country is one thing, but to quantify its impact is a problem of such proportion that it has not been solved to anyone's satisfaction. Four basic approaches[9] have been utilized with varying degrees of accuracy.

The first of these is a simple correlation between some measure of educational activity and an index of economic activity. For example, enrollment ratios have been correlated with GNP per capita, indicating a positive relationship.[10] Finding comparable information on education, not to mention the problems of comparability surrounding GNP, presents formidable data problems. Further, this approach suffers the common malady of all correlational studies, failure to show cause and effect relationships of education.

The second is the residual approach which consists of assessing the total increase in economic output of a country over a period of time, measuring the impact of identifiable inputs (usually capital and labor) and then attributing the residual to unidentifiable inputs, the most important of which is human capital.[11] Over a period from 1889 to 1957, Kendrick found that for the United States economy a combined index of input increased at 1.9 per cent per annum and the output index increased at 3.5 per cent per annum, leaving a residual of 1.6 per cent per annum.[12] Using a percentage of the increase in output per unit of labor input, rather than a percentage increase of the total, Kendrick was able to attribute about 80 per cent of the increased output per unit of labor input to the residual. Massell, relying on data by Solow and using different procedures from Kendrick, found the residual to equal roughly 90 per cent of the increase in output per man-hour in the United States economy between 1915 and 1955.[13] Fabricant found that only 1.0 per cent of an annual increase in GNP of 3.1 per cent could be attributed to capital and labor. He suggested that the residual may be largely explained by investments in education, research and development, and other tangible capital.[14]

Denison carefully studied the growth rate of the GNP between 1929 and 1957 and identified the following factors and percentages: increased employment, 34 percent; increased capital input, 15 per cent; increased education, 23 per cent; increased knowledge, 20 per cent; economies of scale associated with growth of the national market, 9 per cent; and other factors, 8 per cent.[15] Thus increased education and knowledge account for 43 percentage points of a possible 109 for positive and negative factors, or 39 per cent of a total.

While the data show substantial variations, all economists who have seriously examined this issue have concluded that investment in education has a vital effect on economic growth.[16] Defects in the residual approach leave many questions unanswered. To a great extent the residual is difficult to circumscribe because there is interplay between capital inputs and education. Also, the residual may include a product mix created by improvement in the quality of capital assets, certain economies of scale, or reorganizational influences in the economic order.[17] The size of the residual nevertheless signals an interaction which would be inexplicable without the inclusion of education and knowledge as major variables.

A third approach, direct rate of return to education, simply contrasts the future lifetime earnings of people of less education with people of greater educational attainment. The difference in lifetime earnings is usually expressed as a percentage rate of return on the costs incurred in acquiring the education. Analyses of income benefits to education utilize different methodologies, making comparison of results difficult. Miller[18] calculated lifetime income values by level of schooling, which gives a more or less gross measure of returns to education. Refinement was added when Houthakker introduced a discount factor and a productivity factor to adjust for inflation and expected increase in productivity over a period of years.[19] Unfortunately, there is no sure answer to what the discount rate or the productive factors should be, since one cannot accurately predict what the future will hold throughout a lifetime. Both Miller's and Houthakker's methods ignore the costs associated with obtaining an education.

The rate of return approach developed by Hansen[20] may be classified as cost-benefit analysis whereby the costs associated with education are estimated and deducted from the benefits, leaving a more precise estimate of the economic value of education. Of course, the key to the rate of return approach is an accurate determination of the costs of education. Two major variants exist in assessing costs. First are those indicating the total resource costs incurred by society in providing education, which include (1) school costs such as teachers' salaries, supplies, interest, and depreciation on capital, (2) opportunity costs incurred by individuals, primarily from foregone income during school attendance, and (3) incidental school-related costs such as books and travel.[21] Second are private resource costs, including the same basic components with tuition and fees paid by individuals substituted for the costs to society paid through taxation. Additionally, private rates of return usually indicate adjustments for taxation which will tend to shift benefits downward where progressivity of tax rates reduce the benefits of higher income levels.[22]

Opportunity costs or foregone earnings are the income the average student could have expected to earn had he been employed. Income foregone, of course, decreases rapidly toward the lower education grade levels, with income alternative below the eighth grade practically nonexistent. Since income foregone is such a substantial cost of education, the lower levels of education may show unusually high or even infinite rates of return.[23]

Using this methodological approach, Hansen found in 1963 that social or total resource rate of returns provided substantial justification for investment in education. Private rates of return, after taxes, were found to be in excess of alternative investments in physical capital.[24] Schultz reached similar conclusions in summarizing rate of return studies for the National Educational Finance Project.[25] Of the several methods used to assess the returns to education, the rate of return method must be considered the most precise. It has the distinct advantage of not only analyzing economic benefits but also relating costs thereto.

# Unresolved Issues Regarding Investment in Human Capital

Before we review the investment benefits to both state and individual accruing from education, the limitation of the entire concept of investment should be mentioned. Harbison observes that economic costs and benefits may not be a fit measure of the need and desirability for education.[26] He distinguishes between the desirability for developing human resources and the concept of human capital, because human capital's raison d'etre is economic return to investment while the development of human resources should be an end in itself.

Educators will generally deny that the pursuits of education should be controlled by economic determinism. It may be legitimately maintained that education has value in itself, and the knowledge obtained from education is, in fact, the primary reason for its existence. To some it is most logical that "the central purpose of education is to increase the demand for and the supply of more education."[27] Therefore, while education may be a key to the economic development of a country, this role is secondary to its major purpose of obtaining ever increasing amounts of education. Such a rationale as justification for continued and increased public and private investment in education is not in keeping with the traditional standards governing investment decisions by firms.

In a cogent critique of the human capital concept, Shaffer maintains that a career pattern is not always selected to maximize income and the pursuit of education is not necessarily geared to profit.[28] Does a parent expend funds for the education of his child beyond the minimum compulsory educational level in a manner which would suggest maximum return on the marginal dollar invested? The relative significance of consumption versus investment benefits lies at the heart of the question. Can it be that the student selects particular courses and reads certain books merely to increase the monetary return on his investment?

Shaffer has summarized his critique by saying:

> Any attempt to show that rational individuals tend to undertake expenditure on education up to the point where the marginal productivity of the human capital produced by the process of education equals the rate of interest—a point at which the marginal expenditure on education yields a return equal to the return on marginal expenditure for any other factor of production—would be a mockery of economic theory.[29]

Whether the individual consciously chooses his alternatives in an "economically rational" sense after proper consideration or whether he simply reacts in a void of information is unresolved. It may be plausibly maintained that more persons would respond to education with economic incentive if they were simply more knowledgeable of the economic consequences of their actions. Nevertheless, it is uncertain whether people would continue to go into the teaching profession, for example, if they were apprised of its low or negative lifetime economic returns.[30]

Whether education is consumption or investment benefit cannot be simply resolved because it is undoubtedly both, and the precise percentage attributable to each holds the key to the validity of the concept of investment in human capital. As Bowen has observed, rate of return studies do not account for the consumption benefits enjoyed by the student who says that college years are the "best years of his life."[31] To most students education is not necessarily a painful process of joyless development of their own human capital; on the contrary, the educational process may be pleasurable with current satisfaction as its primary reward. The immediate pleasure of being educated may also extend to the parent who has pride in the educational achievement of his off-spring. Beyond this, though, education creates present and future benefits of enjoyment derived from gaining new knowledge and the exploration through learning processes not accessible without education. The basic dilemma then is not to decide whether consumption benefits are present, but to decide how much and what percentage the whole consumption constitutes. Schultz has admitted that the responses of individuals are difficult to classify rationally, but he has sought to circumscribe them in this manner:

(1) that where the capital market does serve human investment, it is subject to more imperfections than in financing physical capital;

(2) that most investment in people, notably in the case of education, is in a long-period capacity, for it has a relatively long life and it is thus subject to the additional uncertainties this implies;

(3) that many individuals face serious uncertainty in assessing their innate talents when it comes to investing in themselves; and

(4) that our laws discriminate against human investments.[32]

Even with these limitations, it may be confidently maintained that the measurement of investment benefits is worthwhile and not entirely eroded by the lack of certainty surrounding consumption benefits. Without assigning percentages, Schultz has sought to enhance the investment argument by noting that there are really two types of consumption, current and future. Current consumption benefits are obviously not an investment, but some future consumption benefits may more properly be classified as such.[33] Future consumption benefits may be of enduring quality as with a house, automobile, or refrigerator. However, this argument does little to determine what portion of benefits are investment, other than to show that it is a little larger than once thought. The relevance of the problem cannot be lightly dismissed. If it is assumed that one-half of all educational costs are consumption oriented, then the rate of return on investment, as suggested by a simple comparison of differential earnings with total educational costs, is doubled.[34]

Amplification of the consumption issue could possible involve assigning investment percentages based on whether a student pursues a liberal arts or a vocational education curriculum. Even though liberal arts undoubtedly has investment benefits, a vocational course in auto mechanics may have more investment and less consumption orientation than an English course which pursues Keats' inner thoughts on a Grecian urn.

There is probably no way out of this dilemma, especially when one recognizes that various aspects of consumption and investment may be complimentary. Society may not really have the option of choosing one over the other, but the significant issue does point up a major and probably insolvable defect in the human capital investment concept. This does not suggest that the theory is useless but rather that it should be applied to educational planning processes only with appropriate admonition.

Reliance on investment in education studies is further impaired by the difficulty of establishing a cause and effect relationship between future income and education. More precisely, can the difference in income between two individuals be attributed to a difference in educational level? Much of the recent research in this area has tried to hold other variables constant to determine the true economic impact of education. The economic value of education is distorted by factors such as intelligence, parent's education, race, sex, urban versus rural, north versus south, health, educational quality, and others too numerous to explore. The most antagonistic of these factors, that of ability or intelligence and its impact on income, has been the subject of several research efforts, none of which is conclusive on the subject. Griliches and Mason found that the bias created by ability was about 100 per cent.[35] Hansen, Weisbrod, and Scanlon found that education was relatively unimportant when a sample of young Selective Service rejects was studied, but their data were peculiar because of the relative youth of the population and the fact that the sample was about 50 per cent black. Rate of return studies usually do not take into account the fact that younger and older people in the work force will not reflect as great an economic advantage to education as those in middle age groups.

Disagreement over the bias in favor of education in determining economic returns also creates uncertainty in placing a precise economic value on education. Hause, for example, has concluded after extensive research that the overstatement of rates of return to a college education attributable to an understatement of ability-related opportunity costs does not appear to be a serious source of bias.[36] On the other hand, Jencks in minimizing the effects of education alleges that education explains only 22 per cent of the variation in income.[37] Bowles' research supports the conclusion that much of the apparent economic return to schooling is in fact attributable to the socio-economic background or income of parents.[38] Such opportunity allows a choice of future employment possibilities with different monetary and nonmonetary configurations. Bowles noted that wealthy, high status parents place great value on nonmonetary aspects of work and lower value on the monetary aspects. This suggests that where one has sufficient income and is accustomed to it he will not opt to maximize his financial returns but is likely to lean toward future nonmonetary rewards.[39]

Becker[40] and Denison[41] refuted the assertion that education is such a minor influence on economic returns. Psacharopoulos in surveying studies on earnings functions found that of 37 studies only 5 showed education to have as minor import as attributed to it by Jencks. The majority of the analyses identified a variance of educational attributes to be in the area of 40 per cent. Psacharopoulos concluded that because of certain omissions which interact positively with education, Jencks' results are biased downwards tending to understate the effect of education on lifetime earnings.[42]

Frailties inherent in measurement, while they do not negate the value of investment in education, do introduce an element of uncertainty which cannot be accounted for and without which absolute precision cannot be attained.

## Commonly Overlooked Benefits

Education benefits cannot be measured solely on the basis of monetary returns to the individual or to society. Justification for investment in education may be found to a great degree in nonmonetary external benefits. Education benefits many people other than the student, including the student's children who receive positive intergenerational transfers of knowledge, neighbors who are affected by favorable social values developed by schooling, and employers who are seeking a trained labor force. These benefits and others are beginning to be quantified and measured by both economists and sociologists. The future of educational investment may depend as much on the research findings in this nebulous area as in the measurement of direct monetary returns. The public is interested in education for benefits external to the student himself. Theoretically, if the values of education could be neatly divided, the public would probably desire to pay for only those benefits it receives over and beyond those accruing to the student. But education is largely an indivisible good, beneficial to society and the student simultaneously, and though each receives benefits the value received by the other is not diminished.

Certain nonmonetary returns to education are well known and largely taken for granted. Ignorant people can be more easily misled and propagandized than the educated. The freedom implicit in a democratic society is premised on an educated citizenry. Yet the impact of education is felt beyond general governmental effects; just as importantly it has direct value to the family, neighbors, employment relationships, crime prevention, and other components of the society.

Family benefits are usually not taken into account in measuring the economic returns to education. Weisbrod estimated that about 25 per cent of the cost of elementary education was returned in the form of child-care services.[43] If one attempts to measure the cost-benefit of a $1,000 expenditure per pupil, $250 is immediately justified for child-care services. This interesting statistic was first forwarded by Weisbrod in 1956 when he estimated that, of the 3.5 million working mothers in the United States with children six to eleven years of age, about one million would not work if there were no schools. Assuming only $2,000 earnings for each mother during the school year, the value of child-care services was figured at $2 billion per year. This was approximately one-fourth of the estimated $7.8 billion expended on public and private elementary schools for that year. An updated estimate is undoubtedly applicable to the United States today.

If one can assume that the household is a small economic enterprise or multiproduct firm which produces many desiderata from which members of the family derive satisfaction—such as good health, physical exercise, and nutrition which are the result of production activities such as convalescing, jogging, and eating—then it is possible to measure the impact of education on the efficiency of the enterprise. In devising this ingenious model, Michael theorized that the introduction of additional education into the household's production process would be analogous to applying new technology to a firm.[44] He concluded that the level of schooling systematically influences consumer behavior independent of the effect of income. His data further suggested that education increases the efficiency of the household's production process.

The general well-being of the family may also be affected by education's role in increasing the individual's capacity to utilize and capitalize on situations which will increase both his consumption and economic benefits. Presumably a more highly educated individual will possess a certain economic serendipity which affects his economic choices. Solmon examined the influence of education on saving behavior over and above the ability to earn more on the job, to consume more efficiently, and to generally enjoy life more fully.[45] From reviewing existing saving and consumption-function theories, Solmon concluded that saving propensities tend to rise with schooling level of the family head. It may be presumed that such tendencies toward frugality will contribute to ordered growth of the income and wealth of society and provide for general economic stability. He further found in studying attitudes that one could infer that additional private benefits of schooling may be found in greater efficiency in portfolio management.

Today's problems created by worldwide overpopulation will certainly have an important impact not only on the socio-economic systems of the world but on the ecological system of the planet. In recent years great controversies have surrounded the desirable goal of zero population growth. Population growth usually starts at home, and its economic aspects can be reduced to the micro level of the household. Familial benefits can be maximized by the proper balance of "child services" passed on to the offspring. It may be theorized that the quality of the child is higher if the time and goods devoted to him are greater. For example, family resources may permit the parent to both purchase a musical instrument and provide music instruction to the child. There is little doubt that positive intergenerational transfers are enhanced by limiting the number of children and increasing the parental time devoted to each child. It has been found that the correlation between education and family size is negative. This may be the result of the impact of schooling on the husband's and wife's preferences or it may be the result of a realistic economic assessment of the household reflecting an increase in the price of children as the educational level of the couple increases.

Where the wife has a high level of education, her time is more valuable; thus time expended raising children is more costly. The level of education has been found to have a consistently high relation with the use of contraceptives.[46] In 1965 the percentage of women who had used oral contraceptives was over three times as high among the highest education group as among the lowest. Ryder and Westoff's data support the argument that education "lowers the psychic and/or transaction costs related to contraception." The educated are more aware of, more receptive to, and more effective in their use and selection of contraceptive techniques.[47] Michael found that the relationship between education of the wife and fertility was negative and statistically significant, indicating that the price of the wife's time accruing from increased education may be an important deterrent against population expansion.[48]

The influence of the education of women on the economy of the family and the nation has not gone unnoticed. Although the rates of return for investment in women's schooling are less than for men's, for several reasons including job discrimination[49] and home care options, the benefits of education are nevertheless substantial.

In his famous analysis of conspicuous consumption, Thorstein Veblen observed that with the decline of servitude it became the respected role of woman to devote her activities to domestic and social amenities associated with household adornment. In his view, such efforts were directed toward acquiring household paraphernalia evidencing conspicuous consumption and providing evidence of the family's vicarious leisure. To Veblen such activity commended itself to "the great economic law of wasted effort."[50] Such expenditure of time and energy on the part of women is not, however, without economic impact. Scott has estimated that at equivalent wage rates the value of women's housework is $13,364 a year.[51] Galbraith maintains that the role of housewife is critical for the expansion of consumption in the modern economy.[52] Yet the value by which women increase consumption is not estimated as a part of national income or product.

The role of the female traditionally required by the economic and social system has become less satisfactory to modern woman. Today, most women are interested in casting off the bonds imposed by menial tasks of the household and more fully developing their economic potential. During the past 30 years the number of married women in the labor force has increased dramatically. In 1940, 15 per cent of the married women were in the labor force; and in 1950, 24 per cent; and in 1972, 41.5 per cent. Before World War II women tended to remain in the labor force until they were married and then drop out more or less permanently.[53] Today women still drop out to a great degree after marriage but reenter between the ages of 45 and 55.[54] This participation of women has not only had a pronounced effect on the age and sex composition of the labor force but has also caused major shifts in the household role of the women. Even though a woman's household activities have economic value, the direct participation in production in the labor force undoubtedly has a more profound impact on increasing the total productivity of the country.[55]

Women's participation in the labor force is accompanied by a striking relationship with the level of education. Better educated women are more likely to be in the labor force.[56] The economic explanation for this is that education raises women's productivity in the labor market more than productivity at home, making it more costly for highly educated women to remain at home. However, labor force participation data for all women show that between the ages of 25 and 40, women, regardless of education level, tend to be present in the home in much greater percentages than at other ages. Of course, this indicates that between these ages a woman's life is most often devoted to child rearing.[57]

The positive impact of education on women is not lost, though, by the time they expend at home. As women become more educated and spend a greater amount of time in the labor force, one might assume that they spend a smaller proportion of their time in home production and that a decrease in home production time will indicate a corresponding decrease in child care activities. The data do not bear out such assumptions. To the contrary, better educated working mothers generally spend more time with their children in effectuating positive intergenerational transfers. Analyzing time inputs for various activities of women, Walker[58] found that the better educated mothers spent more time in "physical care" (bathing, feeding dressing, etc.) and in "other care" (activities related to social and educational development of children, including reading to children, helping with lessons, and taking children to social and educational functions) than did the less educated mothers. Less educated mothers spent more time in activities such as preparing meals and doing the laundry.[59] Husbands of more educated women also spent more time on meal preparation.[60] Further, it was found that children of the more educated had more total time spent on them by adults—mother, father, and others, presumably including other individuals involved in child care. This indicates that, in spite of the greater price of her time, the better educated mother not only extends her own time in caring for her children but incurs a greater expenditure of time from the husband and others for her children. A study in Indiana in 1962 corroborates the findings of the Walker study, reporting that women with college degrees devote more than twice as many hours to child care as women with fewer than twelve years of schooling, 83 per cent more time than high school graduates, and 59 per cent more time than women with one to three years of college.[61]

Similarly, a study of 174 Parisian households showed that professional women (presumably better educated) devoted more time, both absolutely and relatively, to child care and less time to housework on both working and nonworking days than did female white-collar employees and blue-collar workers.[62]

Leibowitz theorized that the above described child care phenomenon is the result of better educated mothers having a greater time preference for the future and thus being willing to make larger investments in their young children to obtain future returns for the children. Better educated mothers more readily recognize the value of human capital and invest their time accordingly.

Intergenerational transfer of knowledge is therefore much more pronounced among the educated households. Educational investments in one generation doubtedly have a profound impact on the succeeding generations.

## Employment-Related Benefits

Even though the value of education as it relates to work has been drawn into the question and an all out attack on credentialism has been launched in recent years,[63] the value of education for employment is readily apparent. The more educated person in the job market receives preferential treatment from the employer. Whether this is justified or right is largely irrelevant if the marketplace responds in this manner. Employers appear to recognize that the educated worker has favorable external effects on other workers and on the firm in general. An interdependence probably exists whereby both the worker and the firm have a financial interest in the education of fellow workers.[64]

Employers apparently, and with some rationale, believe that the education of the employee improves the financial potential of the firm. There is a definite positive relationship between the amount of formal education and on-the-job training received.[65] Firms apparently have found that greater productivity can be gained with less cost by investing in the more educated employees. Greater benefits can be obtained by grafting job training on to the knowledge acquired from formal schooling.[66] Mincer theorized that employers invest in workers with more education because they think education confers greater capacity and motivation for training.[67] It may also be that the employer responds in part to the worker's own willingness to invest in himself, since employer investment in the worker appears to increase in about the same proportion as the worker's self investment in schooling.

The less educated experience a greater amount of unemployment. On the average "job losers" have almost a year and a half less education than "job keepers."[68] Labor turnover and unemployment are related to consumer demand for goods and services. Even though the correlation is rather weak, the more educated, being more generally associated with services, are employed in more stable industries.[69] Some evidence also shows that in some areas of the economy physical capital is more likely to be substituted for unskilled than for skilled labor. Consequently, the less educated labor force is more susceptible to layoffs due to advances in technology and fluctuations in the types of goods produced and the methods of production.[70] Further, inexperienced and uneducated workers whose wages are less than minimum wage have higher unemployment.[71]

Another interesting aspect of education's contribution to the employment relationship is that the duration of unemployment is inversely related to education. This may be attributable to any number of characteristics of the educated, but most certainly it is related to the educated worker's knowledge and increased efficiency in seeking out new employment. Education provides a capacity to acquire information and, because of variations in wages of educated versus uneducated, also provides more incentive to become employed.[72]

Undoubtedly contributing to the relationship between education and employment is the employer's need for employees with specialized knowledge. Employers expend greater resources seeking out workers with certain expertise. Therefore persons with higher educational levels generally benefit from specificity of job training and knowledge.

The aforementioned relationships indicate that the marketplace favors the more educated. This does not imply that more education is the solution to all problems of unemployment. It may be possible as suggested in *Work in America,* that too much education may be inefficient to both the individual and the state. There it was noted that the expansion of professional, technical, and clerical jobs absorbed only 15 per cent of newly educated workers, while the remaining 85 per cent accepted jobs previously performed by individuals with fewer credentials.[73] Such superficial data do not lessen the importance of education to the employer seeking to improve his future productivity by hiring more capable workers. No good evidence currently exists to show that education does not enhance employability, and, though the rates of return to education apparently declined during the first half of the century and have leveled off, the overall picture suggests that education, income, and employability are positively related and interdependent. The dilemma is not simple to decide whether to educate but instead what type and degree of education is required by the social and economic system. Most countries accept the fact that education is an important element in economic development, and many have formalized manpower forecasting systems which reflect the nature of educational development necessary to advance their economies.[74] There is certainly no reason individual states in the United States should not indulge in manpower forecasting to maximize development and minimize unemployment through planned educational processes.

## Benefit to Neighbors and Society

The benefits to an educated citizenry extend beyond the perpetuation of the democratic ideals of our system of government which requires a minimally educated populace to operate properly. More directly, an increment of education reduces government expenditures on crime prevention, fire protection, public health, and medical care.[75] It may be logically argued that education reduces crime primarily because education reduces unemployment and the employed commit fewer crimes.[76] Some portion of criminal behavior can be attributed to a lack of education.[77] With a rise in family income a corresponding decrease in delinquency may be found; since more education and greater income are related, a similar relationship exists between education and crime.[78]

Ehrlich found that inequalities in the distribution of schooling may have an effect on the amount of crime, suggesting that equalization of educational opportunity may be a proper governmental goal in crime reduction. Whether more education will serve as a deterrent to crime may depend, according to Ehrlich, on the extent to which the economic returns to crime are reduced. Whether crime pays or not will thus depend on education coupled with alternative methods of impairing the success of criminals.[79]

Other studies have shown that prisoners have lower educational attainment than the average person[80] and that illiteracy among criminals is much higher than for the population as a whole.[81] A 1955 study of 4,000 inmates in Texas prisons showed that 89 percent had not completed high school; a similar study in New Jersey found that 91 per cent had dropped out before graduating from high school.[82] Bureau of Census data show that in 1970, while 55.2 per cent of the population had educational attainment of grade 12 or beyond, only 25.0 per cent of the prison population had gained an equivalent educational level. The median years of schooling for inmates was 9.8, for the general population 12.2.[83] Low educational attainment seems to increase the likelihood of one's "turning to illegal means to fulfill his social and economic desires."[84] A national commission found in a survey of riot participants that inadequate education and under-employment were among the top four grievances which motivated disorders.[85]

Levin estimated the cost of crime against persons and property in the United States to be $1.1 billion per year, the cost of law enforcement and the judiciary to be $4.2 billion, private costs $1.9 billion, and income foregone by inmates to be $1 billion, a total of $8.2 billion. If one half the costs, an upper limit, is attributable to lack of education, we find that an astonishing $4.1 billion dollars could have been saved by further education. Even with the lower limit of Levin's estimate, 25 percent attributable to inadequate education, over $2 billion in costs of crime could have been prevented by more education.[86]

Some contrary assertions recently suggested that student riots of the late 1960s were evidence that education does not inculcate a respect for the law[87] and that compulsory attendance beyond a certain grade level may lead to antagonism and juvenile delinquency. Nevertheless, the positive relationship between education and crime reduction makes a compelling argument for increased attention to education as a tool of crime prevention.

Recipients of welfare generally have lower educational attainment than the average person. Studies by the U.S. Department of Health, Education, and Welfare have shown that incapacitated and unemployed AFDC fathers have median levels of education far below the average. About 76 per cent of the incapacitated fathers and 61.2 per cent of the unemployed fathers did not have a high school education. Since this high percentage did not reflect the 15.9 per cent of incapacitated and 22.8 per cent of the unemployed for whom no educational data were available, the percentages of inadequate education may be even higher.[88] More recent figures show that 84 per cent of all AFDC unemployed fathers had less than a high school education.[89] Over 82 per cent of the AFDC mothers lacked a high school education.[90] AFDC recipients who did become self-supporting generally had more education than those who did not, regardless of race.[91]

In attempting to quantify the impact of welfare costs on the taxpayer, Levin found that AFDC, medical assistance, and general welfare assistance cost $5.9 billion in 1970, and unemployment compensation amounted to $4.3 billion. Levin estimated that an upper limit of 50 per cent and a lower limit of 25 per cent of public assistance, $2.96 billion and $1.48 billion respectively, could be attributed to low levels of education. With an upper limit of 25 per cent and a lower limit of 15 per cent, he determined the costs of unemployment compensation due to inadequate education to be $1.08 billion and $648 million respectively.[92] Whether these costs are entirely accurate is probably of little consequence; the importance of the data rests on the quantification of an apparently strong relationship between level of education and public expenditure on welfare. Theoretically, the efficiency of the use of public resources may be enhanced by increasing educational levels with a corresponding result of decline in the necessity for welfare.

## Education and Wealth Redistribution

Three aspects of redistribution should be noted. The first is the reduction in the number of persons falling below a predetermined poverty line. The second is the pursuit of equality of income, narrowing the variation in income between rich and poor. Finally, redistribution can be viewed as the value of the various governmental programs which are designed to provide better opportunity.

Ribich, attempting to measure the benefits of education in reducing poverty, found little evidence that federal subventions for the low income were having significant effect.[93] He notes that a lengthy chain of events must transpire in the educational process before the effects on poverty can materialize: (1) spending by government must result in augmented educational resources available to schools, (2) the extra resources must add to learning, (3) the additional learning must lead to increases in the capacity to produce and to earn income, and (4) that capability must result in moving individuals out of poverty or at least mitigating the degree of poverty.[94] He observes that much slippage takes place in this process, reducing education impact at each level.

Other studies have found a strong influence of education on lower income groups. A negative association exists between education and welfare incidence. In analyzing a sample of black women taken by the National Center for Social Statistics in 1969, Owen found that education had a strong welfare-reducing effect. Education retained its influence even when the education and socio-economic level of parents were held constant.[95] Of the sample group, ages 20 to 34, over 22 per cent of those with 11 years or less of schooling were receiving AFDC benefits while less than 5 per cent of those with 13 to 15 years of education were receiving benefits. Educated black women enjoyed better earning opportunities than those with less schooling. Owen concluded that the reduction in welfare incidence among better-educated black women "reflects a meaningful rather than spurious statistical relationship."[96] Bowles theorized that educational level and social class do not determine one's income; rather, they determine one's opportunity.[97] Opportunity provides different configurations of monetary and nonmonetary rewards resulting in many rich, high-status parents placing a greater value on nonmonetary aspects of work and a lower value on the monetary aspects of work than the poorer, lower-status parents.[98]

The chain of events enumerated by Ribich and the frailties involved in the measurement of costs and benefits suggest that much more research will be needed to identify the contribution of education in overcoming poverty. Some maintain that education should reduce the number of persons who are classified as poverty level or below. This presents quantification problems because the poverty line may move upward, and a mere head count of those crossing the poverty line is relatively meaningless if it goes no farther.[99] There is some evidence that education does show certain returns which may tend to move people above a poverty line, wherever the line may be set, and Ribich has found that the payoff from investment in education, although relatively small, is increased by expending public funds in lower expenditure school districts and by placing emphasis on certain types of educational programs.[100] Cost-benefit studies of education and poverty are largely inconclusive.

A quest for eradication of inequality characterizes much of the educational and economic enquiry today. According to Wedgewood, inequality is "not only socially deplorable but an economic defect in the social system."[101] Inequality of incomes is also economically inefficient. Many years ago, Dalton cited scientific foundation for his assertion as to the inefficiency of inequality: "An unequal distribution of a given amount of purchasing power among a given number of people is, therefore, likely to be wasteful distribution from the point of view of economic welfare, and the more unequal the distribution the greater the waste. This is merely an application of the economists' law of diminishing marginal utility."[102]

Inequality is substantially different from the removal of certain numbers of people from the ranks of poverty. Theoretically, the distribution between rich and poor can be very great and yet no one will be in poverty. In 1950 the lowest fifth of income groups of the nation's population had 4.5 per cent of the aggregate income; by 1970 this had increased to 5.5 per cent.[103] This small increase in equality apparently still leaves substantial inequality in the United States, but when the United States is compared with other major countries of the world we find it classified as having one of the lowest levels of inequality. Using pretax income, Ahluwalia shows that in 1970 the lowest 40 per cent income group in the United States has 19.7 per cent of the aggregate income while the highest per cent group has 38.8 per cent, indicating a more equalized system than the United Kingdom with 18.8 per cent and 39.0 per cent, France (1962) with 9.5 per cent and 53.7 per cent, or Spain (1965) with 17.6 per cent and 435.7 per cent. Countries with more socialistic or communistic forms of government generally showed less inequality. For example, Hungary (1969) had 24.0 per cent and 33.5 per cent; Czechoslovakia (1964) had 27.6 per cent and 31.0 per cent, and Poland (1964) had 23.4 per cent and 36.0 per cent.[104] While this equality may be attributable in some degree to form of government, it may also be influenced by the more static nature of a country's population. Countries without a high incidence of poor immigrants have fewer equalization problems. All of the advanced countries mentioned above show high relative levels of equality when compared to Ecuador, for example, where the lowest 40 per cent income level has only 6.5 per cent of the income and the highest 20 per cent has 73.5 per cent.[105] Even so, it has been said and it appears to be generally true that a distinguishing characteristic of the modern age, certainly in more advanced countries, is that equality is a politically attractive and aggressive idea. Kristol has said that "inequality is on the defensive."[106] The extent to which the people of a country desire to further equalize is, of course, a major governmental policy question. When such a desire for equality is demonstrated, a basic question arises as to whether it is better to deliver the equality by means of educational expenditures or through direct financial assistance.

It is certain that public education in the United States has enhanced equality by largely eliminating illiteracy. Johns and Morphet have observed that "the greatest differences in income exist in countries where the mass of the people are illiterate but dominated by a few elites."[107] Education undoubtedly prevents the domination by the elite and the subjugation of the lower economic classes, but to expect education to eliminate inequality by equalizing incomes is a fallacious pursuit. As Johns observes, the incomes of the stone age Indians who inhabited the United States in 1492[108] were almost precisely equal. Those "forensic" social science researchers seeking to relate education and equality of incomes are probably seeking a nirvana neither promised nor contemplated by mass education.[109] Such misconceptions convey a kind of educational nihilism which erodes the public confidence in mass education generally. Johns and Morphet have elucidated the matter as follows:

> It is not the purpose of education to equalize incomes in a country with a political system designed to protect the freedoms of the individual and with a predominately free-enterprise economic system. The educational policy in such a country should be to maximize the development of the talents of each individual by equalizing educational opportunity at a high level. Such a policy will tend to minimize poverty and maximize economic growth, but it will not eliminate differences in income.[110]

There is, therefore, really no argument regarding the impact of education on equalization of income; it does not, beyond certain minimums, erase the variation between high and low income groups. It is undoubtedly more effective for the government to simply give more to the poor in cash transfers if income equalization is the goal. Such transfers, whether wise or not, are already well established in the United States.[111]

The benefits of the alternative governmental redistribution mechanisms may be measured in results as measured in increased income or increased achievement. Do in-kind transfers through food, housing, and medical care increase the individual's future productivity or is a governmental investment in education to increase knowledge of the individual more economically effective and efficient? If the question is put directly, taxpayers have traditionally preferred to redistribute income by providing for educational opportunity. Redistribution would come about by reducing the productivity variance among individuals by expanding educational opportunity of the lower classes.

Public education has been demonstrated to have a high degree of vertical redistributive power in the process of providing equal educational opportunity. Alexander and Melcher show that a family with less than $3,500 yearly income with one child enrolled in the public schools of New York State has nearly a 5 to 1 benefit-tax ratio. In other words, the dollar expenditure received by the poor family through public schools[112] is nearly 5 times its tax liability for that purpose. It is true that poor families generally have greater ratios in wealthier school districts, but in cases examined in 12 states, the poor seldom had less than a 3 to 1 benefit-tax ration.

Redistribution is gained by higher percentages of state and federal funding for the schools and by the progressivity in the tax system; the regressive system impacts on the poor in a greater degree and thereby reduces the benefit-tax redistributional ratio.

Unfortunately, higher education does not show such an impressive redistributive effect. This is largely attributable to the absence of compulsory attendance laws in higher education. Children of poor families do not enroll in higher education as much as do children of middle income and upper income families.[113]

Coleman maintains that neither education nor any other governmental method of redistribution can effectively counter the inequalities created in society by private resources. He says:

To fully counter the inequality of private resources, the publicly-provided resources for the privately disadvantaged must be sufficient to provide to all children the same opportunity as held by the child with the greatest private resources, genetic and environmental. This is obviously impossible.[114]

He doubts that to fully equalize is even desirable, since it would prove a disincentive for parents and would probably reduce the overall level of resources and thus the level of opportunity. In lieu of full equality, he suggests that society must decide what level of inequality it is willing to tolerate and create educational opportunity accordingly. As to how this should be done, Coleman does not elaborate.[115] In short, social research is of little assistance in determining whether education or some other mode of public allocation is most effective in redistributing wealth and creating equality. The equality which education is designed to guarantee is not that of income, but of opportunity. Equal opportunity to develop one's potential to its fullest may not always be related to equal income.

## Option Value of Education

Education is incremental and must be assembled in a precise order and sequence. The amount of education one ultimately receives is thus dependent on the level of education previously received. The decision to obtain a high school education thus involves not only the probability of obtaining additional earnings normally obtainable by a high school graduate but also involves the option value of being able to pursue a college education.[116] At each level of education certain options are available and have economic value if they exceed the rate of return of alternative investments. The value of a high school education given in direct monetary returns understates the true value of the education. In terms of the marketplace, Weisbrod compares the individual to a buyer who purchases a machine now and receives a discount (or option) or a ticket for future redemption. Both the immediate use of the machine and the potential use of the discount ticket have value.[117] The value of the option to pursue additional schooling depends on the probability of its being used and the expected value of the option if exercised. With lower levels of education the option value is great; it may reduce to zero upon completion of graduate school if the education obtained there does not provide for further independent work.

Interdependence among levels of education and their corresponding options increases the value of the lower level of education if the option is exercised. Weisbrod has shown in illustrative calculations that the option value at the elementary level can be quite valuable, possibly increasing the rate of return from 35 to 54 per cent.[118]

Further options are gained from education beyond the monetary returns. In fact, education may be largely justifiable because of the options it provides: job options, leisure options, work condition options, on-the-job learning options, and type of life options. Most of these may be subsumed under the alternatives a person receives from widened job choices. Most people will choose a white collar position as opposed to the job of a laborer, even if the monetary rewards are the same. Options permit the individual to choose among employment conditions which offer not only monetary but, possibly just as importantly, nonmonetary rewards.

Education also provides another type of "option" which enables a person to adjust to changing job opportunities. This "hedging option" gives the individual the capacity to better accommodate technological changes which would otherwise force him to unemployment.[119] Weisbrod suggests that adaptability may be enhanced by a more general educational curriculum.[120] Regardless, the element of job flexibility which education provides is regarded as a viable hedge in the face of technological change.

# Monetary Returns to Education

Even though one can cite many examples of the value of education, sooner or later everyone will ask how much is it worth in dollars. An answer to this question must always be couched in averages which can only broadly predict your chances of having a certain monetary gain over a lifetime. As Miller observes, an investment in education is like buying insurance,[121] insurance companies cannot tell you what will happen to you specifically, but they do know your chances of living to a certain number of years if they know your race, age, sex, and several other things about you. Your chances for gaining certain financial rewards from education can only be estimated actuarially.

Completion of additional levels of schooling is associated with higher average incomes. Elementary school graduates (8th grade) in 1968 averaged $5,096 income per year, high school graduates $7,732, and college graduates $11,257.[122] By 1972 the respective amounts had increased to $6,756, $10,433, and $16,201.

Table 1 shows that the mean annual income for male high school graduates was about 60 per cent of the mean annual income for male college graduates in 1939; the percentage had not increased significantly by 1972 when it was about 64. During the period since 1949 the relative income position of elementary graduates declined, falling to about 64 per cent of the income for high school graduates in 1972. During the fifties and sixties, then, there was an expansion of the difference between elementary and high school graduates, and a very slight narrowing between high school and college graduates.

Among college graduates a differential exists based on the level of degree obtained as well as on the quality of the institution attended. Table 2 shows that among all classes of colleges in 1966, a bachelor's degree was valued at $9,096 per year while a master's was $9,339 and the doctorate or professional degree jumped to $12,900. When quality of the institution was taken into account, it was found that men holding a master's degree from a low ranked institution earned less than one with a bachelor's degree from either a middle or high ranked college. A rather astonishing $4,245

## Table 1
### Relationship of Education to Income, Men Aged 25 and Over

| Schooling completed | Mean annual income | | | | | |
| --- | --- | --- | --- | --- | --- | --- |
| | 1939 | 1949 | 1959 | 1968 | 1969 | 1972 |
| Elementary school | | | | | | |
|   Less than 8 years | NA | $2,062 | $2,551 | $3,333 | $4,242 | $5,235 |
|   8 years | NA | 2,829 | 2,769 | 5,996 | 5,809 | 6,756 |
| High School | | | | | | |
|   1 to 3 years | $1,379 | $3,226 | $4,618 | $6,569 | $7,279 | $8,449 |
|   4 years | 1,661 | 3,784 | 5,567 | 7,731 | 8,827 | 10,433 |
| College | | | | | | |
|   1 to 3 years | $1,931 | $4,423 | $6,966 | $8,618 | $10,387 | $11,867 |
|   4 years or more | 2,607 | 6,179 | 9,206 | 11,257 | 14,079 | 16,201 |

NA = not available

Source: Herman P. Miller, "Annual and Lifetime Income in Relation to Education: 1939–1959," *American Economic Review* (December 1960). Table 1: and U.S. Bureau of the Census, Current Population Reports, Series P. 60, No. 63. Table 4. Also: "Annual Mean Income. Lifetime Income, and Educational Attainment of Men in the United States, for Selected Years. 1956 to 1972." Bureau of the Census, Current Population Reports, Series P. 60. No. 92. 1974. Table 2.

**Table 2**
**Earnings of Male College Graduates by Highest Degree Taken and by Rank of College: 1966**

| Highest degree and rank of college | Median earnings |
|---|---|
| All degrees | |
| All ranks | $9,489 |
| Low rank | 7,881 |
| Medium rank | 9,752 |
| High rank | 11,678 |
| Bachelor's | |
| All ranks | 9,096 |
| Low rank | 7,641 |
| Medium rank | 9,324 |
| High rank | 11,305 |
| Master's | |
| All ranks | 9,339 |
| Low rank | 8,327 |
| Medium rank | 9,407 |
| High rank | 10,555 |
| Doctorate or professional | |
| All ranks | 12,900 |
| Low rank | 11,842 |
| Medium rank | 13,785 |
| High rank | 16,087 |

Source: U.S. Bureau of the Census, "Men with College Degrees: March 1967," *Current Population Reports*, Series P-20, No. 180, From: Herman P. Miller, "Annual and Lifetime Income in Relation to Education," p. 172.

difference existed between the earnings at the doctorate and professional level between the low ranked and the high ranked institution. Thus, to improve the accuracy of the estimates of future earnings it is necessary to determine not only the level of the college degree obtained but just as importantly the quality of the institution awarding the degree.

Education definitely does not pay as well for black males or for women. In 1968, the white male's medium income for a high school education was $7,875 and for nonwhite it was $5,810. The nonwhite was relatively better off in 1968 when his median income was about 73 per cent of the white income as opposed to 1958 when his median income was only 64 per cent of the white median income.[123]

Women's incomes vary substantially because so many are not full-time employees, but for those working full-time, high school graduates' incomes were about 67 per cent of those who had graduated from college. The difference was slightly less than for males.[124] Even though the mean incomes are not equal among white males, nonwhite males, and females, each level of education is accompanied by a substantial rise in income.

Lifetime income is another measure of monetary benefit of educational attainment. From this method can be found the income one can expect to earn in a lifetime by educational level. Insurance techniques utilizing survival ratios and income intervals are employed. In 1972, for example, a man with a high school education could expect a lifetime income of $478,873 while the man with 4 or more years of college could expect $757,923. Table 3 shows the various educational plateaus and the monetary benefits associated thereto in current dollars. Table 4 gives lifetime incomes for the same years, correcting for inflation by using 1972 dollars.

**Table 3**
**Education and Lifetime Income for Men in 1958, 1968, and 1972***
**(in current dollars)**

| Income<br>Schooling Completed | Income<br>1958 | Income<br>1968 | 1972 |
|---|---|---|---|
| Total | $215,784 | $357,552 | $470,795 |
| Elementary School | | | |
| Less than 8 years | 128,861 | 213,505 | 279,997 |
| 8 years | 17,010 | 276,755 | 343,730 |
| High School | | | |
| 1 to 3 years | 203,901 | 308,305 | 389,208 |
| 4 years | 242,480 | 371,094 | 478,873 |
| College | | | |
| 1 to 3 years | 287,3005 | 424,280 | 543,435 |
| 4 years or more | 401,819 | 607,921 | 757,923 |
| 4 years | 363,986 | 584,062 | 710,569 |
| 5 years or more | 440,404 | 636,119 | 823,759 |

*From Age 18 to death.

Source: "Annual Mean Income, Lifetime Income, and Educational Attainment, Men in the United States for Selected Years, 1956 to 1972," Bureau of the Census, *Current Population Report*, Series P-60, No. 92, 1974, Table 6.

The percent increase in lifetime income for males age 18 to death provides a guide as to the increase or decrease in the dollar value of succeeding educational plateaus. In 1972, in current dollars, the level of lifetime income for elementary school graduates was about 72 per cent of the income of high school graduates; the lifetime income for high school graduates was about 67 per cent of that of college graduates. The lifetime income value of the major educational plateaus was rather stable, indicating that the monetary value related to education is relatively constant giving a uniform income advantage to those with higher educational attainment.[125]

# Discount and Productivity Adjustments

When an individual views his lifetime earnings he is concerned not only with the total amount at the end of his lifetime, but also with its distribution throughout the years. Money received earlier is of greater value to him than that which he may receive later in life. Since a person usually cannot choose when he will receive the greatest resources, the value of future income must be reduced to determine its current value. This procedure is known as discounting.[126]

Adjustment in lifetime income is also necessary to account for increase in income due to rising productivity. This factor is added to the equation to allow for increased individual productivity in a growing economy; "every individual may expect an upward trend in his own income, superimposed on the cross-sectional pattern for a given year."[127] It is an adjustment for growth in productivity, not for inflation in prices.[128] Table 5 gives the expected lifetime income for all males 18 years old with income in 1971. This is the present value of the total sum of income received between ages 18 and 64 by educational level.

**Table 4**
**Education and Lifetime Income for Men in 1968 and 1972\* (in 1972 dollars)**

| Schooling Completed | Income 1968 | Income 1972 |
|---|---|---|
| Total | $516,816 | $581,962 |
| Elementary School | | |
| Less than 8 years | 319,251 | 376,417 |
| 8 years | 387,595 | 421,136 |
| High School | | |
| 1 to 3 years | 442,046 | 476,703 |
| 4 years | 511,416 | 563,101 |
| College | | |
| 1 to 3 years | 597,888 | 659,040 |
| 4 years or more | 829,493 | 872,805 |
| 4 years | 796,663 | 824,444 |
| 5 years or more | 870,175 | 975,799 |

\*From Age 18 to death.

Source: "Annual Mean Income. Lifetime Income, and Educational Attainment, Men in the United States for Selected Years, 1956 to 1972." Bureau of Census, *Current Population Report*, Series P-60, No. 92, 1974, Table 7.

Comparison of Tables 4 and 5 shows the impact of the discount rate on lifetime income projections. However, reduction in amounts shown does not affect the relative monetary advantages for those with more education. The man with an eighth grade education can only expect to receive about 43 per cent of the lifetime income of the man with 5 or more years of college.

Taxation plays an important role in the amount of actual dollars one can expect to receive over a lifetime. Progressive income taxes, in particular, will tend to reduce the real income and diminish the relative difference between the higher and lower income categories. As the private monetary benefits are reduced, however, the public benefits from tax revenues are increased with more education. It is therefore essential that the tax benefits of education not be regarded only as a reduction in private benefits from education without awareness of the corresponding public benefit.

Thus far, in this section, it has been shown how education results in a positive monetary benefit. The advantages of being educated are evident when one compares the various levels of education according to annual income and lifetime income, and when adjustments are made for discount rates and productivity increases. The question which now arises is whether the income stream from increased education will remain positive when the costs of the additional education are taken into account.

# Rate of Return on Investment in Education

Several studies have estimated the rate of return to education. As observed above, the rate of return analysis is more precise than total lifetime income or discount and productivity adjusted lifetime income, because it relates the total resource costs of education to income benefits. The result is an estimate of rate of return expressed in percentages. This type of analysis provides for a convenient comparison of education with alternative forms of economic investment characterized as physical capital or, as Psacharopoulos terms it, "investment in steel mills."[129]

### Table 5
### Expected Lifetime Income for all Males 18 Years Old with Income in 1971
**(by years school completed, selected discount rates, and selected annual productivity increase in 1972 dollars)**

| | Expected Lifetime Income | |
| --- | --- | --- |
| Schooling completed | Discount rate of 3 per cent with annual productivity increase of 2 per cent | Discount rate of 5 per cent with annual productivity increase of 4 per cent |
| Elementary School | | |
| Less than 8 years | $177,000 | $176,000 |
| 8 years | 221,00 | 220,000 |
| High School | | |
| 1 to 3 years | 253,000 | 252,000 |
| 4 years | 305,000 | 303,000 |
| College | | |
| 1 to 3 years | 348,000 | 346,000 |
| 4 years or more | 480,000 | 477,000 |
| 4 years | 450,000 | 448,000 |
| 5 years or more | 513,000 | 511,000 |

Source: "Annual Mean Income. Lifetime Income, and Educational Attainment, Men in the United States for Selected Years, 1956 to 1972." Bureau of Census, *Current Population Report*, Series P-60, No. 92, 1974, Table 10.

Rates may be calculated for both private and social costs. Becker published data in 1964 showing that the private rate of return for a college education was 12.5 per cent in 1940 and 10 per cent in 1950. The corresponding social rate of return was 9 per cent for both years.[130] Becker also found that the private rates of return to white male high school graduates, unadjusted for ability, were 16 per cent in 1939, 20 percent in 1949, 25 per cent in 1956, and 28 per cent in 1958.[131] This ascending pattern has not been typical of college education generally. Schultz reported private rate of return estimates of 35 per cent for elementary education, 25 per cent for high school, and 15 per cent for college education.[132] He found social returns to be comparable.[133]

A landmark study in rate of return analysis was performed by Hansen and reported in 1963 in which he estimated the rates of return to both total resource investment and private resource investment, the major difference being between total school costs as opposed to tuition and fees which are funded by the individual.

Assuming an alternative return on physical capital at 10 per cent, an investment in completion of high school and college is well justified. The rate of return to the total resource investment of an eighth grade education is far beyond the other educational levels. Even if a return to investment in physical capital at 12 per cent is assumed, the rate of return for education, even after taxes, is greater for secondary school and commensurate for college graduates. One important finding by Hansen was that the rates of return to education are much higher at the traditional educational plateaus of eighth, twelfth, and college graduate levels. Interval education does not approach these terminal points in payoff.

In what is generally acknowledged to be the most accurate analysis of returns to education, Hanoch found that in 1959 the private rate of return on an eighth grade education for white males exceeded 100 per cent[134] and that the average rate for high school for whites is 16 per cent in the North and 19 per cent in the South.[135] College dropouts showed the relatively low marginal rates of 7 and 9 per cent in North and South respectively. The rate of return for completion of college was 12 and 11 per cent[136] for North and South.[137] Hanoch found the marginal rate of return to graduate school (17 plus years vs. 16 years) to be only 7 per cent. This surprisingly low return could have been affected by Hanoch's methodology which assumed that the direct costs of education equal to the students earnings. As Hanoch points out, this may understate the earnings or overstate the costs because many students in graduate school get tuition scholarships and fellowships which are not reported as earnings.[138] Nevertheless, the graduate rate of return is generally much less than at lower educational levels.

Recently, Hines and colleagues discovered private rates of return of 155.1 per cent for elementary school, 19.5 per cent for secondary, and 13.6 per cent for a college education.[139] Hines was able to obtain total educational cost data which also permitted him to calculate the social rates of return, which he found to be 17.8 per cent for elementary school, 14 per cent for completion of high school, and 9.7 per cent for college graduates. There is a consistent decline in returns as the level of schooling increases, but it is evident from all the studies that the rate of return through college graduation is at least comparable to and generally higher than alternative investment in physical capital.

This generally holds true when international data are analyzed as well. In a review of rate of return studies in 32 countries, Psacharopoulos found that the average social returns to investment in education across countries was 25.1 per cent for primary education, 13.5 per cent for secondary, and 11.3 per cent for higher education.[140] The private returns were 23.7 per cent, 16.3 per cent, and 17.5 per cent for the respective educational levels. Internationally, as well as domestically, higher levels of graduate education tend to produce the lowest rates of return, but Psacharopoulos found that this pattern is not always consistent. In Britain, for example, the return to a master's degree was negative, but the private return to a Ph.D. was higher than even the bachelor's degree. Presumably, more economic value is placed on the terminal graduate degree or the costs are relatively less than intermediate graduate degrees or even the bachelor's degree.[141] Out of 12 countries for which physical capital data were available, a comparison showed that investment in human capital usually exceeded returns to physical capital.[142]

The investment in education was superior from a social point of view, but certain exceptions were noticeable. In the Netherlands and Japan, for example, the returns were higher for physical capital at all levels of education. But generally the social benefits for each educational level were higher than the alternative rate for physical capital.[143] In all cases the social rate of return to elementary school was higher than return to physical capital. Psacharopoulos found in comparing countries according to economic development that the less developed countries showed greater returns to investment in both physical and human capital. He found further that the returns to human capital were much more favorable in less developed countries than in more industrialized countries.[144]

Rate of return studies, while they do not generally lend themselves to definite judgments regarding marginal investment, may provide some suggestion as to investment limits beyond which a country or a state will receive diminishing returns. One may logically assume, for example, that as the costs of higher education increase the rate of return for higher education will diminish. The rate of return for a college graduate will decrease if an oversupply of college graduates leads to a decrease in demand for a college education and if salaries or skilled and blue collar workers with high school educations are able to reduce the college-high school earning differentials as through the power of unionization. A suggested answer to this question is provided in recent data supplied by Raymond and Sesnowitz who reported the marginal private rate of return advantage of a college graduate over a high school graduate to be 17.9 per cent.[145] Adjusting for ability, under the assumption that college graduates may have greater learning capacity to begin with , the rate of return may be reduced to either 16.8 or 15.7 per cent depending on the assumed relationship. Regardless of which rate is used the benefit of a college education over high school clearly justifies investment in education. Social rates of return, although less, still amounted to 15.3 or 14.3 per cent depending on ability adjustment. These recent rates based on the 1970 Census data indicate that neither the private nor the social rate of return has diminished much during the 12 year period since Hansen's study.[146] As indicated by comparing Raymond and Sesnowitz's to earlier studies the private rate of return advantage to a college education does not seem to be diminishing; it may be increasing, in so noting they said: "our results indicate that the increased supply of college-educated males during the 1960s did not cause a significant reduction in the rates of return on a college education."

## Conclusions

Generally, it may be concluded that the economic measures of educational benefits are inadequate to capture the full value of having an educated citizenry. Economic benefits found by rate-of-return analysis or any other economic tool currently in use fall far short of an accurate determination of social benefits accruing to the state and society from investment in education. Returns to individuals can be more adequately assessed by simple macro-estimation of lifetime earnings in relation to costs does not tell the entire story.

Employment benefits, intergenerational transfer of knowledge, and several types of options are all values which are derived by the individual or his family which, if properly measured, increase the estimates of the worth of an education.

Most economists will admit that estimates of social returns to education do not by any stretch of the imagination identify the true value to society of higher levels of education. It is acknowledged that human resources must be developed in order to effectively use physical capital, but the optimum level of education needed is not apparent from the research. Simplistic supply and demand arguments cannot resolve this issue,[147] instead it must be analyzed in terms of the interaction between human and physical capital with appropriate accommodation of the absorption rate created by combining both.[148]

Further complexity is introduced by our inability to place a value on education for its contribution in the prevention of many social problems including crime and poverty, and the value of education in elongating the span of life through more knowledgeable health treatment and care is equally as nebulous. These and other societal benefits cannot be assessed by current economic tools and the result is that the value of education to society is sorely underassessed.

In spite of this downward bias, however, education still appears to possess formidable economic benefits. Rate-of-return analyses consistently show that investment in education returns earnings to both the individual and society in excess of alternative investment in physical capital. Studies have consistently shown that returns from early childhood through college education are of such magnitude as to justify free public education through the bachelor's degree even if we do not add to the return estimate the many nonquantifiable societal benefits. It may be that if these were included the rate-of-return to society would double present estimates.

Some recent adverse opinion suggesting that college education may not be worthwhile economically, notwithstanding, the value of education is apparently as great as ever. Even if the return were decreasing it does not necessarily follow that the value of college education is eroding. On the contrary, it may well mean that elementary and secondary education is increasingly valuable as a result of more efficient and effective education, thereby leaving a narrower difference in returns between high school and college graduates.

Further and increased investment in education by the public is fully justified by current economic analysis. Even though the methods of quantifying educational benefits are inadequate, they nevertheless identify an overwhelming private and public benefit. In view of these benefits, during the present recessed economic condition in which the country finds itself, it would seem to be sound economic policy to invest greater sums in the development of human capital through education.

This paper was prepared for the Florida Department of Education to stimulate discussion of education as an investment in the state and the individual.

# Notes

1. Mark Blaug, ed. *Economics of Education I* (Baltimore: Penguin Books, 1968), p. 11.

2  Alfred Marshall, *Principles of Economics,* 8th ed. (New York: Macmillan Co., 1948).

3. T. W., "Investment in Human Capital," *American Economic Review* 51 (1961): 1–17.

4. R. L. Johns and Edgar L. Morphet. *The Economics and Financing of Education,* 3rd ed. (Englewood Cliffs, N.J.: Prentice-Hall Co., 1975).

5. Frederick H. Harbison. *Human Resources and the Wealth of Nations* (Oxford: Oxford University Press, 1973), p. 3.

6. Ibid., p. 5.

7. B. A. Weisbrod, "Education and Investment in Human Capital," *Journal of Political Economy* 70, no. 5 (Part 2, 1962 Supplement): 106–123.

8. Ibid.

9. W. G. Bowen, "Assessing the Economic Contribution of Education: An Appraisal of Alternative Approaches," *Higher Education, Report of the Committee Under the Chairmanship of Lord Robbins:* 961–63, London, H.M.S.O., 1963, pp. 73–96.

10. "Targets for Education in Europe in 1970," paper prepared for Washington Conference of the O.E.C.D., 1961, p. 75.

11. Bowen, "Assessing the Economic Contribution of Education."

12. John W. Kendrick, *Productivity Trends in the United States,* (Princeton: Princeton University Press, 1961), p. 79.

13. See: B. F. Massell, "Capital Formation and Technological Change in United States Manufacturing," *Review of Economics and Statistics* (May 1960): 182–188.

14. Solomon Fabricant, *Prerequisites for Economic Growth* (New York: National Conference Board, 1959).

15. Edward F. Denison, *The Sources of Economic Growth in the United States and The Alternatives Before Us,* Supplementary Paper No. 13 (Committee for Economic Development, January 1962), pp. 69–70.

16. Johns and Morphet, *Economics and Financing of Education,* p. 98.

17. Bowen, "Assessing the Economic Contribution of Education."

18  .Herman P. Miller, "Annual and Lifetime Income in Relation to Education 1929–1959," *American Economic Review* 50 (1960): 962–986.

19. H. S. Houthakker, "Education and Income," *Review of Economics and Statistics* (February 1959): 26.

20. W. Lee Hansen, "Total and Private Rates of Return to Investment in Schooling," *Journal of Political Economy* 81, no. 2 (1963): 128–141.

21. Ibid.

22. Ibid.

23. Ibid.

24. Ibid.

25. Theodore W. Schultz, "The Human Capital Approach to Education," *Economic Factors Affecting the Financing of Education,* ed. R. L. Johns et al. (Gainsville, Fla: National Educational Finance Project, 1970), p. 48

26. Harbison, *Human Resources and the Wealth of Nations,* pp. 16–17.

27. Ibid.

28. H. G. Shaffer, "Investment in Human Capital: Comment," *American Economic Review* 52, no. 4 (1961): 1026–1035.

29. Ibid.

30. See: Stephen B. Thomas, "Development of a Prototype Teacher Salary Schedule for the State of Florida Based on Rates of Return Analysis" (Ed.D diss., University of Florida, 1974).

31. Bowen, "Assessing the Economic Contribution of Education."

32. T. W., *Investment in Human Capital* (New York: Free Press, 1972). pp. 52–53.

33. Ibid.

34. Bowen, "Assessing the Economic Contribution of Education.": See also: T. W. Schultz, "Investment in Human Capital." *American Economic Review* (March 1961): 12–13.

35. Zvi Griliches and William M. Mason, "Education, Income, and Ability," *Investment in Education,* ed. T. W. Schultz (Chicago: University of Chicago Press, 1971), p. 87.

36. John C. Hause, "Earnings Profile: Ability and Schooling," *Investment in Education,* ed. T. W. Schultz (Chicago: University of Chicago Press, 1971), p. 131.

37. Christopher Jencks et al., *Inequality* (New York: Basic Books, 1972).

38. Samuel Bowles, "Schooling and Inequality From Generation to Generation," *Investment in Education,* ed. T. W. Schultz (Chicago: University of Chicago Press, 1971). pp. 219–251.

39. *Investment in Human Capital.*

40. Gary S. Becker, *Human Capital* (New York: National Bureau of Economic Research, 1964).

41. Denison, *The Sources of Economic Growth in the United States.*

42. George Psacharopoulos, "Jencks and Inequality," *Comparative Education Review* (October 1974): 446–448.

43. Weisbrod, "Education and Investment in Human Capital."

44. Robert T. Michael, "Education and consumption," *Education, Income and Human Behavior,* ed. F. Thomas Juster (New York: McGraw-Hill Book Co., 1975), pp. 235–252.

45. Lewis C. Solmon, "The Relation Between Schooling and Savings Behavior: An Example of Indirect Effects of Education," *Education, Income, and Human Behavior,* ed. F. Thomas Juster (New York: McGraw-Hill Book Co., 1975), pp. 253–293.

46. Norman B. Ryder and Charles F. Westoff, *Reproduction in the United States, 1965* (Princeton, N.J.: Princeton University Press, 1971).

47. Ibid.

48. Robert T. Michael, "Education and Fertility," *Education, Income and Human Behavior,* ed. F. Thomas Juster (New York: McGraw-Hill Book Co., 1975), pp. 339–364.

49. Of late, wage discrimination for comparable employment of males and females has been repeatedly documented. But as early as 1917 E. F. Rathbone implied that communities in England sympathized with and supported male over female unions because the males usually had families to support. "The Remuneration of Women's Services," *Economic Journal* 27 (March 1917): 55–68. In 1922, Edgeworth observed that the pressure of male trade unions appeared to be largely responsible for crowding women into comparatively few, low-paying occupations. F. U. Edgeworth, "Equal Pay to Men and Women for Equal Work," *Economic Journal* 32 (December 1922): 431–457. See also: Gary S. Becker, *The Economics of Discrimination* (Chicago: University of Chicago Press, 1971). Of course, job and wage discrimination against women is much broader than that incurred by organized labor; the foundations of sex discrimination have permeated nearly all aspects of our society.

50. Thorstein Veblen, *The Theory of the Leisure Class* (New York: The Macmillan Company, 1899).

51. Ann Crittenden Scott. "The Value of Housework: For Love or Money," *Ms. Magazine* (July 1972): Recent Reports by the Social Security Administration indicates that the economic value of housework is about $5,500.00 per year (1975).

52. John Kenneth Galbraith, *Economics & The Public Purpose* (Boston: Houghton Mifflin Co., 1973).

53. See: U. S. Bureau of Census, *Current Population Reports*, Series P-50, nos. 22 and 29.

54. Arleen Leibowitz, "Education and the Allocation of Women's Time," *Education, Income and Human Behavior*, ed. F. Thomas Juster (New York: McGraw-Hill Book co., 1975), p. 171.

55. Jacob Mincer, "Labor Force Participation of Married Women: A Study of Labor Supply," *Aspects of Labor Economics*, ed. H. Gregg Lewis, *Universities—National Bureau Conference Series 14* (Princeton, N.J.: Princeton University Press, 1962).

56. Leibowitz, "Education and the Allocation of Women's Time," p. 172.

57. Ibid., p. 174

58. Kathryn Walker, *Definition of Household Activities* (Ithaca, N.Y.: Use of Time Research Project, New York State College of Human Ecology, Cornell University, 1967).

59. Ibid.

60. Ibid.

61. Sarah L. Manning, *Time Use in Household Tasks in Indiana Families* (Lafayette, Ind.: Purdue University Agricultural Experiment Station Research Bulletin, No. 837, January 1968).

62. M. Guilbert, N. Lowit, and J. Creusen, "Les budgets-temps et l'etude des horaires de la vie quotidienne," *Revue Francaise de Sociologe* 8 (1967): 169–183.

63. *Work in America*, Report of a Special Task Force to the Secretary of Health, Education, and Welfare (Cambridge, Mass.: The MIT Press, 1973), pp. 134–152.

64. B. A. Weisbrod, "Education and Investment in Human Capital."

65. Jacob Mincer, "On-the-job Training: Costs, Returns, and Some Implications," *Journal of Political Economy* 70 (October 1962, Supplement).

66. Richard Perlman, *The Economics of Education* (New York: McGraw-Hill Book Co., 1973), p. 32.

67. Jacob Mincer, "Education, Experience, Earnings and Employment," *Education, Income and Human Behavior*, ed. F. Thomas Juster (New York: McGraw-Hill Book Co., 1975), p. 88.

68. John D. Owen, *School Inequality and the Welfare State* (Baltimore: The John Hopkins University Press, 1974), p. 91.

69. Ibid.

70. Ibid.

71. Ibid.

72. Ibid.

73. *Work in America*, Report of a Special Task Force to the Secretary of Health, Education, and Welfare.

74. Maureen Woodhall, *Economic Aspects of Education*, National Foundation for Educational Research in England and Wales, 1972, p. 53.

75. Carl S. Shoup, *Public Finance* (Chicago: Aldine Publishers, 1969), p. 97.

76. B. A. Weisbrod, *External Benefits of Public Education* (Princeton, N. J.: Department of Economics, Princeton University, 1964), p. 31.

77. Werner Hirsch, Elbert W. Segalhorst, and Morton J. Marcus, *Spillover of Public Education Costs and Benefits* (University of California, 1964), p. 342.

78. Belton Fleisher, "The Effect of Income on Delinquency," *American Economic Review* 56, no. 1 (March 1966): 118–137.

79. Isaac Ehrlich, "On the Relation Between Education and Crime," *Education, Income and Human Behavior*, ed. F. Thomas Juster (New York: McGraw-Hill Book Co., 1975), pp. 313–337.

80. Joseph D. Lohman, Lloyd E. Ohlin, and Dietrich C. Retizer, *Description of Convicted Felons as Manpower Resources in a National Emergency*, p. 24, cited by Edwin H. Sutherland and Donald R. Cressey, *Principles of Criminology*, 7th ed. (New York: J. P. Lippincott Co., 1968), p. 251.

81. Price Chenault, "Education," *Contemporary Corrections*, ed. Paul W. Tappan (New York: McGraw-Hill Co., 1951), p. 224.

82. Albert K. Cohen, "The Schools and Juvenile Delinquency," as cited in Sutherland and Cressey, *Principles of Criminology*, p. 251.

83. U.S. Department of Commerce, Bureau of the Census, "Persons in Institutions and Other Group Quarters, July 1973," Table 24, and *Statistical Abstract of the U.S. 94th Annual Edition*, 1974, Table 175.

84. Lillian Dean Webb, "The Development of a Model to Measure Selected Economic Externalities of Education," (Ph.D. diss., University of Florida, 1975).

85. National Commission on the Causes and Prevention of Violence, *Crimes of Violence*, Vol. 11 (Washington, D.C.: Government Printing Office, 1968), p. 394.

86. Henry M. Levin, *The Effects of Dropping Out*, A Report to the Select Committee on Equal Opportunity of the United States Senate (Washington, D.C.: Government Printing Office, 1972).

87. Fritz Machlup, *Education and Economic Growth*, (Lincoln, Neb.: University of Nebraska Press, 1970): pp. 55-56.

88. David B. Epply, "The AFDC Family in the 1960's" *Welfare in Review* 8, no. 5 (September-October 1970): 11-15.

89. Edward Prescott, William Tash, and William Usdane, "Training and Employability: The Effect of MDTA on ADC Recipients." *Welfare in Review* 9, no. 1 (January–February 1971): 2.

90. Perry Levinson, "How Employable are AFDC Women," *Welfare in Review* 8 no. 4 (July–August 1970): 12–13.

91. Webb, "Development of a Model to Measure Selected Economic Externalities," p. 58.

92. Levin, *The Effects of Dropping Out*.

93. Thomas I. Ribich, *Education and Poverty* (Washington, D.C.: The Brookings Institution, 1968).

94. Ibid.

95. Owen, *School Inequality and the Welfare State*, pp. 85–87.

96. Ibid.

97. Samuel Bowles, "Schooling and Inequality," Investment in Education, ed. T.W. Schultz (Chicago: University of Chicago Press, 1971). p. 238.

98. Ibid.

99. See: Ribich, *Education and Poverty*, pp. 19–29.

100. Ibid., pp. 96–97.

101. Josiah Wedgewood, *The Economics of Inheritance* (London: Routledge, 1929), p. 3.

102. Hugh Dalton, *Some Aspects of the Inequality of Incomes in Modern communities* (London: Routledge, 1920), p. 10.

103. Edward R. Fried et al, *Setting National Priorities, The 1974 Budget* (Washington, D. C.: The Brookings Institution, 1973), p. 41.

104. Montek S. Ahluwalia, "Income Inequality: Some Dimensions of the Problem," *Redistribution with growth*, ed. Hollis Chenery et al. (World Bank and the Institute of Development Studies, University of Sussex and Oxford University, 1974), pp. 8–9.

105. Ibid.

106. Irving Kristol, "Equality as an Ideal." *International Encyclopedia of the Social Sciences* (New York: Macmillan company, 1968), pp. 108–111.

107. Johns and Morphet, *Economics and Financing of Education*, p. 100.

108. Ibid.

109. See: Jencks, *Inequality*.

110. Ibid.

111. Presently in the United States 14 cents on every dollar of personal income comes from government cash transfers. "Equality, American Dream—or Nightmare," *U. S. News and World Report*, August 4, 1975, pp. 26–36.

112. Kern Alexander and Thomas Melcher, "Income Redistribution and the Public Schools" *Futures in School Finance*, ed. K. Forbis Jordan and Kern Alexander (Bloomington, Ind.: Phi Delta Kappa, 1974). pp. 60–72.

113. See: W. Lee Hansen and Burton A. Weisbrod, "Who Pays for a Public Expenditure Program," *National Tax Journal* (December, 1971): 515–517; Joseph A. Pechman, "The Distributional Effects of Public Higher Education in California," *Journal of Human Resources* (Summer 1970): 361–370; Douglas W. Windham, *Education, Equality and Income Redistribution* (Lexington, Mass.: D. C. Heath and Co., 1970).

114. James s. Coleman, "Equality of Opportunity and Equality of Results," *Perspectives on Inequality* (Cambridge, Mass.: *Harvard Educational Review*, Reprint No. 8, 1973), pp. 93–101.

115. Ibid.

116. Burton A. Weisbrod. "Education and Investment in Human Capital."

117. Ibid.

118. Ibid.

119. Ibid.

120. Ibid.

121. Herman P. Miller, *Rich Man Poor Man* (New York: Thomas Y. Crowell Co., 1971), p. 167.

122. Ibid.

123. Ibid., p. 172.

124. Ibid., p. 174.

125. Bureau of Census. "Annual Mean Income, Lifetime Income, and Educational Attainment," Table 8.

126. H. S. Houthakker, "Education and Income," *Review of Economic Statistics* (February 1959).

127. Ibid., p. 27.

128. Bureau of Census. "Annual Mean Income, Lifetime Income, and Educational Attainment," (Current Population Reports, Series P-60, no. 92, 1974), p. 9.

129. George Psacharopoulos, *Returns to Education* (San Francisco: Jossey-Bass, Inc., 1973).

130. Gary S. Becker, *Human Capital* (Princeton: Princeton University Press, 1964).

131. Ibid., p. 128.

132. T. W. Schultz, "The Human Capital Approach to Education," *Economic Factors Affecting the Financing of Education*, ed. Johns et al., p. 48.

133. Chambers has noted that college graduates will return in tax payments three dollars for every one society (the state) expends on a student in obtaining his bachelor's degree. M. M. Chambers, "Education Good Investment," *Life*, Illinois State University, 9. no. 9 (May 1975): 4.

134. Giora Hanoch, "An Economic Analysis of Earnings and Schooling," *The Journal of Human Resources* 2, no. 3 (summer 1967): 310–329.

135. Ibid.

136. These returns were for 16 years vs. 13–15 years. Interestingly, the returns for 16 years vs. 12 was about 10 per cent for both regions.

137. Ibid.

138. Ibid.

139. F. Hines, L. Tweeten, and M. Redfern, "Social and Private Rates of Return to Investment in Schooling by Race-Sex Groups and Regions," *Journal of Human Resources* 3 (Summer 1970).

140. Psacharopoulos, *Returns to Education*, p. 65.

141. Ibid., p. 71.

142. Ibid., p. 83.

143. Ibid., p. 62 & p. 82.

144. Ibid., p. 86.

145. Richard Raymond and Michael Sesnowitz, "The Returns to Investment in Higher Education: Some New Evidence," *The Journal of Human Resources* 10, no. 2 (spring 1975): 139–154.

146. W. Lee Hansen and J. H. Hollomon, "The Declining Value of College Going," *Change* 7, no. 7 (1975): 24-31, 62.

147. R. Freeman and J. H. Hollomon, "The Declining Value of College Going," *Change* 7, no. 7 (1975): 24–31, 62.

148. B. Harvat, "The Optimum Rate of Investment," *Economic Journal* 68 (December 1958): 747–767.

# What Determines the Costs of Higher Education? (1980)

HOWARD R. BOWEN

The biography of an American family is written in its canceled checks. A family's life-style as well as its day-to-day events and problems are evidenced by its check stubs: Every birth, marriage, change of residence, change of career, educational decision, illness, and death is recorded there. Similarly, the budget and expenditures of a college or university reveal a great deal about its activities, achievements, and vicissitudes. This book is mainly a study of the behavior of colleges and universities individually and collectively as seen through their financial records.

This first chapter is concerned with the factors that determine the costs of American colleges and universities for educating their students. Some of the determinants operate through society. Others operate through individual institutions. Therefore, both societal and institutional factors— as well as their relationship—are considered.

## The Meaning of Cost in Higher Education

In our thoroughly monetized economy, costs usually appear in the form of expenditures of money. They are payments made to acquire goods and services. For example, as consumers we refer to the cost of a new automobile as the amount of money we must pay for it; producers of automobiles refer to cost as the amount of money paid for the thousands of workers, materials, and services needed to produce automobiles. Similarly, the costs of colleges and universities are usually money payments to acquire the resources needed to operate the institutions. They include cash outlays for the wages and salaries of personnel, the purchase of goods and services, student financial aid, and the acquisition or use of plant and equipment.

The real costs, however, lie beneath the money payments. The products or outcomes of higher education are obtained through the use of scarce resources. These resources consist partly of labor, capital, and land that are employed within the institutions. And they consist partly of goods, services, plant, and equipment purchased from outside vendors. These purchased items are, however, also the product of labor, capital, and land employed by outsiders. Thus, all the expenditures of higher education reduce ultimately to payments for the services of scarce resources.

These same resources, however, could be allocated to alternative purposes. The real cost of higher education, then, consists of the benefits that might have been realized from these resources, but were sacrificed, because these resources were committed to higher education. These alternative benefits might have been in the form of consumer goods—such as food, gasoline, or tennis rackets—and social goods—such as highways, police protection, or environmental improvement. These are the kinds of benefits that are sacrificed when resources are devoted to higher education.

These sacrificed opportunities represent the real costs, or, as they are sometimes called, *opportunity costs*.

Whenever one suggests that more resources should be devoted to higher education, the underlying assumption is that the additional resources so used will produce a greater return than the same resources devoted to other purposes. Or when it is suggested that the resources employed in higher education should be cut back, the implication is that the same resources would produce a greater return if applied to an alternative use. So when one considers how much of the nation's resources should be devoted to higher education, there is an implicit comparison of the benefits that could be obtained from increments of other goods.

As indicated, the costs of higher education are ordinarily expressed in money, which serves reasonably well for the purpose of measuring the relative benefits from different uses of resources. But in some cases, costs expressed in money can lead us astray. For example, in a time of widespread unemployment, the real cost of an increment of higher education may be relatively small because those employed in higher education, either as staff or students, may have no immediate alternative jobs. Similarly, at a time of temporary decline in enrollments due to demographic changes, such as the decline in the early 1950s or the decline widely predicted for the 1980s, higher education may develop idle capacity in both plant and staff. The cost of putting this capacity to work by encouraging increased enrollments or improving educational quality may be negligible if the resources devoted to higher education could not be readily transferred to other productive uses. Also, cost is not adequately measured by money when it takes the form of a deterioration of assets through lack of maintenance or replacement. When this happens, costs are being incurred even though no money payments are being made. The subject of undermaintenance of assets is so important that parts of Chapters Five and Ten will be devoted to it. For these reasons, one must beware of measuring costs solely in terms of money: costs, rather, should be thought of as opportunity costs of the resources employed. Generally, however, money is a reasonably good measure of cost and most of the discussion in this book will be conducted in monetary terms.

Since inflation has become rampant, it is scarcely necessary to mention that when money costs are being compared over time, cost data must be adjusted for changes in the value of the dollar. This adjustment is accomplished with the use of index numbers reflecting changes in the general level of prices. Unfortunately, no price index ever is completely appropriate for the purpose, and these adjustments inevitably introduce distortions.

## Unit Cost

It is not difficult to calculate the total annual dollar cost of operating a college or university. All that is needed is to add up all the expenditures—making sure to include only the costs that are properly allocated to the year in question. But, even when adjusted for changes in the value of the dollar, this total is not meaningful for comparisons over time or among institutions unless it is related to the number of units of service rendered. For example, if the total expenditures of a typical college or university in 1970 and in 1980 were compared, much of the increased cost would be explained simply by the growth of the enterprise over the decade. The cost per unit of service might not have increased at all. But there is a further complication: if the expenditures of two institutions were compared, one of which serves 2,000 students and the other 20,000 students, the difference in expenditures would be explained largely by the contrast in enrollment. Useful cost comparisons, either over time or among institutions, require that expenditures be related to the number of units of service rendered. Given such units, it is then possible to compute cost per unit and thus to make meaningful comparisons.

Traditionally, what passed as cost per unit was computed simply by adding up total institutional expenditures for all purposes and dividing by the number of students. The result was called "cost per student." This method of rough approximation had the virtue of simplicity and worked reasonably well when the education of full-time resident undergraduate students was the predominant business of colleges and universities. However, with the increasing differentiation of institutions by functions—some with substantial expenditures for research, public service, and auxiliary enterprises, and others confining their missions largely to the education of undergraduate commuter students—this rough and ready method of computing unit cost became largely untenable, except for comparisons of institutions having similar missions and student bodies. It became necessary to separate educational expenditures from outlays for non instructional purposes. Only the remainder—after deduction of expenditures for research, public service, and auxiliary enterprises—could be regarded as expenditures for the education of students and properly related to number of students.

But the counting of number of students also had its complications. Some students attend part-time and others full-time. To estimate the effective number of students the concept of "full-time-equivalent student" was devised. With this concept, the number of students was computed by counting full-time students as one each and counting part-time students as a fraction of one according to the number of credit hours for which they are enrolled. But students differ also as to academic level. Some are beginning freshmen and sophomores, some are juniors and seniors, some are advanced graduate and professional students. Costs tend to be higher as students advance up the academic ladder. The educational cost per student therefore tends to be greater in institutions with high proportions of advanced students than in institutions with high proportions of beginners. To standardize the units in which teaching loads are measured, heavier weights must be assigned to advanced students than to beginners. For example, in the present study, doctoral candidates are assigned three times as much weight as entering freshmen. Thus, to obtain a satisfactory measure of the teaching load of an institution it is necessary to express the enrollment in full-time equivalents weighted according to the academic level of students. The resulting adjusted enrollment is expressed in what I shall call "student units"—each unit being the equivalent of one full-time freshman or sophomore student. The unit cost of any institution can then b e calculated by dividing the educational expenditures by the number of student units. Theoretically at least, the educational costs of institutions of all types—from community colleges to major universities—may thus be reduced to the same units and compared.

In a study of institutional costs, it would have been desirable to include the costs of organized research and public service, as well as educational costs, because research and public service are integral and important functions of colleges and universities. To include them, however, would have required units in which the products of research and public service could be measured. Unfortunately, these two activities do not lend themselves to measurement in discrete units. There is simply no known way, except through the broad general judgment of experts, to measure the output of an institution's organized research or public service program. Cost studies, therefore, are usually confined to the educational function for which a tenable measuring unit is available. This unit is a full-time-equivalent student with appropriate adjustment for academic level. The present study is no exception.

Admittedly, the student unit is not an ideal measure of the outputs of the educational process. The student is an input, a resource employed, not an output. The outputs of higher education are results. For individuals, they are mainly learning and personal development; for society, they are mainly advancement of the culture and economic growth. These are the true outcomes in terms of which unit costs ideally should be calculated. But our knowledge of outcomes is so feeble, and even if we had the knowledge, our ability to quantify outcomes would be so limited, that it would be hopeless to count costs in terms of the true outcomes. . . . Therefore, we resort to the expedient of using adjusted number of students as a proxy for the true outcomes. It is an expedient that can be tolerated but not commended. One may hope that as more is learned about the true outcomes, we can do better than merely compute "cost per student unit." Meanwhile, students are our only reliable indicators of the amount of education being conducted and the only tolerable base for establishing unit costs.

# Educational and Noneducational Expenditures

To launch the study of actual costs, I shall present estimates of the combined expenditures of America's colleges and universities in a single year. Table 1 shows the percentage distribution of expenditures by broad functions and by recipient groups for 1974-75. This table may be thought of as representing either the entire American higher educational system or a single college or university. The data are expressed as percentages because the proportions of expenditure in various categories remain fairly constant from year to year whereas the dollar amounts change rapidly with inflation. Table 1 was of necessity constructed by piecing together information from scattered sources; the resulting figures are only estimates but they convey a general view of the way higher educational dollars are spent.

Note that only 33.1 percent of total expenditures are spent directly for instruction and departmental research. When to this 33.1 percent are added student services, scholarships and fellowships, and a *pro rata* share of academic support, institutional support, and operations and maintenance of plant, the percentage that may be allocated to the education of students is 58.9 percent of total expenditures. This 58.9 percent is the part of higher educational expenditures with which this

## Table 1
### Estimated Distribution of Expenditures for all U.S. Institutions of Higher Education, 1974-75

| | Expenditures classified according to recipients (expressed as a percentage of total expenditures) | | | | | | | | | | |
| Expenditures classified by administrative divisions | Employees: salaries, wages, and fringe benefits | | | | | Vendors: purchased goods and services (current) | | | | | |
| | Faculty | Other Professional Staff | Administrative Staff | Other Workers | Subtotal | Equipment and Books | Other | Subtotal | Students: Financial Aid | Capital Costs | Total |
|---|---|---|---|---|---|---|---|---|---|---|---|
| **Education** | | | | | | | | | | | |
| Direct expenditures for instruction and departmental research | 23.8% | 1.5% | — | 1.1% | 26.1% | 0.7% | 1.7% | 2.4% | — | 4.3% | 33.1% |
| Student services | — | — | 2.2 | 1.0 | 3.2 | — | 0.3 | 0.3 | — | 1.0 | 4.5 |
| Scholarships and fellowships | — | — | — | — | — | — | — | — | 3.5 | — | 3.5 |
| Academic support | — | — | 1.8 | 1.5 | 3.3 | 0.6 | 0.1 | 0.7 | — | 0.9 | 4.9 |
| Institutional support | — | — | 1.2 | 1.6 | 2.8 | 0.4 | 2.4 | 2.8 | — | 0.7 | 6.3 |
| Operation and maintenance of plant | — | — | 0.4 | 3.7 | 4.1 | 0.3 | 1.7 | 2.0 | — | 0.5 | 6.6 |
| Subtotal | 23.8 | 1.5 | 5.6 | 8.9 | 39.8 | 2.0 | 6.2 | 8.2 | 3.5 | 7.4 | 58.9 |
| **Organized research and public service** | | | | | | | | | | | |
| Direct expenditures | 1.5 | 4.0 | — | 1.9 | 7.4 | 0.8 | 2.0 | 2.8 | — | 1.5 | 11.7 |
| Academic support | — | — | 0.6 | 0.5 | 1.1 | 0.2 | 0.1 | 0.3 | — | 0.3 | 1.7 |
| Institutional support | — | — | 0.4 | 0.6 | 1.0 | 0.2 | 0.8 | 1.0 | — | 0.2 | 2.2 |
| Operation and maintenance of plant | — | — | 0.1 | 1.3 | 1.4 | 0.1 | 0.6 | 0.7 | — | 0.2 | 2.3 |
| Subtotal | 1.5 | 4.0 | 1.1 | 4.3 | 10.9 | 1.3 | 3.5 | 4.8 | — | 2.2 | 17.9 |
| Auxiliary enterprises | — | — | 0.4 | 2.3 | 2.7 | 1.2 | 6.1 | 7.3 | — | 6.3 | 16.3 |
| Teaching hospitals | — | 1.5 | 0.2 | 2.3 | 4.0 | 0.5 | 1.2 | 1.7 | — | 1.2 | 6.9 |
| Total | 25.3 | 7.0 | 7.3 | 17.8 | 57.4 | 5.0 | 17.0 | 22.0 | 3.5 | 17.1 | 100.0 |

book is concerned. It excludes organized research and public service, auxiliary enterprises, and teaching hospitals—which together account for the balance, 41.1 percent of the total.

Departmental research is distinguished from organized research and public service. Departmental research is the ordinary part-time research that professors pursue as part of their regular work. It is regarded as an essential ingredient of teaching excellence and therefore chargeable to education. Organized research and public service, on the other hand, are less closely linked with education and are separately funded and separately budgeted. . . .

The bottom row of Table 1 shows the distribution of expenditures by recipient groups. All the expenditures of higher education are paid out to staff as wages or salaries, to outside vendors for the purchase of goods and services, to students for financial aid, and to outside vendors and contractors for the purchase of capital goods such as buildings and equipment. The breakdown of expenditures by recipient groups is for many purposes more revealing than the customary classification by functions and this classification will be used to some extent in this study. However, expenditure data are seldom gathered in this way and so the figures in the table are only informed guesses and not accurate amounts. (As an aside, I would recommend that institutions analyze their expenditure data and construct their budgets by recipient groups as well as by functional categories and that the National Center for Education Statistics routinely collect data by recipient groups as well as functional categories.)

As indicated in the bottom row of Table 1, staff compensation accounts for 57.4 percent of total expenditures. This percentage is lower than that usually cited because the total expenditure, of which this figure is a percentage, includes capital costs as well as current operating expenditures. When staff compensation is expressed as a percentage of *current* expenditures excluding capital costs, the figure rises to 69 percent (Millett, 1952, pp. 115-116).

As shown in the top row of Table 1, about one-quarter (26.4 percent) of the total expenditures are for compensation of the people directly engaged in instruction and departmental research. This portion may be thought of as the front-line expenditure to deliver the basic service colleges and universities were created to provide, namely, the education of students. This 26.4 percent is less than half the total expenditures for education which amount to 58.9 percent of the grand total of all expenditures (row seven of right-hand column). The other educational expenditures amounting to 32.5 percent[1] may be thought of as backup or supportive services. Just as an army needs large amounts of personnel, facilities, services to sustain the front-line troops, so colleges and universities need substantial behind-the-lines support to assist the work of the faculty and other front-line staff. The backup expenditures are intended to create the general institutional environment in which the basic service can flourish.

The distinction between "front-line" and "backup" expenditures is by no means precise. The environment created by the backup expenditures may have direct educational effects. For example, student counseling and recreational activities may be influential in shaping the character and aspirations of students. Cultural programs may awaken and develop artistic sensitivity and humane inclinations. Student housing and dining may be a vehicle for meaningful discussion and for valuable experience in human relations. The physical plant through its beauty and careful maintenance may create a serene environment favorable to deep thoughts and high ideals. Even the character of the administration may influence the educative and scholarly capacity of institutions. A college or university is a community whose every part is a potential instrument of learning. Effectiveness in higher education calls for the use of every part of the institution to form an academic community of maximum influence upon its students.

Though all parts of an institution may contribute directly or indirectly to the fulfillment of its purposes, the relative proportions of academic resources devoted to front-line and to backup functions is a matter to which educational leaders cannot be indifferent. The basic educational purposes of colleges and universities are achieved through the work of the people directly engaged in education. That only a quarter of total higher educational expenditures is paid for the compensation of these people is a matter of concern. Indeed, it is a matter of growing concern because . . . the proportion of resources devoted to the front-line functions has been decreasing over recent decades. Given the constraint of fixed total resources, it cannot be denied that every addition to backup expenditures—every additional clerk, accountant, affirmative action  officer, gardener, or security guard or every additional air conditioning system or landscape improvement—may be at the expense of front-line staff. No one would expect a college or university, any more than an army, to operate without behind-the-lines support, yet the trends in this ratio over time may be an important barometer of the progress and health of higher education. Indeed, the ratio of front-line to backup expenditures may be a revealing index of efficiency in higher education.

## The Long Run: Societal Determinants of Cost

The educational expenditures of higher educational institutions in the aggregate are ultimately determined by the amount of money our society is willing to devote to them. However, no single social decision-making authority provides the resources for higher education or regulates the flow of these resources. The sources of funds are widely diffused. They include tuitions and fees paid by millions of students and their families; gifts from numerous donors; endowment income controlled by the governing boards of the institutions; and public appropriations of fifty separate states and several territories, many local authorities, and the federal government. The collective decisions of all these people, organizations, and public authorities determine the amount of money available for higher education. This amount in turn determines the total sum that can be spent, or the aggregate cost, of the colleges and universities.

The broad general characteristics of the higher educational system also are determined by "society." Those who provide the funds all exercise some influence over the scope and organization of the higher educational system and also over its technologies or modes of operation. They influence such characteristics as the number and qualifications of students admitted; the relative emphasis on vocational and liberal studies; the number, types, sizes, and geographic locations of the institutions; and even the modes of instruction as determined by the ratio of students to faculty. "Society" as represented by the several sources of funds usually does not regulate the higher educational system in detail and leaves much scope for the institutions individually. Yet, through widely diffused decisions about the missions and the allocation of funds, considerable influence is exerted over the broad general characteristics of the higher educational system.

These societal decisions are strongly influenced by tradition. At any given moment, concepts of what higher education "ought to be like" have evolved from the past and are accepted widely as part of the general culture. Examples of such concepts are: that colleges and universities should be physically spacious and architecturally beautiful, that they should provide enough staff to give attention and guidance to students individually, that they should extend opportunity to less-privileged social classes, that they should be more or less removed from detailed governmental control, or that they should charge tuitions as low as feasible. These concepts are never universally accepted and are always slowly evolving. For example, in recent decades, controversy has swirled about admissions policies, faculty teaching loads, and tuition. The unsettled questions about what higher education ought to be in the future are the substance of ongoing public debates about higher education. At any given time, however, the general public tends  to hold a set of concepts that define the system and influence decisions about the amount of funds to be devoted to it.

Changes in the amount of funds that the public is willing to allocate to higher education ordinarily occur by small annual increments or decrements. In the past, as higher education has grown, the allocation has usually increased each year. In a possible future stable or declining state, the public may favor decreases. Each increment in expenditure involves an opportunity cost, that is, to allocate additional resources to higher education requires that some amount of another good or goods, which could have been obtained with the same resources, must be forfeited. These sacrifices are the incremental costs of higher education. For example, a small increment in funds devoted to higher education might require a family to decrease personal consumption in another area or might require a state government to forgo a low-priority public project. As successive increments are added for education, they require the abandonment of progressively more important alternative projects. The incremental growth of higher education, relative to other industries, results in a successively increasing opportunity cost. Conversely, each successive decrement of higher education allows increases in the amount of other goods and produces declining opportunity cost, because it allows resources to be used for alternative opportunities of successively lower priority.

An increment of expenditure for higher educational institutions may have either or both of two purposes. It may finance an expansion of the number of students in attendance, or it may be intended to enhance the quality of the service rendered, for example, by raising the ratio of faculty to students or by improving facilities and equipment. Of course, not every addition to cost that is intended to enhance quality will improve the performance of higher education, any more than every increase in private consumption adds to the quality of life. The trade-offs between quality and quantity at any given time are determined by the prevailing ideals for higher education held by those who support colleges and universities.

The cost per student unit results from three societal decisions that reflect the combined influence of the many persons and public authorities who control the flow of funds to higher education. These three decisions pertain to: the total amount to be spent on higher education, the number of units of service to be provided, and the level of quality.

Societal decisions about higher educational institutions are affected not only by cost but also by expectations of benefits to be received from higher education. Higher education, like all other forms of production, is subject to diminishing returns. As expenditures increase, each incremental addition to expenditure may yield fewer or lesser benefits. For example, successive improvements in quality—distinction of faculty, richer faculty-student ratios, elaboration of equipment, additional library resources, architectural refinement—may have a diminishing effect on outcomes until a point is reached at which they have no effect or a negative effect on performance. As higher education expands, it may attract less qualified and less motivated students, which also may eventually bring about reductions in incremental outcomes. Tendencies toward diminishing returns means that as higher education expands, the incremental returns decline and that the amount people are willing to pay for additional units of higher education correspondingly tends to fall.

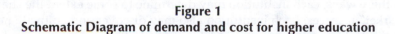

**Figure 1**
**Schematic Diagram of demand and cost for higher education**

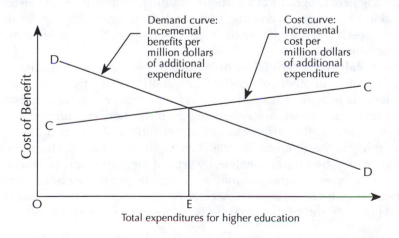

The tendencies of opportunity costs to rise and benefits to fall, as expenditures increase, are illustrated in Figure 1 by an upward-sloping cost curve (CC) and a downward-sloping benefit or demand curve (DD). The point at which the cost curve (CC) intersects the benefit curve (DD) defines the equilibrium position, the amount of expenditure (OE) at which the incremental benefits are equal to the incremental costs (Solomon, 1980). Deviation from this point indicates that higher education is overextended (costs exceed benefits) or that it is underdeveloped (benefits exceed costs).

The two curves are by no means stationary, and the equilibrium position can change. A society may value the returns to higher education more at some times than at others. For example, after the USSR launched Sputnik, the American public called for increased expenditures for education; the demand curve exhibited a sizable, sudden upward shift. In the 1970s, however, the demand curve seems to have shifted downward because of an imminent decline in the number of high school graduates or, possibly, a general decline in the public's valuation of education. The cost curve also may shift upward or downward. For example, the urgency of alternative uses of resources may increase, thus raising the cost curve, as when resources must be diverted to national defense or to environmental purposes. Or the urgency of alternative uses of resources may decline as when unemployment frees resources that could be diverted into higher education at minimal opportunity cost.

The interaction of demand and cost, as conceived by "society" at any given time, determines total expenditures or the amount of resources to be allocated to the operation of higher educational institutions. At the same time, societal influences also affect the kinds of service to be rendered by the institutions and the level of quality of these services. In the long run, the combination of all these decisions or influences determines the expenditure or cost per unit of service.

## The Short Run: Institutional Determinants of Cost

The determinants of cost also may be considered from the point of view of the individual institutions that make up the national system of higher education. They must, of course, operate within the context of societal demand and supply. They are constrained by the broad preferences and decisions underlying societal choices. But the institutions individually do have considerable freedom of action. They are able to exercise some control over their separate destinies. Most institutions exert substantial influence upon the selection of their students, the educational programs they provide, the relative emphasis they place on quantity and quality of services, and the technologies they employ. In these ways, each institution may determine to some extent the share of the higher educational "market" it serves. Each institution also may discover and cultivate new social needs for higher education not previously recognized, for example, by reaching out to adults or minority groups, or by offering new programs of vocational training. Moreover, each can engage in promotional activities akin to selling, advertising, public relations, and lobbying. In these ways, individual institutions—each pursuing its own interests—may in the aggregate affect the societal demand for higher education.

Each institution endeavors to fulfill its own purposes within the constraints set by the social milieu and the competition of other colleges and universities. These purposes vary among institutions. They may include providing needed services for particular clienteles, raising the quality of service; achieving financial security, and enhancing the institutional reputation. It must be said that reputation ranks high among the purposes of most institutions. As an institution pursues its own interests, operating within the given constraints it seeks a niche for itself. The niche may be defined partly by location, by size, by type of clientele, by type of programs, and by level of "quality." The particular niches of the many institutions may vary widely. Some may offer two-year and others four-year programs of instruction, some may cater only to undergraduates and others may have highly developed graduate and professional study. Some may confine themselves strictly to liberal education and others may have elaborate vocational programs. In the competitive race, some institutions may be in the ascendancy and others may be slipping. If some social needs are not being met, new institutions may be established to fill these niches. If some institutions persist in trying to occupy niches for which there is insufficient need, they will disappear.

One of the most striking findings of this study is that institutions of higher education spend their money in very different ways and experience widely different costs per student. The societal influences bearing upon higher education do not enforce standardized patterns in the way institutions are conducted—even among institutions with essentially similar missions. Colleges and universities have no strong incentive to cut costs in quest of profit because they do not seek profit. They are not forced by competition to lower costs in order to survive. This is so partly because they are subsidized by government and philanthropy and partly because they are shielded from competition by geographic location and by differentiation of services. It is so also because institutions know little about the relationship between their expenditures and their educational outcomes, and it is easy to drift into the comfortable belief that increased expenditures will automatically produce commensurately greater outcomes. Under these conditions, the unit costs of operating colleges or universities are set more largely by the amount of money institutions are able to raise per unit of service rendered than by the inherent technical requirements of conducting their work. Within wide limits, institutions can adjust to whatever amount of money they are able to raise. When resources are increased, they find uses for the new funds, and unit costs go up. When resources are decreased, they express keen regret and they protest, but in the end they accept the inevitable, and unit costs go down. This set of generalizations might be called the *revenue theory of cost*; attention is now directed to this theory.

Institutions doubtless are constrained by vague, but nevertheless effective, lower and upper limits to unit cost. The floor is set by prevailing societal concepts of what a college or university ought to be like, by the willingness or unwillingness of students to attend institutions of various characteristics, by the mandate of funding agencies, and by the standards set by accrediting bodies, licensing agencies, and professional societies. In order to function, each institution must attain some bare minimum of funds per unit of service. Otherwise it is not a member of the higher educational community—either because it is not recognized as such or because it does not survive. A ceiling on unit costs is set by aversion to ridiculous waste on the part of institutional leaders and their constituencies. However, as institutions become increasingly affluent, they rarely reject additional funds. Nor do they typically increase unit costs without limit. Rather, they are likely to allow enrollments to grow, take on new and expensive educational programs, expand their research and public service activities, add physical plant, or accumulate endowments.

In explaining the unit cost of higher education, sometimes educators argue that it is determined by the *needs* of institutions. To conduct education of a satisfactory quality, it is said, a certain ratio of faculty to students, or an appropriate salary scale, or funds to pay increased Social Security taxes are needed. This line of argument is common to educators as they plead the case for increased revenues or fend off potential revenue cuts. Because higher education is conducted at so many different levels of expenditures and with so many different allocations of resources, however, there is no precise need that can be objectively defined and defended.

The needs which educators present to legislators and donors are arguments in favor of increased funding, not causes of increased cost. They are often sensible and persuasive arguments but, as every educator knows, they do not automatically bring about increases in unit costs. If arguments persuade and revenues are increased, then costs will rise. But they will rise because revenues grew, not merely because of newly perceived needs. For example, increased energy prices or the demand to expand women's athletics do not automatically bring about increases in appropriations, gifts, or tuitions. The persuasion of educators is, however, one influence on the amount of funds society allocates to higher education. Each educator intends only to influence donors, legislators, and others to be more generous to his or her own institutions; but the combined persuasive effort of all educators may be to increase the total flow of funds to higher education and therefore to increase total expenditures and unit costs.

The obverse of the "needs" argument is the "efficiency" argument. Those who wish to cut the educational costs of institutions often advance proposals for improving the efficiency of operations. A whole array of proposals is offered, for example, to adopt the techniques of modern management, to operate institutions year around, to use classrooms more intensively, to lower the faculty-student ratio, to cut telephone and utility bills. All of these and many more might reduce costs, but they would do so only if revenues were cut commensurately. If revenues were not so reduced, any saving would simply be expended elsewhere in the institution and no net saving would occur. Unit costs are determined not by changes in efficiency but by changes in revenues.

Institutional adjustments to meet perceived needs or to improve efficiency, even though they do not alter overall unit costs, may change the internal allocation of resources and thus alter the overall performance of the institution. It may be possible to meet a need, such as career counseling, by shifting resources from an obsolete academic department without bringing about any increase in overall unit cost. Or it may be possible through improvements in efficiency, for example by simplifying the curriculum, to save resources which can then be shifted to other urgent uses. Given the enrollment of an institution, whether meeting needs or improving efficiency will raise or lower overall unit cost will depend on the amount of revenues. If revenues are changed, there will be a change in overall unit cost, otherwise not. To say that identifying new needs will not raise costs or that achieving efficiency will not lower costs unless revenues rise or fall accordingly does not imply that it is not important or even urgent to meet needs or to improve efficiency. It means only that unit cost will not be affected unless there are corresponding changes in revenue.

## The Revenue Theory of Cost Summarized

The basic concept underlying the revenue theory of cost is that an institution's educational cost per student unit is determined by the revenues available for educational purposes. Given the enrollment, cost per student unit is directly proportional to these revenues. In most institutions, public or private, educational revenues are closely related to enrollment. In most public institutions, educational revenues are derived largely from tuitions and from state appropriations based on "enrollment driven" formulas. In most private institutions, educational revenues come mainly from tuitions. The situation is more complicated in the elite private institutions which potentially have considerable control over the internal allocation of revenues to education and research and over enrollment. But even they depend on tuitions as the major source of revenue available for educational purposes.

On the whole, unit cost is determined neither by rigid technological requirements of delivering educational services nor by some abstract standard of need. It is determined rather by the revenue available for education that can be raised per student unit. Technology and need affect unit cost only as they influence those who control revenues and enrollments.

Given an institution's enrollment, whoever or whatever controls the flow of educational revenue to that institution will determine the unit cost. This control, however, tends to be diffused because revenues are derived from several sources: federal, state, and local appropriations, tuitions, gifts and grants from private individuals and corporations, endowment, and sales of goods and services. Since an institution usually tries to maximize revenues from all sources, one can say that unit costs are determined by the amount of money the institution is able to raise, and that no single person or organization is fully in control of unit costs. In most institutions, the control lies mainly in the hands of state governments as reflected in their willingness to vote appropriations and of students as reflected in their willingness to attend and to pay tuitions. Insofar as institutions have other outside sources of revenue or have endowment income, control is to that extent more widely diffused.

The revenue theory of educational cost is subject to an important qualification. It is a *short-run* theory. It describes what happens practically from year to year in most institutions. In the long run, of course, the amount of revenue institutions receive from public appropriations, gifts and grants, and tuitions will be influenced by such factors as changes in social attitudes toward the value of higher education, by changes in educational technologies that affect resource requirements, by changes in the labor market affecting wages and salaries, by changes in the prices of purchased goods and services, by changes in competitive conditions within the higher educational community, and by any other factors that may affect the willingness of legislators and donors to provide funds and the willingness of students and their families to pay tuitions. Nevertheless, at any given time, the unit cost of education is determined by the amount of revenues currently available for education relative to enrollment. This statement is more than a tautology. It expresses the fundamental fact that unit cost is determined by hard dollars of revenue and only indirectly and remotely by considerations of need, technology, efficiency, and market wages and prices.

## The "Laws" of Higher Educational Costs

From the revenue theory of cost, it is possible to deduce a set of closely interrelated "laws" pertaining to unit costs in colleges and universities. These laws describe the incentives and the behavior of higher educational institutions as they conduct their activities from year to year.

A basic assumption underlying these laws is that the size, type, and mission of each institution is given—having been determined by the unique events of its history. Institutions, of course, change—sometimes drastically. Yet in any short span of years, the great majority have settled into a pattern. Their mission and their enrollment are well established.

Given this assumption, certain laws of higher educational costs may be derived (Bowen, 1970):

1.  The dominant goals of institutions are educational excellence, prestige, and influence.

    The "excellence" or "quality" of institutions are commonly judged by such criteria as faculty-student ratios, faculty salaries, number of Ph.D.s on the faculty, number of books in the library, range of facilities and equipment, and academic qualifications of students. These criteria are resource inputs most of which cost money, not outcomes flowing from the educational process. The true outcomes in the form of learning and personal development of students are on the whole unexamined and only vaguely discerned.

2.  In quest of excellence, prestige, and influence, there is virtually no limit to the amount of money an institution could spend for seemingly fruitful educational ends.

    Whatever level of expenditure is attained is seldom considered enough. Institutions tend, therefore, to spend up to the very limit of their means. As a result, the financial problems of rich institutions are about as severe as those of all but the most impoverished institutions. This is especially so because whatever expenditures are once admitted into the budget become long-term commitments from which it is difficult ever to withdraw.

3.  Each institution raises all the money it can.

    No college or university ever admits to having enough money and all try to increase their resources without limit.

4.  Each institution spends all it raises.

    Many institutions, however, accumulate reserves and endowments. These "savings" are derived primarily from gifts designated for endowment and not from voluntary allocations of current income. In most institutions, the accumulations are of negligible amount. The few institutions that become very affluent, however, are able to save substantial amounts and accumulate significant endowments.

5.    The cumulative effect of the preceding four laws is toward ever-increasing expenditure.

The incentives inherent in the goals of excellence, prestige, and influence are not counter-acted within the higher educational system by incentives leading to parsimony or effi-ciency. The question of what *ought* higher education to cost—what is the minimal amount needed to provide services of acceptable quality—does not enter the process except as it is imposed from the outside. The higher educational system itself provides no guidance of a kind that weighs costs and benefits in terms of the public interest. The duty of setting limits thus falls, by default, upon those who provide the money, mostly legislators and students and their families.

Laws similar to these are applicable to many kinds of not-for-profit organizations other than higher education, such as hospitals, churches, schools, museums, and, not least, governmental agencies. The people committed to these organizations—trustees, administrators, professional persons, and workers—generally share the goals of excellence, prestige, and influence. They have in common a sense of limitless horizons. The field in which they work is to them so vital to human welfare that no effort or resources should be spared. In most cases, this means that the services rendered to each client should be as perfect and complete as possible. Indeed, the sharing of these goals is the very definition of organizational morale, and the success of any organization is dependent upon the commitment of its members to these goals. These aspirations are always tinged with the personal ambitions of the administrators and professional workers involved. This is not all bad. If institutions individually were not ambitious, they would be lethargic, unimagina-tive, and unresponsive to social needs. However, there is nothing in these aspirations and motives that restrains unit cost. From the point of view of institutions, higher unit cost is better almost without qualification. Yet there must be some limit on not-for-profit institutions and governmental agencies including colleges and universities. In the public interest, the economic principle of equi-marginal returns to all areas of expenditure must somehow come into play. According to this principle, the final dollar spent for higher education should yield a return equal to the final dollar spent for health services, national defense, elementary education, environmental improvement, private family consumption, or any other purpose. Yet there are few within higher education, or other not-for-profit organizations, whose purview is the broad public interest. There are only advocates whose purposes and motives are described in the five "laws" of cost.

It is, of course, the political process that we usually depend upon to work out the flow of funds to various fields according to the equi-marginal principle. In the case of higher education, however, no single public agency is responsible for the financing. Funds flow from the federal government, fifty state governments, several territorial governments, and hundreds of local governments. Funds are derived also from tuitions and other fees paid by millions of students and their families, from gifts and grants donated by thousands of donors, and from the income on endowments held by the institutions. The many persons who finance higher education do not speak with a single voice in their estimation of the marginal benefits to be derived from it. Even the fifty states differ widely in their support of higher education. Thus, the allocation of funds to higher education is singularly dependent upon the efforts of the institutions. Each one operates with a sort of hunting license which enables it to gather funds wherever it can find them and to obtain the maximum amount possible. The costs, then, are determined by success in overall fund-raising and they vary widely among institutions.

The hunting licenses vary among institutions in scope and flexibility. For example, most state institutions are largely dependent upon state appropriations and tuitions and rely only marginally on gifts, grants, and endowment income. Most community colleges derive their funds mainly from appropriations of state and local government. Most private institutions are financed mainly by tuitions. Many private and public institutions, however, draw upon varied sources of support. All, however, are free to exert influence on whatever financial sources are accessible to them. They seek appropriations by lobbying and by public relations efforts, they try to maximize tuitions through various admissions and public relations techniques, they assiduously cultivate gifts, and they try to increase endowment income through successful investment policy. All are attempting to increase revenues from whatever sources are available to them. In the end their costs are affected by the degree of their success in fund-raising.

The unit costs of particular institutions are thus determined in large part by the amount of money they are able to raise, not necessarily by some rational determination of the minimal amount needed to provide services of acceptable quality. There are Cadillac institutions and Pinto institutions and all gradations between. Just as Cadillacs and Pintos both provide acceptable transportation, albeit with differing degrees of comfort and prestige, so rich and poor institutions may both provide acceptable education, likewise with differing degrees of excellence and prestige.

There is waste associated with competition among colleges and universities just as there is competitive waste among business firms in the free enterprise system. For example, individual institutions often spend money to enhance their reputations, to attract donors, or to raise the caliber of students attending. Expenditures for such purposes, though they may help to advance the status of some institutions vis a vis their competitors, do not add much to the overall outcomes of higher education. They force competitors to make similar expenditures with the result that all the players are worse off while their relative positions remain about unchanged. There are costs of institutional autonomy in higher education just as there are costs of free enterprise in private business. In the case of higher education, one of the functions of various multi-campus universities or governmental coordinating agencies is to minimize these expenses of competition and to guide the development of the higher educational system through centralized planning. However, it is doubtful whether central planning is superior to institutional initiative and whether the savings achieved through central planning are not obtained at a high cost in loss of local initiative, flexibility, social responsiveness—not to mention erosion of academic freedom.

## Institutional Autonomy

One of the most vexing problems of higher education is to balance the need for control of costs with the need for institutional autonomy. Institutional autonomy is widely acknowledged to be essential to maintaining professional responsibility for academic decisions and to academic freedom in thought and expression. On the other hand, the financing of colleges and universities, especially when public funds are used, cannot be wholly open-ended. There must be some control over costs such that marginal returns to higher education are balanced against marginal returns to other uses of public monies. Even in private institutions that use little or no public funds, governing boards have a responsibility to keep expenditures within reason, relative to those in other parts of the national economy.

In order to bring costs under control, some legislators, state coordinating bodies, boards of trustees, and other governing bodies have tried to regulate educational activities and expenditures in great detail. From this effort have evolved line-item appropriations and detailed supervision by state boards and central offices of multi-campus universities. Excessively detailed financial control brings about a false efficiency and threatens institutional autonomy in academic decisions. For the small sums saved, the much greater efficiency flowing from local initiative and common sense is constrained and discouraged.

The revenue theory of costs suggests that when public agencies or governing boards wish to control costs, they need do only two things: first, to establish in broad general terms the basic scope and mission of the institutions for which they are responsible, and second, to set the total amount of money to be available to each institution each year. With these parameters given for each institution, both total and unit costs will be determined. The individual institutions through their internal decision-making processes can then allocate resources to meet local needs and to protect freedom of thought and expression. The state agencies and governing boards will then be freed from supervision of budgetary line items and they are freed from involvement with supervision of the professional aspects of instruction and research. They may wish to be generally informed on these matters and in particular to make sure that each institution is adhering to its mission. But these goals do not require detailed control of institutional operations. Broad general observation and post-audits are sufficient. To exercise cost control, state agencies and governing boards are obliged to decide only the level of educational revenues in light of the established mission and enrollment of each institution. (Clark, 1978; Harcleroad, 1975).

Such decisions may be based upon simulation studies, comparisons with other institutions, and formulas that take into account enrollments, salary levels, staffing ratios, cost of purchased goods and services; and capital requirements. In the end, however, these decisions are inevitably reached through the political process. Whatever these decisions may turn out to be, they are the ultimate determinants of both total expenditures and unit costs.

## Conclusions

The pattern of American higher education, as it has evolved over three centuries, is part of the national culture. Questions about who should be educated, how the education should be conducted, what level of quality should be maintained, how the system should be organized, what institutions should be responsible for research and public service—all these questions—are largely settled through widely accepted concepts about what higher education should be like. These concepts are at times controversial. They evolve over time. Yet there exists in society at any moment a substantial body of widely-accepted views about higher education.

The services of the institutions of higher education, like most products or services, are subject to increasing unit costs and to diminishing unit benefits as expenditures increase. In the long run, societal decisions about total expenditures will tend toward an equilibrium at which incremental cost per dollar of expenditure equals incremental benefit per dollar of expenditure, that is, at the point of intersection between the cost curve and the demand curve (see Figure 1). Both the cost curve and the demand curve shift from time to time and it is with these shifts that changes in the level of spending occur.

Individual institutions operate within the context of societal decisions concerning total expenditures. Institutions may differ in their responses to the environment in which they operate and they may fare differently. But they are constrained by the societal environment and also by the competition among them? However, their combined activities may affect societal demands for higher education as when they discover new needs or new clienteles or when they launch effective public relations campaigns; and their combined activities may affect overall costs, as when they find ways to reduce expenses or discover ways to enhance outcomes that justify increased costs. Thus, there is constant interplay between societal influences and institutional influences in determining total expenditures. In the long run, however, the broad societal influences are predominant; institutions must accept the parameters laid down by society.

To recognize societal influences on higher educational expenditures does not suggest that somewhere there is a central authority that consciously and overtly articulates public attitudes or regulates the entire higher educational system of the United States. Obviously, there is no such authority. Rather, it suggests that higher education is a relatively stable feature of the culture, that those who control the flow of funds to higher education—students and their families, other users, donors, legislators, and trustees—hold roughly similar concepts of what higher education should be like, and that these concepts provide the context within which the institutions operate and determine both total expenditures and cost per unit of service. As Lord Keynes once said, however, "In the long run, we are all dead." In the short run, which may be very long indeed, costs per student unit for individual colleges and universities are determined by the amount of money they can raise for educational purposes relative to the number of students they are serving.

# Note

1. Total educational expenditures of 58.9 percent of the grand total (row seven of right-hand column in Table 1) minus percentage paid to employees engaged in education of 26.4.

# The Future (1981)

DAVID W. BRENEMAN AND SUSAN C. NELSON

All of higher education faces a difficult and uncertain future in the final decades of this century. Throughout much of the post-World War II era, higher education was a rapid growth industry, experiencing large gains in resources and enrollments. Community colleges in particular increased in number and size at an exceptional rate as they helped to carry out society's commitment to increased postsecondary educational opportunity. The next two decades, however, will witness a very different environment for higher education as enrollments stabilize or decline in response to a 25 percent drop in the traditional college-age population. How community colleges will fare in the intensified competition for enrollments and resources will depend in large measure on general economic trends, policy decisions affecting public support of higher education, and educational decisions made on the nation's campuses. Although the discussion in this chapter is necessarily speculative, focusing on the outlook for community colleges allows us to link the findings and conclusions of earlier chapters to the critical policy decisions that will shape the future of these institutions.

## The Economy and Higher Education

The state of the economy will exert a strong influence on the prospects for higher education in the 1980s. However, the ability to forecast economic trends accurately became increasingly difficult during the 1970s as the economy simultaneously experienced high rates of inflation and unemployment, a phenomenon labeled "stagflation."[1] On very basic matters, such as the causes of inflation or the reasons for declining productivity, there is simply no consensus within the economics profession. Nonetheless, rough agreement does exist on the forces likely to dominate the economy during the next several years, which will clearly influence the prospects of the higher education sector.

First, although disagreement about its causes is rife, there is a broad consensus that inflation in the range of 7 to 10 percent annually will be with us for the foreseeable future, unless the as yet untested new economic program of the Reagan administration produces the changes that are claimed for it.[2] The conventional tools of monetary and fiscal policy have become less effective in constraining inflation without generating an unacceptable cost in reduced investment, lost output, and rising unemployment. If the new administration's cures for inflation are not successful, economic policy may continue to oscillate between restriction and expansion as emphasis shifts from concern for inflation to concern for unemployment. Such a "stop and go" policy would yield a sluggish economy at best, with economic growth well below its potential. The fiscal dividends yielded in the 1960s would not occur, and federal budgets would remain tight.

The declining growth in productivity in recent years is a second factor contributing to both a reduced rate of economic growth and inflation. Productivity gains in real output per hour worked allow workers' wages to increase without contributing to inflation; if workers can produce more, employers can pay them more without having to raise prices. Rising productivity also facilitates real growth in gross national product (GNP). Until the late 1960s, productivity was growing by about 2.4 percent per year. Since then the rate of growth has slowed, averaging only about 1 percent per year in the late 1970s. Productivity actually fell in each year from 1978 through 1980, according to several of the most important measures. While the causes of poor productivity performance are not fully understood, it clearly has the effect of pushing up the costs of production and consequently the rate of inflation.[3] It is too early to tell whether the economic policy of the Reagan administration will succeed in reversing this pattern of limited productivity increases.

The spiraling cost of energy is a third economic force of great significance, for the twelvefold increase in oil prices since 1973 is working a fundamental transformation upon the economy and the way people live. The ramifications of higher energy costs will continue to unfold throughout the next two decades, forcing changes in production techniques and consumer behavior, as well as contributing to inflation and slower economic growth. The effect on oil-importing nations, such as the United States, is a transfer of wealth to oil-producing nations and an associated decline in economic welfare.

Given these negative economic trends in the 1970s and their possible continuance in the 1980s, it is not surprising that taxpayer resistance to further growth in government's share of GNP has developed, with measures passed to limit or cut back the rate of taxation. In fact, as Table 6-1 shows, government's share of GNP peaked in 1975 at 34.9 percent, falling to an estimated 33.1 percent in 1980. State governments' share of GNP has been essentially stable since 1974 at roughly 6 percent, while local governments' share is down from 5.3 percent in 1975 to an estimated 4.4 percent in 1980. Property taxes, the main source of revenue for local governments, have been the principal target of tax limitation measures, with eleven states having such initiatives on the ballot for the November 1980 general election.[4] Recent trends in state and local government expenditures displayed in table 6-1 seem likely to continue, with little growth in state expenditures as a percentage of GNP and a continuing decline in that percentage for local governments. As legislators and local officials look for places to reduce outlays, education will be a likely candidate, particularly if enrollments decline. Thus, limited growth in state and local support for higher education is a fourth factor in this economic outlook.

The changing age distribution of the U.S. population is the final economic force to be noted in this brief review. As college and university leaders well know, the size of the traditional college age group (eighteen to twenty-one) will fall by roughly 25 percent between 1978 and 1997. What this fact portends for college enrollments is subject to much debate. Reasonable estimates center on a decline of 15 percent, depending upon assumptions about the college attendance rate of other age groups and a variety of other factors, such as retention rates, that influence enrollments.[5] The effects of reduced numbers of high school graduates will be felt throughout the economy, as employers and the military services join the colleges and universities in competing for members of this smaller population. Indeed, as the labor market for high school graduates improves, it is possible that the college attendance rate may decline. The competition among colleges and universities for enrollments will clearly intensify, however, with important implications for the structure of the higher education industry. State-level policymakers, as well as college and university officials, will face a number of critical decisions in the next decade that will influence community colleges.

## The States and Higher Education

The most important and far-reaching governmental decisions affecting higher education in the next decade will be made at the state level as legislators, governors, and statewide governing or coordinating boards confront the issues raised by falling enrollments. Not all states will be equally affected by decreases in the number of high school graduates; some states, such as Texas and Utah,

**Table 6-1**
**Government Expenditure as a Percentage of Gross National Product, Selected Years 1929-80**
**Amounts in billions of dollars**

| Calendar Year | Federal | | State | | Local | | Total | | GNP |
|---|---|---|---|---|---|---|---|---|---|
| | Amount | Percent | Amount | Percent | Amount | Percent | Amount | Percent | |
| 1929 | 2.6 | 2.5 | 2.1 | 2.0 | 5.5 | 5.3 | 10.2 | 9.9 | 103.4 |
| 1939 | 8.9 | 9.8 | 3.7 | 4.1 | 4.8 | 5.3 | 17.4 | 19.2 | 90.8 |
| 1949 | 41.3 | 16.0 | 8.9 | 3.4 | 9.1 | 3.5 | 59.3 | 23.0 | 258.0 |
| 1954 | 69.8 | 19.1 | 12.7 | 3.5 | 14.5 | 4.0 | 97.0 | 26.5 | 366.3 |
| 1959 | 91.0 | 18.7 | 18.7 | 3.8 | 21.3 | 4.4 | 131.0 | 26.9 | 486.5 |
| 1964 | 118.2 | 18.6 | 27.3 | 4.3 | 30.8 | 4.8 | 176.3 | 27.7 | 635.7 |
| 1969 | 188.4 | 20.1 | 49.6 | 5.3 | 47.6 | 5.1 | 285.6 | 30.5 | 935.5 |
| 1974 | 299.3 | 21.2 | 85.2 | 6.0 | 73.7 | 5.2 | 458.2 | 32.4 | 1,412.9 |
| 1975 | 356.8 | 23.3 | 95.7 | 6.3 | 80.3 | 5.3 | 532.8 | 34.9 | 1,528.8 |
| 1976 | 385.0 | 22.6 | 103.4 | 6.1 | 85.5 | 5.0 | 573.9 | 33.7 | 1,702.2 |
| 1977 | 421.7 | 22.2 | 111.0 | 5.8 | 93.4 | 4.9 | 626.1 | 33.0 | 1,899.5 |
| 1978 | 459.8 | 21.6 | 124.4 | 5.8 | 101.8 | 4.8 | 686.0 | 32.2 | 2,127.6 |
| 1979 | 509.2 | 21.1 | 136.1 | 5.6 | 107.9 | 4.5 | 753.2 | 31.2 | 2,413.9 |
| 1980 | 601.6 | 22.9 | 150.2 | 5.7 | 116.7 | 4.4 | 868.5 | 33.1 | 2,626.1 |

Sources: Advisory Commission on Intergovernmental Relations, *Significant Features of Fiscal Federalism*, 1979-80 Edition (GPO, 1980), Table 1, p. 4; and unpublished data, ACIR. Expenditure figures are measured on a national income and product accounts basis, which excludes government lending and financial transactions, all transactions in territories of the United States, and other miscellaneous items included in the unified budget accounts, but includes the government contribution for employee retirement benefits, bonuses paid on Outer Continental Shelf land leases, and other miscellaneous items not include in unified budget outlays. Figures are founded.

may experience increases, while others, such as those in the Northeast and upper Midwest, may have sizable losses of 30 percent or more.[6] State-level officials will face a variety of difficult policy decisions as the competition among institutions for resources and enrollments intensifies. State policies will surely influence the outcome of this struggle, either passively by relying on market forces or actively by planning and implementing explicit policies to guide retrenchment.[7] In whatever planning process a state undertakes, community colleges will be treated not in isolation but as one part of a total postsecondary education system.

A passive response by state government would be to ignore the unique circumstances of the 1980s, leaving state educational policies and financing procedures unchanged. Such an approach could result from simple inertia, or could be a conscious decision to let the colleges compete under existing arrangements, with no attempt by the state to influence the outcome. It seems unlikely, however, that such a hands-off policy could be maintained in light of the inevitable political pressures that will be brought on behalf of those institutions that are losing out in the competition for students. Furthermore, state officials may want to maintain an institutional division of labor, which may prove difficult as colleges and universities seek out new and overlapping markets and activities. Pressures to reduce spending on higher education as enrollments decline can also be expected, prompting a search for ways to cut costs by eliminating marginal programs and reducing overlap and duplication among campuses. It seems likely, therefore, that the states will become more active in shaping the system of higher education in the 1980s, operating through strengthened coordinating boards and ad hoc legislative or gubernatorial commissions.

Community colleges will be included in these state planning efforts and will face, together with other colleges and universities, the following types of questions:

—If substantial excess capacity exists in the public sector of higher education, should state policy encourage full-time undergraduate students to enroll in two-year or four-year campuses? Should excess capacity in the system be spread evenly among the campuses, or should it be concentrated in a particular set of institutions?

—How effective are the various campuses in fulfilling their educational missions? How clear are those missions, and how important are they to the state? Are some campuses spreading themselves too thin by trying to serve too many different groups of students?

—Should a strict division of labor among campuses be established by state plan, or should institutions be free to develop new programs in response to market demands? For example, should four-year institutions be allowed to develop two-year associate degree programs and remedial programs, heretofore the province of community colleges in most states?

—Should a tuition differential between two-year and four-year colleges be maintained, and if so, what purpose does it serve? Does the differential reflect cost or quality differences, is it a response to differences in student incomes, or is it intended to attract students to the lower-priced institutions?

—What role, if any, do the private colleges play in the state plan? Should state support be provided for these institutions, either through direct support or through special student aid, or should state support be concentrated solely in public institutions?

—How small can a two-year college become and still be a viable institution? At what point does a small campus cease to be either cost-effective or educationally effective?

Questions of this type at the state level focus on community colleges as only one part of a total higher education system, but the future of two-year colleges will be significantly influenced by the answers each state gives to such questions. Leaders of community colleges, therefore, cannot afford to concentrate exclusively on the financing formula for two-year campuses, but must be concerned with how their institutions fit into the total state system and how that system should evolve. We can construct two scenarios that bracket the realistic possibilities facing community colleges in the 1980s.

# Scenarios of Community College Development

An optimistic scenario for community colleges involves growing demand for their services, continued political support, an ability to control costs while remaining competitive with other sectors, and a favorable fiscal climate. Specific factors of importance are:

- Continued growth of adult and part-time enrollments, coupled with political consensus on how to pay for such programs and the ability of local colleges to maintain their competitive advantage in serving that market;

- Continued growth of vocational-technical programs, coupled with the ability to respond to changes in local labor market conditions;

- Continued growth of remedial education, coupled with consensus that community colleges are the best institutions to provide that service;

- Ability of community colleges to hold their share of full-time, degree-oriented transfer students;

- Growing demand for noncredit community service activities, coupled with political consensus on how to pay for them;

- Increased political support at all levels of government, based on service to broad constituencies, flexibility, and contribution to local economic development;

- Continued financial advantage through ability to keep tuition lower than in other sectors and through cost savings from use of part-time faculty;

- Extension of federal and state student aid programs to students who are currently excluded, such as those enrolled less than half-time or in noncredit courses;

- No more property tax limitations that reduce local support, and an ability to compete effectively for state aid;

- A growing economy able to yield fiscal dividends for growing public outlays.

A pessimistic scenario projects the opposite of the above, with enrollment erosion, diminished political support, failure to remain competitive with other institutions, and the reluctance of taxpayers to underwrite various aspects of lifelong learning. Specific factors that could lead to this pessimistic future are:

- Slow (or no) growth of adult and part-time enrollments because of saturation of demand, effective competition from other sectors, or unwillingness of governments to increase subsidies;

- Shrinking enrollments in vocational-technical programs because of declining quality of equipment and instruction, failure to adapt to changing labor markets, changing student interests, or increased competition from proprietary schools and industry-based training;

- Growing resistance to financing remedial education: "How many times does the taxpayer have to pay for seventh grade-level work?"

- Erosion of full-time, transfer enrollments, lost to four-year institutions that recruit aggressively and change their admission requirements, and made financially possible by the growth of need-based student aid;

- Inability to establish community services and noncredit courses on other than a "pay-as-you-go" basis;

- Failure to sell the comprehensive community service mission, coupled with a tendency for states to treat community colleges as overflow institutions needed during the years of rapid enrollment growth but less necessary now;

- Erosion of cost and tuition advantages, hence a less competitive position relative to other institutions;

- Inability to broaden coverage of student aid and other forms of financial support needed for lifelong learning;

- Absence of political clout in state legislatures and the damaging effects of poor public relations, as evidenced by attacks on courses in macrame, poodle grooming, cake decorating, and belly dancing;

- Slow economic growth and a shrinking public-sector pie to be distributed among a growing number of claimants.

We make no attempt to forecast which of these scenarios is more likely to occur because the outcome will differ among the states and even among the colleges within a state; as the title of a recent Carnegie Council publication suggests,[8] each campus in the nation faces a unique combination of problems and possibilities in the next two decades. The future for community colleges is not predetermined, but will be influenced by actions and decisions yet to be taken by community college leaders and others.

# Summary of Findings

In the balance of this chapter, we draw together our findings, conclusions, and recommendations about the financing of community colleges, relating our analyses to the two scenarios above. Our conclusions fall into three categories: a first set based on economic criteria of equity and efficiency; a second set based on site visits and empirical analyses of federal, state, and local government policies; and a third set based on analyses of the National Longitudinal Study and other studies of educational outcomes, as well as our own judgments about the educational strengths and weaknesses of community colleges.

Discussion of efficient pricing of community college offerings in chapter 2 yielded the following conclusions:

1. No single best system of financing community colleges can be derived from efficiency considerations, for determinations of efficiency depend upon value judgments about public benefits and upon voter preferences, both of which are as diverse as the colleges themselves.

2. Tuition for academic courses and most vocational-technical offerings should be well above zero but less than full cost, with subsidies provided by both state and local governments.

3. Remedial courses, including adult basic education, should be tuition free, with full state and local subsidy.

4. Vocational programs providing highly specific training for particular firms should receive support from those firms. An exception would occur if the course offerings are part of a state's economic development plan designed to attract employers to an area or convince them to stay.

5. Community service programs that are noncredit and primarily for personal enrichment should be self-supporting from user fees or subsidized from local funds if public benefits are judged to be present.

6. In the absence of political consensus regarding the mission of community colleges, disagreements over financing patterns and policies can be expected to persist. Many of the disputes over financing can be traced to disagreements over mission.

Conclusions based on efficiency must be supplemented with considerations of equity. Several types of equity were examined . . . and it was shown that the approach often used in finance studies—computation of net benefits, or subsidies minus tax payments by income class—can give misleading results for policy purposes. Consequently, our analysis focused on the educational opportunities made possible by community colleges and the ways in which those opportunities are affected by financing procedures, rather than on the equity to taxpayers of various local, state, and federal taxes used to support the colleges. Our principal conclusions included the following:

1. The policy of low (or no) tuition traditionally advocated for community colleges is not necessarily equitable. Given the last decade's increases in federal and state student aid, a policy of higher tuition coupled with increased need-based aid can be more equitable in supporting educational opportunity. At a minimum, the assumption that low (or no) tuition is superior on equity grounds should be questioned and this policy compared to what might be accomplished through one of higher tuition and increased aid.

2. A comparison of public expenditures for two-year and four-year colleges and universities does not support the claim that community college students are systematically receiving less support than their lower division counterparts in other public institutions. Meaningful

comparisons of expenditure differences are difficult to make because of the different functions performed by the various institutions, but when adjustments are made for those differences, educational expenditures per lower division student are generally similar.

3.  In states where community colleges receive local property tax support, there may be expenditure differences among colleges attributable to local wealth differentials. Although the significance of interdistrict equity is not nearly as great at the community college level as it is for elementary-secondary education, state support formulas should be designed to offset these local wealth differentials to some extent.

Equity in the distribution of federal student aid dollars was the central concern of chapter 4. After detailed analysis of the distribution of federal student aid among students and institutions of higher education, we were not able to give conclusive and unambiguous answers to assertions that the federal programs are underutilized (or overutilized) by two-year colleges and their students. The provisions of the various aid programs that may have contributed to some underutilization of federal aid in the 1970s include the following: (1) the half-of-cost limitation in the Pell grant (formerly the basic educational opportunity grant) program; (2) the provisions in the Pell grant program that treat independent students (both with and without dependents) more stringently than dependent students; (3) the system of institutional requests and panel reviews of the campus-based aid allocations; and (4) the provisions that limit aid to students enrolled at least half-time in degree-credit courses.

Each of these provisions was addressed in the Education Amendments of 1980 in ways that promised to help community colleges and their students. The maximum Pell grant was authorized to increase by stages to $2,600 for academic year 1985-86, with the half-of-cost limitation raised by 5 percent intervals as the maximum awards increased, allowing grants equal to 70 percent of costs when the maximum grant reached $2,600. Independent students with dependents were to be treated exactly the same as dependent students under the Pell grant program, a major gain for the older students that make up such a large share of community college enrollments. The allocation process for campus-based funds would no longer include graduate enrollments in the interstate allocation, and the intrastate distributions should be less arbitrary and more predictable now that a formula approach has replaced the panel review process. Finally, students enrolled less than half-time would be aided by the provision that allows up to 10 percent of an institution's supplemental educational opportunity grant funds to be allocated to such students.

To a remarkable degree, the interests of community colleges and their students were well served by the Education Amendments of 1980. However, the Reagan administration has introduced considerable uncertainty into the future of student aid with numerous legislative proposals designed to reduce federal outlays, particularly in the Pell grant and guaranteed student loan programs. From the standpoint of community colleges and their students, restoration and full funding of the Education Amendments of 1980 (particularly the Pell grant provisions) should be the main priority at the federal level for the 1980s.

Chapter 5 discussed state and local issues, emphasizing practical questions that arise regarding financing formulas currently in use. Definitive conclusions are difficult to reach because the choice of policies depends upon objectives sought and because great diversity exists among the states in financing procedures; nonetheless, we were able to advance the following conclusions:

1.  Although simplicity in a finance plan is desirable, complex plans are necessary if a state seeks to achieve multiple objectives, such as efficiency and equity.

2.  Considerations of efficiency favor a combination of state and local tax support, but greater equity can be achieved through full state funding alone. The efficiency gains appear to outweigh the equity losses, however, arguing for continued local tax support.

3.  For states with local financial support, differences in property wealth among community college districts do give rise to inequities in resources per student, which can be offset to some degree by state equalization formulas. Although such formulas are complex, equalization is a desirable objective to include in a state financing plan.

4.  Finance plans that recognize differences in program costs (for example, between allied health programs and general studies) are a definite improvement over simple unit rate or flat grant formulas.

5.  Although no precise way exists to determine what share of educational costs should be borne by tuition, the presence of private as well as public benefits, coupled with recent increases in need-based student aid, suggests that policies of low (or no) tuition may no longer be either efficient or equitable. We suggest that tuition in community colleges should not exceed 33 percent of current operating costs, but urge each state and college to review tuition policies in light of changing economic circumstances.

6.  Formula budgets are likely to be more equitable than negotiated budgets that follow no guidelines and are politically determined.

7.  There is no strong economic case for state support of most noncredit courses. Analysis of courses in this category suggests that financing should be provided either through user fees or payments by local government or private agencies.

8.  Although it is tempting to link the level of support for community colleges to that provided to four-year public colleges and universities, differences in purposes served, instructional programs, and allocation of faculty time suggest that such linkages would serve little purpose other than to force an undesirable uniformity.

9.  As enrollments stabilize or decline, the use of enrollment-driven formulas based on average costs per student needs to be reconsidered. Such formulas served the institutions well during a time of growth but will be damaging during a period of decline. The cost structure of community colleges should be analyzed and financed in terms of fixed and variable costs, not by a single average cost per student.

10. Analysis of how community college costs vary with size indicates the presence of both economies and diseconomics of scale; in other words, over a certain range unit costs fall, but beyond a certain size, unit costs rise. Financing formulas should reflect this fact, for in most instances it will not be possible to increase or decrease college size to the optimal (or least-cost) level of operations.

## Implications of the Findings

If these economic conclusions about financing were incorporated into local, state, and federal policies, the effect would be, on balance, to tilt the institutions toward the pessimistic scenario. Analysis in preceding chapters, based on criteria of equity and efficiency, leads to recommendations for:

- Increased tuition, coupled with increased student aid;

- Increased local support (as opposed to state support) for community college programs;[9]

- User charges that cover costs of most community service activities;

- Caution in assessing (and acting upon) claims that states provide more support for lower division students in four-year colleges and universities than for comparable students in community colleges;

- Continued restriction of the federal Pell grant program to students enrolled for at least a half-time course of study.

Recommendations such as these contribute to the pessimistic scenario largely because they emphasize circumstances in which students can be expected to pay a higher share of their educational costs than thought desirable by many community college leaders. Indeed, some leaders argue that virtually any activity undertaken by a community college should be fully subsidized, an extreme position not supported here. Furthermore, our analysis does not lead to recommendations for state or federal subsidies that would encourage the evolution of two-year colleges into community-based learning centers; to the extent that such development is desirable, we would look to local subsidies and private support as the principal sources of funds. The dilemma facing community colleges is that the share of support provided by local government is declining at the very time that their direction of development calls for increased local aid. The case for state or federal subsidy of community-based learning centers is hard to make and does not derive much support from economic analysis. The primary state interest in community colleges is likely to remain in the more traditional functions of academic transfer and vocational-technical programs unless the growth in numbers of people participating in noncredit community activities swings the political balance in favor of increased state support for such programs. It is entirely possible that some states may never reach that position.

Other recommendations stemming from our analyses support the optimistic scenario:

- Remedial courses (adult basic education) should be fully subsidized;

- In states with local tax support, the state formula should include equalization provisions that reduce disparities in resources per student;

- The limitation of Pell grants to a maximum payment of half of cost should be liberalized (as was done in the Education Amendments of 1980), for its impact falls primarily on very poor students attending low-cost institutions;

- Finance formulas should reflect differences in program costs;

- Formulas based on fixed and variable costs should replace those that use only average costs;

- Formulas should reflect the fact that unit costs differ with college size.

Recommendations such as these are largely intended to improve current funding formulas by linking the formulas more closely to the actual cost structure of community colleges. In most cases, the changes proposed are in effect in one or more states and thus seem realistic. Their implementation could be viewed as simply the extension of "best practice" to a larger number of colleges. On the other hand, these are not the types of changes that would radically transform the nature of community colleges or alter their competitive position vis-à-vis other institutions. They are incremental steps that promise modest improvements in the financing of two-year colleges, and as such it seems likely that more states will adopt them. But these recommendations would have a marginal effect at best in determining the future of community colleges.

Thus, economic analysis yields a number of modest improvements that could be made in state financing formulas and federal programs, but provides little support for the more striking changes in policy that would hasten the conversion of two-year colleges into community-based centers for lifelong learning. Writing as economists, we end our story here; however, as individuals greatly interested in higher education, we continue with a brief discussion of educational issues that affect community colleges and the strategic choices facing these institutions in the 1980s. Public policy toward community colleges—or higher education in general—cannot be determined solely by economic considerations. The future of community colleges will be determined through a mixture of economic, political, and educational considerations.

# Educational Considerations for Public Policy

We have seen in . . . the difficulties encountered in defining, measuring, and evaluating the educational, social, and economic outcomes of two-year college programs. Despite these difficulties, however, the demands of an era of limited growth or retrenchment in higher education will force state policymakers to consider institutional performance carefully in allocating limited resources for education. One area within the community colleges that is likely to be examined critically is the educational performance and productivity of academic transfer programs. If these programs are expected to contribute significantly to the production of college degrees, then the performance data in many states are troubling. The proportion of students who actually complete a two-year degree within two to five years is very low; numerous studies have documented completion rates of roughly 10 percent. In our analysis of the National Longitudinal Study of the High School Class of 1972, we found that only 16 percent of two-year college students enrolled in academic programs had earned a bachelor's degree four and one-half years later, compared to 44 percent who began in a four-year college or university. Even after controlling for a wide range of background characteristics, including educational aspirations, enrolling in a community college was a significant—and negative—factor in determining bachelor's degree completion. The analysis suggested that a majority of students would have a better chance of earning a bachelor's degree if they start at a four-year rather than a two-year college.[10] These findings raise an important question for state educational policy in the 1980s, particularly for those states where excess capacity is anticipated in the higher education system. Should states continue to encourage transfer enrollments in community colleges, or instead pursue policies to assist as many full-time, degree-seeking students as possible to enroll directly in four-year colleges?

One way to approach this question is to consider those areas in which a particular type of institution may have an educational comparative advantage over others. It has been argued that two-year colleges lack a comparative advantage in academic transfer programs populated by full-time, degree-seeking students aged eighteen and nineteen. Drawing on extensive survey research of student performance, Alexander Astin concluded that

> While these institutions [community colleges] provide important services to adults, part-time students, and those pursuing technical courses that are not offered by four-year institutions, the results of this and other studies suggest that they may not really serve the interests of students coming directly from high school to pursue careers requiring baccalaureate degrees. . . .Lack of residential facilities and the low student involvement in campus life partly explain low persistence rates, but even when these factors are considered, students have less chance of persisting at a community college than they do at some other kind of institution. . . . Whatever the explanation, for the eighteen-year-old going directly to college from high school, the public community college does not represent an "equal educational opportunity" compared with other types of institutions."[11]

Arthur M. Cohen and Florence B. Brawer, of the center for the Study of Community Colleges at UCLA, have developed another dimension of this argument through research that documents the declining status and support for liberal arts disciplines in community colleges that increasingly emphasize career, compensatory, and community education.[12] Acknowledging the severity of this problem, the American Association of Community and Junior Colleges recently organized a national assembly to discuss ways to strengthen the humanities in two-year colleges.[13] Cohen and Brawer's work suggests, however, that community colleges may no longer serve the academic needs of traditional college transfer students as well as did the junior colleges of twenty years ago. As the mission of two-year colleges has grown to include nontraditional clienteles, increased emphasis on vocational-technical training, and stronger community orientation, it is not surprising that traditional collegiate programs have suffered.

A further consideration derives, paradoxically, from one of the strengths of the two-year college: its strong community orientation. As we pursued our campus visits, it became apparent that two-year colleges are very much products and reflections of the communities where they are located. Public two-year colleges are truly community institutions, or, to use Edmund Gleazer's phrase, the "community's college."[14] This fact explains the great diversity one finds among two-year colleges, for they are as different as the towns and cities in which they are located. Educationally, this trait is a positive factor for many students and programs: for older part-time students who might find a university intimidating, for vocational-technical programs geared to the local labor market, and for community service activities. In these areas, the colleges can truly act as local service agencies or community-based learning centers. In our view, this local orientation is a disadvantage primarily for one group of students—those of traditional college age who are enrolled full-time in academic transfer programs and intend to obtain a four-year degree. It is for this group of students that the benefits of going away to college are most often stressed, for an important part of the educational process in residential colleges is the exposure to a diverse student body drawn from many areas beyond the student's local community.[15] Apart from the quality of classroom instruction (which is undoubtedly better in some community college classes than in some university classes), the residential student gains out-of-class experience that is denied the commuting student. Community colleges are invaluable in providing educational opportunities for place-bound adults; however, traditional college-age students are a less place-bound group for whom experiences beyond the local community are particularly valuable. As the eighteen-year-old population declines throughout the 1980s and into the 1990s, it will be possible to provide a four-year residential college experience for a growing percentage of college-bound youth. State policymakers have an opportunity to decide whether to encourage such enrollment, with financial aid provided as necessary to assist with higher tuition and residential charges.

Four-year colleges and universities may have a comparative advantage over community colleges in traditional undergraduate education; however, it can be argued that community colleges have a comparative advantage over four-year schools in virtually every other area of education in which the two-year colleges are heavily involved, including vocational-technical programs; remedial education, and noncredit community services. Community colleges have been engaged in these activities by choice for a longer time than most four-year institutions; their faculties are generally more experienced in, and receptive to, teaching highly diverse groups of students; and their strong local orientation is a source of strength for community services. Increased numbers of four-year colleges and universities are expressing interest in moving into these activities as a way of expanding the markets that they serve and enlarging their clienteles. Whether state policy should encourage or discourage these developments within the four-year sector is an equally important issue for each state to decide.

We favor an educational division of labor among institutions in the 1980s that would result in the community colleges enrolling fewer full-time academic transfer students of traditional college age and retaining a dominant position in those activities that four-year institutions have not undertaken traditionally and are likely to do less well. To a considerable degree, this rough division of labor reflects trends and tendencies already under way: four-year residential institutions are working very hard to maintain full-time undergraduate enrollments, while community colleges continue to evolve away from the junior college emphasis on transfer programs toward service to new clienteles. Of course, this division of labor among institutions will never be absolute, nor should it be. For some undergraduates, the community college will still be the best option, just as the university will be better for some older students returning to school part-time. We do recommend, however, that state education officials play an active role in supporting these natural directions of development through statewide planning that encourages and strengthens institutional division of labor, and that they accordingly review and change as necessary the incentives built into financing formulas. Increased competition among institutions for enrollments and resources could be healthy and lead to educational improvements or could be damaging and wasteful. We believe the worst outcome will occur if competition turns into a free-for-all, with each institution trying to enter as many educational markets as possible, regardless of educational capability. Responsible state leadership can prevent that outcome by establishing educational and financial policies that support a division of labor based on the relative strengths and weaknesses of the colleges and universities within each state.

## Strategic Choices Facing Community Colleges

The future of community colleges is hard to predict because the range of choice regarding what to emphasize—and even what to become—is wider for community colleges than for other institutions of higher learning.[16] Throughout this book we have stressed the tension between institutional mission and finance as the central theme or issue in the financing of two-year colleges. This tension promises to grow during the next two decades, as higher education adjusts to a 25 percent drop in the traditional college-age population and as the promise of expanding adult markets through programs of lifelong learning is either realized or falls short of expectations. In the face of considerable uncertainty regarding the future contours of post-secondary education and training, community college leaders must decide which direction of development is best for their institutions. Broadly speaking, three general strategies are possible.

First, the commitment to a comprehensive mission could be maintained, giving equal priority to academic, vocational-technical, and community service programs. For this comprehensive approach to be a realistic option for the difficult times ahead, a college must have reasonable assurance of gaining (or retaining) both the resources required to mount a comprehensive program and the enrollment necessary to justify it. As noted above, community colleges in most states are likely to face increased competition from other institutions in each of these program areas, particularly for full-time academic transfer students. Perhaps the greatest risk of an unflinching commitment to the comprehensive mission is that sufficient financial support will not materialize, and the college will suffer across the board, becoming less competitive and less distinctive in all program areas. To opt for comprehensiveness is to gamble that sufficient support will be forthcoming to render unnecessary hard choices among program priorities.

If our campus visits were representative, this approach appears to be most common: we found little evidence of procedures for setting priorities or examples of studied decisions to deemphasize or withdraw from specific activities. The dominant administrative objective on most campuses seems to be to maximize enrollments (or the number of people involved in some college-related program). If the financing formula does not pay for a certain type of activity, every effort is made to reclassify programs into the fundable category; however, there appears to be a simple faith in the long run benefit of maximizing head counts (or the proportion of the population served) regardless of the finance mechanism. This policy has generally served two-year colleges well in the past. As open door institutions with comprehensive missions, virtually no educational need within the community was off limits, which generated a great deal of goodwill for the colleges. We are reluctant to suggest that an educational philosophy so successful in the past may fail in the 1980s, but there does seem to be a distinct possibility of that happening in a time of tight budgets and increased scrutiny of the value of all publicly supported activities. The most searching questions for two-year colleges will come from state officials as both the amount and percentage of state support increase. Colleges that lack the capacity to set limits on themselves and to establish and defend clear priorities among activities may see their state support diminish.

A second strategic approach would be to drop the strong community service orientation, placing renewed emphasis on the traditional collegiate functions—shifting the focus, in other words, from *community* to *college*. Resources would be concentrated on degree-credit programs in both the academic transfer and vocational-technical areas, with a general education core curriculum required for all students.[17] Under this strategy, community service activities would be relegated to the fringe of campus life. A strong case can be made for the wisdom of such a course, for it emphasizes the more traditional values associated with higher education, it puts the stress on quality programs with clear investment value, it moves away from such classes as belly dancing or fly-tying that are easily held up to ridicule, and it responds to the preferences of many state officials who still see community colleges as junior colleges, very much a part of traditional higher education. As one state director of community colleges observed, "Academic and vocational programs are in the center ring, while community services are the sideshow. States will support the center ring, but not the sideshow." It is hard to argue against this approach, for as we have seen, most state financing formulas were designed with college programs and full-time students in mind. From a financial perspective, a decision to move back to the basics may appear to be the safest strategy, but this conclusion holds only if the two-year college can compete successfully for full-time undergraduates. Colleges that want to maintain or strengthen their academic transfer programs would be advised to adopt this strategy, concentrating resources on academic quality. To the extent that higher education is a declining industry in the 1980s and 1990s, however, there is limited appeal to tying the community college future narrowly to that enterprise. The risk of moving farther away from traditional higher education, though, is that adequate public support for programs of lifelong learning may fail to materialize. This is the dilemma facing community colleges.

The third approach, advocated by Edmund Gleazer and others, is for the colleges to become community-based learning centers.[18] . . . The emphasis in this model is on *community*, not *college*. The vision laid out by Gleazer is in many ways the logical next step in the evolution of community colleges, with a diminished role for traditional college programs and students and an expanded role for part-time, non-degree seeking, adult learners. The appeal of this model is that it seems to be moving with the times, opening up new areas for educational effort just as the traditional college-age population begins to decline. The potential market for lifelong learning is immense and only partially tapped, and community colleges are well placed geographically and philosophically to develop further this educational frontier. A shift in this direction is also consistent with our earlier observations about the comparative educational strengths and weaknesses of the two-year and four-year sectors of higher education. The only drawback is the distinct possibility that the necessary financial support for community learning centers will not be forthcoming. And, as this book has indicated, proponents of such centers will not find in economic analysis strong support for heavy federal or state subsidies of the centers and their students. Arguments stressing other than economic values will have to be developed and sold politically before this vision of the community college becomes reality.

None of these three broad strategies charts an obvious or easy course for the future. We expect community colleges to respond to the uncertainty and challenges ahead in diverse ways, depending upon which direction appears most suited to each institution's particular circumstances. Community college leaders must draw upon the unique strengths of their own institution as they seek to resolve the inevitable dilemma posed by changing missions and restrictive financing.

# Notes

1. For an excellent survey of the economic dilemmas of the 1970s, see James Tobin, "Stabilization Policy Ten Years After," *Brookings Papers on Economic Activity, 1:1980*, pp. 19-71.

2. Office of Management and Budget, *America's New Beginning: A Program for Economic Recovery* (OMB, February 18, 1981).

3. Edward F. Denison, *Accounting for Slower Economic Growth: The United States in the 1970s* (Brookings Institution, 1979).

4. Initiatives passed in only three states: Arkansas, Massachusetts, and Missouri.

5. For a good discussion of enrollment projections, see *Three Thousand Futures: The Next Twenty Years for Higher Education*, final report of the Carnegie Council on Policy Studies in Higher Education (Jossey-Bass, 1980).

For contrasting views, see the articles by Fred E. Crossland, "Learning to Cope with a Downward Slope," and Carol Frances, "Apocalyptic vs. Strategic Planning," *Change*, vol. 12 (July-August 1980), pp. 18, 20-25, and 19, 39-44.

6. William R. McConnell, *High School Graduates: Projections for the Fifty States*, Western Interstate Commission for Higher Education, National Institute of Independent Colleges and Universities, and the Teachers Insurance and Annuity Association (Boulder, Colo.: WICHE, 1979).

7. For discussion of these options, see David W. Breneman, "Policy Strategies for the 1980s," in James R. Mingle and associates, *Challenges of Retrenchment: Strategies for Consolidating Programs, Cutting Costs, and Reallocating Resources* (Jossey-Bass, forthcoming).

8. *Three Thousand Futures.*

9. There are, of course, some states in which tuition already covers a substantial percentage of costs and others that have ample local support. Thus these first two recommendations would not apply in every case.

10. See chapter 2. Some community college leaders argue that their institutions should not be evaluated by such data, and we agree that the figures have to be interpreted cautiously. We do not agree, however, that such data are irrelevant or completely misleading and thus should be ignored.

11. Alexander W. Astin, *Four Critical Years* (Jossey-Bass, 1977), p. 247.

12. See the series of special reports on *The Humanities in Two-Year Colleges* (Center for the Study of Community Colleges and ERIC Clearinghouse for Junior Colleges, University of California-Los Angeles, 1975-1978).

13. Roger Yarrington, ed., *Strengthening Humanities in Community Colleges: National Assembly Report* (Washington, D.C.: AACJC, 1980).

14. Edmund J. Gleazer, Jr., *The Community College: Values, Vision, and Vitality* (Washington, D.C.: AACJC, 1980), p. 38.

15. Astin, *Four Critical Years*, pp. 220-21. Of course, many students attending urban universities also live at home.

16. See the interesting articles by K. Patricia Cross, "Community Colleges on the Plateau," *Journal of Higher Education*, vol. 52 (March-April 1981), pp. 113-23; and Mary Lou Zoglin, "Community College Responsiveness: Myth or Reality?" *Journal of Higher Education*, vol. 52 (July-August 1981), pp. 415-26.

17. Miami-Dade Community College is among the leaders nationally in developing such a general education program, emphasizing basic skill requirements for all students, together with standards of academic progress. Jeffrey D. Lukenbill and Robert H. McCabe, *General Education in a Changing Society: General Education Program, Basic Skills Requirements, Standards of Academic Progress at Miami-Dade Community College* (Kendall/Hunt for Miami-Dade Community College, 1978).

18. Gleazer, *The Community College*, chaps. 1, 2.

# Pricing Public Sector Services:
## The Tuition Gap (1981)

REGINA E. HERZLINGER AND FRANCES JONES

## Abstract

*The large gap between the tuition charged by public colleges and universities and private ones is likely to cause severe disruptions to the private sector institutions of higher education. If it continues, private sector institutions may once again become bastions for students who can afford their services, rather than for those who merit them, and these institutions will diminish in size and diversity as well. Public sector institutions will become relatively stronger—not solely for reasons of effectiveness, efficiency, or equity—but because of the competitive advantage that the tuition gap affords them. This paper explores the feasibility and desirability of the three methods of correcting this problem, using real cost and demand data from the University of Massachusetts for illustrative purposes. It concludes the subsidization of students (rather than institutions) and raising public sector tuitions are two possible alternatives to the present "tuition gap."*

## Tuition Gap

The American higher education industry grew dramatically in the past quarter century. Between 1950 and 1975, expenditure grew from $2 billion to over $32 billion annually; but public and private sector expenditures on higher education grew at substantially different rates. While in 1950 both sectors had equal annual operating expenses of $1.2 billion, by 1974 public sector expenses had grown to be double those of the private sector.

By the mid-1970s, the period of intense growth ended. In its place, the American college and university system now faces a period of retrenchment. The sharp decline in the birth rate of this country in the 1960s and 1970s will result in a corresponding drop in 18–21 year olds in the 1980s and 1990s. The Census Bureau projects that that population will decrease from 17.2 million in 1979 to 13.0 million in 1995. While in the past colleges and universities shared in an ever-growing market, they are now forced to compete with each other for students.

The competition, however, will not be decided purely on quality of education; the market is skewed in favor of public sector schools because of their state-subsidized tuition. The tuition for attending a four-year public college in 1974 was $470. At a private four-year college, the tuition averaged $2,131. Thus, average tuition at the private colleges is over four times that at public ones, a factor that has come to be known as the tuition gap.

In the period 1956 through 1974, the gap between the average private and public sector tuition steadily increased from $755 to $1,668 (in constant 1974 dollars). While the rise in median family income has so far kept pace with that increase, and the ratio of private to public tuition has not become larger over time, in the future the absolute dollar difference in tuitions is likely to present a graver threat to the survival of private institutions. As Breneman and Finn (1978: 30–31) describe it:

> . . . during the years of rapid enrollment growth, non-price factors, such as geographic accessibility, diversity of curriculum offerings, and the vast expansion of community colleges, played a more important role than the widening tuition gap between the two sectors. While such factors will continue to be important, the tuition gap is likely to be of greater significance in an era of stable or declining enrollments.

Administrators of private institutions have recently focused national attention on the issue, arguing that the tuition gap not only threatens the viability of the private sector, but also defies rational justification. John Silber, President of Boston University and one of the most outspoken critics of the public sector's tuition policies, put the argument this way in a 1975 address to the Massachusetts legislature:

> Here in Massachusetts, we are constantly told that there are two kinds of education. One of these, we are told, is called private, and it is said to be costly, elitist, and not truly in the interest of the public; the other, we are told, is called public, and it is said to be inexpensive, populist, and responsive to the public interest. This distinction is false and dangerously misleading.
>
> All higher education is *public* higher education for the simple reason that there is nothing but the public to educate. One sector of public higher education, better called *independent*, provides the cost of education through substantial tuition charges, fees, and outside income in the form of gifts and grants. The other sector, more accurately called *state-owned* or *state-subsidized*, assigns the cost of education to the taxpayer; its operating expenses are provided in annual appropriations; its facilities are financed by bond issues of the Commonwealth; and tuition payments by the student are minimal.
>
> Both sectors educate the public; both are public education. They are differentiated only by the mechanisms each uses to pay the costs. A low tuition does not mean a low cost of education; it merely means that someone else, the taxpayer, is meeting the bills. A high tuition does not imply an undemocratic philosophy; it merely demonstrates that, where there is no Santa Claus, deficits are synonymous with bankruptcy.

In response, advocates of state-subsidized schools have argued that fundamental differences in the missions of, and services provided by, the two kinds of institutions justify a difference in financing strategy: both sectors may, as Silber argues, educate the public, but they are very different publics.

## History of Public and Private Financing of Higher Education

The ambiguity about the roles of the public and private sectors dates back to the origins of this country. In the century before the Revolution, American institutions of higher education were all "private"; nevertheless, they still had substantial governmental aid. In his history of American higher education institutions, Frederick Rudolph writes:

> The crucial support by the state has often been clouded by the highly romantic regard held by Americans for unaided effort and by the confusion introduced by the use of such terms as "public" and "private" to describe institutions in a world that was itself in the process of defining the meaning of such terms.
>
> . . . On over one hundred occasions before 1789, the General Court of Massachusetts appropriated funds for Harvard College. Indeed. Harvard, Yale, and Columbia could not have survived the colonial period without support of the state (Rudolph, 1962: 185).

In colonial times, access to a college education was limited by social status, religion, race, and sex. The rise of state universities in the south in the 19th century and their rapid expansion in the midwest after the Civil War, arose from a desire to foster a meritocracy in which those who were able would have the opportunity to attend a college, regardless of family background and ability to pay. As free public high school education became generally available late in the 19th century, enrollments in public institutions burgeoned.

Over the first half of the 20th century, private institutions were gradually won over the notion of a meritocracy. While still giving some preferential treatment based on birth status, they began to admit increasing numbers of students from the same "public" served by the state systems, and to provide the financial aid that made it possible for those students to enroll. But if the originally distinct mandates for private and public universities were beginning to converge, it was not a source of concern to either sector. Between 1890 and 1925, higher education enrollments grew almost five times as quickly as the population, and the combined "supply" of the private and public sectors was still not sufficient to meet the ever-increasing "demand."

Generally, academic or athletic merit remained the criterion for financial assistance at public and private institutions until after World War II, when the GI Bill offered assistance to all veterans—a foretaste of changes to come. In the 1960s and 1970s, the long-entrenched notion of a meritocracy gave way to the theme of equal opportunity. What had been done for veterans was now extended to the population as a whole, through an elaborate entitlement system of low-cost loans and basic education grants available to students in any school, and an expanded system of public, low-tuition, four- and two-year colleges with liberal admissions policies. The implicit reasoning behind the expansion seems to have been that the "public" served by the two sectors was once again diverging. While private universities could be relied on to maintain their commitment to equality based on merit, they were not likely to embrace this new broader notion of equality. If the *entire* population—many of whom had not yet had a chance to prove merit—was to be served, it appeared it would once more fall to the public sector to do so.

## The Massachusetts Example

Massachusetts offers a vivid illustration of this pattern. Until the early sixties, the state-supported higher education system was limited to the University of Massachusetts at Amherst and a system of ten small state colleges, which primarily trained teachers. In 1979, there were 15 regional community colleges and five university campuses, in addition to the state colleges. State appropriations for annual maintenance of the institutions had risen from $17.2 million in 1960 to $220.6 million in 1976.

In many states, the rapid growth of the public sector coincided with political shifts in the electorate; Massachusetts is once more a case in point. Until the late fifties, political power in Massachusetts was held mostly by the Republican party whose ties were to the prestigious private colleges and universities in the state. Then the political leadership shifted to the Democratic party with its strong ethnic base. Senator Gerard D'Amico, Chairman of the Joint Committee on Education in the state legislature, gave the following political analysis of the growth of the public higher education sector:

> In the late fifties and sixties, the Democratic party determined the political power in Massachusetts. The voters in the Democratic party had strong ethnic group identities. Many were second and third generation Americans, working class people, and they wanted their children to have a chance to really make it in America. That means a college education.
>
> But what did they have? The Catholic institutions were very selective and tuitions were high. The private institutions were seen as bastions of Brahmin tradition that wouldn't let these kids in.
>
> So, the public institutions were developed by the legislature to provide access to higher education for the working class in the state. Of course, legislators like to have something concrete to point to —the "edifice complex" that built the public campuses is a legislative tool. It's part of our pork barrel policy. Each side, the voters and the legislators, benefitted from the buildup of the system.

## Recent History of the Tuition Gap

Until the mid-1970s, the unique mission of the rapidly expanding public sector was not seriously questioned, and the growing tuition gap was accepted as necessary to fulfill that mission. But in the past few years, several factors have conspired to change that climate of public acceptance. First, in an era of "back-to-basics" in education, the wisdom of entitlement itself has been debated. Critics have argued that open enrollment, rather than guaranteeing all students a worthwhile college education, has merely guaranteed them an increasingly worthless college degree. Secondly, in an era of Proposition 13 fever, all public expenditures have come under scrutiny, and the expenditures of public universities, albeit obscured by inadequate accounting systems, are at least beginning to emerge into the public eye.

Finally, and most importantly, in an era of declining college enrollments, publicly subsidized schools have taken on an entirely new significance. As suggested above, a public and private sectors are forced increasingly to compete for the same shrinking applicant pool, the tuition gap will weigh far more heavily in the balance. However socially justified policy-makers may find a subsidized public sector to be, they will have to reckon with its severe economic repercussions for the private sector. Beyond that, the very fact that the two sectors *are* now competing for the same applicant pool makes it harder to supply that social justification. All but a few colleges and universities in this country may be forced to accept a higher and higher proportion their applicants, as the absolute number of applicants decreases. The implications this trend are not hard to deduce, although administrators like Silber have been understandably reluctant to do so in public. To remain solvent, private colleges and universities may be inclined to consider everyone entitled to a higher education who can afford to finance it, and every service worth providing that the government considers worth subsidizing.

Because of this, the government will have increasing leverage to eradicate those differences that still exist in the missions of the two sectors, either by adopting comprehensive tuition financing plan for which every student in the country would be eligible, or by offering conditional subsidies to private institutions. If it chooses not to exercise that leverage, the differences in the missions of the two sectors are likely to intensify, but in a direction wholly antithetical to the spirit of public education: the two sectors will become almost entirely segregated by the personal wealth of their student body.

## Differences Between Public and Private Institutions

Defenders of the tuition gap have necessarily argued their case not on future prospects, but on past and present differences in the missions fulfilled and services provided by the two kinds of institutions. One way to test the validity of their argument is to examine the patterns of expenditures in the two sectors. As shown in Table 1, which traces college and university expenditures from 1929 through 1976, the two sectors do not vary critically in the way they expend their resources. Indeed, over that almost fifty-year period, the two sectors have become increasingly similar. The most striking example is in the extension and public service category. While that function traditionally has been of negligible importance in private institutions, it accounted almost 10% of expenditures in public institutions in 1939. But by 1973 public institutions spent only 3.3% of their resources on public service, with the public sector apparently shifting its focus toward more sponsored research, like the private sector.

However similar those expenditures may be, the sources of revenues differ substantially in the two sectors. While public institutions receive 63% of their funds from government sources, private institutions receive only 22%. This difference governmental funding between them must be made up through private gifts, endowment and tuition. Thus, private institutions finance 36% of their expenses through tuition and fees; public institutions, only 13%.

What differences there are in expenditure patterns between the two sectors are explained for the most part by their different sources of revenues Student aid costs are proportionately lower at public colleges and universities because their lower tuition creates less need for student aid. General administrative costs tend to be lower at public institutions, first because some administrative functions, such as pension administration and auditing, are often assumed by the state, and second, because private institutions must spend more to manage their diverse sources of revenue, including substantial sums spent to generate current and deferred gifts.

The remaining costs of higher education, whether in a public or a private institution, are roughly the same. Public sector university faculty salaries and benefits are equivalent to those in the private ones, while public four-year college salaries, as well as nonfaculty salaries, are on the average better than those in the private institutions. Nonsalary expenses, such as the cost of heat,

## Table 1
## Percentage Distributions of College and University Expenditures by Sector 1929–1976

|  | '29–'30 | '39–'40 | '47–'48 | '59–'60 | '69–'70 | '71–'72 | '73–'74 | '74–'75[1] | '75–'76 |
|---|---|---|---|---|---|---|---|---|---|
| **Public Institutions** | | | | | | | | | |
| Total current funds exp. (millions of dollars) | 238 | 328 | 952 | 3,154 | 13,250 | 16,484 | 20,336 | 23,490 | 26,212 |
| Total education and general | 81.1 | 82.0 | 74.9 | 82.4 | 80.7 | 81.2 | 80.3 | 80.5 | |
| General administration | 6.8 | 7.0 | 7.0 | 8.6 | 11.6 | 12.3 | 13.0 | 18.0 | 18.0 |
| Instruction and dept. research | 46.3 | 41.5 | 35.7 | 34.1 | 35.7 | 36.3 | 36.3 | 36.5 | 36.4 |
| Libraries | 1.4 | 2.7 | 2.2 | 2.4 | 3.1 | 3.0 | 3.1 | 2.9 | 3.0 |
| Plant operation | 12.4 | 10.3 | 10.0 | 8.6 | 7.5 | 7.8 | 8.4 | 8.2 | 8.6 |
| Extension and public service | 8.5 | 9.8 | 6.5 | 6.2 | 3.6 | 3.4 | 3.3 | 3.9 | 4.0 |
| Other including org. research[2] | 5.7 | 10.6 | 13.6 | 22.5 | 19.1 | 18.0 | 17.0 | 10.8 | 10.5 |
| Auxilliary enterprises | 17.4 | 15.9 | 23.3 | 15.6 | 12.3 | 11.6 | 10.9 | 10.8 | 10.7 |
| Other noneducational | 1.5 | 2.1 | 1.8 | 2.0 | 7.0 | 7.7 | 8.0 | 8.9 | 8.8 |
| student aid | n.a. | n.a. | n.a. | 2.0 | 3.4 | 3.8 | 3.5 | 3.1 | 3.1 |
| **Private institutions** | | | | | | | | | |
| Total current funds exp. (millions of dollars) | 167 | 346 | 932 | 2,474 | 7,794 | 9,075 | 10,377 | 11,568 | 12,674 |
| Total education and general | 68.7 | 72.9 | 72.9 | 78.3 | 75.1 | 75.2 | 74.5 | 71.9 | 71.8 |
| General administration | 9.8 | 11.5 | 11.4 | 12.8 | 14.0 | 14.5 | 15.0 | 17.8 | 17.8 |
| Instruction and dept. research | 42.1 | 41.5 | 34.1 | 29.4 | 27.6 | 27.2 | 27.4 | 27.9 | 27.6 |
| Libraries | 2.5 | 3.0 | 2.5 | 2.5 | 3.0 | 2.9 | 2.9 | 2.8 | 2.8 |
| Plant operation | 11.4 | 10.4 | 11.5 | 8.1 | 6.9 | 7.1 | 7.5 | 7.4 | 7.5 |
| Extension and public service | 1.0 | .9 | .9 | .5 | .6 | .6 | .7 | 1.5 | 1.6 |
| Other, including org. research[2] | 1.9 | 5.6 | 12.4 | 24.9 | 22.9 | 23.0 | 21.0 | 14.5 | 14.6 |
| Auxiliary enterprises | 24.3 | 20.8 | 23.3 | 17.2 | 14.7 | 14.0 | 13.5 | 13.3 | 13.0 |
| Other non-educational | 7.0 | 6.3 | 3.8 | 4.5 | 10.2 | 10.8 | 12.0 | 14.8 | 15.0 |
| student aid | n.a. | n.a. | n.a | 4.5 | 6.8 | 6.8 | 6.7 | 6.3 | 6.3 |

1. Expenditure category definitions changed in 1974, making several administrative cost categories shift markedly, 1975–76 data are estimated from preliminary figures.

2. Includes organized or sponsored research, related activities, and other. Categories may not be strictly comparable for both sources.

utilities, and supplies, do not vary for the two sectors. The apparent cost differences are mostly explained by differences in reporting: private institutions account for all of their costs, while public institutions frequently have portions of their costs sequestered in other accounts. Pension expenses and capital costs are usually maintained in funds separate from that of the public institution. Some public costs, such as the opportunity costs of financing working capital and depreciation expenses, are never accounted for at all in the grossly inadequate reporting system employed by the public sector.

## Effects of the Tuition Gap

The tuition gap, coupled with a decline in enrollments, makes the financial situation of many private colleges and universities precarious. Those private institutions with other sources of funds, such as endowment income or significant amounts of gifts and unrestricted grants, will survive. But fewer than twenty percent of private institutions have endowments or current gifts of any magnitude, and the remainder will be extremely vulnerable.

There vulnerability will be exacerbated by the increasing unionization of higher education employees, the high proportion of tenured faculty, and the increasing need for capital and equipment for teaching and research. These trends tend to make expenses which were formerly variable now fixed. And so as the number of students declines, institutions will be unable to vary their costs proportionally. The costs that can be varied are in areas such as student aid. In 1974, the private sector provided an average of $560 in student aid to every student over a four-year period. As financial pressures mount, this number will decline, leading to homogeneity of students unless the government provides alternate sources of aid.

Generally, private institutions will be unable to match their cost increases with an increase in tuition because their competition, the public sector, can pass on these increased costs to the taxpayer rather than to the students. Too many of these private institutions may be unable to find any other revenue to meet increased costs and may be forced into bankruptcy. One expert concluded that there is a fifty-fifty chance that sometime during the 1980s there will be a year in which one college closes a week (Behn, 1979).

The students who would have enrolled in these schools will either not attend college, or more likely, enroll in public institutions. Thus, as suggested above, the tuition gap will concentrate the private sector into a far smaller number of well-endowed, high-priced private institutions and enlarge further the public sector. The net result of such a trend will be to *decrease* diversity and choice and to harden the boundaries between those who attend the public institutions and the elite who attend the private ones. There is danger of a giant step backwards into the 17th and 18th century, when access to private higher education was dictated by birth status and not be merit.

A managerial consequence of the tuition gap is that public institutions have less incentive to be efficient because they do not need to generate the external revenues to match their budget. Whatever their expenditures, they can generally rely on state legislatures to cover them .And the actual magnitude of these expenditures is dependable obscured by poor cost accounting, decreasing even further any incentives to control costs.

The heavy public subsidization of these institutions also leads to major social inequities. Parents whose children attend private institutions pay for *both* the private and public sectors. Further, in states that tax income at a flat percentage, lower-income people subsidize the children of higher income people attending the public institutions. At the same time, there is a large percentage of above middle-income students in public institutions, as shown in Table 2. Over the last ten-year period, the relative income of students at public universities and four-year colleges has tended to rise, while in the private institutions—except for universities—it has fallen. By 1975, over half of the students in public four-year colleges and universities had incomes above the national median.

**Table 2**
**Income Class of Freshman, 1966, 1970, 1975**
**Percentage of Median Income and Above**

| | Public | | | | Private | | |
|---|---|---|---|---|---|---|---|
| | **1966** | **1970** | **1975** | | **1966** | **1970** | **1975** |
| Universities | 62 | 67 | 65 | | 73 | 71 | 75 |
| Four-year | 47 | 51 | 52 | | 67 | 64 | 57 |
| Two-year | 54 | 42 | 43 | | 55 | 55 | 39 |

# Closing the Tuition Gap

The central policy question, then, is whether the current public-private tuition gap is necessary to encourage access to higher education by all citizens. The data do not support the contention that it currently is, and as the student population decreases, it will become even less likely that financially hard-pressed private institutions will bar government-funded students from their doors. Further, from a social and economic perspective, the current system is socially inequitable and inefficient.

Three alternatives exist to narrow the tuition gap:

- Use public funds to subsidize the private sector institutions directly;
- Use public funds to subsidize students directly and permit them to choose among private and public sector institutions;
- Raise public sector tuitions.

The consequences of these three alternatives will be explored below.

## Subsidizing the Private Sector

The first approach, government aid to the private sector, currently exists in a variety of forms. Most states offer indirect aid to the private sector in the form of property tax exemptions. Contracting for services at private colleges has also become a means for states to avoid costly program duplication in the public sector. Thus far it has been a limited solution, however, with funding for such programs amounting to about $40-million in 1977–78.

One drawback to a widespread adoption of this solution is that private colleges and universities run the risk of losing their protection from political intervention when they become dependent on direct state aid. The "Bundy aid" in New York provides an interesting example. The state makes payments directly to institutions on a formula basis, involving the number and types of degrees awarded. Sectarian institutions are, by state law, barred from receiving state aid. When the program began in 1969, just over half of one hundred institutions were certified as eligible: the remainder had sectarian affiliations. In 1976, ninety-one out of one hundred fifteen were eligible. Although it is clear that the Bundy aid was not the only incentive for sectarian institutions to change their status, it was quite likely a strong one. Another such example is provided by a large private university whose employees went out on strike. The university chose not to meet employee demands, because it found its labor agreements increasingly one-sided and onerous. The state legislature, however, found the university anti-labor, and cut back severely on its appropriations. In effect, it caused the university to settle a strike it did not wish to settle, to compromise principle for principal.

In addition to compromising the independence of the private sector, the subsidization of *both* the public and private sectors is extremely inefficient. As enrollments decline, total costs will stay the same; as a result, either taxpayers will be required to pay an ever-increasing amount per student attending either kind of institution, or the amount taxpayers provide will cover an ever decreasing and inadequate percentage of the institutions' costs. Neither possibility offers an attractive long range solution.

## Subsidizing Students

The bulk of federal subsidies to higher education comes in the form of student financial assistance. In FY 77, students received almost $8 billion in federal aid; state scholarship and loan programs contributed an additional $650 million. Although students used approximately 40% of their federal assistance at private institutions, the level of aid has not been sufficient to bridge the tuition gap. The largest federal entitlement grant, the Basic Educational Opportunity Grant, limits payment to one-half of the cost of attendance.

One recent proposal is the tuition tax credit plan introduced in Congress by Senators Moynihan and Packwood. The plan is most unusual, and most controversial in its provision of aid to students at the elementary and secondary levels, which would have the effect of assisting parochial as well as independent schools. The plan, to go into effect gradually over three years, would provide income tax credits in the amount of fifty percent of tuition and fees, up to $250 per year for students at private elementary and secondary schools and up to $500 for undergraduate students at all postsecondary institutions, by the year 1982.

The Moynihan-Packwood plan would foster considerable heterogeneity and choice among public and private institutions of higher learning. However, the amount of student aid needed to reduce significantly the tuition gap is enormous and could result in an income transfer that would be politically and socially undesirable. Some voters response will surely be, "Why should I pay for someone else's child to attend Yale?" Further, although increased subsidies would allow students the greatest degree of choice, the policy has the potential for *increasing* the differences in socio-economic status of students in the two sectors. A survey conducted for the Association of Independent Colleges and Universities in Massachusetts indicates that parental preference for private sector institutions increases as income increases (although the data in Table 2 indicate that this trend is abating somewhat).

## Raising Public Sector Tuition

The third alternative of raising public sector tuitions gives rise to the claim that higher tuitions would limit access, a claim reinforced by the institutions and student organizations that have lobbied strongly for low tuition: for example, in the last few years, the American Association of State Colleges and Universities has circulated widely the "Low Tuition Fact Book,' which asserts that increased tuition would greatly cut enrollment.

However, because the first two alternatives have severe equity or implementation problems, the alternative of increasing public sector tuition deserves closer study. It may well be the most feasible response to the problems created by the tuition gap.

The alternative would raise public tuition to a level closer to that of private institutions. The increased revenues thus generated could be used to increase financial aid to the public institution's lower income students. Proponents of this alternative claim that it would increase the competitive viability of the private sector and the revenues of the public sector, even with generous student aid formulas, without severely changing the composition of the student body. How is this possible? It occurs because a substantial number of students in public universities come from middle and upper class families whose children would attend college with or without low-cost tuition. Raising their tuition would result in a policy that delivers the student aid to those most in need of it, rather than to all the students in the public institutions.

Initially, a higher tuition would undoubtedly discourage applicants, regardless of the generosity of the student aid accompanying it. But as the Education Commission of the States reported, as lower income people become more familiar with higher education, they become increasingly aware of the variety of financial aid options existing to assist the student who cannot pay the full tuition price. At any rate, this tuition policy should be accompanied by a substantial outreach program and promotion of the student aid policies.

Some observers claim that the immense investment in public higher education needs to be supported with low cost tuition. The argument is fallacious on two counts. First, the costs of *past* investments are irrelevant to *future* decisions. Secondly, from the perspective of the economy as a whole, the likely decay of the private sector ought to be of equal concern to that of the public one. A dollar has no idealogical affiliation.

## The Example of the University of Massachusetts

The University of Massachusetts at Amherst (U. Mass) illustrates both the problem of the tuition gap and some alternative solutions.

The growth of the U. Mass/Amherst campus shows in microcosm the recent history of American higher education. A land-grant institution founded as the Massachusetts Agricultural College in 1863, the university remained quite small until after the second World War, when enrollment doubled, increasing from 1,000 to 2,000 students from the fall of 1945 to 1946. From 1947 through 1960, the number of students rose an average of 9.3% per year, to 6,500. The most rapid growth, however, occurred after 1960, when the philosophy of entitlement was implemented through growing state and federal appropriations. Enrollment at U. Mass/Amherst rose to 24,000 in 1977; the faculty increased from 366 to 1,465; the budget increased from $9.4 million to $69.5 million. The University itself expanded to two more campuses, a liberal arts school in Boston and a medical school in Worcester.

At the same time, there are eighty-five private institutions of higher education in Massachusetts, ranging in size from small, local-market junior colleges to large research universities. Most of these institutions enroll fewer than 3,000 students. In the fall of 1977, when the private sector enrolled 211,500 students (56% of the total student population), Massachusetts remained the only state in the union with more students enrolled in the private sector than the public. While no one has estimated the full economic impact of these institutions, a 1974 study of the Boston metropolitan area found that Boston postsecondary education—public and private—was a $1.3 billion enterprise.

While Massachusetts's private colleges and universities have been a significant educational and economic resource for the state, they are now finding themselves squeezed by a fast-growing public sector. A few have folded and many find themselves in the unenviable position of Boston University, competing with the public system for an ever decreasing student population and saddled with the need for rapidly increasing tuitions .

Of the three alternatives open to the Commonwealth of Massachusetts to close the tuition gap, raising public institution tuition is probably the most feasible. Direct subsidy of private institutions is politically and economically unattractive, except for very small programs. The state presently funds a student scholarship program which provides $300 to students attending public institutions and $900 to those attending private institutions in the state. But, at $15 million in support for the program, it does not now begin to fill the need, and is not likely to do so in the future without an increase in taxes or a shift in spending priorities. Since the state is nicknamed "Taxachusetts" and has recently enacted a stringent ceiling on taxes, the prospect for such increased state revenues is dim.

The third alternative, raising public tuition, is one which, at least unofficially, is presently being used. The tuition at U. Mass/Amherst has risen steadily over the last several years, from $300 in 1976 to $625 in the fall of 1979 because the legislature has been unwilling to support as large a proportion of costs of operation as it had previously.

Unfortunately, the decisions to raise tuition seem to have come about solely as a result of political pressure rather than as part of a carefully considered pricing and student aid policy. There seems to have been no analysis of the various approaches available that would have enabled the state to make the best of its private and public education resources and generate financial support for those who need it. Tuition charges can be based on cost, or on the value that higher education provides, or on the market charges for tuition. For illustrative purposes, we will examine the implications of tuition policies based on all three of these factors for U. Mass and for the Commonwealth.

## Value Added and Tuition Pricing

Some people argue that the tuition for a public sector institution should reflect the private benefits which accrue to individuals from attending the institution, the value added to their lifetime incomes. The argument is supported by the establishment of the 18-year-old majority in this country and the suggestion that students, and not their parents, should be responsible for paying the costs of a higher education. The fact that many older adults are now students at colleges and universities, both full time and part time, has bolstered that argument.

Two proposed tuition payment plans, one an optional percentage-of-subsequent earnings plan at Yale and the other a government-sponsored Tuition Advance Fund proposed by Boston University's President, John Silber, are pragmatic applications of this concept. Both of these plans assume that there is an economic reward to higher education, an assumption superficially supported by the U.S. Census data. Between ages 25 and 64, a person with four years of college could expect to earn $229,000 more (in 1972 dollars) than someone with only fours years of high school education. The additional year of college thus yields a significant amount of value added to a person's income potential. Tuition prices could be set at a level proportional to this gain. These data, however, overstate the value added by a college education because a person who chooses to attend college is intrinsically likelier to earn a higher income than one who does not.

Yale University's Tuition Postponement Option began in 1971. Students could borrow from the university; all students who borrowed at a given time became part of a loan pool. The loan was to be repaid by the borrower at the rate of 0.4% per thousand dollars borrowed times his/her annual income, until the group debt was repaid to a maximum of 35 years. That plan has since been replaced by a similar Contingent Repayment Option, in which the student borrows through the Federally Insured Student Loan Program rather than through the University and the University repays those loans when the student graduates. The maximum repayment time is 25 years rather than 35. In both instances, payment is contingent upon income. Yale has recently decided to discontinue the plans because the rate of interest the university must pay to finance its loan pool has increased so much in recent years. Silber's Tuition Advance Fund proposal is an application of the Yale plan at a national level, with the Federal government managing the loan fund.

One objection to this approach is that it attributes all benefits to the student and does not account for the benefits to society that accrue from higher education. These social benefits should be funded by society, not by the student; but measuring their magnitude is an infeasible task. In the following discussion, we will note the existence of public and private benefits, but will decline to specify their magnitude.

## Cost Based Tuition Pricing

Tuition based on costs has an intuitive and logical appeal. Yet, as with most government programs, measuring cost is difficult because:

(1) The accounting and statistical systems of most governmental agencies are notoriously poor. Thus the source expense and output data are erratic and inconsistently maintained.

(2) Governmental organizations define expenditures as monies spent, or committed to be spent, against an appropriation. Unlike private institutions, they do *not* measure the value of the resources *used* to provide educational services.

(3) Not all of the costs of providing higher education services are included in the books of account of the public sector. For example, pension expenses are frequently accounted for only in the state's pension fund and not allocated back to the institution. Similarly, the costs of financing the physical plant are usually kept in accounts that are separate from those of the public college or university. The cost of using the physical plant, depreciation, is usually not accounted for at all in public institutions.

The difficulty obtaining accurate cost data is frequently cited as a reason for not using cost-based pricing in public sector institutions. As we shall demonstrate below, using the University of Massachusetts as an example, the data problems can be solved with reasonable, if not total, accuracy.

In 1975, the operating budget for the Amherst campus was $67.44 million. Pension, insurance and cost of living adjustment costs, accounted for elsewhere, amounted to $8.52 million. A fuel deficiency appropriation to the university added another $2.09 million to the cost of operating the Amherst campus. Thus the total operating expenses were $78.05 million.

The capital expenditures associated with the institution must be included in this cost estimate. The state does not depreciate its capital investment, thus neglecting to account for the use of that investment over time. The best information of the capital investment in Amherst comes from a twenty-year summary (1953–72) of U. Mass capital budgets compiled from state financial reports. Since this period includes the years of rapid growth of the university, the figure of $177.02 million of capital expenditures is not a bad estimate. Given a 50 year-life to the investment, yearly straight-line depreciation cost is $3.54 million.

Next, we need to account for the cost of the capital used to finance these investments Massachusetts, like most other states, uses its bonding power to generate capital funds. However, debt service costs are not necessarily accurate measures of capital costs, since they reflect a payment plan rather than the opportunity cost to society of capital invested in the public sector. The Federal Office of Management and Budget uses an interest rate of 10% per year, a rate which is an approximation of the *opportunity* cost to society of having funds used by the public rather than the private sector [1]. Applying this rate to the value of capital investment at U. Mass/Amherst, we get a cost of capital of $17.70 million, 10% of $177.02 million. While out-of-pocket costs are lower because municipal interest rates are tax-sheltered, the opportunity cost gives us the better measure of the consumption of resources from a social perspective.

Table 3 aggregates these individual items to obtain the full cost for FY 1975. It should be noted that of the total expenses of nearly $100 million, $33 million (pension, fuel deficiency, and the capital expenses) are not usually identified with the university.

In the 1974–75 academic year, U. Mass/Amherst's full-time equivalent (FTE) student body was 22,035. Dividing the total costs in Table 3 by that figure leads to an average full cost per student of $4,506. This measures the total value of the resources consumed in order to provide one FTE student with the educational services of U. Mass. Tuition could be set equal to this cost.

**Table 3**
**Annual Expenses, University of Massachusetts, Amherst**
**(in millions)**

| | | |
|---|---|---|
| Operating Budget | $67.44 | |
| Pension, Insurance and | | |
| Cost of Living Adjustments | 8.52 | |
| Fuel Deficiency | 2.09 | |
| Operating Expenses | | $78.05 |
| Depreciation Expense | 3.54 | |
| Interest Expense | 17.70 | |
| Capital Expenses | | 21.24 |
| Total Expenses | | $99.29 |

However, from a social perspective, average full cost may well not be an appropriate measure; if there were no students, the state would still be responsible for millions of dollars in fixed costs. Marginal cost, the cost of producing one more unit of output, measures the resource cost to society of producing that unit. If the state assumes that there are significant private benefits to higher education, then marginal cost should be the minimum price. The point where the marginal cost exceeds price represents an inefficient use of societal resources because the cost of the resources exceeds the value consumers place on them.

Several methods are available for calculating marginal cost. The simplest is to assume that educational costs vary directly with volume of students and that marginal and variable costs are therefore identical. In a university where personnel costs are the major part of operating expenses, the percentage of faculty with tenure is a good proxy for fixed costs. For U. Mass, that ratio is 69.5%. Therefore, for FY 1975:

| | |
|---|---|
| Operating expenses | $78.05 million |
| Less 69.5% | $54.24 million |
| Variable expense | $23.81 million |
| Divided by FTE students | 22,035 |
| Variable expenses/FTE | $1,080 |

This estimate of marginal cost per full-time equivalent student, $1,080, does not reflect the costs of one extra FTE student, which are likely to be zero or very small, but rather the cost per FTE of the next large increase in enrollments.

Another perspective on marginal cost is provided by calculating the effect on institutional operations not of *one* student, but of a group of students. Institutional managers can use internal data on faculty costs, teaching loads in various departments, and costs of support services to calculate the increase in faculty and other costs needed to maintain a level of service if the institution were to grow by a given increment, for example, one hundred students. Using this approach to marginal cost for U. Mass/Amherst, we derive an effective marginal cost of approximately $1,600 per FTE student [2]. Therefore, it seems reasonable that the tuition at U. Mass be raised at least to $1,080, the lower of the two marginal cost figures.

## Market Price for Tuition

The market price can often be a useful approximation of marginal cost in a well-functioning market; but the market in this case is an imperfect one with heavy subsidization of tuition in both public and private sectors. Further, because the data show that public sector tuition tend to be lower than the marginal cost of $1,080, it is clear that this is not a well-functioning market. In 1975, the tuition and fees at U. Mass were $549. The average tuition and fee charged at the eight private universities in the state was $3,812; the mean for all New England universities was $833; and at public universities in comparable states, $712.

## Effect of Tuition Price Changes

For illustrative purposes, we will explore the effect if U. Mass tuition were raised to $1,080.

The increase would be likely to have several consequences:

- it would generate more revenue for the state;

- lower-income students would be eligible for increased federal Basic Educational Opportunity Grant funds, which in 1975 provided up to $1,400 to cover half the costs of attending a college or university.

- some students would choose to attend private institutions, increasing revenue to the private colleges or universities. Some would choose not to attend college at all.

The response of individuals to changes in higher education price, or the price elasticity, has been studied in a varied of ways in the last dozen years. Although these studies used a variety of methodologies, the results were surprisingly similar; they found that a $100 increase in public tuition would induce between 0.06% and 1.9% of individuals to choose not to attend the institution. Fifty-seven percent of those students would choose to enroll instead at a private institution (Jackson and Weathersley, 1975) [3]. Of course, these elasticities vary widely across income and institutions; out, we will use these averages for illustrative purposes.

Table 4 analyzes the possible effects on the state and the institutions of setting tuition at four different levels: marginal costs of $1,080 and $1,600; average full cost of $4,506; the private sector market price of $3,812; and the total sector market price of $833. For the purposes of this analysis, we assume that all students with parental incomes of $15,000 or under would be eligible for increased Basic Grant awards that would cover one-half of the tuition, up to $700. For example, if tuition were set at $1,080, the net increase in tuition for the lower-income students would be, we assume, $390, and for higher-income students, $780.

At a price of $1,080, we find that an average of 1,243 students will leave U. Mass and 705 students will enroll in private institutions. The effects of the increase are to increase public institution revenues by $15 million and to increase private institution revenues by $2.7 million, as shown in the last two rows of Table 4, for the column headed $1,080.

Yet, were the state to follow such a policy, the goal of access would not be served because 534 (1243–709) students would leave the higher educational system as a result of the price increase. However, were the state to use 50% of the increased revenues generated, $7.9 million, for student financial aid, the number of students leaving the institution because of the price increase would be significantly lower. Alternatively, if students with parental incomes under $15,000 receive 65% of the new state aid and those with parental incomes between $15,000 and $25,000 35% of that aid, the increase in public revenues would be about $8.8 million and the increase in private sector revenues about $1 million. This method of calculation was employed for each of the four prices whose consequences are examined in Table 4.

Clearly, some of the alternatives, such as average full cost, would limit access severely, an unacceptable consequence, unless they were coupled with some kind of comprehensive Tuition Advancement Plan. On the other hand, the marginal cost and market alternatives can generate additional revenues of up to $10 million with a net reduction of only 200 students on the average.

## Table 4
### Effect of Alternative Prxices of Enrollment and Revenues
Year = FY 75; U.S. Mass Tuition and Fees = $549; (Tuition = $300); FTE = 22,035

| | With no change in financial aid | | | | | With 50% redistribution of revenues to financial aid | | | | |
|---|---|---|---|---|---|---|---|---|---|---|
| | Marginal costs | | Average full cost | Market (private) | Market (public) | Marginal costs | | Average full cost | Market (private) | Market (public) |
| | A | B | | | | A | B | | | |
| Tuition | $1080 | $1600 | $4506 | $3812 | $833 | $1080 | $1600 | $4506 | $3812 | $833 |
| Increase over $300 | $780 | $1300 | $4206 | $3512 | $533 | $780 | $1300 | $4206 | $3512 | $533 |
| Financial aid increase | up to $540 | up to $650 | up to $700 | up to $700 | up to $417 (state aid $380–453) | up to $993 (state aid $609–727) | up to $1377 (state aid $1314–1569) | up to $2269 (state aid $1238–1478) | up to $2178 (state aid $264–315) | up to $732 |
| Net tuition increase | $390 to $780 | $650–1300 | $3644–$4206 | $2962–$3512 | $266–$533 | $(-63)–$780 | $223–$1300 | $2086–$2891 | $1484–$3512 | $(-49)–$533 |
| Decline in public enrollment @ 0.06% per $100  Low | (-77) | (-127) | (-516) | (-425) | (-52) | (-29) | (-71) | (-351) | (-269) | (-19) |
| @ 1.90% per $100  High | (-2409) | (04014) | (-16334) | (-13444) | (-1644) | (-906) | (-2250) | (-11137) | (-8525) | (-597) |
| Mean | (-1243) | (-20710) | (-8425) | (-6761) | (-849) | (-467) | (-1161) | (-5745) | (-4397) | (-308) |
| Increase in private enrollment @ 57% substitution of private for public enrollment  Low | +44 | +72 | +294 | +342 | +29 | +17 | +40 | +200 | +153 | +11 |
| High | +1373 | +2288 | +9310 | +7663 | +937 | +617 | +1283 | +6348 | +4860 | +340 |
| Mean | +709 | +1180 | +4082 | +3854 | +484 | +266 | -662 | +3275 | +2506 | +175 |
| Increase in public revenue | $15,844,860 | $25,331,900 | $54,716,160 | $51,613,988 | $11,037,438 | $8.8 million | $14.1 million | $39.4 million | $34.8 million | $6.0 million |
| $3812 (mean tuition and fees) X (increase in students) | $2,696,708 | $4,498,160 | $18,305,224 | $14,691,448 | $1,845,008 | $1,013,992 | $2,523,544 | $12,484,300 | $9,552,872 | $667,100 |

This analysis is crude and limited. It assumes that behavior is similar across income levels, whereas most studies show that lower income students are more responsive to price. Also, the financial aid to each student from federal grants and loans cannot be predicted exactly. Nevertheless, this analysis is much preferable to no analysis at all and it allows us to conceptualize clearly the consequences of pricing strategies.

The analysis highlights the fact that raising tuition in a public institution can improve the position of both the state and the private institutions, with much less effect on access than initially thought. If tuitions in public institutions were raised, public institutions would be less vulnerable to political budget maneuvers and more inclined to be efficient in their use of resources. Private institutions would be in a more competitive position and more likely to be able to survive the 1980s. Further, states would be able to target their financial assistance to those who need it and thus improve the method of redistributing societal resources.

## Implications

Public higher education grew rapidly in the 1960s and 1970s primarily because higher education came to be viewed as a right to which all were entitled. Private universities could be relied on to provide equality of access based on merit, but they could not be relied on to provide equality of access based solely on the desire for the services. To insure this definition of equality of access, tuitions at public sector institutions were maintained at a low level, substantially below average and even marginal cost. Although the low tuitions did help to maintain access, they had three peculiar, unanticipated efficiency and equity effects:

1.  A substantial proportion of the student population attending public institutions did not require a subsidy of the magnitude granted by the flat, subsidized tuition policy.

2.  If the present tuition gap between private and public colleges and universities continues, it is quite likely that the private sector will become severely diminished in size and diversity. This will occur in part because the low tuition rates at public institutions provide a competitive disadvantage for private sector institutions, particularly those with small endowment and research grants. The effects will be notable in the recessionary economy with a decreasing number of students that is likely to characterize this decade. The retrenchment in the private sector will not occur solely because of the superiority of public education over private services, but partially because of the competitive advantage that their subsidized prices bestow.

3.  The subsidization of tuition shelters the public sector institutions and may motivate inefficient behavior on their part.

These problems can be most efficiently and equitable remedied by subsidizing students, rather than institutions. However, for reasons of cost and political preferences, a substantial "tuition voucher" plan seems infeasible. Alternatively, raising public sector tuition seems to solve many of the problems caused by the present tuition gap without leading to a severe diminution of the numbers of students attending institutions of higher education; for example, if tuition at U. Mass were raised to $1,080, only 200 of the 22,000 students presently enrolled would choose not to attend either a public or private sector institution. Their departure must be weighed against the increase in public and public revenues from raising tuition of nearly $10 million.

It is not the purpose of this paper to specify the shape of the reduced access-increased revenue curves that would result from a decision to raise tuition at public sector institutions. It is our purpose, however, to illustrate that such tradeoffs can be analyzed in a clear and articulate manner. The University of Massachusetts example illustrates that it is feasible in the recessionary economy with a decreasing number of students for a state government to develop a set of rational pricing strategies for its public institutions; to analyze the effects of those strategies on the enrollments and revenues of the private sector and the revenues and costs of the state; and to delineate a policy that could lead to a wiser allocation of societal resources, without cutting deeply into the number of students attending institutions of higher education.

## Notes

1. The federal rate can be used as regional opportunity cost if one assumes that capital moves efficiently.

2. In FY 1975, the University had 1,293 full-time faculty with an average salary of $21,787. Adding 20% for fringe benefits, the average cost per faculty member is $25,530. In order to maintain a student faculty ratio of 17 to 1 [22035 FTE ÷ 1293 faculty] an increase in 100 students would require that six faculty members be hired, at cost of $153,180, or $1,532 per student. This simple calculation probably errs on the high side, because the 1,293 faculty includes those on research and effective student-faculty ratios are therefore higher. It errs on the low side, however, because it does not include the cost of additional services, such as counselors and clerical staff, who will be needed to support the increased enrollment.

3. Each of the methodologies used in he demand studies has its limitations. The cross-sectional analyses, which examine many institutions at the same time, assume that all institutions are the same: time series analyses which look at price changes over time assume that the world has not changed as time went on; a questionnaire methodology is only as good as the instrument itself. Further, the data are merely point estimates on an elasticity curve. While results obtained on the basis of these data are not widely unrealistic, an institution or a state policy agency conducting a similar analysis would obviously have access to data relevant to its own situation. However, for purposes of illustration, these data are useful in allowing us to examine the consequences of a variety of pricing strategies.

## References

Behn, Robert D. (1979). "The End of the Growth Era in Higher Education." Working Paper. Durham, North Carolina: Duke University, Center for Education Policy, June 7.

Breneman, David W. and Finn, Chester G., Jr. (1978). *Public Policy and Private Higher Education.* Washington, D.C.: Brookings Institution.

Jackson, Gregory A. and Weathersby, George B. (1975). "Individual Demand for higher education," *Journal of Higher Education* 46: 623–652.

Rudolph, Frederick (1962). *The American College and University: A History.* New York: Vintage Press.

# PART B
## *CONTEMPORARY ARTICLES*

*This section presents articles written in the 1980s and early 1990s, covering current issues and policy discussions of student and institutional finance.*

# FINANCIAL TRENDS FOR INSTITUTIONS OF HIGHER EDUCATION

# Changing Patterns of College Finance and Enrollment (1991)

Michael S. McPherson and Morton Owen Schapiro

This chapter summarizes the principal trends in the finance of undergraduate higher education and the pattern of postsecondary enrollment over the last half century. By taking a long view, some dramatic developments emerge. These include substantial growth in the share of enrollment at public institutions, a considerable increase in the fraction of young people who attend some kind of college, and a major increase in the role of the federal government in financing higher education. Over the long haul, though, it has been the growth in federal research support, rather than in federal student aid, that has been most prominent. Only in more recent decades has federal student aid come to play a more significant role.[1]

The first part of this chapter takes the long view, reviewing college finance and enrollment patterns since 1939. Later sections focus more closely on developments since the introduction of the major federal student aid programs in 1965 and 1972.

## A Long-Run Perspective on College Finance

Tables 2-1 through 2-3 provide a schematic overview of the principal changes in college finance and enrollment since 1939. Table 2-1 shows how colleges' principal sources of revenue have changed over the last fifty years.[2] For public institutions, state and local government spending has been the most important source of support, and has plainly helped keep tuitions relatively low—with gross tuition (inclusive of student aid) providing between 13 percent and 25 percent of revenue at public colleges and universities. Both the state and local government share and the tuition share have been fairly stable over the period, although a gradual rise in the share of public tuition can be observed starting about 1959.[3]

For private institutions, the most important source of revenue has been tuition. As with public institutions, the share of tuition in total revenue is fairly stable, with a gradual upward trend visible from 1965 on. A decline in the share of support that private institutions derive from gifts and endowment earnings is evident in the table. The importance of federal support has varied considerably for private institutions, accounting for just 1 percent of revenue in 1939, 30 percent of revenue in 1965, and 22 percent in 1985. The share of federal support in public institutional revenue has shown a similar but more muted pattern of change.[4] Notice that in the table, student aid is reported under gross tuition and not under the government revenue figures—these latter figures include appropriations, gifts, grants, and contracts for colleges and universities.

**Table 2-1**

**Shares of Educational and General Revenue, Public and Private Institutions, Selected Academic Years, 1939–86[a]**

| Year | Gross tuition | Government | | Gifts and endowment earnings | Other |
|---|---|---|---|---|---|
| | | Federal | State and local | | |
| | | Public institutions | | | |
| 1939–40 | 0.20 | 0.13 | 0.61 | 0.04 | 0.01 |
| 1949–50 | 0.25 | 0.13 | 0.56 | 0.03 | 0.03 |
| 1955–56 | 0.13 | 0.17 | 0.62 | 0.04 | 0.04 |
| 1959–60 | 0.13 | 0.21 | 0.59 | 0.04 | 0.03 |
| 1965–66 | 0.14 | 0.23 | 0.54 | 0.03 | 0.05 |
| 1969–70 | 0.15 | 0.19 | 0.57 | 0.03 | 0.05 |
| 1975–76 | 0.16 | 0.18 | 0.61 | 0.03 | 0.02 |
| 1979–80 | 0.15 | 0.16 | 0.62 | 0.04 | 0.03 |
| 1985–86 | 0.18 | 0.13 | 0.61 | 0.05 | 0.03 |
| | | Private institutions | | | |
| 1939–40 | 0.55 | 0.01 | 0.03 | 0.38 | 0.03 |
| 1949–50 | 0.57 | 0.12 | 0.04 | 0.23 | 0.05 |
| 1955–56 | 0.45 | 0.18 | 0.02 | 0.28 | 0.06 |
| 1959–60 | 0.43 | 0.25 | 0.02 | 0.25 | 0.05 |
| 1965–66 | 0.43 | 0.30 | 0.02 | 0.18 | 0.06 |
| 1969–70 | 0.44 | 0.26 | 0.03 | 0.19 | 0.08 |
| 1975–76 | 0.48 | 0.25 | 0.04 | 0.19 | 0.04 |
| 1979–80 | 0.47 | 0.25 | 0.04 | 0.19 | 0.05 |
| 1985–86 | 0.50 | 0.22 | 0.03 | 0.19 | 0.06 |

Sources: Data for 1939–66 are from Susan A. Nelson, "Financial Trends and Issues," in Breneman and Finn (1978, table 2-1, pp. 70–71). Data for 1969–86 are from National Center for Education Statistics (1989, tables 270 and 271, pp. 293–94).

[a]Figures in table do not include revenue from auxiliary enterprises or from sales and services.

[b]Government figures do not include student aid. Such aid is counted under gross tuition.

While these figures in table 2-1 point to considerable stability in the funding sources of public and private institutions, enrollment patterns have not been nearly so stable. As table 2-2 shows, the shares of enrollment in the two sectors have changed markedly over the last half-century. In 1949, enrollment was divided almost equally between the public and private sectors, but by 1975, the public share had grown to 79 percent of all enrollment. Much of the growth in public enrollment during the 1960s occurred at two-year institutions. These institutions accounted for only 24 percent of public enrollment in 1963, but for 43 percent in 1975.[5] Interestingly, over this period of rapid growth in public enrollment relative to total enrollment, the level of private college enrollments continued to grow—it was simply the case that public institutions absorbed more of the rising enrollment. By the mid-1970s, rapid enrollment growth had subsided. Since then, the shares of enrollment in public and private higher education have been stable.

Yet, the swing that did occur in enrollment shares has major implications for overall financing patterns. Table 2-3 uses the enrollment weights reported in table 2-2 to examine the sources of higher-education revenue since 1939. Table 2-3 reports revenue shares for the major categories given in table 2-1, averaged over public and private institutions, and also breaks down gross tuition

## Table 2-2
### Enrollment at Public and Private Nonprofit Institutions, Selected Academic Years, 1939–88[a]

| Year | Total enrollment | Share Public | Share Private |
|---|---|---|---|
| 1939 | 1,494 | 0.53 | 0.47 |
| 1949 | 2,659 | 0.51 | 0.49 |
| 1959 | 3,640 | 0.60 | 0.40 |
| 1965 | 5,921 | 0.67 | 0.33 |
| 1969 | 8,005 | 0.74 | 0.26 |
| 1975 | 11,185 | 0.79 | 0.21 |
| 1979 | 11,570 | 0.78 | 0.22 |
| 1985 | 12,247 | 0.77 | 0.23 |
| 1988 | 12,849 | 0.78 | 0.22 |

Source: National Center for Education Statistics (1989, table 3, p. 10).

[a]For 1939 and 1949, data include all resident degree-credit students enrolled at any time during the academic year. Beginning in 1959, data include all resident and extension students enrolled at the beginning of the fall term. Data for 1988 are based on "early estimates."

## Table 2-3
### Shares of Higher-Education Revenue, by Source, Selected Academic Years, 1939–86

| Year | Gross tuition | Tuition paid by Families | Tuition paid by Insti-tuitions | Tuition paid by Government Federal | Tuition paid by Government State | Nontuition revenue Federal | Nontuition revenue State and local | Nontuition revenue Gifts and endowment earnings |
|---|---|---|---|---|---|---|---|---|
| 1939–40 | 0.37 | 0.35 | 0.02[b] | 0.00 | 0.00[b] | 0.07 | 0.33 | 0.21 |
| 1949–50 | 0.40 | 0.37 | 0.03 | 0.00 | 0.00[b] | 0.12 | 0.32 | 0.12 |
| 1959–60 | 0.26 | 0.22 | 0.03 | 0.00 | 0.01 | 0.23 | 0.34 | 0.13 |
| 1965–66 | 0.26 | 0.21 | 0.04 | 0.00 | 0.01 | 0.26 | 0.33 | 0.09 |
| 1969–70 | 0.25 | 0.20 | 0.04 | 0.00 | 0.01 | 0.22 | 0.38 | 0.08 |
| 1975–76 | 0.26 | 0.16 | 0.04 | 0.04 | 0.02 | 0.20 | 0.43 | 0.08 |
| 1979–80 | 0.26 | 0.14 | 0.04 | 0.06 | 0.02 | 0.19 | 0.43 | 0.09 |
| 1985–86 | 0.29 | 0.18 | 0.05 | 0.05 | 0.02 | 0.16 | 0.41 | 0.10 |

Sources: Gross tuition and nontuition revenue are calculated from tables 2-1 and 2-2. Distribution of revenue among tuition-payers is calculated from tables 2-1 and 2-2 as well as from data in O'Neill (1973, table A-1, pp. 28–29); O'Neill (1971, tables 9 and 10, pp. 18–19), Gillespie and Carlson (1983, table A-1, p. 30), and College Board (1989b, table 1, p. 6).

[a]Both veteran's educational benefits and social security benefits paid to qualified college students are excluded from federal tuition payments.

[b]Figure is authors' estimate.

by its sources—showing the share paid by families directly and the shares paid by various forms of student aid.

The most striking trend in table 2-3 is the steady decline through 1979 in the overall share of tuition that is paid by families.[6] This decline was brought on by several forces. First, as the enrollment share of public institutions grew until the mid-1970s, the share of state and local spending grew along with it. Consequently, there was little pressure on tuitions and tuition payments as a share of total institutional revenue fell over the period. Second, the growth of federal grant and contract revenue from the end of the 1930s through the mid-1960s helped lower the share of gross tuition in overall revenue. Most of these federal funds were directed toward financing research, although there were significant federal subsidies for dormitory construction in the 1960s. These vastly expanded research expenditures might be seen as largely separate from undergraduate instruction and finance, but we later present evidence that changes in federal grant and contract spending influence several aspects of institutional behavior, including the pricing of tuition and the spending on instruction.

A third reason for the declining share of family payments is that institutions and state governments gradually increased their student aid spending as a share of revenue. Thus the net tuition paid by families formed a decreasing share of total revenue. In addition, an even greater change in student aid spending was brought about by new federal programs. While federal student aid grants began to contribute to tuition payments in 1965, with the introduction of the educational opportunity grant program, it was not until 1972, with the launching of what is now the Pell program, that federal student aid grants made enough of a difference to show up in table 2-3. Since the 1975–76 academic year, the Pell program's impact has been substantial, reducing the share of higher education revenue provided by families by between 4 and 6 percentage points in each year.[7]

The cumulative effect of all these changes has been substantial. Over the period 1939–80, the educational and general revenue of colleges and universities has grown at 1.9 percent annually in real terms—a pace that roughly matches the growth in family incomes. However, because government payments covered a growing share of institutional revenue, real tuition grew at just 1.0 percent annually until about 1980. Government and institutional subsidies of tuition payments have further reduced the rate of growth in the burden on families. This shifting of burdens—through the expansion of public higher education and through a larger federal role—has substantially increased the affordability of college over the last fifty years for a wide segment of the American population, changing the nation's conception of higher education from that of a luxury available only to the elite to a normal experience for all qualified young adults.

The steady decline in the share of higher education revenue provided by families came to an abrupt halt after 1979, with the family share increasing by 4 percentage points in the 1979–86 period. Most of this increase is explained by the increasing reliance on tuition in the finance of both public and private institutions in the 1980s—a trend whose counterpart is a modest decline in the share provided by state and local government and a more substantial decline in the share provided by federal grant and contract payments. Links between changes in external funding and internal adjustments by institutions are the major topic of chapter 4.

As we look ahead, it seems unlikely that the steadily expanding government subsidies to higher education, which came to a halt at the end of the 1970s, are likely to resume. First, the public share of total enrollment cannot expand much further: the expanded role for state subsidies that accompanied a growing share of public enrollment is nearing its end. Second, postsecondary enrollments have grown so large that expanding the total government subsidy per student has become a very expensive proposition. These facts raise broad questions about future college affordability. . . . More immediately, these same facts underline the importance of examining how existing higher-education subsidies have been targeted and how effective they have been in meeting governmental goals.

# College Financing Trends Since 1965

In 1965, when Congress passed and President Lyndon Johnson signed the Higher Education Act, the principle that the federal government should bear an important share of responsibility for ensuring college opportunity for disadvantaged students was enacted into law. Although state governments were and have remained the largest financial contributors to public institutions (indeed, their share of total revenue grew as the community college movement expanded public enrollments during the 1960s and early 1970s), policy discussion has come increasingly to focus on defining and financing the changing federal role.

Table 2-4 shows the overall magnitudes of federal and other forms of student aid, expressed in constant dollars, for selected years since 1963. The overall change from the 1970s to the 1980s is dominated by so-called specially directed aid, funds provided to veterans and to children of social security recipients. However, it is not entirely clear whether the veterans' programs should be regarded as "student aid," since they might instead be seen as a form of deferred compensation. Moreover, although awards in both the veterans' and social security programs are contingent on college attendance, neither was designed with the principal aim of promoting higher education, and neither fits the model of need-based student aid, which dominates other federal student aid programs. Both programs were large in the mid-1970s, and have dwindled to almost nothing in the 1980s.[8]

When these programs are ignored, the "generally available" student aid programs administered by the Office (later Department) of Education predominate. The campus-based programs . . . have not grown much in real terms since their inception in the mid-1960s, with the result that the guaranteed student loan (GSL) programs and the basic educational opportunity (later Pell) grant program have gradually become the main sources of federal student aid.

With respect to how federal funding has developed, the period from 1965 to the present can be usefully divided into four subperiods. From 1965 to 1973, a fairly modest total of "generally available" aid was divided between the GSL and the campus-based programs.[9] From 1973 to 1980, the federal aid budget grew rapidly, with expenditures on the newly introduced Pell program roughly keeping pace in percentage terms with the growing number of dollars lent through the GSL program. From about 1980 through about 1984, GSL growth continued to be substantial, while real growth in the Pell grant and the campus-based programs declined. In 1979, new guaranteed loans represented about 49 percent of the total volume of generally available federal student aid; in 1985, they were about 62 percent.[10] Since 1985, the Pell program has grown by 12 percent and guaranteed loans by 20 percent in real terms.

The targeting of these federal programs, across both students and institutions, has varied considerably. The following section examines the targeting of federal aid by income groups in some detail, focusing on that group of full-time students in "traditional" colleges and universities who are dependent upon their parents for financial support. Although when the programs were launched, this group constituted the largest set of aid recipients, and they remain an important group, the participation of other groups of students and institutions in federal student aid programs has grown substantially.

Table 2-5 illustrates this point through an examination of how Pell funds have been distributed in the 1970s and 1980s. While, in the early years of the program, the bulk of grant recipients were traditional-aged college students supported by their parents, this has changed so much that in recent years the majority of recipients are independent students, many of whom are adults.[11] An equally striking change has occurred in the distribution of Pell funds among institution types. Currently, as table 2-5 shows, students at proprietary vocational and technical institutions, most of which offer nondegree programs of less than two years, receive more than a quarter of all Pell grant funds—a figure that is up from only 11 percent in 1979–80. Yet, proprietary institutions enroll fewer than 7 percent of undergraduate students. While comparable figures for the distribution of loan

Table 2-4
Aid Awarded to Students, by Source of Aid,
Selected Academic Years, 1963–89
Millions of 1989–90 dollars

| Source | 1963–64 | 1970–71 | 1975–76 | 1979–80 | 1981–82 | 1983–84 | 1985–86 | 1987–88[a] | 1988–89[b] |
|---|---|---|---|---|---|---|---|---|---|
| Federal programs | | | | | | | | | |
| Generally available aid | | | | | | | | | |
| Pell grants | 0 | 0 | 2,154 | 4,108 | 3,114 | 3,491 | 4,176 | 4,103 | 4,679 |
| Supplemental educational opportunity grants | 0 | 429 | 463 | 546 | 490 | 451 | 480 | 460 | 412 |
| State student incentive grants[c] | 0 | 0 | 46 | 125 | 104 | 75 | 89 | 82 | 77 |
| Work-study | 0 | 727 | 679 | 976 | 845 | 854 | 768 | 697 | 741 |
| Perkins loans | 469 | 768 | 1,059 | 1,059 | 786 | 853 | 823 | 883 | 901 |
| GSL, PLUS, and SLS[d] | 0 | 3,249 | 2,915 | 6,438 | 9,782 | 9,472 | 10,348 | 12,500 | 12,461 |
| Subtotal | 469 | 5,173 | 7,315 | 13,251 | 15,121 | 15,196 | 16,684 | 18,726 | 19,270 |
| Specially directed aid | | | | | | | | | |
| Social security | 0 | 1,597 | 2,515 | 2,602 | 2,703 | 275 | 0 | 0 | 0 |
| Veterans | 276 | 3,588 | 9,619 | 2,925 | 1,830 | 1,435 | 994 | 837 | 779 |
| Other grants | 37 | 51 | 147 | 189 | 462 | 454 | 484 | 476 | 474 |
| Other loans | 0 | 134 | 104 | 69 | 148 | 329 | 436 | 322 | 315 |
| Subtotal | 313 | 5,371 | 12,384 | 5,785 | 5,143 | 2,493 | 1,913 | 1,635 | 1,568 |
| Total federal aid | 782 | 10,544 | 19,700 | 19,037 | 20,264 | 17,690 | 18,597 | 20,361 | 20,839 |
| State grant programs | 230 | 755 | 1,128 | 1,292 | 1,247 | 1,383 | 1,535 | 1,649 | 1,723 |
| Institutionally awarded aid | 1,234 | 3,089 | 3,302 | 3,096 | 3,043 | 3,602 | 4,301 | 5,006 | 5,409 |
| Total federal, state, and institutional aid | 2,247 | 14,389 | 24,129 | 23,425 | 24,555 | 22,675 | 24,433 | 27,016 | 27,970 |

Sources: Gillespie and Carlson (1983, table A-1, p. 30), Lewis (1988, table 1, p. 6), and College Board (1989b, table 1, p. 6).
aFigures are estimated.
bFigures are preliminary.
cState student incentive grants, or SSIGs, are federal matching funds for state and need-based aid programs.
dThe acronyms represent guaranteed student loans, parent loans for undergraduate students, and supplemental loans for students, respectively.

**Table 2-5**
**Distribution of Pell Grant Funds to Independent Students and**
**Proprietary Schools, Selected Academic Years, 1973–88**
**Percent**

| Year | Pell recipients who are independent students | Pell revenue going to students at proprietary institutions |
|---|---|---|
| 1973–74 | 13.3 | 7.0 |
| 1975–76 | 29.8 | 9.0 |
| 1977–78 | 38.5 | 8.9 |
| 1979–80 | 33.8 | 10.5 |
| 1981–82 | 41.9 | 13.5 |
| 1983–84 | 47.5 | 18.8 |
| 1985–86 | 50.4 | 22.1 |
| 1987–88 | 57.6 | 26.6[a] |

Sources: Gillespie and Carlson (1983, table 9, p. 26, and table A-12, p. 41); and College Board (1989b, tables 7 and 8, p. 12).

[a]Figure is an estimate.

funds are not available, they would probably show a similar pattern. These remarkable changes in the targeting of federal subsidies obviously raise major policy questions both about the suitability of traditional student aid programs as vehicles for aiding adult and vocational students, as well as about the drain on resources available for traditional students that results from the increased participation of other groups.

Student aid from state governments and institutions adds to the funds provided to families to subsidize tuitions. (The states, it should be remembered, contribute mostly through direct operating subsidies to state-run colleges and universities.) The data in table 2-4 indicate that these nonfederal sources of financial support have also fluctuated. Both state and institutional grants grew substantially from the 1960s to the 1970s. From 1975 to 1989, state programs grew by 53 percent, while institution-based aid, after holding steady in real terms in the 1970s, grew by 78 percent in real terms from 1981 to 1989. The bulk of the institution-based aid is awarded by private institutions, with much of it taking the form of tuition discounts.

This changing picture of federal and other forms of student aid must finally be seen against a background of changing tuition prices in higher education. Figure 2-1 shows the course of public and private tuition charges from 1966 to 1988. Here, three rough periods suggest themselves: from 1966 to the early 1970s tuitions rose relative to the price level, at a fairly modest rate; from the early 1970s until around 1980, they fell behind the rapid inflation of those years; and from 1980 to 1986, they rose rapidly in real terms, especially in private higher education. The fact that tuitions and federal student aid levels have tended to move in opposite directions over the past twenty years or so (with aid levels rising most rapidly in periods when tuition has been rising slowly) makes it difficult to determine the relative importance of different factors in influencing "affordability" as well as in detecting the enrollment effects of aid, since it is hard to distinguish between the effects of lower tuition and those of higher aid. . . .

**Figure 2–1**
**Costs of Attendance at Public and Private Institutions, 1966–88**
**Thousands of 1989–90 dollars**

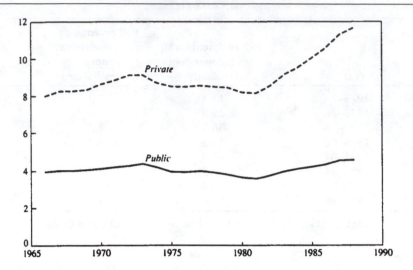

Source: National Center for Educational Statistics (1989).

# A Detailed Look at Financing Trends Since 1974

These aggregate data mask a good deal of variation both in the cost and in the availability of aid at different types of institutions and for different socioeconomic groups of students. A more detailed picture of trends in the level and the distribution of generally available aid can be derived from the American Freshman Survey, an instrument administered yearly to freshmen enrolling at a large number of colleges and universities. Since 1974, the managers of the American Freshman Survey have included detailed questions on the sources and amounts of financial assistance received by surveyed freshmen. These responses provide a fairly complete picture of freshmen's *own percep-tions* of how their education is being financed. These numbers should be interpreted cautiously, since students may be unclear not only about the amount but especially about the form (grant versus loan) and source (federal government versus state government versus institution) of the aid they receive.[12] Despite these limitations, however, the American Freshman Survey data, which are used extensively below, provide a helpful baseline for years after 1974—a baseline that is not otherwise available on an annual basis.

The figures that follow focus on a limited subgroup of American undergraduates: young (ages 18–24), full-time freshmen in residence at traditional two-year and four-year colleges. This is the population that is most reliably sampled in the survey, and it provides a fairly well defined universe for comparisons over time.[13] Still, as noted above, a great many students—and an increasing portion of aided students—are outside this "traditional" category, because they are older or part-time, because they attend nontraditional institutions, or because they commute. Note that all data are reported in 1990 constant dollars, including the income classifications. The figures are adjusted using the consumer price index, or CPI, as the deflator.

Figure 2-2 summarizes trends in federal grant and loan awards received by full-time freshmen in public and private institutions. (Notice that the reported numbers are averages over *all* fresh-men, including both recipients and nonrecipients of aid.) What stands out is the increase in per-student borrowing and the decrease in the real value of grants per student in the 1980s. It should be

**Figure 2–2**
**Federal Aid per Student at Public and Private Institutions, 1974–84**
1990 dollars per student

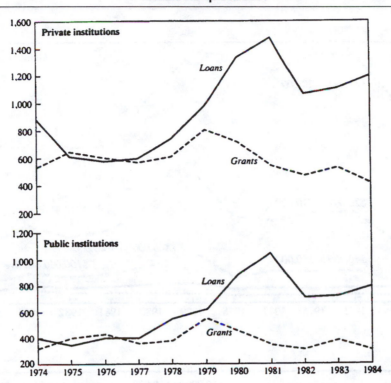

Source: Authors' calculations from *American Freshman Survey*. The data include both aided and nonaided students.

noted that the decrease in grants is more pronounced for this group of young full-time freshmen than it would be for a more broadly defined group, since an increasing percentage of federal grant money is going to older and part-time students as well as to students at "nontraditional," proprietary institutions.

Organizing the data by real family income allows us to trace changes in college affordability. The distribution of federal aid among income classes has by no means been constant over time. Figure 2-3 shows the variations in grants and loans according to income. One sees the substantial effects of the Middle Income Student Assistance Act (MISAA) of 1978 in increasing the grant and loan money available to middle- and (in the case of loans) upper-income students. During the years 1980 to 1981, when subsidized loans were available to all full-time students, regardless of income and need, the average student from a family with income over $100,000 (in 1990 dollars) borrowed more than $800 (in 1990 dollars).

Since 1981, the availability of subsidized loans to upper-income students has been sharply reduced. Moreover, the first half of the 1980s saw a substantial real decrease in the federal grants available to lower-income students. This partly reflects a squeeze on those federal dollars awarded in the Pell grant program, which (as shown in table 2-4) fell in real terms in the early 1980s before returning to roughly its 1979–80 level by 1985–86, and partly the awarding of more Pell grant funds to independent students and students at proprietary institutions. As figure 2-3 shows, the decrease in real grant money for lower-income students was accompanied by a rapid increase in the amount they borrowed.

**Figure 2–3**
**Federal Grant and Loan Aid, by Family Income, 1974–84**
**1990 dollars per student**

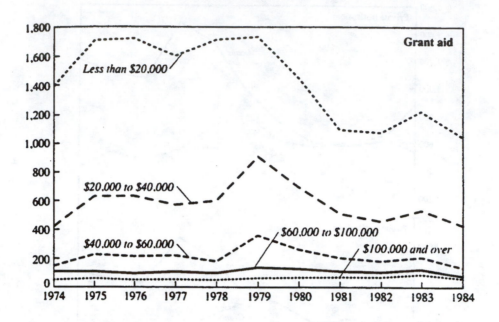

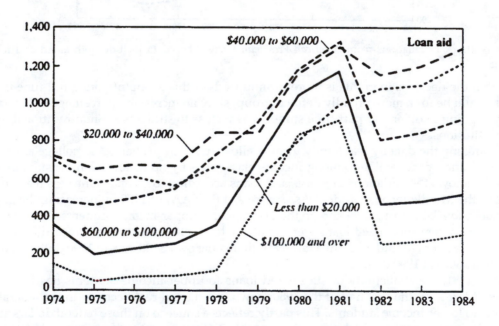

Source: Authors' calculations from *American Freshman Survey.*

Student opportunities throughout this period were affected not only by changes in federal student aid policy but by changes in the schools' tuition charges and in the aid available from nonfederal sources as well. Data that report the amount of nonfederal grant aid that lower-income students have received each year suggest that nonfederal aid comes mostly from the institutions. Not surprisingly, the amount of aid varies by the form of institutional control, such aid being especially important at private universities. Moreover, it is not only lower-income students who benefit from nonfederal grant aid. At private universities, for example, students with incomes between $20,000 and $40,000 receive almost as much nonfederal grant aid per student as the lowest income group.

Although no one measure can fully reflect the impact of aid on affordability, it is helpful to boil down the changes in tuition and in the various forms of aid to a manageable index. One way to construct such an index is to estimate the subsidy value of the aid received by a particular subclass of students, recognizing that the subsidy value of a loan is less than that of a grant. Per-student subsidies, combining all sources of aid, and putting the subsidy value of a federal loan at half the amount lent, can be combined with estimates of the cost of attendance (including books, room and board, and tuition) to come up with an estimate of the "net cost" or "net price" of attending college.[14] Figure 2-4 reports these net cost figures for students of different income levels at public and private institutions.

The figure shows that for students at both public and private institutions, and at all income levels, net costs for the 1970s and 1980s have followed a similar U-shaped pattern. Costs in general fell for all groups of students in the latter part of the 1970s and rose in the 1980s, and in many cases, the dollar amounts of the changes have been roughly similar for different groups. In other words, the overall student aid system did not succeed in insulating needier students from changes in the cost of college; the changes affected needy and affluent alike.

Still, there are some notable differences in the experiences of various groups. First, even when the dollar amounts of the changes in cost are similar for students at different income levels, percent changes in cost sometimes differ. Thus, for public institutions as a whole the difference in net costs for the lowest-income student group in the "best" year (1979) and the "worst" year (1984) was 33 percent, while for the highest-income group, the best-worst comparison (1979 and 1984) yields a difference of just 19 percent. For private institutions, the picture is somewhat different. As net prices at private institutions fell from 1974 to 1980, the net cost for the lowest-income students dropped by just over 30 percent, while for the most affluent students the drop from their worst (1974) to their best year (1979) was just 11 percent. In the first half of the 1980s, net prices have risen: the lowest-income students have seen prices rise by 42 percent, while the most affluent students have experienced exactly the same 42 percent increase.

This figure also implies that over time there have been some significant changes in the relative prices of different institution types. For the lowest-income students ($0–20,000 in 1990 dollars), the ratio of the net price of a private institution to that of a public four-year institution has actually fallen from 1974 to 1984 (from 1.75 to 1.52), mainly because of the importance of institution-based aid in private schools. On the other hand, for both the highest-income students (above $100,000) and for the "upper-middle" income group ($60–100,000) the ratio of the private to public price rose—from 1.67 to 2.01 for the top group and from 1.61 to 1.85 for the "upper-middle" group. This picture of private colleges becoming relatively more accessible to the very lowest income group and relatively less accessible to the more affluent has come in for considerable discussion as a possible threat to the representation of middle-income students in private institutions.

In fact, looking at the 1974–84 period as a whole, it is apparent that relatively more affluent students have faced significant cost increases at private institutions. For families in the $40–60,000 bracket, this increase is moderate—about 10 percent over ten years—but for families earning more than $60,000 in 1990 dollars, the increase is more substantial—on the order of 25 percent or more. Many of these families, though relatively affluent compared to the population as a whole, would

**Figure 2–4**
**Net Cost per Student at Public and Private Institutions, by Family Income, 1974–84**
1990 dollars per student

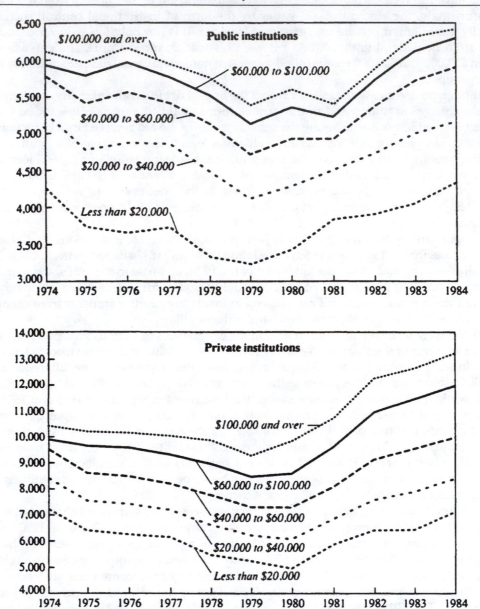

Source: Authors' calculations from *American Freshman Survey*.

still be classified as "middle class." While it could not be said that this increase has damaged this group's access to college—since costs facing these families remain moderate at public institutions—there may well be an impact on "choice." This increase may well be related to the worries about "middle-class enrollment melt" at private institutions. . . .

# Enrollment Patterns Over Time

Trends in enrollment may also shed light on trends in affordability. Certainly over the very long run, from the 1930s to the present, the remarkable increase in participation rates and the broadening of the range of social groups represented in higher education are testimony to gains in affordability, gains that have been urged on by the expansion of public higher education and increased federal aid.

In examining the more recent era, it is useful to divide the historical data on the enrollment effects of government financing into three periods: that before 1974, preceding the introduction of the basic grants program; that from 1974 to 1980, when federal funding for student aid grew sharply in real terms; and that following 1980, when federal student aid funding first failed to keep pace with inflation and then later grew only slowly.

The pre-1974 evidence is scattered. Data on the distribution of student aid by income class are very hard to come by. Evidence on enrollment distributions is also shaky, partly owing to data availability problems, but also owing to the fact that large swings in military personnel levels and changes in recruitment policies during the Vietnam era complicate the interpretation of available data.

Nonetheless, fragmentary evidence suggests that the late 1960s and early 1970s were a period of rapid change in the socioeconomic composition of the United States college population. Davis and Johns have examined data on the distribution of college freshmen by income class, using the American Freshman Survey.[15] They found a marked increase in the fraction of students from families below the median and from within the bottom quartile of U.S. incomes in those years. Similar findings, relying partly on other data, are reported by the Carnegie Council and by Larry Leslie and Paul Brinkman.[16]

It seems implausible to attribute very much of this important change to the direct effects of federal student aid policy. The federal commitment of dollars to the main Office of Education programs (the campus-based programs and the guaranteed student loans) remained modest through the late 1960s and early 1970s. Moreover, a large fraction of this federal support was in the form of guaranteed loans, which were not at that time targeted at the neediest students.

More likely, the proximate causes of the change in enrollment patterns can be found in changed policies at the state and institutional levels and in changed social attitudes. The most prominent state-level effort was the dramatic expansion in community colleges and urban state-run four-year colleges in the 1960s. These institutions were geographically closer to disadvantaged populations than traditional state universities and often adopted open admissions policies that encouraged the enrollment of educationally disadvantaged students, who are disproportionately from poor economic backgrounds. For many such students, the opportunity to conserve on spending by living at home has provided a dramatic increase in college affordability. Meanwhile, private colleges and universities expanded their own student aid efforts substantially in the late 1960s—by a factor of more than two from 1963 through 1971 after adjusting for inflation—and it may be that they targeted their funds more heavily at lower-income students. Finally, the strong society-wide concern in the late 1960s for combating poverty and promoting racial equality should not be neglected. These forces led to stronger recruiting efforts directed toward disadvantaged youth and probably had effects as well on the college-going aspirations of minority and lower-income students.

While these effects probably outweighed any direct impact that federal student aid had on increasing lower-income enrollments in the 1965–74 period, the indirect effects of federal aid policy should not be overlooked. States and private institutions may well have been encouraged to strengthen their commitment to the higher education of disadvantaged students by the knowledge that the federal government was supporting those efforts, and seemed likely to increase that support. Student expectations may have been similarly affected. The anticipation of an expanded federal role in student finance in the 1970s may have produced some effect on enrollments even before the actual programs came into being; this effect, however, is unmeasurable.

The period 1974–85 saw an expanded federal aid commitment followed by a decline, as well as a shift in emphasis from grants to loans. As noted earlier, the period of expanding student aid was also a period of declining tuition (in real terms), while in the 1980s tuitions rose as aid fell. As a result, all groups of students faced lower costs in the second half of the 1970s and higher ones in the 1980s.

Can we detect the effect of these swings in net costs on enrollment patterns and levels? Figure 2-5 shows enrollment rates, expressed as a percentage of the eligible population, for students of different income levels over the 1974–85 period.[17] In these enrollment graphs, there is no evident effect of net costs on enrollment for families with incomes above $60,000 (1990 dollars)—from 1974 through 1980, their enrollment rate averaged 56 percent, while from 1981 through 1985, it averaged 58 percent. For families with incomes between $20,000 and $60,000, there again appears to be virtually no effect from the increase in net price—the enrollment rate fell from 41 percent to 40 percent over the two periods.

A more distinct swing, however, is evident for the lowest income group, those with incomes below $20,000 in 1990 terms. This group's enrollment rate averaged 33 percent from 1974 through 1980 but fell to 28 percent from 1981 through 1985.

This general pattern is consistent with the theory that student aid changes have played a significant role in either encouraging or discouraging the enrollment of lower-income students. As noted, net cost changes in percent terms were somewhat larger for lower-income students, and econometric studies . . . lead us to expect that that group will respond more sensitively to relative price changes of a given magnitude. It thus seems plausible, on the basis simply of examining these enrollment trends, that the change in federal student aid policy, which contributed significantly to the changes in the net cost facing lower-income students, played a substantial role in reducing lower-income enrollment rates in the 1980s.

It may well be that factors additional to changes in the net price facing lower-income students contributed to the enrollment trends described. The 1980s saw a greater emphasis on admissions selectivity at postsecondary institutions and a less aggressive federal stance toward supporting affirmative action in admissions. Both trends may work against students from educationally and socially disadvantaged backgrounds.

A slightly different way of looking at these data may also prove illuminating. W. Lee Hansen has suggested that a look at relative enrollment rates of more- and less-affluent students may help gauge the impact of federal student aid—on the grounds that federal student aid is the most obvious factor that should affect the enrollment behavior of these two groups differentially.[18] He used Current Population Survey (CPS) data to examine the enrollment rates for students from families with dependents aged 18 through 24 for two, separate academic years, 1971–72 and 1978–79. He then calculated the ratio of the enrollment rates of below-median-income to above-median-income families for the two years and found that between 1971 and 1979 the ratios declined for whites, blacks, men, and women. When a weighted average was taken for whites and blacks and for men and women, the ratios again fell between the two years.

The conclusion from this study is well known among researchers and policymakers: these data force one to conclude that the greater availability of student financial aid, targeted largely toward students from below-median-income families, did little, if anything, to increase access. The results

**Figure 2–5**
**Enrollment Rates, by Income Group, 1974–85**

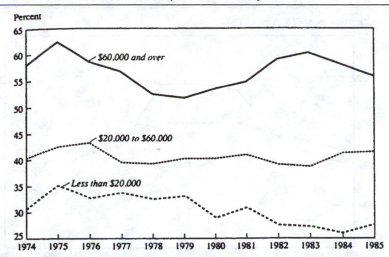

Source: Authors' calculations from *Current Population Survey*. Incomes are measured in 1990 dollars.

certainly do not accord with expectations that access would increase for lower-income dependents relative to higher-income dependents."[19]

There are some obvious limitations in interpreting this kind of snapshot comparison at two points in time. First, year-to-year fluctuations may obscure underlying trends, so that increasing the number of years in the comparison is helpful. Second, controlling for variation in other factors that affect the demand for enrollment is not possible using this methodology. Such factors as overall economic conditions, changes in the rate of return to higher education, and changes in the opportunity costs of college enrollment (as produced, for example, by changes in the draft law) may influence the comparison if they affect income groups differently. Finally, this kind of comparison is not responsive to changes in the targeting of student aid. As noted, over the 1970s, the total amount of federal student aid not only increased substantially but also changed significantly in its distribution. A larger fraction of available aid was targeted at middle- and upper-income students in the late 1970s, tending to obscure any effect on differential enrollment rates that might have occurred.

Some of these limitations can be dealt with by extending the analysis to more years and by relating the enrollment fluctuations to what we know about year-to-year fluctuations in the amounts and direction of aid. Figure 2-6 presents data for the extended period 1975–84 and displays a three-year moving average of the ratio of the enrollment rates for the lowest (below $20,000) and highest (above $60,000) income groups (in 1990 dollars). The figure looks separately at white and black students. Although the trends are similar for both racial groups, the changes are much sharper for blacks than whites. The late 1970s saw a relative increase in the ratio of lower-income to higher-income enrollment, and the 1980s saw a decrease, with some recovery quite recently. For blacks the swing is marked—lower-income blacks enrolled at almost 70 percent of the higher-income black rate in 1979; by 1982 the ratio was only around 40 percent. For whites the change in the ratio was from about 60 percent to under 50 percent.

This narrowing of differences between upper-income and lower-income participation rates in the late 1970s was importantly influenced by a decline in upper-income enrollment rates in the late 1970s, a decline for which there is no obvious explanation. (It certainly was not caused by the federal student aid policy, which was becoming more generous to affluent students in those years.)

**Figure 2–6**
**Ratio of Low- to High-Income Enrollment Rates, by Race, 1975–84**

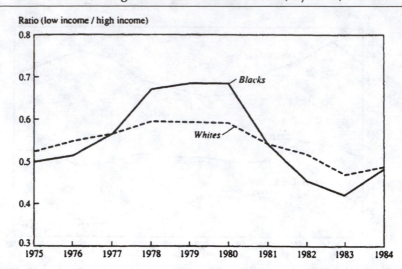

Source: Authors' calculations from *Current Population Survey.* Incomes below $20,000 in 1990 dollars are considered low. Incomes above $60,000 are considered high. Figures are calculated using three-year moving averages.

Lower-income students did not share in that decline, possibly because substantial federal student aid was available to them. The underlying reasoning behind that supposition is that the forces (whatever they were) pressing down on higher-income enrollments should have applied across the board; therefore, the failure of lower-income enrollments to decline in the late 1970s is backhanded evidence of the effectiveness of aid in bolstering enrollments in that group. This is a plausible, but not a very strong, argument. The fact that in the 1980s a real decline in federal aid was accompanied by a distinct drop in the lower-income enrollment rate, while the upper-income rate stayed more or less constant, seems considerably more convincing.

These data suggest that extending the Hansen time-series analysis to more years, and taking closer account of changes in federal aid targeting, raises questions about the strong conclusion that federal aid has been without effect. These extensions do not, however, deal adequately with one of the most important empirical concerns about such data: the need for an estimation method in which the strength of the relationship between cost variation and enrollment variation is systematically measured. . . .

# Footnotes

1. In addition, that role has been subject to substantial fluctuations, both in the level of support and in the distribution of support among families and institutions.

2. Data after the 1985–86 academic year have not yet been released by the federal government.

3. For the 1949–50 academic year, the unusually high share of public tuition, 25 percent of public institution revenue, was the result of the GI Bill. Federal tuition payments for veterans are counted under gross tuition.

4. For the 1939–40 academic year, the surprisingly high figure for the federal share of public revenue, 13 percent, reflects the fact that the military academies are counted as public institutions.

5. National Center for Education Statistics (1989, table 149, p. 168).

6. Recall that payments made under the GI Bill caused the tuition share in the 1949–50 academic year to be unusually high. The figures in table 2-3 report GI Bill tuition payments as if they were made by families rather than by the federal government. When veterans' tuition payments are treated differently, the share of revenue provided by families is dramatically reduced in 1949–50 as well as in 1969–70 and 1975–76, when Vietnam veterans received federal support. Our treatment here is based partly on the premise that trends stand out more clearly if we do not include these episodic events. Moreover, there may be a case for treating educational payments to veterans as deferred compensation rather than as student aid.

7. Table 2-3 does not take into account the federally financed educational loans provided to families—such loans are treated as part of the family's payments.

8. The social security benefit was being phased out by 1982. As for the GI Bill, the lower spending results both from changes in the program and from the reduced number of young veterans claiming benefits after the Vietnam War ended.

9. The original GSL program (now called the Stafford loan program) has been, and still is, considerably larger than the other two components of the federal guaranteed loan program, PLUS and SLS. In table 2-4, we sum the three types of loans.

10. The shift toward loans is more dramatic when social security benefits and the GI Bill are included. In 1979, new guaranteed loans comprised about 34 percent of total federal aid, compared with 57 percent in 1985.

11. Although the share of college students who are adult or independent has grown, it has not grown as fast as the share of Pell recipients who are independent. Chapter 7 discusses in greater detail the participation of adult students in government loan programs.

12. The survey is also forced to rely on self-reported family incomes. This survey is administered by institutions that elect to participate, and the setting in which it is administered may vary among institutions. As such, the sample of institutions is self-selected rather than random (institutions are only included in the sample if they survey a large fraction of their freshmen); as a result, the survey substantially underrepresents two-year colleges. Note also that we focus on data for full-time resident students, who are more likely to be enrolled at public and private four-year institutions than at public two-year institutions. Proprietary institutions, mostly vocational and technical institutions, are not included. The survey is conducted annually by Alexander W. Astin and (varying) other authors and published under the title *The American Freshman: National Norms for Fall.*

13. The specially directed aid programs (principally the GI Bill and the social security program) do not appear important in these data, apparently for two reasons. First, much of this money probably went to students outside the subsample reported here, which is limited to first-time, full-time freshmen who reside on campus, who are dependent on their parents for support, and who are 24 years old or younger. Second, many students who were recipients either of social security survivor benefits or of GI Bill assistance may not have reported it as student aid.

14. The estimate that the subsidy value of a loan is half of its face value is consistent with findings reported by Bosworth, Carron, and Rhyne (1987) and Hauptman (1985).

15. Davis and Johns (1982).

16. Carnegie Council (1980); Leslie and Brinkman (1988).

17. These data are derived from the Current Population Survey. The figures include only students who are enrolled full time; the figures do not include most proprietary or vocational enrollment. Our sample is further limited to persons who are 18 to 24 years old, are financially dependent on their parents, and have completed less than four years of college.

18. Hansen (1983).

19. Hansen (1983, p. 93).

# The Impact of Changing Levels of Financial Resources on the Structure of Colleges and Universities (1990)

## Joseph Froomkin

There is no right level of resources required by American colleges and universities because these institutions do not have a clearly defined mission: They accommodate under one roof a teaching function and a scientific function, and no clear-cut standard has been set for the desirable level of activity for either function. No uniform curriculum is mandated in the United States for baccalaureate or advanced degrees. Higher education institutions set their requirements for graduation and decide on the level of resources to be expended for instruction. Nor is there any consensus about the level, content, and quality of research that colleges and universities are expected to perform. For an individual institution, the research and development effort is evaluated by fellow academics and, for the sector as a whole, it is judged by academia's ability to meet national goals for the advancement of scientific knowledge.

In this unstructured environment, it is not possible to set absolute standards for financial resources needed by American colleges and universities. Instead, one can only compare levels of resources which were available to higher education in the recent past and document where university administrators economized when the level of these resources diminished.

## Trends in Resources

### An Overview of the Past Forty Years

From the end of World War II until 1970, the higher education sector experienced very rapid growth. The number of degree-credit students quadrupled between 1946 and 1970—from 2.0 million in 1946 to 3.6 million in 1960 and 7.9 million in 1970. Enrollments grew at some 6 percent a year compounded during this period. Since 1970, the growth rate has decelerated to 2.4 percent, on the average. Between 1980 and 1984, the number of students in this category was practically stable, and in 1984 their number declined to 11.0 million.*

Non-degree-credit student enrollment grew at an even faster pace than degree-credit enrollment during the forty years since World War II. Although there were so few nondegree students in the late 1940s that it was believed inessential to count them, by the end of the 1950s they made up five percent of the total enrollment. By 1960, nondegree students numbered two hundred thousand and accounted for eight percent of the enrollment of higher education. Their share of enrollment is currently ten percent of the total. In 1984, 1.2 million nondegree students were enrolled in colleges and universities.

The growth in enrollments during the past forty years was made possible by a spectacular growth in the current resources made available to higher education. These increased some seventy-fold, in current dollars, between 1946 and 1984. In 1946, the total current revenues of institutions of higher education were reported to be $1.2 billion. In 1984, they were $86.1 billion. In constant prices, the increase was also impressive. We estimate that the 1946 revenues are the equivalent of $9.4 billion in 1984 prices. Thus the growth of revenues in real terms was more than nine-fold.

The resources expended per student on education have kept up very well despite the fast rate of growth. A number of studies have documented that the amount spent per full-time equivalent (FTE) student (a statistic derived by counting three part-time students as the equivalent of one full-time student) did not change significantly during the period of rapid growth or the current period of stable enrollments for 1966 to 1974, see Froomkin, 1978.

Tuition and fees receipts grew at a more modest pace, from $925 million in 1946 (some $8 billion in current prices) to $19.7 billion in 1984, a mere 2.5-fold increase in the face of six-fold increase in total enrollment. Average tuition and fees grew more slowly than enrollments as a higher proportion of students attended low-tuition schools. Starting with the end of World War II, the high-tuition private sector enrolled a lower proportion of students every year until 1970. While half of the student in American colleges and universities were enrolled in private institutions in 1946, roughly one in four attend private institutions today.

After the end of World War II, states stepped up their appropriations to public colleges and universities thus enabling state schools to provide the majority of new places for a growing enrollment. State appropriations for the operation of colleges and universities increased from $225 million (around $2.0 billion in today's purchasing power) in 1946 to $23 billion in 1984.

Research and development and related contract work performed predominantly by universities grew even faster than other items of current revenue. In 1946 higher education institutions were paid $87 million, representing eight percent of their current revenues, to do research. In 1984, $12.0 billion of current revenues were derived from this source. After adjustment for the intervening price change, research receipts grew sixteen times in constant prices during that time.

Comparisons of income statements of colleges and universities for 1946 and 1984 cannot be made with great precision because until 1966 financial statistics were not collected carefully and the earlier data may be incomplete or inaccurate.

## Recent Trends in Revenue Sources of Higher Education

The revenues of postsecondary institutions are conventionally reported under the following headings: tuition and fees, appropriations of different levels of government (the most important of these are state appropriations to higher education institutions), research and development grants and contracts from different levels of government (the federal government provides the lion's share of these), private gifts and contracts, and endowment income. In addition, the revenues from sales related to education (mostly dormitory income), sales and services of auxiliary enterprises, the revenue from university-run hospitals, and from miscellaneous activities are also listed as revenue sources.

Revenue trends of institutions of higher education come into sharper focus if revenues from peripheral activities, such as dormitories, hospitals, and miscellaneous activities are netted out from the total. What remains are the moneys used for the principal functions of colleges and universities: instruction and research. For convenience, we call this figure adjusted current revenues (ACRs). The ACRs are further disaggregated into two parts: the money received for contract research, and the rest.

**Table 1**
**Tuition and Fees per FTE Student in Current and Constant Dollars**
**and Percent of per-Capita Disposable Income**

|  | 1966 | 1970 | 1976 | 1979 | 1984 |
|---|---|---|---|---|---|
| Current Dollars FTE |  |  |  |  |  |
| All | 573 | 749 | 1,043 | 1,233 | 2,175 |
| Public | 280 | 379 | 533 | 690 | 1,197 |
| Private | 1,148 | 1,537 | 2,392 | 3,005 | 5,381 |
| Constant 1967 Dollars per FTE |  |  |  |  |  |
| All | 603 | 578 | 589 | 568 | 668 |
| Public | 302 | 313 | 301 | 318 | 368 |
| Private | 1,208 | 1,270 | 1,350 | 1,385 | 1,653 |
| Percent of per Capita Disposable Income |  |  |  |  |  |
| All | 22.0 | 21.0 | 19.5 | 17.6 | 20.8* |
| Public | 10.7 | 11.4 | 10.8 | 9.9 | 11.5 |
| Private | 44.1 | 46.1 | 46.6 | 43.0 | 51.6 |

Source: See footnote, p. 198, and The National Income and Product Accounts of the United States.

## Tuition and Fee Receipts:

The average level of tuition charged to students depends upon (1) the share of students in public or private enrollment, since tuition levels are much lower in the public sector, and (2) the proportion of students attending part-time, since these students pay less tuition per capita.

In the twenty years since 1966, the year when sufficiently detailed data became available to calculate meaningful ratios, the amount of tuition charged per FTE student has been highly correlated to the level of per-capita disposable income (the regression equation for the whole period has an $R^2$ of over .9). Throughout most of the period, the average tuition was equal to twenty percent of the per-capita disposable income, with private institutions charging around forty-six percent and public institutions eleven percent of the income (see Table 1).

The four-fold increase in tuition per FTE student in the eighteen years between 1966 and 1984 brought the institution only ten percent more resources per student. In 1979 the institutions did not anticipate the high rate of inflation and set the tuitions and fees to low. In 1984 private schools may have set their tuition higher than was warranted by past trends, possibly because they anticipated a higher rate of inflation.

The contribution of tuition and fees to adjusted institutional revenues net of receipts of grants and contracts for research and development is extremely stable over the years. The share of tuition and fees has remained practically constant as a percent of nonresearch ACRs in each type of institution. In public institutions it accounted for seventeen to twenty percent, and in private schools it neared or exceeded sixty percent of that figure (see Table 2).

The net contribution of tuition to institutional resources is reduced by awards of scholarships from unrestricted funds (other scholarship moneys from either state or government moneys channeled through institutions or specially endowed funds for this purpose cannot be used for any other purpose). In public schools, scholarships paid with unrestricted funds eroded the tuition and fees receipts by nearly four percent in 1966 and six percent in 1984. In 1976 and 1979, scholarships constituted a higher proportion of tuition than in 1984. This implies that in 1984 state schools were short of funds and cut down on scholarships. In private schools, scholarship funds from unrestricted sources increased consistently from under 8 to 10.5 percent during the same period. The

**Table 2**
**Tuition and Fees as Proportion (in percent) of Non-Research Revenues**

|  | 1966 | 1970 | 1976 | 1979 | 1984 |
|---|---|---|---|---|---|
| All | 35 | 33 | 29 | 30 | 33 |
| Public | 19 | 19 | 18 | 17 | 20 |
| Private | 61 | 61 | 59 | 61 | 60 |

Source: See footnote, p. 198.

**Table 3**
**Tuition Remission from Unrestricted Funds by Type of Higher Education Institution for Selected Years, 1966 to 1984**

|  | Millions of Dollars | | | Percent of Tuition Revenue | | |
|---|---|---|---|---|---|---|
|  | All | Public | Private | All | Public | Private |
| 1966 | 184 | 39 | 145 | 6.7 | 4.4 | 7.8 |
| 1970 | 326 | 105 | 220 | 7.3 | 6.0 | 8.2 |
| 1976 | 687 | 276 | 410 | 8.2 | 7.9 | 8.8 |
| 1979 | 887 | 328 | 559 | 8.2 | 7.4 | 8.7 |
| 1984 | 1,738 | 518 | 1,220 | 8.8 | 6.4 | 10.5 |

Source: See footnote, p. 198.

percentage of tuition and fees remitted increased especially rapidly during the last five years (see Table 3).

The future level of tuition and fee receipts depend upon the rate of growth of the economy, the share of personal income taken by taxes, and, of course, enrollment levels. If and when the U.S. economy reduces unemployment levels to around four percent and the productivity of the labor force resumes in its historical upward trend, some of the decline in tuition and fees caused by projected future declines in enrollment may be made up.

## Government Appropriations

One and half times as much current revenue comes from government appropriations as from tuition and fees. Nine out of ten dollars provided by governments come from state sources and benefit state schools almost exclusively. Between 1966 and 1984, state appropriations to higher education increased nearly nine-fold. After taking account of the intervening inflation, the purchasing power of the state appropriation (deflated by the Higher Education Price Index) was still two-and-half times higher in 1984 than it was in 1946.

State appropriations since 1966 averaged roughly $1,000 in constant 1967 dollars ($3,500 in 1984 prices) per FTE student in public institutions. This level of support has increasingly taxed the resources of the states. Slightly under seven percent of the total revenue of states, or ten percent of the tax revenues, was allotted to higher education during the 1946-1984 period (see Table 4).

This rather impressive record failed to meet the expectations of administrators of institutions of higher education who hoped that the share of revenues, which rose from 2.6 to 4.9 percent between 1946 and 1966 and finally leveled off at 6.7 percent in 1976, would continue rising to meet the growing needs and aspirations of state schools. An increasing number of state legislatures have be-

**Table 4**
**Proportion of State Revenues Allocated to Higher Education Institutions,**
**Total and per FTE Student, Selected Years 1946-1984**

|        | Percent of total rev. | Appropriation in current $ | Appropriation in 1967 $ | Per FTE |
|--------|-----------------------|----------------------------|-------------------------|---------|
| 1946   | n.a.                  | 225                        | 600                     | n.a.    |
| 1966   | 4.9                   | 2,707                      | 2,854                   | 793     |
| 1970   | 6.5                   | 5,669                      | 4,782                   | 933     |
| 1976   | 6.7                   | 11,741                     | 6,626                   | 1,018   |
| 1979   | 6.7                   | 15,837                     | 7,301                   | 1,073   |
| 1984   | 6.7                   | 23,635                     | 7,172                   | 1,071   |

Source: U.S. Bureau of the Census, *State Government Finances*: see also footnote, p. 198.

come more niggardly with respect to their allocations to colleges and universities. Hard pressed for resources to fund other programs, states with declining revenues did not hesitate to cut appropriations to higher education during the last recession.

National averages fail to depict the plight of institutions in roughly half the states. Between 1979 and 1985, twenty-eight states and the District of Columbia reduced their subsidy per FTE student in higher education. In five jurisdictions, Alabama, the District of Columbia, Florida, South Carolina, and Virginia, an increase in tuition more than offset the decline in the purchasing power of the state appropriations. The table below reproduces statistics for twenty-three states where appropriations per FTE decline as well. But in roughly half of the rest of the states tuition increases closed the gap only partially. In some states, tuition remained constant (see Table 5).

Generally the decline in support did not come about as a result of a significant cut in the proportion of tax resources allocated to higher education. Most states with declining support to higher education were either in the Northeast, in the industrial Midwest, or the agricultural Midwest. The three exceptions were Alaska, California, and Nevada, where local politics either put a ceiling on tax revenues or cut support to higher education. The reasons state appropriations per FTE student declined were that (1) states where economic activity was low reduced their appropriations, (2) states that benefited from the oil boom raised their appropriations very little or not at all, and (3) catch-up increases in low-expenditure Southern states failed to make up for losses elsewhere.

The variation of state appropriations for higher education in the past few years has highlighted once again these institutions' vulnerability to economic conditions. The proportion of state resources allocated to educational institutions has remained pretty constant. Thus, such states as Texas, which experienced dramatic increases in well-being, did not increase the proportion of revenue allocated to education during the period when oil prices were high, although their total funds for education increased. During the current funding cycle, as the price of oil declined causing a drop in state revenues, Texas impose the same proportional funding cuts on institutions of higher education as it did on other functions of the state government.

Government appropriations other than those by states play a very minor role in the current revenues of institutions of higher education. The major share of federal appropriations goes to Howard, Gallaudet College, and U.S. Service Schools. From 1979 on, these appropriations amounted to half a billion dollars a year in 1967 prices, a small fraction of the federal funds channelled to universities. About fifteen percent of these moneys, seventy-five million dollars a year, went to private schools. Federal moneys accounted for eight percent of the net revenues of public colleges and universities. Their share in private budgets was insignificant, a little over one percent.

### Table 5
### Trends in State Allocations per FTE Student to Higher Education
### (in 1985 dollars) in States with Declining Support, 1979/80-1984/5

| | Decline of Appropriation | Decline after Tuition Change | Percent Change in Tax Revenues |
|---|---|---|---|
| Alaska | 502 | 113 | -5.2 |
| Arkansas | 135 | 112 | +0.1 |
| California | 298 | — | -0.07 |
| Florida | 130 | — | -0.4 |
| Idaho | 450 | 554 | -0.3 |
| Iowa | 486 | 487 | +0.1 |
| Massachusetts | 836 | 836 | +0.4 |
| Michigan | 546 | 289 | -1.2 |
| Minnesota | 623 | 368 | -1.4 |
| Nebraska | 541 | 626 | -0.09 |
| Nevada | 854 | 802 | -0.8 |
| New Hampshire | 338 | 114 | -0.5 |
| North Dakota | 585 | 570 | -1.4 |
| Ohio | 311 | 125 | -0.7 |
| Oregon | 164 | 31 | -1.5 |
| Pennsylvania | 586 | 403 | -0.1 |
| South Carolina | 266 | — | +0.9 |
| South Dakota | 988 | 1,002 | -2.1 |
| Virginia | 33 | — | -0.5 |
| Washington | 426 | 487 | -3.5 |
| Wisconsin | 737 | 924 | -0.8 |
| Washington, D.C. | 211 | 126 | -0.9 |
| Wyoming | 506 | 810 | -2.4 |
| United States | 112 | 186 | -0.1 |

Source: Halstead (1985b).

Local expenditures, which include the District of Columbia's outlays for its higher education institutions, grew during the immediate post-war period when enrollment was booming, but they actually declined in real terms between 1976 and 1979. The decline was caused by the increased responsibility for higher education assumed by the states in New York, Illinois, Michigan, and California. The financial difficulties of big cities in these states caused states to take over city-controlled institutions.

By 1979, local expenditures, which were mostly for junior colleges, had stabilized in real terms. In real terms they were slightly lower in 1984 than in 1979 (see Table 6).

## Gifts and Endowments

There is no way to estimate precisely the amount of resources form private gifts which add to the current income of colleges and universities. In the first place, the National Center for Education statistics changed the definition of Higher Education General Information Survey (HEGIS) survey of revenues included under the rubric of gifts. In some years, gift moneys only were reported, in others, gifts and private contracts for research and development were lumped under this heading. In addition, a number of state-supported schools have established special foundations which are

**Table 6**
**Federal and Local Government Appropriations**
**(in Millions of Dollars) for Selected Years, 1946-1984**

| | Federal | | | Local | | |
|---|---|---|---|---|---|---|
| | All | Public | Private | All | Public | Private |
| **Current Dollars** | | | | | | |
| 1946 | 197 | n.a. | n.a. | 31 | n.a. | n.a. |
| 1966 | 560 | 460 | 100 | 296 | 295 | 1 |
| 1970 | 511 | 417 | 94 | 727 | 706 | 22 |
| 1976 | 906 | 782 | 185 | 1,419 | 1,419 | 3 |
| 1979 | 1,173 | 1,000 | 173 | 1,336 | 1,334 | 2 |
| 1984 | 1,426 | 1,216 | 210 | 1,826 | 1,824 | 2 |
| **Constant 1967 Dollars** | | | | | | |
| 1946 | 524 | n.a. | n.a. | 82 | n.a. | n.a. |
| 1966 | 589 | 484 | 105 | 311 | 310 | 1 |
| 1970 | 457 | 374 | 84 | 651 | 632 | 19 |
| 1976 | 511 | 441 | 71 | 801 | 799 | 2 |
| 1979 | 540 | 461 | 80 | 615 | 615 | * |
| 1984 | 438 | 374 | 64 | 561 | 561 | * |

*=less than one million dollars.

Source: See footnote, p. 198.

the principle recipients of private gifts, thus hiding them effectively from the scrutiny of state legislators.

There is no good way to obtain independent estimates for all of higher education. Statistics provided by a special private source, the Council For Financial Aid to Private Education and the Association of Independent Schools collect information from only half of all institutions. In 1969/70, a year when the National Center published statistics on a comparable basis, the council reported $825 million dollars in gifts to support current operations. That same year, the National Center for educational Statistics reported a total of $671 million in gifts in their statistics of current revenue. The survey listed $147 million in gifts to public schools for current operations, while HEGIS statistics put this figure at $58 million. The survey's figure of $524 million in gifts to private schools was relatively close to the $559 million reported by the private sector.

In 1984, the council reported that $1,014 million of gifts for current operations was received by public institutions. This figure is close to the one reported by HEGIS which claims to include private contract revenues. In the case of private institutions, the council's $1,694 million figure is much lower than the one in HEGIS. One suspects that the reports of the council are not consistent from year to year.

The figures for private gifts shown in Table 7 were derived by subtracting from private gifts and contracts listed in HEGIS the amounts reported by the National Science Foundation for private sources for research and development for the years 1966, 1976, 1979 and 1984. HEGIS lumped private gifts and contracts under one heading in those years. In 1970, the actual amount reported in HEGIS can be used, this being the year when only gifts were supposed to be reported. It is possible that our figures may include some moneys for training or research, and they certainly do not include moneys collected by public institutions through separate foundations.

In all probability, gifts to public institutions should be doubled to take into account moneys which are channeled through alumni foundations outside of state control. Even so, these gifts do not account for more than three percent of adjusted revenue in 1970 and four percent today. It should be noted, however, that the public schools' share of total gifts to schools increased from ten to eleven percent during the 1970s to twenty-eight percent in 1984. State schools were successful in convincing donors that their needs were no longer being met by public funds alone and that they were deserving of private support. Is this the beginning of a trend?

Gifts to private schools doubled in real terms in the past eighteen years, a rate which exceeded the 1.5-times growth in real gross national product. This growth is consistent with what was reported in the past and should continue in the future. Roughly one dollar in six which is spent on instruction in the private sector comes from gifts. This ratio has remained fairly constant over time (see Table 7).

## Endowment Income

That part of endowment income which is used to pay for current expenses has grown more slowly than gift income. Nevertheless, it nearly doubled in real terms between 1966 and 1984. Although it grew most rapidly in both current and constant dollars in the public sector, its part of the budget is still less than one percent, even after research is netted out. In private institutions, endowment income in most years contributed slightly more than nine percent of current revenues, and thus played a more important part in the finances of these institutions (see Table 8).

### Table 7
**Private Gifts to Institutions of Higher Education (in millions of dollars) for Selected Years, 1966-1984**

|      | Current Dollars | | | | Constant 1967 Dollars | | |
|------|------|--------|---------|---|------|---------|--------|
|      | **All** | **Public** | **Private** | | **All** | **Private** | **Public** |
| 1966 | 463   | 65  | 327   | | 486   | 68  | 343 |
| 1970 | 617   | 58  | 559   | | 510   | 48  | 462 |
| 1976 | 1,512 | 116 | 1,396 | | 853   | 66  | 787 |
| 1979 | 1,924 | 480 | 1,414 | | 887   | 184 | 652 |
| 1984 | 3,328 | 937 | 2,391 | | 1,022 | 287 | 734 |

### Table 8
**Endowment Income of Higher Education Institutions (in millions of dollars) for Selected Years 1966-1984**

|      | Current Dollars | | | | Constant 1967 Dollars | | |
|------|------|--------|---------|---|------|--------|---------|
|      | **All** | **Public** | **Private** | | **All** | **Public** | **Private** |
| 1966 | 276   | 24  | 253   | | 290 | 25 | 266 |
| 1970 | 447   | 57  | 590   | | 401 | 51 | 529 |
| 1976 | 687   | 96  | 591   | | 387 | 54 | 333 |
| 1979 | 986   | 154 | 832   | | 455 | 71 | 383 |
| 1984 | 1,874 | 315 | 1,559 | | 575 | 97 | 478 |

Source: See footnote, p. 198.

In the past few years, the contribution of endowment to current revenues has grown apace. This is due to the way these contributions are programmed by institutions of higher education. Starting in 1966, institutions increasingly adopted a formula for withdrawals from endowment which took into account the erosion of the endowments' purchasing power because of the increase in prices and allowed transfers on the basis of a set percentage of the average change in the value of the endowment in the past five years.

What with inflation moderating, the stock market booming, and interest rates declining between 1982 and 1987, the value of most endowments has increased substantially, doubling on the average. Of course, they declined somewhat during the October 1987 market crash. Nevertheless, having scaled down their provisions for future inflation, most private school financial officers now anticipate that their endowments will provide one and a half times as much money to current revenue as they did in the past few years.

## Other Revenue

Very little can be said about other revenue. This chapter will not deal with the revenues from auxiliary enterprises or hospitals which roughly equal expenses. The reporting of other revenue items is probably not consistent from year to year. Revenues from educational departments, auxiliary services, and other miscellaneous sources grew at roughly the same rate as the other revenues—8.7 times in current dollars and 2.5 times in constant dollars—between 1967 and 1984.

Such revenues increased somewhat faster in private institutions than in public colleges and universities. The share of other revenue in private institutions doubled—from 7.5 percent to 14.6 percent of adjusted current revenues. It fluctuated around the six percent level in public institutions. More recently, from 1979 to 1984, these revenues increased a little faster than the prices paid by institutions.

## Grants and Contracts and Research and Development

Grants and contracts play a lesser role in the current revenues of institutions of higher education today than they did in the 1950s and 1960s. Their share of revenue decreased from twenty-two to sixteen percent in all institutions. This decline in importance is due primarily to the failure of grants and contracts to grow at the same pace as other parts of the adjusted current revenues of higher education institutions.

The slow-down in research and development outlays by the federal government, the main provider of funds in this area, was first noted with alarm at the end of the 1960s. What was deplored then was the stabilization of the level of grants, rather than their decline. Since then, the purchasing power of the research and development moneys available to higher education institutions did decline slightly in some years, but generally these declines were made up during the following budget cycle.

Current concerns of the higher education research community fall under two headings: (1) In the administration budget, defense research and development is scheduled to increase faster than nondefense activities. The Reagan administration policies to fund generously military development, test, and evaluation and to curtail development in nondefense areas is causing some apprehension; (2) The possible across-the-board cuts which may be made to balance the budget could have serious consequences for the research effort at colleges and universities. Despite the lip service to basic research, there is a general feeling on the campuses that the situation of academic research and development in science and engineering is likely to get worse rather than better as the administration's projections are not likely to be translated into appropriations.

Two series are often cited in describing the role of research and development in university budgets, one from the Financial HEGIS, the other from the National Science Foundation, Survey of Science Resources Series, *Academic Science, R&D Funds*. HEGIS reports moneys both for research

## Table 9
### Grants and Contracts in Current and Constant (1967) Prices (in millions of dollars) and Share of Science Research and Development for Selected Years, 1966-1984

|      | Current | Constant | Share of Science R&D |
|------|---------|----------|----------------------|
| 1966 | 2,419   | 2,565    | 58                   |
| 1970 | 3,263   | 2,735    | 58                   |
| 1976 | 5,225   | 3,009    | 61                   |
| 1979 | 7,198   | 3,401    | 64                   |
| 1984 | 12,000  | 3,858    | 59                   |

Source: See footnote, p. 198.

## Table 10
### Amounts (in millions of current dollars) of Grants and Contracts and Research and Development and Reported Percentage of Federal Share

|      | Grants and Contracts | | Research and Development | |
|------|---------------|-----------|---------------|-----------|
|      | Millions of $ | % Federal | Millions of $ | % Federal |
| 1970 | 2,643         | 81        | 1,647         | 71        |
| 1976 | 4,525         | 86        | 2,511         | 67        |
| 1979 | 5,715         | 79        | 3,595         | 67        |
| 1984 | 9,475         | 79        | 4,096         | 67        |

Source: Research and development figures are from National Science Foundation (1981). Figures for 1984 are from an advance release of the same series. See also footnote, p. 198.

and development in science and nonscience fields and for other government services, such as traineeships and nonresearch activities. The survey of science resources reports separately on research and development expenditures by institutions of higher education. A comparison of the two series for the past ten years reveals that, on the average, sixty percent of grants and contracts are for scientific research and development (see Table 9).

The federal government dominates both the contract and grant funds reported by colleges and universities and the research and development expenditures of colleges and universities reported by the National Science Foundation. Nearly eighty percent of contracts and grants come from federal sources, and the federal government contributes nearly seventy percent of research and development moneys (see Table 10).

By contrast, state and local government shares declined. The proportion of research and development financed by the institutions' own funds remains constant. And industry's contribution increased faster than funds from other sources. Nevertheless, the role of industry in research and development at universities is still minor: Its shares grew from three to five percent of the science research and development budget between 1973 and 1984.

In the fifteen years since 1970, the share of different disciplines in sciences and engineering in the research and development budgets has remained fairly constant. The life sciences—the principal interest of the National Institutes of Health and a field where there is a great deal of excitement—claimed more than half of the resources in each of the last fifteen years. Engineering,

**Table 11**
**Percent of Total Research and Development Outlays by Discipline for Selected Years 1970-1984**

|  | 1970 | 1976 | 1979 | 1984 |
|---|---|---|---|---|
| Engineering | 13.4 | 11.6 | 14.3 | 14.2 |
| Physical sciences | 13.2 | 10.1 | 11.2 | 11.7 |
| Environmental sciences | 5.4 | 7.7 | 8.4 | 7.6 |
| Mathematics | — | 1.4 | 1.5 | 1.5 |
| Computer sciences | 3.0 | 1.5 | 1.8 | 2.6 |
| Life sciences | 51.3 | 56.5 | 52.8 | 54.2 |
| Psychology | 2.5 | 2.1 | 1.9 | 1.7 |
| Social & other sciences N.E.C. | 11.0 | 9.5 | 8.0 | 6.4 |

Source: Research and development figures are from National Science Foundation (1981). Figures for 1984 are from an advance release of the same series.

somewhat neglected in the mid-1970s, has staged a comeback since that time: fourteen percent of the research and development budget was allocated to engineering disciplines both in 1970 and now.

A somewhat larger share of research and development budgets went to environmental sciences in 1984 than in 1970. The fastest growing item was computer sciences, though it still takes up only a small share of the budget. The proportion of the budget allocated to physical sciences declined between 1970 and 1976. It has gained since then, but by 1984 it had not yet regained the share of funding it commanded in 1970. The big losers were psychology, social sciences, and other sciences not separately listed, whose share declined substantially after 1970 (see Table 11).

The same source reports that despite the drastic restructuring of federal priorities in the last five years, the share of university research devoted to basic research, as contrasted to research and development, hardly changed at all: two-thirds of the higher education institutions' activities were devoted to basic research both in 1979 and 1984.

The scientific community's contention that research and development budgets are inadequate is based on the slow growth of these budgets, rather than their decline. In constant dollars, the scientific research and development activity funded by moneys other than those provided by the university itself increased some fifty percent in the years 1966 to 1984. During the period 1979 to 1984, the level of research appears to have maintained, in constant prices, in all disciplines except the social sciences not elsewhere classified.

## Why There Is Talk of a Financial Crises

A superficial summary of the financial trends in the current revenues of higher education belies the pervasive talk of a financial crisis. Most items of current revenue has not changed substantially. Nor are there any grounds for alarm when one looks at the financial conditions of higher education in another way, comparing the current revenues available per FTE student in 1966 and 1984. The resources available per FTE student have remained relatively level ever since 1970 in the public sector and have actually increased in the private sector (see Table 12).

**Table 12**

**Resources Net of Research per FTE Student by Type of Institution, for Selected Years, 1966-1980**

|  | 1966 | 1970 | 1976 | 1979 | 1980 |
|---|---|---|---|---|---|
| All Institutions |  |  |  |  |  |
| Current dollars | 1,548 | 1,982 | 3,223 | 4,339 | 6,401 |
| Constant 1967 $ | 1,625 | 1,775 | 1,919 | 2,000 | 1,967 |
| Public Institutions |  |  |  |  |  |
| Current dollars | 1,391 | 1,832 | 2,965 | 4,017 | 5,747 |
| Constant 1976 $ | 1,464 | 1,642 | 1,673 | 1,852 | 1,766 |
| Private Institutions |  |  |  |  |  |
| Current dollars | 1,876 | 2,385 | 4,075 | 5,286 | 8,251 |
| Constant 1967 $ | 1,975 | 2,370 | 2,300 | 2,437 | 2,535 |

Source: See footnote, p. 198.

**Table 13**

**Professional Wages in Higher Education, Selected Years 1970-1984 (index 1967 = 100)**

|  | 1970 | 1976 | 1980 | 1984 |
|---|---|---|---|---|
| Professional Wages | 121.4 | 161.6 | 202.1 | 266.6 |
| Nonagricultural Wages | 117.7 | 172.2 | 230.8 | 288.7 |
| Consumer price index | 116.3 | 170.5 | 246.8 | 311.1 |

Source: Halstead (1985a) and U.S. Department of Labor (1986).

The reason for the unease among administrators and faculty lies not in the resources they command, but in the prices which they pay for resources whose prices the university can influence: wage and salaries to professional staff.

## Trends in Prices Paid for Inputs

During the years after World War II, educational institutions' costs increased faster than such common indicators of price change as the consumer price index (CPI) or the deflator used to calculate constant dollar values of the gross national product. This is no longer the case. Since 1971, the price of goods and services purchased by institutions and the CPI have tracked each other very closely. This was achieved by keeping down the salaries of the professional staff. These lagged behind the CPI by nearly twenty percent by the end of 1984. Professional salaries also fell behind total nonagricultural earnings during the past ten years (see Table 13). Since 1985 professionals in higher education have received wage increases which exceeded the rise in consumer prices.

Shrinking real incomes of professional staffs made it possible for both the resources per student and the level of research to be safeguarded, on the average, during this difficult decade. From 1979 to 1984, as enrollments grew very slowly, the amount of money available to colleges and universities remained fairly constant in real terms. Those institutions and state-wide systems that had to learn to operate with less money each year found this a particularly difficult period. Even institutions whose current revenues increased did not feel affluent, since hardly any of them experienced an influx of funds at all comparable to that of the 1960s.

## Slower Enrollment Growth

The financial adjustments required by a slow-down in the growth of enrollments in the late 1960s and early 1970s were documented in two studies by Earl F. Cheit (1971 and 1973). The first study documented the financial difficulties of a number of public and private institutions which were running deficits and did not cover current expenses. The surprising finding of the second study was that all the higher education institutions surveyed, including those that had been in financial difficulties two years previously, had managed to bring their expenditures and revenues into a state of precarious balance. This balance was achieved through an unprecedented cut in the rate of growth of expenditures per student, down, in real terms, from 4.0 percent a year, to 0.5 percent.

Clark Kerr, the former Chancellor of the University of California and then-Chairman of the Carnegie Commission on Higher Education, noted in his introduction to Cheit's (1973) study that this low rate on growth could not be sustained indefinitely without loss of quality. Cheit documented that these savings were through (1) the elimination of possibly marginal programs, (2) selective cutbacks in the number of faculty positions, and, (3) most important, general parsimony, especially in setting levels of faculty remuneration.

These conditions appeared to have prevailed over the next twelve years. Between 1979 and 1984, the most recent five-year period for which financial data are available, instructional costs per student did not increase at all terms, and as the first part of this study documented, resources per student devoted to instruction remained constant. This 'miracle' was achieved by keeping faculty wages down.

Faculty wages had failed to keep up with average earnings in the United States since the early 1970s. Until then, the challenge facing administrators and department chairmen was to recruit sufficient suitable staff to accommodate an increasing number of students. In the mid-1970s, enrollments began to grow at a slower pace, and the demand for faculty slackened. Just as tuition receipts failed to reach expected levels, utility bills made unexpected demands upon institutions' budgets. The increase in the price of energy added one to two percent to the current expense budgets of colleges and universities.

Concurrently, tighter rules for reimbursement of overhead for government contracts reduced the resources available for faculty salaries or the maintenance of support activities. At the University of Chicago, one of the few institutions forthright enough to report the share of faculty salaries paid by government grants and contracts, the proportion of faculty salaries paid by this source of income declined from twenty-five percent of faculty compensation in 1972 to fourteen percent in 1980 (Gray, 1986a).

## Impact of Slowdown in Economic Growth

The recent period of high unemployment and slow economic growth in the nation impacted educational institutions even more seriously. In 1977, a study I directed projected revenues for the period 1980 to 1985 for higher education institutions (Froomkin and McCully). In the public sector the projected tuition level per FTE student for 1985 was expected to amount to $1,328 (in 1984 prices), and state aid per FTE student was projected at $4,594 (also in 1984 prices) for a full-employment economy where productivity grew at two and a half percent a year. The actual amounts for that year were $1,197 and $3,530 respectively. The difference between the total of projected tuition and state aid and the actual receipts amounted to twenty-five percent of public institutions' budgets. These two revenue sources depend upon the level of economic activity and, while their relationship to economic variables did not change significantly, the shortfall was due to the poor performance of the economy.

The growth of tuition levels (in real terms) in private institutions was also kept down by high unemployment and the failure of productivity to increase. The average tuition level per FTE student was $5,750 in 1984, 6.4 percent less than projected. The shortfall reduced instructional revenues of private colleges and universities by 4 percent of their current revenue. An equal amount was lost because of the shortfall in gifts and endowment income.

## Patterns of Cutbacks

It is possible to describe a pattern for cutbacks in institutions with shrinking resources. In those cases where resources were reduced less than twenty-five percent per FTE student: (1) Either the number of faculty members was frozen or the size of the faculty was allowed to shrink through attrition; (2) faculty salaries were allowed to lag behind the increase in the price level or the increase in real salaries of all professional workers; (3) tighter cost controls were introduced for all parts of the college and university budgets; (4) auxiliary enterprises, such as dormitories, bookstores, and university presses were made to break even or to contribute to the general revenue of universities; (5) maintenance was reduced to the extent that professors were forced to empty their own wastepaper baskets; and (6) some renovation of facilities was delayed and capital maintenance was deferred.

These measures were taken by all institutions. As a general rule the research universities, both public and private, did not reduce the number of course offerings, although in certain instances, especially in the graduate area, they deemphasized or eliminated graduate programs in their weak fields. For instance, Princeton's biology department reduced the scope of its graduate offerings to the four areas where it was traditionally strong. Georgetown University discontinued its graduate physics program. Simultaneous with the cutbacks, research universities established new programs. Princeton started an impressive computer science program, and Georgetown moved more resources into its graduate chemistry program.

Even public universities which are dependent on the fortunes of the state financial system are able to convince state legislators that some needs cannot be deferred. For instance, the University of California at Berkeley was the only institution to be given a waiver during the freeze on all construction projects decreed by Governor Edmund G. Brown, Jr., in 1982. It was allowed to build a new microelectronic research facility (McDonald, 1982). The following year, the chancellor of the university successfully lobbied the legislature to release construction funds for a new biology building that was needed to reorganize the biology department on that campus (Trow, 1983). Recognizing that one of its departments was in trouble, Berkeley took extraordinary and successful means to obtain resources to correct the situation.

The less selective institutions changed their character by discontinuing unpopular courses and offering others that were more likely to appeal to students. Many started undergraduate business programs, while other grafted a graduate business program onto their undergraduate offerings. It is not clear to what extent these innovations maintained enrollments in individual schools.

We have few documented instances of declines in revenue of more than twenty-five percent. The only publicized occurrence is that of the City University of New York. In this instance, one-sixth of the full-time faculty was dismissed. The scope of course offerings for the system as a whole did not shrink, but some students were forced to register in more than one undergraduate college to get the courses they wanted. In at least one of the four-year colleges, there was a long wait for registration in the science courses required for applicants to medical schools.

During the financial crisis of the 1970s and early 1980s in the New York City, difficult decisions were made to keep the schools responsive to the needs of students: According to key documents about adjustments (kindly provided by Dean J. Magner of the Central Administration of the City University), Tenured faculty members in underenrolled programs were dismissed, while more junior staff members were retained in programs which the individual schools believed to be important and viable. Similarly in the Illinois higher education system, when total resources remained unchanged in constant dollars during the eight years 1974 to 1982, the resources allocated to computer sciences were allowed to triple and the health professions' budget was allowed to grow by 41 percent. These and other selective increases in professional courses were achieved with only slight declines in the budget of biological (5.9 percent) and physical sciences (1.2 percent) while mathematics and engineering budgets increased modestly in real terms. Programs in the humanities bore the brunt of the losses.

## Impact of Cutbacks on Location of Science Research

The reluctance of institutions to drop departments or change the scope of graduate instruction translates into relative stability of the location of research. The universities with the highest dollar grants for research in 1970 were almost identical to those in 1982. Nevertheless, the share of research, region by region, has changed significantly during the past fifteen years. (National Science Foundation, 1972-81).

Three states, Arizona, Maryland, and Texas, significantly strengthened the research capabilities of their public systems. In Arizona, both the University of Arizona and the remainder of the system spent considerably more on research and development during the mid-1980s than in any earlier period. In Maryland, between 1977 and 1984, the University of Maryland at College Park moved twenty notches up in the ranking of all colleges and universities, based on their expenditures on research and development. It now ranks nineteenth. In Texas, both the University of Texas in Austin and Texas A&M University increased their research and development outlays faster than the national average, and a new network of medical schools, such as the University of Texas Health Sciences Center at Dallas, became important research centers in the course of the past ten years. The proportion of federal funds in research and development outlays declined in both Maryland and Texas and remained relatively constant in Arizona. The University of Maryland was particularly successful in attracting industry funds for its research program. Industry now contributes nearly ten percent of the College Park research and development budget, double its share ten years ago.

All three states financed their institutions generously enough to allow internal funds to finance part of the growth in research and development. It is not clear how long this trend will continue. In 1985 and 1986, economic conditions in Texas deteriorated and the University was scheduled to have its budget cut just as much as the other functions in the state. Its revenues were further affected by a decline in royalties from offshore wells which benefited the university. Since the final appropriation for the institution was not set at the time of writing this report, it is too early to pass any judgment on the effect of these cuts on the Austin campus. As to the Arizona campus, no published information on long-range plans is available.

On the other hand, institutions in the so-called rust belt of Illinois, Indiana, Michigan, Ohio, and the Pennsylvania lost a share in the total research and development outlays. Their doctoral-granting institution's share, which declined slowly from 19 to 18 to 17 percent in 1970, 1975, and 1980, took a sharp drop to 14 percent in 1984. A significant part of this decline was due to a shift in federal funding away from the social sciences. The Universities of Chicago, Michigan and Pennsylvania State University were important performers of social science research and suffered from these cuts. In Michigan, the depression in the automobile industry resulted in no increase in research and development contributions from industry during the last five years, and, of course, translated itself into a decline in activity in real terms.

## Conclusion

All higher education institutions experienced difficulties in balancing their income and expenditures during the five years ending in 1984. These difficulties were caused mainly by the slowdown in the economy. During this period of penury, budgets were balanced mostly at the expense of faculty compensation. Other functions of the university, such as construction, renovation of facilities, and maintenance also suffered. Most institutions managed to protect their instructional programs and, as far as we could determine, shifted resources from declining programs to new, emerging fields, mostly in the hard sciences.

On the whole, scientists and engineers fared quite well during this period of slow growth and shortages of money. The number of full-time scientists (including social scientists) and engineers did not decline significantly in any institution and increased slowly in others. Much of the credit for this is due to the federal government which maintained research and development funding at a fairly high level. During the next decade, if the resources earmarked for instruction fail to accommodate the size of the current postsecondary establishment, the vitality of research universities will have to be maintained by generous infusions of research moneys. Other means will have to be found to preserve the science and engineering capabilities of teaching institutions.

## Will There Be Another Crisis?

The next expected threat to university finances is the decline in overall enrollments which started in 1984 and is likely to continue for close to a decade. There is no consensus on the possible magnitude of the decline in enrollments. A number of state boards of higher education have projected either level or slowly rising numbers of students, justifying these projections by assumptions of either higher participation rates of young persons 18 to 24, or growing rates of attendance of mature, mostly part-time, students.

These projections are highly optimistic. Current demographic projections do not anticipate the number of 18-24 year olds to increase until 1996, and a rather optimistic projection of enrollment places the number of FTE students in the year 2000 ten percent below the level of 1984. Decreases in enrollment due to demographic causes may be accentuated by a decline in interest in college education because the financial return for this investment is declining.

The decline in enrollment will affect higher education institutions unevenly, it is agreed. The most vulnerable ones are: (1) institutions in states where the number of 18–21 year olds has declined most, i.e. states in e Northeast and the upper Midwest ; (2) nonselective institutions which do not have much prestige; and (3) smaller, isolated, liberal arts colleges. By contrast, private institutions which are highly selective, such as Harvard, Yale, Chicago, etc., do not expect to have any trouble filling their freshmen classes, and neither do most of the flagship schools of state colleges, e.g. Berkeley in the University of California system, the University of Michigan at Ann Arbor, or the Austin campus of the University of Texas. By contrast, less-distinguished state universities and colleges and some liberal arts colleges have already experienced enrollment declines.

The prospect that enrollments may decline drastically are especially real for liberal arts schools. Among the current crop of freshmen, an increasing proportion shun such liberal arts majors as history or English and favor business or other practical subjects. The proportion of freshmen who planned to major in liberal arts subjects declined from 12 percent in 1975 to 8 percent in 1984. The proportion of freshmen planning to be physical science majors has remained relatively constant—18 percent in 1975 and 19 percent in 1984.

Institutional planners hesitate to forecast enrollment declines for individual institutions for fear of receiving the treatment usually given the messenger who brings bad news. As Frederick Balderston has stated repeatedly, most institutions prefer to devise schemes to beggar their neighbors rather than to plan for an orderly contraction.

The expected contraction of enrollments, two to four percent a year, and the consequent decline in tuition revenue and possibly state support, which is often calculated on a per-student basis, are not likely to affect the college and university budgets any more than the slow-down in economic growth in the early 1980s. However, the beggar-thy-neighbor policies of some schools may exacerbate some institutions' enrollment problems.

In Minnesota, where a twenty-three-percent decline in enrollment is anticipated, the Board of Higher Education convinced the state legislature to set appropriations for colleges and universities based on their enrollments two years before the budget cycle in question. This measure was designed to allow for an orderly contradiction of staffs and facilities on campuses with declining enrollments.

If university resources depend mainly on the number of students, a prolonged depression will be experienced by higher education, more serious than anything in the past fifty years. Retrenchment to meet temporary difficulties has a very different impact than permanent retrenchment to accommodate conditions of a declining industry.

No models of higher education finances is easily available for the next decade when enrollments are likely to decline. In preparing such simulations, a number of alternative scenarios would have to be considered. Will the price of resources in higher education rise faster than the cost of living? From 1930 to 1967, the cost of these resources increased two-and-a-half percent per year in real terms (O'Neill, 1973). Between the early 1970s and the mid 1980s, the increase in the price of these resources has been close to zero.

If resource costs resume their upward trend, it is possible to anticipate a postsecondary sector where (1) the wages of staff increase as fast as earnings in the total economy, and employment declines in proportion to enrollment, or (2) the wages of staff remain stagnant and the employment stabilizes at current levels.

The fewer students and the scantier resources will be distributed among roughly the same number of institutions. If past experience is any guide, it is highly unlikely that public sector institutions will close. Even in New York City, which experienced the most serious financial crisis of any system, with its budget cut by some thirty percent during the financial crisis of 1976 and 1977, local politics made it impossible to implement the City University administration's proposal to close one of the four-year schools and downgrade others to two-year status. In California, where community college enrollment declined by one-third after tuition was imposed, not one of the colleges closed its doors.

One would expect some closings among private-sector schools, especially those that are dependent on tuition. During the past decade, one four-year institution closed its doors or merged with another institution each year. Most of these institutions were small, with enrollments under five hundred students. None offered engineering programs. It appears that there is unbelievable tenacity among private institutions, and as long as they can attract a minimum number of students, their doors will remain open.

The staying power of weak or unpopular institutions may have an undesirable effect on the rest of the postsecondary sector. Fewer students are likely to enroll in the stronger institutions, and these institutions may find it more difficult to shift resources to meet students' changing demands for new majors. In the recent past, when resources were tight but enrollments were still rising, some institutions could no longer accommodate the demand for certain programs. Thus, Berkeley placed a ceiling on the number of students in engineering, and Iowa tried a novel approach to discouraging applications: the university extended the engineering bachelor's curriculum to five years.

Among administrators of research universities there is an abiding conviction that students follow resources for research and development. As long as the lion's share of funds for research and development comes from the federal government, the prospects of leading universities depend more on federal policy than on whether they are privately controlled or state institutions. Institutions with the most prestige and the leading research universities are generally believed to have a competitive edge in attracting both undergraduate and graduate students. But it is not certain that this advantage will hold during a prolonged period of decline in enrollments. No one wishes to discuss the circumstances which may weaken these institutions: a prolonged depression, federal fiscal austerity translated into cuts for research and development funds, and the decreased attractiveness of academic programs due to aging and disgruntled faculty.

The viability of public research universities will continue to depend on the level of state appropriations, determined by the levels of economic activity. Private research institutions also would benefit from prosperity. But in the final analysis it is the volume of federal funds which will determine whether all research universities prosper. The failure of either the executive or Congress to offer a convincing plan to balance the budget does not augur well for the long-range science policy of the government and, consequently, the health of these institutions.

It may not be enough for the prestigious schools, which have had less trouble attracting students, to maintain current enrollment levels. In her report to the faculty, Hanna H. Gray, the President of the University of Chicago, mentioned the university's plans to increase its under-graduate enrollment and also attempt to attract more students to its graduate programs (Gray, 1986b). The University of Chicago has the highest proportion of tenured instructional staff in arts and sciences of the six leading private universities: 82 percent, compared to 81 percent at Stanford, 69 percent at Princeton, 64 percent at Harvard, 59 percent at Columbia, and 57 percent at Yale. To afford an infusion of new blood, the university is forced to expand.

The high proportion of tenured faculty, and the consequently high costs, are as real a threat as any of the others to research university finances. The intellectual imperatives by which these universities live will force them to hire new staff to make sure that their research capability is preserved. These new hires may very well destroy the newly achieved balance between revenues and expenses.

A financial crisis in higher education is likely to come about as enrollments decline and schools start competing with each other. The united front of college presidents may disintegrate, and, horrors of horrors, both state and federal lawmakers may dare to look at the costs and benefits of instruction beyond high school.

## Note

* In this chapter all financial and enrollment figures are for the academic year ending in June of the year cited. Statistics prior to 1966 are from the U.S. Bureau of the Census, *Historical Statistics*. For later years data are based on U.S. Department of Health, Education and Welfare, *Higher Education General Information Survey*, 1966-79, and U.S. Department of Education, *Higher Education General Information Survey*, 1980-85. Enrollment figures are from the opening fall enrollment of that year. Income statistics are from the U.S. Department of Commerce, *Survey of Current Business* for each appropriate year. The higher education price indexes, developed by D. Kent Halstead (Halstead, 1985a) were used to convert current to constant dollars. The series is updated and published currently by Research Associates of Washington, D.C. Additional sources are listed with the tables and described in the text.

# The Economic Prospects for American Higher Education (1992)

## Arthur M. Hauptman

## Introduction

For American higher education, the 1980s—particularly the latter half of the decade—were marked by moderate enrollment increases and rapid resource growth. But there is good reason to believe this growth will not continue during the first half of the 1990s. And although enrollments probably will increase in the latter half of the 1990s with renewed growth in the traditional college-age population, the prospects for resource growth throughout the decade are not so bright.

This paper assesses the level of resources that colleges and universities might reasonably expect to have access to over the next 30 years. Such a forecasting exercise can be a daunting task, however, in that the track record of predicting trends in American higher education over the past several decades has not been stellar. Many observers in the 1970s and 1980s, for example, missed the mark on the demand for faculty and the growth in enrollments. Past estimates of future resource availability have been similarly inaccurate. With such a record, how much credence can one reasonably give to predictions regarding the economic state of higher education some three decades hence? To provide some cover for this forecasting exercise, this paper presents future resource level estimates based on several possibilities regarding national economic activity, the degree of public confidence in higher education, and enrollment growth.

The bottom line conclusion of this paper is that the resources available to higher education will depend principally on the economy's overall growth. If, for example, the American economy does well over the next 30 years, American higher education can reasonably expect to share in the additional resources created through sustained economic growth. Even if public confidence in higher education is not high, robust overall economic growth will still funnel more resources to higher education. If, instead, the economy limps along at a modest pace, the resources available to higher education can be expected to be sluggish as well. And if some of the ominous signs on the macroeconomic horizon materialize, then colleges and universities, like many other sectors of the American economy, will be in for a rude awakening, as contraction and readjustment will replace the economics and politics of growth that have characterized the nation since the end of World War II.

Many economists expect that America, at best, will experience modest economic growth in the future. If these predictions are accurate, then higher education must think hard about how it can better use its resources. Colleges and universities will no longer be able to depend on a growing economy to bring in more resources. But neither should they view the economy as something totally outside of their control. Instead, institutions should now be considering ways in which they can enhance the rate of national economic growth—through the quality of their graduates and the research they sponsor, to mention two. More and better college graduates will lead to a more productive economy. The research and knowledge advances made in campus laboratories and classrooms typically translate into technological and economic progress.

More than macroeconomic conditions affect resource levels of higher education, however. Resource levels also will be heavily influenced by the degree of public confidence in higher education. If legislators and the public believe that higher education is doing a good job, colleges and universities will be able to charge higher tuitions and receive a larger portion of the public-resources pie than if the recent concerns about the direction of American higher education intensify over the next several decades.

To address these issues, this paper is organized in three sections. First, it examines some historical relationships between higher education and general economic trends. For example, changes in higher education resources and enrollments since 1920 indicate that over time higher education growth has been uneven. The second section projects possible resource levels available to higher education over the next 30 years based on various projections of macroeconomic conditions, public confidence levels, and enrollment growth. The final section describes how higher education might best prepare itself for the future, given the uncertainty over resources, and examines what higher education can do to affect both the future growth of the economy and the level of public confidence in the enterprise. An appendix, which looks at the accuracy of past higher education forecasts, is provided to remind the reader of the fragility of these predictions.

# Section 1

## Patterns of Enrollments and Resources Since 1920

The growth of the American higher education enterprise, in terms of both resource levels and the number of students, has been highly variable over time. From one decade to the next, growth has not been uniform. (This section, and the paper generally, examines patterns in terms of decades, not because events occur neatly in ten-year increments but because this demarcation seems to be helpful in discerning general trends.) In predicting what future resource levels may be, the uneven patterns of past growth make it inadvisable simply to look at the immediately preceding period of time and then extrapolate into the future.

Chart 1 . . . compares the growth in faculty and enrollments in each decade since 1920. As the chart indicates, the numbers of students and faculty have not grown at similar rates in each decade. For example, in the 1960s, enrollments more than doubled, while the number of faculty members grew by less than one-fifth. The number of faculty clearly did not keep up with the growth in students in the 1960s, which may help to explain the large-scale expansion in federal fellowships for graduate students during that time. Other than the 1960s, enrollments grew fastest in the 1920s and 1940s (after the end of World War II). By contrast, in the 1930s and 1950s, the number of faculty grew much faster than the number of students, with a resultant decrease in student-faculty ratios. In the 1970s and 1980s, the number of students and faculty grew at roughly comparable rates. (One important trend missed in this highly simplified accounting of students and faculty is the increased proportion of both part-time students and part-time faculty. Thus, one should not put too much credence in these changes in student-faculty ratios without making some adjustment for full-time equivalency.)

Chart 2 . . . indicates the growth in revenues for each decade between 1920 and 1990. As the chart shows, the growth in resources has been erratic over time. In the 1960s, revenues in current dollars and in real terms grew fastest, consistent with the notion that the 1960s represented a "golden age" for American higher education. The 1920s, 1940s and the 1950s also represented periods of substantial revenue growth in real terms.

Charts 3 and 4 . . . indicate the growth in resources per student and per faculty member. Revenues per student in real terms grew fastest in the 1950s; the 1980s had the next highest rate of growth. This contrasts to the 1970s and the 1930s when resources per student actually declined in real terms. Revenues per faculty member grew fastest in the 1960s, with the 1980s once again being the decade with the second fastest growth, and the 1970s and the 1930s showing real declines.

Another way to examine these patterns is to compare the relative growth in the numbers of students with the number of degrees granted, as indicated in Table 1 (page 9). In the 1920s, 1930s, and 1940s, the growth in degrees far outpaced the growth in the number of students. In the 1950s, enrollments grew faster than degrees—at least at the bachelor's degree level. Since the 1960s, the growth in enrollments and degrees have tracked fairly closely.

How do these trends in higher education relate to what is happening in the economy? The most typical way to relate higher education to overall economic activity is to calculate higher education expenditures or revenues as a percentage of the Gross National Product. This measure provides a perspective of the size of higher education as a part of the overall economy. Higher education's share of the economy also provides a rough sense of both the degree of public confidence and the relative level of participation in higher education. The higher the proportion of GNP that is spent on higher education, the greater confidence there is in what higher education is doing and/or the larger the percentage of the population that is enrolled in higher education

Since 1970, higher education expenditures have constituted at least 2.5 percent of the GNP, as Table 2 . . . indicates. Before the 1970s, this figure was decidedly lower, but not because there was

### Table 1
### Trends in Faculty, Students, and Degrees, 1920 to 1990
#### (numbers in thousands)

|      | Faculty | Enrollment | Student/ Faculty Ratio | Bachelor's | Master's | Doctorates |
|------|---------|-----------|------------------------|-----------|----------|-----------|
| 1920 | 49      | 598       | 12.2                   | 49        | 4        | 0.6       |
| 1930 | 82      | 1101      | 13.4                   | 122       | 15       | 2.3       |
| 1940 | 147     | 1494      | 10.2                   | 186       | 27       | 3.3       |
| 1950 | 247     | 2659      | 10.8                   | 432       | 58       | 6.4       |
| 1960 | 381     | 3640      | 9.6                    | 392       | 74       | 9.8       |
| 1970 | 450     | 8004      | 17.8                   | 793       | 208      | 29.9      |
| 1980 | 675     | 11570     | 17.1                   | 929       | 298      | 32.6      |
| 1990 | 755     | 13715     | 17.8                   | 1050      | 324      | 38        |

#### Percentage Change, Decade to Decade

|       | Faculty | Enrollment | Student/ Faculty Ratio | Bachelor's | Master's | Doctorates |
|-------|---------|-----------|------------------------|-----------|----------|-----------|
| 1920s | 67%     | 84%       | 10%                    | 149%      | 275%     | 283%      |
| 1930s | 79%     | 36%       | -24%                   | 52%       | 80%      | 43%       |
| 1940s | 68%     | 78%       | 6%                     | 132%      | 115%     | 94%       |
| 1950s | 54%     | 37%       | -11%                   | -9%       | 28%      | 53%       |
| 1960s | 18%     | 120%      | 86%                    | 102%      | 181%     | 205%      |
| 1970s | 50%     | 45%       | -4%                    | 17%       | 43%      | 9%        |
| 1980s | 12%     | 16%       | 4%                     | 12%       | 7%       | 17%       |

**Chart 1**
**Average Annual Change in Enrollments and Number of Faculty, by Decade from 1920 to 1990**

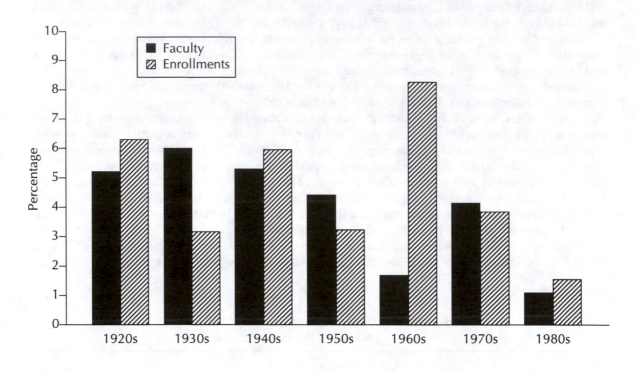

**Chart 2**
**Average Annual Change in Higher Education Revenues, by Decade from 1920 to 1990**

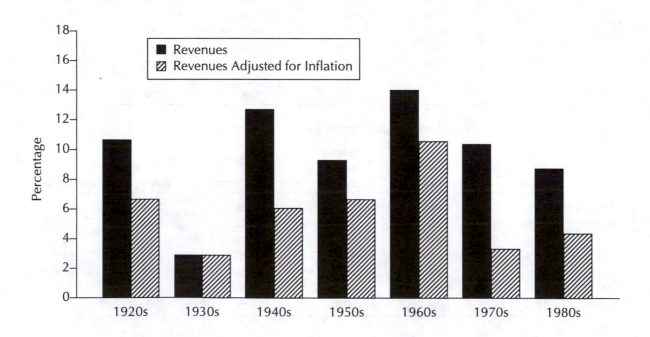

**Chart 3**
**Average Annual Change in Revenues Per Student and Per Faculty Member, by Decade from 1920 to 1990**

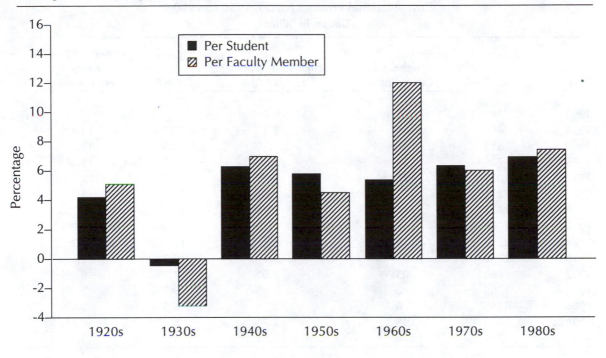

**Chart 4**
**Average Annual Change in Revenues Per Student and Per Faculty Member, Adjusted for Inflation, by Decade from 1920 to 1990**

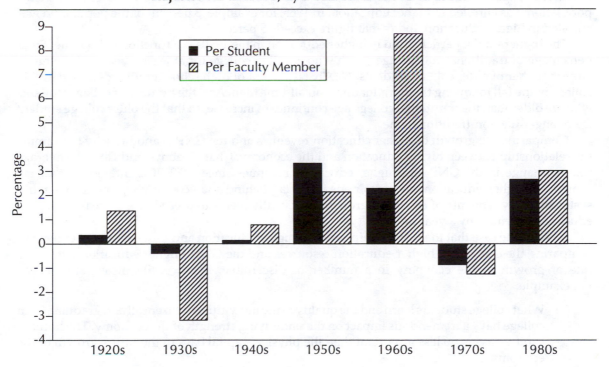

**Table 2**
**Higher Education Expenditures and**
**Gross National Product (GNP), 1950 to 1990**
**(Dollars in Billions)**

| Year | GNP | Higher Ed Expenditures | Higher Ed Spending as % of GNP | Annual Percentage Change In: GNP | Annual Percentage Change In: HE Revenues |
|------|-----|------------------------|-------------------------------|-----|-----|
| 1950 | 288 | 2 | 0.8% | | |
| 1955 | 406 | 5 | 1.1% | 7.1% | 13.4% |
| 1960 | 515 | 8 | 1.6% | 4.9% | 12.2% |
| 1965 | 705 | 16 | 2.2% | 6.5% | 14.3% |
| 1970 | 1015 | 28 | 2.7% | 7.6% | 12.0% |
| 1972 | 1213 | 32 | 2.6% | 9.3% | 7.7% |
| 1974 | 1473 | 40 | 2.7% | 10.2% | 11.7% |
| 1976 | 1782 | 47 | 2.6% | 10.0% | 8.9% |
| 1978 | 2250 | 55 | 2.5% | 12.4% | 8.2% |
| 1980 | 2732 | 71 | 2.6% | 10.2% | 12.9% |
| 1982 | 3166 | 83 | 2.6% | 7.7% | 8.8% |
| 1984 | 3765 | 98 | 2.6% | 9.1% | 8.6% |
| 1986 | 4268 | 116 | 2.7% | 6.5% | 8.6% |
| 1988 | 5010 | 135 | 2.7% | 8.3% | 7.9% |
| 1990 | 5527 | 148 | 2.7% | 5.0% | 5.4% |

less confidence in higher education—if anything, public confidence in higher education was greater in the 1960s than it is today. More important in explaining the lower proportion of GNP' devoted to higher education in the 1960s and before is that a much smaller percentage of the population was enrolled in higher education. In 1965, for example, 3 percent of the population was enrolled in higher education; today that figure exceeds 5 percent.

The higher rate of participation in higher education in the 1990s is a function of both the larger percentage of traditional college-age youth who enroll in college for at least a year and the much larger number of older college students. Nearly 60 percent of high school graduates now enroll in college in the fall following their graduation—an all-time high. And the number of college students who are older than the traditional college age continues to increase, so that the older college student is no longer the non-traditional one.

Comparing the growth of higher education revenues and the GNP is another way to examine the relationship between higher education and the economy. Chart 5, above, indicates the average rate of change in the GNP and higher education revenues since 1972. It is interesting that the growth in higher education revenues appears to lag behind the economy's growth in a fairly systematic way. The rate of economic growth consistently seems to precede the increase in higher education revenues by a year or two.

It is also the case that the relationship between higher education and the economy goes beyond comparing the changes in higher education resources and the GNP. Higher education affects the rate of growth in the economy in a number of discernible, if not easily measurable, ways. For example:

- What college students learn and the quality of the individuals who enroll and graduate from college have a tremendous impact on the underlying strength of the economy. The human-capital base is no less important than the physical-capital base to the future growth of the economy.

- Colleges and universities employ several million individuals, including more than 700,000 faculty members, representing 2 to 3 percent of the total work force. In many localities, colleges and universities are the largest employers and a major economic force in the community.

- More than half of all basic research in the country is conducted on university campuses or with university affiliation. The list of discoveries and inventions stemming from this research is staggering.

## Section II

### The Resource Prospects for the Next Three Decades

This section explores the question of how fast the resources available to higher education are likely to grow over the next 30 years. The short and overly simplistic answer to this question is: It depends critically on the future economy, which affects all of the major sources of financing for higher education. The state of the economy, for example, largely determines the level of state financial support, which remains the single largest source of funding for higher education. Roughly 30 percent of all higher education revenues currently comes from the states, mostly as general support to public institutions. (A much smaller proportion of state funds for higher education is devoted to

**Chart 5**
**Annual Percentage Change in GNP and Higher Education Revenues, 1970 to 1990**

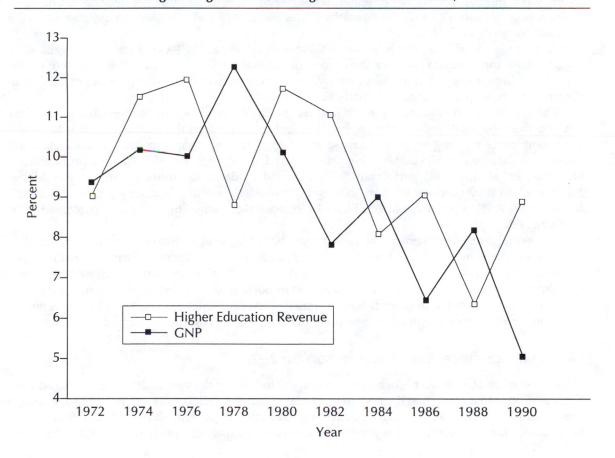

state student-aid programs, support for independent institutions, support of research, and other appropriations for designated purposes.)

When the economy performs well, state revenues tend to rise faster, and higher education benefits. Because public college tuitions are the bridge between what the state provides and institutional budgets, tuitions at public colleges tend to rise less sharply during good economic times when state funds are more available. The basic problem with the current system of state finance of higher education arises when the economy goes sour. During a recession, state funds tend to shrink, accelerating tuition increases. The unfortunate consequence is that public college tuitions increase most when students and their families can least afford to pay the higher prices.

The economy, of course, also substantially affects the growth of federal revenues and spending, including expenditures for higher education. For the past several decades, policy makers have depended on a strong economy to "grow" out of the federal budget deficit. Projections of a federal surplus sometime in the future have been regularly produced based on an assumption of a strong economy. Yet, despite the robust economy for most of the 1980s, the deficit grew by historic proportions.

Economic growth also determines the growth in family incomes, which affects the ability of parents and students to pay for college. Presumably, the more that income grows, the greater the ability of parents and students to pay and the higher that colleges and universities can set tuitions.

A good economy also can affect the willingness of students to pay, since a good economy usually means a better job market for college graduates. One reason families may have been willing to pay higher tuitions in the 1980s was that the wage premium between college and high school graduates widened considerably, serving as an indicator that attending college was worth the financial outlay. Also, a healthy economy usually translates into more voluntary giving and a strong stock market, both of which enhance the size of college endowments over time. The other major source of funding for higher education, sales and services, also is likely to increase when the national economy does well.

As was discussed in the introduction to this paper, however, the level of resources available to higher education depends on more than economic growth. Another factor is the degree of public confidence in higher education. Additionally, enrollment growth over time plays a critical role in determining how much money is provided to each student.

The link between resources growth and the public's confidence in higher education is less obvious than the relationship between funding and the growth in the economy, but it is no less important. State funding tends to increase at a higher rate when governors and legislators are satisfied with the education that is being provided and when there is confidence in administrators' and trustees' abilities and performance. Parents and students are more willing to pay higher tuitions when they perceive they are getting their money's worth. Voluntary giving by alumni, foundations, and corporations also is likely to increase more when the system is perceived to be working well.

The pattern of enrollments over time affects both the level of overall funding provided to higher education and the amount provided to each student. Formal funding formulas that incorporate enrollment levels as a critical variable are used in more than half the states; in most other states, enrollments are a more informal, but nonetheless important, component in the funding equation. Thus, at the state level, enrollments tend to translate directly into dollars. The growth in enrollments in turn becomes a critical component in determining the resources available per student.

## Simulating Resource Availability in the Year 2020

What level of resources can higher education expect to have in the year 2020? One way to address this question is to assume that the resources available to higher education will rise in proportion to the economy's growth so that higher education maintains its current share of the economy over time. Using this fairly simplistic approach, if the economy grows at a fairly robust rate of 3 percent per year in real terms, then the total spending for higher education would grow from about $150 billion in 1990 to roughly $365 billion (in 1990 dollars) by 2020. By the same token, if the economy does not grow at all in real terms over the next 30 years, then higher education would still have the same $150 billion in 1990 dollars when the year 2020 rolls around.

But the share of the economy devoted to higher education may well change for a variety of reasons, including possible shifts in public confidence in higher education and changing enrollment patterns. One way to factor each of these considerations into the calculation of future resource levels is to make an educated guess on the economy's future growth, the level of public confidence, and the growth of enrollments over the next three decades, and to estimate the level of resources produced. Given the degree of uncertainty regarding each of these three factors, however, it is more reasonable to use a range of possibilities than to rely on a single point estimate.

To this end, a simple model is presented here that estimates the level of resources per student for higher education under three different scenarios of economic growth, public confidence, and enrollment growth.

The three overall economic scenarios used in the model are as follows

- "The Sky's the Limit" projects robust economic growth of 3 percent per year in real terms throughout the next three decades. Such growth would be high relative to the average in this country over the last 50 years.

- "Muddling Through" projects an average real economic growth rate throughout the three decades of roughly 1.5 percent per year. This scenario assumes periods of robust growth interspersed with several severe recessions.

- "The Roof Caves In" projects no economic growth over the 30-year period as a result of intensified global competition and the consequence of years of federal deficit financing.

The level of resources devoted to higher education also will depend on the degree of public confidence in the effectiveness of colleges and universities. This also can be expressed in terms of high, medium, and low scenarios.

- A high level of confidence would be reminiscent of the early and mid-1960s, prior to the protests later in that decade. Some observers refer to this period as the so-called golden age of American higher education.

- A medium level of confidence describes the current situation, where American higher education is regarded as the best in the world, but nagging doubts about its future direction have driven down confidence.

- A low level of confidence may result if the current barrage of concerns remains largely unaddressed, and the traditional American faith in the value of higher education diminishes.

It is difficult, however, to quantify these different degrees of public confidence in higher education. After all, no single index is available that measures changes in the nation's attitude toward its colleges and universities.

One possible gauge of public confidence, however, is the percentage of GNP devoted to higher education. For example, it might be the case that in an era of good feeling toward higher education, such as the early 1960s, a higher-than-average share of GNP was devoted to higher education. Regrettably, this was not the case, as the percentage of GNP for higher education was substantially lower in the 1960s than it has been in the last two decades. As noted earlier, this is largely a function of a smaller percentage of the population being enrolled in higher education at that time.

What is needed, then, is a measure of higher education's share of the economy that takes into account changes in enrollment patterns over time. One such measure is higher education spending per student as a percent of GNP per capita. This percentage, which should be viewed more as an index than as a real measure of anything, correlates nicely with the perceived changes in the

**Table 3**
**Higher Education Spending Per Student as a Percentage of GNP Per Capita**

| Year | GNP Per Capita | HE Spending Per FTE Student | Higher Ed Spending per Student as % of GNP per Capital |
|------|----------------|----------------------------|--------------------------------------------------------|
| 1950 | 1907 | 1412 | 74% |
| 1955 | 2461 | 1667 | 68% |
| 1960 | 2861 | 1933 | 68% |
| 1965 | 3653 | 2660 | 73% |
| 1970 | 4951 | 3707 | 75% |
| 1972 | 5804 | 3575 | 62% |
| 1974 | 6915 | 4255 | 62% |
| 1976 | 8212 | 4671 | 57% |
| 1978 | 10181 | 5595 | 55% |
| 1980 | 12088 | 6882 | 57% |
| 1982 | 13706 | 8022 | 59% |
| 1984 | 15953 | 9204 | 58% |
| 1986 | 17783 | 11230 | 63% |
| 1988 | 20533 | 12325 | 60% |
| 1990 | 22100 | 14200 | 64% |

public's perception of higher education. As Table 3 indicates, from 1950 to 1970, higher education spending per student ranged between 65 and 75 percent of GNP per capita. Since 1970, the figure has ranged between 55 and 65 percent. Thus, in this simulation, we use 75 percent as a measure of a high degree of public confidence in higher education, 60 percent as a medium level, and 50 percent as a low level.

In terms of enrollment growth, the three scenarios used are:

- High enrollment growth is 2 percent per year—a figure at the high range of what can happen in the future given present participation rates among both traditional-age and older college students.

- Moderate enrollment growth is assumed to be 1 percent per year—akin to 1980s gains in the numbers of college students.

- For this exercise, we have assumed that a low rate of growth is no enrollment increase at all.

Possible future resource levels for American higher education can therefore be analyzed and projected according to changes in each of these three factors, as indicated in Tables 4, 5, and 6. For purposes of this discussion, current fund expenditures per full-time-equivalent (FTE) student are used as the measure of the current level of resources, rather than an aggregate level of resources. This measure shows the effect of enrollment growth on the amount of resources available per student. In these estimates, the real rate of growth in GNP per capita is the indicator of possible growth in the economy. Assuming 1 percent per year growth in population, annual growth in GNP per capita will be roughly 1 percent less than the growth in the GNP.

Table 4 indicates the results of the simulation that assumes a moderate rate of increase in enrollments of 1 percent per year over the next 30 years. Several interesting trends emerge from this simulation. First and foremost, the future path of the economy appears to be a far more important factor in determining the future level of resources available to higher education than the foreseeable changes in levels of public confidence.

As the table shows, no matter what level of public confidence is assumed, the amount of resources per student for higher education will increase in real terms if the economy grows robustly over the next 30 years. If public confidence levels are also high, then the amount of resources per student will more than double in real terms between 1990 and 2020, from the 1990 level of $14,200 to nearly $30,000 in 2020 (an increase of 110 percent in real terms). But even if public confidence in higher education is low at that time, the amount of resources per student (roughly $20,000) would be 40 percent higher than current levels.

Conversely, what happens if economic growth is nonexistent over the next three decades? Resources per student will decline no matter how high the level of public confidence is in higher education. If low economic growth combines with low levels of public confidence, the amount of resources per student would drop by 42 percent by the year 2020 in real terms. If public confidence is high, however, with no economic growth, resources per student will still be 13 percent lower in 2020 than in 1990.

Tables 5 and 6 . . . indicate the future level of resources per student under the alternative enrollment growth scenarios of 2 percent per year and no enrollment growth, respectively. Although the dollar figures differ from the projections using moderate enrollment growth assumptions, the relative influence of the economy and public confidence levels on resource availability is similar. If enrollment growth is high, as shown in Table 5, economic growth and public confidence in higher education would both have to be at least moderate for resources per student to grow over time. Low levels of either public confidence or economic growth would lead to a real reduction in resources per student.

With no growth in enrollment, the amount of resources per student naturally would be higher (see Table 6 . . .) than under higher enrollment scenarios. With high economic growth and high levels of public confidence in higher education, resources per student would nearly triple in real terms to more than $40,000 by 2020 if enrollments do not increase. Unlike the other enrollment scenerios, however, with no growth in enrollment, resources per student would grow even if there were no economic growth, as long as public confidence is high. But a combination of low or moderate levels of economic growth and public confidence will result in only modest increases or possibly decreases in resources per student, if enrollments do not grow.

The importance of the economy to the future growth of higher education resources is confirmed by projections made by Michael McPherson and Morton Schapiro in *Keeping College Affordable*, a book recently published by the Brookings Institution. The authors produce estimates of the tuition dependence of different types of institutions under a variety of assumptions, including the economy's performance. For public four-year institutions, tuition dependence grows from the current 20 percent of total revenues to more than 40 percent by the year 2010 if the economy is weak. If the economy is strong over the 20-year period, however, McPherson and Schapiro estimate that tuition dependence will drop to 12 percent. Similarly, for private four-year institutions, a weak economy increases tuition dependence from 60 percent in 1990 to 68 percent in 2010, while tuition dependence drops to 53 percent in a strong economy.

McPherson and Schapiro provide similar projections for the affordability of college under a variety of economic assumptions. They estimate that the ratio of net price to family income for students at public four-year institutions would rise from 9 percent in 1990 to 15 percent in 2010 if the economy is weak over the next 20 years, but the ratio declines by roughly half, to 4.6 percent, if the economy is strong. At private four-year institutions, where affordability is obviously of greater concern, this ratio would increase from 18 percent in 1990 to 28 percent in 2010 with a weak economy, but drops to 13 percent in a strong economy.

One final note on the level of future resource needs: It may well be the case that the necessary amount of resources to educate a student is higher now than what was needed previously. A number of observers have argued that the changing characteristics of college students—more of them now are lower income, older, and part-time—have led over time to higher costs per student as

**Table 4**
**Resource Levels Available to Higher Education in the**
**Year 2020 Assuming 1 Percent Per Year Growth in Enrollments**
(Stated in terms of 1990 Dollars)

| | |
|---|---|
| 1990 Resources per Student | $14,200 |
| 1990 GNP per Capita | $22,100 |
| Enrollment Growth per Year | 1% |

**Economic Growth Projections—Annual Real Rate of Growth in GNP per Capita**

| | | High | Medium | Low |
|---|---|---|---|---|
| Public Confidence Levels<br>Resources per Student<br>as a % of GNP per Capita | | 3% | 1.50% | 0% |
| High | 75% | $29,849 | $19,222 | $12,297 |
| Medium | 60% | $23,879 | $15,377 | $ 9,838 |
| Low | 50% | $19,899 | $12,815 | $ 8,198 |

*Change from 1990 Levels*
**Economic Growth Projections—Annual Real Rate of Growth in GNP per Capita**

| | | High | Medium | Low |
|---|---|---|---|---|
| Public Confidence Levels<br>Resources per Student<br>as a % of GNP per Capita | | 3% | 1 50% | 0% |
| High | 75% | 110% | 35% | -1 3% |
| Medium | 60% | 68% | 8% | -31% |
| Low | 50% | 40% | -10% | - 42% |

colleges have sought to meet their need for enhanced services. To the extent these trends in student characteristics continue, one can surmise that the level of resources needed to provide the same education will increase over time. If this is true, it will not be sufficient to maintain the current level of resources per student in real terms simply to ensure that the quality of the education provided remains the same. Additional resources over current levels may be required just to stay even in terms of educational quality.

It also is possible, however, that the opposite result could occur. Colleges and universities, faced with pressures from all sides, could react by slashing the amount of resources invested per student, increasing class sizes, increasing faculty teaching loads, keeping faculty and other personnel salary increases below inflation, and cutting many of the services that were expanded during the 1980s. In short, adversity in the 1990s could reverse the increased resources gained in the mid- to late-1980s.

# Section III

## Preparing For the Future

Uncertainty over the level of resources that will be available to higher education in the future should have at least two effects on the thinking of college trustees, administrators, and others involved in higher education. One effect is that colleges and universities should be doing more in

## Table 5
## Resource Levels Available to Higher Education in the
## Year 2020 Assuming 2 Percent Per Year Growth in Enrollments
### (Stated in terms of 1990 Dollars)

| | |
|---|---|
| 1990 Resources per Student | $14,200 |
| 1990 GNP per Capita | $22,100 |
| Enrollment Growth per Year | 2% |

### Economic Growth Projections—Annual Real Rate of Growth in GNP per Capita

| | | High | Medium | Low |
|---|---|---|---|---|
| Public Confidence Levels Resources per Student as a % of GNP per Capital | | 3% | 1.50% | 0% |
| High | 75% | $22,211 | $14,303 | $ 9,151 |
| Medium | 60% | $17,769 | $11,442 | $ 7,320 |
| Low | 50% | $14,807 | $ 9,535 | $ 6,100 |

### Change from 1990 Levels
### Economic Growth Projections—Annual Real Rate of Growth in GNP per Capita

| | | High | Medium | Low |
|---|---|---|---|---|
| Public Confidence Levels Resources per Student as a % of GNP per Capita | | 3% | 1.50% | 0% |
| High | 75% | 56% | 1% | -36% |
| Medium | 60% | 25% | -19% | -48% |
| Low | 50% | 4% | -33% | -57% |

the way of long-range planning based on the wide range of possible resource levels that may be available in the future. The other is that colleges and universities should be giving greater consideration to how they can increase their resources, either by fueling economic growth or by taking steps to improve the level of public confidence in higher education, thereby paving the way for more substantial future levels of resources.

It seems clear that higher education cannot plan on enjoying in the near term or in the foreseeable future the same growth in resources that occurred in the 1980s. In the short term, the economic recession and the continuing criticisms of higher education are likely to limit resource growth. In the longer term, resource constraints will be imposed through heightened global economic competition, more demands on both federal and state dollars, and an unwillingness or inability of an increasing number of families and students to pay increasing tuitions, among other reasons.

In the face of these fiscal realities, college officials should be thinking harder about better ways to use available resources. The next several decades will most likely entail making more difficult choices than in the past. To help in making these choices, it will be critical to plan ahead, not to be caught off guard by developments that could have been predicted many years before. Most colleges and universities no doubt have long range plans of one form or another, but it is worth asking: How seriously are these plans developed and debated within the institution? I expect in far too many cases the answer is: Not very much.

### Table 6
### Resource Levels Available to Higher Education in
### the Year 2020 Assuming No Growth in Enrollments
#### (Stated in terms of 1990 Dollars)

| | |
|---|---|
| 1990 Resources per Student | $14,200 |
| 1990 GNP per Capita | $22,100 |
| Enrollment Growth per Year | 0% |

#### Economic Growth Projections—Annual Real Rate of Growth in GNP per Capital

| | | High | Medium | Low |
|---|---|---|---|---|
| Public Confidence Levels Resources per Student as a % of GNP per Capita | | 3% | 1.50% | 0% |
| High | 75% | $40,232 | $25,908 | $16,575 |
| Medium | 60% | $32,186 | $20,726 | $13,260 |
| Low | 50% | $26,821 | $17,272 | $11,050 |

#### *Change from 1990 Levels*
#### Economic Growth Projections—Annual Real Rate of Growth in GNP per Capital

| | | High | Medium | Low |
|---|---|---|---|---|
| Public Confidence Levels Resources per Student as a % of GNP per Capital | | 3% | 1.50% | 0% |
| High | 75% | 183% | 82% | 17% |
| Medium | 60% | 126% | 46% | -7% |
| Low | 50% | 89% | 22% | -22% |

# Appendix

## The Perils of Forecasting in Higher Education

Analysts of higher education in the second half of the 20th century cannot take great pride in their ability to predict the path which the enterprise took in recent decades. Several major trends have either not been predicted or the predicted results have been quite contrary to what actually happened. These mispredicted trends include the rate of growth in enrollments beginning after the Second World War and continuing through the 1960s; the oversupply of faculty which occurred in the 1970s; and the unexpected growth in resources in the second half of the 1980s.

The purpose of this appendix is to remind the reader of the fragility of these forecasts by comparing some predictions for the condition of higher education in 1990 that were made at the beginning of the 1980s and comparing them to what actually happened in 1990. In this context, the following charts compare the forecasts for the 1990 academic year that were made in 1982 by the Department of Education's National Center for Education Statistics with the actual numbers. These projections included high, intermediate, and low alternative estimates for enrollments, faculty, degrees granted, and current fund expenditures. The analysis presented here also touches upon 1990 projections that were made by the Department of Education as recently as 1985.

What the charts indicate is that in several cases, and particularly in the area of finance, the actual 1990 numbers fell outside of any of the projected ranges. In other instances, the actual numbers were in the range of prediction, but not particularly close to the mid-point estimate.

## Full-Time Equivalent Enrollment

The actual full-time equivalent enrollment of 9.9 million in 1990 fell closest to the 1982 high alternative estimate for 1990 of 10.4 million. Interestingly, 1982 predictions for enrollments in 1990 ended up being far more accurate than projections that were made three years later in 1985. The 1985 range of projections was between 7.6 million and 9.6 million, which were exceeded by the actual 1990 FTE enrollments.

## Faculty

The actual number of 1990 faculty, 762,000, fell between the 1982 projection's low and intermediate ranges (723,000–799,000), while the high alternative projection of 986,000 exceeded the actual faculty total by 225,000. In this case, the 1985 high projection of 764,000 almost exactly equaled the actual 1990 total.

## Degrees Granted

In projecting the number of *bachelor's degrees* granted, the 1982 projections for 1990 were slightly more accurate than those made in 1985, although both were reasonably close to the actual figures. The 1982 high alternative of 1,054,000 was very close to the actual 1,050,000 degrees awarded and the 1985 high alternative of 1,038,000 slightly undershot the actual 1990 total.

The 1982 and 1985 predictions of 1990 *master's degrees* granted were quite accurate. The 324,000 masters degrees granted in 1990 matched the 1985 predicted high alternative of 322,000 and fell between the 1982 intermediate and high projections (303,000 and 367,000).

The low, intermediate, and high 1990 projections from 1982 and 1985 for *doctorates* granted differed little. The actual number granted in 1990, 38,000, fell between the intermediate and high estimates.

## Current Fund Expenditures

The 1982 projections for 1990 current fund expenditures turned out to be highly inaccurate. (The 1985 projection report did not include current fund expenditures). The low and high estimates were $53 billion and $74 billion, but the actual 1990 current fund expenditures stated in terms of 1980 dollars were $92 billion, far exceeding projected levels. The many variables involved in forecasting make it an inexact science, and this variance is the reason why high, intermediate, and low alternatives are presented. But the fact that many actual 1990 numbers fell outside of projected ranges is testimony to the uncertainty of the future state of higher education and should give great pause to those who attempt to predict future trends.

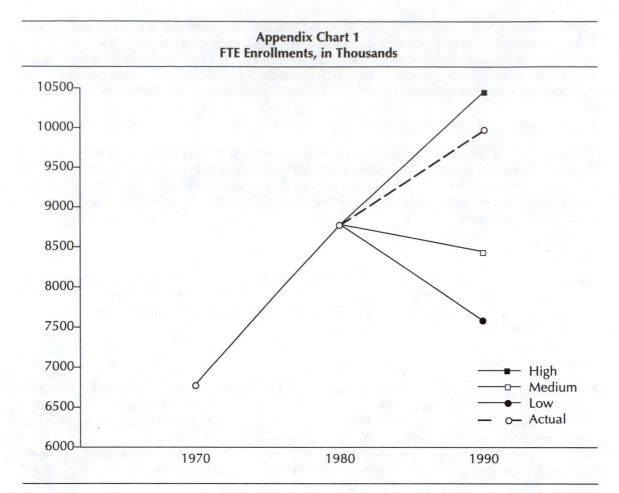

**Appendix Chart 1**
**FTE Enrollments, in Thousands**

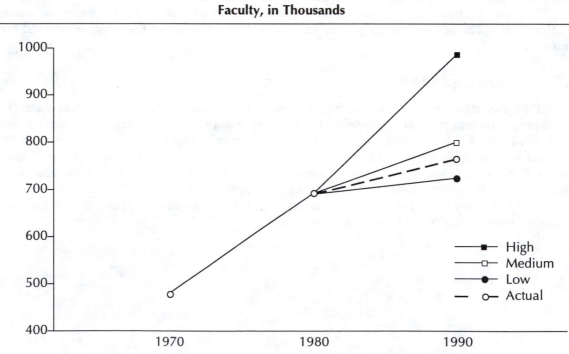

**Faculty, in Thousands**

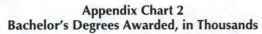

## Appendix Chart 2
## Bachelor's Degrees Awarded, in Thousands

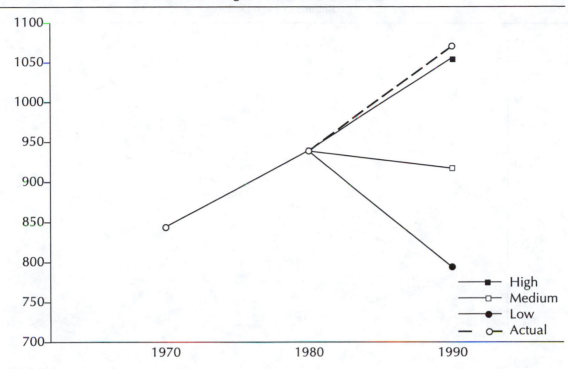

## Master's Degrees Awarded, in Thousands

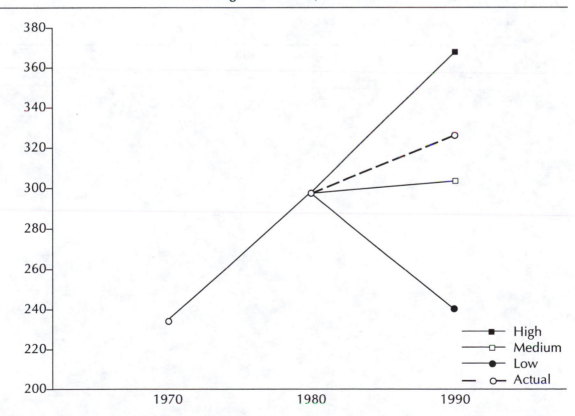

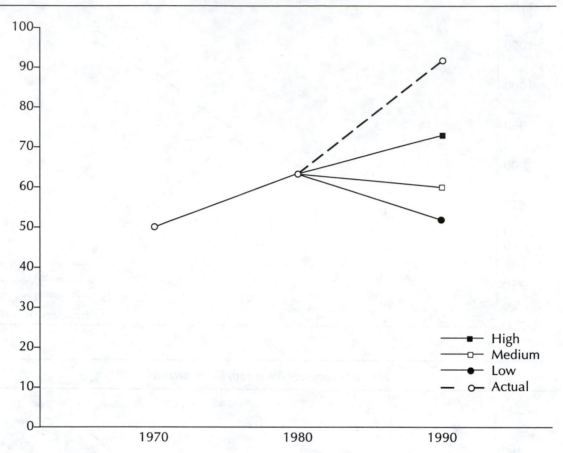

**Appendix Chart 3**
**Current Funds Expenditures**
**(in Billions of 1980 Dollars)**

# Why Are Capital Costs Ignored by Colleges and Universities and What Are the Prospects for Change?[1] (1993)

## GORDON C. WINSTON

An important part of the cost of education in US colleges and universities is ignored in the economic information used by policy makers, the public, and the colleges themselves. We try to understand and manage the educational enterprise with only crude and incomplete information about the costs of the plant and equipment services used in education. At Williams, as a convenient if extreme example, the cost of producing a year of education for a student in 1991 appears to be $33,600 but accounting for the use of capital, it is a bit more than $51,000. Put differently, leaving some $18,000 of capital costs[2] out of calculation of the educational cost of a student's year at Williams has the same effect, almost to the dollar, as would leaving out *all* personnel costs—the total costs of the faculty, administration, and hourly workers, including their fringe benefits ($18,051 per student).

The distorted view of actual costs that comes from neglecting capital at a school like Williams is especially severe because, oddly, the degree of neglect and distortion depends primarily not on how much capital a school uses in its activities, but on the accident of how it pays for that plant and equipment. Williams' costs are understated a great deal because the school owns its capital stock, outright. If Williams were to sell its campus to a private real estate entrepreneur, lock, stock and barrel, and rent it back at a competitive rate, its apparent current costs per student would rise by almost 60% and reflect its true costs. But of course nothing real would be changed, economically. So inconsistency in the treatment of capital costs among schools compounds the problems of their understatement, *per se*, since it becomes impossible to compare educational costs meaningfully except among schools that have very similar financial arrangements in using their plant and equipment. By the same token, it is impossible to estimate how much of the estimated $31 billion of capital costs in 1988-89 (based on an estimated $258 billion capital stock) is neglected in measuring the yearly cost of US higher education.

None of this is news, of course; economists have acknowledged it since Schultz [1960] made explicit correction for the absence of capital cost data and it has since become routine in studies of educational costs to estimate and add in imputed capital costs (see O'Neil, 1971; James, 1978, etc.).

It is, though, still important to ask "So what?—the cost figures are quirky, but what real difference does that make?" There are, I think, five pieces to the answer:

1. We simply don't know the real costs of higher education—as those costs enter into issues of public policy, into comparisons among schools, into tracking educational costs over time.

2.  We can't make informed choices about how best to *do* what we have to do—how many people to use with how much space and equipment; what it really costs, for instance, to equip everyone with a personal computer or a space in a parking garage.

3.  Redundant, duplicated facilities and equipment—between departments and between campuses—are hard to avoid if we don't know what that added convenience really costs us; library collections and research equipment include a lot of convenience-costs of unknown size that carry faint incentives to economize.

4.  Gifts are accepted—or, more generally, long term commitments are made to projects and programs—with an incomplete recognition of their real future cost implications.

5.  It's hard to recognize capital costs that vary over the day or week or season—like classrooms outside the popular period from ten o'clock to two—so chronic shortages (from ten to two) will coexist with idle facilities (at other hours).

6.  Borrowing decisions are distorted as debt financing requires, while self-financing does not allow, recognition of the opportunity costs of capital.

Neglect of capital costs appears, for one or more of these reasons, to be non-trivial.

So the questions of the title remain: Why don't nonprofit enterprises explicitly and routinely recognize the considerable cost (and contribution to production) of their physical capital stocks and what, after all this time during which the distortion has been recognized, is likely to come of it?

# A. Why Don't Nonprofits Recognize Capital Costs?

Intermediate microeconomic theory—as taught to undergraduates and in the nation's MBA programs—provides an effective way to organize understanding of the role and costs of capital in higher education. The theory of the firm distills out the essential elements of technology, costs, and prices that characterize production processes, including those of colleges and universities. Though it is easy to misapply the economic model of the for-profit firm—to be glib and careless in transferring it to nonprofit activities—used with care and modesty it can serve many purposes well.

## 1. The Tradition—Capital Costs in the For-Profit Firm

The past couple of decades have seen significant clarification of the theory of productive capital in *for*-profit firms with the work of Haavelmo (1960) and Jorgenson and Grilliches (1967) and, with particular respect to capital utilization, my own efforts of a few years ago (1982). Capital costs are conceptually slippery for two related reasons: because a firm's capital stocks are *durable*, purchased in one period for use well into the future, and because capital services enter the production process *from within* the firm, unlike the typical flow of inputs to production that are purchased from outside agents. A firm buys a year's labor services and fuel and raw materials from outside suppliers, but it gets the complementary flow of capital services from the durable buildings and machinery that it owns itself. Those characteristics need generate no special conundrums in modeling the production technology but they do create problems in measuring capital costs and responding to them.

The costs of using plant and equipment that is already owned by the firm have, broadly, two dimensions.[3] The first rests on the value of the capital stock used in production: the number of "machines," $K$, in a stylized example, times the price paid, $P_m$, for each machine[4] measures the value of the firm's capital stock, $P_m K$. The other dimension of capital cost recognizes its durability and the fact that it wears out and becomes obsolete (depreciates) over time and use.

The value of the capital stock measures the scarce resources that are tied up in capital assets (factories and classrooms and libraries and lab equipment) for a long time. Income is foregone by the owner of those capital assets since those resources would have been earning interest income if they'd been invested, instead, in financial assets. The cost of those lost earnings—the "opportunity cost" of owning long lived plant and equipment instead of owning financial assets—is usually the largest cost of using capital in production. If, for instance, the interest rate (rate of return) on financial assets is 10% percent per year, the yearly opportunity cost of a plant worth $1 million is $100,000.

Real deterioration or depreciation is the other and typically smaller component of capital cost—the fact that when it's used in production, the capital stock is partially worn out and becomes obsolete and that, too, is a cost of using durable capital. With the conservative figure of 2% real depreciation each year,[5] a $1 million plant looses $20,000 of its value through wear and tear.

Putting depreciation (d) and opportunity cost (r) together, the total cost of using K of capital in production for a year will be $(r + d)P_mK$: with 2% depreciation and a 10% rate of interest, the cost of the $1 million plant is $120,000 a year. That's the full, economic cost of using those capital services in production. It is the "user cost" or "rental rate" of capital, the price that would have to be charged to rent a unit of capital for a year in a highly competitive environment.

## 2. Transplanting Capital Costs

That specification of capital costs is quite universal—it describes the economic costs of using capital in production whether in a for-profit or a nonprofit enterprise.[6] So it effectively structures the understanding of total capital cost in colleges and universities.

But *accounting* for those capital costs in a nonprofit firm hits a serious snag. Accounting traditions were developed primarily for for-profit firms and applied to nonprofits like colleges and universities only secondarily. What makes sense for a nonprofit firm, in this case, seems quite strange in the for-profit tradition. Intuition, nurtured by for-profits, makes it very awkward to do the right thing about capital costs in nonprofit firms. Furthermore, part of capital costs—depreciation, the smaller part—more easily and often is recognized in nonprofit accounts[7] while the larger part—opportunity cost—continues to cause problems.

The hitch comes from the fact that in western capitalist economies, the distinctly different roles of (a) owner of the productive capital stock and (b) entrepreneur/organizer of the firm have been merged in the private archetypal firm so their functionally quite different rewards—the costs of capital services and the residual profits that reward entrepreneurial risk—have been mixed up too. Ownership of capital carries with it rights and responsibilities—and rewards—of management. In the typical for-profit firm like that of Economics 101, these roles are joined in a single owner (or a group of stockholder-owners), so Econ 101 instructors routinely insist that their students disentangle these two things. The "accounting profits" earned by an owner-entrepreneur are shown to be an amalgam of, on the one hand, payments to him as the owner for the use of his capital, $(r + d)P_mK$, and, on the other hand, any additional payment or "economic profits" he might earn as entrepreneur—residual payment for his organizing-managing-risk-taking function. It's unlikely that that distinction lasts in the minds of the students much beyond the final exam, but the effort at clarity satisfies the instructor.

But if capital costs are mixed in with entrepreneurial profits in the accounting concepts of the private, for-profit firm, what happens to capital costs when those accounting concepts are transplanted to nonprofit firms? The answer has been that capital costs have largely disappeared along with the accounting profits of which they were part. No accounting conventions exist to report the costs of capital separately from entrepreneurial profits because separation wasn't needed in the capitalist for-profit firm. The owner got the residual over current costs: economic profits, capital costs, and all.

With no way to recognize the opportunity cost of owned productive capital in its own right— even mixed in with profits—the treatment of capital costs in college and university accounting has depended on the accident of its financing. Specifically:

- if *capital is not owned* by the school but is *rented* from outside agents, its full cost, $(r + d) P_m K$, will be recognized as a cost of production because it is explicitly paid to an outside agent.

- if *capital is owned* by the school but is *financed by borrowing*, its opportunity cost will be recognized because interest costs, $(rP_m K)$ are, again, explicitly paid to an agent outside the institution. The depreciation component of its capital costs, $(dP_m K)$ need not be recognized.

- if *capital is owned* by the school but was *purchased from its own funds*, neither its depreciation nor its opportunity costs will be recognized as a current cost $((r + d)P_m K = 0)$. This is why the Williams illustration in the introduction is an extreme case of cost distortion.

But if the theory of the for-profit firm—with its implied accounting logic and the accumulated weight of tradition—has eliminated most of capital costs from the economics of production in nonprofit firms, it also provides the conceptual structure through which to put them back.

## 3. Capital Costs in a Nonprofit Firm

A nonprofit firm has three relevant characteristics that differentiate it from the for-profit firm and tangle any simple effort to transplant the logic of for-profit accounts to nonprofit firms. They are important to why a nonprofit is a nonprofit.

First, the nonprofit firm has no "owners" (entrepreneurial or stockholder), either inside or outside, separable from the firm itself; no one who has, in capitalist tradition, invested in the capital stock and therefore become entitled to be paid its returns. This underlies the "nondistributional constraint" that Hansmann saw as distinguishing nonprofit from for-profit firms: nonprofits can and do earn profits, but they can't distribute them to anyone (Hansmann, 1986).

Second, the nonprofit firm usually earns *negative* economic profits when those are defined as they are for the typical for-profit firm, as proceeds from the sale of its products less the costs of their production: total revenues minus total costs in Econ 101. In colleges and universities, this is manifested in the fact that the sticker price (tuition) is typically a good deal less than the average cost of production. Each student-customer is subsidized: with a tuition charge of $20,760, a Williams student got a subsidy of at least $29,000 in 1991.

But third, the nonprofit firm very often does earn profits; it can run at a loss in conventional terms but accumulate regular "surpluses" because its *sales* revenues are augmented by other non-product sources of income—notably gifts, endowment earnings, and indirect cost recovery. So that its total or "global" income exceeds total expenditures. These sources of income are, of course, absent from the typical for-profit firm.[8]

So for a nonprofit firm, then, current accounting stymies incorporation of capital costs in three ways: (a) there normally *is* no conventional profit to act as a carrier for the cost of capital services, (b) though there often *are* positive global profits, they can't legally be distributed outside the firm but (c) the capital stock is owned by the firm itself so any explicit payment of capital service costs will involve the disconcerting practice of the firm's making payments to itself, increasing both its expenditures and its income, the one as a cost of its production and the other as a return on its invested wealth.

Despite the Looking Glass nature of the accounting procedures by which a nonprofit firm can accurately reflect the cost of capital services, how it *should* be done seems clear. To recognize the opportunity cost of capital, the nonprofit firm would estimate the current value of its physical capital stock, $(P_m K)$, it would estimate yearly earnings lost by diverting a dollar of that wealth from financial investments, $(r)$; and it would include the resulting opportunity costs of capital, $(rP_m K)$ in both its current production costs and its asset income. To recognize depreciation costs, it would estimate yearly real depreciation, $(dP_m K)$ and add to current production costs any excess of that over current maintenance spending.

What may be jarring about the treatment of capital costs is the addition of the same, imputed, opportunity cost to both spending and income. "Why not," it is reasonable to ask, "leave things alone?" If the neglect of these capital costs misstates the income and expenditures of a nonprofit firm by equal amounts, the bottom line—their difference—won't be affected."

But that is a question framed for the for-profit firm where the bottom line is *profits*, literally the difference between income and expenditures. Which isn't affected. But of greater importance to the nonprofit firm is the *composition* of costs and income. Where do the resources to pay for education come from, for instance, and where do they go? What is the total cost of education? How and how well are various resources used in producing education? Do the inevitable tradeoffs between use of capital and non-capital resources—computers and teachers, for instance—reflect their costs to the institution? To society? These are questions that simply can't be answered without an accounting of capital costs. They are far different from questions about profit levels.

But even the procedure that would correctly measure the opportunity cost of capital is not as unconventional as it might appear. Rental income from owner-occupied houses is routinely estimated and simultaneously imputed to home owners as both income and expenditures in the national income accounts. That convention involves the same thing as does a correct accounting of capital costs in a college, and for the same reason: it captures the value of an economically significant flow of capital services that are hidden within the accounting-ownership unit. So we impute the value of that flow of capital services. The same entity both spends and receives the imputed money flow—it spends as a *user* of capital services and receives as an *owner* of the capital stock. Samuelson and Nordhaus put it this way:[9]

> "*Rent* income of persons [in the national accounts] includes rents received by landlords. In addition, if you own your own house, you are treated as *paying rent to yourself*. This is a so-called imputed item and makes sense if we really want to measure the housing services the American people are enjoying and do not want the estimate to change when people decide to own a home rather than renting it. This imputed item has to be estimated, since people do not report rental receipts on their own homes." [p. 115]

## B. What Are the Prospects for Change?

Which leads to the second question in the title: how likely is it that there will, in the future, be something more than repeatedly *ad hoc* recognition and incorporation of the costs of capital services in studies of higher education? What are the chances, in other words, that the kinds of procedures needed to measure and report capital service costs will be incorporated into the *routine* economic information generated by and for colleges and universities?

One can only speculate, of course, but speculation leads me to doubt that recognition of capital costs will become widespread in the accounts of institutions of higher education. Imputation of income seems too much of a departure from the conventions of for-profit firms and those firms provide the framing that practical people—like Trustees and accountants and auditors—will use to define what's sensible. The reasons, rehearsed here, why for-profit accounting conventions don't serve nonprofit firms well are a bit arcane—dealing with grand issues like the Traditions of Western Capitalism—and it's unreasonable to expect that they'll be widely appreciated by those outside of nonprofit firms themselves. And those inside may well be so accustomed to neglecting capital costs that few can be expected to find these suggestions anything but baffling. Their appeal is not increased, either, by the fact that the most important of capital costs leave the bottom line unchanged—that it is, for a nonprofit firm, an irrelevant bottom line may escape notice.

Nor does the recent mandate—from the Financial Accounting Standards Board ("FASB," the official arbiter of accounting practices)—that nonprofit organizations report depreciation costs turn out to be as encouraging as it first appears. Despite the clarity with which they recognize at least part of the problem ("Omitting depreciation produces results that do not reflect all costs of services provided" [FASB, p. 13]), their new standards will not alter the reported Operating Budgets or "Educational and General" spending or Current Fund spending on the basis of which "the costs of higher education" will usually be judged by managers and policy makers and scholars. Instead, the depreciation costs that FASB requires are to be hidden away as an obscure accounting adjustment to "Plant Fund Balances." Nor does the Board give any guidance on how to measure depreciation, leaving the method up to the individual institution with the requirement only that it be based on historical asset costs and that it be made explicit.[10] It appears that when all colleges are in full compliance with the FASB depreciation reporting requirement it will still be just as necessary as it is now to estimate and impute both the depreciation and opportunity costs of capital if one wants to know the costs of higher education.[11]

There is, however, one quite heartening development with respect to an accurate treatment of depreciation. It is Harvard's recent decision both to calculate depreciation of their capital on its replacement value and to recognize that depreciation is an important cost of current operation [Harvard]. The result of 1990-91 was a more realistic addition of $77 million in operating costs—and a $43 million operating deficit. Because Harvard is Harvard, other schools may be emboldened to follow suit.

And it should be noted, in fairness, that other schools have long tried to account for some depreciation costs, one way or another [Collins and Forrester, Ch. 8]. Like Islamic banking where capital costs have to be zero by doctrinal mandate, colleges have found ways to acknowledge depreciation costs simply to avoid kidding themselves. Local option, of course, makes comparisons between schools even more dicey.

But there remains a major reason to be pessimistic about future recognition of capital costs in, simply, the very large dollar figures involved for colleges that own their own capital stocks. The full recognition of capital costs in reported financial data, however it might improve our understanding, will sharply increase reported costs—the 60% increase at Williams is not extreme for a wealthy private institution. And Harvard's $77 million increase in operating costs would have been more like $400 million had they recognized, too, the opportunity cost of capital. In itself, therefore, the very importance of capital costs in higher education will discourage their recognition as it makes candor politically so unattractive to administrators.

But, of course, the *fact* will remain. Those real capital costs *are* being incurred in the production of higher education at the same time that colleges *are* earning implicit returns on their capital stocks. And decisions *are* being made about efficient use of capital and other resources and schools' efficiency *is* being judged. And all of this is done in the absence of explicit information about the very considerable costs of capital.

## Notes

1. To appear in *NACUBO Business Officer*, forthcoming. Work on this paper was supported by the Andrew Mellon Foundation through its support, in turn, of the Williams Project in the Economics of Higher Education. Michael McPherson, David Healy and Saeed Mughul made helpful comments on an earlier draft and Collin Roche provided research assistance.

2. A $300 million plant at 10% interest rate and 2% depreciation spread over 2000 students. This is conservative: total return on endowment has been 12% in the recent past and the plant size and real depreciation are probably understated.

3. A third dimension that is not of immediate relevance to this discussion is the utilization of a capital stock, most simply the proportion of the total 8760 hours a year it is used in production. That issue does, though, motivate some collegiate schemes like Dartmouth's "trimester" system and the extensive use of campuses in attractive settings like Williams's for "summer conferences."

4. This raises a familiar but sticky issue since most accounting records will show the "historical costs" of capital—its value at the prices originally paid—but what is relevant is what the capital is worth now—its replacement or market cost.

5. The figure normally used by economists (Schultz, O'Neill, James) though Dunn's much more detailed analysis makes a strong case that as much as 4.5% of replacement value may depreciate each year when both "renewal" and "adaption" (obsolescence) are recognized [Dunn].

6. Despite some caveats necessitated by restricted funds.

7. Though it falls short of a full accounting of depreciation, an effort is often made by nonprofit hospitals, foundations, and some colleges; a similar (and similarly inadequate) depreciation accounting has been mandated—as discussed below—for colleges and universities starting this year [FASB].

8. For a more detailed discussion, see Winston (1991).

9. A more official statement is found in U.S. Department of Commerce, 1987, p. 2.

10. They acknowledge that using historical values for capital assets creates inherent inaccuracies, but since that problem plagues all of capital asset valuation—of for-profit and nonprofit alike—they sensibly argue that the nonprofit context is not an appropriate one in which to take that issue on.

11. It is significant that neither the FASB discussion of depreciation nor the much longer analysis done for the National Association of College and University Business Officers (NACUBO) by Collins and Forrester has even a passing reference to the larger part of capital service costs represented by their opportunity costs.

# Bibliography

Bezeau, Lawrence. "The Treatment of Capital Costs in Educational Projects." *Educational Planning*, Vol. 1, No. 4 (March, 1975) 11-18.

Collins, Stephen J., and Robert T. Forrester. *Recognition of Depreciation by Not-for-profit Institutions.* (Washington: the National Association of College and University Business Officers, 1988.)

Dunn, John A., Jr. *Financial Planning Guidelines for Facilities Renewal and Adaption.* (Ann Arbor: The Society for College and University Planning, 1989.)

Financial Accounting Standards Board. "Statement of Financial Accounting Standards No. 93: Recognition of Depreciation by Not-for-Profit Organizations." *Financial Accounting Series. No. 047.* (Stamford, CT: FASB, 1987.)

Haavelmo, Trygve. *A Study in the Theory of Investment.* (Chicago: The University of Chicago Press, 1960.)

Hansmann, Henry. "The Role of Nonprofit Enterprise," Chapter 3 in Susan Rose-Ackerman, ed. *The Economics of Nonprofit Institutions.* (New York: Oxford University Press, 1986.)

Harvard University, *Financial Report to the Board of Overseers of Harvard College: For the Fiscal Year 1990-1991.* (Cambridge: Harvard University; 1992).

James, Estelle. "Product Mix and Cost Disaggregation: A Reinterpretation of the Economics of Higher Education." *The Journal of Human Resources*, Vol XII, No. 2., 1978.

Jorgenson, D. W., and Z. Griliches. "The Explanation of Productivity Change." *Review of Economic Studies*, Vol. 34, 1967, 249-83.

O'Neill, June. *Resource Use in Higher Education: Trends in Output and Inputs, 1930 to 1967.* A Technical Report Sponsored by the Carnegie Commission on Higher Education. (Berkeley: The Carnegie Commission on Higher Education, 1971.)

Samuelson, Paul A. and William D. Nordhaus. *Economics*. 13th ed. (New York: McGraw-Hill Book Company, 1989.)

Schultz, Theodore W. "Capital Formation by Education," *Journal of Political Economy*, Vol. 68, No. 6 (December, 1960), 571-83.

U.S. Department of Commerce. Bureau of Economic Analysis. "GNP: An Overview of Source Data and Estimating Methods." *Methodology Papers: U.S. National Income and Product Accounts*. Washington, D.C.: GPO, 1987.

Winston, Gordon C. *The Timing of Economic Activities: Firms, Households, and Markets in Time-specific Analysis*. (New York: Cambridge University Press, 1982.)

Winston, Gordon C. "Maintaining a College's Wealth: Endowment Spending Rules, Plant and Equipment, and Global Accounts," Williams College, January, 1991.

# FINANCING STUDENTS:
## ACCESS AND CHOICE

# The United States (1986)

D. Bruce Johnstone

## Higher Education in the United States

Higher education in the United States differs from its counterpart institutions and systems in Europe in a number of ways that are particularly germane to higher educational finance and the sharing of costs among parents, students, and taxpayers. The principal differences, constituting, in essence, the defining characteristics of American higher education in the mid-1980s, are: (1) its enormous size; (2) egalitarianism and the resulting diversity (e.g., in academic preparedness and socioeconomic status) of the student population; (3) a strong and diverse private sector; (4) the absence of a national ministry and the consequent relegation of all coordination and regulation to the states and to voluntary associations; (5) a revenue base that relies relatively less on the taxpayer and relatively more on students, parents, and philanthropists; and (6) aggressive marketing and price competition. This section will portray higher education in the United States by elaborating on each of these six points of difference.

## The Size of the Enterprise

The enormity of the higher educational enterprize in the United States is more than a function of the nation's large size and considerable wealth. U.S. higher education is large not only in sheer numbers of students and institutions, but also in the proportion of youth going on to college, in the extent of part-time and nontraditional participation, in the size of its very large universities and the number of its very small colleges, in the cost per student, in research support per faculty member, and even in the proportion of GNP consumed by the enterprise. American higher education in 1985–86, for example, includes:

- an estimated 12,247,000 students;[1]

- 3,330 institutions (1,497 public and 1,833 private or independent);[2]

- 694,000 faculty (454,000 full-time);[3]

- $9.6 billion in campus-based research, more than 75 percent of which is sponsored;[4]

- more than $100 billion in total expenditures, counting institutional operating budgets and the costs of student maintenance;[5]

- approximately $18 billion in grants, loans, and work-study assistance from governmental and institutional sources to help students and parents (particularly low- and middle-income) meet the expenses of tuitions and student living costs;[6] and

- 63 percent of 1980 high school graduates in college by the spring of 1982;[7] 32 percent of all American adults in 1981 claiming to have had some college and 22 percent claiming to have degrees.[8]

## Egalitarianism and Diversity of the Student Body

Probably no national character trait so epitomizes the United States as the belief in both the possibility and the desirability of bettering the socioeconomic station into which one was born. By hard work, right living, *and education,* it is believed that every American can and should make the very most of his or her natural abilities. Education, including college and even graduate school, is not just for the brilliant, but is, in some fashion at least, for nearly everyone. Education in the United States is thought to be the great engine of both social mobility and economic growth as well as the major cure for the ills of poverty, structural unemployment, idle youth, and mid-career boredom. It is considered a sound investment, even for its great cost, both for society (i.e., the taxpayer) and for the individual student and his or her family.[9]

There remains in the United States, as in all countries, an association between the socioeconomic status of the family and the higher educational participation of children as measured by entrance rates, completion rates, probability of postbaccalaureate study, and prestige of college attended. Young people from low socioeconomic backgrounds—which includes a large proportion of black, Hispanic, and Native American youth—are less likely to complete high school, and those who do are less likely to enter a four-year college, to graduate, or to go on to graduate study. Nevertheless, these associations are less pronounced than in most, if not all other, countries, if only because of the very great proportion of youth from all socioeconomic strata who finish secondary school with at least some college-preparatory work and the great percentage of those who go on to some form of higher education.[10]

Some part of American higher education is within reach of nearly anyone with a modicum of learning ability and enough interest to sign up for a course or two, perhaps in the evenings or on weekends only, with or without academic credit, related or unrelated to career aspiration. In fact, the idea of limiting the number of students to some governmentally predicted number of future openings in a certain kind of job is anathema to most Americans: better to give people a chance to win the available jobs, to create new jobs and opportunities unforeseeable by yesterday's manpower planners, or at the very worst to take a job for which they are educationally overqualified, with the satisfaction of the college education anyway, and with the enhanced ability to forge a new career sometime in the future.

Thus, there exists in American higher education the almost perpetual "second chance": the ability to try again, perhaps at a different and less rigorous college, in the event of failure. Similarly, there exists almost complete horizontal mobility, that is, the ability to transfer into a new academic field, even one so rigorous as medicine or law, at almost any point in an academic track, even from a totally unrelated field of study and with usually no more than some loss of time and academic credit.

With this great openness, accessibility, and mobility, of course, comes a great diversity in traditional academic preparedness and motivation. The United States has students in some colleges and even in some graduate schools who would not be admitted to, and probably would not succeed in, even the less selective institutions in most European higher education sectors. Academic failure and dropout rates among such students are high, and they tend to be found disproportionately in the least selective institutions, in the most vocational programs, and in the two-year programs. But America's egalitarian ethic and its great faith in education, coupled with special programs to enhance college-going among minorities and motivated by the financial need to maintain enrollments, combine to encourage students with a very wide range of abilities to try to find a place in American higher education.

## The Importance of the Private (Independent) Sector

In the 1985–86 academic year some 1,833 colleges and universities, or nearly 50 percent of the total number in the United States, educating some 2,656,000 students, or just under 22 percent of the total fall 1985 enrollment, comprise that sector designated "private" or "independent." But the importance of this sector to American higher education is even greater than these statistics indicate. Many of the top-ranked research universities and nearly all of the most selective liberal arts colleges are private, and a disproportionate number of the nation's leading business executives, physicians, lawyers, and political and governmental leaders have come out of private higher education and have worked to keep the sector basically strong through charitable donations and public subsidies.

Although there is a relatively small but robust subsector of private proprietary, or for-profit, colleges and institutes, the term "private college" generally means a not-for-profit corporation, chartered under applicable state and federal laws and controlled by its trustees. The trustees are usually prominent alumni or other prominent citizens (often clergy in the case of a church-affiliated college), who serve without pay and who maintain fiduciary custody over the assets of the institution, select a president as chief executive officer to run the college, give and raise money, and select their successors according to the by-laws of the corporation. (Many such institutions prefer the designation "independent" to "private," in part out of a fear that the latter designation mistakenly suggests elitism and the absence of public accountability, and in part out of recognition that they, too, have become heavily reliant on taxpayer-borne subsidies as well as subject to a host of state and federal regulations that have blurred very substantially the difference between "private" and "public.")

The most significant characteristic of the private sector to this study as its dependence on tuition for nearly all the institution's basic operating expenses that cannot be met by endowment earnings, current annual giving, and, in a few states, unrestricted governmental grants for operating expenses. This does not, however, mean that tuition is lower in colleges with larger endowments and better fund-raising capability. Tuition, rather, is set more nearly according to what the market will bear, with the more prestigious colleges, generally also the more heavily endowed, usually able to charge higher tuition as well as to spend more nontuition revenue.[11] Thus, tuition in 1985–86 can range from $4,500 at a relatively low-cost, nonselective regional private college, which amount may also constitute 90 percent or more of the per-student instructional costs, to $10,000 or more at a prestigious college like Harvard or Stanford, which sum may also be supplemented by at least as much endowment income and current giving, reflecting actual per-student instructional costs of $20,000 or more.

At the same time, the very extensive financial aid available to students in the private sector, from both philanthropic and taxpayer sources, makes it impossible to determine who or what is actually bearing the cost from the figures on tuition alone. Grants from the state and federal government, both to the student directly and at times to the institution on the student's behalf, combined with the institution's own funds, either from endowment or current operations, can bring what at first glance may look to be the absolutely insurmountable cost of a private-college education down to within reach of some students from very low-income families.

Thus, the United States at both the state and federal levels has made public policy decisions to support financially the large and very diverse private/independent sector, not for the most part by direct institutional grants (as per the university grants in the United Kingdom, for example), but by grants to students on the basis of financial need, allowing (or forcing) such institutions to set a tuition rate high enough to bring in sufficient revenue but with the assurance that needy students will get some assistance in meeting these tuitions as well as room, board, and other expenses.

## Decentralization and Autonomy

Education in the United States, insofar as government is involved, is reserved by the U.S. Constitution to the 50 states. Thus, with only a few exceptions such as the armed-services academies, the 1,500 public colleges and universities educating almost 9,600,000 students are owned and operated by the states, by municipalities under state regulations, or by special state-chartered public-benefit corporations. Furthermore, even at the state level, the existence of a large private sector, whose curriculums and degree standards are very nearly beyond governmental reach anyway, coupled with the traditional of lay boards of trustees, strong presidential offices, and a general political preference for decentralized government, have combined to assure that governmental control of higher education in the United States from any level of government is minimal by the standards of Europe or, for that matter, of most of the rest of the world.

This is not to say that the federal government is unimportant to higher education in the United States. Its importance, however, is overwhelmingly in the provision of financial support to students, including grants, loans, and work-study subsidies, and in the support of basic research, mainly to the top 100 or so research universities. Although there is now a cabinet-level Department of Education, the principal leverage it has over the nation's 3,330 colleges and universities is its ability to win sufficient congressional appropriations to maintain (and desirably, to increase) the federal student-assistance funds of approximately $8 billion. The significance to this study is that budgets, tuitions, grants, and nearly all the other basic ingredients that go into the cost of higher education and their impact on students and families, as well as many of the policies and programs of student financial assistance, are set by states, by individual institutions, by independent voluntary associations such as the College Scholarship Service of the College Board, and of course to some degree by the forces of supply and demand rather than by any central authority, as is the case in the European nations within this comparative study.

## Use of Other-Than-Taxpayer Sources of Revenue

Compared to the other nations in this study, and probably to all other nations in the world, U.S. colleges and universities rely on more diverse sources of revenue and especially on more nongovernmental (or nontaxpayer) sources. Parents contribute very heavily at high income levels, although less than their French or German counterparts at low levels of income. Students contribute substantially, through both summer and term-time work and through borrowing. Philanthropy, from alumni, foundations, corporations, and friends, is a significant source of revenue to the private sector and increasingly to the public sector. Finally, businesses, sometimes through collective-bargaining agreements, are becoming a potentially significant "bearer of costs" for their own employees in further, or continuing, education and sometimes in undergraduate and graduate degree-oriented education as well.

## Aggressive Marketing and Price Discounting

All U.S. colleges and universities are financially dependent on enrollments: private colleges because enrollments bring tuition revenue, and public colleges because enrollments drive their state budget formulas. The immediate financial threat is the sharp decline in the number of 18-22-year-olds—the traditional college-going age cohort—that began in 1978 and that will extend at least through the mid 1990s, ultimately reducing this traditional cohort by some 25 percent. This loss will exceed 40 percent in the Northeast, where the effects of declining birth rates in the 1960s are exacerbated by population out-migration in the 1970s and 1980s.[12]

Most industrialized nations are experiencing the same demographic phenomenon. What makes the downturn especially frightening to many U.S. colleges and universities is that this market may already be nearly saturated: that is, nearly all the young people who have the academic aptitude and interests appropriate at least to the more traditional, selective colleges are already college bound. Adult and part-time students have taken up much of the slack at many colleges; but this pool, too, certainly has a saturation point, even if that point is not yet known. To make matters even worse, the demand for the "bread-and-butter" traditional four-year liberal arts education has been softening for some time, quite apart from the diminution of the number of potential students. In short, most enrollment projections call for a decline in the number of students at U.S. colleges and universities and a very substantial decline at institutions that have little depth in their applicant pools, little access to adult and part-time students, and limited competitive advantage vis-à-vis other providers.

A nearly universal response to these pressures has been enhanced attention to marketing: research into the wants and preferences of potential students and of those, such as parents and school guidance counselors, who influence them; attractive college recruiting publications; radio, TV, and newspaper advertising; direct mail; and price discounting. Private institutions with high tuitions have always discounted their price via financial aid for those able students with demonstrated need—that is, whose parents are unable to cover the full costs—but have discouraged price cutting for marketing purposes only. By the mid-1980s, with enrollments beginning to turn down, with excess capacity driving the marginal costs of another student to the college down near zero, and with a burgeoning "excellence movement" craving symbols and gestures for the very able, the old college cartel is weakening, and price warfare seems imminent.

## Sharing the Costs Among Parents, Taxpayers, Students, and Institutions/Philanthropists

### Costs to the Students and Family

Costs to the student and family in the United States vary principally by the magnitude of tuition and fees, which can range from a few hundred dollars at some public colleges to upwards of $10,000 at high-priced, selective private institutions. The variation in tuition and fee charges is almost as great among the institutions wholly within the private sector, with 6 percent of four-year private colleges reporting tuitions of less than $2,500, 44.3 percent less than $5,000, and nearly 4 percent more than $10,000.[13]

The other major source of variation is the difference between commuter and resident costs of room and board, which may be from as low as $1,000–$1,100 "out-of-pocket" to the family for the student living at home to well over $3,000 for a college residence with a complete meal plan, to far higher amounts for independent students, older students, and students supported more generously by their parents.

College costs for U.S. undergraduates are generally presented for the nine-month academic year only; most students still return home to live with parents for the three-month summer break. Adults and independent youths attending college must, of course, meet living expenses for summers and vacations, generally through summer employment.

A range of nine-month costs for 1985–86 is presented in Table 6.1, extending from costs for a low-cost public college in a commuting situation ($3,150), to the average costs of attending a public ($5,314) or a private institution ($9,659), to a high-cost example typified by an Ivy League college at $15,000.

**Table 6.1**

**Cost Facing Undergraduate Students and Families, Nine Months, United States, 1985–86**

|  | Low-cost public (commuter) | Average public (resident) | Average private (resident) | High-cost private (resident) |
|---|---|---|---|---|
| Tuition and fees | $800 | $1,242 | $5,418 | $10,000 |
| Room and board | 1,030 | 2,473 | 2,781 | 3,400 |
| All other | 1,320 | 1,599 | 1,460 | 1,600 |
| Total | $3,150 | $5,314 | $9,659 | $15,000 |

Average public and private costs are from actual survey data as reported in *he College Board News*, Fall 1985; also in *The Chronicle of Higher Education*, vol. 30, no. 24, 14 August 1985, p. 1.

The low-cost public commuter budget is based on the commuting students' "option two" expense estimate guideline for 1985–86 from the College Scholarship Service. The room-and-board estimate is for "at-home" costs only. See *CSS Need Analysis: Theory and Computation Procedures for the 1985–86 FAF* (New York: The College Board, 1984), pp. 52–53.

The high-cost private resident budget was drawn from catalogs of selective private colleges. Total costs at such institutions reach $17,000 for the highest-cost undergraduate institutions.

## The Parental Contribution

The U.S. system begins with an assumption of parental responsibility for meeting a portion of the costs of higher education, at least through the undergraduate years or until the child has left the house and become financially independent. The expected parental contribution is determined primarily by the family income, of course, but also includes an expected contribution from some portion of assets, including home equity. Special considerations that diminish the ability of a family to contribute to the costs of college and that are not immediately controllable by the family—such as number of dependent children and their educational expenses, if any, unusually high medical and dental bills, and taxes—as well as the ages of the parents and the number of parents working are factored into the calculation of the expected parental contribution.[14]

The expected contributions from a two-parent family with one child in college and another not yet of college age, with no net assets and no unusual expense, is shown in Table 6.2 as a function of adjusted gross income. Expected contributions begin when the annual income reaches about $15,000, taking about 15 percent of annual income above $15,000, with what is in effect a "marginal tax rate" increasing to about 25 percent on income in excess of $35,000. Since the median income of families with college-age children is close to $30,000, it is clear that U.S. parents contribute very substantially to the costs of their children's higher education, with contributions of $10,000 a year and up common for more affluent parents of children attending high-priced private colleges.

The American system of need analysis assumes that parents can and should devote a noticeable proportion of their current annual income, requiring some sacrifices, as well as some proportion of their net discretionary worth (net assets less a provision for retirement) to the costs of their children's higher education. For most families, this means cutting back substantially on discretionary spending, perhaps forgoing or deferring vacations, entertainment, new autos, home improvements, and the like. Most expected contributions, particularly if based to any substantial degree on assets, will also involve either liquidation of a portion of these assets or else the assumption of new debt, perhaps in the form of a second mortgage or a home equity loan, to preserve intact the primary asset holdings. Finally, a family may prefer to meet the expected contribution not just by

### Table 6.2
### Expected Parental Contribution for Academic Year 1985–86 as a Function of 1984 Family Income
#### (Adjusted Gross)

Assume a family of four with two parents, the student, and one additional dependent child.

| Adjusted gross income | Expected contribution |
|---|---|
| $15,000 | 0 |
| 20,000 | 700 |
| 25,000 | 1,430 |
| 30,000 | 2,230 |
| 35,000 | 3,210 |
| 40,000 | 4,500 |
| 45,000 | 5,890 |
| 50,000 | 7,270 |
| 55,000 | 8,540 |
| 60,000 | 9,810 |
| 65,000 | 11,060 |
| 70,000 | 12,230 |
| 75,000 | 13,410 |
| 80,000 | 14,580 |

Based on 1985–86 uniform methodology and excluding any special considerations or home equity. The expected contribution at the adjusted gross income level of $15,000 by CSS suggestion is actually a *minus* $60, but the federal government does not recognize negative expected parental contributions. See College Scholarship Service, *CSS Need Analysis: Theory and Computation Procedures for the 1985–86 FAF* (New York: The College Board, 1984). See also *Federal Register*, vol. 50, no. 67, April 1985, pp. 13,919–13,923.

cutting current consumption and depleting savings, but by extending the burden into the future through a PLUS loan (Parent Loan for Undergraduate Students), available to a maximum of $3,000 per year per student, guaranteed by the state and federal governments and carrying an interest rate of 12 percent.

## The Student Contribution

The U.S. student is also assumed to bear some responsibility for the costs of his or her college education through summer and term-time work and subsidized loans, as well as through a portion of his or her own assets or savings. This expectation, termed self-help, is considerably higher for students at high-priced private or independent colleges, particularly where little aid is available, but it exists at all colleges and is expected of students from all socioeconomic backgrounds.

*Loans.* Undergraduate students borrow through two principal governmentally sponsored programs: Guaranteed Student Loans (GSLs) and National Direct Student Loans (NDSLS). Guaranteed Student Loans are made by private lenders, usually banks, and are guaranteed by the federal government. Undergraduates can borrow up to $2,500 a year and up to $12,500 for all undergraduate years. Students whose parents earned less than $30,000 in the preceding year can borrow up to the cost of education, not to exceed the limit. Students whose parents earned more than $30,000 must show a remaining financial need after the expected family contribution and other sources of income have been subtracted from the total cost of attendance at the particular college.

The interest rate to the student is zero percent while in school (or in certain other endeavors) and during a six-month grace period; for new borrowers in 1985–86, it is 8 percent during the 10-year repayment period. The private lenders are paid the 8 percent by the government (taxpayer) while the borrower is in school, plus an additional interest supplement designed to bring the total return to the lender up to a market rate, set every 180 days by the federal government. (The supplement for the quarter ending September 1985, on GSL loans made after October 1981 was 2.84 percentage points, bringing the return to the lender at that time to 10.84 percent [8 + 2.84]).

National Direct Student Loans are made by the college from a revolving loan fund that has been capitalized by direct appropriations from the federal government and supplemented increasingly by repayments. As in the GSL program, NDSLs carry no interest during the in-school years or the six-month grace period after graduation. The interest rate thereafter is 5 percent. Because of the greater subsidy and easier access of these loans, they are to be targeted at low-income students.

Considering all forms of student loans—GSLs, NDSLS, and the several much smaller state and federal sponsored student loans,[15] it has been estimated that more than 3.3 million students in 1985–86 will borrow nearly $9 billion, with new loans averaging almost $2,300.[16] This amount of lending is up from 1.5 million students borrowing $3 billion in 1979, reinforcing the conclusion that the past decade has seen a substantial shift of higher educational costs from parents and taxpayers to the student, largely in the form of more students borrowing larger amounts. The College Board in 1984 reported ". . . the continuation of a trend that began in the mid-1970s: the ever-increasing emphasis on loans over grants"—an observation buttressed by the decline of grants from 80 percent of all federal student assistance in 1975–76 to just under 45 percent in 1984–85, with the proportion of federal assistance in the form of loans increasing in those years from 17 percent to 52 percent.[17] Total accumulated debts at the end of four years of undergraduate education are being reported commonly in the neighborhood of $10,000, and debts for students completing medical and other advanced professional schools can easily top $30,000.

As explained in Appendix B and in the earlier chapters on the German and Swedish loan plans, a subsidized loan can be divided into a true loan and an effective grant, the former being the present value of the actual repayment stream at some appropriate discount rate and the latter, the difference between this present-value calculation and the actual principal amount borrowed—or, equally valid, the present value of the stream of subsidies measured as the differences between each payment and what the payment would have been had the loan carried a more realistic rate of interest. Table 6.3 shows the present value of the repayment stream for a $1,000 Guaranteed Student Loan to be $854 with a discount rate of 8 percent, $753 discounted at 10 percent, and only $667 discounted at 12 percent. The corresponding effective grants are thus $146, $247, or $333 per $1,000 borrowed. By this perspective, if a student takes a $2,000 GSL toward the annual cost of his or her college education, and if 10 percent is an appropriate discount rate, that student may be credited with $1,506 in true loan, or a real student-borne contribution to costs, with $494 being credited to the taxpayer, who will bear the cost of the loan subsidies.

Another adjustment that can be made to refine the actual burden of U.S. student loans is an estimate of that proportion of student lending that is actually repaid by the parents and that in some cases was originally a substitute for a portion of the expected parental contribution. Particularly during the late 1970s and early 1980s, when prime interest rates in the United States were above 15 percent and when the 1978 Middle Income Student Assistance Act opened the federal subsidized GSL program to all students regardless of need, and before a series of amendments in the mid-1980s began to "close the loan window" to children of very affluent parents, it was legal and clearly rational for parents to substitute their children's borrowing (at effective annual interest rates below 5 percent) for their own contribution (which could earn 12 percent in any bank) to the maximum extent possible. In addition, some parents believe that their children should end at least their undergraduate years debt free and therefore formally or informally assume some or all of the repayment burdens on undergraduate student debt. In 1981, however, the GSL program guidelines

### Table 6.3
**Student Loan Terms (Guaranteed Student Loan Program) and Present Value of Repayments, United States**

| | |
|---|---|
| Initial loan | $1,000 |
| In-school period[a] | 1.5 years |
| Grace period[b] | 0.5 years |
| Interest rate, in-school and grade periods | 0% |
| Debt at beginning of repayment | $1,000 |
| Interest rate in repayment[c] | 8% |
| Repayment period[d] | 10 years |
| Repayment mode | equal quarterly payments of $36.56 |

| | | |
|---|---|---|
| | Discount rate 8% | $854 |
| Present value of repayments[e] | Discount rate 10% | $753 |
| | Discount rate 12% | $667 |

[a] Period between origination of loan end of schooling; assumed here to be 1.5 years for purposes of simplification and comparison.

[b] Period between end of schooling and beginning of first repayment period: six months by law, but extensions are possible for, e.g., military service.

[c] For loans taken out since 1984; earlier loans carry other rates.

[d] Ten years maximum.

[e] See Appendix B.

changed and began to require that all students from families earning more than $30,000 a year borrowing under the GSL program must show need—that is, a gap in funds required to meet the costs of college *after* assuming a full expected family contribution. The reauthorization of the basic GSL legislation expected to take place in 1986 may well extend this needs test to all students applying for federally guaranteed student loans. Thus, we will not in this chapter attribute any part of new student borrowing to parents, but readers may be alert to the possibility that student debts accumulated during the period of the "open GSL window" may in fact represent a combination of student and parental debt, with the federal subsidy effectively shifting a portion of each over to the federal taxpayer.

*Summer and Term-Time Employment.* "Working one's way through college" is almost legend in the United States. Christoffel reports a study of high school seniors who began college in the fall of 1980: Two-thirds of the part-time and 52 percent of the full-time students had jobs. By 1981, 75 percent of the part time and 55 percent of the full-time students were working during term time. Eighty percent of adult part-time students in 1981 were employed. In 1983–84, some 850,000 students worked part-time through the assistance of the federal College Work Study Program, which picks up 80 percent of the expenses of hiring college students. In summary, Christoffel's findings suggest that a majority of American students work at least part time.[18]

Amounts earned vary widely. The uniform methodology for determining financial need assumes a summer savings contribution of $700 for new students and $900 thereafter. A work-study job during the course of the academic year can earn $1,200 or more, and many students earn a great deal more, particularly if they hold down an outside, non-work-study job.[19] Term-time earnings above $1,500, however, would be discouraged by most campus financial aid officers as encroaching too much on study time. However, earnings of $2,000 and even much higher are not at all uncommon, particularly for older students and for students at less selective, community-oriented institutions where students frequently maintain both a full-time job and full-time (i.e., 12 credit-hours) study or else alternate between semesters of full-time study and part-time work and then part-time study and full-time work. Counting both summer savings and term-time earnings, U.S. students commonly earn in the range of $1,000–$2,000.

## The Taxpayer's Contribution

Because the European countries in this comparative analysis for all practical purposes charge no tuition, the costs of higher education that have been distributed among the British, French, German, and Swedish parents, students, and taxpayers have been almost entirely the students' costs of living plus those costs of education such as books, travel, and equipment that are typically met by the student or his or her family, even with the assistance of governmental or institutional grants. The *full* taxpayer-borne costs, of course, would be the taxpayer's share of these expenses, on a per-student basis, plus the per-student direct costs of undergraduate instruction as might be revealed in the institutions' operating budgets were such data to be available.[20]

The U.S. situation is considerably complicated by the fact that the costs faced by students and their families include both the costs of student living and that portion of institutional, or instructional, costs that are passed on as tuition or fees. It is even further complicated by the great variation within the United States in actual unit costs of instruction among different institutions as well as the very great difference in the taxpayer's share of these costs, as between the public and the private sectors. To the student and his or her family, there is probably no significant difference between their share of instructional costs as reflected in tuition and their share of the costs of student living as reflected in the charges for room and board and other expenses, less whatever aid is received to defray these costs. Nor do government grants distinguish, for most purposes, between tuition and other costs. However, the need for students and parents in the United States to meet some portion of instructional costs, as well as all student maintenance costs, with or without assistance from government or from the institution itself, means that taxpayer-borne, need-based grants in the United States will be inflated relative to similar grants in Europe—only slightly in the case of public institutions, for which tuitions and fees typically constitute only 20–30 percent of the actual costs of undergraduate instruction, but very greatly in the case of private institutions, in which tuitions may constitute 70 to 90 percent of such costs.[21] (This does not, of course, mean that the total per-student taxpayer contribution in the United States is necessarily higher. On the contrary, because all the tuition revenue goes to support university operations, the taxpayer contributions to the institutions' operating budgets are reduced by the presence of tuitions—at least those that can be paid by more well-to-do parents or industrious students and that therefore do not need to be covered by a taxpayer-borne grant.)

With these caveats in mind, the principal, generally available, taxpayer-borne, need-based grants to undergraduates (excluding work study and the true value of loans, which are considered in this analysis to be student-borne revenues) are Pell Grants, Supplemental Education Opportunity Grants, the implicit grants of the subsidized loan programs at the federal level, and various need-based grant programs at the level of the 50 states.

*Pell Grants.* These are awarded to students on the basis of need as determined by their own and parents' income and assets. Except for the requirement to show satisfactory progress toward the degree and at least a half-time course load, the Pell Grant is given as an entitlement without regard to ability, achievement, the particular institution attended, or the major program of study. The maximum award in 1985–86 by the authorizing statute is $2,600, but the Pell Grant Program is not an automatic entitlement, and the actual awards depend upon the amount appropriated by the Congress each year and the number and needs of potential recipients. In 1985–86 the actual maximum award is $2,100, which is given to students from families (two parents and one additional nonstudent dependent child) with incomes of about $9,860 and below; the minimum grant is $250, just before the awards phase out entirely at a 1984 family income of about $26,500. Pell Grants cannot be more than 60 percent of the federally determined cost at a particular institution. At the low-cost institution portrayed in Table 6.1, for example, with a tuition of $800, the government allows a consideration of an additional $1,100 for a commuting student's room and board plus only $400 for all other costs, for a total allowable cost of education of $2,300, 60 percent of which is $1,380—the maximum Pell Grant for a student of such an institution. The Pell Grants rise as tuition and the actual room-and-board charges rise up to the maximum award for the particular income and number of dependents. Beyond this point, Pell Grants are insensitive to increases in tuition and give no more to a student at a very high-priced private college than to a student from a similar family financial background in residence at an average-cost public college. In 1984–85, some 2,853,000 students received Pell Grants at an estimated average award of $1,105.[22]

*Federal Supplemental Educational Opportunity Grants.* These are awarded to needy students at the discretion of the college financial aid office, whose allotment of federal SEOG funds is determined by the number of students from low-income families enrolled in recent years. SEOGs range from $200 to $2,000 and may take into account the student's full need, including tuition charges. Supplemental grants, together with the subsidies inherent in the governmental loan programs, represent the principal contribution of the federal government toward the goal of bringing more expensive private higher education more nearly into reach for young people from low-income families. In 1984–85, some 655,000 students received SEOGs, averaging an estimated $550.[23]

*State Need-Based Grants*: All states provide some form of need-based financial aid to under-graduates, although there is wide variation in generosity and mechanics. The total state grant dollars for 1984–85 were estimated at $1,257 billion—almost 40 percent of the combined general federal grant programs of Pell and SEOG.[24] Some states provide "portable" grants, good for attending colleges out-of-state as well as in-state; other grants are good only in-state. Most state grant programs are designed avowedly to provide some extra assistance to needy students attend-ing private colleges, thereby reducing somewhat the so-called tuition gap between the lower-tuition public sector and the higher-tuition private sector.

The most generous of the state need-based financial aid programs is New York State's Tuition Assistance Program, or TAP. TAP provides a maximum academic-year undergraduate grant of $2,700 or tuition, whichever is less (i.e., reducing the maximum grant to undergraduate students in New York's public colleges and universities to the State University tuition, or $1,375), with the maximum award reduced according to parents' income, beginning the reduction at a net taxable annual income of $5,000 and phasing out the award altogether for net taxable incomes above $29,000 (equivalent to an adjusted gross income of $34–$35,000). New York State TAP awards for full-time undergraduates in private nonprofit and public colleges are shown in Table 6.4. Awards are reduced by $500 if the college attended is private proprietary, or profit-making. There are also TAP awards for graduate and advanced professional study, as well as special schedules for students who can prove financial independence from their parents. A state need-based grant program such as New York's TAP thus supplements the federal Pell Grant Program for students for a wide range of college costs, and it also goes beyond Pell in providing some additional aid to cover the higher costs of attending a private college.

*Federal Loan Subsidies*: As explained above and in Appendix B, governmentally subsidized and guaranteed loans can be viewed as being composed of a true loan, which is that principal amount that the expected repayment stream would actually amortize at a rate of interest closer to the market rate, and an effective grant, or subsidy, which is the difference between the principal amount received and the true loan. As shown in Table 6.3, a conservatively assumed discount rate of 10 percent suggests that at least 25 percent of the amount borrowed under federal GSL terms should be considered an effective grant from the taxpayer to the student, realized in the stream of subsidies that lower the eventual repayments. In 1984–85, an estimated 3,403,000 students took out Guaranteed Student Loans averaging $2,326, for an average effective subsidy of $580, or about 25 percent of the principal amount borrowed, and an average true loan of $1,746, assuming the 25–75 division suggested by the 10-percent discount rate assumption.[25]

### Table 6.4
### New York State Tuition Assistance Program (TAP) Grants for Undergraduates
### at New York State Public and Private Colleges, 1985–86

| New York State net taxable income of family[a] | Estimated TAP award at private college | Estimated TAP award at public college[b] |
|---|---|---|
| $29,000 | $300 | $300 |
| 27,500 | 453 | 300 |
| 25,000 | 740 | 300 |
| 22,500 | 1,015 | 300 |
| 20,000 | 1,290 | 300 |
| 17,500 | 1,565 | 300 |
| 15,000 | 1,840 | 515 |
| 12,500 | 2,100 | 775 |
| 10,000 | 2,330 | 1,005 |
| 7,500 | 2,525 | 1,200 |
| below 5,000 | 2,700 | 1,375 |

Source: Standard Descriptions of State and Federal Student Assistance Programs for Use by Postsecondary Institutions in Complying with Part 53 of the Regulations of the Commissioner of Education (Albany: The State Education Department, April 1985).

[a] Net taxable income is adjusted gross income less exemptions and deductions, or appropriately 15–20 percent under adjusted gross.

[b] The public-college award uses the 1985–86 State University tuition and college fee of $1,375 as the maximum TAP award for the public sector. Upon receipt of four or more semester payments, the annual award is reduced by $200. The provisions in the legislation allow for a minimum award of $300 per year.

The actual award is $2,700 minus:

| Net taxable family income | Reduction |
|---|---|
| $5,000 or less | no reduction |
| 5,001 – 8,000 | 7% of excess over $5,000 |
| 8,001 – 11,000 | $210 + 8% of excess over $8,000 |
| 11,001 – 14,000 | $450 + 10% of excess over $11,000 |
| 14,001 – 25,000 | $750 + 11% of excess over $14,000 |
| 25,001 – 29,000 | $1,960 + 11.5% of excess over $25,000 |
| 29,001 or more | no award |

*Other Federal and State Assistance to Students*: In 1975–76, veteran's education benefits and education benefits to children of social security recipients (i.e., persons drawing federal retirement or disability allowances) totaled 5.273 billion dollars: nearly one-half of all federal higher education assistance and more than 80 percent of all federal grant aid. Strictly speaking, neither program was need-based or means-tested, although it was assumed that most of these benefits went to students who were either independent from parental support (e.g., veterans' education benefits) or whose parents' resources would have been limited anyway (e.g., dependent children of social security recipients). By the mid-1980s few veterans were still drawing on higher education benefits, and grants to children of social security recipients had been phased out as allegedly duplicative of the Pell Grants and other truly need-based programs. Federal benefits, thus, are estimated by Wagner to have fallen to about $746 million in 1985–86, or less than 5 percent of all federal student assistance.[26] Other federal and state assistance includes special state grants to educationally and economically disadvantaged students and to Native American students, special grants to students in certain underserved professions (e.g., nursing), and various smaller state- and federally subsidized loan programs to supplement the major Guaranteed Student Loan Program. These federal and state awards are not, however, generally available to U.S. undergraduates and are not considered further in this analysis.

*Summarizing the Per-Student Taxpayer Contribution to the Costs of Higher Education.* Taxpayer-borne assistance to students in the United States is difficult to summarize because the range of awards is so great and because each student's total taxpayer-borne assistance, from both federal and state sources, is a complex function of:

- parents' income;

- own income;

- "family factors," such as the number of other dependent children both in and out of college;

- the tuition charges at the particular college attended, which may range from a few hundred to ten thousand dollars; and

- decisions of the campus financial aid officers in awarding federal supplemental grants.

Consequently, average awards derived by dividing total expenditures by the estimated number of recipients are not particularly useful because they ignore this range. Furthermore, published federal- and state-aid data is always by program, and program averages are not additive. Empirical studies that take aided students themselves as the units of observation and that then determine, by student and/or parental reports, the grants that have actually been obtained are much more useful for our purpose. Unfortunately, such studies often aggregate dissimilar types of aid (e.g., Supplemental Educational Opportunity Grants and Campus Work Study) and contain such variation, and probably such reporting error, that they are also not particularly useful for an international comparative study, such as this one, that must compare similar data.[27]

Therefore, this study employs the concept of "representative" awards, based on financial aid practices and consistent with empirical data but not drawn from any single source. Such representative taxpayer-borne awards—for low- and middle-income students at high- and low-cost colleges—are shown in Table 6.5. Note that the Pell Grants, except for a reduction at the very lowest-cost colleges, do not vary by the cost of the college for a given family income. On the other hand, federal SEOGs, which are awarded by the campus aid officers, and the state grants, most of which are also tuition sensitive, do reflect the variation in costs, particularly in tuitions and living costs. By design, the federal and state taxpayers provide larger awards to equally needy students at more expensive institutions. However, these awards lessen but do not eliminate the cost (price) differentials, particularly between the private and public sectors.

## Institutional/Philanthropic Contributions

Historically, some students and their families have been given financial assistance in meeting the costs of college by the institution itself from funds made available through philanthropic donations, principally by alumni. Institutional, or philanthropic, support comes from three sources. The first is endowment, or income from past philanthropy. The second is current donations from alumni, businesses, and friends of the college. The third, found only in private colleges and much less prevalent, is generated by charging and getting tuitions from some students and families that are above and beyond the amounts necessary to cover all costs, thus generating some budgetary surpluses with which to grant aid in the form of tuition discounts to some needy students.

## Table 6.5

**Representative Taxpayer-Borne (Federal and State), Need-Based Assistance to Students in the United States for Low- and Middle-Income Students Attending High- and Low-Cost Institutions, 1985–86ᵃ**

| Principal federal and state grant programs | Maximum award | Students from low-incomeᵇ families at: | | | | Students from middle-incomeᶜ families at: | | | |
|---|---|---|---|---|---|---|---|---|---|
| | | Lowest-cost public ($3,150)ᵈ | Average-cost public ($5,314) | Average-cost private ($9,659) | High-cost private ($15,000) | Lowest-cost public ($3,150) | Average-cost public ($5,314) | Average-cost private ($9,659) | High-cost private ($15,000) |
| Federal Pell grantsᵉ | $2,100 | $1,290 | $1,650 | $1,650 | $1,650 | $0 | $0 | $0 | $0 |
| Federal supplemental grants | 625+ | 125 | 375 | 550 | 800 | 125 | 375 | 625 | 800 |
| State need-based grantsᶠ | 2,700 | 500 | 800 | 1,500 | 1,500 | 0 | 200 | 300 | 300 |
| Subtotal taxpayer-borne cash grants | $6,800 | $1,790 | $2,900 | $3,950 | $4,150 | $125 | $575 | $1,200 | $1,500 |
| Federal loan subsidiesᵍ | 625+ | 125 | 375 | 550 | 800 | 125 | 375 | 625 | 800 |
| Total taxpayer-borne assistanceʰ | $7,425 | $1,915 | $3,275 | $4,500 | $4,950 | $125 | $575 | $1,825 | $2,300 |

a The figures in Table 6.5 are "representative," i.e., are consistent with U.S. financial aid policies and with available data, but do not come from any particular empirical study or single source. The chart considers only those costs that are faced by the student and the family—not the instructional costs that, particularly for public colleges, are also borne in part by the taxpayer.

b The "low-income" range is approximately $10,000–$15,000 taxable (adjusted gross) income.

c The "middle-income" range is approximately $30,000–$35,000 taxable (adjusted gross) income.

d The four representative cost figures are from Table 6.1.

e An adjusted gross family income of $15,000 with no assets gives a family of four a Pell index of 490 and a maximum grant of $1,650. The low-cost public commuter situation described in Tale 6.1, however, presents a cost-of-education ceiling, for the purpose of grant calculations, of only $2,150 ($800 tuition, $1,100 maximum allowable room and board, and $400 maximum allowable "all other"), 60 percent of which is $1,380.

f The maximum generally available, need-based state grant in New York State's TAP maximum. Most states are considerably smaller, however, and the estimates here seek a representative-size state grant program.

g The federal-loan-subsidy estimates assume a 10-percent discount rate per Table 6.3, or 75 percent "true loan" and 25 percent subsidy or "effective grant." It is assumed that borrowing reaches the maximum $2,500 GSL, at the "average private" college but is supplemented by as much as $700 NDSL, for a total of $3,200, at the "high-cost private" college.

h Federal College Work Study is an important component of the total federal student assistance program, but is not included in these totals on the grounds that the costs are borne by students and that the recipients of the taxpayer-borne subsidies are the institutions which receive the labor, rather than the students.

Institutionally awarded student aid, mainly originating with one of these philanthropic sources, was reported to total $2,634,000,000 in 1984–85—or just under the total of all federal Pell Grants.[28] This total, however, includes some graduate fellowships as well as undergraduate aid and includes both merit aid, given without regard to need and mainly for the purpose of attracting a particular student to a particular campus, and need-based or means-tested aid, given for the ostensible purpose of supplanting funds that the family is financially unable to provide and thus making the selection of a particular college at least financially feasible. The Miller and Hexter studies reported that about 40 percent of low-income students and more than 50 percent of middle-income students at private colleges receive college-provided aid averaging around $2,000; only 4 percent of low-income students and 5 percent of middle-income students at public colleges received any college-provided aid, and the average awards were under $800.[29] Given the reasonable assumption that the combination of low tuition and public need-based grants (e.g., Pell, SEOG, and state grants) have removed the financial barrier to attending the nation's public colleges even for children from the lowest-income families, it is likely that most of the institutionally awarded grants in the public sector are based on criteria other than need and provide the student with some extra purchasing power rather than supplant or relieve any other source of financial support. In the private sector, however, the role of philanthropically originated, institutionally awarded grants is very significant for most students from low- or middle-income families faced with yearly college costs ranging from $7,500 to $15,000 and up. Institutionally awarded aid in most cases makes up the difference between the total costs faced by the student and his or her family and the sum of all resources available from the three primary sources of family (i.e., the expected family contribution as revealed by need-analysis procedures), taxpayer or government (e.g., Pell, SEOG, and state grants), and the student (through savings, term-time work, and loans). This institutionally awarded grant may be less than $1,000 or may, at a well-endowed expensive college, and particularly for a student whom the college wishes very much to enroll, be in excess of $5,000.

## The Financial Aid Package

The cost of higher education faced by students and families in the United States—tuition and fees, room and board, and all other expenses—is shared by the parents of dependent students, to the extent of their financial abilities; by the students themselves, through their own assets, through summer and term-time earnings, and through governmentally subsidized loans; by the taxpayers, through federal and state grants and through loan subsidies; and by philanthropists or donors, through gifts to particular (primarily private) colleges that in turn allow those colleges to grant scholarships to needy students. Except for those students and families whose resources are sufficient to meet all expenses without the need for governmental grants, subsidized loans, or college grants, each student's mix of resources is individually "packaged" by the financial aid officer of his or her particular college. This packaging proceeds essentially through the following steps:

**Step 1.** The total expenses faced by the student and his or her family are determined. These would correspond to the expenses illustrated in Table 6.1 and generally represent a "modest-but-adequate" budget, exceeded by those students whose parents contribute more than the minimum expected or needed, or who contribute more themselves through savings, earnings, or loans.

**Step 2.** Governmental grants to which the student is entitled (i.e., apart from any decision by the college's financial aid officer) are estimated, and the student is assumed to have applied for them and to receive them. These principally include federal Pell Grants and any state entitlement aid.

**Step 3.** The parents' expected contribution is calculated, generally through one of the independent need-analysis agencies (e.g., College Scholarship Service or American

## Table 6.6
### Sources of Revenue to Meet College Costs at High- and Low-Cost Institutions for High-, Middle-, and Low-Income Families, United States, 1985–86

| Sources of revenue | Lowest-cost public ($3,150)ᵃ Family incomeᵇ | | | Average-cost public ($5,314)ᵃ Family incomeᵇ | | | Average-cost private ($9,659)ᵃ Family incomeᵇ | | | High-cost private ($15,000)ᵃ Family incomeᵇ | | |
|---|---|---|---|---|---|---|---|---|---|---|---|---|
| | low | middle | high | low | middle | high | low | middle | high | low | middle | high |
| **Student:** | | | | | | | | | | | | |
| Term-time and summer work | $860 | $1,075 | $800 | $914 | $1,114 | $600 | $1,659 | $1,600 | $1,000 | $2,100 | $2,100 | $1,100 |
| Loans | 500 | 500 | 0 | 1,500 | 1500ᶜ | 600 | 2,200 | 2,500 | 0 | 3,200 | 3,200 | 1,100 |
| Total gross student contribution | 1,360 | 1,575 | 800 | 2,414 | 2,614 | 0 | 3,859 | 4,100 | 1,000 | 5,300 | 5,300 | 2,200 |
| (less loan subsidies)ᵈ | (125) | (125) | 0 | (375) | (375) | 0 | (550) | (625) | 0 | (800) | (800) | (275) |
| Total net student contribution | 1,235 | 1,450 | 800 | 2,039 | 2,239 | 1,200 | 3,309 | 3,475 | 1,000 | 4,500 | 4,500 | 1,925 |
| **Parents: from current income, savings, and Loans** | 0 | 1,575 | 2,350 | 0 | 2,500 | 4,114 | 150 | 2,759 | 8,659 | 150 | 3,200 | 12,800 |
| **Taxpayer:** | | | | | | | | | | | | |
| Federal and state need-based grants | 1,790 | 0 | 0 | 2,900 | 200 | 0 | 3,950 | 1,200 | 0 | 4,150 | 1,500 | 0 |
| plus loan subsidiesᵈ | 125 | 125 | 0 | 375 | 375 | 0 | 550 | 625 | 0 | 800 | 800 | 275 |
| Total net taxpayer contribution | 1,915 | 125 | 0 | 3,275 | 575 | 0 | 4,500 | 1,825 | 0 | 4,950 | 2,300 | 275 |
| **Institutional/philanthropic:** College grants | 0 | 0 | 0 | 0 | 0 | 0 | 1,700 | 1,600 | 0 | 5,400 | 5,000 | 0 |
| **TOTAL** | $3,150 | $3,150 | $3,150 | $5,314 | $5,314 | $5,314 | $9,659 | $9,659 | $9,659 | $15,000 | $15,000 | $15,000 |

aThis chart considers only those costs faced by the student and the family—not the institutional costs that, particularly for the public institutions, are also borne in part by the taxpayer. Actual numbers are "representative" and conform in total to the cost estimates from Table 6.1, but the numbers are derived as explained below and do not come from any one empirical study.

b"Low" family income would be in the $10,000–$15,000 adjusted gross annual income range; "middle income" is in the range of $30,000–$35,000, or just within reach of some college-based federal aid at private institutions, but not at public ones; "high income" is more than $75,000.

cThe taxpayer's share is from Table 6.5; "subtotal taxpayer-borne cash grants." The parent's share from the low-income family is assumed to be zero, with very small amounts, however, to help with very high private college costs. Parents' share from the middle-income family is from Table 6.1, with a bit extra for the high-cost, a bit less for the average public, and exactly one-half the total cost for the low-cost public college. Parents' share from the high-income family is the remaining need after some minimal self help. The student's share and the institutional and philanthropic share balance to cover the rest of the costs, with loans and work being essentially interchangeable, and with total "self-help" rising to a maximum of $5,300 at the high-cost private college, assuming a $3,200 loan package made up of $2,500 GSL and $700 NDSL.

dThe taxpayer-borne loan subsidy estimate is 25 percent of the principal, per Table 6.3 with a 10 percent discount rate assumption. The subsidy estimate is netted out of the student's gross contribution and added to the taxpayers' share.

College Testing Program) or through a procedure of the college's own choosing. Students may apply to be considered financially independent of their parents. Such status generally requires three conditions for both the current and the prior years: (1) living no more than six weeks a year with the parents; (2) not being claimed by parents as an income-tax exemption; and (3) receiving no more than $750 in support from parents. (Independent status for the purpose of qualifying for institutionally given aid is granted by the college at its own discretion. Eligibility for independent status for the purpose of receiving federal Pell or state need-based grants is similarly based, but is an entitlement should the student qualify.)

**Step 4.**   A student self-help expectation is added, composed of expected prior summer savings and some combination of term-time work (often subsidized in part by the federal government's College Work Study Program) and loans, including either a National Direct Student Loan offered by the college or a Guaranteed Student Loan that the student must secure from a private lender with the college certifying need. This self-help total may be $3,000 to $5,000 or even more at an expensive private college where the parental, institutional, and taxpayer-borne shares fall far short of meeting the full need. The self-help expectation may be a great deal lower, however, at a less expensive college, or where the parental contribution is sufficient to meet most of the need, or where a college wants so much to attract a particular student that it is willing to make up the shortfall from a very low self-help by a very high institutional grant (Step 5).

**Step 5.**   The remaining need—that is, the difference between the budget and all the revenue sources assumed in Steps 2–4—must be made up by institutional sources, at the discretion of the college financial aid officer. Some of these sources, such as the federal Supplemental Educational Opportunity Grant, are taxpayer-based. Others are from endowment earnings or current gifts from donors earmarked for aid. Some may come from college operating budgets, constituting a kind of "differential pricing."

**Step 6.**   Should the amounts still be inadequate (which would be the case only for private colleges and generally for those without substantial endowments), the college may help meet the gap either by providing a bit more self help (e.g., a larger NDSL loan or more assured work study) than was originally assumed or by admitting the student but passing the problem of seemingly inadequate assistance on to the student and his or her family. (Some states, for example, have established special nonfederally guaranteed loan programs to help parents borrow more than the officially expected parental contribution.) In fact, although some aid officers might deny the practice, students whose needs are too great and who lack special highly sought-after qualities may be denied admittance on the grounds that the student's academic credentials are not strong enough to warrant the devotion of more institutional resources and the further belief that there is no point in admitting a student who could not attend without extraordinary personal and family hardship.

The resulting aid packages are almost infinitely variable. They cannot be predicted precisely from governmental or college policies, discerned from published averages, or necessarily revealed by student or family self-reporting. Representative aid packages can, however, be illustrated, disaggregated by the cost of the college (e.g., as typified by the range of costs in Table 6.1) and by the income level of the family. Such representative packages are shown in Table 6.6. Student shares, including summer savings, term-time earnings, and loans, range from $800 for a student from a high-income family at a low-cost college to a $5,300 gross, or a $4,500 net, contribution for low- and middle-income students at a high-cost private college. Parental shares, a function of income, assets, and other considerations, range from a low of no contribution at all to a high of an estimated $12,800 for the high-income family with a student at a high-cost college. Taxpayer-borne grants—counting only the taxpayers' share of tuition, room, board, and other expenses, and omitting their share of direct instructional or institutional expenses—range from a low of zero for most high-income families and even for middle-income families at low-cost colleges to a high of more than $4,000 for low-income students at high-cost colleges.

## Trends, Issues, and Summary Observations

The 1980s in the United States have seen an erosion of both the parental and the taxpayer share and a resulting increase in the share borne by the student. These three trends are obviously related, yet are also to some degree independent of one another.

*The Erosion of the Parental Contribution.* The erosion of the parental contribution is due to three principal factors. First is the increasing proportion of undergraduate students who are adult and genuinely independent financially from their parents, the increasing proportion who want to establish a claim of financial independence, plus some whose parents refuse to support them and who have thus forced the issue of independence. Second is the increasing proportion of students, even in the traditional college-going age group, whose parents have divorced or separated, greatly complicating the process of determining need or ability to pay, not to mention actually getting the expected contribution from the estranged parent. A final factor is the apparent diminution of parental willingness to sacrifice for their children's college education, perhaps akin to the growing American disinclination to save, give, or be taxed even for supposedly worthy goals.

The expected parental contribution works best with reasonably affluent parents who have never been divorced, who value higher education for their children and are willing to sacrifice to make it possible, and whose children enter college right after high school and attend full time for four years until graduation. Unfortunately, this no longer describes the overwhelming majority of student-family situations, and the expected parental contribution, while far too significant to be abandoned, may continue to be strained and even eroded.

*A Lessening of Taxpayer (Especially Federal) Support in the Form of Need-Based Grants.* Federal grant aid has declined both in real value and as a proportion of total financial resources available to students during the 1980s. From 1980–81 to 1984–85, federal student aid of all sorts declined 18.9 percent in constant dollars, while federal loan aid and state aid of all forms was increasing.[30] A report by the National Institute of Independent Colleges and Universities on student aid packages between 1979–80 and 1983–84 found the Pell Grant aid to students at independent colleges, for example, falling by 34.5 percent in constant dollars.[31]

Much of the decline in federal grants has been in entitlement programs that were not necessarily need-based, e.g., the phasing out of federal aid to dependent survivors of social security contributions and the phasing down of veteran's benefits. But the need-based grants—principally Pell and Supplemental Educational Opportunity Grants—have also declined in real terms: by 5.7 percent and 17.2 percent respectively.[32] Reasons for the decline in federal student aid, and in grant aid in particular, may be partly economic—that is, a need to reduce all public expenditures in the face of soaring federal budgets—but are more fundamentally ideological. The conservative sentiment represented by the administration of President Ronald Reagan and the Republican majority in the U.S. Senate (and shared by some fiscally conservative Democrats and by others who are otherwise strong supporters of measures to help the truly needy) is that federal need-based aid had become excessive, wasteful, and beyond the levels necessary to assure higher educational opportunities for the children of the needy. Such a sentiment assumes that a diminution of federal aid may indeed lead to a restoration of some lost parental support, to a curtailment of higher educational costs, to more appropriately frugal student living standards, to more student self help, to a greater role for the states vis-à-vis the federal government, or at worst to a return to the work force of those who may not be particularly academically prepared or inclined anyway—any or all of the above consequences being quite acceptable to American conservative ideology.

On the other hand, the erosion of federal grant aid is directly related to the increase in student-debt levels and may be a partial cause of the decline in the proportion of low-income youth, especially minorities, beginning, and especially continuing in, college. College attendance and completion rates for black students, for example, actually dropped between the mid-1970s and the mid-1980s, despite the fact that their high school graduation rates continued to improve.[33]

*Increasing Reliance on Student Loans.* The Guaranteed Student Loan Program increased from 1980–81 to 1984–85 by nearly 26 percent in number of loans, 8.4 percent in size of average loan, and (with other loan programs) from 40.7 to 51.7 percent of all aid in those two benchmark years.[34] This increasing reliance on loans was reported with alarm by Frank Newman in his 1985 report sponsored by the Carnegie Foundation for the Advancement of Teaching. Although corroborating evidence is very thin, Newman echoed concerns held by many American higher education observers as he speculated that the increasing reliance on loans might:

- affect career choices by driving students toward high-paying jobs and away from socially important but less remunerative ones

- discourage students, particularly from low-income and minority backgrounds, from entering or continuing in college

- undercut traditional values such as working one's way through college (with the help of family, philanthropy, or taxpayer) and then starting a career or profession "even" and relatively unburdened, and

- prove to be economically inefficient for the government, which incurs repayment subsidy commitments far into the future, and economically damaging to the private sector, which must compete with students in the capital market and which will find future student purchasing power diminished by repayment obligations.[35]

Newman's speculations about the possible detrimental effects of heavy loan burdens have been disputed by other researchers.[36] Definitive answers are unavailable in 1986. Clearly, though, debt loads, by any historic comparison, are getting very high for some students, and there is as of 1986 no reason to predict any change in this trend.

*The Increasing Practice of Awarding Grants and Price Discounts without Regard to Need.* Not long ago, nearly all American colleges operated under one or more formal or informal compacts that agreed, in essence, to avoid price warfare and to concentrate available aid resources on bringing college within financial reach of the needy rather than to compete for students through offers of financial aid. Like any cartel, these compacts survived as long as the members controlled the supply and as long as demand was high. However, as enrollments in the United States are finally beginning to fall in response to the declining number of college-bound high school graduates (with worse yet to come), and as the marginal costs of educating a student in an underenrolled college falls to near zero, colleges are beginning to cut prices through selective discounts—not just to the needy, who pay relatively little anyway, but to those families who could probably afford to pay all costs but who might be induced to alter their choice of college with a relatively small grant. In addition, the United States in the mid-1980s is in the midst of an "excellence" movement in education that looks with favor on rewards for merit and with disinterest, at best, on public money spent on the nonmeritorious poor. Although the amount of so-called merit aid is still small relative to the amount given on the basis of need, such expenditures do divert resources that might otherwise go either to needy students, to additional operating expenditures, or to curbing the next round of tuition increases. More serious to the critics of non-need-based aid is the observation that any enrollment-altering effect must be short-lived at best, as institutions are forced to match the price discounts of their competitors. "The result," writes Wagner, "is that an increasing proportion of resources will be devoted to price inducements that do nothing to increase access to higher education generally, let alone enrollments at individual institutions."[37]

*Cost Sharing in U.S. Higher Education.*[38] Despite continuing downward pressures on all public expenditures, and despite the increasing proportion of nontraditional college students who may no longer have access to parental resources, it is difficult to imagine a fundamental, massive shift away from the current balance of cost sharing in the United States among parents, taxpayers, and students. To begin with, it is unlikely that the next decade will see any significant change in the underlying costs of instruction, that is, the production function that links inputs such as faculty, staff, books, laboratories, and classrooms with outputs such as students served, research produced, or learning added. Without such a change, these costs must still be borne by the same three or perhaps four parties that bear them today: students, parents, taxpayers, and to a lesser extent institutions or philanthropists. Any further diminution of the taxpayers' share must, then, be taken up by a commensurate increase either in the students' share, which for many students is already the heaviest of any nation, or in the parents' share, which is also already very high by most comparative measures and which is furthermore exceptionally visible and thus vulnerable—either shift being increasingly unpopular politically and thus increasingly unlikely.

It is true that the taxpayer burden could be lessened and the student and the parental burdens at least not increased through a significant reduction in the size and cost of the overall higher educational enterprise itself. For example, if the proportion of youth going on to college, already far higher than in any of the other nations in this study, could only be stabilized, the extension into nontraditional populations ceased or even rolled back, and the amount of time spent in college and graduate school also frozen or even reduced, then enrollments—and presumably costs—could be reduced very significantly, if only temporarily, just by the decline in the number of 18–22 year olds in the United States over the next decade. However, the nation's commitment both to education and to equal opportunity is far too high, and the nation's wealth too great, to permit such a significant abandonment of the principles that underlie the public taxpayer support of higher education. A continued shift of the taxpayer burden from the federal to the state level is possible, although even that trend may soon run its course. The students' share may continue to broaden to embrace even more students than it does now, but it is unlikely to increase significantly when it is now the heaviest. Parents will continue to have a primary and substantial obligation. In short, the costs of U.S. higher education will almost certainly continue to be borne by students, parents, taxpayers, and donors, with each segment alert to resist any attempt on the part of another sector to shift the burden onto it.

# Stresses in the Student Financial Aid System (1991)

MARTIN KRAMER

Thirty-five years ago the leading colleges and universities of the United States reached a consensus that student aid should be awarded ordinarily on the basis of measured financial need alone. That consensus has displayed remarkable staying qualities. Its neutrality toward the sources of aid funds has made it highly flexible as the sources of those funds have changed over time. In addition, the consensus has been able to deal—or appear to deal—with changing student budgets. Because of the apparent adaptability of the need-based financial aid system, it has been easy to assume that the aid system remains unchanged in all essentials, even though its role in financing college attendance has become much larger and more complicated.

This assumption is valid to a very important extent. Affluent parents usually do pay most of the educational bills of their dependent offspring. Students from low-income families usually do have most of their bills paid with aid funds. This income-relatedness of aid holds for most types of colleges and for most students, regardless of their differing talents, academic preparation, gender, and ethnicity.

Yet, of course, times do change. Some of the implicit premises of the need-based aid model would seem much less self-evident if the task of creating such a model from scratch had fallen to a group of knowledgeable people in the 1980s rather than to those who took on the task in the 1950s.

## The Context of the 1950s

A pressing problem for many colleges in the 1950s was to suppress the practice of bidding for desirable students with competing aid offers. This was largely a problem for the private colleges, which then had most of the very limited aid funds available. Enrollments at these institutions were threatened by the rapid decline in the number of veterans with unused GI Bill entitlements. The private institutions also found themselves competing with each other for academic prestige. Then, as now, the issues of enrollments and prestige were related. More students want to enroll in institutions with "elite" reputations. Using aid to recruit the most desirable students thus could attract other students as well.

Although the motivation for the bidding wars was rational, it introduced chaos. Before the bidding wars colleges had awarded most of their aid on the basis of academic or other special promise— often, but not necessarily, with a preference for students who could not otherwise afford to attend college. A scholarship awarded to a student who did not need the money made egalitarians uneasy, but an institution that made such awards usually could say with a clear conscience that its methods for judging merit were fair at any rate. But the bidding wars could have the result that one student would get less money than another of equal merit merely because more colleges were eager to recruit the second student. This seemed unfair by any standard, academic or egalitarian.

The heart of the new consensus that emerged from the bidding wars was to limit aid awards to the difference between what the student's family could afford and what attending the college cost. If all colleges used the same method of measuring family ability to pay, then there could be no bidding wars. Colleges that cost more were allowed to make larger offers of aid, but the assessed family contribution would be the same at any college, so the student's choice among colleges would be financially neutral. This approach also required and enforced intramural fairness: the less a student needed aid to attend, the less the student could get, and students with the same need would get the same amounts.

One measure of the sense of urgency, financial and moral, that brought this need-based consensus into being is that the colleges were willing to impair a long-standing tradition of honoring the intent of philanthropic donors. When a nineteenth-century millionaire left a bequest to a college to provide scholarships to graduates of a particular high school, there was usually an intent that these graduates would be better off than others because of the benefaction. To honor bequests legally and still make the new consensus work, a college first would have to distribute earmarked aid to its designated beneficiaries and then use its unrestricted aid funds to bring the awards of equally needy but undesignated students up to something approaching parity. The tradition of special preferences for designated beneficiaries of trust funds was thus effectively overridden by the new consensus.

The procedure of evening-up, or packaging, as it came to be known, had an important consequence for policy: aid from public sources could be distributed according to the federal or state rules, and then any preference given by those rules could be offset by the distribution of the institution's own unrestricted funds. The continuity of the need-based aid system over thirty-five years of great change in the sources of aid funding owes much to this adaptability of packaging procedures, as well as to the strength of its ideas of equity across families and across institutions.

## Sources of Strain in the Need-Based System

For all its adaptability, the need-based financial aid system is under increasing strain, and the lines of stress are exactly where one would expect to find them—in the areas where the consensus of the 1950s took for granted assumptions that are now considerably less valid. The discussion below focuses on four of these assumptions:

1. that the source of most aid funding would be philanthropy—either restricted or unrestricted and in the control of colleges and universities;

2. that the number of students eligible for need-based aid would be small relative to total enrollments;

3. that the bulk of aid would take the form of grants or scholarships, not loans; and

4. that the recipients of aid would be young full-time students dependent on supportive families.

### The Changing Sources of Aid Funds

The packaging concepts of the need-based aid systems readily allowed the incorporation of aid from nonphilanthropic sources. However, they were not designed to accommodate a predominant reliance on such sources. For example, in most states almost all aid to community-college students comes from public programs. There was virtually no aid of any kind at these institutions before the growth of the public programs. This growth unquestionably represented an increase in financial support for educational opportunities. But the result has also been that the amount of financial aid received by community-college students has rarely been determined by a calculation of need and a packaging procedure of the sort prescribed by the consensus. There has simply not been enough discretionary aid to even up the distribution. At high-tuition private institutions the award of aid according to the consensus model has not been similarly constrained. Federal and state aid awards do not constitute the entire aid package, leaving room for other sources of aid.

However, the consensus did not anticipate that much of the discretionary aid used to even up aid packages often now comes not from philanthropy in the ordinary sense but from the tuition revenues of the institution—that is, from tuitions and fees paid by other students, aided and unaided. The consensus model did not anticipate the growing importance of aid from this source and has nothing to say about it. Yet it is clear that this Robin Hood aid potentially endangers the financial well-being of the institution. Some colleges can be sure of enrolling enough students no matter how much they charge. But others must try to calculate the effects of their decisions about tuition levels, admission policies, and aid awards simultaneously. Tuition must not be so high that the college loses too many affluent students who do not receive offsetting aid. Colleges must admit enough students from higher-income families, who will pay most of the tuition they are nominally charged, to raise enough aid money to support the lower-income students they also want to enroll.

The consensus model is compatible with many different solutions to the problems posed by trying to make tuition, admissions, and aid decisions simultaneously. Some of these solutions, however, can reintroduce the bidding wars of the 1950s through the back door: what is now called "merit" aid is often no more than a way of sanctioning grants to relatively affluent students to make sure that enough of them enroll to make the combined tuition, admissions, and aid policies of the institution work out as planned.

Another source of confusion and strain arising from the changing sources of aid funds is in the set of rules for estimating the ability of families to pay for a college education. The initial formulas of the need-based system expressed what private colleges would expect from middle-class parents who were willing to make substantial sacrifices of the family's standard of living to make a "good" college possible for their children. There was not, and could not be, a demonstrable basis for the validity of such expectations and formulas. They necessarily depended on the experience and judgment of college administrators. It was therefore difficult for colleges to resist growing pressures from state and federal governments to have a say in, and ultimately control over, the measurement of need once these public funding sources had come to provide a preponderant share of the aid available. Much of the empiricism, discretion, and self-governance of the original consensus has thereby been lost. Now, with the 1986 amendments to the Higher Education Act, Congress has prescribed in detail how financial need will be measured for all generally available federal aid programs.

## The Growing Proportion of Aided Students

In the 1950s students receiving aid from all sources were seldom more than one-third of an institution's enrollment, and this only at private colleges with strongly egalitarian admissions policies. Now, at such institutions, the fraction is commonly more than one-half and quite often more than two-thirds. At public institutions the aided fraction usually was, and is, smaller, except for the community colleges, where the fraction aided was negligible in the 1950s and now can be as high as for expensive private colleges, although these students are almost entirely dependent on public resources.

Increases over time in the proportion of students who receive aid mean that student financial aid is no longer a marginal charitable activity of colleges and universities. This also means that aid administration has become a much more mechanical task. The consensus of the 1950 envisioned aid administration as a job depending on administrators' judgments about individual student situations in the application of rules, consisting as much in counseling as in calculation. That is not, and cannot be, the case now. Computers make it much easier to calculate eligibility for aid in large numbers of cases and to estimate the aggregate consequences of changes in the rules. But they also lead to much more inflexible application of the rules, because even the best-staffed aid offices cannot deal individually with large numbers of exceptional cases. In community colleges, where the aid function is often grossly understaffed, almost none of the hand-tailoring of aid packages envisioned by the original consensus is possible.

## Grants Versus Loans

The consensus of the 1950s assumed that most aid would be in the form of grants and scholarships. It has been an abiding assumption in the ideology of aid that grants equalize educational opportunity by taking the place of the financial support a low-income student's parents cannot provide.

Growing reliance on student loans—now about half of all aid—is undermining the validity of this assumption. Grant programs reduce inequality of resources, but loan programs perpetuate it when low-income graduates owe more than do their affluent contemporaries. Although educational opportunities and students' future incomes are equalized no less by loans than by grants, making low-income students dependent on loans undermines the rationale of leveling-up that was central to the consensus of the 1950s. With the growth in loans, student financial aid becomes more financial and less aid. In addition, because the sources of aid are less likely to be philanthropic, and the colleges now are less likely to act financially in loco parentis toward students, a sense of reciprocal obligation is undermined.

The foregoing perhaps suggests that the shift to reliance on credit only affects the "atmosphere" of the aid system. Far from it. Credit, unlike grant aid, does not have to depend on a legislature, college, or foundation appropriating a given amount of money for student aid, with the needs of students competing among other priorities. In a financial system such as that of the United States, the rationing of credit is by the market, and market forces are easily overwhelmed by the kinds of interest subsidies that are available under the federal student loan programs. As a result, credit has expanded into all the gaps, old and new, in the student aid system. Indeed, this is why more than half of a much larger total amount of aid is now in the form of loans. And, until recently, at least a portion of the credit under the Guaranteed Student Loan (GSL) program was outside the need-based system altogether. Federal legislation has traditionally exempted expected parental contributions from consideration in determining the amount of GSL eligibility, on the ground that these loans should be available to serve as loans of convenience for families that could, but would rather not, pay for education out of current resources.

Rationed neither by a appropriation process nor by a system of need-based awards, student loans have been made both to middle-income students who needed no aid and to low-income students for whom grants would have been the aid of choice. It has become easy to find "abuses" in the GSL program—students who are using GSL funds to subsidize consumer purchases or who later contrive reasons to default. Indeed, the loan program often has given all student aid a bad name. It has become hard to remember that in the early days of the need-based system the relatively small loan programs run by individual colleges with philanthropic funding were regarded as a character-building alternative to grants—a way for students to commit themselves to paying their own way, at least in part, on a par with "working your way through college."

The failure of the need-based system to come to terms with student loans has left a loophole that allows a college to comply with the letter of the system but to evade its spirit. The spirit is that like cases should be treated alike financially. But the consensus spoke to the total amount of permissible aid in individual packages, not to the kinds of aid making up the total. It is thus consistent with the consensus (although, many would say, not with "good practice") to include more grant aid and less loan aid in the package offered a less meritorious or desirable student. To do so is not treating like cases alike, because loans represent a less valuable kind of aid. Even when subsidies and inflation make student loans a bargain, they are plainly less valuable than grants. It is hard to believe that the consensus of the 1950s would have taken hold as it did without addressing this possibility of evasion, if loans had been as important then as they are now.

## The Increase in "Nontraditional" Students

The aspect of the need-based system that has shown the greatest degree of strain is the assumption that the task of the aid system is to make college financially possible for dependent, young, and full-time students. At many colleges and universities most students do not now match this description in one or more respects.

The reasons why students arrive at college not dependent, not young, or not full-time are infinitely varied. Students may be independent because they have a successful small business or because their divorced parents simply refuse to provide help. In addition, they may or may not have a spouse with financial resources, who may or may not be willing to pay for education. Students may be older because they are returning to an education career after several or many years in full-time jobs. They may be part-time because they want to hold on to their jobs and to the living standards that their employment has made possible. Other students, although young, prefer a higher standard of living than the meager one an aid administrator would allow and also make the same choice of part-time enrollment.

The educational goals of nontraditional students vary as widely as their background circumstances. The education sought may lead to a credential of immediate cash value and therefore may be self-financing over the short term. Or the education may be recreational for someone living on social security and little else. Even people of the same age may have vastly different financial situations—for example, a successful teacher who is married to a physician and wants an Ed.D. and a welfare mother who wants a first postsecondary technical qualification. Their situations are as different from each other as either is from that of the young dependent student at a liberal arts college.

The concepts of the need-based aid system have been elaborated to try to take all this variety into account. But the problems of bending so many and such extreme variations in circumstances to fit the consensus model are probably insuperable as a practical matter. The need-based system contemplates a neat marshaling of student expenses on one side and student resources on the other. The difference between the two is "financial need," and the role of aid is to bring up the resources to equal (and only equal) the expenses. But for nontraditional students, there are tremendous problems in defining both expenses and resources. On the expense side, there are great differences in the standard of living that is reasonably regarded as "subsistence." The costs of this standard of living are commonly so inextricably mixed with the costs of the habitual and appropriate standard of living of the student's family—parents, siblings, spouse, and children—that just isolating the student's expenses can be impossible. There are too many joint products.

On the resource side, there can be large differences in what students earn in the year before they enroll and large differences in what they may be expected to earn during the academic year. There are also great differences in how much they will earn immediately after they leave school and therefore in their debt-service capacities. There are also great differences in what relatives and spouses, if any, can be expected to contribute.

Of course, standard amounts of expenses and resources can be imputed to impose some degree of uniformity on this variety. Such amounts will be highly arbitrary, however. Further, to the extent that these standard amounts provide generously for real hardship cases of students with large expenses and small resources, they will tend to bleed off aid funds at a rapid rate. Generous treatment of a welfare mother can cost as much as supporting a dozen average aid-eligible traditional students attending the same institution.

Almost from the beginning the need-based system recognized a category of independent students consisting of those whose parents were not expected to make a financial contribution. The problem was—and is—to define the characteristics of such students that make it reasonable to accord them this status. The enormous variability in the situations of nontraditional students in itself would assure the difficulty of the task. Moreover, the changes in family relationships that lead to real independence are usually subtle, private, and gradual, making the task harder still. Add further the difficulty in differentiating intentions from verifiable conditions, and the process of conferring independent status is bound to become more contentious. Finally, the fact that independent status can be enormously advantageous financially—making aid available to relieve parents of educational expenses—creates much room for bad faith, concealment, and contrived compliance with whatever criteria are adopted.

Even when independent status has been accorded, only one set of complications has been confronted. It does not follow from any of the general criteria of independence tried over the years that such a student can be expected to provide a given contribution from his or her own earnings. Even if previously attached to the labor force, students going back to school, especially full-time, will find their earnings shrinking or vanishing. It is for this reason that full-time versus part-time enrollment can be critical, with part-time allowing a greater contribution from earnings. Yet, when the reason for part-time enrollment is the responsibility to care for young children, part-time enrollment still may permit no earnings.

This case brings us to another difficulty: Should the subsistence costs of the children of a student be part of the student's budget, just as much as are the room and board of a younger student with no family responsibilities? The need-based system traditionally has allowed the inclusion of such costs in student budgets, but even if student aid funding were ample enough to cover them, the issue remains of whether a low-income family should be better off than others simply because one member is a student.

## A Second System of Support

The maze of issues raised by the variety in the situations of nontraditional students makes it seem as though no human agency could ever resolve them. That may well be true if we approach the problem of aid for nontraditional students by starting from the concepts and procedures of the need-based system. There are simply too many permutations. But if we look instead at how postsecondary education is financed in fact, the problem is simplified. Actually, there are two distinct patterns for financing educational participation beyond high school. One is the pattern for students who fit the assumptions of the need-based system with only minor and plausible elaborations. For these students, aid does indeed take the place—and only the place—of the parental support received by students from affluent families. The other pattern is that of most nontraditional students. Enormously different as their situations are from each other, they tend to finance their educations by one or another combination of the following resources: earnings from full- or part-time jobs; room and board provided in kind by parents, spouses, or friends; Guaranteed Student Loans; and grants, subject to the rules of the need-based aid consensus.

The reason for placing conventional student aid at the end of this list is that the forms of support higher on the list tend to eliminate or greatly reduce aid eligibility when quantified under the applicable need-analysis formulas. Living at home and part-time enrollment also often have the effect of reducing eligible costs of attendance.

To many, this result seems unfair—especially to representatives of institutions (such as community colleges) that enroll a high proportion of nontraditional students. It is difficult to attend a meeting on student aid policy of any size where there will not be at least one person who decries the neglect of nontraditional students by the need-based system. There is seldom a reply, for everyone present knows that these students often make heroic sacrifices to complete their educations. They also often lack the parental support and future prospects of students who receive substantial support from the need-based system.

Before we are overwhelmed by such comparisons, however, we should recognize that nontraditional students tend to lead considerably more complicated lives than do young full-time undergraduates. Many of the complications are the result of choice—for example, a decision to postpone college until after forming a family or to go to college part-time because of an immediate employment opportunity that holds out the prospect of a higher standard of living. It is not a reproach to the student aid system that it makes one path easier, but not all paths.

Moreover, we may ask whether the student aid system should be responsible when a student's path, chosen or not, turns out to be rockier than one would hope. The need-based aid system tends, by its own ideology and rhetoric, to suggest that the answer is yes. It is commonplace for student aid to be spoken of as removing "obstacles" to college attendance. The evening-up procedures of the need-based system emphasize compensation for disadvantage, and this makes it seem that *every* disadvantage may be grist for the student aid mill. But perhaps this tendency should be resisted. Think about the puzzles to which it leads: if student aid should be available to deal with the difficulties of someone who postponed college in favor of taking a job or starting a family, isn't it unfair to do something about the problem only if, and because, the person becomes a student? What about others in exactly the same situation who have decided not to go to college? And it surely does not make sense to do something for all nontraditional students who have made similar choices *whether or not* they have encountered difficulties along the way.

We can avoid some of these confusions and still maintain reasonable sympathy by thinking of how nontraditional students finance educational participation as a second, alternative system, alongside the need-based system. The main categories of support for nontraditional students were noted above, in an order that represented a set of guesses about the amount of financial support each provides. But another way of ordering them makes it possible to speak of a system—an order of preference. For example, with good reason, most nontraditional students probably would like to be able to depend more on student grants and in-kind support provided by relations and friends and less on earnings and GSL loans. What nontraditional students actually are doing, on their own or with advice, is working out their own packaging process. They see what need-based aid they can get, if any, and how much they can count on relations and friends, and then they figure out how much they must earn and borrow to pay fees and maintain themselves and their families. Some prospective students are able to add in support from employer-sponsored education programs or public income-maintenance programs. Then they decide whether to go ahead with postsecondary education, depending in part on whether they feel they can live with the results of their own packaging.

What the growth of student aid has done over the past two decades for nontraditional students is to add more sources of support to the list—Pell Grants and GSL loans most conspicuously. Student aid *has* made the situation of these students better, although not exactly in the way articulated by the need-based system and although there is a catch: the more they depend on increasing their earnings and reducing their educational expenses (by commuting from home especially), the less need-based aid they will qualify for. The resources they least prefer tend to disqualify them from precisely the aid they most prefer.

There are other ironies when we look at things from the point of view of the "second system." The continuing popularity and political appeal of the College Work-Study program depends on the high regard for the tradition of "working your way through college." Yet the students who best exemplify that tradition, the "nontraditional" students, tend to be excluded from the program if they have jobs in the unsubsidized private sector. Moreover, if they are awarded work-study jobs, they face a 100 percent tax rate on their earnings, because work-study is counted as a resource in the need-based system.

When the GSL program was made part of the need-based system in the 1986 amendments to the Higher Education Act, this was widely regarded as reform unalloyed. In the context of the need-based consensus, it certainly was a reform, because the subsidies provided by the program often were not used to meet measured need. But in the second system the fact that GSL loans previously had escaped need analysis gave them much of their value. They represented resources available for educational participation even if a student's costs were low and earnings high. Now the need-based catch applies to GSL loans as well as to grants and work-study.

## Conclusion

Several observations are in order on how policies may be altered to relieve the stresses and bolster the effectiveness of the student aid system. When innovative financing mechanisms are considered, it is important to think about how they would fit in with the mechanisms of the existing system as it is, and not only as it is supposed to be or as one would wish it to be.

First, it should be recognized that at institutions (such as community colleges) whose aided students are almost entirely dependent on public programs, the packaging process can do very little to smooth out anomalies created by new programs. Although coordination between new and old programs is desirable in principle for all students, it is critical for these students.

Second, institutional interests need to be seen clearly. Private institutions have an enormous stake in programs that increase the availability of aid funds coming from outside the institution. They also have an enormous stake in any program that will tend to reduce measured financial need among their students, such as some of the proposed savings plans.

Third, the new dependence on student loans is proving very troublesome, and it is disquieting that many of the proposals for new loan programs are aimed at, or are consistent with, persuading students to depend on credit even more. This is usually to be done by lengthening repayment periods, making installments proportionate to income, or both. Attention should be paid to alternatives that would relate the amount of borrowing to student characteristics, such as costs of attendance, measured financial need, or year in college—formulas that might restrain dependence on loans rather than increase it.

Because of the continuing influence of the need-based model, it is easy to focus exclusively on the role new programs would play in the need-analysis and packaging process. Yet attention also should be given to how they might make the second system stronger or weaker. For example, some proposals for aid in compensation for public service would cut back on other aid in order to drive students into a service program. But for many students who rely on the second system, the public service approach would be a cruel absurdity. For example, what about a teacher's aide and mother of four who wants to go to college to get a bachelor's degree and a teaching credential and who is going to earn all the money she can in part-time jobs? Is this someone whose grant and loan entitlements, such as they are, should be constrained to force her participation in designated "public service?"

The extraordinary achievements of the need-based system should be recognized, and the system should not be interfered with lightly where it is working well. However, the strains that are disguised by these achievements also should be recognized and taken into account as innovations in college financing are developed.

# The Effects of Student Financial Aid (1988)

LARRY LESLIE AND PAUL BRINKMAN

The explicit goal of need-based student financial aid is to ensure that, given a minimal level of academic competence, all students have an equal opportunity to participate in higher education. Specifically, the intent of such aid is to remove financial barriers that could prevent individuals from enrolling in college, unduly restrict their choice of institution, or bring about their premature departure from college. The questions for policymakers, taxpayers, and those who work in higher education are whether student financial aid is effective in achieving these goals and, if so, to what extent.

Government-sponsored student financial aid as we know it began in the mid-1960s. By the mid-1980s, the Federal effort alone had leveled off at around $10 billion annually, including about $1 billion in veterans benefits. Federal subsidies of Guaranteed Student Loans (GSL) are part of that $10 billion. Although the amount borrowed through the GSL and other government loan programs is included in some analyses under the rubric of student aid, in fact only the government subsidy constitutes aid, with the remainder representing a student rather than a government expenditure. The states contribute approximately another $1 billion, and the institutions at least another $3 billion (differences among reporting procedures across the nation make the latter figure difficult to determine precisely), making the total package about $14 billion.

These billions of dollars affect student demand for higher education by lowering the net price students must pay. Whereas in the previous chapter we examined the effects of increases in the cost of college, here, by implication, we examine the effects of cost decreases that come about through the student aid mechanism. Theoretically, there is little mystery about the effects of student aid. Aid recipients should enroll in large numbers, attend higher-cost institutions more often, and complete their education with greater frequency than comparable nonrecipients because their net, or true, costs are lower.

In practice, however, determining the actual effects of student aid is a formidable task, due to a variety of methodological problems ranging from mundane data issues to the subtleties of econometric modeling. The data problems are substantial. As of the mid-1980s, a comprehensive, national student aid data base did not exist, making it impossible to determine, for example, how much total aid a given individual received or the magnitude of the net price faced by the student after aid has been awarded.

Other methodological problems stem from the sheer complexity of human behavior. Researchers have had difficulty in isolating the effects of student aid from a myriad of other influences. In all likelihood, the aid effects are relatively weak compared to factors known to be important, such as parents' education. It would be surprising, would it not, if nothing more than a reduction in the net price of attendance could overcome years of relative deprivation of many kinds experienced by typical low-income families? Furthermore, there is evidence to suggest that the college attendance decision routinely occurs early in the high school years, well before at least the specifics of the student aid picture could be expected to have much effect (Hearn, 1980).

Student aid itself is complicated. It can take the form of an outright grant, a job, a loan with varying degrees of interest subsidy, or, quite often, some combination thereof. Conceivably, the effectiveness of student aid could be related to its form as well as its amount.

The supply side of the equation is not without is problems, too. Student aid researchers usually assume that the number of enrollment places expands indefinitely to meet any level of demand. Serious conceptual and statistical problems may arise if the assumption does not hold. However, in reality, phenomena such as enrollment caps at major public universities and even the deliberate downsizing of a few such universities have occurred during the last decade, and many of the elite private institutions have traditionally maintained enrollment ceilings. Institutional budget cuts, which were common during the late 1970s and early 1980s, reduced the outreach efforts and the availability of services that are vital in stimulating and maintaining the enrollment of low-income students. Strictly speaking, then, the assumption of unlimited supply of enrollment places is probably invalid. The quantitative relationships are murky, however, and it is conceivable that supply limitations, although real, have little material effect.

In what follows we first discuss briefly the various approaches that have been used to analyze the effects of student aid. Then we review what has been learned about the effectiveness of student aid with respect to each of its three purpose: improving access, providing choice, and contributing to persistence. Each goal is examined individually because that is how researchers typically deal with them, but interaction effects are also noted.

## Analytical Approaches

Three distinct approaches have been used to measure the impact of student aid: econometric analyses of enrollment behavior, surveys of student opinions on the impact of student aid, and calculations of higher education participation rates. Findings based on all of the approaches will be examined in this chapter. None of the three is without its weaknesses, but taken together they do provide a reasonably sound basis for evaluating the effects of student aid.

In the econometric approach, researchers typically use multivariate statistical techniques. As is generally true of statistical modeling of complex phenomena, this method is subject to various threats to the accuracy and reliability of the estimated effects. These threats include biased parameter estimates resulting from omission of a variable that belongs in the model, misleading measures of statistical significance resulting from collinearity among the independent variables, misinterpretations of estimated effects because of a failure to "identify" the model properly, and so on. Still, all things considered, this is the preferred method for determining the effects of student aid because the econometric approach affords the researcher the best opportunity to control systematically the influence of intervening variables (i.e., events or characteristics that mask the true relationship between student aid and enrollment).

A second approach to assessing the impact of student aid is to ask students how they perceive that impact on their own attendance decisions. Unfortunately, there is a good chance that these impressions of the effect of student aid will be biased upward. Students have an obvious interest in keeping their cost of attendance as low as possible, and they are likely to be prone to exaggerating the effects of financial factors on their decision to enroll or remain in college.

The participation rate studies are similar to the econometric analyses in that they examine actual behavior, but they resemble the impressionistic studies in the simplicity of their methodology. They address the following question: Do changes in higher education participation rates for target populations move in the same direction as changes in the overall amount of student aid? Often, this approach is the form of practical political test used to assess public policy initiatives. If participation rates and student aid amounts move in the same direction, then one has *prima facie* evidence that the student aid initiative is working, whereas a lack of such correlation may be viewed as a policy failure.

Although popular and seemingly straightforward, this approach is the most seriously flawed because, in effect, it fails to recognize the complexity of the phenomena being investigated. Although one can readily observe participation rates over time along with changes in the amount of student aid, one cannot readily ascertain the extent to which other socioeconomic dynamics (including the composition or type of aid) may have caused whatever rate behaviors are observed. Typically the studies include no formal control over the influence of these other factors, apart from an occasional adjustment of the income categories to reflect the movement of prices in the economy.

Not only the methodology, but the underlying assumption of this approach can be challenged. Carlson (1976) reasons as follows:

> Equality of opportunity in higher education does not imply equality of demand. That is, there is no reason to expect or even desire that all types of individuals should enroll in colleges and universities in equal proportions. Because of varied preferences across segments of the population, the usefulness of enrollment rates as measures of access and choice is very limited and without any solid foundation. (p. 10).

Of course, this reasoning is not beyond question either, as it assumes that in these matters one safely can ignore the reasons for varied preferences. It is not within the scope of this book, however, to pursue issues of social and political philosophy. Our task is to assemble the evidence that will indicate whether student aid does what it purports to do. Many individuals consider participation rates to be an important part of that evidence, so it is appropriate to discuss them in this chapter.

In reviewing the findings of the studies that comprise each of these approaches, two questions will be addressed: Does student aid have any effect? If it does, what is the magnitude of that effect? As might be imagined, the first of the two questions is by far the easier to answer. Indeed, for the second question we shall have to be content with "ballpark" figures in most instances. To the extent that such figures can be firmly established, however, we will have accomplished something of value, given the current scarcity of even rough estimates.

The emphasis throughout this discussion will be on the impact of aid on low-income students, the primary target population of most need-based student aid. Low-income students are either independent students with low incomes or, more often, dependent students from families with low incomes. The effects of student aid on middle-income and high-income students will occasionally be discussed as well. The former have at times been the target of aid policies, and the later often serve as a benchmark for gauging the effects of student aid programs on lower-income groups.

## Integrative Review Results

In examining the effects of student aid, varying degrees of integration will be achievable. We are, after all, examining three issues—access, choice, and persistence—from the perspective of three methodological approaches. In some instances, the studies to be reviewed generate results that, when standardized, can be the basis for meaningful measures of central tendency, such as mean or modal values. In other instances, the review will be able to go no further than assembling results in a manner that makes it possible for patterns to be observed.

## Access

Student aid either lowers the cost of attendance through grants or makes additional funds available to students through loans or work opportunities. Either way, student aid makes it easier financially to attend college. But does student aid do more than that? Is it at least partly responsible for the fact that some students attend at all? What proportion of students now attending college are doing so partly because of student aid? What proportion would not have entered college in the absence of student aid, or some portion thereof? These are the questions addressed in the studies reviewed in this section.

The review will be organized around the three methodologies described above. Findings from econometric analyses will be examined first, followed by those from student opinion surveys and participation rate calculations. This way of proceeding is desirable because the nature of the evidence varies so greatly among the three approaches. In a concluding section, and occasionally before then, the summary findings are compared across methodologies.

## Econometric Analyses

Nine econometric studies were found. Data on the seven studies used for the integrative review as shown in Table 8.1 (additional details can be found in Appendix Table 7). The data show the percentage of full-time low-income enrollment that is dependent on student aid—that is, the percentage of students who would not be enrolled without aid. As expected, the effect on students from low-income families is by far the strongest. Without aid, mostly in the form of nonrepayable grants, the enrollment of low-income students would be reduced by about 20-40 percent, depending on the estimate. The estimated effect on middle-income students is much smaller: The range across five studies is 7.4-19.5 percent. Other results of the econometric studies are that the magnitude of the impact of student aid varies by type of aid, sex, race, and level of academic achievement. The seven studies differ in important respects: the manner in which income categories are delineated, the type of aid whose effects are examined, and the assumptions about the rules governing the awarding of aid (e.g., whether an award can be treated as a substitute for other aid). These differences limit the comparability of the results shown.

Four of the studies (Carroll, Mori, Relles, and Weinschrott, 1977; Jackson, 1978; Manski and Wise, 1983; Blakemore and Low, 1985) are based on data from the National Longitudinal Study (NLS) of 1972, which surveyed approximately 22,000 high school seniors across the nation. All four studies use complex statistical techniques and a great deal of control over factors that might be expected to influence the decision to enroll, factors such as characteristics of the students themselves, their families, or the high schools they attended, and the costs and other features of the colleges they plan to attend. It is important to note that the Basic Educational Opportunity Grant (BEOG) program was not yet funded in 1972. (BEOGs were renamed Pell Grants in 1980; the original name will be used in this chapter for studies that examine effects of this aid program in the 1970s, while the current name will be used for studies involving grant aid from 1980 onward.) The federal programs operated by the Office of Education in 1972 consisted of loans, College Work Study, and Supplemental Educational Opportunity Grants (SEOG). Veterans assistance, the largest program at that time, was not a factor in the NLS because this survey was administered to students before they had the opportunity to be in military service. In contrast, another large grant program, Social Security benefits for 18-22-year-olds with deceased or disabled parents, was a factor even though it was not need-based. Grants were also available form the institutions, of course, as they had been from the early years of higher education in this country, but the focus of this type of aid has traditionally included merit as well as need. The same is true for Merit Scholarships, which came into existence long before the 1970s.

Blakemore and Low (1985) found that financial aid offers in the form of grants have a significantly different impact on students of varying ethnic background, level of academic achievement, and family income. They estimated that a 30 percent drop in total grant aid per capita would result in the following percentage enrollment declines: white males, 5.2; white females, 7.1; black males, 8.5; and black females, 4.7. Among students with a 2.75 grade point average (GPA) and a family income of $11,000 or less (1982 dollars), the percentage declines were as follows: white males, 8.3; white females, 12.0; black males, 6.3; and black females, 3.5. The percentage declines

**Table 8.1**
**The Impact of Student Aid on Access: Econometric Studies**
**Estimated Percentage of Full-Time Enrollment Dependent on Grant Aid (by Level of Family Income)**

| | Family Income | | |
| --- | --- | --- | --- |
| | **Low** | **Middle** | **High** |
| Range of Effects as | 41.5 | 19.5 | 3.5 |
| Estimated in Various Studies | 37.3 | 14.1 | 3.0 |
| | 37.0 | 12.4 | 2.4 |
| | 34.4 | 11.1 | |
| | 32.1 | 7.4 | |
| | 30.8 | | |
| | 20.6 | | |
| | 19.5 | | |
| Mean | 31.7 | 12.9 | 3.0 |

were estimated to be much greater for students with lower (2.25) GPAs, but much smaller for students with higher (3.5) GPAs. For example, enrollment among low-income, low-GPA white males would decline 13.6 percent, compared to only 3.5 percent for low-income, high-GPA black males. Blakemore and Low did not provide aggregate data. To derive the composite figures shown in Table 8.1, we used their estimated rates for students with average GPAs along with weighted averages reflecting the relative number of enrolled students by sex and race, and we assumed that the effects of totally eliminating grant aid would be a linear extension of the effects of eliminating 30 percent of such aid. Race and gender differences in response to grant aid are explored in greater detail in an earlier study of Blakemore and Low (1983), with results similar to those reported here.

Manski and Wise (1983) used data from the NLS to built a simulation model that predicted the impact of the federal BEOG program on 1979-1980 freshmen enrollment in postsecondary education institutions. They derived alternative estimates based on whether BEOGs would replace or be complementary to other aid awards. Under the assumption that BEOGs would be substituted for other aid, their model estimates that low-income enrollment would decline by 37.3 percent in the absence of the BEOG awards. Enrollment of middle- and upper-income students, who together received 40 percent of all BEOG money in 1979-1980, would decrease by 11 percent and 2 percent, respectively, without the BEOG awards. The estimated effects of BEOGs on enrollment are of course more positive assuming that they complement other aid.

Manski and Wise concluded that the BEOG program is indeed effective in increasing access, but that a significant fraction of BEOG funds is spent as a pure subsidy. They calculated that in 1979-1980 only about 25 percent of BEOG awards went to students who would not otherwise have enrolled, compared to 39 percent in 1977-1978, when the BEOG program had less liberal income-eligibility requirements (i.e., it was limited more to low-income students). Since then, those requirements have been tightened again.

Carroll et al. (1977) also used data from the NLS to stimulate the enrollment effects of BEOGs, but their approach differed from that of Manski and Wise in several important respects, including statistical techniques and objectives. The purpose of the Carroll et al. analysis was to investigate how various ways of implementing the BEOG program would affect the number of students induced to attend college. Among the policy alternatives examined were award ceilings, the percentage of cost covered by the grant, the percentage of need covered by the grant, and so on. The estimated enrollment effect of 20.6 percent, which is shown in Table 8.1, is the mean value for ten different simulations based on variations in these award rules.[1]

Carroll et al. found that none of the BEOG policies they considered had much effect on the enrollment behavior of nonwhite males. Nonwhite and white females were about equally responsive to aid. White males were more responsive to aid than were nonwhite males, but less responsive than were the females of either ethnic group. The results reported by Carroll et al. differ most from those of Blakemore and Low with respect to nonwhite males. Taken together, the results of the two studies suggest that the ethnic background and gender of students make a difference in the impact of student aid, but that more research needs to be done to sort out what is apparently a complex set of relationships and interactions among ethnicity, gender, and economic status.

Carroll and colleagues' findings are more congruent with Blakemore and Low's with respect to the differential impact of aid on students on differing academic abilities. The latter investigators found that low-income students of low ability were nearly four times as sensitive to aid offers in deciding whether to attend college than were low-income students of higher ability. For students of all income levels, Carroll et al. estimated that students in the lowest ability quartile were about twice as responsive to BEOG awards as students in the highest quartile. As these authors point out, high-ability students will attend college in relatively large numbers regardless of aid, but the same is not true for low-ability students. Many of the latter apparently require a cost reduction in order to achieve a favorable cost-benefit ratio for attending college.

One of the ways in which Jackson's (1978) study differs from the other three NLS based studies is that he compared the impact of the awarding of aid with the impact of the amount of aid awarded. He found that the offer of aid has a much greater impact on access than does the amount of the award. This result is not totally surprising. The amount of aid, given some level of family income, is largely a function of the cost of attending a particular institution. Thus, for many students the amount of aid may have more effect on the choice of institution than on the basic decision to attend college.

In contrast to Jackson, Carlson (1975) reported that the amount of aid did have a statistically significant effect on enrollment. Carlson also estimated that loans and work study were only about half as effective as grants in stimulating enrollment of low-income students. Interestingly, loans were more effective than grants with respect to the enrollment of middle-income students.

One other econometric study, Berne's (1980) analysis of factors affecting enrollment at community colleges, examined the effect of the award amount. In this case, one would expect the amount to influence access because at this type of institution, typically the lowest-cost alternative, many students are likely to be deciding between higher education enrollment and some other option. As expected, Berne found that the greater the amount of grant aid, the greater the positive effect on enrollment.

Crawford (1966) calculated that the presence of student aid led to an increase of 14.8 percent in the enrollment of financial needy National Merit Scholars of 1958-1959. The students involved, both those awarded as well as those denied aid, were highly talented (for example, both groups had average combined Scholastic Aptitude Test [SAT] scores of about 1250). Inasmuch as the work of Blakemore and Low and Carroll et al. shows that the impact of grant aid on high-ability students is much less than on those with low or medium ability, and given the known correlation between academic performance and family income plus the greater response to aid by low-income youth, it is reasonable to assume that Crawford's estimate understates substantially the effect of aid on students overall, and especially on low-income students. If one adjusts Crawford's finding to reflect the impact of ability, by using the mean of the relationship estimated in the Carroll et al. and Blakemore and Low studies, the result is a low-income enrollment effect of about 37 percent.

The eighth econometric study did not contain sufficient data to present findings in the form required for inclusion in Table 8.1, but, in general, the results support those of the other studies. In this study, Weinschrott (1978) simulated the effects of grants and loans on the enrollment of students at several income levels, using data from the NLS. He found that grant aid induced additional enrollment of low-income students, while loans increased the enrollment of middle-income students. The average effects for loans, expressed as elasticities, were about 88 percent as large as the average effects for grants.

Finally, in simulating various effects of the Tuition Assistance Program (TAP) in New York, Mullen (1982) estimated that for every additional $100 in the average grant award (1982 dollars), low-income enrollment in New York higher education would increase by about 1.2 percent. Mullen suggests that the enrollment gain would have been larger had it not been for the presence of substantial amounts of aid available prior to the inception of the TAP.

Several studies presented usable data on the relative impact on enrollment of a decrease in tuition versus an increase of the same amount in grant aid. Theoretically, one would expect there to be little difference except that tuition tends to be known further in advance and is more definite. Despite the attention given to student aid in the media and, presumably, by high school counselors and college admissions recruiters, knowledge about student aid is anything but universal within the target population. For example, Olson and Rosenfeld (1984) reported that 52 percent of surveyed parents of high school seniors in 1980 know nothing about BEOG/Pell Grants. Given a lack of knowledge about the availability of aid, tuition should have a slightly greater impact than a comparable amount of grant aid (Hyde, 1978).

The empirical evidence in the access studies is inconclusive. Manski and Wise (1983) found that the estimated parameters for tuition, dormitory costs, and discretionary grant aid (not including (BEOGs) were roughly similar for 4-year colleges and vocational-technical schools, but grant aid was nearly four times as potent as tuition at 2-year colleges—a relationship that the authors could not explain in terms of their model. In Blakemore and Low's (1985) model, a change in tuition was, on average, about three time as effective as a comparable change in grant aid. The difference in impact was smaller for males and greater for females, favoring tuition in both instances. Carlson (1975) estimated that a $100 increase in grant aid was just slightly less effective (.86, to be precise) than a $100 decrease in tuition as a way of increasing enrollment. In a study that will be discussed in more detail in the section on choice, Schwartz (1985) estimated that grant aid had more than twice the impact of a comparable amount of tuition at 4-year institutions, but warned of estimation problems. Only Carlson's finding and some of the estimates in Manski and Wise would seem to be plausible, but no more than that can be said on the basis of the available studies. Clearly, more research is warranted on this important question.

## Surveys of Student Opinions

A second approach to assessing the impact of student aid on access is to ask students how they perceive that impact on their own attendance decisions. Table 8.2 shows the results of asking aid recipients whether they would attend college without a particular form of grant aid. All aid was need-based except in the Springer (1976) study of the Social Security program. Typically about one-fourth to one-half of those asked indicated that they would not attend either full-time or part-time without the aid. The 22 data points range from 22.5 percent to 67.1, with a mean value of 42.6 percent. As expected, the reported effects are greater for students from low-income families: The mean values were 45.4 percent for the lowest-income group and 35.1 percent for the middle-income group.

The results obtained by Fence, Boyd, and Maxey (1979) for the Illinois state student aid program show an increasing effect of the program over the decade in which surveys were conducted. (The results of the first survey, in 1967, were exceptionally low; they are not included in Table 8.2 but can be found in Appendix Table 7.) The reason for this growth in the perceived impact of the Illinois aid programs is not apparent, nor do the authors of the study venture an opinion on the matter. They also found a larger effect for those awarded grants as opposed to merit-based scholarships. This was to be expected, they indicated, because the latter individuals presumably have greater motivation to attend and more options for financing their college education without

**Table 8.2**
**The Impact of Student Aid on Access: Student Opinion Surveys**
**Estimated Percentage of Full-Time Enrollment Dependent on Grant Aid,**
**Based on Surveys of Student Aid Recipients (by Level of Family Income)**

|  | Family Income | | |
|---|---|---|---|
|  | Low | Middle | Others |
| Range of Effects as | 67.1 | 44.9 | 36.0* |
| Estimated in Various Studies | 65.3 | 43.7 |  |
|  | 53.8 | 37.1 |  |
|  | 50.9 | 27.5 |  |
|  | 50.5 | 22.5 |  |
|  | 50.4 |  |  |
|  | 50.3 |  |  |
|  | 46.5 |  |  |
|  | 45.8 |  |  |
|  | 44.6 |  |  |
|  | 43.4 |  |  |
|  | 37.5 |  |  |
|  | 36.5 |  |  |
|  | 32.8 |  |  |
|  | 26.9 |  |  |
|  | 23.7 |  |  |
| Mean | 45.4 | 35.1 | 36.0 |
| Overall mean = 42.6 |  |  |  |

*Social Security beneficiaries (Springer, 1976).

state student aid. However, mixed results were obtained by Fife and Leslie (1976) in their analysis of the grant and scholarship programs in New Jersey, perhaps because of differences in regulations governing the two types of aid.

In commenting on the differences among the states in their study, Fife and Leslie attributed the relatively small effects in California, 36.5 percent for low-income and 22.5 for middle-income recipients, to the availability of an inexpensive alternative should aid not be forthcoming. At that time, the state's community college system had no tuition.

The studies shown in Table 8.2 reflect the views of student aid recipients only. There are several student surveys that assess more broadly the effect of student aid on access. In a survey of high school seniors, Leslie et al. (1977) found that among those planning to attend college, 43.5 percent of low-income students, 27.7 percent of middle-income students, and 15.0 percent of high-income students said they could not attend without student aid. In a survey of Kentucky high school seniors who were eligible for need-based state aid but were denied assistance because of a shortage of funds in the aid program, Foreman, Lunceford, and Elton (1984) found that 44.8 percent of those who subsequently did not attend college attributed their failure to insufficient student aid. During the 1950s and early 1960s, there was concern about the loss of talent represented by very able, low-income high school graduates who did not go on to college. A series of studies was done to estimate the portion of that loss that could be attributed to a lack of financial resources. Crawford (1966) reviewed five of those studies: The mean of the effects he reported was 47 percent. That is, an average of 47 percent of nonenrolled, highly talented recent high school graduates indicated that lack of money was the primary reason for their decision not to enroll in college.

How do the results of the student opinion studies in Table 8.2 compare with the results from econometric studies? Because the aid-recipient surveys address the effect of state grant programs only, as opposed to that of all grant aid in the econometric studies, a straightforward comparison is not fully appropriate. Nonetheless, the results from the two sets of studies appear to be reasonably similar. For example, if we assume that two-thirds of low-income students receive grant aid, then according to the aid-recipient surveys the amount of enrollment dependent on grant aid would be .67 x .454 (from Table 8.2), or 30.4 percent. This figures is at the midpoint of the 20-40 percent range obtained from the econometric studies. If 33 percent of middle-income students are awarded grant aid, then .33 x .351, or 11.6 percent, of middle-income enrollment would be lost if grant aid were eliminated. The comparable range in the econometric studies was 7.4-19.5 percent.[2]

. . .

## Summary for Access

Overall, the results for access are as follows. All of the econometric analyses and student opinion surveys indicate that student aid, at least in the form of grants, does increase the enrollment of low-income individuals. The results of the participation rate studies do not lend themselves to unambiguous interpretation, but most studies indicate that a greater proportion of eligible low-income individuals were participating in higher education in the early 1980s than prior to the advent of the major grant program (BEOG/Pell).

The econometric analyses suggest that about 20-40 percent of low-income enrollment is the result of grant aid. How many students do these percentages represent? Rough estimates, pegged to 1982-1983, can be developed as follows. Data on the number of full-time, low-income students in higher education are not readily available. The most recent data available are for 1978-1979 (in Frances, 1982). If $12,000 in 1978 dollars is chosen as the cutoff point for low-income families—median income in calendar year 1978 was $17,640—then 37.4 percent of all full-time students in higher education in 1978-1979 came from low-income families. If the proportion of low-income students remained about the same into the 1980s, and given that higher education enrolled about 7 million full-time students per year during that time, then the full-time, low-income group would have numbered about 2.6 million. Given that number, the econometric results indicate that in 1982-1983 about 500,000 to 1 million low-income students were enrolled in college because of grant aid. If 45.9 percent of all full-time students continued to come from middle-income families (defined as families with incomes from $12,000 to $30,000 in 1978), as they did in 1978, and the enrollment of 13 percent of such students is dependent on grant aid (the mean value from Table 8.1), then grant aid accounted for the enrollment of 415,000 middle-income students. In all, then, the econometric studies suggest that in 1982-1983 about 900,000 to 1.4 million full-time students were enrolled because of student aid in the form of grants. The midpoint of those figures, 1.15 million, is about 45 percent of the annual number of Pell Grants awards and represents roughly 16.4 percent of all full-time students in that year.

Comparable estimates based on the student opinion surveys in Table 8.2 lead to rather similar conclusions. About 51 percent of all full-time students receive some student aid, not counting Guaranteed Student Loans (Anderson, 1984). If we assume that about 10 percent of the recipients received no grant aid in 1982-1983, that would leave about 3 million students receiving grant aid of some kind (an assumption is required because of the lack of recipient information that cuts across types of aid). In any case, 3 million would seem to be a conservative estimate, given that the Pell Grant program alone accounted for 2.5 million recipients. Multiplying 3 million by 42.6 percent (the overall mean value from Table 8.2) yields an estimate of 1.3 million students whose enrollment in 1982-1983 depended on grant aid.

A third estimate can be generated using the results of the student demand studies in Chapter 7. The modal result from those studies was that a $100 decrease in tuition is accompanied by a 1.8 percent increase in enrollment. Let us assume, for the sake of argument, the correctness of Carlson's (1975) estimate that $100 dollars in grant aid is .86 times as effective as $100 in tuition. Then for every $100 in the average grant aid offer, we would expect a 1.55 percent enrollment increase among those offered aid. To obtain a rough estimate of the amount of grant aid available for low- and middle-income students, the target population, let us assume that they received all of Pell, SEOG, veterans benefits, and state grants, plus $1 billion in institutional grants, for a total of $7.3 billion in grant aid (as of 1982-1983). The number of full-time low- and middle-income students is 5.3 million, based on the data from Frances (1982) previously cited. Dividing the total amount of grant aid by the total number of students results in an estimate of $1400 as the average aid offer. The arithmetic, then, is simply 14 x .0155 x 5.3 million, and the result is an estimate that grant aid was responsible for the enrollment of roughly 1.5 million full-time students. In reality, of course, students will be offered aid that is less than or more than the average, or they will not be offered any aid, so the arithmetic is a considerable simplification. The assumption is that these phenomena will have a tendency to cancel on another, so that the simplification can stand as a reasonable estimate. For example, if some students do not receive aid, then the average award to those who do will increase, which in turn will result in a larger portion of the aid recipients enrolling than would have been the case with smaller average awards.

Whether readers will attribute the similarity of these three estimates to the discovery of truth, to chance, or to the ingenuity of the authors of this book will depend, perhaps, on the extent to which they are comfortable with the numerous assumptions and intermediate estimates used. From our perspective, the estimate that best reflects the studies reviewed is that in 1982-1983 the enrollment of about 1-1.3 million full-time students was dependent on grant aid.

## Choice

By lowering the cost of attendance, student aid helps make it possible for individuals of limited financial means to participate in higher education in some form. The question addressed in this section is whether student aid also helps make it possible for those same individuals to attend the full range of higher education institutions.

Student aid achieves its purpose to the extent that it reduces the number of occasions when income dictates where a student enrolls. The issue is sometimes framed as though it were a matter of ensuring that students can attend their first-choice institution. This is a less satisfactory way of defining the objective. It is highly probable that student and family income play an important role in shaping the initial choice set, that is, the range of institutions initially considered to be viable options. If disproportionately large numbers of low-income students have low cost and less prestigious institutions as their first choices, and there is some evidence for this suggestion (Munday, 1976), then realizing those choices would not achieve the goal of equal opportunity.

With few exceptions, the research studies reviewed in this section focus on the enrollment distribution of students from different income levels. The distributions considered important are those between high cost and low cost institutions, public and private institutions, and institutions that differ by status: 2-year and 4-year colleges, and universities. Because control (public versus private) and status typically are correlated with price, most studies are in effect examining enrollment choices in relation to the price of attendance. Nonetheless, the other distinctions are important in their own right. There is evidence to suggest that an individual's postschooling economic and social position in society is heavily influenced by the type and caliber of college he or she attends (Trusheim and Crouse, 1981). Other interests are at stake as well. Allowing students a wide range of choices has the secondary effects of promoting institutional diversity. Appropriately configured, student aid will reduce the tuition gap between public and private institutions, thereby helping the latter institutions remain competitive, especially among low-income students.

For expository purposes, the studies reviewed are again organized by their general investigatory approach: econometric analyses, student opinion surveys, and compilations of participation rates (in the form of enrollment shares by type of institution). As was true for access, the number of studies concerning the effects of student aid on student choice is modest given the complexity of the issue. Nonetheless, the studies are sufficient to show beyond any reasonable doubt that student aid does help ensure choice. They also provide some idea of the magnitude of that effect.

## Econometric Analyses

A total of 23 econometric analyses were found that analyze how student financial aid impacts on student choice. No one analytic approach was used in all of them; instead, three distinct approaches predominated. In the first set of studies to be reviewed, the focus is on choice effects as viewed from an institutional perspective. In the second set of studies, the research centers on the choice effects of federal and state student aid programs. In the third set of studies, student choice patterns are examined without reference to specific institutions or aid programs. Only one of the three approaches leads to results that can be synthesized quantitatively, but each approach leads to findings that are of some interest. A brief outline of several important findings will serve to organize the presentation that follows. Further details on the individual studies can be found in Appendix Table 7.

The econometric studies converge around the following results:

1.  Institutions can improve their ability to recruit students by using student aid. In situations in which students are clearly choosing between two or more institutions, student aid that reduces the net price difference by $100 will have a positive enrollment effect of about 1.8 percent on the higher cost institutions.

2.  The effect of Pell Grants on student choice is unclear. The studies that have examined this issue have come up with conflicting results. The positive choice effects of state student aid programs have been more clearly established.

3.  Application and enrollment patterns for a variety of students at least hint that student aid has had a beneficial effect on student choice.

In addition to these findings, some patterns mentioned in the previous section again appear. Students from low-income families are the most sensitive to the price of attendance and to the awarding of student aid. Aid in the form of grants has the largest effect on the enrollment behavior of students from low-income families.

The largest group of studies, 10 in all, examined the choice effects of student aid from the perspective of institutions in direct competition for students. The estimate of the effect of a $100 decrease in the net price difference between competing institutions is based on 4 of those studies (Berne, 1980; Tierney, 1980; Tierney, 1982; Tierney and Davis, 1985). The methodology used in these studies was standard regression or logit analysis of the choice behavior of students who had applied to more than one type of institution. The choices examined were between public and private institutions, different types of public and private institutions, and between community colleges and other types of institutions. In all of the studies, a great deal of control was exercised statistically over student and institutional characteristics. The net price variables consistently performed as one would expect theoretically.

The four studies produced 11 data points. The data initially took the form of changes in enrollment probabilities. These data were standardized to reflect the percentage change in enrollment that would be experienced by the higher cost institution (in the various institutional pairings) if it reduced the price differential with the lower cost institution by $100 (in 1982 dollars). The value of 1.8 percent is both the median and the mean value for the results distribution, although the range is large (.8 percent to 3.6 percent).

By extrapolation from the 1.8 percent figure, the impact of aid that changes the net price difference by $1000 would have a positive low-income enrollment effect on the higher cost, aid-awarding institution of 18 percent. In other words, for every 100 low-income applicants who would have chosen an institution with significantly lower costs, the higher cost institution would enroll 18 additional students, from the 100 applicants, by raising its average aid award by $1000. This figure should be used with caution, however. In two of the studies (Tierney, 1982b; Tierney and Davis, 1985) the authors warn that the certainty of the estimated effects are inversely related to the size of the change in the net-price differential, and, of course linear extrapolation typically carries some risk. Still, some comfort can be taken in the fact that the estimate does not seem out of line when viewed from the perspective of the results of the studies on access and, more generally, the results of the student demand studies in Chapter 7. In addition, in Tierney's (1980) study in which he examined the choice between attending a public and private institution, nearly 18 percent of the enrollment choice behavior of students from low-income families was explained by student aid after controlling for a variety of student and institutional characteristics. These two virtually identical percentage figures, while they address the same underlying issue, do so in fundamentally different ways. Thus, the most that one can say of their similarity is that it suggests that these studies may have given us a reasonably good fix on the order of magnitude of the effects in question.

The remaining studies from the institutional perspective offer some additional support for the direction if not the magnitude of the preceding results. In one segment of a study by Astin, Christian, and Henson (1980), the focus was again on students who had applied to, and been accepted by, more than one institution. In these situations, it was found that grants generally were the most influential form of aid. For students choosing between two private institutions, the size of the difference in grant aid offers was highly correlated with subsequent student choice, with students favoring the institution that offered the most aid. For the choice between a public and a private institution, the most important variable was the net cost at the private institution.

In a study by Jackson (1977), using a different methodology, an institution that offered some aid to all its applicants could expect to increase its matriculation rate of accepted freshmen by nearly 17 percent (although increasing the average aid award had only a minuscule effect on enrollment). At a public university, Fields and LeMay (1973) compared matched samples of individuals who had applied and been accepted for admission and who had applied for aid. Some of the students subsequently were awarded aid and some were not. Among those awarded aid, the matriculation rate was 33 percent higher than among those denied aid. A difficulty in interpreting this result is that no control was exercised in the analysis over aid offers that may have come from other institutions. Hoenack and Weiler (1979) found positive choice effects for student aid at a public flagship university. Miller (1981) showed that loans and work study have a negative impact on enrollment when substituted for grants in the aid award packages at an elite private institution.

In a simulation study of college-specific grants and loans, Weinschrott (1978) found significant positive effects and negative cross effects for grants. That is, college-specific grants tended to increase enrollments at the institutions awarding them, and the increases came at the expense of other institutions. Most of the effects occurred for low- or middle-income students. Four-year institutions at various cost levels were able to attract additional students. College specific loans did not have widespread effects, but there was some evidence that loans from medium to high cost institutions attracted some students away from low cost 2-year and 4-year institutions.

In the section on access, we reviewed strong and fairly consistent evidence that grant aid, often in the form of Pell Grants, induced additional enrollment in higher education. One of the issues addressed in a second set of choice studies is whether Pell Grants, known as BEOGs at the time when most of the studies were conducted, and designed primarily as a means of ensuring access, also have a demonstrable effect on the overall distribution of students by institutional type. To be more specific, has the Pell Grant program resulted in a shift from 2-year to 4-year institutions, or from public to private institutions, or from less costly to more costly institutions? An affirmative answer to one or more of these options could be taken as evidence that Pell Grants do contribute to choice as well as to access. Similar questions can be asked about state student aid programs.

The evidence with respect to BEOG/Pell Grants is conflicting, to say the least. As noted in the discussion of access, Carroll et al. (1977) used a simulation model to examine how the predicted effects of the BEOG program would change depending on the award rules. They found that in almost all cases enrollments at higher cost institutions were enhanced the most, in comparison to enrollments at lower cost institutions, by the presence of BEOGs, regardless of the rules. Carroll et al. examined 10 different policy sets for BEOGs. Measured by the increase in low-income enrollment, the average effect for public institutions was 23.6 percent compared to 40.6 percent for private institutions, an advantage for the latter of 17 percentage points. The differences were even greater for institutional segments within the sectors. For example, public 2-year colleges gained only 14.5 percent compared to a 49.4 percent gain at high tuition public 4-year institutions. Medium and high tuition private institutions gained the most, 135 and 115 percent, respectively. Low tuition private institutions were the one exception to the general trend of these results; their low income enrollment gain was only 3.2 percent. The relative percentages reflect in part, of course, the original (pregrant) enrollment of low-income students. The small low-income enrollment at higher cost private institutions contributed to the extremely large percentage increases in the simulation exercise.

In Weinschrott's (1978) study, general grants, that is, grants that can be spent at any institution, were found to increase enrollments at several types of institutions. The largest increases were predicted to occur at low cost 2-year colleges and low cost 4-year colleges. Smaller increases were predicted for middle and high cost 4-year colleges. The pattern was nearly identical for loans, except that grants influenced low-income students, while loans had their effect on middle-income students.

Weinschrott's findings are, in a sense, somewhere between those of Carroll et al. and those of Manski and Wise (1983). As indicated, Carroll et al. found very strong choice effects, in that BEOGs dramatically increased low-income enrollments at middle and high cost 4-year institutions. Weinschrott found that public grants and loans led to only modest increases of that kind, while Manski and Wise found almost no increases at all at 4-year institutions in their study of the BEOG program. In the Manski and Wise study, almost all of the enrollment increases occurred at 2-year colleges or vocational-technical schools. The Astin et al. (1980) results seem to support those of Manski and Wise and of Weinschrott: Receiving a BEOG tended to be associated with enrolling in less selective institutions, including less selective private institutions. Astin et al. cautioned against drawing conclusions about causal effects, however, citing the possibility that some institutions may actively encourage students to apply for BEOGs after the students have already applied and been accepted.

Schwartz (1986) found that public grants (including Pell Grants) accounted for about 22 percent of the low-income enrollment, 12 percent of the middle-income enrollment, and 3 percent of the high-income enrollment in 4-year colleges. Schwarz looked for but did not find evidence that either loan subsidies or private grants affected enrollment at these institutions. Confirmation of the direction of these effects for public grants can be found in Carlson (1980). He found that when tuition and the percentage of federal aid in the form of grants were held constant, an increase in federal aid was accompanied by an increase in the enrollment rate for students of all income levels in 4-year public institutions. Both the Schwartz and Carlson data included SEOGs as well as BEOGs. Since SEOGs are used predominantly by higher cost institutions, this could help account for the positive effects of public grants on enrollments at 4-year institutions.

The Schwartz and Carlson findings appear to represent fairly strong support for the beneficial effects of grant aid on choice, given the tendency of low-income students to be underrepresented in 4 year colleges. Schwartz's study is especially important because he used a data sample, the High School and Beyond survey of high school seniors of 1980, that is a better representation of the aid picture in the 1980s than is the NLS, which is used in so many of the other econometric studies. His results, however, as well as Carlson's do not indicate how the overall pattern of enrollment is being affected by grants. Conceivably, the enrollment gains at public 4-year colleges could have come at the expense of 2-year colleges, which typically would be viewed as a gain for choice, or at the expense of private colleges, which typically would be viewed as a loss for choice, or at the expense of neither, which could be interpreted as a gain for choice and probably access as well. (In a related analysis of the same data, Schwartz [1985] concludes that whereas public grants led to an increase in wealth neutrality with respect to enrollment in public 4-year colleges, a decrease in tuition would lead to a decrease in wealth neutrality.)

Kehoe (1981)) found that state grants had greater power to discriminate between students' institutional choices than did BEOGs. His analysis focused on in-state versus out-of-state institutional choices.

All this adds up to a complex and somewhat confusing picture of the effects of BEOG/Pell Grants, which have come to be the most ubiquitous form of grant aid. Low-income students can qualify for a Pell Grant by attending virtually any type of higher education institution. Because Pell Grants are so widespread, it may be difficult to determine accurately their differential effects on different types of institutions. In many, if not most, instances Pell Grants are the base upon which an aid package is built. Thus, it is not surprising that although Pell Grants *may* tend to be associated with enrollment at less expensive institutions, SEOGs have been associated with enrollment at more expensive institutions (Astin et al., 1980). Pell Grants suffice at the former institutions. Supplemental aid is me often needed at the higher priced institutions where a Pell Grant is not sufficient, even if it is a larger award than would be given at a lower priced school. Financial aid officers commonly employ campus-based aid (SEOGs, NDSLs, and CWS) and then the institution's own funds to "fill out" the student aid package after the Pell Grant amount is known. Perhaps, therefore, it is not surprising that it is easier to assess the relationship of Pell Grants to access than to choice.

Using a very different approach than in any of the previously mentioned studies, Zollinger (1984) constructed hypothetical college choice sets for a sample of Illinois state scholarship recipients. The choice set for each student consisted of institutions that the student might reasonably attend given the student's academic ability. He found that financial aid increased the proportion of students who were able to afford the least costly one-quarter of the institutions in their choice set from 13 percent to 44 percent, a gain of 31 percentage points. Generally, there was little difference in the impact of aid with respect to male versus female students or students of low versus high academic ability. By contrast, although aid increased college choice for minorities, blacks and other minorities were still not able, on average, to attend colleges in their choice sets as frequently as white students. The amount of available aid apparently was not enough to compensate fully for generally lower family income among the minority students, especially blacks. Zollinger concluded that aid is helping to enhance choice, but that college choice remains linked to family income.

The first set of studies in this section examined choice effects from the institutional perspective. The second set investigated the extent to which the Pell Grant program can impact or has impacted on choice, as well as the effects of state grant aid programs. A third set of studies consists of analyses that, while they are less cohesive than the previous two sets with respect to method or central focus, collectively at least hint at the beneficial effects of aid. The common feature among these studies is analysis of student application and enrollment patterns.

In a replication of an earlier study (1973), Spies (1978) found that in 1976 the effects of family income on the enrollment choices of high-ability students were smaller than those he observed in 1971. Taken together, the results of Spies's two studies suggest that the advent of additional student aid in the early 1970s had increased choice. In the 1978 study, controlling for family income, parental education, and academic ability, he also found that students applying for aid were more likely than nonapplicants to apply to high cost institutions and that low-income minority students were more likely then their nonminority counterparts to apply to high cost institutions.

In a broad-based analysis of the effects of student aid on enrollments in the private sector, Leslie (1978) found that about one half of the change from 1965 to 1975 in the private college enrollment share could be explained by changes in public (federal and state) aid expenditures. Using several estimation methods, he concluded that public student aid has added about 250,000 students to private collegiate enrollments in 1975, or about 11 percent of total private enrollments in that year.

Among SAT takers in 1981, Baird (1984) found that family income had no apparent effect on the percentage of students who were able to attend their first-choice college. Although the percentage attending 4-year colleges generally increased with family income, the lowest-income category was an exception. Students from low-income families had a relatively high rate of attendance at 4-year colleges. Shaut and Rizzo (1980) examined the enrollment behavior of students who received 1973-1974 Tuition Assistance Program (TAP) grants in New York. Differences in family income were not a factor in students choosing high cost versus low cost institutions. Mullen (1982) simulated the effects of the TAP and found that private institutions experienced enrollment gains at the expense of public institutions. Munday (1976) examined a national sample of 1972 freshmen aid applicants and found that they tended to enroll at colleges whose students were, on average, different from them in terms of educational development (ACT scores) and family income. This was not the case for students generally. Munday attributed the difference in behavior to the effects of student aid.

. . .

## Summary for Choice

The impact of student aid on student choice is difficult to analyze, perhaps more so than its impact on access. The process of choosing an institution is complex. There are several points in the process when student aid, or the likelihood thereof, could be influential. For instance, general notions about the availability of aid would be important at the time when students and their families initially think about the range of attendance possibilities. The attendance decision itself would more likely be affected by actual offers of aid from specific institutions.

The aid picture also is complex. At least two things happen with the introduction of aid, other things being equal. On the one hand, more institutions become affordable to low-income and, to a lesser extent, middle-income students. At the same time, relative prices, or price differentials, change. One or the other may be the more important development in a given situation. For example, aid can be an enabling device for students who very much want to attend a particular institution. With aid they will enroll at that institution, and the relative prices of other options will make little difference. On other occasions, perhaps when personal preferences are not strong, relative prices become more critical and the best aid offer is likely to influence the attendance decision.

The evidence assembled in this section, at least with respect to the econometric and student opinion results, provides confirmation for what one would expect theoretically. Student aid is an effective way of changing net-price differentials among competing institutions. An institution can increase its enrollment share by increasing the amount of aid it offers, other things staying the same.

There is less agreement in the studies about the effects of the federal government's BEOG/Pell Grant program. Much depends, it would seem, on how the institutions react to such aid. More institutions become affordable because of the aid, presuming that they do not raise prices commensurately in concert with the aid. If they do raise prices, they may end up with the same number of students as before the aid but with more revenue per student. This helps the institutions but does little for choice; that is, it does not lead to a redistribution of students. Although the evidence would be circumstantial at best, we may be seeing something of this situation in the disparity between the results of the opinion studies and most of the econometric studies, on the one hand, and the enrollment share studies on the other. The results from the latter studies are ambiguous at best. The former tell us that aid does work. The resolution may be that aid has worked well enough to maintain the distribution of students, more or less, while helping to strengthen the financial position of the institutions. The enrollment share of private institutions, for example, is essentially unchanged since the early 1970s, when the rapid growth in aid began, after precipitous declines in the 1950s and 1960s.

. . .

## Summary for Persistence

The effect of student aid on persistence in college can be summarized as follows. One, the overall effect is to permit aid recipients to persist about as well as nonrecipients. Two, the effect differs along several dimensions, the most important of which would seem to be that (1) the size of the effect has grown in a positive direction in recent years; (2) nonwhite aid recipients do not persist as well as white aid recipients; (3) persistence is enhanced by larger amounts of aid; and (4) when aid forms are compared to one another, grant and scholarship aid have more positive effect on persistence than do loans.

The conventional wisdom among those who have examined attrition in higher education is that students typically do not drop out of school because of financial problems (for example, see Noel, 1985). The predominant paradigm for the study of attrition, formulated by Tinto in 1975, models a student's chances of remaining in school as a function of the degree of social and intellectual integration he or she achieves. The paradigm does not include any explicit reference to student aid or student financial status. At a later point (1982), Tinto does cite the lack of attention to a student's financial condition as a weakness of the current approach to studying attrition. The findings we have presented neither confirm nor deny either the conventional wisdom or the research paradigm, but these findings do suggest the reason why both were so dominant during the 1970s and into the 1980s. The meta-analysis results indicate that aid allows recipients to hold their own when compared to students who "officially" have no need, that is, do not qualify for aid. In a word, student aid has apparently worked well enough that those concerned about attrition could legitimately focus on noneconomic dimensions of student life. A substantial decline in aid, particularly in the form of grants, might well require a change in the conventional outlook and in the research paradigm.

## Conclusion

Student financial aid has become a major tool for social policy. The evidence assembled and presented in this chapter shows that it is an effective tool. Student aid does work on behalf of the equal opportunity goal. Because of aid, more low-income individuals have been able to study at the college level, attend relatively costly and prestigious institutions, and stay in school longer than would otherwise have been the case. Having said that, it must also be said that aid clearly is not all powerful. It has not removed all of the effects that are associated with variations in income and other aspects of a person's upbringing and overall environment. To put it another way, as a tool for social policy, student aid is not a viable substitute for nurturing home life and a solid primary and secondary education. Still, at the margin, student aid is helping very considerable numbers of students.

It will have been obvious in reading through the chapter that we know much more about the effects of student aid in the form of grants than in the form of loans. Virtually everything about which we could be definite in the integrative review had to do with grant aid. Yet loans have become an increasingly important part of the overall aid picture. More must be learned soon about their effect on access, choice, and persistence. The long-term, socioeconomic effects of greater reliance on loans must also be examined.

Finally, there is the matter of the cost effectiveness of student aid. We have said nothing at all about it in the chapter. A few studies touch on it, but essentially this is fallow ground. We are not referring to the broader question of student aid versus, say, health care or national defense, but rather to the less value-laden issue of how best to ensure equal higher education opportunities. Presuming that student aid is part of the answer, the relative cost effectiveness of different forms of aid, particularly grants versus loans, is an issue that deserves more attention than it has thus far received.

## Notes

1. The percentages shown in Table 8.1 reflect the estimated percentage of students who would leave higher education without grant aid. The data in Carroll et al. (1977) is presented in the form of additional enrollment. For example, the mean effect for the 10 policy alternatives is a 26 percent increase in enrollment over the amount that would be present without the aid. That translates into a 20.6 percent drop in enrollment if the aid were to disappear. Given that aid is a fact of life, the latter mode of presenting the results seems more appropriate.

2. The number of students who are in a particular income category and who receive aid can only be estimated. The .67 figure for low-income students is probably conservative. The number of Pell Grants awarded annually, around 2.5 to 2.9 million, is about the same as the number of full-time low-income students (see the summary at the conclusion of the access section). In 1981-1982, 67 percent of Pell Grants went to students with individual or family incomes of $15,000 or less (Gillespie and Carlson, 1983, p. 17). Although a Pell Grant is the cornerstone for most need-based aid, it is fair to assume that some low-income students who do not receive Pell Grants receive some other form of grant aid. Thus, 0.67 is a conservative estimate of the proportion of low-income students receiving grant aid. The .33 figure for middle-income students is less certain. In 1981-1982, about 860,000 Pell Grants went to students from families with incomes over $15,000. Based on an estimated 3.2 million full-time middle-income students, that translates into 26 percent of receiving the most basic form of grant aid. Presumably there are middle-income students who receive grant aid, but not in the form of a Pell Grant. According to an analysis of the High School and Beyond survey (Carroll, 1984), the percent of middle-income students in 1981-1982 receiving grant aid in some form averaged 38 percent (unweighted) across four institutional types. Presumably, some of these students received merit rather than need-based grants, so the figure needed for the calculation in question is probably somewhat less than 38 percent but more than 26 percent. The 33 percent figure used to calculate the middle-income enrollment effect is simply a "ballpark" estimate. In any case, any figure within 10 percentage points of 33 percent would still result in estimated enrollment effects within the 7.4-19.5 range established in the econometric studies.

## References

Astin, A.W., Christian, C.E., and Henson, J.W. (1980). *The Impact of Student Financial Aid Programs on Student Choice*. Final Report to the U.S. Office of Education. Los Angeles: Higher Education Research Institute, University of California at Los Angeles.

Baird, L.L. (1984) . "Relationships Between Ability, College Attendance, and Family Income." *Research in Higher Education*, 21, 4, 373–396.

Berne, R. (1980). "Net Price Effects on Two-year College Attendance Decisions." *Journal of Education Finance*, 5, 4, pp. 391–414.

Blakemore, A.E., and Low, S.A. (1983). "Scholarship Policy and Race-Sex Differences in the Demand for Higher Education." *Economic Inquiry*, 21, pp. 504–519.

Blakemore, A.E., and Low, S.A. (1985). "Public Expenditures on Higher Education and Their Impact on Enrollment Patterns." *Applied Economics*, 17, pp. 331–340.

Carlson, D.E. (1975). *A Flow of Funds Model for Assessing the Impact of Alternative Student Aid Programs.* Menlo Park, CA: Stanford Research Institutes.

Carlson, D.E. (1976). *Access and Choice in Higher Education: Alternative Measures and Implications for Planning.* Davis, CA: Department of Agriculture, University of California at Davis.

Carlson, D.E. (1980). *Student Access to Postsecondary Education: Comparative Analysis of Federal and State Aid Programs.* Summary of SISFAP Study D. Washington, DC: Office of Education, HEW.

Carroll, S.J., Mori, B.M., Relles, D.A., and Weinschrott, D.J. (1977). *The Enrollment Effects of Federal Student Aid Policies.* Rand Report R-2192. Santa Monica, CA: Rand Corporation.

Crawford, N.C. (1966). *Effects of Offers of Financial Assistance on the College-Going Decisions of Talented Students with Limited Financial Means.* (ED 017000). Evanston, IL: National Merit Scholarship Corporation.

Fenske, R.H., Boyd, J.D., and Maxey, E.J. (1979). "State Financial Aid to Students: A Trend Analysis of Access and Choice of Public and or Private Colleges." *College and University*, 54, pp. 139–155.

Fields, C.R., and LeMay, M.L. (1973). "Student Financial Aid: Effects on Educational Decisions and Academic Achievement." *Journal of College Student Personnel*, 14 (February), pp. 425–429.

Fife, J.D., and Leslie, L.L. (1976). "The College Student Grant Study: The Effectiveness of Student Grant and Scholarship Programs in Promoting Equal Educational Opportunity." *Research in Higher Education*, 4, pp. 317–333.

Foreman, D.W., Lunceford, B.E., and Elton, C.F. (1984). *The Kentucky Grant Study: The Effect of State Grants on Access and Choice in Higher Education.* Frankfort, KY: Kentucky Higher Education Assistance Authority.

Frances, C. (1982). *Basic Facts on College-Going Rates by Income, Race, Sex, and Age, 1970 to 1980.* Washington, DC: National Commission on Student Financial Assistance.

Hearn, J.C. (1980). "Effects on Enrollment of Changes in Student Aid Policies and Programs." In J.B. Henry (Ed.), *The Impact of Student Financial Aid on Institutions.* New Directions for Institutional Research, No. 25. San Francisco: Jossey-Bass.

Hoenack, S.A., and Weiler, W.C. (1979). "The Demand for Higher Education and Institutional Enrollment Forecasting." *Economic Inquiry*, 17 (January), 89–113.

Hyde, W.D., Jr. (1978). *The Effect of Tuition and Financial Aid on Access and Choice in Postsecondary Education.* Papers in Education Finance, No. 1. Denver: Education Commission of the State.

Jackson, G.B. (1978). *Methods for Reviewing and Integrating Research in the Social Sciences.* Final report to the National Science Foundation for Grant No. DIS 76-20309. Washington, DC: George Washington University, Social Research Group.

Kehoe, J.J. (1981). "Migrational Choice Patterns in Financial Aid Policy Making." *Research in Higher Education*, 14, 1, 57–69.

Leslie, L.L. (1978). *The Role of Public Student Aid in Financing Private Higher Education.* Topical Paper No. 10. Tucson, AZ: Higher Education Program, University of Arizona.

Leslie L.L., Johnson, G.P., and Carlson, J. (1977). "The Impact of Need-Based Student Aid Upon the College Attendance Decision." *Journal of Education Finance*, 2, pp. 269–285.

Manski, C.F., and Wise, D.A. (1983). *College Choice in America.* Cambridge, MA: Harvard University Press.

Miller, L.S. (1981). "College Admissions and Financial Aid Policies as Revealed by Institutional Practices." *Economic Inquiry*, 19 (January), pp. 177–131.

Mullen, J.K. (1982). "Implications of Tuition Grants in Higher Education: The Case of a Prior Need-Based Aid Program." *Economics of Education Review*, 2, 1, 49–65.

Munday, L.A. (1976). *Impact of Educational Development, Family Income, College Costs, and Financial Aid in Student Choice and Enrollment in College.* Report No. 7. Iowa City, IA: American College Testing Service.

Noel, L. (1985). Increasing Student Retention: New Challenges and Potential. In L. Noel, R. Levitz, D. Saluri, and Associates, *Increasing Student Retention.* San Francisco: Jossey-Bass, pp. 1–27.

Olson, L., and Rosenfeld, R. (1984). "Parents and the Process of Gaining Access to Student Financial Aid." *Journal of Higher Education*, 55 (July/August), pp. 455–480.

Schwartz, J.B. (1985). "Student Financial Aid and the College Enrollment Decision: The Effects of Public and Private Grants and Interest Subsidies." *Economics of Education Review*, 4, 7, 129–144.

Schwartz, J.B. (1986). "Wealth Neutrality in Higher Education; The Effects of Student Grants." *Economics of Education Review*, 5, 2, 107–117.

Shaut, W.E., and Rizzo, L.M. (1980). "Impact of a Tuition Assistance Program on Students' Freedom of Choice and College Selection." *Journal of Student Financial Aid*, 10, 1, pp. 34–42.

Spies, R.R. (1978). *The Effect of Rising Costs on College Choice.* New York: College Entrance Examination Board.

Springer, P. (1976). "Characteristics of Student OASDI Beneficiaries in 1973: An Overview." *Social Security Bulletin, November.* (ERIC Document Reproduction Service No. ED 072 877).

Tierney, M.L. (1980). "Student Martriculation Decision and Financial Aid." *Review of Higher Education*, 3, pp. 14–25.

Tierney, M.L. (1982a). *Trends in College Participation Rates.* Boulder, CO: National Center for Higher Education Management Systems.

Tierney, M.L. (1982b). "The Impact of Institutional Net Price of Student Demand for Public and Private Higher Education." *Economics of Education Review*, 2, 4, pp. 363–384.

Tierney, M.L. and Davis, J.S. (1985). "The Impact of Student Financial Aid and Institutional Net Price on the College Choice Decisions of In-State Seniors." *Journal of Student Financial Aid*, 15, 1, pp. 3–20.

Tinto, V. (1982). "Limits of Theory and Practice in Student Attrition." *Journal of Higher Education*, 53, 6, pp. 687–700.

Trusheim, D., and Crouse, J. (1981). "Effects of College Prestige in Men's Occupational Status and Income." *Research in Higher Education*, 14, 4, 283–304.

Weinschrott, D.J. (1978). "Private Demand for Higher Education: The Effect of Financial Aid and College Location on Enrollment and College Choice." Doctoral dissertation, University of California at Los Angeles.

Zollinger, R.A. (1984). "Financial Aid and Equity of College Choice: The Illinois Experience." *Journal of Education Finance*, 10, 1, pp. 121–131.

# Enrollment Effects of Alternative Postsecondary Pricing Policies (1985)

JAMES C. HEARN AND DAVID LONGANECKER

The last few years have been marked by heightened public debate over the financing of postsecondary education in the United States [6, 7, 22, 29]. Many states and the federal government have begun to reexamine how public resources should be used to subsidize education. The primary impetus for these deliberations has been pragmatism. The obvious constraints on public resources in an era of enduring economic malaise, the increasing costs of providing basic postsecondary services, and the daunting price tags attached to maintaining quality education in a technological age have made it virtually imperative to reexamine current approaches. Necessarily, however, long-disputed, more fundamental, and less pragmatic issues of public policy have come to play an important part: what are the societal benefits of higher education for individuals? How are public subsides best employed to achieve the goals of equity and efficiency in education?

The controversy has been evident at both the federal and the state levels. One significant aspect at the federal level has been the perception that the middle class is being forced out of higher education by rising tuition costs and by a federal government that pays real attention only to poorer students' financial needs [e.g., see 50]. Although the heavily funded Middle Income Student Assistance Act of 1978 (MISAA) initially quieted this debate, arguments about the validity of the "middle income squeeze" have once again come to dominate congressional debates on student aid [see 24]. At the state level (and in individual private institutions as well), the financing battles have been primarily over tuition increases and have been as fierce as those at the federal level. Powerful public pressures to restrain rises in tuition in order to maintain commitments to educational opportunity [9, 44, 63] have come into direct conflict with financial constraints and concerns for quality, often making resistance to tuition rises extremely difficult for administrations and legislators [12].

In the public sector of American higher education, these debates have crystallized rather neatly into two divergent approaches to financing—the traditional approach of distributing public subsidies broadly by maintaining low tuition and an emerging approach that relies on more targeted public subsidies, achieved through a combination of higher tuition and more generous financial aid aimed squarely at those with financial need. The traditional approach, which seeks to subsidize the education of all able citizens regardless of financial need, is a logical outgrowth of the public school movement and reflects the general belief that the returns to society from a highly educated citizenry justify significant public expenditures on education. In contrast, the targeted approach reflects two "revisionist" philosophical premises quite out of step with the exultant rhetoric of earlier educational leaders: first, because both the individual and society benefit appreciably from education, both should share a substantial portion of the cost of providing that education; second, public expenditures for education should be provided so as to maximize the difference between public returns and costs.

To some extent, arguments over these two distinct approaches express largely irreconcilable values. Statehouses, student rallies, and the popular press are fertile and appropriate ground for debating concepts of freedom, social justice, and proper public policy. But the arguments are also arguments about facts, the focus of this article. Divergent approaches to financing have resulted, in part, from different perceptions of how to effectively achieve goals about which there is very little disagreement. Virtually everyone accepts educational opportunity and equity as critically important goals for public postsecondary education, but they disagree about how best to achieve them. On the one hand, advocates of the traditional broad-subsidy approach argue that the surest way is to keep the cost of education low through large tuition subsidies [e.g., see 37, 63, 66]. Advocates of the more targeted approach, on the other hand, contend that true opportunity and equity will most likely be achieved by focusing subsidies on those lacking financial resources [e.g., see 23, 67]. The vagueness of the terms notwithstanding, the choice of the most productive path to equity and opportunity is centered on a concrete, empirical issue over which the two approaches dispute.

The central issue is how changes in college costs affect college attendance. The two approaches have different hypotheses about student reactions to financing scenarios: will tuition rises of $X$ dollars (or $Y$ percent) a year, accompanied by certain parallel changes in student aid financing (often the raising of student aid for lower-income students), cause deleterious declines or shifts in a state's enrollment patterns? Will a tuition rise of $400 at "State U" really cut enrollment by 20 percent? Will dollar-for-dollar balancing of financial aid increases for lower-income students against tuition rises really preserve attendance rates among the disadvantaged? These are factual questions for which there exists a coherent body of research, and that knowledge is too seldom being heard above the din of current debates.

Accordingly, we shall review here what researchers know, and do not know, about the effects of raising costs for postsecondary education. Particular, but not exclusive, attention is paid to one aspect very much in the public eye: raising tuition at state-supported institutions. Revisionists argue that when a state moves toward higher tuition and higher, more targeted student aid, it is moving toward responsible, progressive public policy. Traditionalists argue that when a state does so, it is in fact (if not in intent) acting to constrain educational equity and opportunity for the poor and middle class: students will begin to downgrade their educational choices or to opt out of education altogether. Each side has its eloquent champions. For example, consider the following statement by Theodore Mitau:

> [A]s Steven Bailey wrote in *Ethics and the Politician*, "The ultimate ethical postulate of a democratic society is not that man is good but that he is capable of good. Not that man is free from corruption but that he is desperately sick of it; not that man has created the good society but that he has caught a glimpse of it." This is not the time to abandon the tuition policy which has made it possible to provide increasing numbers of Americans with something of an unforgettable glimpse of what a good society could be all about. [46, pp. 155–56]

Unfortunately, moving claims of this kind, and the equally appealing counterclaims of revisionist policymakers and analysts, have too seldom been backed up by systematic empirical analysis. Our intent is not only to contribute to the public debate on postsecondary financing but also to propose an agenda for further research on this highly visible aspect of the nation's educational system.

## The Rationale for Targeting Postsecondary Subsidies

As discussed above, the dispute over postsecondary financing is both pragmatically and philosophically driven. Thus, the case for targeting subsidies by increasing public tuition and increasing financial aid is based not only on the strains on the public purse but also on a particular conception of appropriate public policy. This conception, often referred to as the "market rationalization model," is not unique to education. It lies at the heart of a number of recent reforms in government housing policies, consumer protection policies, and airline regulatory policies [see, for example, 13, 14]. Its core is that the public is best served by policies that strengthen market forces in consumer decision making. In postsecondary financing, a number of prominent economists and policy analysts of the rationalization school have argued that providing low postsecondary tuition as public policy is both inefficient and inequitable.[1]

It is inefficient because a large number of students can afford to pay more than the going rate of tuition and are thus getting an unneeded state subsidy. Many of these students would attend college anyway, profitting in later income and status, so why should a state pay them out of its constrained resources without receiving anything new in return? Some of these students would no doubt choose not to attend college at higher prices, but is it efficient to provide a service to those who value it so little? These arguments gain more force when one considers the paucity of evidence for measurable societal (as opposed to individual) benefits from higher education. Although such "externalities" form a prime defense for subsidizing the education of the relatively affluent [5, 63], research has found little evidence of significant benefits to society in general [see 21, 67, and various chapters of 62]. Therefore, a supply and demand model governed by market forces and characterized by targeted subsidies makes sense. The general subsidy of reduced tuitions should be more modest than it is today and should more closely approximate social benefits believed to be received. More substantial targeted assistance should be provided for those who cannot afford to attend without it.

Low tuition is said to be inequitable because it spends more money on the middle class and the rich than on the poor. Even though the financial needs of the relatively affluent are less than those of the poor and their state taxes are not all that much higher than those of the poor (because of generally regressive state taxes), the relatively affluent are far more likely to receive the benefit of subsidized tuition than the poor are because they are far more likely to send their offspring to college (including state-supported institutions). Therefore, the benefits and costs of low tuition do not seem to add up quite as favorably for the poor as they do for the other segments of a state's population.[2]

From this "tuition rationalization" perspective, matching educational costs with societal benefits and individual financial needs removes inequity and inefficiency by adjusting costs for different income groups. In Figure 1, it is apparent that as the amount of the blanket state subsidy ($C$ minus $T$) falls, the amount of targeted aid for lower-income students ($A_L$) rises essentially in tandem with tuition and fees. Thus, the cost to lower-income students ($T$ minus $A_L$) remains unchanged. The costs to upper-income students ($T$ minus $A_U$) and to middle-income students ($T$ minus $A_M$) rise, however. Ostensibly, a well-planned tuition rationalization approach should have few negative effects on attendance patterns. Families facing a net increase in educational costs (that is, middle- and upper-income families) are exactly those believed most indifferent to changes in costs. Those changes that do occur may, in fact, reflect appropriate consumer behavior—that is, some students may change their educational plans because of the value, or lack thereof, of the education to them.

In two ways, research findings support tuition rationalization as a policy that does not radically alter attendance patterns. First, a series of studies in the early and mid-1970s indicate that changes in price have only a modest impact on college attendance.[3] Jackson and Weathersby [33] and McPherson [41] examined the various studies of price effects and developed summary estimates of the average price elasticity of enrollments. Adjusting their estimates for inflation suggests that a rise in net price of $100 (in 1984 dollars) would, on average, conversely affect enrollments by about 1.25 to 1.5 percent. As demonstrated in *The Price of Admission*, a study by the California Postsecondary Education Commission [8], this scenario could affect tens of thousands of students in a large state, yet the proportionate effects on overall enrollment must be considered small.

Second, existing research demonstrates that changes in price have their most significant effects on the very population protected from price changes under tuition rationalization: the lower-income students. Though the studies disagree somewhat in their estimates of how students from

**Figure 1**
**State Subsidies for Postsecondary Students—Blanket Versus Targeted Systems**

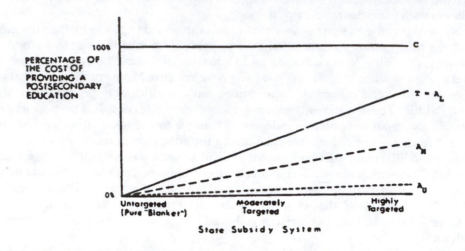

Note: Although state financial aid generally covers more than basic tuition and fees, this hypothetical scenario has been simplified to focus on the relationships among costs, tuition and fees, and student aid.

Key:   C = Cost of providing a postsecondary education
       T = Tuition and fees
       $A_L$ = Financial aid for lower-income students
       $A_M$ = Financial aid for middle-income students
       $A_U$ = Financial aid for upper-income students

various incomes would respond to rising prices, all studies suggest that family income is inversely correlated with responsiveness to price. The California Postsecondary Education Commission study [8] estimates that "lower-income students are approximately twice as price responsive as middle-income students" and "high-income students are about two-thirds as responsive as middle-income students." Figure 2 illustrates this principle: the greater negative slope for the lower-income groups conveys their greater sensitivity to prices. Among the upper-income groups, however, virtually no changes appear in their college attendance when higher education costs rise. In other words, a price rise from $P_1$ to $P_2$ lowers attendance more among lower-income groups than among middle-income groups and lowers attendance more among middle-income groups than among upper-income groups (i.e., $X_L > X_M > X_U$). Reflecting the axiom that it takes a larger amount to noticeably dent the disposable income and liquid assets of the relatively affluent, the results show that it takes a larger increase to affect their attendance decisions.

These two sets of research findings combine to support the general position that tuition rationalization has little overall impact on postsecondary attendance. Reasonable increases in tuition, unaccompanied by more student aid, are unlikely to have large impacts on many students. Moreover, whatever modest impacts "raw" tuition rises are likely to have will be strongly muted by the parallel targeting of increased student aid for the students most likely to be sensitive to higher prices. A critical assumption for targeted subsidies is that financial aid is a perfect substitute for low tuition for the poor. In other words, this approach assumes that educational decisions, to the extent that they are affected by educational costs, are affected only by the net price facing the students and their families, and are not affected by the composition or form of the subsidies. Because the actual price is costs minus whatever financial aid is available, exchanging low tuition for equally generous financial aid should not alter attendance decisions. In Figure 2, for example, there would be no rise in the actual price of attendance for the lower-income groups and thus no fall

## Figure 2
### A Simplified Model of Postsecondary Attendance Patterns for Different Income Groups

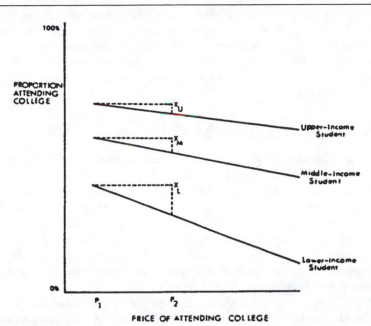

Note: This simplified model assumes that students in all income groups are high school graduates with equivalent aspirations, abilities, and preparation and that there is only one pricing scheme.

in attendance. The state, by substituting student aid in direct proportion to the lost subsidy, can make the poor theoretically indifferent to the tuition rise. Their college attendance rates, as well as their specific institutional choices, should be unaffected by the changes in tuition and student aid.

The middle class, from this perspective, will experience a rise in the price of their attendance at state institutions because this group would receive less under the reduced tuition subsidy (see Figure 1). The upper-income group would receive no new student aid to offset higher prices. The number of lost middle- and upper-income students ($X_M$ and $X_U$), however, is expected to remain relatively constant in the face of the rises. Indeed, any loss would logically result from rational economic decisions by some consumers not to purchase a service (in this case, education) that has little value for them. So goes the theoretical and philosophical argument for targeted subsidies. But what are the pragmatic considerations? If the approach proves sound, there is much to be gained. Public funds will be allocated more efficiently, without jeopardizing the goals of equity and equality. But more importantly, the additional resources garnered can be used to enhance the quality of education in public institutions, thereby keeping public postsecondary education competitive in a rapidly changing environment. Without these resources, public postsecondary education simply may not be able to provide more than mediocrity.

If the approach fails, however, the costs to individuals and society will be great. If significantly lower proportions of high-school graduates attend public institutions, as the opponents of targeted subsidies argue, not only educational equity but also the well-being of the state may be of concern. Two effects on the state treasury will be quickly felt: the state will have lower student aid and lower educational and tuition subsidies than if attendance had remained constant, but it will also take in fewer than forecast levels of revenues (from both tuition payments and federal sources). Furthermore, revenue and outlays will be similarly affected by the extent to which students might attend lower-cost state institutions in lieu of the "flagship" public campuses. Beyond these possible short-term effects on the states, the quality of the work force may eventually be affected as well, potentially leading to declines in future income tax revenues. Thus, tuition and student aid changes could affect college attendance, which indirectly may affect the financial future of the state. The dispute over targeted subsidies is not, therefore, over trivialities, either from the social or the economic perspective. A state's decision to move toward targeted subsidization has extremely wide-ranging implications. Our focus is to discuss its initial effects on student enrollment patterns (i.e., who goes to college and where they go). The research evidence and the theoretical and pragmatic reasoning in favor of targeting state subsidies, as outlined above, are quite strong, but there are a number of questions to analyze.

## Questioning the Targeted Subsidy Model

Proponents of targeted subsidies assume that tuition rationalization, if undertaken responsibly, will have minimal effects on student attendance patterns. We agree, in general, that tuition rationalization makes sense on the grounds of both equity and efficiency, but we have reservations about three underlying assumptions: that students will act in a particular knowledgeable, orderly way (the *rational actor* assumption), that other factors will not disturb the effects of the price changes (the *ceteris paribus* assumption), and that a revised financing scheme relying more on student aid than on tuition subsidies can be made to work well (the *efficient delivery* assumption). Each of these assumptions involves areas that might "go wrong," increasing exponentially the chance for policy failure, and each needs closer scrutiny.

*The Rational Actor Assumption.* Seriously questions can be raised about the model's underlying conception from classic economics of the "rational man." As usually conceived, "homo economicus" is assumed to have perfect knowledge about the prices in question and their associated returns, to be infinitely sensitive to differences in the prices, and to make decisions in a "rational" (i.e., an economic) manner [see 15]. The conception suggests that the prospective student bases his or her decision primarily on the "net price" of the product or products under consideration (i.e., on the personal costs of attendance minus any subsidies from state, federal, or private student aid). If the net price, so calculated, exceeds his or her expected benefits as a consumer or investor, the prospective student will not choose education at that price.[4] This *rational actor* conception is assumed both for the choice between institutions and for the choice between college attendance and nonattendance.

When this conception is contrasted with the interpretations and experiences of most college students, some important contradictions arise. Students and their families may seek and even achieve rationality in many ways, but they do not always do so in the sense posited by the model. First, consider the usual chronology of students' decisions about college. That chronology is substantially more chaotic than the targeted subsidy model usually assumes, leading to serious doubts about the meaningfulness and importance of net price in college attendance. For example, public tuition rises are often not announced until just prior to the academic year, too late to play a central role in fundamental decisions about feasible choices. Even when tuition levels are known, there can be a "messiness" about college decisions quite different from the assumptions of the model:

> Now student and family face the series of crises-acceptance or rejection letters. Comparatively, rejections are easy; acceptances cause the trouble. Some colleges use a continual admissions policy, giving accepted students two or three weeks in which to reply. Others have a fixed date for notifying students. Obviously, these methods conflict, leaving the student with the dilemma of having to tell college X yes or no before hearing from college Y or Z. And even when Y and Z announce their decisions, the various financial aid packages are so complex that trying to determine what it will really cost to send a student to Podunk State or Old Ivy is like predicting the weather for March. [4, p. 13]

The essay cited above was written by a parent who is also a college professor. For parents less well educated or less familiar with the college setting, the indeterminacy of the admissions, acceptance, and attendance decisions must be even more trying. There may never exist, at any given time, a set of known net prices for students and their families to judge in the precise fashion suggested by the classic conception.

Second, it is not only the chronology of decision making that thwarts parents and students reasoning along net price lines: recent research indicates that the knowledge of students and their parents about the forms and terms of student aid is sadly inadequate. For example, Olson and Rosenfeld [51] found that in 1980, 55 percent of the parents of high school seniors knew nothing of the Guaranteed Student Loan program, and 52 percent knew nothing of the Basic Educational Opportunity Grant (BEOG) program (now the Pell Grant program). Even among parents with incomes under $10,000 a year, over half knew nothing of the BEOG program. On top of this lack of basic information, the public has often been misled by press reports of exorbitant tuition increases and slashes in financial aid, according to Gladieux [19] and others. Such stories no doubt cloud the already vague knowledge of many about postsecondary financing. It was such misperceptions that helped pass the Middle Income Student Assistance Act of 1978. Thus, the twin spectres of disorderly chronology and inadequate information interfere with the "real world" applicability of the net price concept.

Third, Goggin [20] argues that the net price idea, as it is usually conceptualized and researched for policy, is seriously flawed because it does not differentiate between students and their families as decision makers. The value of college attendance as a consumer expenditure or as an investment cannot be equated between parents and children. This problem is more a flaw of current policy research than of mainstream econometric research because economists have long realized the role of individualized and time-discounted returns on investment in purchase decisions. When growing numbers of students are claiming independence from their parents [45] and reliance on student loans is increasing [61], the notion that college decisions are made by the family as a whole is questionable. Yet some policy makers at various levels continue to see the prime criterion of a successful financing policy to be equalized, undiscounted net prices across family income groups.

A fourth, related point is that, even if net price does in some way drive college decision making (and it is hard to imagine it not having some role), it seems questionable to assume that parents or students decide using net prices undifferentiated by source. In other words, a loan represents something different from a grant. Reviewing the literature, Rosenfeld [57] reports that students do indeed react differently to different kinds of aid when deciding to attend or drop-out [also see 3]. When a needed subsidy disappears, an alternative source of aid must be found to continue attendance. Thus, the effects of changes in state tuition policies toward the targeted subsidy model will depend, in part, on what kinds of aid are available as substitutes for the lost subsidy and how students respond to packages of those kinds of aid. For example, a significant unknown factor is how middle-income students will respond to an increased need for loans because loans, unlike grants, represent a claim on future income in an uncertain economic climate. Research and policy efforts not taking these subtleties into account run the risk of miscalculating student responses to specific kinds of changes in state subsidy policies.

Fifth, people may not "process" information in the ways posited by the targeted subsidy model. In other words, reactions to various prices and subsidies may not always be economically rational in the classic sense. Jackson [31] reports that students may react just as strongly to receiving a grant as to the actual amount of that grant. Related research suggests that loans are not always accepted as a valued source of aid and may, in fact, be culturally shunned or, among the risk-averse, feared [3, 57]. These reactions may occur regardless of the precise financial implications of specific loan arrangements.

Findings of this kind have clear policy implications. Recent experiences in Washington suggest that, in the extreme short term (six months to one year), tuition rises prompt attendance losses out of proportion to the actual dollar effects of those rises on discretionary incomes. Although such reactions tend to fade as accurate information spreads, they are of fundamental significance for governmental policy making and budget forecasting. One may hypothesize that there may very well be a "halo effect" in financing, such that widely publicized cuts in federal student aid occurring simultaneously with rises in state tuition levels will create a perception more dire than the economist or policy analyst working from the usual rationalist model and research perspective would deem warranted. The precise changes in aid dollars, tuition levels, and net prices may not be very clear to the public, but the tone of the changes as a whole may alter behavior in ways not predicted by the standard model. Just as the "mood" of the American public plays a big role in the profitability of consumer products, so the "mood" of the prospective college student may play a big role in the fate of reforms in postsecondary pricing.

Obviously, educational research and policy making that does not assess the possible role of noneconomic factors (e.g., sociocultural values, psychological tendencies) in student decision patterns risks imprecision. Those involved in policy can benefit immensely from familiarity with the growing body of knowledge on the limits of human rationality. The seminal work remains that of Simon and his many colleagues [see especially 60], but others have made major contributions as well [see 34, 36, 42]. The fundamental message of this research has been summarized by psychologists Edwards and Tversky: "Apparently, the most serious deficiencies in human decision making behavior arise in processing information, not in making decisions" [16, p. 123].

That message continues to be elaborated. Recently, Tversky presented new evidence to the National Academy of Sciences supporting the conclusion that "actual human behavior departs in very radical ways from rational theory," despite the fact that the principle of rational choice has long been a cornerstone of traditional economic theory [10]. In his study of cognitive and psychophysical determinants of choice, Tversky found strong evidence that the way options are presented can produce a decidedly nonrational choice. Intelligent people may be highly averse to one option and highly favorable to another, even though they are simply restatements of the identical alternative. Specifically, Tversky found people are more averse to loss than they are attracted to gain, and this tendency can lead them to disparate behaviors that are largely dependent on whether options are presented in terms of gains or loss. Extending these conclusions to higher education financing, one can hypothesize that cost rises (a "loss" to the consumer) may be more often publicized and more easily visible to the public than student aid rises (a "gain" to the consumer), and people's behavior may be accordingly less rational in the economic sense. Certainly this possibility merits further research.[5]

Another intriguing qualification of rational information processing derives from one of the more durable psycho-physiological concepts of the nineteenth century, the notion of "just noticeable differences." Sometimes stated mathematically as Weber's Law, the concept aims to specify the point at which any of the human sensory organs (tongue, skin, ear, eye, or nose) becomes aware of a change in an external stimulus. In essence, the law states that the higher the intensity, the greater the change needed to be noticeable [69]. In pricing, the law implies that a change of $100 will be more noticed in lower-priced items than in higher priced items and that having many price lines confuses consumers' perceptions [43, 47]. The relevance of Weber's Law to postsecondary finance lies in viewing various postsecondary prices and aid as stimuli. Given the rising prices and rampant noise and misinformation of financing, it may very well be impossible for students and their families to "pick up" some of the signals being sent to them by policy makers. Yet the rational model assumes decision makers to be infinitely sensitive to stimulus changes [see 15]. The research has not yet seriously delved into the sensory thresholds of students as they are given financial signals or into the variations in those thresholds across different socioeconomic classes, but it is clear that Weber's Law suggests significant qualifications to the *rational actor* assumption.

A sixth qualification relates not so much to the public's information as to the information about the public used in policy modeling. Even when one considers only the economic factors in decision making, and even when one assumes that families are perfectly knowledgeable about college prices and aid, it must be borne in mind that students and their families will not always interpret their own financial situations in ways policy analysts working with government data sets believe they do or should. Research at the national and state levels consistently suggests that the much talked about "middle-income squeeze" in college financing in the late 1970s was as much a matter of public perception as reality [see 24, 40]. Thus, it is sometimes hard for the empirically minded policy analyst to see much more than inexplicable, seemingly irrational attitudinal changes behind the concerns of the relatively affluent about tuition rises.

Yet it can be argued that those perceptions are not only rational under some expectations of future economic conditions, but are also the driving force behind most family behavior, rather than accounting-style analyses of the highlights of family finances. What one considers rational behavior in another person is bounded by time and levels of information. By necessity, researchers and policy makers must rely on only partial accounts of family finances and choices, rather than the total picture as known and felt by the family. Smith [61] reports that Minnesota high-school juniors are increasingly citing financial reasons for not planning to enroll in college. One must be very cautious about such self-reported data, but it would be fallacious to assume these perceptions are based on ignorance or awkward chronology alone. Perceptions, whether based in fact or in myth, may affect attendance patterns among the relatively affluent more than the targeted subsidy model predicts.

Seventh, the *rational actor* assumption, as usually activated in policy decisions, tends to disregard the noneconomic aspects of the differentiation among institutions and students, as well as the unique attachments and loyalties between certain kinds of institutions and certain kinds of students. Recent research by Tierney [64], Litten et al. [38], Litten et al. [39], and Zemsky and Oedel [71] on the preferred institutional "choice sets" of students suggests, at least indirectly, that there are "sticky" and "fluid" parts of the college attendance market. In other words, some parts of the market may be marked by fairly inelastic demand (prices do not much matter), whereas others may show highly elastic demand (prices matter a good deal). Subsidy policies designed without close attention to these irregularities in the market (e.g., policies considering only family income as a factor in forecasting price elasticity of attendance responses) may be destined for surprise endings.

*The Ceteris Paribus Assumption.* Assuming *ceteris paribus* (i.e., all else remains equal) is a convenient convention in forecasting the impacts of various public policy options, but it may not accurately reflect reality. The world cannot be assumed to stand still for long; "all else" is not usually equal or stable. One true test of any policy is how well it can stand up to the unpredictables that can thwart its intents. There are several "wild cards" that can threaten the success of the targeted subsidy approach to funding postsecondary education.

The first involves the possible effects of future economic developments and whether the returns of a college education will remain stable, rise, or fall. If the income gains from college are indeed on a downslope,[6] there is no reason to believe the price responsiveness of different groups will remain the same. College attendance has aspects of both a consumer expenditure, on the order of a car or a stereo set, and an investment, akin to a stock market purchase. Its price is thus weighed not only against the current assets available to pay for it but also against its likely income returns after graduation. When external factors affect the demand for education, enrollments will be affected regardless of cost. For a state, the issue then becomes one of determining the appropriate public commitment to postsecondary education in such an environment. Is the logical extension of the targeted subsidy approach not only to differentiate tuition levels by the cost of providing programs but also by the likely economic returns to the participants? If we accept the need to make tuition into a price in the true economic sense [see 49], such a move might be considered an aspect of market rationalization.

A second set of "wild cards" affecting enrollments in a state involves future governmental policy changes. It is well-known that individual states and institutions can do much to effectively neutralize federal policy in student financing [2]. One way this has been accomplished in the past is for a state to raise public tuition levels by amounts roughly in line with new increases in federal grant programs for students. The result is a transfer of federal funds to the state; the new funds may pass through student hands but do not necessarily accrue to their benefit. The other side, of course, is the ability of the federal government to support or undercut state policies. How the two governmental sides mutually adjust to each other's actions will play a big role in the actual prices faced by students. In turn, these developments can affect the attendance decisions of students.[7]

A third set of "wild cards" affecting state enrollment forecasts involves changes in the supply of postsecondary education. In many states, it is not too difficult to construct a scenario for the next decade in which demographically induced declines in enrollment, along with pressures on enrollment rates fed by student doubts about the value of postsecondary education, force closings of both public and private institutions. These demand-induced changes in the supply of postsecondary education would in turn affect prices paid by students for their educations. In the end, these price changes would presumably affect enrollment patterns.[8]

Within such an environment, what public policy options are available? Do states close institutions to achieve efficiency but in so doing potentially jeopardize access for some students? Or do they attempt to maintain constant offerings despite fewer students? Neither alternative appears very attractive. Either more money will be needed to educate each student or the level of educational services will have to decline. To garner additional money requires either increased public appropriations, which seem unlikely given current fiscal constraints, or increased tuitions, even beyond those urged by the targeted subsidy approach, which would result in net increases in costs for all students and thus undermine the goal of equal opportunity. Without additional resources, however, essential levels of educational services cannot be maintained, let alone enhanced, and public education will sink into mediocrity. In summary, regardless of what strategy (targeted or traditional) is used for funding public postsecondary education, a declining market for this service may have an impact on the overall level of service provided. The choice of the putatively more cost-effective targeted approach does not immunize states from the dangers of exogenous market influences.

Fourth, the nature of information available to students and their families is not constant. Earlier, we stressed that misinformation, misprocessing of information, and lack of information are features of students' college decision making. Given those facts, exogenous changes in flows of information to students can have major effects. Knowledge may have changed appreciably since earlier studies estimated price responsiveness coefficients. At the urging of a number of analysts, the federal government and many states have made concerted efforts in the last few years to improve materials describing prices and aid [see 3, 31, 52]. Conceivably, the injection of extra information about college prices and aid could raise or lower price responsiveness significantly. All research is bound partially by its time and place, and price-responsiveness research is no exception. Consumer information about college net prices may be viewed as a set of continua, each continuum corresponding to knowledge about a certain category (e.g., student loans, Pell Grants, and so on). Movements along the continua are critical determinants to responses to public policies, yet these movements are often unknown to state policy makers and out of their control.

*The Efficient Delivery Assumption.* It is generally assumed that the targeted subsidy approach, relying more on student aid than on tuition subsidies, will more efficiently direct scarce resources. Nevertheless, there are at least three factors which may work to counteract the projected efficiencies. First, there is worry about whether the targeted subsidy approach may be an especially precarious means for assuring aid to the most needy students. Pechman [53, p. 369] has argued that "grant-loan systems, combined with full-cost tuition fees, may appear to be more 'efficient' in principle," but may in fact jeopardize the primary goal of equity because they may prove to be more subject to political machinations than the simpler low-tuition systems. After all, aid costs are a relatively clear-cut item for legislators debating a state budget, whereas tuition subsidies are a less politically visible (more indirect) aspect of state budgeting deliberations. What is more, from the standpoint of the public, visibility is reversed: it is the low tuition that is more known and often best supported. Thus, aid may be the more debatable expenditure from both the public's and politicians' perspectives.

Second, there is also some question about how effectively student assistance programs can be managed. Economies of scale clearly should make it very cost-effective to operate large, state-wide financial aid systems, and a centralized delivery system may be essential to preserve the integrity of this funding approach. Yet research for the U.S. Department of Education [1] suggests that, at least at the federal level, the prevention of errors in student aid (e.g., incorrect income reports, institutional errors in awards, and so on) is a monumentally difficult and expensive task. More inefficiencies can result from the fact that the knowledge of students and their parents about the forms and terms of aid is sadly inadequate, as discussed earlier. Without knowledgeable consumers and efficient processing, the vaunted merits of targeting may be severely tested.

Third, the data and the technology policy makers use to predict the impact of price changes on attendance patterns may not be specified and developed enough to apply precisely to all policy situations that might arise. Our data, for example, are often based in historical behaviors taking place within a limited context of past price ranges, price sets, and price changes. Our models generally assume a linear relationship between price and attendance. Yet is it reasonable to assume that the first dollar change would have the same impact as the last dollar of change? We know that each person has a threshold, beyond which his or her behavior will be affected, but what is that threshold? We know that the most likely response to price changes, if there is one, is to change one's choice of a college rather than to change one's choice about attending [e.g., see 26, 31, 64], but at what point do such decisions to shift to lower-cost institutions occur? Policy making with the targeted subsidy plan is made more risky by the lack of better knowledge of such phenomena.

## Implications

The empirical results reviewed here support the view of many policymakers and econometricians that tuition rises serve to enhance rather then diminish equity when they are offset by rises in need-based financial aid. We label as myth, therefore, the view that such rises *per se* threaten equality of educational opportunity. On the basis of existing research, there is strong evidence that responsible movement toward targeted subsidization of postsecondary education should not appreciably affect enrollment rates in the long run. Several effects of a lower order of magnitude will often be felt, however. Price changes of the magnitude and type usually planned by states are not powerful enough to change the minds of many students about whether or not to seek postsecondary education [for supportive evidence, see 31; 41]. It is unlikely that many students who planned to attend will be deterred. It is nonetheless more likely that some redistribution of enrollments will occur. Logically, some students attending more costly public institutions might choose to attend lower-cost schools, and likewise some students attending public institutions might choose to attend higher-cost private institutions because of decreased tuition differentials. Finally, any precipitous move towards a targeted subsidy approach will almost certainly have a short-time impact because of misleading public perceptions resulting from a lack of full understanding and information. Articles in the popular press about families struggling to cope with the changes feed the misperceptions of the lay community. Such unfortunate consequences should fade perceptively after the public becomes more knowledgeable and accustomed to the changes.[9]

These conclusions are based on what we know, however. They do not address the many elements we do not know. The concerns that there are too many unknowns and that our guiding assumptions may prove to be false suggest that efforts to move towards targeted subsidization must be monitored closely. Great caution should be exercised in utilizing policy research based strongly on assumptions of consistently rational human behavior; on stable markets, expectations, and policies; and on fluid movement of funds, people, and information. The extent to which these concerns are significant depends on specific policy or research situations. At the very least, the public debate over these issues should be informed by knowledge of both the uses and limits of existing research.

Some rather urgent questions demand further research. Many of these questions relate to one little-understood domain: the social psychology of reactions to price changes in postsecondary education. To the extent that people perceive the current and future financing scene and their own current and future financial situation in ways distinct from the expectations of the standard policy model, they will behave differently from the model's expectations. The greatest research imperative in postsecondary financing thus relates to the ways people process information. The world of perceptions and knowledge in postsecondary finance is as yet little explored by researchers. Standard models do not always predict behaviors well, and the need to find additional explanations is clear. Some analysts are already conducting intriguing research in this domain using longitudinal data from the national High School and Beyond Survey funded by the U.S. Department of Education [see 51]. At the state level, the changes in postsecondary financing currently being instituted in California, Minnesota, Washington, and several other states will provide valuable laboratories to explore new understandings of postsecondary enrollment patterns.

How much does the public know about actual postsecondary prices? How is this knowledge used? How do individuals in different income groups weight their own ability to pay? Is there strong student willingness to undertake debt as a substitute for a tuition subsidy? How much can a state raise tuition without changing the attendance patterns of the relatively affluent and possibly creating a drain into the private sector? Finding at least tentative answers to questions of these kinds could make educational policy making far more informed and straightforward in the future.

An earlier version of this article was presented at the annual meeting of the American Educational Research Association, New Orleans, April 1984. The authors very much appreciate the comments of Robert Fenske, Rachel Rosenfeld, Jay Stampen, Richard Yanikoski, and various staff members of the Minnesota Higher Education Coordinating Board. Nevertheless, the views presented here, and any errors, are the responsibility of the authors alone. Address any communications to James C. Hearn, Department of Educational Policy and Administration, University of Minnesota, 275 Peik Hall, 159 Pillsbury Drive, S.E., Minnesota, MN 55455.

## Notes

1. See, for example, Hansen and Weisbrod [23], Hoenack [30], Windham [67, 68], and Jackson [32]. The arguments of these economists are simplified here in some respects. Space and the reader's patience prevent a recounting of the many subtleties and technicalities involved.

2. This argument has been quantitatively defended by analysis of state tax sources and outlays, broken down by different income groups. State taxes across the country tend to be regressive, so although the poor are attending postsecondary schools at lower rates than other segments of the population [see 29, 55], they may be paying for the states' postsecondary expenditures at rates equal to or greater than those segments [23, 68]. Thus, the poor's taxes may be paying for the rich's attendance. These findings have been hotly disputed, however, and the tax-flow equity debate is far from closed [see 25, 48, 53, 54, 63].

3. The series of studies examining the effects of price changes on college attendance differ considerably in focus, methodology, and rigor. Two of the most methodologically sophisticated studies are Radner and Miller's *Demand and Supply in U.S. Higher Education* [56], a 1974 study for the Carnegie Commission on Higher Education, and Kohn, Manski, and Mundel's *Empirical Investigation of Factors Which Influence College-Going Behavior* [35], a 1974 Rand Corporation study. The results of these studies and others are summarized by Jackson and Weathersby [33] and McPherson [41].

4. Both costs and benefits are calculated in present-value terms in the more sophisticated analyses.

5. For some parallel comments by economists, see [36] and [42]. Economist Albert O. Hirschman [11] has said, "As economics has grown more ambitious, it becomes of increasing importance to appreciate that the means-end, cost-benefit model is far from covering all aspects of human activity and experience."

6. See Freeman [17]; see Rumberger [59] for a critique of this view.

7. Gillespie and Carlson's [18] summary of recent federal student aid patterns and the conclusions of Smith [61], Gladieux [19], and others regarding the likely funding patterns in the near future suggests continuing pressure on students' ability to finance postsecondary attendance. The recent resurgence of federal interest in education matters, however, may counter that conclusion somewhat.

8.  For an intriguing description of this and other possible scenarios for higher education in the 1980s, see Heydinger and Zentner [28].

9.  Supportive (albeit early) evidence for these expectations may also be found in the analyses of institutional researchers at the University of Minnesota [65]. Similarly, in a 1984 personal communication with the first author, Richard Yanikoski reported support for the "shortwave dip" hypothesis from DePaul University: "When we dramatically increased tuition in our School of Music, enrollment dropped substantially for one year and then rebounded to above its prior level." Yanikoski noted that such dislocations might be avoided by greater attention to the "just noticeable differences" concept as it relates to efforts to differentiate tuition prices at the undergraduate level [see 70]: gross price increases might be masked by smaller price adjustments at the credit unit or course level because those smaller changes might fall under consumers' thresholds.

# References

1.  Advanced Technology, Inc. "Quality in the Basic Grants Delivery System: Final Report." Report prepared for the U.S. Department of Education, Office of Student Financial Aid, Division of Quality Assurance, Reston: Advanced Technology, 1982.

2.  American Council on Education. *Tuition and Student Aid: Their Relation to College Enrollment Decisions.* Special Report by the Policy Analysis Service. Washington, D.C.: ACE, 1978.

3.  Astin, A. "SISFAP-Study A: The Impact of Student Financial Aid Programs on Student Choice." Report of research supported by the Office of Planning, Budgeting, and Evaluation, U.S. Office of Education, Department of Health, Education, and Welfare, under U.S.O.E. Contract 300-75-0382, 1978.

4.  Baldwin, D. "The College Admissions Torture." *Newsweek*, 6 June 1983, 13–14.

5.  Bowen, H. R. *Investment in Learning: The Individual and Social Value of American Higher Education.* San Francisco: Jossey-Bass, 1977.

6.  Breneman, D. W. "Comments on Lee Hansen's Paper: Economic Growth and Equal Opportunity: Conflicting or Complementary Goals in Higher Education." Paper presented at the NIE Conference on Education, Productivity, and the American Economy, Leesburg, Virginia, 12 November 1982.

7.  Breneman, D. W., and C. E. Finn, Jr. (eds.). *Public Policy and Private Higher Education.* Washington, D.C.: Brookings Institution, 1978.

8.  California Postsecondary Education Commission. *The Price of Admission: An Assessment of the Impact of Student Charges on Enrollments and Revenues in California Public Higher Education.* Sacramento: CPEC, 1980.

9.  *Chronicle of Higher Education.* "California Governor Cuts College Aid by $381 Million." 3 August 1983, 1, 10.

10.  _____. "Research Notes." 7 December 1983, 8.

11.  _____. "Research Notes." 9 January 1984, 12.

12.  _____. "Tuition Increases Slow But Are Likely To Outpace Inflation." 29 February 1984, 3.

13.  Congressional Budget Office. *Charging for Federal Services.* Washington, D.C.: U.S. Government Printing Office, 1983a.

14.  _____. *The Industrial Policy Debate.* Washington, D.C.: U.S. Government Printing Office, 1983b.

15.  Edwards, W. "The Theory of Decision Making." *Psychological Bulletin,* 51 (1954), 380–417.

16. Edwards, W., and A. Tversky. "Utility and Subjective Probability." In *Decision Making*, edited by W. Edwards and A. Tversky, pp. 121–23. Harmondsworth: Penguin, 1967.

17. Freeman, R. B. *The Overeducated American*, New York: Academic Press, 1976.

18. Gillespie, D. A., and N. Carlson. *Trends in Student Aid: 1963 to 1983*. Washington, D.C.: The College Board, 1983.

19. Gladieux, L. E. "The Future of Student Financial Aid." *The College Board Review*, 126 (Winter 1983), 2–12.

20. Goggin, W. "Some Thoughts on the Misspecification of Net Price Student Aid Models and Their Policy Relevance." Paper presented at the Annual Meeting of the American Educational Research Association, San Francisco, April 1979.

21. Halstead, D. K. *Statewide Planning in Higher Education*. Washington, D.C.: U.S. Government Printing Office, 1974.

22. Hansen, W. L. "Economic Growth and Equal Opportunity: Conflicting or Complementary Goals in Higher Education." Discussion Paper #706-82. Institute for Research on Poverty, University of Wisconsin, 1982.

23. Hansen, W. L., and B. A. Weisbrod. *Benefits, Costs, and Finance of Public Higher Education*. Chicago: Markham, 1969.

24. Hartle, T., and R. Wabnick. "Discretionary Income and College Costs." Paper prepared for the National Commission on Student Financial Assistance, 6 August 1982.

25. Hartman, R. W. "A Comment on the Pechman-Hansen-Weisbrod Controversy." *Journal of Human Resources*, 5 (1970), 519–23.

26. Hearn, J. C. "Effects on Enrollment of Changes in Student Aid Policies and Programs." *New Directions in Institutional Research*, 25 (1980), 1–14.

27. _____. "The Role of Academic, Ascribed, and Socioeconomic Characteristics in College Destinations." *Sociology of Education*, 57 (1984), 22–30.

28. Heydinger, R., and R. D. Zentner. "Multiple Scenario Analysis as a Tool for Introducing Uncertainty into the Planning Process." In *New Directions in Institutional Research: Applying Methods and Techniques of Future Research*, edited by J.L. Morrison, W.L. Renfro, and W.T. Boucher, 29 (1983), pp. 51–68.

29. Heyns, B., and B. O'Meara. "Access to Higher Education and Federal Policy." Paper presented at the Annual Meeting of the American Sociological Association, San Francisco, September 1982.

30. Hoenack, S. A. "The Efficient Allocation of Subsidies to College Students." *The American Economic Review*, 61 (1971), 308–11.

31. Jackson, G. A. "Financial Aid and Student Enrollment." *Journal of Higher Education*, 49 (November/December 1978), 548–74.

32. _____. "Public Efficiency and Private Choice in Higher Education." *Educational Evaluation and Policy Analysis*, 4 (1982), 237–47.

33. Jackson, G. A., and G. B. Weathersby,. "Individual Demand for Higher Education: A Review and Analysis of Recent Empirical Studies." *Journal of Higher /Education* 46 (November/December 1975), 623–52.

34. Kahneman, D., P. Slovic, and A. Tversky (eds.). *Judgment Under Uncertainty: Heuristics and Biases.* Cambridge: Cambridge University Press, 1982.

35. Kohn, M. G., C. F. Manski, and D. S. Mundel. *An Empirical Investigation of Factors Which Influence College-Going Behavior.* Rand Report R-1470-NSF. Santa Monica: Rand Corporation, 1974.

36. Leibenstein, H. *Beyond Economic Man: A New Foundation for Microeconomics.* Cambridge: Harvard University Press, 1980.

37. Leslie, L. L., and G. P. Johnson. "Equity and the Middle-class." In *Exploring the Case for Low Tuition in Public Higher Education,* edited by K. Young, pp. 105–37, Iowa City: American College Testing Program, 1974.

38. Litten, L. H., E. Jahoda, and D. Morris. "His Mother's Son and Her Father's Daughter: Parents, Children, and the Marketing of Colleges." Unpublished paper, Consortium on the Financing of Higher Education (COFHE), February 1980.

39. Litten, L. H., D. Sullivan, and D. L. Brodigan. *Applying Market Research in College Admissions.* New York: The College Board, 1983.

40. Longanecker, D. "Ability to Pay for Student Costs of Higher Education Taking Into Account Family Income After Taxes." Paper presented at the Research/Analysis Seminar of the American Council on Education, Washington, D.C., 7 July 1978.

41. McPherson, M. S. "The Demand for Higher Education." In *Public Policy and Private Higher Education,* edited by D. W. Breneman and C. E. Finn, Jr., pp. 143–96. Washington, D.C.: Brookings Institution, 1978.

42. Maital, S. *Minds, Markets, and Money: Psychological Foundations of Economic Behavior,* New York: Basic Books, 1982.

43. Miller, R. L. "Dr. Weber and the Consumer." *Journal of Marketing,* 26 (January 1962), 57–61.

44. *Minneapolis Star and Tribune.* "Sharply Higher Tuition Ahead for State's Public Colleges." 7 May 1983, 1.

45. Minnesota Higher Education Coordinating Board. "Student Financial Aid in the 1980s: Roles and Responsibilities." Policy paper, January 1982.

46. Mitau, G. T. "A State Chancellor: Some Preliminary Comments on State Tuition Levels." In *Exploring the Case for Low Tuition in Public Higher Education,* edited by K. Young, pp. 153–56. Iowa City: American College Testing Program, 1974.

47. Myers, J. H., and W. H. Reynolds. *Consumer Behavior and Marketing Management.* Boston: Houghton-Mifflin, 1967.

48. Nelson, S. C. *The Equity of Public Subsidies for Higher Education: Some Thoughts on the Literature.* Papers is Education Finance No. 5. Denver: Education Finance Center, Education Commission of the States, 1978.

49. Nerlove, M. "On Tuition and the Costs of Higher Education: Prolegomena to a Conceptual Framework." *Journal of Political Economy,* 80 (1972), Part II, s178–218.

50. O'Hara, J. G. "It's Time to Blow the Whistle." In *Exploring the Case for Low Tuition in Public Higher Education,* edited by K. Young, pp. 141–50, Iowa City: American College Testing Program, 1974.

51. Olson, L., and R. Rosenfeld, "Parents and the Process of Gaining Access to Student Financial Aid." *Journal of Higher Education,* 55 (July/August 1984), 455–80.

52. Packer, J. "Student Aid and Student Needs on Campus." In *New Directions in Institutional Research: Impact of Student Financial Aid on Institutions,* edited by J. B. Henry, 25 (1980), 75–87.

53. Pechman, J. A. "The Distributional Effects of Public Higher Education in California." *Journal of Human Resources,* 5 (1970), 361–70.

54. _____. "Note on the Intergenerational Transfer of Higher Education Benefits." *Journal of Political Economy,* 80 (1972), Part II, s256–59.

55. Peng, S. S., J. P. Bailey, and B. K. Eckland. "Access to Higher Education: Results from the National Longitudinal Study of the High-School Class of 1972." *Educational Researcher,* 6 (December 1977), 3–7.

56. Radner, R., and L. S. Miller. *Demand and Supply in U.S. Higher Education.* New York: McGraw-Hill, 1975.

57. Rosenfeld, R. "Family Influence on Students' Postsecondary Decisions." Paper presented at the Annual Meeting of the Mid-South Sociological Association, Little Rock, Arkansas, October, 1980.

58. Rosenfeld, R., and J. C. Hearn. "Sex Differences in the Significance of Economic Resources for Choosing and Attending a College." In *The Undergraduate Woman: Issues in Educational Equity,* edited by P. Perun, pp. 127–57. Lexington: Lexington (Heath), 1982.

59. Rumberger, R. W. "The Economic Decline of College Graduates: Fact or Fallacy?" *Journal of Human Resources,* 15 (1980), 99–112.

60. Simon, H. A. *Models of Man.* New York: Wiley, 1957.

61. Smith, B. "Slip Sliding Way: Student Aid in Minnesota: Analysis and Recommendations." Minnesota Public Interest Research Group, undated.

62. Solmon, L. C., and P. J. Taubman (eds.), *Does College Matter?: Some Evidence on the Impacts of Higher Education.* New York: Academic Press, 1973.

63. Stampen, J. *The Financing of Public Higher Education.* AAHE/ERIC Report No. 9, Washington, D.C.: American Association for Higher Education, 1980.

64. Tierney, M. "Student College Choice Sets: Toward an Empirical Characterization," 1980.

65. University of Minnesota. "Rising Tuition Hasn't Cut Into Enrollment." *University of Minnesota Report,* January 1984, 1.

66. Van Alstyne, C. "Tuition: Analysis of Recent Policy Recommendations." In *Exploring the Case for Low Tuition in Public Higher Education,* edited by K. Young, pp. 35–103. Iowa City: American College Testing Program, 1974.

67. Windham, D. "Social Benefits and the Subsidization of Higher Education: A Critique." *Higher Education,* 5 (1976), 237–52.

68. _____. "The Benefits and Financing of American Higher Education: Theory, Research, and Policy." Project Report Number 80-A19. Stanford: Institute for Research on Educational Finance and Governance, School of Education, Stanford University, November 1980.

69. Woodworth, R. S., and H. Schlosberg. *Experimental Psychology.* New York: Holt, 1960.

70. Yanikoski, R. A., and R. F. Wilson. "Differential Pricing of Undergraduate Education." *Journal of Higher Education,* 55 (November/December 1984), 735–50.

71. Zemsky, R., and P. Oedel. *The Structure of College Choice.* New York: The College Board, 1983.

# The Financial Squeeze on Higher Education Institutions and Students:
## Balancing Quality and Access in the Financing of Higher Education (1989)

W. Lee Hansen and Jacob O. Stampen

## Introduction

This paper illuminates recent discussions about the tremendous financial pressures experienced by students, their parents, and colleges and universities in paying the costs of higher education.[1] It does this by placing these developments in the context of long-run, pendulum-like swings in society's interest in promoting greater access to higher education and enhancing the quality of the higher education enterprise. These swings are made apparent by using a new approach to organizing and analyzing the data on higher education finance.[2]

The conclusion that emerges from this analysis is that higher education is currently in a transitional period, with a growing emphasis on improving quality after a long period that emphasized equity and access. This current shift in emphasis toward quality is surrounded by an intense struggle over how the costs of quality improvements are to be shared among students, their parents, state and local taxpayers, voluntary contributors, and in the case of student financial aid, the federal government.[3]

Goal setting in higher education is influenced by a wide variety of internal and external forces. That is, goals do not emerge exclusively or even principally from internal analysis and deliberation. Rather, they grow out of external forces and events. This pattern is reflected in the common practice among educators of moving toward new goals and pushing for increased levels of funding in the wake of external political events (e.g., increased institutional support after Sputnik, new student financial aid programs after the beginning of the War on Poverty). This is followed by some new event that sets off a reaction in another direction.

Precedent for this view emerges from the research of historians and scholars from other disciplines who have tried to capture these alternating patterns of change, with terms such as tensions, cycles, pendulums, spirals, and dialectics.[4] Observers generally agree about the nature and identity of these cycles whose life spans average between twelve and seventeen years.[5] They also agree that these political cycles alternate between emphasizing public action versus private interest, described by Hirschman as the "frustrations of public life," or by others as "liberal versus conservative" traditions. Whatever the term, the meaning is generally the same. The most active exponent of the cycles view is Schlesinger, who notes that each cycle "must flow out of the conditions and contradictions of the phase before and then itself prepare the way for the next recurrence."[6]

Schlesinger's analysis provides a useful framework for sharpening the research questions in analyzing recent changes in higher education goals and financing. The principal questions that guide this analysis are:

1) How have the goals of higher education and levels of investment in it changed over the past forty years? What were the key turning points during this period?

2) Do the turning points in higher education reflect cyclical mandates for change in higher education? If so, what were these mandates?

3) Did changes in the goals of higher education affect the level of investment in instructional programs, the sharing of costs between students and society, and the ability of students and their families to finance college attendance? How did these effects show themselves?

4) Can these cycles and patterns in the financing of higher education help assess past progress and better understand issues affecting the future of higher education?

The data available for identifying finance-related changes are not ideal. Routinely gathered federal statistics on higher education finance are not highly detailed, and the definition of key variables change over time. This makes it difficult to document in consistent fashion both the financial trends and the changes they produce. Thus, the variables selected for observation are necessarily broad and, of course, reflect to a considerable degree personal judgments. Nonetheless, the general patterns that emerge offer explanations of changes in higher education that are directly pertinent to the current policy debate on the issues of quality and access in higher education.

## Cross Currents in Higher Education

American higher education has been buffeted by numerous forces over the past half-century. Perhaps the most dramatic force was demography. With the depression of the 1930s, college enrollments grew more slowly than they had in the past, and with the beginning of World War II, they plummeted dramatically. This was followed by an enrollment surge after World War II resulting from the GI Bill; some observers have viewed this surge as "making up" for the slower enrollment growth of the 1930s and early 1940s.[7] With the passage of World War II veterans through the system, enrollment levels remained relatively stable until the late 1950s. After a gradual increase into the early 1960s, an explosion of enrollments occurred by the mid-1960s as the post-World War II "baby-boom" population reached maturity. Enrollments rose even more sharply as interest heightened about increasing the enrollment of previously underrepresented ethnic minorities and women. Enrollments continued to increase through the 1970s, although the rate of growth slowed considerably. By the early to mid-1980s, overall enrollment growth came to a virtual halt and has remained relatively unchanged since then. College participation rates for most minority groups have declined since the mid-1970s, as they have for males generally; meanwhile, significant gains have occurred for females.

Political forces have also exerted a powerful influence on the growth of higher education in the United States. These forces are revealed most immediately in governmental action. Ultimately, however, these actions reflect an even more powerful force: namely, the changing priorities of the citizenry who determine the focus of political action and the availability of resources for higher education. The rhetoric of having to compete with the Soviets after Sputnik and of broadening access to minorities in the late 1960s and early 1970s proved effective in galvanizing public opinion and bringing about the allocation of more resources to higher education. The impact of student unrest in the early 1970s no doubt had an opposite effect. Whether the current view, that higher education can be an effective instrument for enhancing our international competitive situation and actually produce some shift in resource allocation, is a valid one remains unclear.

Still another factor is the higher education sector's efforts to chart its own course, as reflected in a long series of recent reports that articulate the goals and aspirations of academic institutions. Closely related are the efforts of economists, historians, and other social scientists to periodically offer new ideas that stir the air and stimulate thinking about the course of higher education.

## Periods of Analysis

To facilitate this analysis, four distinct periods are defined. This study begins in 1947, shortly after the end of World War II. This period embraces the years between 1947-48 and 1967-68 but the period appears to have two distinct phases. The first from 1947-48 to 1957-58 represents a period of readjustment following World War II and the playing out of the effect of the GI Bill. The second phase from 1957-58 to 1967-68 captures the enormous expansion of the higher education sector and the emphasis on that elusive dimension of quality, spurred by concern that American technology was falling behind the Soviets and resting on widely publicized studies establishing the link between investment in education and economic growth.

The third period from 1967-68 to 1980-81 reflects the search for ways to expand opportunities for students to attend college. This phase began with the initiation of certain federal student aid programs in 1965 and culminated with the federal decision in 1972 to establish a national need-based student aid system of Basic Educational Opportunity Grants (BEOG), later renamed Pell Grants. This was followed by what can best be described as a period of consolidating the financial aid system and confronting other equity-related problems; a prime example is the Middle Income Student Assistance Act of 1978. The fourth period from 1980-81 to 1985-86 (and perhaps to the present as well) reflects the beginning of a sharp swing in the opposite direction, with concerns about the quality of instruction, the efficient use of resources, and economic growth rising to the forefront once again.

These periods and their alternating swings between quality and equity (or access) closely correspond with the pendulum-like political cycles mentioned earlier. That is, when society promotes public action on equity issues, higher education is asked to expand access; when it promotes private interest, higher education is mandated to improve quality.

It should be noted that the various trends do not emerge full-blown. Rather, they reflect the aggregation of not only changes in individual attitudes and behavior but also the perceptions of change emerging within higher education institutions and the actions these perceptions generate. These micro-level developments are not dwelt upon, even though they constitute an important part of the story.

## Analytical Framework

Having established the time periods for this analysis, the data are now examined in hopes of learning whether changing political-social-economic conditions and the accompanying mandates exerted any lasting effect on higher education. First described are the changing dimensions of the nation's investment in higher education institutions. Examined next are higher education's expenditures in an effort to highlight major trends and reveal the interplay between the external and internal forces affecting resource allocation within the higher education sector. This information paves the way for measuring the burden of higher education costs and how these costs are shared among students/parents, state and local taxpayers, private donors, and also federal taxpayers through federal student financial aid programs.

Official data from the Department of Education and its predecessor, the U.S. Office of Education, were utilized. Because of changes in the data collection systems, as well as periodic alterations in the definitions of expenditures and revenues, the detailed data are not completely comparable over the forty-year period under study. Nonetheless, the broad categories employed here are generally consistent. The analysis begins with 1947-48 because data from 1946-47 are incomplete. Readers are cautioned that this analysis for all of higher education obscures differences between public and private independent institutions; these differences are to be examined in subsequent work.

## Enrollment Growth

Enrollment growth is described by two different sets of data. One is total head count enrollment, for which the data are readily available. The other is full-time equivalent (FTE) enrollment, which often must be estimated. Both of these series are shown in Table 1 (columns 1 and 2).

Total enrollment edged up only slightly between the late 1940s (to 2.6 million) and the late 1950s (to 3.0 million), doubled by the late 1960s (to 6.9 million), almost doubled again by 1980-81 (to 12.0 million), and then increased at a much slower pace in the early 1980s (to 12.2 million). Continued enrollment increases in the 1980s are at odds with many projections from the 1970s that had anticipated enrollment declines by the early 1980s because of declining numbers of high school graduates.

An appreciation for the implications of enrollment growth is provided by examining total enrollments as a percentage of the adult population. The total percentage enrolled from the civilian noninstitutional population age 16 and above increased from 2.7 percent in 1947-48 to 6.9 percent in 1985-86. In short, a substantial expansion in demand for higher education occurred, but its uneven rate of growth was heavily influenced by demographic forces.

Full-time equivalent enrollment has grown progressively more slowly because of the steadily increasing proportion of part-time students; their numbers increased from 22 percent of all students in 1947-48 to 41 percent in 1985-86. Relative to the civilian noninstitutional population age 16 and over, the FTE enrollment percentage rose from 2.1 to 5.0 percent. Then large rise in part-timers is attributable to several developments, the most important being the substantial increase of older students, those age 25 and over, who for occupational or family reasons typically cannot attend full time.

## Total Resources for Higher Education

Providing for the ever-growing numbers of students required raising substantial amounts of new revenue from taxpayers, private donors, students, supporters of research and others who purchase services from higher education institutions. Current revenues and expenditures grew rapidly and

### Table 1
### Enrollment in Higher Education Institutions

| Year | Total Head Count Enrolled (000) (1) | Total FTE Count Enrolled (000) (2) | Percent Civilian Non-Institutional Population Age 16+ | | Current Fund Exp. As % GNP (5) | Instr-Related Exp As % of GNP (6) |
| --- | --- | --- | --- | --- | --- | --- |
| | | | Head (3) | FTE (4) | | |
| 1947-48 | 2,616 | 2,222 | 2.6 | 2.2 | 0.8 | 0.5 |
| 1957-58 | 3,068 | 2,395 | 2.7 | 2.1 | 1.0 | 0.6 |
| 1967-68 | 6,912 | 4,591 | 5.3 | 3.5 | 2.0 | 1.3 |
| 1972-73 | 9,298 | 6,973 | 6.5 | 4.8 | 2.3 | 1.5 |
| 1980-81 | 12,097 | 8,819 | 7.2 | 5.3 | 2.3 | 1.5 |
| 1985-86 | 12,247 | 8,943 | 6.9 | 5.0 | 2.4 | 1.5 |

Source: Derived from Hansen and Stampen (1987) and updated to 1985-86.

at identical average annual rates ranging between 9 and 14 percent. (Note that this analysis excludes capital expenditures and revenues.) This pattern of growth is not surprising because the level of expenditures is conditioned by the amount of revenues available. As Howard R. Bowen explains,[8] higher education institutions are essentially nonprofit organizations that must live within their available resources. However, in contrast with most European nations, governmental authority is decentralized and custom permits colleges to independently advocate increases in public investment in order to better serve their students and society.

## Higher Education Revenues

Of interest in this study is the relationship between higher education's revenue growth and the economy's capacity to support higher education. As shown in column 5 of Table 1, total current fund revenues averaged about 1 percent of GNP in the 1940s and the 1950s, rose to slightly over 2 percent during the late 1960s and early 1970s, and then stabilized at about 2-1/2 percent of GNP in the 1980s. (Since current fund expenditures are approximately equal to current fund revenues, the percentages shown here can be applied to either measure.) These results demonstrate the close connection between enrollment levels and the proportion of the nation's total resources allocated to support higher education. This connection exists in considerable part because of funding formulas that, at least in the public sector, give considerable weight to enrollments.

The revenue component of particular interest here is the tuition and fee payments by students. These payments represent an important component of student costs, in fact, the only one captured in the institutional revenue data.

## Higher Education Expenditures

The pattern of increase in total current fund expenditures parallel that of revenues inasmuch as higher education institutions typically cannot operate for any length of time with deficits. In any case, the overall expenditure data are not particularly helpful in understanding the impact of changes on the quality of higher education. One reason is that total expenditures include funds allocated to carry out many other activities that are not central to the instruction-related activities of colleges and universities; among these activities are public service, research, and auxiliary enterprises.

How are estimates of what have been referred to as instruction-related expenditures constructed? Several categories of expenditures need to be excluded from total current fund expenditures to arrive at instruction-related expenditures. The first category includes self-financing activities, such as hospitals, dormitories, and related activities. (In fact, expenditures on these activities grew at a somewhat faster pace in recent periods than did total expenditures.)

A second category includes research expenditures, which are heavily financed by outside sources, and public service expenditures. Research expenditures prove to be a substantial component of total expenditures and grew rapidly in the 1950s and 1960s; since then their growth has slowed appreciably. Research activity builds new knowledge that is subsequently disseminated through classroom instruction and published journal articles and books. While research is an integral element in the mission of universities and many colleges, it is not directly related to instruction, especially at the undergraduate level and hence it is excluded.

A third category, institutional-awarded student financial aid expenditures, is also not central to the instructional activity of institutions, even though it may be highly important in promoting access. By way of illustration, student financial aid expenditures from institutional sources may affect not only the mix of students at individual institutions, but also overall enrollment levels; this does not imply that such expenditures are in any way related to instruction.

If these three categories of expenditures are excluded, something that can be identified as instruction-related costs is derived. These costs represent approximately 60 percent of total current fund expenditures, as shown in Table 1. If some part of research activities were viewed as an essential component of instruction, the percentage figure would be higher.

## Student Aid

As noted above, a small portion of student aid is provided directly by higher education institutions in the form of what are called "scholarships and fellowships." But this leaves out student aid provided under various federal programs, such as Pell Grants, Guaranteed Student Loans, etc. The remaining student aid funds—those provided through federal programs—do not flow to institutions, but rather are distributed directly to students through federal and state grant and loan programs. To capture fully the impact of student financial aid, federal student aid funds also must be considered. This financial aid, as well as aid provided by institutions, is allocated primarily on the basis of student financial need; hence, not all students receive student financial aid.

## Instruction-Related Costs, Tuition and Fees, and Student Aid

For purposes of this analysis, instruction-related costs are viewed as an indicator of efforts to promote quality. Tuition and fees less student financial aid funds are viewed as indicators of efforts to improve access. These are at best crude proxies for the inability to measure that portion of aid that enables young people from lower income families to attend and persist in higher education. Also, focusing only on instruction-related expenditures does not capture the benefit from those expenditures that "make a difference" in quality (i.e., that which produces greater and more lasting increments of student learning).

Even more important is the extent to which changes in these categories of expenditure affect quality and access. Spending more or less would change the dollar totals, but whether, for example, additional expenditures would enhance quality or improve access is more difficult to say. Nonetheless, for purposes of this analysis, the dollar totals and changes in these totals will be taken as crude indicators of the relative priority given to quality and access in higher education.

## Sharing the Costs of Higher Education

The institutional costs of higher education, as well as the costs of student financial aid, are shared by students (and their parents) through the tuition and fees they pay, by those who provide the underlying support to higher education institutions (which comes through taxes and voluntary contributions), and by federal taxpayers who fund student financial aid programs. The student share reflected by tuition payments can be described as the *gross student share* because it is not offset by student financial aid. One offset is institutionally-awarded student financial aid, which is described as the student share net of institutionally-awarded aid. Another more important offset is federal student financial aid. When these two sources of aid are subtracted from tuition and fees, the remainder is the *net student share*. This net student share reflects the impact of society's commitment to offset the costs of instruction through what are commonly described as "tuition subsidies" (the non-student share) and student financial aid.

Of interest is how instruction-related costs are shared between students through their tuition and fee payments (their gross share) and nonstudents, namely state and local taxpayers, as well as those who make voluntary contributions to institutions of higher education. As shown in Table 2, except for 1947-48 and 1985-86, the shares paid by these two groups are relatively constant. The 1947-48 data reflect in part the special financing arrangements of the GI Bill. By 1985-86, however, the gross student share rose to more than 38 percent, a change that can be given at least two interpretations. One is that colleges and universities found it relatively easy, in light of the strong demand for higher education, to increase their total revenue by raising tuition and fees. An alternative explanation is that the student share of costs was forced up by the slow growth of support from the non-student sector, a point examined below.

The gross share paid by students is offset by institutionally awarded student financial aid and federal student aid. The former plays a relatively minor role because institutions have traditionally tried to promote access via low tuition rates. The latter has come to play an increasingly important role through the provision of federally guaranteed loans and need-based grants.

When these two sources of aid are subtracted from the gross student share, a significant drop in the net student share of the costs occurs. (It is recognized that student aid funds can help pay for more than tuition and fees; they can also help pay for other costs of attendance, such as room, board, books, and incidental expenses.) The net student share is negative in 1947-48 because of the large infusion of educational benefits arising from the GI Bill. Despite the diminishing effects of the GI Bill by 1957-58, the magnitude of this aid was still sufficient to keep the net student share well below the gross student share.

By 1967-68, the net student share rose to roughly one-half the gross share, largely because of the phasing out of the GI Bill. However, by 1972-73, the dramatic effects of rapidly expanded federal need-based student aid programs are evident. In fact, total student financial aid funds grew so rapidly that by 1972-73 they exceeded the total amount of tuition and fees paid by students. This situation continued through the 1970s, so that by 1980-81, student aid exceeded tuition and fees by an even larger relative margin. This pattern reversed itself in the early 1980s as a result of efforts to control federal spending. By 1985-86, the net student share rose, but remained far below the 1967-68 level.

This change in the net student share hides two noteworthy shifts. One is the sharp rise in tuition and fees as a percentage of total instruction-related costs. The other is an almost equally large percentage point increase in the student share net of institutionally-awarded financial aid; this change indicates that only a small part of the added tuition and fee income was redistributed in the form of student aid.

## How Burdensome Were These Costs?

Nothing has been said yet about the burden of college attendance costs or the ability of students and their families to pay for higher education; nor has anything been said about the adequacy of the resources available to higher education institutions to carry out their mission.

**Table 2**
**Sharing the Costs of Higher Education:**
**Percentage Shares of Total Instruction-Related Expenditures**

| Year | Total Instruction-Related Costs (1) | Nonstudent: Gross Student State-Local Share: Taxpayers and Private Donors (2) | Tuition and Fees (3) | Student Share Net Institutional Awarded Aid (4) | Net Student Share: Net of All Financial Aid (5) |
|---|---|---|---|---|---|
| 1947-48 | 100.0 | 72.8 | 27.2 | 23.6 | -36.3 |
| 1957-58 | 100.0 | 65.4 | 34.6 | 29.8 | 13.1 |
| 1967-68 | 100.0 | 67.0 | 33.0 | 26.1 | 16.9 |
| 1972-73 | 100.0 | 66.7 | 33.3 | 25.9 | -1.0 |
| 1980-81 | 100.0 | 65.4 | 34.6 | 28.3 | -8.2 |
| 1985-86 | 100.0 | 61.7 | 38.3 | 31.4 | 4.0 |

Sources: Derived from Hansen and Stampen (1987) and updated to 1985-86.

One straightforward approach to answering these questions calls for comparing instruction-related costs with some comprehensive measure of the nation's capacity to finance higher education costs. Such a comparison avoids the need to convert any of the data from nominal to real values to correct for price level changes. Thus, rather than working with the total dollar values, the desire was to show how, over the period of analysis, instruction-related costs per student compare with a similar measure of the public's capacity to support higher education, but expressed on an individual or personal basis. Because gross national product (GNP) provides such a convenient and well-understood measure of aggregate output and hence aggregate capacity to pay, GNP per member of the labor force was used as an indicator of individual capacity to pay. GNP is preferable to other widely used measures because it reflects the value of all goods and services produced in the economy; it can also be related more directly to frequently made comparisons of higher education expenditures with GNP (i.e., higher education expenditures as a percent of GNP). Moreover, using GNP per member of the labor force gives a measure of the output produced by the average person, including those people who want jobs but are unable to find them. It can therefore be viewed as reflecting the capacity of the average member of the labor force to provide tax and non-tax support for higher education.[9]

The patterns representing the two measures selected, instruction-related costs per student and GNP per member of the civilian labor force, are shown below based on 1985-86 data:

$$\frac{\text{Instruction-related Cost per FTE Student}}{\text{GNP Output per Member CLF}} = \frac{\$6,755 \text{ each for 8.9 m. FTE Students}}{\$34,733 \text{ each for 115 m. Members CLF}} = 19.4\%$$

|  | Based on |
|---|---|
| Instruction-related Cost (expenditure for instruction less expenditures for research, public service, scholarships and fellowships, and auxiliary enterprises) | = 1.5% GNP |
| Instruction-related and scholarships and fellowship (what are called institutional-awarded aid) | = 2.1% GNP |
| Total Institution Current Fund Expenditures | = 2.6% GNP |
| Total Institution Current Fund Expenditures and All Other Student Financial Aid | = 3.2% GNP |

Note that the 19.4 percent figure in the third column of Table 3 is in a sense equivalent to the 1.5 percent in the last column of Table 1. The GNP-oriented measure (GNP/CLF) highlights the relationship between the level of instruction-related costs, who pays for them, and how financial aid affects the student share of these costs. Most immediately apparent is the small variations in the gross student share (tuition and fees), the much more pronounced variation in instruction-related costs and net student share, and the remarkably parallel movement on instruction-related costs and net student share. Thus, measures of quality and access move in quite opposite ways.

In Table 3, instruction-related costs per student as a percentage of the GNP measure rose sharply until 1967-68, hitting a peak of 21.1 in 1967-68. It then declined sharply until 1972-73 and remained virtually unchanged through 1980-81. Since then, it rose again to 19.4 percent in 1985-86. The non-student share of costs as a percentage of the GNP measure showed less variation, increasing through 1967-68, declining through 1980-81, and increasingly only modestly since then. Meanwhile, the gross student share, reflected by tuition and fees, after remaining constant from 1972-73 to 1980-81, increased by 1.3 percentage points to its 1985-86 near-high level of 7.4 percent.

What many students actually pay differs from the gross student share, as already noted, because institutionally-awarded aid reduces the student share as a percentage of the GNP measure. This share has remained approximately constant since 1957-58, varying within a narrow range. After dropping between 1967-68 and 1972-73, it began increasing again, and jumped substantially from 1980-81 to 1985-86.

The net share paid by students was, on average, strongly affected by the greatly increased amounts of student financial aid that became available during the past two decades. The net student share starts out negative in 1947-48 because of the GI Bill. By 1957-58, the percentage turns positive but remains lower than the gross student share because a considerable number of veterans were still receiving GI Bill benefits. During 1967-68, the net share rose even more because of declines in federal support, despite accelerating increases in funding for new federal student aid programs; this increase would have been even greater were it not for the rapid expansion of institutionally awarded financial aid.

The substantial growth in student aid between 1967-68 and 1972-73, the year before funding for the BEOG program (now called the Pell program) took effect, is illustrated by the drop in the net student share from 3.8 to -0.2 percent. Put another way, total student aid in 1972-73, for the first time since 1947-48, exceeded total tuition and fees. With the expansion of the Pell program, and as a result of the relaxed standards applying to federal grant and loan programs as a consequence of the 1978 Middle Income Student Assistance Act, student aid resources expanded greatly. The net student share in 1980-81 exceeded total tuition and fees by an even greater margin, -1.1 percent. But, by 1985-86 the net student share had become positive once again, at 0.8 percent.

What explains the reversal of efforts to promote greater access through low tuition and abundant financial aid since 1980-81? One explanation may be a belated realization that the decline in instruction-related costs since 1967-68 brought with it some erosion in quality, an erosion that could be halted only with increased spending for instruction. Another explanation emerges from desegregating the components of the change. Recall that instruction-related costs increased by 1.7 percentage points from 1980-81 to 1985-86. However, the share of these costs financed by traditional sources of support—state and local taxes as well as voluntary contributions—rose by only 0.4

## Table 3
### The Burden of the Costs of Higher Education

| Year | Instruction Related Costs Per FTE Student (1) | GNP per Member of the Civilian Labor (2) | Instruction Related Costs (3) | Non-student (Total Instruction-Related Exps. Less Tuition & Fees (4) | Gross Student Share: Tuition & Fees (5) | Student Share: Net of Institutional-Awarded Aid (6) | Net Student Share: Net of All Student Aid (7) |
|---|---|---|---|---|---|---|---|
| 1947-48 | 505 | 3,963 | 12.7 | 9.2 | 3.5 | 3.0 | -4.6 |
| 1957-58 | 1,128 | 6,738 | 16.7 | 10.9 | 5.8 | 5.0 | 2.2 |
| 1967-68 | 2,229 | 10,555 | 21.1 | 13.3 | 7.8 | 5.5 | 3.8 |
| 1972-73 | 2,483 | 13,935 | 17.8 | 11.9 | 5.9 | 4.6 | -0.2 |
| 1980-81 | 4,519 | 25,547 | 17.7 | 11.6 | 6.1 | 5.0 | -1.1 |
| 1985-86 | 6,755 | 34,733 | 19.4 | 12.0 | 7.4 | 6.1 | 0.8 |

Source: Derived from Hansen and Stampen and updated to 1985-86.

percentage points. This means that the gross student share had to make up the gap of 1.3 percentage points. The only source of revenue was increased tuition and fee charges.

Put another way, increases in instruction-related costs had to be met largely by higher student charges because no other support was available. At the same time the gross student share after adjusting for institutionally awarded aid rose 1.3 percentage points, meaning that increases in institutionally-awarded aid were not large enough to offset increases in tuition and fees. But the bottom line, the net student share, rose by 1.9 percentage points, from -1.1 to 0.8. The fact that the net student share increased by more than either the gross student share or the student share net of institutionally awarded aid indicates that federal aid grew more slowly than either instruction-related costs or tuition and fees. What remains most striking is that the net student share of 0.8 percent in 1985-86 still constitutes little more than 10 percent of the gross share of 7.3 percent. This means that the commitment to access continues to be strong despite some erosion of efforts in the 1980s.

The key to understanding what happened lies in knowing what caused instruction-related expenditures to rise so sharply (by 1.7 percentage points from 1980-81 to 1985-86). A key factor was the need to raise faculty salaries, which had lagged seriously throughout the 1970s. Early in the 1980s, it became evident that higher salaries were required to attract young people into the academic profession and to retain faculty members who were becoming increasingly receptive to outside offers, particularly for nonacademic jobs. At the same time, the costs of goods and services had escalated because of the largely unanticipated price increases of the late 1970s. In addition, maintenance expenditures that had been deferred because of the tight budgets of the 1970s needed to be financed. Changes in technology, perhaps best represented by the expanded use of computers, required extensive expenditures.

For these reasons, institutions found it necessary to augment their revenues to meet these cost increases. They presumably concluded that it would be easier to pass on these costs to students via increased tuition and fee charges than to win substantial additional support from traditional sources, namely, state and local taxpayers and private donors. This is not to suggest any lack of effort to raise additional public revenues. Rather, the depressed state of the economy, indicated by the relative stability of real GNP through the early 1980s, combined with the pressure on tax revenues from other programs, made it difficult to generate additional revenues from the public. Student demand, however, continued to be strong as a result of growing concern among the youngest cohorts of the baby boomers about getting good jobs.

One other important explanation needs to be mentioned. Higher education institutions, often in response to state mandates to improve the quality of education, argued that tuition increases were required to improve the quality of the education they were providing. By paying higher faculty salaries, increasing expenditures to update equipment and facilities, and introducing new technology to the classroom, institutions believed they were improving quality. Most institutions would have preferred to find other ways of meeting these increased cost s; they would have liked to receive more state and local revenue as well as larger voluntary contributions. Despite the much-publicized fact that tuition and fees increased so sharply, public reaction against these increases has not been noticeably strong enough to elicit additional support from other sources.

## Summary and Conclusions

In examining the course of events—the goals and the financing of higher education—over the past four decades, systematic patterns of change were found. These changes reflect political cycles similar to those noted by Schlesinger, cycles that no doubt exist for a variety of public policy issues. For higher education, however, these cycles translate into essentially two alternating mandates, one to improve quality and the other to improve access.

What is particularly interesting is how changes in the goals of higher education affected quality, access, and the sharing of costs between students and society. The relative constancy of the gross student share, represented by tuition and fees, in contrast to fluctuations in instruction-related costs and the net student share, is remarkable. The fact that these other two measures displayed such variation is an interesting commentary on the changing priorities in higher education finance. Equally surprising is the fact that total student financial aid exceeded total tuition and fee revenues in two quite different time periods—through most of the 1970s and much earlier, just after World War II.

In the late 1980s, a shift in public and institutional priorities appears to be underway: away from access and toward quality. This shift toward quality, at least so far, is being financed largely by students through tuition increases, rather than by the traditional sources of support such as state and local taxpayers and private donors, or federal taxpayers. In a sense, institutions, by trying to be responsive to the growing concern about quality, had to find whatever financial support they could. In the absence of other support, tuition and fees had to be raised.[10]

At the same time, careful consideration needs to be given to how much the emphasis on access in the 1970s contributed to the nation's goal of enhancing equal educational opportunity. Since the net cost of college attendance did decline sharply for young people with incomes low enough to quality for student aid, this proved to be a major accomplishment. While college participation rates for low income students did not increase,[11] evidence for the early 1980s shows that low family income was not by itself an important determinant of dropping out of college and that the availability of financial aid largely offset the effect of low family income.[12] Increasingly, it appears that academic ability, as reflected by academic performance in high school and by performance on standardized tests, constitutes the most important remaining barrier to expanding access to college.[13] This finding suggests that access will be difficult to increase without improving quality. In other words, current efforts to improve the quality of instruction could be effective if in the process academic performance improves among low income and ethnic minority students. As larger proportions of these students enter college with better preparation and are able to perform well in college, student financial aid will become even more effective for ensuring greater equality of opportunity in higher education.

The moral of this analysis is that while pursuing the current and much-needed mandate to improve quality, adequate amounts of targeted student financial aid support must be maintained. Concurrently, efforts are needed to enhance the academic performance of students, particularly minority students, in their pre-college years. Only in this way can they have a reasonable chance of performing adequately in college. The need for improved college preparation will be even greater as higher education institutions accentuate their emphasis on quality. In this meantime, increased reliance on tuition to finance improvements in quality, along with reductions in need-based student aid, will resurrect financial barriers. Perhaps even more important, these factors will undercut incentives for young people, especially those from low income families, to adequately prepare for college by taking full advantage of learning opportunities in the elementary and secondary schools.

# Notes

1. This paper draws on a longer paper by the authors: "Balancing Quality and Access in Financing Higher Education." December 1987.

2. For other recent discussions of higher education finance, see the papers from a recent conference on College and University Adjustment to a Changing Financial Environment, sponsored by the National Science Foundation in the summer of 1986: Paul T. Brinkman and Dennis P. Jones, *College and University Adjustment to Changing Financial and Enrollment Condition* (Boulder, CO: National Center for Higher Education Management Systems, 1986); Joseph Froomkin, *The Impact of Changing Levels of Financial Resources on the*

*Structure of Colleges and Universities* (Washington, DC: Joseph Froomkin, Inc. 1986). Also, see Durward Long, "Financing Public Universities and Colleges in the Year 2000" in Leslie W. Koepplin and David A. Wilson, eds., *The Future of State Universities: Issues in Teaching, Research, and Public Service* (New Brunswick, NJ: Rutgers University Press, 1983).

3.  The results reported here are part of a larger study of higher education finance, one that is motivated by curiosity about how higher education goals are formed and how this process influences the financing of higher education.

4.  The importance of cycles has been emphasized primarily by the Schlesingers: see Arthur M. Schlesinger, Jr., *The Cycles of American History* (Boston, MA.: Houghton Mifflin, 1986), and Arthur M. Schlesinger, *Paths to the Present* (New York: 1949). Also see, Herbert McClosky and John Zaller, *The American Ethos: Public Attitudes Toward Capitalism and Democracy* (Cambridge: Harvard University Press, 1984); Carl Kaestle, "Social Reform and Urban Schools," *History of Education Quarterly* 2 (Summer 1972): 211-228; A. O. Hirschman, *Shifting Involvements: Private Interest and Public Action* (Princeton, NJ: Princeton University Press, 1982); George Hegel, *Encyclopedia of the Philosophical Sciences in Outline* (Heidelberg, 1817).

5.  Arthur M. Schlesinger, Jr., *American History*, 24.

6.  Schlesinger goes on to say that such cycles "cannot be determined, short of catastrophe, by external events. Wars, depression, inflation may heighten and complicate moods, but the cycle itself rolls on, self-contained and self sufficient." (pp. 27-29). Hegel might have characterized each cycle as part of a dialectical process wherein each asserts a thesis which as time passes draws opposition resulting in the formation of an anti-thesis, causing a new cycle to begin. However, surviving elements of a previous cycle's thesis become permanent parts of a presumably richer and higher array of public policies.

7.  John F. Folger and Charles Nam, *Education of the American People* (Washington, DC.: Bureau of Census, 1960).

8.  Howard R. Bowen, *The Costs of Higher Education* (San Francisco: Jossey-Bass, 1980).

9.  This approach contrasts sharply with studies of how individual families meet the nontax costs of college (e.g., tuition, room and board, etc.) Such studies typically use family income or disposable personal income. It also contrasts with comparisons that use per capita measures, such as disposable personal income per capita. All per capita measures are sensitive to demographic shifts, and such shifts have been substantial over this period. For example, the nonworking population has changed considerably over the past forty years, reflecting not only altered patterns of labor force behavior among the older population, but also shifts in the youth population (under age 18). The latter group in particular was relatively small in 1947, increased substantially over the next two decades as a result of the baby boom, and gradually diminished in relative size during the late 1970s and early 1980s. Put another way, changes in GNP per capita include the very effects we seek to identify.

10. W. Lee Hansen, "Cost Containment in Higher Education," forthcoming in *The High and Rising Costs of College: Is There A Problem?* ed. John Lee (College Park, Md.: National Center for Postsecondary Governance and Finance, 1988), 22 pages.

11. W. Lee Hansen, "Economic Growth and Equal Educational Opportunity: Conflicting or Complementary Goals in Higher Education," in *Education and Economic Growth* ed. Edward Dean (Boston, MA.: Ballinger Publishing Co., 1984).

12. Jacob O. Stampen and Alberto F. Cabrera, "Exploring the Effects of Student Aid on Attrition," *Journal of Student Financial Aid* 16 (Spring 1986).

13. Stampen and Cabrera, "Exploring the Effects," and Stampen and Cabrera, "The Targeting and Packaging of Student Aid and Its Effects on Attrition," *Economics of Education Review* 7 (1988).

# Student Aid:
## Price Discount or Educational Investment?
## (1992)

WILLIAM G. BOWEN AND DAVID W. BRENEMAN

In his recent decision finding the Massachusetts Institute of Technology guilty of price-fixing for joining with the Ivy League universities in an agreement to award financial aid solely on the basis of need, Judge Louis C. Bechtle accepts the Justice Department's description of student aid as a "discount" from tuition. In the case of MIT, that was a serious error. While student aid sometimes functions as a price discount, at MIT it functions very differently—as an "educational investment."

This is far from a semantic quibble. The answer to the question of how student aid should be viewed is (as is true of most interesting questions): "it all depends." Much confusion has been caused by thinking of the student aid that colleges provide as either always a price discount or always an educational investment. In fact, it can be either—or both—*depending* on the ability of the college in question to attract enough students to fill its entering class without offering any price discounts (if it were to choose to do so). It is instructive to consider polar cases.

## Filling Desks or Encouraging Diversity?

At the non-MIT end of the spectrum are hard-pressed colleges that struggle to enroll enough students to meet their essential financial obligations. While some students who seek to enroll at these colleges will be willing to pay full tuition, there are not enough of them, of sufficient academic quality, to fill the entering class. Others will come only if offered a price discount in the form of a scholarship. So long as the "net revenue" contributed by this latter group of students (defined as the tuition they pay less the financial aid provided by the institution) exceeds the marginal cost of enrolling them, it is to the *financial* advantage of such colleges to provide price discounts in the form of scholarships.

The viability of this strategy depends on both the shape of the college's cost curve and the size of the discount, relative to tuition, needed to attract additional students. Colleges have substantial fixed costs and choose numerical enrollment targets consistent with reasonably full use of their physical plant and faculty resources; within some range on either side of the enrollment target, the incremental cost of enrolling an additional student is very low. Of course, discounts can be so large that the resulting net revenue falls below marginal cost. This is an important reason why colleges in these situations cannot be expected to provide "full scholarships" from the general funds of the institution; they are much more likely to provide many partial scholarships. Providing students aid discounts to increase net revenue is analogous to the practice of merchants in many fields—and, for that matter, to that of for-profit educational institutions.

At the other (MIT) end of the spectrum are highly selective colleges that could, if they chose to, meet their enrollment targets without offering any institutionally provided financial aid. Their applicant pools contain more than enough candidates who are qualified *and* willing to pay full tuition to fill all available places. Notwithstanding the understandable public perception of tuition levels as very high, institutions such as MIT could even charge a higher rate of tuition than they do. In point of fact, however, these colleges keep their tuition charges below the market-clearing level (thus conferring benefits on the student body at large) and also provide financial aid from their own resources—even though it is not to their financial advantage to do so. Why? To achieve what they perceive to be their educational objectives.

In sharp contrast to the first set of cases, student aid is not given to affect the size of the entering class, which would be the same whether or not aid was provided; rather, it is provided to affect the *composition* of the class. For MIT and similarly situated institutions, student aid enables the college to attract qualified students who could not afford to come otherwise, including students who will contribute to the diversity of the student population and, ultimately, to the needs of the nation for more well-educated students from racial minorities and disadvantaged backgrounds. Decisions to spend some of the college's own resources in this way are analogous to decisions to increase spending on the library, on faculty positions, on scientific equipment, or on any number of other worthwhile activities. For institutions at this end of the spectrum, student aid outlays are discretionary and therefore represent educational investments.

Of course, there are strong internal and external pressures to provide student aid, and therefore one might argue that the true degree of discretion is limited. But that is true of every major category of expenditure, such as library acquisitions. In all such cases, discretion exists—on the margin, and certainly in times of financial adversity, as much recent experience demonstrates. And the key distinction remains: in MIT-like situations, the pressures to award student aid do not stem primarily from financial considerations related to the overall number of students who will be enrolled (indeed, the short-term financial effects will be negative); rather, they stem from a sense of what constitutes the *educational* objectives—even the educational obligations—of the institution.

## How to Tell the Difference

A simple (conceptually at least) test allows us to tell whether student aid is a price discount or an educational investment. The key question is: does providing student aid increase or decrease the net resources available to the college to spend on other purposes?

When student aid functions as a price discount, because it is needed to enroll enough students to achieve a financial objective, it increases the net resources available for other purposes by providing some incremental tuition revenue above marginal costs. Here we assume that the enrollment target would not have been met in the absence of institutionally provided student aid.

On the other hand, when the college could meet its enrollment target without providing student aid, "gross" tuition revenue is a fixed amount, and the aid provided by the college represents a discretionary educational investment that has been chosen over other claims on the revenues of the institution. Here student aid is a source of budgetary strain, which is why some colleges (Columbia University is a recent example) have felt compelled to cut back on financial aid when faced with deficits.

From a budgetary perspective, the proper treatment of student aid also differs in the two situations. When student aid functions as a price discount, it should not be shown as an outlay on the expenditure side of the budget of the college (as it often is). Rather, it should be treated as a deduction from gross tuition revenue and in that way taken into account in calculating net tuition revenue on the income side of the ledger. After all, the college could not have earned the full amount of gross tuition revenue without the student aid discounts. In contrast, when total enrollment is unaffected by student aid, gross tuition revenue will be the same regardless of student aid outlays, and all of it should be regarded as income. Here, student aid is appropriately treated as an expenditure—along with the other types of spending with which it competes for resources.

Ironically, "full-ride athletic scholarships," including those provided by schools that are highly selective, also need to be understood as price discounts intended to increase revenue—only here it is mainly TV revenue generated by highly publicized teams that makes it "profitable" to provide these athletic scholarships, not increased enrollment. If it were not for NCAA rules which limit the amount of financial aid that can be provided, outstanding athletes would be able to command even larger scholarships than they do now, with no attention paid to financial need.

Of course, many colleges and universities occupy intermediate positions along what is a continuum. Consider, for example, the circumstances of a strong liberal arts college that does not, however, have the drawing power of an Oberlin or a Swarthmore. This liberal arts college may not be able to fill all its places without some use of student aid as a price discount, but it may spend considerably more on student aid than it would need to spend if it were concerned only with meeting an enrollment target. Many colleges invest some of their limited institutional resources in student aid to achieve a stronger and more diverse student body than they could attract otherwise. They are able to exercise *some* discretion, and the amount that they choose to invest in student aid will reflect institutional priorities. In mixed cases of this kind, student aid functions partly as price discount and partly as an educational investment. Real-world situations are still more complex in that investing in student aid to increase diversity and to attract some absolutely outstanding students who might otherwise go elsewhere can in turn affect total enrollment by increasing the appeal of the college to more full-tuition-paying students; and it can also increase revenues in the long run by increasing contributed income.

It should be emphasized that a college's place along this continuum depends on its academic reputation and financial resources. While institutions surely vary in the priorities they assign to making educational investments in student aid, almost all would *like* to make such investments if they could. Thus, we are not talking here about differences in educational philosophies or about purity of intentions, but rather about harsh realities: the degree to which a particular institution can afford to make a genuine choice concerning its investment in student aid.

## Making Policy Inside the Academy—and Out

Being clear about the function of student aid in different contexts is important both for wise decision making within educational institutions and for broader issues of public policy. Most educational decision makers naturally *want* to think of student aid outlays as educational investments, but this tendency can lead to serious errors. For instance, student aid may be "capped" at an artificially low level (say, 30 percent of gross tuition revenues) because the college doesn't believe that it can "afford" to spend more on student aid—when, in point of fact, offering some additional aid (discounts) might add to net revenues by increasing enrollment. When student aid is a discount, the focus should be on the comparison of marginal changes in net revenues and in institutional costs, not on the absolute amount of aid. In highly selective institutions, on the other hand, it is correct to think of student aid as one of many competing claims on scarce resources, and some limit may have to be placed on the amount that can be spent for this purpose if other educational goals are also to be achieved.

From the standpoint of public policy, it is important to note, first, that the very situations in which one might be most concerned about "restraints on trade" (where student aid functions as a pure price discount) are those in which agreements to follow a common approach to providing financial aid are highly unlikely. Colleges that need to use discounts to meet enrollment targets would be ill-advised to constrain their ability to compete for students by agreeing with other schools on some formulaic basis for awarding scholarships. These colleges cannot afford to collaborate, and there would seem little reason to worry about any inappropriate spread of collaborative agreements to base student aid solely on need.

At the other extreme, colleges that can fill their classes without offering discounts and that (properly) view student aid as an educational investment will have a quite different perspective. For them, student aid is a discretionary outlay, and their objective will be to make the most effective possible use of the scarce institutional funds that they have chosen to devote to this purpose. This can lead, as in the MIT case, to an agreement to award aid only on the basis of demonstrated need defined in a common way. Otherwise, scarce scholarship funds could be used "inefficiently" by being assigned to a well-to-do student who might have enrolled anyway.

One could accept the distinction between price discounts and educational investments presented here and still argue against collaborative student aid programs on the grounds that they are intended to allow participating institutions to purchase a desired "service" (for example, diversity) more cheaply than would be possible otherwise—by, in effect, making it harder for students to "shop around" for the best possible financial aid package. If student aid funds were unlimited, this way of thinking would have more appeal than it does in real-life situations in which the pressures on outlays of all kinds, including student aid outlays, are enormous. The practical consequences of making it more difficult for educational institutions to concentrate limited resources on students with demonstrated need are likely to include less financial aid for needy students—and perhaps for all students, since the general appeal of student aid, as a budgetary outlay, is likely to be reduced if it no longer serves the principle of equal opportunity in a clearly cost-effective way.

We would argue that whatever cost is borne by students who have less opportunity to "sell themselves to the highest bidder" is more than compensated by the benefits enjoyed by other students who have greater need for limited student aid resources. Presumably this is one reason why the government itself insists on a single, need-based standard in administering federal programs such as Pell grants. In any case, this is at bottom an issue of fairness and of social policy, as well as of efficient use of scarce institutional funds. From a public policy perspective, it is hard to see the social gain to be achieved by prohibiting trustees from making those choices that seem to them most consistent with the missions of the nonprofit institutions for which they are responsible.

## MIT as "Big Steel"?

Recognizing that, for an institution such as MIT, student aid is to be understood as a discretionary educational investment by a nonprofit entity makes it much easier to see the inapplicability of the traditional argument used to demonstrate the harmful consequences of collaborative price-setting in profit-making contexts. There, collaborative behavior serves to reduce output and to raise price. In the MIT context, on the other hand, providing need-based aid defined according to a common methodology has no effect whatever on "output" (enrollment), which is determined independently. Moreover, net revenue is reduced, not increased, by providing student aid in any form. Options for "consumers" (students) are increased, since awarding a budgeted amount of aid strictly on the basis of need gives more students a chance to attend an expensive institution.

In the case of these institutions, the correct analogy is not with "Big Steel," in the days before the Sherman and Clayton antitrust acts were passed. Rather, the apt analogy is with other collaborative efforts by these same educational institutions to use scarce resources as effectively as possible. Examples include agreements among institutions to divide responsibility for subscribing to high-priced scientific journals, to collaborate in providing expensive educational programs, and to share the costs of expensive laboratories. Like the need-based aid program followed by MIT, all these practices are agreements among potential "competitors," but they hardly seem "antisocial." They surely do not call for the opprobrium associated with price-fixing as understood by the framers of the antitrust laws.

# Trustbusting, 1990s-Style

*In 1989 the Antitrust Division of the U.S. Department of Justice began an investigation into the activities of some 60 colleges and universities. The investigation touched on a number of practices, including coordination of financial aid practices. The focus of the investigation eventually narrowed to the eight Ivy League universities and the Massachusetts Institute of Technology.*

*On May 22, 1991, the Justice Department filed a complaint against the nine schools in the U.S. District Court for the Eastern District of Pennsylvania, challenging, under the Sherman Antitrust Act, certain longstanding financial aid practices, generally known as "Overlap," in which the schools engaged. Simultaneously, the Justice Department filed a consent judgment signed by the eight Ivy League schools, but not by MIT, in which the schools agreed to cease the challenged activities, and to satisfy reporting, inspection, and compliance requirements, without admitting to liability. MIT alone continued to defend the challenged conduct in a trial on the merits that took place last summer.*

*The cornerstone of Overlap was an agreement by the schools not to award aid beyond a student's demonstrated need (that is, no "merit aid"). The schools also attempted to agree on appropriate approaches for determining a given student's need and to resolve differential need assessments on a case-by-case basis. The schools claim that need-based aid is necessary to maintain their unique policy of admitting students without regard to their ability to pay and funding all of the need of students who are admitted. Such "need-blind" admissions policies are rare and have become increasingly threatened as budget constraints have increased pressure on financial aid resources.*

*A central issue presented by the case is whether the Sherman Antitrust Act, enacted in 1890 to regulate behavior in the commercial marketplace, applies to the financial aid practices of nonprofit educational institutions.*

*In arguing that it should not, the schools have pointed out that almost all colleges and universities are qualified as charitable institutions under the Internal Revenue Code. As such they are exempted from federal taxes, and charitable donors to the schools are allowed to deduct donations from their federal income taxes.*

*The Justice Department's position is that the Sherman Act applies to the schools' Overlap agreement, which violates the act by virtue of the fact that some students—those who would have received no-need aid in the absence of the agreement—paid more for a college education than they would have in the absence of Overlap. Last September the District Court ruled in favor of the Justice Department. The appeal in the case is currently pending.*

# STATE BUDGETING AND POLICY

# Budgeting for Higher Education at the State Level:
## Enigma, Paradox, and Ritual[1] (1990)

DANIEL T. LAYZELL AND JAN W. LYDDON

## I. Introduction

Winston Churchill once described Russia as a riddle wrapped in a mystery inside an enigma. To many in higher education, the state budget process is their Russia. Many in higher education suffer from myopia when it comes to the budget process in that they only see the parts that directly affect them. This narrow focus tends to enhance the enigmatic nature of the budget process. The objective of this paper is to broaden the focus and to analyze this topic cohesively and comprehensively by first presenting a conceptual overview of the broad elements of the process (context, procedure, and outcome), followed by a systematic analysis of this conceptual framework through a review of the literature, and finally a discussion of the implications of the framework and literature.

## II. Conceptual Overview of State Budgeting

Once people looked to the stars to tell what the future would bring; today they look at the budget. The budget spans the distance between present choices and future options (Caiden 1988). State governments bear the principal responsibility for budgeting for public higher education operations. Thus, they are the principal participants in shaping both the present and the future of higher education.

A basic framework is the starting point for understanding state budgeting. Such a framework is illustrated on the following page.

Although the elements are disaggregated for the purpose of analysis, there is much overlap within the state budget process for higher education. The budget framework illustrated here is based on the Easton (1957) model of inputs (context) flowing through a 'black box' (process) and to final outputs (product).

Examination of the state higher education budget process begins with the external environment of a state, which includes its history, politics, economy, and demography. Historical factors include past state budgeting practices and the past higher education share of the state's budget as well as less tangible historical factors such as state culture and traditions. One important historical tradition is". . . that last year's allocation is the absolute minimum to be expected from the state this

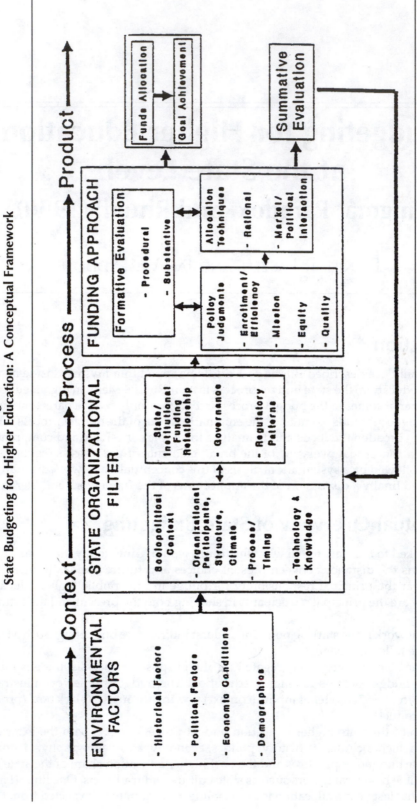

Figure 1

State Budgeting for Higher Education: A Conceptual Framework

Source: Lyddon, Fonte, & Miller (1986).

year" (Jones 1984 p. 64). This inviolability of the base is frequently referred to as *incrementalism*; that is, a gradual progression building on previous decisions. Incrementalism as both budgetary theory and practice is eroding, however, in part because of the significant effects of other environmental factors on the process such as the economy. Wildavsky (1986) noted that federal budgets, for example, experienced "shift points" during the 1947-63 period where changes were not simple linear progressions. Lyddon (1989) noted that state spending for higher education, while largely incremental, did not progress forward in steady, predictable jumps.

LeLoup (1988) noted that budgeting has changed in recent years from a process that is primarily concerned with bottom-up and line-item decisions (micro-budgeting) to a process focused on high level decisions on spending relative budget shares, and a top-down approach (macro-budgeting). LeLoup's study, however, was conducted on the federal budget, not states. Nonetheless, states are showing evidence of budgetary decision making among competing areas of state spending by holding some areas at the same levels and increasing (or cutting) spending in others.

Other environmental factors are economic, political, and demographic variables. Studies have shown clear, direct relationships between the economy of a state and its spending on higher education. For example, Garms (1986) found a significant positive relationship between personal income per capita and state higher education expenditures per capita. General revenue availability in a state has also been shown to be very closely associated with state spending for higher education (Coughlin & Erekson 1986; Garms 1986). Overall, quantitative analyses of demographic and political variables have been shown to have weak relationships with total spending for higher education. However, intuitively we know that individual variables within each of these categories relate to the process in qualitative ways that create intervening effects on the final outcome. Moving farther through the model one comes to the state organizational filter which is the first portion of the state response to the external environment. It has two major components: the broad socio-political context and the more specific relationships between the state and its higher education community. The state filters the various components of the external environment somewhat as it responds to, or ignores, environmental factors. The effect of environmental variables on the budgetary outcome for higher education has been shown to vary because different states have different environmental conditions and different responses to these conditions (Layzell 1988). One set of actors in the process may respond while others do not respond at all to certain conditions. For example, one state's tax structure may be based largely on sales taxes (e.g., Florida). Since the yield of an income tax varies more over the business cycle than the yield of a general sales tax, a state with an income tax system may react more quickly to economic changes than one with a sales tax-based revenue system (Mikesell 1984). Similarly, a state may decide in a case of declining (or rising) revenues to treat higher education the same as all other state funded activities, or may leave it protected (or unprotected) from revenue changes because of factors in the full state organizational filter.

The roles of various organizational participants depend on the state in which they are working. In most states, the Governor sets the broad agenda or parameters of the state's budget, and the legislature modifies the distribution of the budget (Adler & Lane 1988). In contrast to governors' roles in broad agenda setting, legislatures more typically see their roles as parochial, directed most toward assisting constituents. Thus, the legislature tends to operate more narrowly on distributive and redistributive matters (Brandl 1988). Budgets operate on several time schedules, including four phases in a single budget cycle. The phases include preparation, approval, execution, and audit of a budget (Lee & Johnson 1983). Each of these phases is being affected by changes in technology and knowledge, the most obvious of which is the spreading use of computers. Budget preparation and allocation involves using various funding techniques, such as formulas, which are the most common approach used by states (Lamb 1986). A phase which is undergoing substantial change is the evaluative/feedback (audit) phase. States are increasingly using this phase of the budget process as a means to promote and study quality and effectiveness in higher education.

The state-institutional funding relationship includes both the governance structure and regulatory patterns. With respect to these aspects of the relationship, the most direct and tangible link between state government and higher education is the allocation for higher education in the state budget. The governance relationship between state government and higher education institutions shapes both the structure of the budget and its purposes (Jones 1984). Curry, Fischer, and Jons (1982) suggested a spectrum of state-institutional funding relationships which they termed "financial governance" to distinguish it from structural governance. The spectrum ranges from educational institutions treated very much like state agencies to institutions which function like independent, non-profit organizations which get funds via contract-for-service. In between the two extremes are state-controlled institutions and state-aided institutions. States may have more than one financial governance model for different types of institutions. Additionally, the relationship within a state may change as a state loosens or tightens its control over institutions and their spending patterns (Hines 1988).

The funding approach itself is another major segment of the conceptual framework. Within any funding approach there are policy judgments that shape the particular allocation technique used, and some sort of evaluation of the utility of the approach. Policy judgment categories include 1) efficiency and enrollment linkage, 2) mission diversity, 3) equity and fair share, and 4) quality, outcomes, and effectiveness. Policy makers choose among their values and set priorities as they develop—or use—an allocation approach that handles the issues in these categories. Further, policy makers may emphasize one or more policy judgment categories in response to changes in environmental conditions or changes in values of the predominant decision making parties. Whether objective (i.e., quantitative) procedures and data are used in a funding approach does not alter the fact that subjective (i.e., political) value decisions are made by policy makers (Wirt, Mitchell, & Marshall 1988).

Resources are allocated to higher education based on policy judgments, which in turn are influenced by the various factors in the state organizational filter and the environment of the state. Allocation techniques are divided into two basic and competing approaches: 1) the political or interest group interaction model, and 2) the "rational school" models. The former includes incrementalism and political log rolling. The "rational school" models include formula funding as well as lesser used approaches like Zero Base Budgeting (ZBB), and performance budgeting (Morgan 1984). A recent survey found that of 46 respondent states, 29 used a formula or guideline to request and/or allocate state general funds for public higher education (Maryland Higher Education Commission 1988). Despite its inclusion in the "rationalist" group, formulas are often "adjusted" for political reasons. Meisinger (1976) has called funding formulas "a combination of technical judgments and political agreements" (p. 2).

Formative and summative evaluation provide opportunities to assess both the process and the outcomes, and to make modifications to either or both. Much evaluation is informal, though increasingly evaluation, particularly of outcomes or results, is formal. There are three broad criteria for evaluating a funding approach: 1) technical expertise: Does the formal allocation technique measure, weight, identify or qualify effectively what it purports to measure, weight, identify, or qualify?; 2) two way feedback: Is the allocation process "open" and does it encourage and facilitate participation and the communication of views on institutional needs and state priorities among all actors in the process, i.e., legislature, governor, higher education agency, institutions, and the general public?; 3) values and issues clarification: To what extent does the allocation process highlight the value choices and the facts involved in any choices? (Miller 1964).

**Table 1**
**Major Components of State General Fund Spending**
**(Percent of Total)**

| Budget Area | FY 1992 | FY 1992 | Change |
|---|---|---|---|
| Higher Eduction | 13.5% | 13.0% | (0.5)% |
| Medicaid | 10.1 | 12.0 | 1.9 |
| Corrections | 4.5 | 5.0 | 0.5 |
| K-12 Education | 35.5 | 36.9 | 1.4 |
| All other | 36.4 | 33.1 | (3.3) |
| TOTAL | 100.0% | 100.0% | — |

Source: Eckl, Hutchinson, and Snell (1990) and (1991).

# III. Review of the Literature

## The Environmental Context of Budgeting

Why do some states allocate more of their budget to higher education than others? One factor contributing to wide variations among states is the external environment affecting each state including the historical traditions, politics, economy, and demography of a state. The impact of the external environment on state appropriations for higher education is significant, although it does not fully explain the variations in funding for higher education (Layzell 1988; Lyddon 1989).

## Historical Traditions

A central function of all political systems is to allocate resources among competing preferences for their use (Wirt, Mitchell, & Marshall 1988). Values and policy preferences are at the heart of all state budget processes. Participants in a state's budget process bring with them the values and policy preferences of their constituencies—state agencies, interest groups, and of course private citizens—which are both conflicting or complementary, narrowly defined or wide ranging. In short, the spectrum of values and policy preferences represented in the state budget process mirrors that within the state's citizenry, and is a result of the historical development of the state.

Further, the share of the state budget going to higher education versus other segments of the budget is related to, among other factors, these historical traditions. In recent years, the share of the state budget going to higher education has declined in the face of competing demands from other service areas, especially health (Medicaid), corrections, and K-12 education (see Table 1).

This shift is perhaps more reflective of the tendency for political systems to respond to immediate crises (e.g., the health care problem, prison overcrowding from mandatory sentencing laws, declining federal dollars in all areas, etc.) than it is of a decline in the value placed by states on higher education. This also reflects higher education's "discretionary" status in the state budget.

## The Political Context

Closely related to the context of historical traditions is the political context. "The social life of a citizen is interwoven into the political life, and the mediating factor that makes [it] possible is culture" (Wirt, et al. 1988, p. 271). Higher education and state politics in this country have been intertwined since the Massachusetts legislature began making direct legislative grants to Harvard in the 1600s (Brubacher & Rudy 1976). In later years, the passage of the Morrill Act ensured that higher education would remain within the realm of state politics indefinitely (Hines & Hartmark 1980). Three aspects of the changing political environment as it relates to state budgeting for higher education include the structure of higher education, gubernatorial influence, and legislative influence.

The structure of higher education. During the 1960s and 1970s, most of the states established coordinating agencies to handle the massive expansion higher education was experiencing at the time (McGuinness 1988). With the formation of these state agencies, many powers that were previously the sole domain of institutional governing boards were at least shared with these agencies, including (but not limited to) planning, budgetary, and financial functions. Of those states, 43 have statutory authority to review and/or recommend budgets for higher education to the governor or legislature (McGuinness 1988).

Gubernatorial influence. Over time, governors have begun to take a more active role in the formation of policy for higher education (Herzik 1988). Over the past several years, the impetus for creating policy for higher education has shifted from institutions to the executive mansion (Adler & Lane 1988). In essence, the governor's main role in the budget process is that of chief facilitator. In fact, some have asserted that "it is the governor who has the greatest potential to become the initiator as well as the catalyst for policy changes" in higher education (Adler & Lane 1988, p. 17). While the intensity of the role may vary from state to state, it is generally true that the governor has the formal authority to veto or sign legislation, appoint his or her own people to coordinating and governing boards, and to recommend a budget for higher education (Beyle 1983).

Legislative influence. The relationship between higher education and state government became increasingly complex in the 1980s, resulting in legislatures that are more sophisticated in matters of higher education policy than their predecessors (McGuinness 1986). With this sophistication, the legislature has moved from a minor to a major player in the formation of higher education policy. One reason cited for this is the fact that for many states, higher education has become the largest discretionary item in the budget (Zusman 1986). This increase in state expenditures on higher education has increased the interest of legislatures in how and where those funds are spent. The legislature serves a dual role in the higher education budget process. As watchers of the public purse, legislators act as stewards of funds for higher education, ensuring that public funds are spent efficiently. On the other hand, the legislature also serves as the forum for constituents (including institutions of higher education) and the party's policy preferences. In a sense, these roles are mutually exclusive in that one role requires that rational spending decisions be made while the other is often irrational, forsaking sound fiscal policy in an effort to satisfy a multitude of needs and desires (Brandl 1988). Research on legislatures and their policy outputs is limited, partly because of the difficulty of building generalizations on 50 diverse settings (Oppenheimer 1985). One important factor is the increasing number and professionalism of legislative staffs (Davis 1984) and their impact on the process. One such study noted that staff is crucial in reducing the reliance of legislators on lobbyists (BeVier 1979).

## The Economic Context

If historical traditions set the stage and politics provides the actors, then the economic context is the script that frames the budget outcomes for higher education at the state level. During the 1980s states with the greatest increase in state tax support for higher education were located in regions of the country with the strongest economies (Hines, Hickrod, & Pruyne 1989). Three interrelated aspects of the economic context affect state budgeting for higher education: general economic conditions, state tax capacity, and availability of state revenues.

State economies can change rapidly.[2] Public support for higher education is directly related to the general condition of a state's economy (Wittstruck & Bragg 1988). Nationally, the economy enjoyed a period of sustained expansion from 1982 until 1990, with just a few states as exceptions.

In the wake of this expansion, the nation has been involved in a balancing act, trying to keep inflation in check and recession from occurring (Anderson & Massy 1989). Either one of these events could trigger severe budget problems for higher education. High inflation lowers real salaries, lowers available federal funds for research and student aid, and adversely affects endowments (Anderson 1988). The onset of recession reduces state tax revenues resulting in tight budgets (Carnevale 1988). This could lead to a new period of fiscal stringency and retrenchment for higher education.

State tax capacity is defined as the amount of state revenue that would be generated if the revenue base were taxed at the maximum allowable tax and service fee rates (Berne & Schramm 1986). Revenue bases include the volume of general sales, licenses issued, corporate income, personal income, property value, and oil and gas production (Halstead 1989). The most important variable in determining the level of a state's tax capacity is not the nominal tax rates but the underlying economic condition of the revenue base. And, "state governments face no more severe handicap in their task of adequately supporting public services than the near permanent burden of low tax capacity" (Halstead 1989, p. 22). Not surprisingly, states with higher tax capacities have been shown to allot more state revenue to higher education than states with low tax capacities (Garms 1986).

Closely related to state tax capacity is the availability of state revenues. The principal difference between strong and weak state support of higher education is the availability of state revenue (Hines, Hickrod, & Pruyne 1989). Availability of revenues is simply the amount of current and projected revenue growth expected in the next budget period. A survey of state-level budget officers in five western states indicated that a majority felt that the availability of revenues was the major factor affecting budget decisions in their states (Duncombe & Kinney 1985). Further, although revenue availability is important, the willingness of lawmakers to spend it on higher education is even more crucial (Hines, Hickrod, & Pruyne 1989). Additional state revenues do not benefit higher education if they are not directed toward higher education.

## The Demographic Context

A state's demographic context affects the state budget outcome in that the mix of population and overall growth or decline directly affects services required. State demographics affect higher education at both a macro- and micro-level. At the macro-level, changes in overall population and in the composition of the population, such as age and minority distribution, affect the demand for different types of public services, such as higher education. At a micro-level, changes in enrollment patterns and participation rates in higher education affect policy makers' perceived need for higher education.

Some have argued that changes in overall state population affect state budgeting in general (Wildavsky 1986) and state budgeting for higher education in particular (Lyddon, Fonte, & Miller 1987; Volkwein 1987). If population levels increase, the need for state services increases correspondingly. If population levels decrease, corresponding economic difficulties usually require stagnant or declining state services. An analysis of two-year changes in state higher education appropriations indicated that states in high growth areas such as the Sunbelt tended to show large increases in appropriations for higher education and vice versa (Nines 1988).

Changes in the composition of the population also affect the state budget process, particularly the age distribution of the population and the percentage of the minorities within the population. Over a 30-year period, the numbers of a state's residents aged 5 to 17 and 18 to 20 were significant determinants of public revenues allocated to K-12 and higher education in years when those age groups constituted a large percentage of the state's total population (Garms 1986). On the other hand, as older, "nontraditional" students become the new majority in higher education, service delivery systems will need to be changed (e.g., odd-hours and weekend courses) resulting in different kinds and levels of costs (Brinkman 1988). Similar pressures will come from an increasingly diverse student population.

Traditionally, funding for higher education, at least as far as the operating budget is concerned, has been linked to enrollments (Leslie & Ramey 1986). However, despite conventional wisdom, there is evidence that this relationship may not be so clear cut. A recent analysis found that increasing enrollments in public colleges and universities typically resulted in a net loss in state appropriations per FTE student (Leslie & Ramey 1986). Related to enrollment levels is the state higher education participation rate, generally defined as the proportion of student enrollment to the state population. It is a proxy measure for resident demand for higher education. Available data suggest that states with high participation in public higher education allocate a larger portion of their budget to public higher education (Halstead 1989).

## The Budgetary Process

As we have seen, contextual factors in state budgeting for higher education are changing. The process itself is also changing. Process changes include an increasing number of actors and changes in the roles they play. Changes also include structural issues such as state level governance and coordination of higher education, timing issues such as the advent of mid-year reductions and supplemental appropriations, creative financing techniques, and resource allocation strategies. Many of these issues have been referenced in the description of the budgeting framework and also with regard to the environmental context. Portions of the process illustrated in the framework, however, are distinctive and deserve further discussion. Some portions of the higher education budgeting process at the state level are poorly supported with empirical research. We must, then, rely on research about other levels of government (such as federal or municipal governments) or research about budgeting for other state functions (such as elementary and secondary education, or general government).

Drawing precise conclusions about the nature of the state budgeting process for higher education is difficult for several reasons. Relying on studies conducted primarily about other levels of government is faulty because the nature of authority is different in each level of government. For example, state governors usually have line item veto power, allowing them to annul certain legislative decisions. The President lacks this authority in his relations with the U.S. Congress. Mayors or municipal managers are usually the dominant figure in their arenas, working with a weak or unassuming council (Wildavsky 1986).

Another difficulty with "borrowing" research is the nature of the relationship between state governments and higher education institutions. In some states, the institutions may be treated for budgetary purposes much like other state departments. In other states, however, public colleges and universities operate much more like private institutions with which the state contracts for services (Curry & Fischer 1986). Clearly, the processes of budgeting for institutions under disparate conditions differs. Even within a single state, one system of higher education may be governed differently from another.

Budgetary processes are not static, so a study conducted 10 years ago may have little bearing on current budgeting processes. Changing conditions sometimes cause changes in budgeting processes, or vice versa. For example, budgeting under severe economic constraints differs from budgeting under conditions of greater flexibility because "The most important variable in determining the behavior of participants is the adequacy of revenues" (Wildavsky 1986, p. 240). Most budget cuts resulting from revenue shortfalls occur under emergency conditions; thus, an opportunity rarely occurs for planning by either states or institutions (National Conference of State Legislatures 1982). Perhaps the emergency nature of such cutting also inhibits sharing of information about changes in the budgetary processes as well.

## The Link Between the Environmental Context and the Budget Process

Changing public attitudes about government spending in general and higher education in particular have an obvious effect on the process of budgeting. These attitudes shifted in the 1970s toward higher education as a personal asset rather than a societal one, resulting in a much tighter fiscal environment. Furthermore, taxpayer revolts have added pressure for increased institutional accountability (Munitz & Lawless 1986, p. 67). One significant process change has been use of ". . . expedients—one-time ad hoc taxing and spending measures—which provide no lasting basis for sustained financial capacity . . . the budget is made and remade throughout the fiscal year in a desperate game of catch up to make figures come out even at the end" (Caiden & Chapman 1982, p. 118). Another direct effect of revenue constraints on higher education is the increase in tuition rates—and the increased attention of state officials on them.

Changes in the political environment also puts pressure on state decision makers to change their budgeting approaches. Various budgeting techniques, including formula budgeting, Program Planning and Budgeting Systems (PPBS), Zero Base Budgeting (ZBB), and the current interest in budgeting for quality outcomes are, at least in part, results of political pressures. Incentives for enhancing quality in higher education are a current approach used in a number of states, though there is a shift in the focus of such efforts. According to Berdahl & Studds (1989), "during the last decade, some states have intensified efforts to make quality improvement a key public policy agenda item by employing assorted techniques to associate financing with performance objectives or quality measures." One consequence of this is a destabilization of the budget process and funding amounts (Folger 1989).

## State Organizational Filter

Legislatures have been asserting themselves more strongly, and many have developed strong professional staffs to assist them. The effect of this on budgeting is not yet fully measured, but may result in greater use of data in decision making about budgeting.

The timing of budgeting is changing; where once budgets were written and enacted in a more or less regular cycle, this is less and less the case. Legislatures are meeting with greater frequency, economic conditions are shifting, and demands for state dollars have increased in number and intensity, necessitating more frequent budgeting. Even still, there are different time frame perspectives for state officials and for higher education institutions. A typical politician focuses on election-to-election cycles; a state budget officer focuses on the budget on which he or she is working at the moment with an eye to the previous one for comparisons; higher education institutional officials must have a longer time frame focus for operations. Difficulty arises when elected officials expect a "quick fix" solution to problems that are long term and complex.

Allocation techniques vary between and even within states. Several states use funding formulas for at least part of the higher education budget. Those states that use formulas to fund higher education have been adding even greater complexity to the formulas in recent years. Despite this increased sophistication, however, the differentiation or lack or differentiation between higher education institutions in a state remains a perennial concern with regard to funding formulas.

# Budgetary Outcomes

The state budget document is more than a book of numbers and rhetoric. In the larger context of state government and politics, the budget may be seen as a unique product shaped by a unique environment interacting with a dynamic process. The budget reflects the "state of the state," as well as setting forth the major policy preferences of state government within these external constraints. As Wildavsky has noted, "If politics is regarded as conflict over whose preferences are to prevail in the determination of policy, then the budget records the outcomes of this struggle" (1986, p. 9).

Higher education, although it performs a valued function in the state, is not immune from the political economy of the state budget process; there is only a finite amount of state revenue to be distributed among state services for their operations. Therefore higher education is subject to the same environmental forces and dynamic processes as other state services. Moreover, the state higher education budget sets forth the major state policy preferences for higher education and budgeting is the process for bringing these higher education policy concerns to fruition. These policy areas include accountability; costs, productivity, and quality (including fiscal incentives); affordability; economic development; minority and non-traditional students; and independent higher education. Although some of these areas may not be directly identified as budget items per se, all have budgetary implications for the state and higher education.

## Accountability

An often used term with respect to higher education in recent years is accountability. Only recently, however, has accountability been tied directly to the budget process. The advent of fiscal incentive programs, for example, is representative of an attempt by policy makers to tie funding to specific outcomes. As noted by one observer, "The utility of the budget as a device for accountability . . . depends heavily on the extent to which it reflects state priorities and ties this funding to performance" (Jones 1984, p. 16).

Although much used by state policy makers and in higher education circles, an exact definition of accountability remains elusive. Accountability is hard to define because the term refers to a process rather than a product (Hartmark 1978). Accountability has also been viewed as a means as opposed to an end in achieving greater efficiency and administrative control in higher education (Mines 1988). Further, between the 1960s and 1980s, the focus of accountability evolved from a fiduciary orientation to an outcome orientation (Mingle & Lenth 1989). In essence, the concept of accountability refers to the responsibility of higher education to report on its failures and achievements to state government.

The current view of accountability is as a concept having several dimensions occurring within different policy domains (Hartmark & Hines 1986). These dimensions are: 1) systemic accountability: dealing with the fundamental purposes of higher education; 2) substantive accountability: dealing with the values and norms within higher education; 3) programmatic accountability: dealing with academic and other programs; 4) procedural accountability: dealing with institutional and administrative procedures; 5) fiduciary accountability: dealing with the finance of higher education.

## Costs, Productivity, and Quality

Like accountability, three terms which we increasingly hear being used together in higher education circles are costs (institutional), productivity, and quality. These three terms have almost become a litany recited by state policy makers to the leaders of the higher education community: costs should be kept down and productivity should be increased while maintaining (or improving) quality in higher education.

The term 'cost' is usually thought of in terms of what we spend in order to acquire some good or service. Higher education incurs costs in two senses: once for the item it bought (its monetary cost) and once for the item it could not buy because of the one it did (the opportunity cost), (Bowen 1980). Opportunity costs are inherent in any budgetary decision given limited resources and seemingly unlimited demands. As resources grow scarcer, opportunity costs become almost as important as actual costs.

According to one observer, there are three reasons why costs in higher education have been increasing at such a rapid rate: "cost disease," the "growth force," and "organizational slack"

(Massy 1989) "Cost disease" refers to the fact that higher education is highly labor intensive. Because of this, higher education and other "non-progressive industries" do not benefit from the adoption of labor-saving technologies in order to reduce costs. So, assuming the productivity of higher education remains constant, higher education costs will grow at about the same rate as the general productivity increase in the economy, which is slightly above the rate of inflation. "Growth force" refers to the fact that in its desire to improve or maintain quality, colleges and universities add new programs and services while maintaining all existing programs and services. Thus, institutions are consistently in a net growth mode. Finally, "organizational slack" refers to simple waste and inefficiency that occurs in all organizations. Resources are not being used to their greatest potential. When slack remains within an organization, as it often does within colleges and universities, additional costs are incurred in order to deal with the problems caused by the slack.

Closely related to higher education costs is the concept of productivity. In simple terms, productivity refers to the ratio of outputs to inputs, where higher ratios reflect greater "productivity" and vice versa. In industrial settings, productivity is relatively easy to measure. One would only need to take the total product (output) of a company and divide the input of choice: per worker, per dollar spent, etc. Measuring productivity in higher education is a much more messy proposition. In higher education, although inputs are relatively easy to identify (i.e., land, labor, and capital costs), ". . . outcomes are diffuse and difficult to measure . . ." (Mingle & Lenth 1989, p. 13).

For many years, especially in states where formula funding was used to finance higher education, productivity in higher education was seen in terms of enrollments. Institutions which were able to increase their enrollments were the beneficiaries of increased funding through the formula (Leslie & Ramey 1986). Much of this had to do with the meritocratic goal of state and federal governments in maintaining access to higher education for all eligible citizens. Institutions that were increasing their enrollments were seen as meeting that goal, and were rewarded as such. In recent years, however, much has been said of the declining productivity of American higher education. Part of this debate hinges on the seemingly unending dilemma surrounding the measurement of higher education's productivity. Steeply rising costs combined with the trend toward an outcomes orientation in higher education have led many state policy makers to question the results of public expenditures. Enrollment increases are no longer automatically assumed to be desirable ends and thus are no longer rewarded with increased funding. In fact, enrollment increases sometimes result in decreased funding for higher education (Leslie & Ramey 1986). Further, state level efforts to assess higher education outcomes are often seen as ineffective or intrusive.

Even more ambiguous than the definition and measurement of higher education's productivity is that of the quality of higher education. These ambiguities aside, there are some central tenets of the quality movement in higher education include:

1.  College students should take, and faculty should teach college-level courses—remediation detracts from the quality of the institution;

2.  The public sector should be stratified—the integrity of the "flagship" must be maintained through toughened admissions standards even at the expense of "lesser" institutions;

3.  Institutions should serve the cause of economic development—a "quality" institution is a big draw in economic development (Mingle 1989).

For policy makers, "quality" higher education has become a political maypole around which few can afford not to dance.

The interrelationships between cost, productivity, and quality are relatively clear. The achievement of desired budgetary ends related to these concepts is less than clear. "When external constituents complain about the high costs of higher education or its lack of productivity, they seldom wish to see societal commitment reduced in absolute terms" (Mingle & Lenth 1989, p. 14). It is evident, however, that state budgeting for higher education will need to change in order to address increased costs, lagging productivity, and the need to enhance quality. Three steps increasingly cited by researchers and policy makers alike include: 1) become more goal-driven; 2) use resource constraints; and, 3) make better use of incentives in the budget process.

## Affordability

During the 1980s, the affordability of higher education began to develop as a significant issue for state policy makers. Between fiscal year 1981 and 1988, average tuition at public institutions increased by 83%, average tuition at private institutions grew by 95%, while the Consumer Price Index and median family income grew by 34% and 50% respectively (Halstead 1989). Further, increased income inequality among American families has led to a "vanishing" middle class, and a nation of "haves" and "have nots" resulting from the growing income gap between individuals with high school and college diplomas (Levy 1989). The traditional policy levers available to state higher education policy makers for dealing with the affordability question include the setting of public tuition levels and providing student financial aid.

Traditionally, tuition in the public sector has been seen as a way to plug the gap between state appropriations and expected expenditures for the coming fiscal year, leading to an inverse relationship between the two sources of funds. During the 1980s, the rapid rise in institutional costs/expenditures coupled with a decline in state appropriations led to the substantial growth in public institution tuition (Wittstruck & Bragg 1988). Further, there is empirical evidence that increases in tuition adversely affect enrollments (approximately 1.8 to 2.4% decline for every $100 price increase) (Leslie & Brinkman 1988). An added complication has been the increased focus on the quality of higher education in the midst of the rising costs of attendance. As noted by one observer, "Nobody likes higher prices; that's a given. But if higher prices are linked to lower quality, the result can be devastating" (Rosensweig 1990, p. 44).

A related policy lever which addresses the issue of affordability is state-funded need-based grant and scholarship programs. Student aid has been shown to increase access to higher education, promote choice, and improve persistence among recipients (Leslie & Brinkman 1988). Every state has some form of need-based student aid program for undergraduate students, and although the amount spent by states on student financial aid pales in comparison with that of the federal government, it remains an important policy lever.

## Economic Development

For state policy makers, the potential use of higher education in state economic development efforts has become a major issue for the 1980s and beyond. For most states, economic development is synonymous with the attraction of high technology industries, which involves higher education. "Economic planners increasingly regard academic institutions as critical resources in strategies to reinvigorate mature industries and stimulate new, "sunrise" industries" (Johnson 1984, p. i). Consequently, some states have begun to implement new economic development programs through the higher education budget process. Interestingly, one study found that states that have promoted themselves as preferential sites for business development also tended to have expanded governmental investment in higher education (Slaughter & Silva 1985). The primary ways that higher education has become involved in economic development efforts have been in the forms of research activities, work force education and training, and business partnerships with higher education.

## Minority and Non-Traditional Students

Two policy issues which have gained importance in the past decade are the issues of minority student achievement and the accommodation of non-traditional students. These issues have gained significantly in importance at the state level, while at the same time, higher education has come under fire for failing to meet the needs of these two groups. While many states have attempted to address these problems through the budget, little information exists to evaluate the effectiveness of such initiatives.

## The State and Independent Higher Education

State policy makers have long realized that the independent sector of higher education represents an important component of the diversity of higher education and that it also provides a number of economic, cultural, and other quality of life benefits to the state. One important direct benefit to some states has been the avoidance of costs to educate residents who choose to attend independent colleges and universities (Brinkman 1988). Consequently, some states have chosen to make a significant investment in the independent sector. The significance of independent higher education varies considerably as to its physical presence and historical traditions from state to state. As a result, the importance of the independent sector in the state higher education budget process varies from state to state as well.

For states that have chosen to take a proactive policy stance toward independent higher education, the primary budgetary mechanisms have been student aid and direct institutional grant programs. All states except Wyoming (which has no independent institutions) now have at least one student aid program in which students from the independent sector can participate. In addition, 17 states have separate tuition equalization grant programs for students attending private institutions (Zumeta 1988). In general, there is a strong correlation between the proportion of a state's enrollment in private institutions and the level of funding for state student aid (Zumeta & Green 1987). Given the decrease over time in federal financial aid and the significant increase in institutional aid expenditures within the independent sector, state student financial aid programs (when linked with public university tuition policy) have probably become the most important policy lever available to state policy makers with regard to the private sector. Twenty-one states also have direct institutional grant programs to private colleges and universities. The programs take the form of general aid (six states), support for health related programs (22 states), support for other educational programs (12 states), research and technology support (10 states), support for programs for under served students (six states), support for cooperative ventures (four states), and capital grant programs (three states). The cumulative policy effect of direct institutional aid to the independent sector is less clear than that of state student aid, although direct state aid is reported to be highly valued by the independent sector (Zumeta 1988).

# IV. Analysis and Implications

As we have illustrated previously, state budgeting for higher education is a complex, multifaceted process involving a number of players and factors. Within the framework presented, the environmental context frames the state higher education budget process resulting in a "product" (i.e., budget) which in turn provides a number of outcomes. In synthesizing the literature on this and related topics, we now have a sense of the knowledge gaps related to state budgeting for higher education.

## Analysis and Implications for Research

We began by presenting and illustrating a framework of the budgetary process. It provides a start-to-finish, external environment-to-completed budget outcomes means of understanding what occurs in budgeting. The major weakness in the framework is empirical research to affirm (or disaffirm) portions of it. There is, for example, research about the relationship between specific environmental factors and total state spending for higher education. There is little research about the interactions among some of the environmental variables themselves and their combined effects on higher education budgets.

Within the scheme of state budgeting for higher education, contextual factors such as a state's historical traditions, political culture, demography, and economy all affect the process and outcome, albeit in different ways. The historical traditions and political culture within a state provide the ground rules in the budget process while demographics and the economy serve as immediate indicators of demand and supply for state services. A state's traditions and political culture indicate how importantly higher education is and has been viewed as a state priority and also the relative importance of the players within the budget process, including the governor, legislature, state coordinating board, and individual campuses. On the other hand, demographics provide an indicator of the demand for state services and the economy provides a measure of resource availability to meet these needs.

As we move into the 1990s, it appears that the most critical contextual factor will be a state's economy, while other factors will moderate the effect of the economy on the process and outcome. In the last decade the prosperity of higher education has both risen and fallen with state economies. Since both the timing and size of these changes vary from state to state, we argue that historical traditions, political culture, and demographics moderate the effects of the economy to some extent. To what degree these contextual factors interact separately and with the budget process is essentially unknown.

The culture and traditions of states is probably the most promising area for looking at the effects of historical or political variables. As we noted earlier, the research on the relationship between political variables and spending for higher education shows frustratingly inconclusive results. It is obvious to any observer of the political scene that variables such as voter participation, public opinion, or partisan control of the legislature influence state spending priorities. The traditional ways of measuring these factors' effects is clearly unsatisfactory. Concluding qualitative research on the culture and traditions, particularly some of the political traditions, may be a means of clarifying some of these relationships.

Closely related to the culture and traditions of states is the *process* of budgeting. This is clearly an area needing more research attention. Budgeting and budgets cannot be captured entirely through numerical descriptions or quantitative studies. One might think that a budget is cut and dried. It is not. It is a representation of a wide spectrum of personalities, organizations, priorities, and needs. The study of budgeting does not fully support the English scientist Lord Kelvin's thesis (paraphrased) that "if it can be measured it can be understood." Merely measuring the budget or its context in quantitative terms is not sufficient to tell the whole story of budgeting.

Because of this, and because of numerous environmental changes, budgeting cannot be described as simple incrementalism. By understanding deviations from incrementalism, one can begin to examine the events that occurred near that time which might be used to help explain the deviations. The shift from incrementalism, in which budgets are largely based on what was decided in the past—to a market model of budgeting, in which budgets are adjusted to accommodate changing conditions, may vary from one state to another. This variation may happen as much because of the variation of economic conditions as because of political culture and traditions. It is not well understood what traditions govern why higher education in particular gets its "share" in good times or in bad. Are there traditions or patterns of organizational types with respect to state budgeting for higher education? Fisher (1988a & b) has done some important work in this area that needs to be extended to other states and to specific state budgeting situations.

Considerable research on budgeting processes has occurred at the federal level. Such research models could be applied to states—individually or several at a time. For example, Kingdon (1984) examined agenda setting in health care policy and transportation at the federal level. One could apply his approach to states and examine who sets agendas for different areas of the budget. There is research about the governor's role in budgeting (typically setting the parameters—or the agenda—for the state budget for higher education) (Adler & Lane 1988). To what extent, and under what circumstances, are higher education leaders able to set the agenda or influence the agenda for higher education budgeting? Further, how is this agenda affected by the presence of special interest groups? In many states the advent of faculty unions and state-level student associations has become an addition to the equation. Though these interests are typically narrow (e.g., faculty salaries and tuition costs), these groups have become another force tugging at the budget from different directions. Other increasingly powerful interest groups include community college associations and private college federations. A less organized, though quite potent force is public opinion. Public opinion polls help governors, legislators, and some interest groups gauge citizens' reactions to policy and budgetary initiatives, and therefore further affect parameters of budgeting. Knowing who sets agendas and how within the political process can greatly enhance higher education's chances by influencing those agendas.

Research on the process of budgeting could draw heavily on decision theory, and on organizational theory. There is much literature in public administration about aspects of budgeting, including the budgeting process. It could be drawn together to assist in conducting research on state budgeting for higher education specifically. As we have already pointed out, we do not believe that the research literature on state budgeting for other areas is completely applicable to state budgeting for higher education. Higher education has special relationships with states that sometimes creates completely different budgeting processes from other state government entities.

Another line of research is the effect of tight economic times on the budget process. We know that the outcomes have changed during economic distress: there is less money available generally, and higher education has been viewed as a more discretionary item than other areas of the state budget. Literature already exists about the effect of limited resources on institutions of higher education. In general, their budgeting becomes more centralized. Does the same phenomenon occur at the state level? What specifically goes into the decisions made by state officials to reduce spending for higher education, (or to maintain its level) in tight economic times? Does the previous experience that higher education is more discretionary continue to hold true? Higher education is being incorporated into many states' economic revitalization efforts. Will this help insulate the institutions from budget cuts in tight economic times?

To many state policy makers, the state higher education budget is a way to link state higher education policy priorities with the resources needed to meet those goals and objectives. In the past, higher education funding has also been used by some policy makers to further their own political goals. Their political goals include both broad state wide initiatives like involvement in economic development and assisting parents in saving for college, and narrower goals such as supporting the campus within one's home district (or withholding support from the campus in another's district). Some of the state higher education policy areas addressed through the budget include: accountability; costs, productivity, and quality; affordability; economic development; minority and non-traditional student; and independent higher education.

In essence, the state higher education budget as policy document has begun to shift its orientation over time from that of providing resources to institutions through base budgets to a newer focus on designing categorical programs to meet state higher education policy goals. Part of the reason may be that the increased state/legislative presence in higher education policy making has created this new emphasis on distinct programs. Part of this may be purely political in that as legislators become more professional and attuned to the educational needs of their constituencies, they may realize the value of being able to point out their particular contribution to a popular program. The relative merit of using categorical programs versus base budgets to achieve state policy goals has not been evaluated, and thus remain inconclusive. Similarly, there is little to suggest the source of the pressure to shift the focus from increasing the base to spreading funds into categoricals. Initially, it appears that institutions prefer funds to flow into the base budget with few strings attached. However, as growth in the base budgets slowed and emphasis increased for categoricals, some institutions have become quite adept at garnering resources through this mechanism. What impact does this have on other institutions that are not so adept?

In general, then, it is evident that the potential for policy research on state budgeting for higher education is enormous. There is literature in public administration and political science, but little of it refers specifically either to states or to state budgeting for higher education. We have shied away from anecdotal information in this monograph. Such information however, is a mother lode from which to start research. Like the dictum of former U.S. House Speaker Tip O'Neill, "all politics is local," such information is generally localized to a state, a time span, or a particular budget area. It must then be tested and broadened beyond pure localism.

## State Budgeting for Higher Education as Enigma, Paradox, and Ritual

Through the title of this article, we suggested that state budgeting for higher education is an enigma, a paradox, and a ritual. As we come to the end of our journey through this process, it seems necessary for the purpose of closure to visit these concepts. For many, budgeting in general is an enigma. Certainly for the uninitiated, it is. As each of us began our own professional journeys into state budgeting for higher education, we found that there were few guideposts. There is literature about outcomes of budgeting. There is limited literature about the process. Mostly, however, there are millions of anecdotal tales from experienced professionals. Some are willing to share the stories, and they enabled us to begin piecing together a more complete understanding of budgeting. That, combined with further reading and work within the field has helped. In the process, we have learned that budgeting is not merely a set of numbers and charts. It is not cut-and-dried; it has many interwoven parts.

Budgeting is paradoxical. Traditional budgeteers have approached the subject as a set of columns and rows of numbers that must properly add up within limited state revenues. More recently, however, persons with other disciplinary backgrounds have begun noting that budgeting is much more than that. It instead is both simple and complex. The simple parts of budgeting, in our experience, can be represented as a broad framework with inputs, a process of manipulating those inputs, and outputs. The complexities are the details. A more important paradox is that although both practitioners and scholars insist that the primary purpose of state budgeting for higher education is to link state intentions with desired policy outcomes, little evidence exists to suggest that this purpose is being met.

We have tried both to simplify some aspects of the budgeting process and product, and to represent fairly the many complexities of it. At the same time, we have also tried to note that the outcomes are not always as they seem. For example, state legislators quickly look to the bottom line percentage increase for each institution. They compare the increase of "their" institution with those of others. The percentage increase from year to year is a simple means of assessing how well an institution is doing. The legislators all know, however, that the simple percentage increase from year to year has greater implications. The percentage increase can appeal to voters back home; it can include mostly general operating funds or funds with considerable strings attached; it can represent a large percentage built on a small base, or a smaller percentage on a large base, and so on.

Finally, budgeting is a ritual, albeit a ritual with changing externalities, participants, and desired outcomes. Like the theme music in a symphony, certain budgeting actions are repeated in the same or a slightly different form throughout the process. The cycles of the budget process described earlier are repeated again and again for many years. In many cases, the outcomes are the same from year to year as well. To some extent this is a result of comfortable rituals. Budgeting is a process, and despite changes in externalities, participants, and desired policy outcomes, it always will be a process. Given this, state budgeting for higher education will remain inherently ritualistic.

As we move through the 1990s, higher education policy makers and practitioners at both the state and institutional level will be facing significant pressures to improve upon the ways higher education addresses the needs of citizens within the state. Clearly, the state budget process should be the means by which improvements are made in both policy outcomes and service delivery to the citizenry. Given that the process is demonstrably complex and that we need to know much more about it, it is evident that there is great potential for an improved level of consciousness about state budgeting for higher education through a strengthened linkage between research and practice.

## Notes

1. This is a condensed version of *Budgeting for Higher Education at the State Level: Enigma, Paradox, and Ritual.* ASHE-ERIC Higher Education Report No. 4. Washington, D.C.: The George Washington University, School of Education and Human Development. 1990.

2. National and state economic conditions have changed for the worse since the time the monograph was originally written, with subsequent adverse consequences for higher education.

## References

Adler, M. W. and F.S Lane. 1988. "Governors and Public Policy Leadership." In *Governors and Higher Education*, S. Gove and T. Beyle Eds. Denver, CO: Education Commission of the States. pp. 2-15.

Anderson, Richard E. 1988. "The Economy and Higher Education." *Capital Ideas*, 1(3), 1-11.

Anderson, Richard E. and William Massy. 1989. "The Economic Outlook and What it Means for Colleges and Universities." *Capital Ideas* 4(3): 1-10.

Berdahl, Robert 0. and Susan M. Studds. November 1989. "The Tension of Excellence and Equity: The Florida Enhancement Programs." Denver: Paper presented at National Center for Postsecondary Governance and Finance Conference on State Fiscal Incentives.

Berne, Robert and Richard Schramm. 1986. *The Financial Analysis of Governments.* Englewood Cliffs, NJ: Prentice-Hall.

BeVier, M. J. 1979. *Politics Backstage: Inside the California Legislature.* Philadelphia: Temple University Press.

Beyle, Thad L. 1983. "Governors." In *Politics in the American States: A Comparative Analysis.* V. Gray, H. Jacob, and K. Vines, Eds. 4th edition. Boston: Scott, Foresman and Co.

Bowen, Howard R. 1980. The Costs of Higher Education. San Francisco: Jossey-Bass

Brandl, John E. 1988. "The Legislative Role in Policy Making for Higher Education." In *Governors and Higher Education.* S. Gove and T. Beyle Eds. Denver, CO: Education Commission of the States. pp. 17-19.

Brinkman, Paul. June 1988. "The Costs of Providing Higher Education: A Conceptual Overview." Denver: State Higher Education Executive Officers.

Brubacher, John S. and Willis Rudy. 1976. *Higher Education in Transition.* 3rd revised edition. New York: Harper and Row.

Caiden, Naomi. 1988. " Shaping Things to Come: Super-Budgeters as Heroes (and Heroines) In the Late-Twentieth Century." *New Directions in Budget Theory.* I.S. Rubin, Ed. Albany: State University of New York Press. pp. 43-58.

Caiden, Naomi and J. Chapman. 1982. "Constraint and Uncertainty: Budgeting in California." *Public Budgeting and Finance* 2(4): 111-129.

Carnevale, John T. 1988. "Recent Trends In the Finances of the State and Local Sector." *State and Local Finances*. pp. 33-48.

Coughlin, Cletus C. and O. Homer Erekson. 1986. "Determinants of State Aid and Voluntary Support of Higher Education." *Economics of Education Review*, 5(2): 179-190.

Curry, Denis J and Norman Fischer. February 1986. "Public Higher Education and the State: Models for Financing Budgeting and Accountability." San Antonio, TX: Paper presented at the Annual Meeting of the Association for the Study of Higher Education.

Curry, Denis J., Norman Fischer and Tom Jons. 1982. *State Policy Options for Financing Higher Education and Related Accountability Objectives: Summary and Conclusions*. Olympia, WA: State of Washington Council for Postsecondary Education.

Davis, N. M. 1984. "Legislative Staff Careers." *State Legislatures*, 10(10): 11-18.

Duncombe, Sydney and Richard Kinney. 1986. "The Politics of State Appropriation Increases: The Perspective of Budget Officers in Five Western States." *The Journal of State Government*, 59(3): 113-123.

Easton, D. 1957. "An Approach to the Analysis of Political Systems." *World Politics*, 9: 383-400.

Eckl, C.L., A.M. Hutchison, and R.K. Snell 1990. *State Budget and Tax Actions, 1990*. Legislative Finance Paper #74. Denver, CO: National Conference of State Legislatures.

_____. 1991. *State Budget and Tax Actions 1991*. Legislative Finance Paper #79. Denver, CO: National Conference of State Legislatures.

Fisher, Lois A. November 1988a. "External Political Traditions: Their Development and Continuing Impact On the Nature of Two Public Systems of Higher Education." St. Louis: Paper presented at the 1988 Annual Meeting of the Association for the Study of Higher Education.

_____. 1988b. " State Legislatures and the Autonomy of Colleges and Universities: A Comparative Study of Legislation in Four States, 1900-1979." *Journal of Higher Education*, 59(2): 133-162.

Folger, John. November 1989. "Designing State Incentive Programs the Work in Higher Education" Denver: Paper presented at National Center for Postsecondary Governance and Finance Conference on State Fiscal Incentives.

Garms, Walter I. 1986. "The Determinants of Public Revenues for Higher and Lower Education: A Thirty Year Perspective." *Educational Evaluation and Policy Analysis*, 8(3): 277-293.

Halstead, Kent. 1989. *State Profiles: Financing Public Higher Education, 1978-1989*. Washington, D.C.: Research Associates of Washington.

Hartmark, Leif S. 1978. "The Effect of Rationalistic Budgeting and Legislative Staff upon University Policy-Making Independence: The Wisconsin Experience." Ph.D. dissertation, State Univ. of New York at Albany.

Hartmark, Leif S. and Edward R. Hines. 1986. "Politics and Policy in Higher Education: Reflections on the Status of the Field." In *Policy Controversies In Higher Education*. S. Gove and T. Stauffer, Eds. New York: Greenwood Press.

Herzik, Eric B. 1988. "The Expanding Gubernatorial Role in Education Policymaking." In *Governors and Higher Education*, S. Gove and T. Beyle, Eds., pp. 61-67. Denver: Education Commission of the States.

Hines, Edward R. 1988. *Higher Education and State Governments: Renewed Partnership, Cooperation, or Competition?* ASHE-ERIC Higher Education Report No. 5. Washington: Association for the Study of Higher Education.

Hines, Edward R. and Leif Hartmark. 1980. *Politics of Higher Education.* ASHE-ERIC Higher Education Report No. 7. Washington: American Association for Higher Education.

Hines, Edward R., G. Alan Hickrod, and Gwen B. Pruyne. March 1989. *State Support of Higher Education From Expansion to Steady State to Decline, 1969 to 1989.* MacArthur/Spencer Series Number 9. Normal, IL: Center for Education Finance and Higher Education.

Johnson, Lynn G. 1984. *The High Technology Connection: Academic/Industrial Cooperation for Economic Growth.* ASHE-ERIC Higher Education Research Report No. 6. Washington: Association for the Study of Higher Education.

Jones, Dennis. 1984. *Higher Education Budgeting at the State Level: Concepts and Principles.* Boulder, CO: National Center for Higher Education Management Systems.

Kingdon, John W. 1984. *Agendas Alternatives and Public Policies.* Boston: Little, Brown and Company.

Lamb, Jane A. 1986. "An Analysis of the Structure of 1985 State Budget Formulas for Public Higher Education with a Comparison of 1973, 1979, and 1985 Data." Ed.D. dissertation, Univ. of Tennessee.

Layzell Daniel T. 1988. "The Relationship Between Demographic, Economic, and Socio-Political Factors And State Appropriations To Public Four-Year Colleges and Universities in Florida, Illinois, and Virginia: 1965- 1985." Ph.D Dissertation, The Florida State University.

Lee, R. D., Jr. and R.W. Johnson. 1983. *Public Budgeting Systems.* 3rd ed. Baltimore: University Park Press.

LeLoup, Lance T. 1988. "From Microbudgeting to Macrobudgeting: Evolution in Theory and Practice." In *New Directions in Budget Theory.* I. S. Rubin, Ed. Albany: State University of New York Press. pp. 19-42.

Leslie, Larry L. and Paul T. Brinkman. 1988. *The Economic Value of Higher Education.* New York: ACE-Macmillan Publishing Co.

Leslie, Larry L. and Garey Ramey. 1986. "State Appropriations and Enrollments: Does Enrollment Growth Still Pay?" *The Journal of Higher Education,* 57: 1-19.

Levy, Frank 1989. "Paying for College: A New Look at Family Income Trends." *College Board Review,* 152: 18+

Lyddon, Jan W. 1989. "Incrementalism and Economic, Demographic, and Political Conditions Related to State Appropriations to Higher Education: A Study of the Fifty States from 1960 to 1985." Ph.D. dissertation. The University of Michigan.

Lyddon, Jan W., Richard Fonte, and James L. Miller. February 1986. "Toward a Framework to Analyze State Funding of Higher Education." San Diego: Paper presented at the Association for the Study of Higher Education.

Maryland Higher Education Commission. 1988. "Guideline Use in Other States." Annapolis, MD: Author.

Massy, William F. October 1989. "A Strategy for Productivity Improvement in College and University Academic Departments." Santa Fe, NM: Paper presented at the Forum for Postsecondary Governance.

McGuinness, Aims C. 1988. *State Postsecondary Education Structures Handbook, 1988.* Publication No. PS-87-2. Denver: Education Commission of the States.

Meisinger, R. J., Jr. 1976. *State Budgeting for Higher Education: The Uses of Formulas.* Berkeley: Center for Research and Development in Higher Education, University of California..

Mikesell, John L. 1984. "The Cyclical Sensitivity of State and Local Taxes." *Public Budgeting and Finance,* 4(1): 32-39.

Miller, James L., Jr. 1964. *State Budgeting for Higher Education: The Use of Formulas and Cost Analysis.* Ann Arbor: Univ. of Michigan, Institute of Public Administration.

Mingle, James R. 1988. "Survey on Tuition Policy, Costs and Student Aid." Denver: State Higher Education Executive Officers.

Mingle, James R. and Charles S. Lenth. 1989. "A New Approach to Accountability and Productivity in Higher Education." Denver: State Higher Education Executive Officers.

Morgan, Anthony. W. 1984. "The New Strategies: Roots, Context, and Overview." In *Responding to New Realities in Funding.* L. L. Leslie, Ed. San Francisco: Jossey-Bass, Inc.

Munitz, B. and R. Lawless. 1986. "Resource Allocation Policies for the Eighties." *Policy Controversies in Higher Education.* S. K. Gove and T. M. Stauffer, Eds. New York: Greenwood Press.

National Conference of State Legislatures. 1982. *Higher education finance issues for the 1980s and 1990s: A Legislators' handbook.* Denver, CO.

Oppenheimer, B. I. 1985. Legislative influence on policy and budgets. *Handbook of Legislative Research.* Gerhard Leowenberg, Samuel C. Patterson, and Malcolm E. Jewell (Eds.). Cambridge, MA: Harvard University Press. pp. 621-667.

Rosensweig, Robert M. 28 February 1990. "Challenges to Test the Mettle of Academe's Best Leaders." *The Chronicle of Higher Education,* 36(25): 44.

Slaughter, Sheila and E.T. Silva. 1985. "Towards a Political Economy of Retrenchment." *The Review of Higher Education,* 8: 295-318.

Volkwein, J. Fredericks. February 1987. "State Regulation and Institutional Autonomy." San Diego: Paper presented at the ASHE Annual Meeting.

Wildavsky, Aaron. 1986. *Budgeting: A Comparative Theory of Budgetary Processes.* 2nd Edition. New Brunswick, NJ: Transaction Books.

Wirt, Frederick, Douglas Mitchell, and Catherine Marshall. 1988. "Culture and Education Policy: Analyzing Values in State Policy Systems." *Educational Evaluation and Policy Analysis* 10(4): 271-284.

Wittstruck, John R. and Stephen Bragg. 1988. "Focus on Price: Trends in Public Higher Education, Tuition and State Support." Denver: State Higher Education Executive Officers.

Zumeta, William. 1988. "Survey of State Policies that May Affect Independent Higher Education." Denver: Education Commission of the States.

Zumeta, William, and Kenneth C. Green. 1987. "State Policies and Independent Higher Education: A Conceptual Framework and Some Empirical findings, or Can the States Help the Private Sector Survive?" Paper presented at an annual meeting of the Association for the Study of Higher Education, February, San Diego, California. ED 281 454. 89 pp. MF-01; PC-04.

Zusman, Ami. 1986. "Legislature and University Conflict: The Case of California." *The Review of Higher Education,* 9(4): 397-418.

# An Analysis of State Formula Budgeting in Higher Education (1990)

## Martin M. Ahumada

It is no coincidence that the increasingly new economic, political, and demographic realities facing U.S. higher education all have worked to heighten concern around the viability of state formula budgeting—the prevalent approach to allocating state resources to colleges and universities. One must recall that formula budgeting became widespread during the growth period of the '60s and '70s, when it was broadly heralded as a universal panacea for addressing the problems and challenges of managing the explosive growth of the nation's higher education enterprise. Indeed, we are all familiar with the unique conditions, challenges and concerns of that period—the general fiscal prosperity of the states, the tremendous increase in the public demands on and expectations for higher education; and the desire for a simple, objective and equitable public policy device to fund the growing number of new institutions of higher learning. And we are all well attuned to the various arguments as to why formula budgets were ideally suited to meet the challenges of growth that were experienced in that era. But as Gross (1979) had warned us a decade ago.

> While the use of formulas during the growth period of the last two decades may have been a temporary panacea for the funding problems of state-supported institutions, continued reliance upon budget formulas as they now exist may prove to be public higher education's nemesis during the no-growth or declining periods ahead. The real test for the medicinal utility of budget formulas will be in their application to accommodate the major trends of the 1980s and their ability to preserve the quality of public higher education and the existence of the state institutions under their purview (p. 5).

In looking back over the '80s and forward into the impending decade of the '90s, few of us might question the validity and wisdom of the above warning. Indeed, the apparent dilemmas of using formula budgets (as they were originally designed) in the 1990s are becoming abundantly clear. First, while state resources for higher education continue to be formulaically tied very closely to enrollments, changes in enrollment patterns are arguably the most significant of the new realities facing U.S. higher education. Second, while higher education is confronted with what Jones (1984a) calls "the legacy of a growth mentality—one that has been instilled in educators, administrators and legislators alike and, in turn, has been embodied in the procedures and mechanisms they utilize to determine levels of support for state colleges and universities—the social forces and environmental conditions in most states have called on colleges and universities to do much more with less and to do it much better."

How, then, and to what extent have budget formulas been reformed to remain viable in the constantly changing reality within which they must function? In states where formula budgets have undergone review or reform in some major way, What are the major concerns under discussion? And on what bases might states best examine these concerns and the alternative solutions to them? Whereas the primary aim of this chapter is to provide an informed response to these questions, two key objectives are pursued. The first is to uncover how and for what reasons the role of formula budgets in the financing of higher education has changed over time, with particular attention to the issues and rationales underlying the most recent developments in formula budgeting. As a logical extension to this effort, a second objective is to frame and analyze some contemporary issues of formula review—an effort carried out in this chapter through an in-depth case study of California's formula budgeting approach to funding instructional workload in the University of California. The current viability of the California approach is examined in light of changes over time in the University's enrollment patterns by level of instruction and academic discipline. As part of the case study analysis, a review of the pertinent research literature is conducted (vis-à-vis the critical connection between costing and formulas), and a conceptual framework is offered for examining the instructional cost and resource issues of formula review under discussion in many states. Because this analytical framework is offered for studying the topic of state formula budgeting within a national context, the California case study is deemed an appropriate foundation for its development, owing largely to the state's political and demographic complexity as well as its large and heterogeneous higher education enterprise.

## I. The Evolving Role of Formula Budgets in Higher Education

State formula budgeting in higher education can be traced to 1951 (Gross, 1979) when only a handful of states (California, Indiana, Oklahoma, and Texas) were developing or utilizing a formula approach. Yet Morgan (1984) informs us that the origins of the formula budgeting strategy can be found in much earlier developments in public budgeting, namely, in the drive toward greater efficiency or what Schick (1966) referred to as the "management movement in budgeting." As Morgan states: "Touted by presidential commissions for public budgeting in 1912, 1947, and 1955, this strategy was developing simultaneously in higher education" (p. 11).

The most prolific adoption of state formula budgets to establish the funding levels for public colleges and universities occurred between 1963 and 1973. In that decade alone, the number of states using formulas increased from six to twenty-five (Gross, 1979). Thus, despite the fact that formulas continue to be a significant factor in about half of the states, it must be acknowledged that formula budgeting is a legacy of a unique period in American higher education, when student enrollments burgeoned from coast to coast—beginning in the 1950s and ending in the mid 1970s— and when the general public was eager to invest generously in the rapid expansion of its higher education enterprise. The concerns and challenges of that era, which clearly are much unlike those of today, were centered, for example, on constructing new classrooms, buildings, and campuses; on creating new academic programs; and on hiring new faculty. Pertaining to those challenges, Cross (1979) astutely observes that formula budgets may be considered the "offspring of necessity":

> Faced with a variety of state-created higher educational institutions, the failure of available state resources to keep up with growth patterns and the public demand for services, the advent of accountability and cost-effectiveness, and the groundswell of public opinion for greater equity in the appropriation of state funds among colleges and universities, it is easy to understand why many states decided to develop budget formulas to "feed the tigers" (p. 1)

The nature of formulas and their role in the financing of higher education at various times has been viewed from various perspectives. Taken together, these different perspectives have served to uncover the multifaceted role that formulas have played in the budgeting and funding process. Beginning with Miller's (1964) state-by-state account of developments in formula budgeting, formulas have consistently been defined as strategies for anticipating or projecting the future resource needs or expenditures of the institutions, based on prices, expected loads, and other factors. And today many still embrace Miller's (1964) view, which was articulated 25 years ago, that formulas serve to secure an equitable distribution of funds among the institutions as well as to provide sufficiently objective budget justifications to satisfy state budget offices and legislatures.

Formula budgets have been more recently defined as: subjective judgments that are expressed in mathematical terms (Meisinger, 1975); a combination of technical judgments and political agreements (Meisinger, 1976); a mathematical approach to linking the workload of a public institution to its state appropriations (Pickens, 1981); a rational calculation of funding needs based upon standards of cost of doing business (Morgan, 1984); mathematical statements that link state appropriations to institutional characteristics such as workload, costs, and output (Brinkman, 1984); and a standard as much as an instrument for resource allocation, wherein the basic intent is to relate workload to appropriations, however, objectively, subjectively, technically, or politically that workload may be determined (Brinkman, 1984).

Notwithstanding the multidimensional aspects of state budget formulas, recent formulas display several common characteristics and attributes. According to Jones (1984b), for example, the structure of formulas has two basic forms:

> The first calculates allocations by multiplying some workload measure, such as the square feet of space to be maintained or the number of students to be served, by a rate that can be normative (negotiated or traditionally accepted) or analytically derived (a technical judgment based on cost studies). This method can translate base factors directly into dollars, or it can introduce an intermediate step that converts workload measures into physical resource needs, such as full-time-equivalent faculty, to which dollar amounts are then attached. The other form establishes a base for key functions, such as instruction, by one of the approaches just described. It then funds other functions, such as administration or library service, as a percentage of that base (p. 23).

## Assessing the Strengths and Weaknesses of Budget Formulas

Much of the advocacy for formula budgeting has to do with the salutary effect of formulas on the budgetary process (Brinkman, 1984). Attention has been called therefore to how formulas enhance the uniformity and ease of budget preparation and presentation (Hale and Rawson, 1976); how they routinize the decisionmaking process, thereby minimizing conflict between institutions and state budget officials (Caruthers and Orwig, 1979); how they curtail politics from the decision process once the formula is established (Jones, 1984); how they provide a good method for the equitable distribution of funds among institutions (Miller, 1964; Hale and Rawson, 1976; and Moss and Gaither, 1976); how they establish the areas of discretion and the limits of debate (Meisinger, 1975); and how they reduce uncertainty in the decision allocation process by simplifying budgetary standards, by accommodating different organizations, and by establishing limits in the size of base budget increments or decrements, and by providing an "objective" basis for determining each institution's "fair share" of the budget (Meisinger, 1975). And as Millett (1974, pp. 11-12) pointed out, the advantages identified by formula advocates includes:

1. The lessening of the political warfare among, and open lobbying by, state-supported institutions for scarce funds.

2. The assurance of annual operating appropriations for institutions based on quantifiable objective measures.

3. The provision to state officials of a reasonably simple and understandable basis for deciding upon the appropriation requests of individual institutions.

4. The representation of a reasonable compromise between state control over line-item budgeting and institutional fiscal autonomy.

Criticisms of formula budgets, on the other hand, have centered on how formulas do not-self-adjust so as to ensure a proper level of funding (University of Wisconsin, 1982); how they fail to reflect the qualitative dimensions of educational activities (such as changes in students' knowledge and skills) (Pickens, 1982); how they ignore economies of scale and fixed costs versus variable costs (Boutwell, 1973); and how they tend to reproduce past costs and behavior—irrespective of changes in program needs or priorities—instead of truly predicting the budgetary requirements of institutions. In sum, however, effective formulas were as means for managing the growth of higher education in the '60s and '70s, the "uncritical" reliance on formula budgeting as the basis for making appropriations to higher education is obviously a questionable course of action.

## Recent Developments in Formula Budgeting

Many recent reforms in formula budgeting involve strategies for countering what seem to be the major pitfalls or undesirable tendencies of formula budgets, such as their linear approach to estimating institutions' resource requirements (the size/cost relationship) and their "leveling" effect on the quality and diversity of programs and institutions. Yet, the obvious concern underlying these developments is the viability of formula budgeting in the new context of higher education: steady-state or declining enrollments; economic recessions at the state and national levels; significant changes in the composition of the student body with regard to age, ethnicity, and academic and career orientations; increasing competition among public agencies for limited state resources; major shifts in the priorities of public policy from access to achievement; and the fuller internalization by colleges and universities of what Howard Bowen (1980, pp. 76-100) called the "socially imposed costs" of higher education, which include protection for the handicapped, antidiscrimination laws, public information, and workers' pensions. It would appear, then, that formula budgets must assume a completely new role in assisting the states to manage change and decline in higher education. As Jones (1984a, p. 7) puts it:

> Be they formula or incremental approaches, funding mechanisms are devices for bringing some measure of certainty and stability to resource allocation. They are not geared to respond to rapid change or to reallocate funds swiftly among shifting state priorities. Change, however, has been the hallmark of the last decade. Many of the resource-allocation mechanisms now in place were developed at a time when the baby-boom cohort was reaching college age. At that time, the primary state objective was accommodating the horde of new students. Clearly, conditions and objectives have changed. Enrollments are now increasing slowing, if at all. Today, states are more concerned with maintaining the quality of their institutions and promoting the economic development of their region than with expanding their capacity to serve more students.

In his chapter for the New Directions for Institutional Research series: "Formula Budgeting: The Fourth Decade," Paul Brinkman (1984) offers what is arguably the most significant of the recent analyses of state formula budgeting in higher education. As Leslie (1984) puts it, "Brinkman has collected in one brief chapter all that is noteworthy in the existing literature in regard to the allocation formula as a public policy device and to what is new in formula design and implementation; (p. 89). The following review of recent developments in state formula budgeting therefore draws considerably from Brinkman's (1984) important contributions to the topic.

### Buffering and Decoupling

In order to protect state funding levels from the vagaries of enrollment shifts, several states have developed strategies to loosen or weaken the linear relationship between enrollment and appropriations. These strategies are referred to as "buffering" and "decoupling." Decoupling serves to limit the amount of an institution's appropriation that is driven by enrollment (Jones, 1984), or, as Brinkman (1984) puts it, decoupling "simply eliminates the connection altogether for one or more formulas in the set that comprises the funding mechanism" (p. 30). As Jones (1984a) explains:

> This is accomplished by altering the structure of the formula or other resource-allocation guidelines so that a relatively smaller proportion of funding is driven by enrollment-related factors. For example, library funding can be determined by the number of programs supported rather than by the number of students served. Likewise, maintenance and operation of the physical plant can be related to campus size rather than student population. In other words, decoupling affords institutions the opportunity to support centralized services in a way that is not directly affected by yearly enrollment fluctuations (pp. 76-77).

Most formula budgeting states are using the decoupling strategy in one way or another (Spence and Weathersby, 1981), indicating therefore that enrollments and appropriations do not operate in a linear fashion. Decoupling in Kentucky and Minnesota, where enrollments are declining, is done using an "average of enrollments" for the biennium (or a longer period) immediately preceding the year being funded in order to determine funding levels. In this use of decoupling, then, a lag factor is adopted to mitigate against major funding declines due to enrollment loss. As in the case of Minnesota, the purpose of this lag factor is to "provide the systems and governing boards the time to implement staffing and funding changes in a smoother and well-considered fashion" (Ahumada, 1985, p. 12).

With respect to the "buffering" strategy, the states have taken a variety of approaches. In Ohio, for example, the approach serves to ensure that institutions receive between 96 and 99 percent of the previous year's appropriations, irrespective of shifts in enrollment. In Minnesota, a "bulge funding" policy was adopted in 1977 as a temporary solution to the problem of long-term projected enrollment declines, wherein state funding levels would decline only when enrollments dropped below their 1977 levels—the "bulge area" (Ahumada, 1985). Buffering approaches in other states are described by Brinkman (1984) as follows:

> Tennessee uses what might be called a corridor or threshold approach. Any enrollment change that is no larger than plus or minus 2 percent elicits no change at all in funding; and 2 percent is subtracted from any larger change before the funding request is made (for example, a 6 percent change is treated as if it were only 4 percent). In Florida, the amount that the funding level may change in any given year is restricted to a certain range irrespective of what happens to enrollment. In Pennsylvania, a "hold-harmless" clause allows institutions experiencing enrollment declines to be allocated more funds than they would have been entitled to on the basis of formula calculations (p. 30).

Yet another notable approach to buffering is the one taken in Missouri. As Brinkman points out, "In Missouri, buffering is accomplished in the instructional formula by recognizing only 90 percent of the actual percentage change in enrollment for institutions with an enrollment increase. For institutions experiencing a decrease in enrollment, the 'marginal adjustment' is 70 percent" (1984, pp. 30-31).

## Recognizing Changes in Part-Time Enrollments

Another strategy to control the impact of enrollment changes on funding levels is concerned not with diminishing the strict linear dependence of appropriation on enrollments but with better recognizing the fiscal consequences of changes in the mix of full-time versus part-time enrollments. In Maryland, for example, community colleges receive a small additional amount of funds over and above the basic formula amount for each part-time student enrolled (Brinkman, 1984). This strategy has apparently become more widespread as systems of institutions have experienced dramatic shifts in their full-time versus part-time enrollments. No doubt, the need to recognize the funding implications of these enrollment shifts is a critical issue in the current and future financing of colleges, across all areas of the country.

## Improving Cost Calculations

In order to overcome what Gross (1979) refers to as the "linear-cost syndrome" in formula budgeting (that is, the underlying presumption in formula budgeting that average costs behave in a linear fashion irrespective of the scale of operations), many states have reformed their formulas by improving cost calculations. As Brinkman (1984, p. 32) points out: "Average costs will in fact be nonlinear under two conditions: if marginal costs (the change in the total cost that accompanies an additional unit of output) are greater or less than average costs, or if at least some costs are fixed (that is, not related to the level of output)."

Because colleges and universities do have economies and diseconomies of scale, a solution to the linear-cost syndrome in formulas is to use the marginal-cost method rather than the average-cost method for estimating institutions' future resource requirements. As Jones (1984, p. 76) puts it, "By utilizing marginal cost concepts, the state or institution considers the 'extra' costs associated with adding an 'extra' student (or the increment of cost savings associated with decreasing the student body by one)." The marginal cost method, then, serves to more accurately reflect the actual cost behavior of institutions and, therefore, to better determine the actual resource implications of the changing enrollment trends in higher education. In simulating a variety of marginal costing formulas, Monical and Schoenecker (1980, p. 79) found that:

1. Marginal-costing formulas are sensitive to enrollment changes, but not as sensitive as linear funding formulas.

2. Under all marginal simulations, fewer resources will be added and fewer reduced than with linear funding. As enrollment increases, resources will be added at the marginal rate. As enrollment decreases, they will be withdrawn at a marginal rate. The net effect is to "flatten" the resource-requirement curve during a period of enrollment fluctuation.

3. With respect to the base year, marginal funding will bring in more total dollars and lower dollars per student in periods of enrollment growth, and fewer total dollars and higher dollars per student in periods of enrollment decline. There can be an overall lowering of appropriations, even though the appropriations per student will be undergoing a "real" increase over the base.

In light of the economic and demographic realities of most states, one can easily appreciate the conceptual soundness of the marginal costing approach as well as it superiority over the historically popular average cost method to estimating institutions' resource needs. As Allen and Brinkman (1983) point out:

> Funding and pricing schemes based on marginal-cost principles can directly address the weakness of techniques that are based on average costs. By focusing directly on the cost implications of changing enrollment levels, marginal costing allows the state or federal government and the institution to base their actions on estimates of actual cost behavior rather than on a static calculation of costs at a particular enrollment level that is no longer applicable (p. 4).

Yet, in spite of the obviously desirable characteristics of marginal costing techniques only a few states (most notably California and Indiana) have incorporated them into their resource allocation process (Brinkman, 1984; Jones, 1984a). For some time, appropriations for additional students in California's community colleges have been based on a rate that is one-third less than the average cost per student in the state. This approach operates on the assumption that the marginal costs are constantly equivalent to two-thirds the average costs. Thus, when enrollments decline, it is assumed that the marginal savings will be less than the average cost by about one-third, and that is the basis upon which appropriations are adjusted. Indiana's efforts to incorporate marginal costing principles into the budget process are notable for unique reasons. As Brinkman (1984) informs us, "Although not a formula budgeting state, Indiana uses a formula-like relationship between enrollment change and change in the appropriations request. Marginal costs are assumed to be less than average costs (based on cost studies done in the mid 1970s), but, unlike California, in Indiana the difference is made a function of the extent of enrollment change" (1984, p. 32). Jones (1984a) contends that the reasonableness of the Indiana approach stems, in part, from the fact that although Indiana remained faithful to the concept of marginal costing, it "determined which factors should be applied not through empirical analyses but through consensus and negotiation" (pp. 79-80).

What is underscored in Jones' (1984a) observations on the Indiana approach to marginal costing, is the growing recognition that a number of technical and political factors have inhibited the widespread implementation of marginal costing techniques. First, unlike average costs, it is extremely difficult to calculate marginal costs, particularly for every type of institution, level of enrollment, and academic program (Allen and Brinkman, 1983). For the most part, the use of marginal costs in higher education has been primarily in academic research on cost behavior, with some budgeting applications (Brinkman and Allen, 1986). And as Jones (1984a) points out, "Since marginal costs for numerous individual institutions have not been calculated, a body of conventional wisdom has yet to emerge about reasonable and realistic marginal costs for different kinds of institutions at different enrollment levels. Further, complications exist because higher education lacks a known or standard set of production relationships" (p. 78).

There are, of course, several political liabilities associated with the use of marginal cost methods. First, not only are these methods complex and subject to error but they also produce information that is difficult for legislators and administrators to interpret (Jones, 1984a). Moreover, in the view of some state officials, because the institutions themselves have the most to gain through the adoption of these methods, they can therefore be suspected of being "self-serving"—of conveniently changing the rules of the budgeting game. After all, as Clark Kerr (1983) observed at a national conference focused on the future financing of higher education:

> Officials in other states think it is only fair that formulas that were advantageous to higher education in a period of growth should be maintained in a period of decline even though they then become disadvantageous—it all balances out; and higher education, it is quickly noted, did not complain when it made a profit on these past formulas (p. 4).

In light of the above problems with marginal costing techniques, how, then, are states making the marginal adjustments (in their appropriations) that are appropriate for their changing economic and demographic realities? In what might be the most accurate response to this question, Brinkman (1984, p. 32) contends that the states are opting for decoupling and buffering procedures that, in effect, operate like an indirect approach to marginal costing. As he specifies:

> A direct marginal-cost approach entails changing the formula rates from average to marginal; the indirect approach to marginal costing leaves the rates as they were but changes the base factor. In buffering, for instance, the actual enrollment figure, when would normally constitute the base, may be replaced by an average (or some previous) enrollment figure, thus dampening the effect of the most recent enrollment change. Decoupling has a similar effect, since the funding response to an enrollment change becomes a composite of a (possibly linear) response for some components plus no response at all for the decoupled components, adding up to a dampened, or marginal, response overall (1984, pp. 32-33).

Some states are modifying their formula budgets through other than marginal costing strategies, namely, by explicitly recognizing "fixed" or "variable" costs. Fixed costs are those that do not vary with changes in the volume of output (e.g., enrollment levels) whereas variable costs change as the volume of output changes. According to Jones (1984a), the usefulness of fixed and variable costs stems from two propositions:

> First, there are certain institutional capacities that must be put in place if one is to have an institution. Among these capacities are a critical mass of faculty, an administrative core, and a certain minimum complement of academic and student support functions. Second, this core component can differ

depending on the mission of the institution. A broader institutional mission requires a larger core capacity (pp. 80-81).

As noted in McKeown (1982), of 28 states found to be using formula budgets, 13 reported they were using a fixed-cost component in at least one of their formulas. Yet, Wisconsin's experiment with fixed and variable costs is perhaps the most significant, owing largely to its explicit recognition of (1) the state's responsibility to fund the "critical mass" required for institutions to perform their missions; and (2) the conventional wisdom that institutions with different missions have different needs. Wisconsin integrated the concept of fixed and variable costs into the budgetary system based on the assumption that institutions were currently operating in accordance with desirable missions (Jones, 1984a).

In other states (i.e., Alabama, Florida, Louisiana, and Virginia) differences between fixed and variable costs are recognized by establishing a standard "base" funding level. For example, in Alabama and Florida, the smaller institutions get the base amount and the larger institutions get funding above and beyond the base amount. The amount of extra funds received is determined on a per-student rate that varies with institutional size. Brinkman (1984, p. 33) describes the approach in other states: "In Virginia, separate funding floors have been established for four-year institutions (2,500 students) and for two-year institutions (1,000), implying that fixed costs are substantially different in the two sectors. In Louisiana, all institutions receive a base appropriation of approximately $1.3 million in recognition of fixed costs and diseconomies of scale."

However successful the above experiences with fixed and variable costing might be, some observers (e.g., Jones, 1984a) contend that, owing to the limited state and institutional experience in using these types of costs to calculate allocations, it is difficult to achieve broad agreement on what should constitute fixed costs for different sizes and types of institutions and what can be most reasonably viewed as a variable cost. Brinkman and Allen (1986) argue there are no widely accepted procedures for separating fixed from variable costs, although "ingenious" methods have been proposed (e.g., Baughman and Young, 1982). In fact, Brinkman and Allen (1983) hold that because fixed and variable costing inevitable involves policy determinations and the political process, "anyone who is asked to do this type of costing should concentrate on people and decision processes rather than on costing techniques" (p. 4).

Yet, notwithstanding the problems in implementing a budgeting approach that utilizes the concept of fixed and variable costs, it is difficult to argue against the conceptual soundness of such an approach. As Jones (1984a) contends, "It encourages states to consider resource allocations in terms of institutional quality and viability, not merely operation. In so doing, it explicitly recognizes key state priorities in the field of higher education while simultaneously allowing institutions greater control over day-to-day operations" (p. 83).

## Increasing the Complexity of Formula Budgets

Formula budgets have also been evolving to better recognize differences in cost behavior and experiences among different types of institutions (e.g., research universities versus teaching colleges) and between different institutional functions and operations (i.e., instruction, research, and student services). On this phenomenon, Pickens (1981) noted that the "clear trend is toward applying a different state formula to each of the (program) classifications or to clusters of them (p. 2). As noted in McKeown (1982), in 1980 17 states were found to be using at least one distinct formula for each of five functions (instruction, administration, library, student services, and plant operations and maintenance). And within particular formulas, there is often differentiation by discipline, levels of enrollment, and type of institution, especially in the instructional area (Brinkman, 1984). A useful review of this practice can be found in Lamb (1986).

A key objective in making formula budgeting more complex is to counter the "leveling" tendencies of formulas through the more explicit recognition of institutional differences

(Brinkman, 1984). In Tennessee, for instance, a new method of funding research serves to promote a varying research emphasis among the state's institutions. With respect to the Tennessee method, Jones (1984a) points out that:

> The state's allocation for academic research is determined by an institution's success in acquiring research support from other sources. An institution receives state research funds acquired by all institutions in the state. Under this arrangement, already well established research institutions are able to reinforce their missions in a way that does not require research funds to flow to institutions that do not have a demonstrated research capacity (p. 87).

## Promoting Quality Through Formulas

Viewed as a longstanding limitation of formula budgeting approaches is their quantitative orientation (that is, their tendency to focus on input measures) to the detriment of quality considerations (Brinkman, 1984). Yet, one must acknowledge that some states were addressing the quality issue with formulas long before this issue was catapulted to center stage on the public policy agenda. In California and Texas, for example, a longstanding approach to funding quality has been to provide a higher level of funding to an institution or system of institutions (usually the "flagship" institution) relative to the other institutions in the state. These varying levels of funding are arrived at through the use of differential rates (e.g., dollars per student).

Until recently, most states have preferred to fund "innovations" or "quality initiatives" through special allocations separate from the general budget formula rather than changing or limiting the formulas themselves. Among the few exceptions to this tendency are the Georgia initiative which adds one percent to the total budget at each institution for the purpose of supporting quality, and the Tennessee Performance Funding Program—the most ambitious of its kind in the nation—that incorporates state dollars to individual institutions beyond their regular formula funding. The Tennessee program uses six criteria to allocate a certain share of state dollars to these institutions:

1. The percentage of programs eligible for accreditation that are accredited;

2. The percentage of programs that have undergone peer review;

3. The percentage of programs that administer a comprehensive examination to their majors;

4. The value added by the general education component of the curriculum, as demonstrated by students' scores on the College Outcome Measures Project examination of the American College Testing Program;

5. Demonstration that specific improvements in campus programs and services have been stemmed from evidence about the quality of academic programs or services derived from survey of enrolled students, alumni, community members, and employers; and

6. The implementation of a campus-wide plan for instructional improvement based on findings derived from the above procedures (California Postsecondary Education Commission, 1987, p. 9).

Some observers of the Tennessee plan suspect that the "new funds for higher education appropriated by the legislature for allocation through the performance-funding program are actually funds that would otherwise have gone into the general budget of Tennessee's colleges and universities. Yet, officials of those institutions that have received the maximum award—an add-on of up to 5 percent of their budget—believe that these funds are indeed "new" money. (More information about the Tennessee strategy can be found in Banta, 1985).

The other major state approaches to funding quality, which are commonly referred to as "challenge grant" and "competitive grant" programs, both set aside funds aimed at encouraging institutional practices that will improve institutional performance in areas important to the institution or the state. Among the states using this approach are California, Colorado, Connecticut, Florida, Kentucky, Ohio, and Virginia. These approaches, however, are basically unrelated to the states' formula budgeting process.

In summary, a number of states have developed new strategies in formula budgeting to deal more effectively with the changed conditions of American higher education: steady-state or declining enrollments, general financial exigency, and increased public demands for evidence that public funds for educational purposes are used effectively. The direct effects of changes in enrollment levels and patterns are being weakened to protect institutions from major losses in funding. "Costing procedures and techniques, which underlie many formulas, are getting a bit more sophisticated perhaps, but indirect approaches (for example, conventional average costs plus enrollment averaging) outnumber pure forms" (Brinkman, 1984, p. 39). And concerns about quality and diversity are being addressed through new formulas that differentiate between types of institutions and functions.

## II. Issues of Formula Review: A Case Study of the University of California's Faculty Workload Formula

Between 1972-73 and 1977-78, budgeted undergraduate enrollment at the University of California grew by 9.9 percent while budgeted graduate enrollment grew by 8.4 percent, keeping the composite ratio pretty much in balance. However, between 1977-78 and 1986-87, budgeted undergraduate enrollment grew by 21 percent while budgeted graduate enrollment grew by only 1.6 percent. Understandably, state officials in California believe that this differential in enrollment growth over the last nine years has caused a distortion in the workload measure that drives the states formula used to fund the university, wherein excess instructional resources have been generated for the campuses. This is because undergraduate students require less work for the faculty (and therefore less resources) than that required for graduate students. State officials further believe that this may be the reason why the university has been able to overenroll graduate students for the past several years.

The above concerns of California officials raise several subtle but important issues of formula review that, quite clearly, have relevance within a national context. First, what should the state's policy be for budgeting faculty instructional resources in the university? Second, what method of budgeting resources in the university is most likely to serve the state's best interest over the long run? And thirdly, on what basis should the state review its policy and methods for budgeting instructional resources at the university if it is to (1) provide adequate levels of annual appropriations to support the university's instructional requirements, (2) eliminate or minimize undesirable spending incentives for the university that are inconsistent with the state's long-range goals for higher education, and (3) preserve the university's flexibility to accommodate inevitable fluctuations in its enrollment mix—that is, its enrollment by level on instruction and academic discipline?

### Background on the University's Instructional Resources Formula

The University of California has historically received instructional resources from the state on a formula basis, wherein new funds are provided to the system when enrollments increase. The new resources for instruction are given in the form of new faculty positions, and the state maintains position control for these positions, which are allocated to the central administration on the basis of systemwide student-faculty ratios, undifferentiated by campus, or level of instruction, or discipline where the enrollments actually occurred. The central administration then allocates the positions and the resources to the campuses, using student-faculty ratios and other criteria to make the internal allocation decisions.

Prior to 1971, the state funded faculty workload at the university through a budget formula that applied a weighted student value schedule designed to recognize the differential cost in faculty time for different levels of instruction. The formula interpreted one lower-division undergraduate student to be equal to 2.5 first-year graduate students and to 3.5 full-time third-year Ph.D. students. This meant that 3.5 times as many resources were generated for each advanced doctoral student than for each lower-division student or, in general terms, that proportionately a greater number of faculty were funded for the same number of graduate students than for undergraduates.

Since 1972, the state has used a different formula for funding the university's faculty resources. That formula is based on a composite index that does not distinguish undergraduate from graduate workload and that funds or adds one full-time faculty position for every 17.61 undergraduate or graduate students. In other words, the state uses the composite student-faculty ratio of 17.61:1 to calculate the instructional resource requirements of additional enrollments at the university. (Although the current formula does not use a weighted student value schedule, student weights are used to calculate full-time-equivalent enrollment at different levels of instruction. For instance, full-time undergraduate students are enrolled for 15 units per quarter while full-time first-stage and second-stage graduate students are enrolled for 12 and 9 units, respectively.)

The university contends that its student-faculty ratio increased steadily during the late 1960s and early '70s—from 14.71 in 1966-67 to 17.49 in 1974-75, as shown in Display 1—primarily because of a series of state budget cuts in the early '70s. Display 1 might suggest that the formula used before 1971 generated more instructional resources than the current formula, but in the absence of an understanding of how students are counted and of a detailed analysis of changes in the university's enrollment mix by academic department and level of instruction and of the cost implications of these changes, it is difficult to ascertain whether the university has gained or lost resources since then.

It should be noted that throughout the various stages of resource allocation from its system-wide office to the campuses and then to the colleges and departments, the university exercises a considerable amount of flexibility to recognize the unique philosophy, role, and scope of each of its campuses, colleges, and departments. It bases this approach on the principles that the budget process should neither dictate program priorities at the campus level nor attempt to homogenize campuses or programs and that the allocation process should protect campus participation in governance by maximizing the ability of campus leaders to pursue and protect local needs and interests.

## Shifts in Enrollment at the University

Changes have occurred in the university's enrollment by level of instruction. Display 2 shows that over two seven-year periods—1971-72 to 1978-79 and 1978-79 to 1985-86—actual annual full-time equivalent undergraduate enrollments increased at a faster rate than graduate enrollments. During the first period, undergraduate enrollments grew 18.9 percent, compared with 5.4 percent for graduate students; while similar increases of 15.6 and 6.5 percent occurred over the second period. These trends in actual enrollments show the recent steady growth in non-budgeted graduate enrollments at the university. According to California officials, the number of graduate students enrolled in 1986-87 was 1,180 above the budgeted level—the highest number recorded in the past 15 years. The state's officials contend that this discrepancy is evidence that the university has obtained from the formula the additional resources needed to enroll more graduate students than had been budgeted for.

**Display 1**
**Budgeted General Campus Student-Faculty Ratios of the**
**University of California, Fiscal Years 1966-67 through 1986-87**

| Fiscal Year | Student/Faculty Ratio |
|-------------|----------------------|
| 1966-67 | 14.71:1 |
| 1967-68 | 15.35:1 |
| 1968-69 | 15.43:1 |
| 1969-70 | 15.88:1 |
| 1970-71 | 16.48:1 |
| 1971-72 | 17.40:1 |
| 1972-73 | 17.42:1 |
| 1973-74 | 17.41:1 |
| 1974-75 | 17.49:1 |
| 1975-76 | 17.49:1 |
| 1976-77 | 17.49:1 |
| 1977-78 | 17.48:1 |
| 1978-79 | 17.48:1 |
| 1979-80 | 17.48:1 |
| 1980-81 | 17.48:1 |
| 1981-82 | 17.48:1 |
| 1982-83 | 17.48:1 |
| 1983-84 | 17.48:1[a] |
| 1983-84 | 17.61:1[b] |
| 1984-85 | 17.61:1 |
| 1985-86 | 17.61:1 |
| 1986-87 | 17.61:1 |

[a]Historical calculation method used prior to 1983-84.

[b]New calculation method introduced in 1983-84, thereby increasing full-time-equivalent graduate enrollment base by 873 students. (No additional resources involved.)

Source: Office of the President, University of California.

One has to agree that the state's formula appears to generate additional resources for the university when more students are added at the lower end of the cost scale while faculty are provided at the average. But while it is plausible that the formula has provided the university with "additional instructional resources" in recent years, such a conclusion cannot be drawn without consideration of the instructional costs associated with the changes in the university's overall enrollment mix. One cannot ascertain whether or not "additional" resources are generated without knowing if the university has experienced faculty turnover in areas of decreasing demand to allow the reallocation of resources to areas with increasing enrollments. If turnover has not occurred, or if there have been internal enrollment shifts to areas of relatively higher cost, then no "excess" resources have been generated.

Specifically, what is required is an examination of the enrollment changes by both academic discipline and level of instruction—approached with a broader understanding of some of the inherent functional differences among the academic disciplines of the university. Hence, before proceeding with an analysis of the changes in the university's enrollment by discipline, it appears necessary to first develop a conceptual framework for interpreting the differences in costs among

**Display 2**
**Actual Annual Full-Time-Equivalent Enrollments by Level of Instruction at the**
**Eight General Campuses of the University of California, 1971-72, 1978-79, and 1985-86**

| Period | Undergraduate | Graduate | Total |
|--------|--------------|----------|-------|
| 1971-72 | 70,573 | 22,559 | 93,132 |
| 1978-79 | 83,931 | 23,779 | 107,710 |
| 1985-86 | 99,392 | 25,440 | 124,440 |
| Percent Growth | | | |
| 1971-72—1978-79 | 18.9% | 5.4% | 15.7% |
| Percent Growth | | | |
| 1978-79—1985-86 | 15.6 | 6.5 | 15.5 |

Source: Governor's Budgets for 1987-1988, 1980-1981, and 1973-1974.

its various academic levels and programs. In addition, a review of the literature on formula budgeting and on costing concepts and methods is important in interpreting the university's resource requirements in a more informed manner.

## Framework for Considering Instructional Cost and Resource Issues

This review of the California formula used to fund workload at the University of California is approached with the realization that it is not possible to evaluate the effectiveness or the quality of the learning environments created by the university's campuses, colleges, and departments. A plausible option, however, is to examine those factors that, required for the creation of a learning environment, can be viewed in quantitative terms.

For example, it is possible to quantify the number of faculty or the student-faculty ratio involved in the learning environment of a department or college. These factors provide a rough measure of the "inputs" or resource requirements of an academic unit. A corresponding output (proxy) educational outcome, then, could be the number of full-time-equivalent students taught by a mathematics department or a college of engineering. The process that transforms input factors into educational outcomes has been described by Cohn (1979, p. 164) as the "production function of higher education."

Some of the earlier landmark studies on higher education costing, such as the California and Western Conference Cost and Statistical Study (Middlebrook, 1955), were built solely on a production function framework. However, in the more recent literature, such as in Carlson (1972), Robinson, Roy, and Turk (1977), and Leslie and Brinkman (1980), somewhat broader conceptual frameworks have been used. These broader frameworks have focused not only on the "production function" of an institution or academic program but on its "cost function" as well. The latter, which is described in the following paragraph, evolved from microeconomic cost theory. An important contention in such frameworks is that sufficient similarities exist between a business firm and a college or university to permit the use of microeconomics in examining university costs (a more detailed explanation can be obtained from Maynard, 1971, and Carlson, 1972).

Within a microeconomics context, the "cost function" of the university's academic programs, which describes the relationship between their costs (resource requirements) and output levels, is dependent not only on the university's production function but upon its "market supply function" as well. According to Brigham and Pappas (1972, p. 211), the market supply function specifies the prices of the inputs used in the production process. The average salaries paid to full-time faculty or to department heads are examples of related "input prices."

What the broader conceptual frameworks connote for this case study, then, is that variations in the instructional costs or resource needs among the university's academic units or disciplines can be interpreted as departmental or "academic discipline" differences in the production and market supply functions. A major objective for this case study analysis, therefore, is to provide an enhanced understanding of the costs or resource implications associated with the production and market supply functions of the university's academic programs.

## Research Literature on Instructional Costs and State Formula Budgeting Methods

In the United States, considerable attention has been given to cost information and cost analysis in higher education, as evidenced by an existing body of literature that spans more than 85 years. Issues of costs and efficiency in educational institutions have attracted the attention not only of college and business administrators but of educators, researchers, and state higher education and political leaders. As a result, the contributions made to the field of cost analysis in higher education have been numerous and diverse. Considering the diversity of methods and objectives involved in the higher education costing process, this review of the literature on costing is approached with caveats. The following review focuses on those costing studies that are directly relevant to the purpose of this case study analysis, especially to identify consistent differences in instructional costs by level in instruction and academic discipline.

One of the better known and more widely quoted unit cost studies has been the *California and western Conference Cost and Statistical Study for the Year 1954-55* (Middlebrook, 1955). This study examined the variations in instructional costs among institutions, levels of instruction, and subject fields. Moreover, this study aimed at determining the relationship of these variations to variations in the factors presumed to affect institutional costs, namely (1) size of class, (2) method of instruction (laboratory or non-laboratory), (3) total volume of teaching activity, (4) faculty teaching assignment, (5) faculty salaries, and (6) teaching expenditures other than teaching salaries (e.g., expenditures for secretarial assistance, supplies, and others). Among the conclusions arrived at for the instructional part of this study were the following (pp. 30-31):

- In the institutions studied, the number of weekly student-class-hours per full-time-equivalent teaching-staff member is the most important factor in explaining variations in unit costs. This is basically a measure of teaching assignment; it also reflects class size. A generalized conclusion may be drawn that unit costs can be most easily changed by changing the ratio of students to staff in the specific subject field. The effect of such changes upon the learning environment is not, however, taken into account.

- Total volume of teaching activity, if extremely low, prevents much increase in class size or teaching load, thus making cost adjustments difficult.

- Cost per student is affected not only by the number of students, but also by the composition of the student body in terms of instructional level, curriculum, and so on: the so-called "student mix."

- Methods of instruction definitely affect cost. Their effect, however, is in terms of their influence upon class size, teaching load, and other factors bearing upon costs. Where the measure of costs is indicated in terms of the student-class-hour per week, attention must also be given to the number of weekly meetings of the class.

The Middlebrook study found that although costs varied among subject fields, levels of instruction, and institutions, it was possible "to isolate the causes of these variations and explain them in terms of influences which exerted themselves regardless of subjects of institutions" (p. 31).

As indicated in this study, it was also possible to examine the effects of various policies upon the costs of a specific type of learning environment. This policy issue is addressed in a few of the more current studies reviewed below.

In much of the unit cost literature published since World War II, considerable interest has been shown in knowing the cost associated with the education of one student in a specific academic level or subject field. Moreover, much of this literature has given particular attention to economy of scale issues. Williams' (1961) study reported that at the University of Michigan the mean cost ratios among freshmen, juniors, and graduate students averaged about 1:2:6, respectively. He found that, depending upon the school or college the student was enrolled in, the cost of one freshman and sophomore student ranged from $534 to $1,865 and averaged $656, while the cost of one junior and senior student ranged from $686 to $1,877 and averaged $990 (p. 324). In his study titled "Proved at Last: One Physics Major Equals 1.34 Chemistry Major or 1.66 Economics Major," Hyde (1974) reported that, when compared with the costs of producing an upper-division FTE chemistry or economics major, the high cost of an upper-division FTE physics major was chiefly a diseconomy of scale problem since student enrollment in this major was usually small. The high cost of a physics major, he added, may be explained by the high diversity in some physics departments, resulting in numerous specialties with low enrollment.

The studies by Beatty, Gulko, and Sheehan (1974) and Leslie and Brinkman (1980) are among the most recent to examine the factors accounting for instructional cost differences among levels of instruction, academic disciplines, and methods of instruction. An overview of these studies provides an understanding of the numerous factors influencing unit instructional costs in higher education.

Beatty, Gulko, and Sheehan (1974) pointed out that the minimum set of policy variables required for an analysis of direct instructional costs included (1) faculty compensation, (2) relative faculty effort, (3) class section size, (4) faculty teaching load, and (5) instructional support programs. The authors contended that by assigning a numerical value to these variables, it was possible to characterize institutional academic and resource allocation policies that influenced the direct cost of instruction. They added that the purpose of the policy variables was "to provide numerical information to help decision makers focus on probable causes of differences in instructional cost indices" (p. 8). Beatty et al. demonstrated the application of an instructional cost index using data collected from five sample academic departments (business, biological sciences, humanities, engineering, and social sciences) from the University of Massachusetts at Amherst. Their work served to identify the policy variables causing major differences in the instructional cost indices:

> For example, the Instructional Cost Index for Engineering is approximately 2.5 times greater than for Humanities. The average class size in Engineering is approximately one-half that of Humanities, and can be identified as a major cause of the index differential. Although slight differences are discernible in faculty load, relative faculty effort, and faculty compensation, the two largest contributors to the differential are class size and support expense (pp. 16-17).

In one of the few major unit cost studies carried out in the 1980s, Leslie and Brinkman (1980) explored the reasons for cost variations among 20 public and 11 private institutions designed as "Research Universities I" by the Carnegie Commission on Higher Education (1976). The author is reported that among the variables having the highest influence on unit instructional costs were average faculty compensation, percent of graduate students, curriculum breadth, and the student-faculty ratio. Unfortunately, the authors did not report differences in cost ratios among the academic disciplines.

Costing information and cost analysis have been essential properties of the formula budgeting approaches taken by various states to determine funding levels for their public colleges and universities. About half of the states have been known to base their appropriations on formula budgets. Because most formula budgets have been based on costs, they therefore have tended to be based heavily either on past behavior or on meeting current fiscal needs—irrespective of changes in program needs or priorities—rather than truly predicting budgetary requirements. Yet in spite of the linear approach used in most formulas to estimate resource requirements—one based on the linear relationship between enrollments and appropriations—formulas have been reformed in recent years so as to buffer the effects of enrollment fluctuations and to contend with the problems of fixed and variable costs in certain programs. As noted earlier in this chapter, among the newest trends in formula budgeting is differentiation by academic discipline and levels of enrollment. For example, at the core of the Minnesota formula is a differential, buffered, average-cost funding approach. Brinkman (1984, p. 38) elaborates on this:

> The buffering is accomplished by relating requested resources to a previous level of full-year equivalent enrollments. The enrollment figures used are those recorded two years prior to the year being funded; for example, 183 enrollments are used in determining the funding level for 1985. Costs and enrollments are differentiated by program type (12 categories) and by level of instruction (four categories).

Minnesota's formula budgeting method is based on instructional funding matrices in which average costs are differentiated on the basis of low, medium, and high cost academic programs and levels of instruction in each of the state's four segments of public higher education. The method combines enrollments with average costs to determine future instructional funding levels. For example, in 1985, the University of Minnesota's "medium cost" programs averaged $3,725 per full-time-equivalent lower-division student, with 2,765 students enrolled in those programs in that year. By combining these enrollments and average per-student costs, a future (1987) instructional funding level of $10,295,900 for the programs was estimated.

Lamb (1986) conducted perhaps the most recent review of budget formulas used by other states to estimate the instructional resource requirements of their institutions of higher learning. From this study, the following are a few examples of those formulas that use student-faculty ratios as a mathematical means of linking state appropriations to the instructional workload of the institutions' varied academic programs at the undergraduate and graduate levels.

In Connecticut, the state budget formula funds instructional workload according to different categories of institutions, academic programs, and instructional levels. For example, in the "social science" programs at the "four-year institutions," the state formula recognized student-faculty ratios of 30.0:1 at the "lower-division" level, 21.0:1 at the "upper-division" level, 14.0:1 at the "master's only" level, and 8.0:1 at the "master's and doctoral" level. By contrast, in the category of programs containing the engineering and physical sciences disciplines, the ratios by instructional level were 19.0:1, 12.0:1, 10.0:1, and 8.0:1, respectively. These differences in the ratios would indicate that, at the lower-division level, workload in engineering and the physical sciences is about 33 percent greater than workload in the social sciences, with the latter's workload being almost half as much at the upper-division level. While the social sciences have a 40 percent lighter workload at the "master's only" level, they have the same workload as engineering and physical sciences at the "master's and doctoral" level.

In Kentucky's universities [which are classified as "other universities" by Lamb (1986) because Kentucky State University is not included] the student-faculty ratio at the "lower-division" level ranged from a high of 22.5:1 in the liberal arts and education programs to a low of 7.5:1 in the health sciences. In these institutions, the "doctoral" level ratios were highest in education (5.2:1) and lowest in fine arts and in pharmacy (3.0:1). For the engineering programs, the student-faculty ratio was 14.1:1 at the lower-division level, 11.7:1 at the upper-division level, 9.0:1 at the master's level, and 3.8:1 at the doctoral level.

In a final example, at the South Carolina institutions conferring the doctoral degree (Clemson University, the University of South Carolina at Columbia, and the Medical University) the student/faculty ratios used in the formula were highest in the business and management disciplines—

**Display 3**
**Undergraduate Workload by Academic Discipline as Measured by**
**Full-Time-Equivalent Undergraduate Enrollments, 1971-72 and 1986-87**

| Period | Engineering and Sciences | Social Sciences | Arts and Humanities | Total |
|---|---|---|---|---|
| Workload | | | | |
| 1971-72 | 20,319 | 23,068 | 19,988 | 63,375 |
| 1986-87 | 29,921 | 30,316 | 24,408 | 84,645 |
| Increase | 9,602 | 7,248 | 4,420 | 21,270 |
| | | | | |
| Workload as Percent of Total | | | | |
| 1971-72 | 32.77% | 36.40% | 31.54% | 100.00% |
| 1986-87 | 35.35 | 35.82 | 28.84 | 100.00 |
| Increase | 47.26 | 31.42 | 22.11 | 33.56 |

Note: "Workload equals the three-quarter average of actual credits accrued in undergraduate courses divided by 15 to determine full-time-equivalent undergraduate students. Two general campuses, Irvine and Santa Cruz, are omitted from this table because comparable data for 1971-72 were not available for them. Postbaccalaureate credential student enrollments are not included.

Source: Adapted from 1988-89 Budget for *Current Operations,* Office of the President, University of California, September 1987, p. 43.

at both the undergraduate level (24.0:1) and the graduate level 17.0:1). By way of comparison, engineering had an undergraduate ratio of 19.0:1 and a first-level graduate ratio of 11.0:1, which connotes that the latter's instructional workload is about one-fourth greater at the undergraduate level and about one-third greater at the graduate level.

The above research on costing and formula budgeting in higher education provides evidence that instructional workload requirements, as measured in per-student costs, vary considerably among academic levels, subject fields, and types of institutions. The Middlebrook (1955) study, which was the first to focus on the technical relationships in the production process in higher education, noted that unit cost variations among campuses, level of instruction, and subject filed were influenced by variations in such production factors as size of class, faculty teaching assignment, and faculty salaries. The more recent studies have provided an enhanced understanding of the production function in higher education by stressing that the market supply function, as reflected by market-based faculty salaries, must be taken into account. The literature shows that state formula budgeting approaches rely heavily on costing information to determine funding levels for higher education institutions. These formulas frequently use a student-faculty ratio to link state appropriations to the differential workload needs of the states' varied institutions and their varied academic programs at the undergraduate and graduate levels.

Based on these differences in workload, the tentative assertions can be made that *collectively* (1) graduate instruction is likely to be two to three times as expensive as undergraduate instruction, (2) at the undergraduate level the hard sciences can be about 33 percent to 55 percent more costly than the social sciences, and (3) while average unit costs among subject fields vary the least at the graduate level, engineering and the hard sciences are the most costly.

## Shifts in the University's Enrollment Mix Over Time

Display 3 shows the university's undergraduate workload (as represented by full-time-equivalent enrollments) by academic discipline category from 1971-72 to 1986-87 as well as the percentage of these disciplines' workload as a share of total workload and their percentage increase in workload over the 15 years. As it shows, between 1971-72 and 1986-87, the largest increase in workload—9,602 students, or 47.26 percent—was in engineering and the sciences where instructional resource requirements are typically high, followed by the social sciences with an increase of 7,248 students, or 31.42 percent. The increase in engineering and the sciences was more than one-third greater than in the social sciences and double that in the arts and humanities.

In other words, in response to student demand the university has had to provide a growing amount of instructional services in academic areas known to be expensive because of small average class sizes, low student-faculty ratios, and a separate salary schedule in engineering. Furthermore, this shift in enrollments has increased the university's need for support for teaching assistants and often expensive instructional laboratory equipment. Thus, within the context of the production function in higher education, it is clear that the university has required additional instructional resources for its undergraduate programs, although the exact amount cannot be determined without more costing information.

Paralleling the changes in the university's undergraduate instructional resources over time, its graduate enrollments have shifted toward the comparatively more costly disciplines such as engineering and computer sciences. Display 4 shows the university's graduate headcount enrollment by academic discipline for Fall 1969 and Fall 1986, indicating that while its greatest percentage increases have been in architecture and environmental design (89.2 percent) and business and management (52.6 percent), its largest numerical growth—1,187 headcount students—has been in engineering and the computer sciences. Major percentage decreases have occurred in physical education (-52.4 percent), fine and applied arts (-30.9 percent); education (-30.6 percent), social sciences (-22.5 percent), and social work (-21.2 percent).

In short, although the imbalance in the university's mix of undergraduates and graduate students has generated additional instructional resources, these resources have most likely been absorbed to some extent by enrollment increases in costly disciplines at both the undergraduate and graduate levels.

## Concluding Comments Regarding the California Approach

Based on the examination conducted herein of changes over time in the university's enrollment by level of instruction and academic discipline and of the research literature on state budgeting approaches and costing in higher education, a number of general conclusions can be appropriately drawn.

First, additional instruction resources are not necessarily generated when the university's enrollments shift toward the less expensive undergraduate level, nor do insufficient resources necessarily result as its enrollments shift toward the costlier disciplines.

Second, the state's priorities in budgeting instructional resources in the university should be (1) to protect against unintended spending incentives aimed solely at obtaining more state revenues, (2) to protect local autonomy and flexibility to allocate resources according to new program needs and priorities, (3) to contain costs over time while appropriately reflecting actual costs, and (4) to promote program stability and quality by helping maintain the needed cadre of full-time permanent faculty.

Third, the advantages of formulas that aggregate enrollment at undergraduate and graduate levels and across academic disciplines might outweigh those of differentiated formulas because they avoid institutional incentives to over enroll students in high-cost areas as a means of obtaining more state revenues and to transform normally low-cost programs into high-cost programs.

Fourth, the available evidence indicates that the state's interest is served best over the long run if faculty instructional resources in the University of California continue to be funded through the current formula budget approach that provides the university with aggregate, lump-sum appropriations without differentiating by discipline area or program level. Not only is this funding

**Display 4**
**Graduate Headcount Enrollment by Academic Discipline at the**
**Eight General Campuses of the University of California, Fall 1969 and Fall 1986**

| Discipline | Fall 1969 | Fall 1986 | Percent Change |
|---|---|---|---|
| Agriculture and Natural Resources | 957 | 1,169 | +22.2% |
| Architecture and Environmental Design | 379 | 717 | +89.2 |
| Biological Sciences | 1,592 | 1,919 | +20.5 |
| Business and Management | 1,526 | 2,328 | +52.6 |
| Engineering and Computer Sciences | 3,223 | 4,410 | +36.8 |
| Fine and Applied Arts | 1,249 | 1,383 | +10.7 |
| Journalism | 79 | 74 | -6.3 |
| Law | 1,878 | 2,311 | +23.1 |
| Letters | 3,502 | 2,421 | -30.9 |
| Library Sciences | 349 | 365 | +4.6 |
| Mathematics | 949 | 798 | -15.9 |
| Physical Education | 84 | 40 | -52.4 |
| Physical Sciences | 2,392 | 2,934 | +22.7 |
| Psychology | 629 | 583 | -7.3 |
| Social Sciences | 4,045 | 3,133 | -22.5 |
| Social Work | 523 | 412 | -21.2 |
| Other (a) | 223 | 530 | — |
| Total | 26,546 | 27,587 | +3.9% |

[a]Unclassified and Interdisciplinary majors.

Source: Office of the President, University of California.

approach least likely to provide the university with unintended incentives to overenroll students in high-cost programs, it also provides the university with some flexibility to accommodate short-term fluctuations in its enrollment mix while reallocating instructional resources that are invested over longer periods.

Fifth, without more complete data on the university's changing resource needs, no adjustment should be made in the state's current ratio of 17.61 full-time-equivalent students for every full-time faculty position at the university. Among the data needed for any change would be faculty data disaggregated by subject area and level of instruction regarding teaching assignment loads, rank, salary levels, and student-faculty ratios.

Sixth, like other states, California uses workload formulas based on student-faculty ratios as a relatively expedient and objective basis for linking state funding levels with its universities' resource requirements but this practice lacks the support of clear and explicit assumptions about (1) what budgeting methods and objectives best serve the state's long-term interests, (2) how the state's budgeting approach can and should influence institutional decisions, and (3) what state issues should *not* be addressed through the budgeting mechanism. Concerns by state officials about controlling imbalances in undergraduate and graduate enrollments at the university might best be addressed apart from the formula for funding instructional resources. The complexity of those issues requires solutions that go beyond simply manipulating the mechanism for linking state appropriations to institutional resource requirements.

Finally, the state should preserve the university's flexibility to determine its instructional resource needs and carry out needed internal allocation or reallocation of resources as dictated by funding realities and its long-range plans. The state also has a legitimate interest in understanding how the university plans to correct the imbalances that develop over time in its faculty resources by program areas and levels of instruction. This understanding should be based largely on cost data—developed through more sophisticated costing procedures and techniques—on the university's programs and on the university's long-range plan for meeting student demand and accommodating needed workload adjustments. Because there should be at least a plausible relationship between state appropriation levels and resource requirements in the university, the state should establish a process for periodically reviewing every five to seven years the effectiveness of its formula (the student-faculty ratio for budgeting instructional resources in the university. Obviously, this review process requires the support of reliable costing information.

## III. Some Considerations for Future Inquiry

Although the public priorities and demographic circumstances facing U.S. higher education have been radically transformed over the past twenty years, the basic design of state budget formulas has been only marginally modified. And whereas the presumptions of growth and stability upon which formulas were originally designed have been proved totally invalid in all but a few situations, the underlying assumptions that were originally incorporated into formulas have remained largely intact. Thus, it is as remarkable as it is unsettling that formula budgets remain today one of the most important and widespread mechanisms for funding public higher education.

Yet, the current conditions of decline and financial exigency are expected to continue, if not worsen, throughout the decade of the '90s. As a result, much new study is needed to develop truly viable formula and non-formula approaches to funding higher education throughout the difficult times that lay ahead. The following are some considerations for future study in this regard.

First, a subtle but important development emerging from the national debate about excellence in higher education is the increasingly assertive role of the states, and particularly of the states' budgeting strategies, as the eminent impetus for achieving public priorities related to educational excellence. Indeed, faced with major fiscal constraints, state legislators, citizen groups, and other constituents of higher education will continue to seek evidence that public funds for educational purposes are targeted strategically and used effectively. Thus, state leaders will likely seek new funding approaches that will provide institutions the types of incentives that are effective in addressing some of the new priorities facing higher education, such as minority student achievement in college.

Special consideration should be given, then, to state budgeting strategies that serve as important tools or means to achieving state policy goals for higher education, rather than as ends in themselves. A reasonable beginning point is to increase our understanding of the viability of the three major types of state-level funding approaches currently in use throughout the nation for promoting quality: (1) "performance based funding," which ties appropriations directly to measurable outcomes or demonstrated results, such as the increased percentage of academic programs that have undergone peer review; (2) "challenge grants programs," which set aside a small amount of state funds aimed at encouraging institutional practices that improve institutional performance in areas important to the state (these programs are often operated on a non-competitive basis, and are funded on a multi year basis to address specific needs); and (3) "competitive grants programs," which are largely modeled after the federal Fund for the Improvement of Postsecondary Education (FIPSE), provides one-time seed money awarded totally on a competitive basis to encourage a select or limited number of institutions to develop model programs that could later be adopted on a broader scale.

A second area for further research relates to the critical role of costing in formula budgeting. Because there should be at least a plausible relationship between state appropriation levels and resource requirements in the institutions, not only will the desire for costing information always exist but state legislatures will with almost predictive regularity commission studies to determine the costs of programs and institutions. All the evidence suggests that formula budgeting decisions will remain based in one way or another on costing information, as was evidenced in the California case study conducted in this chapter.

Much worthy research can still be conducted in the area of costing in higher education. For instance, to overcome the linear cost syndrome in formula budgeting (the underlying presumption in formula budgeting that average costs behave in a linear fashion irrespective of the scale of operations), additional efforts are needed to improve the calculations of marginal, fixed and variable costs that should be used as formula factors. Notable efforts exist to improve these sorts of cost calculations (i.e., Indiana and Wisconsin), but many more are obviously needed since preliminary indications are that the future viability of costing techniques and information remains discouragingly uncertain.

Finally, the time is ripe for a new examination of state and local formula budgeting approaches vis-à-vis the nation's community colleges, where the changing realities of U.S. higher education are undoubtedly the most complex and challenging. The formula budgeting issues facing community colleges merit new and ambitious research efforts. Consider the following: Can viable formulas be found to accommodate the changing patterns of state and local funding of community colleges? How can formulas deal effectively and equitably with the increasing complexity of funding the various community college services (i.e., remedial education, transfer education, occupational/ vocational training, and community service)? And what are the most effective formula budgeting strategies for better recognizing the fiscal consequences of changes in the mix of full-time versus part-time enrollments in the community colleges?

# References

Ahumada, M. M. (1985). *Tuition and Student Aid Policy in Minnesota: A Case Study*. Denver, CO: Education Commission of the States.

Allen, R. H., and Brinkman, P. (1983). *Marginal Costing Techniques for Higher Education*, Boulder, CO: National Center for Higher Education Management Systems.

Banta, T. W. (1985). Use of Outcomes Information at the University of Tennessee, Knoxville, in Peter T. Ewell (ed.), *Assessing Educational Outcomes: New Directions for Institutional Research*, No. 47, pp. 19-32. San Francisco: Jossey-Bass.

Baughman, G. W., and Young, M. E. (May 1982). A Method for Incorporating Fixed and Variable Costing Concepts in Student-Based Models for State Funding of Higher Education in Ohio. Paper presented at the Association for Institutional Research Forum, Denver.

Beatty, G. Jr., Gulko, W. W., and Sheehan, S. B. (July 1974). The Instructional Cost Index: A Simplified Approach to Interinstitutional Cost Comparisons. Paper presented at the Ninth Annual Meeting of the Society for College and University Planning, Denver. (ERIC Document ED 112 818).

Boutwell, W. K. (1973). Formula budgeting on the down side. In G. Kaludis, (ed.), *Strategies for Budgeting: New Directions for Higher Education* No. 2 San Francisco: Jossey-Bass.

Bowen, H. R. (1980). *The Costs of Higher Education: How Much Do Colleges and Universities Spend Per Student and How Much Should They Spend?* San Francisco: Jossey-Bass

Brigham, E. F. and Pappas, J. L. (1972). *Managerial Economics*. Hinsdale, IL: The Dryden Press.

Brinkman, Paul T. (1984). Formula budgeting: the fourth decade. In L. L. Leslie (ed.), *Responding to New Realities in Funding: New Directions for Institutional Research* No. 43, pp. 21-24. San Francisco: Jossey-Bass.

Brinkman, Paul T., and Allen, R. H. (1986). Concepts of cost and cost analysis for higher education. *AIR Professional File* 23: 1-8.

California Postsecondary Education Commission. (1987). *Funding Excellence in California Higher Education: A Report in Response to Assembly Concurrent Resolutions* 141 (1986). Commission Report 87-18. Sacramento: The Commission.

Carlson, D. E. (1972). *The Production and Cost Behavior of Higher Education Institutions.* Ford Foundation Program for Research in University Administration. Berkeley: University of California (ERIC Document ED 081 375, 1972).

Carnegie Commission on Higher Education. (1976). *A Classification of Institutions of Higher Education.* The Carnegie Foundation for the Advancement of Teaching.

Caruthers, J. K., and Orwig, J. (1979). *Budgeting in Higher Education.* ERIC/AAHE Research Report No. 3. Washington, DC: American Association for Higher Education.

Cohn, E. (1979). *The Economics of Education.* Cambridge, MA: Ballinger.

Governor's Budget for 1980-81. (1981). Sacramento: Office of the Governor, State of California.

Governor's Budget for 1987-88. (1987). Sacramento: Office of the Governor, State of California.

Gross, F. M. (1973). *A Comparative Analysis of the Existing Budget Formulas Used for Justifying Budget Requests or Allocating Funds for the Operating Expenses of State-Supported Colleges and Universities.* Monograph No. 9. Knoxville: University of Tennessee Office of Institutional Research.

Gross, F. M. (1979). Formula budgeting and the financing of public higher education: panacea or nemesis for the 1980s? AIR Professional File 3: 1-6.

Hale, J. A., and Rawson, T. M. (1976). Developing statewide higher education funding formulas for use in a limited growth environment. *Journal of Education Finance* 2: 16-32.

Hyde, W. L. (1974). Proved at last: one physics major equals 1.34 chemistry major or 1.66 economics major," *Educational Record* 286-290.

Jones, D. P. (1984). *Higher-Education Budgeting at the State Level: Concepts and Principles.* Boulder, CO.: National Center for Higher Education Management Systems.

Jones, D. P. (1984). Budgeting for academic quality: structures and strategies. In John Folger (ed.), *Financial Incentives for Academic Quality: New Directions for Higher Education* No. 48. San Francisco: Jossey-Bass.

Kerr, C. (1983). Survival in the 1980s: quality, mission, and financing options. In R. A. Wilson (ed.) *Survival in the 1980s: Quality, Mission, and Financing Options.* Tucson: Center for the Study of Higher Education, University of Arizona.

Lamb, J. A. (1986) An analysis of the structure of 1985 state budget formulas for public higher education with a comparison of 1973, 1979, and 1985 data. Doctoral dissertation, University of Tennessee.

Legislative Analyst. (1987). *Analysis of the Budget Bill for the Fiscal Year July 1, 1987 to June 30, 1987.* Sacramento: Office of the Legislative Analyst.

Leslie, L. L. (1984). Bringing the Issues Together. In L. L. Leslie (ed.), *Responding to New Realities in Funding: New directions for Institutional Research* No. 43. San Francisco: Jossey-Bass.

Leslie, L. L., and P. T. Brinkman. (1980). Instructional costs at research universities I. *Financing and Budgeting Postsecondary Education in the 1980s.* Tucson, AZ: University of Arizona, College of Education, Center for the Study of Higher Education.

Maynard, J. (1971). *Some Microeconomics of Higher Education.* Lincoln: University of Nebraska Press.

McKeown, M. P. (1982). The use of formulas for state funding of higher education. *Journal of Education Finance* 7: 277-300.

Meisinger, R. J., Jr. (1975). The politics of formula budgeting: the determination of tolerable levels of inequality through objective incrementalism in public higher education. Doctoral dissertation, University of California, Berkeley.

Meisinger, R. J., Jr. (1976). *State Budgeting For Higher Education: the Uses of Formulas.* Berkeley: University of California, Center for Research and Development in Higher Education.

Middlebrook, W. T. (1955). *California and Western Conference Cost and Statistical Study for the Year 1954-1955.* Berkeley: University of California.

Miller, J. L., Jr. (1964). *State Budgeting for Higher Education: The Use of Formulas and Cost Analysis.* Michigan Governmental Studies, No. 45. Ann Arbor: University of Michigan Institute of Public Administration.

Millett, J. D. (1974). *The Budget Formula as the Basis for State Appropriations in Support of Higher Education.* New York: Management Division, Academy for Educational Development, Inc.

Monical, D. G., and Schoenecker, C. V. (1980). Marginal funding: a difference that makes a difference? *Research in Higher Education* 12(1): 67-82.

Morgan, A. T. (1984). The new strategies: roots, context, and overview. In L. L. Leslie (ed.), *Responding to New Realities in Funding: New Directions for Institutional Research* No. 43, pp. 5-20. San Francisco: Jossey-Bass.

Moss, C. E., and Gaither, G. H. (1976). Formula budgeting: requiem or renaissance? *Journal of Higher Education* 47(5): 543-563.

Pickens, W. H. (1981). Statewide formulas to support higher education. *Legislator's Guide to Higher Education Issues of the 1980s.* Washington, DC: National Conference of State Legislatures.

Pickens, W. H. (1982). What's ahead for higher education? *Journal of the National Association of College Auxiliary Services* (April): 8-12.

Robinson, D. D., Ray, H. W., and Turk, F. F. (1977). Cost behavior analysis for planning in higher education. *NABUCO Professional File 9* No. 5.

Schick, A. The road to PPB: the stages of budget reform. *Public Administration Review* 26: 243-258.

Spence, D. S., and Weathersby, G. B. (1981). Changing patterns of state funding. In J. R. Mingle and Associates (eds.), *Challenges of Retrenchment: Strategies for Consolidating Programs, Cutting Costs, and Reallocating Resources.* San Francisco: Jossey-Bass.

State of California Budget Supplement for Health and Welfare Education for 1973-74, Volume II. (1974). Sacramento: Office of the Governor, State of California.

University of California. (1986). *University of California Faculty Workload Policies.* Berkeley: Office of President, University of California.

University of Wisconsin System. (1982). *Instructional Funding Report.* Madison: University of Wisconsin System.

Williams, R. L. (1961). The cost of educating one college student. *The Education Record* 42(4): 322-329.

# Financial and Tuition Trends in the 1980s:
## A Review (1991)

GLEN R. STINE

## Abstract:

*In this essay, Glen R. Stine extends an analysis of financial issues in higher education that was first presented as a "Profiles" essay in this publication ("The 1980s: A Financial Retrospective," Policy Perspectives, September 1989). Six data profiles were used to track expenditure growth in administrative and academic functions. Data were drawn from 157 institutions and classified in categories based on public or private status, level of initial tuition charges, research or non-research status, and primary higher education association membership. Stine's further analysis of these data concentrates on tuition pricing and room and board rates for each academic year from 1983 to 1990.*

While agreeing that tuition increases progressed at a rate above inflation, Stine shows that this general trend contains a complex pattern of pricing strategies among individual institutions. He argues that identifying and recognizing these patterns within a pattern is helpful in understanding institutional behavior.

Analysis of the data leads to several general conclusions. Private institutions had a smooth rate of annual increase during the period studied. State colleges and universities, however, had rates of increase for tuition that varied sharply from year to year; and within a single state, total price change among public institutions did not vary as much as could be expected. Generalizable and predictive factors were difficult to identify. Room and board information showed that these rates increased faster at private institutions than at institutions in the public sector. Further, those institutions that had the highest tuition increases in both sectors also tended to have the largest increase in room and board charges.

Stine also discusses four models describing how public institutions set tuition rates. The models emphasize that institutional activity takes place in the context of a state government's appropriations for and attitude toward higher education.

Stine reminds readers that the economic trends of the 1980s created a bifurcated financial path, with increasing wealth for groups that traditionally consider higher education to be a necessity and increasing hardship for groups that have more frequently chosen immediate employment over continued education. These differing financial experiences make high tuitions an even more compelling barrier for non-traditional students. For these students, Stine asserts, the question of "Who pays?" centers on activities of state government policymaking.

## Excerpt:

[I]t is useful to review four models that delineate the ways in which public institutions set their tuition rates. It should be remembered, however, that no matter what statutory or constitutional provisions exist in a given state for setting tuition, it is clearly a complex political process.

1. An institution or a set of institutions within a state has relative statutory or constitutional autonomy to set tuition rates.

This authority often differs by sector within any given state. For example, in Pennsylvania, the four state universities (Pennsylvania State University, University of Pittsburgh, Temple University, and Lincoln University) have more authority to set their own tuitions than do the other public institutions in the state college and university system. During most years, those institutions with relatively greater autonomy may set their tuitions at any rate of growth that they choose. However, as was seen with the Michigan institutions in academic year 1983-84, the three constitutional institutions (University of Michigan, Michigan State, and Wayne State) held their tuition rate increases to zero percent at a time when their state appropriation increased by zero percent. Thus, such institutions are not fully insulated from the political process. In the case of the Michigan schools, the state threatened to withhold or reduce state appropriations for every dollar that the universities increased tuition. It is very interesting to note that states in which the greatest institutional autonomy exists are typically viewed as being high-tuition states with very weak coordinating boards. Lastly, these states generally encourage high out-of-state tuitions.

2. A state framework exists for coordination in setting tuitions.

Two slightly different examples of this type of state situation are Ohio and Colorado. In Ohio, the maximum tuition is calculated as a percentage of cost, based on a formula that determines the percentage of revenue that should come from tuition and from state appropriations. Thus, a price cap is put on the institutions through the formula, although a given institution may charge less. In Colorado, the state coordinating board sets a percentage increase cap that cannot be exceeded but gives the governing boards autonomy to set the rate of tuition increase within the cap. In some cases, institutions also have their tuition income appropriated back to them by the legislature. Generally, these appropriations do not have to be returned if tuition revenues exceed the revenues anticipated in the appropriations bill. Thus, rate-setting can be uncoupled from the appropriation process. In Colorado in 1987, the legislature used this appropriation authority to set specific tuition increases. Again, out-of-state tuition is less regulated for all the states in this category.

3. Tuition-setting is regulated.

In New York, tuitions may not be set until after the legislature passes the annual appropriations bill. Thus, all tuition discussions are essentially established as parameters of the appropriations bill. In such regulated states, tuition revenues are appropriated, and any revenues received from tuition that exceed the appropriation estimate must be returned to the states, often for reappropriation.

4. Tuition-setting is unrelated to institutional revenue.

In a few states (e.g., Massachusetts), the tuition revenue traditionally has gone into state revenue coffers and does not appear as an appropriation or a revenue to the institution itself. Until recent years, when Massachusetts found itself short of income, it would raise tuition in order to raise state revenue. The educational institutions, which had the autonomy technically to set their own rate of tuition, were unable to control the state process. Obviously, the incentive here is for the institution to hold down tuition charges because it has no stake in the actual revenue process. . . .

Overall, certain conclusions can be drawn from the information presented by these data. For public institutions, the role of state politics in tuition-setting is significant, and situations within the state set some very basic price parameters. For example, the state government essentially decides whether it is going to be a high-tuition or low-tuition state. Some of the factors (outside the statutory requirements) that help form this determination are the relative strengths of the legislature versus the governor, constitutional provisions, current state income growth, successful tax limitation efforts, and the state view of the role of higher education. In addition, a number of institutional factors seem to be critical, including the mission of a given institution, its regional location, and its prestige. It is typical for the flagship institution or major state campus to have a higher rate of in-state tuition than other state institutions. In a number of the states, room and board increasingly seems to be a factor in marketing.

For private institutions, market principles seem to hold. The more selective an institution is or wants to be, the higher its tuition rate. It is clear that some institutions have sought to raise their tuitions as part of a considered strategy to improve the perceived quality of their student bodies and of the institution overall.

During the last decade, the overall rate of growth in tuition is alarming if inflation is used as the only comparative guide. The increases are less dramatic, however, if the growth of personal income or per capita income is taken into account. Moreover, when all changes on total charges are taken into account during the last several years, little or no real growth has occurred for most institutions.

What is problematic about this analysis is that changes in personal income have developed a bifurcated path over the decade. Professional and managerial employees have had substantial relative growth in personal income, while blue collar and lower-middle income earners have typically lost relative income. Thus, individuals from economic and social backgrounds that are the least likely to see higher education as an alternative choice to beginning employment are even more likely to view high rates of tuition growth and total cost increases as barriers.

As the Roundtable seeks to address the questions that surround the issue of "Who pays?" it cannot fail to acknowledge state political behavior as the primary determinant of this policy question for over 75 percent of the students in the United States. For these students the discussion does not center on the student or parents, but rather the relative contribution of the states.

# State Financing of Higher Education:
## A New Look at an Old Problem (1990)

FREDERICK J. FISCHER

> Establish the law for educating the common people. This it is the business of the state to effect and on a general plan.
>
> —Thomas Jefferson

Virtually all students of higher education would agree that there is no "general plan" that guides the public sector (the federal government and the states) in providing subsidies to "educate the common people," at least at the postsecondary level. Some would go further and assert that no such plan should exist. Larry Gladieux and Tom Wolanin noted years ago in their instructive study, *Congress and the Colleges*:

> Another historical assumption of federal higher education policy is that there is *no* policy in the sense of an integrated, coordinated and comprehensive blueprint. . . . Also, because the federal role is supplementary to that of the states, an aspect of the consensus is that a comprehensive federal policy is unnecessary. Indeed, if such a comprehensive policy were formulated, it might violate the understanding of the proper federal and state roles because it would imply a primary federal responsibility.

But a comprehensive policy or "general plan" is important, as Jefferson realized, because it is usually the "common people" who are excluded or left worst off when complex public policies are poorly coordinated and lack an overall strategy. These people have limited political clout. They cannot afford expensive lobbyists and lack the resources to avoid the consequences for them of retrogressive policies. The litany of powerlessness is familiar, I know. But improving the lot of these people should, in my view, be the major goal of policymakers; it is the principal domestic business of the state.

In this article, then, I will advance a general plan of public responsibility for the finance of higher education. More precisely, I will review the current state approach to higher education finance, analyzing state policy on its own merits and the appropriateness of the federal response thereto, and then commenting on the resulting level of policy coherence. I will argue specifically that:

- contrary to popular wisdom, there *is* an implicit general plan currently uniting federal and state financing policies;

- this general plan is inefficient, inequitable, and ineffective, involving obsolete state financing policies and mistaken federal responses thereto;

- another general plan is available that addresses most of the problems with the current plan; and

- implementation of this plan would almost certainly require federal intervention in state financing policies.

Much of what follows is hardly new; readers may find, for example, cogent discussion of the issues raised here in a seminal 1971 paper by Lee Hansen and Burton Weisbrod and in the Carnegie Commission's lucid 1973 study, *Higher Education: Who Pays? Who Benefits? Who Should Pay? . . .* Little has been written on this topic in the last decade, however, and the issues are important enough to deserve consideration anew.

Let us begin by recalling Willie Sutton, the infamous bank robber, caught once more and asked by a judge, "Willie, why do you keep robbing banks?" Sutton replied, supposedly in all innocence, "Because that's where they keep the money."

Sutton's point about concentrating on where the money is a useful one in thinking about public policy. Looking for big money is often how we discover what the underlying policies are, how we get pointed to real sources of problems. A big money focus can also help us avoid Washington-based myopia about public purses that matter. Many people, misled by the determinedly federal focus of many higher education lobbyists and by frequent media attention to battles about federal student aid, have come to believe that the federal government is the principal public-sector contributor to the general financing of higher education.

Not only is this perception wrong, it is badly so. For the most recent year for which the National Center on Education Statistics has published actual data (1985), direct state and local government contributions to current-fund revenues of institutions of higher education were $30.6 billion, while federal appropriations for the title IV student-aid programs were $9.0 billion. That is, *state and local dollars were more than three times the federal dollars*; the big money, without question, is at the state level. What are the states doing, and why?

## Current State Practice

There is great diversity across the states in policies toward financing higher education. Some charge relatively high tuitions at public colleges; others keep tuitions low. Some provide substantial need-based aid to students; others relatively little. Most provide direct aid to students at private institutions, though in most cases the amount is small.

These differences have important implications for how states would react politically to a change in federal financing policy; they make it difficult to fashion a single, coherent federal policy in the first place. They need not, however, distract us from analyzing the dominant thrust of state policy.

That policy is unambiguous and essentially unchanged for more than a century: provide direct appropriations to public institutions to allow those institutions to charge tuitions for all students that are low in absolute terms. The resulting charges are also, importantly, low relative to the cost of providing education services at these institutions, and low relative to charges by comparable private institutions. That direct appropriations to reduce tuition for all is the basic financing policy is clear from figures developed by Tom Mortenson of the American College Testing Program: in recent years only about 5 percent of state support for higher education has been in the form of need-based financial aid—95 percent goes to colleges as a direct tuition subsidy for all students.

Seven basic reasons have been advanced over the years in support of this direct-aid-to-institutions approach.

First, higher education is a public good that should be free—or at least very easily accessible financially—to all qualified users. It produces general benefits to society and should, therefore, like public elementary and secondary education, be financed to a great if not exclusive extent by taxpayers. Economists making this argument would say that the approach is "efficient," priced as it ought to be.

Second, a related argument views higher education as an entitlement: everyone (who can gain admission academically) should be able to afford and have access to a college education, and therefore it should be essentially free for everyone.

The third reason is a parochial version of the first: a state needs to provide a subsidy to keep its most able students from leaving the state, from attending college elsewhere and perhaps not returning; future state benefits in the form of economic growth and intellectual, cultural, and political vitality are said to depend on this.

Fourth, low tuition promotes equal opportunity by making it easier for able students from lower-income families to afford college. The approach is equity-enhancing among the college-bound. There are two subtle variations of this argument. One is that a low-tuition "sticker price," as opposed to a high sticker price offset by need-based aid, prevents "sticker shock" and reduced enrollment by low-income students (I use this latter phrase as shorthand, with regard to dependent students, for "students from low-income families"). The other variation is that making low tuitions available for all makes it easier for the political process to make them available for students from poor families.

Fifth, direct appropriations by the state legislature affecting all students maintain needed public control over what goes on at public institutions; accountability is ensured.

Sixth, direct state appropriations is a simple mechanism that means much less paperwork and red tape for the state, for public schools, and, importantly, for students.

The seventh reason needs mention only in passing. The low-tuition approach basically extracts money from parents (and other state taxpayers) via the tax system rather than relying on a voluntary parental contribution to a student's education. This "forced-payment" approach makes students more independent and, in essence, prevents well-off parents from preventing their children from going to college by refusing to help pay the bills. This argument seems too cynical about the relations of parents and children. Even if there were, however, large numbers of well-off parents unwilling to help financially (poor parents would not be expected to help in any case), there is sufficient aid-officer discretion in the current system of determining need and awarding aid to allow the situation of children of such parents to be addressed. This argument is not discussed further.

## Arguments Against Current State Practice

The first six arguments are, at first glance, plausible and persuasive. Yet on closer inspection, I believe, we will find none of them—with the exception of administrative simplicity—very compelling.

- Postsecondary education as public good. It is more difficult to make a case for the general (or social, or public) benefits of a *college* education, and for the corresponding general subsidy approach, than it is for elementary and secondary eduction.

If a student is literate, for example, he will be able to read street signs and be a safe driver, which benefits pedestrians and other drivers. Or, at another level, he will be able to comprehend newspapers and other basic written materials, which will help him be a better citizen by improving his understanding of events around him. Similar arguments apply to basic numeracy. This is not to deny that these basic skills create substantial private benefits—they clearly do—but only to argue that a significant share of lower school benefits is public.

It is much harder to identify benefits that clearly accrue to society, *above and beyond what accrues to the student*, from going to college and learning to be an engineer. English teacher, businessman, or computer programmer. One can say that society needs and values engineers, which is certainly true, but that is just another way of saying that the salary the student (not society!) comes to enjoy as an engineer reflects the usefulness of his or her skills.

Although I am better off because engineers exist, the degree to which I am better off is measured by how much I am willing to pay for engineering services. That is, I will be just indifferent at the margin between keeping my money and buying engineering services. If I buy those services, my well-being will be *unchanged*: I will have increased my well-being by some amount by acquiring the services, but decreased it by an equal amount by giving up money.

A common objection to this line of argument is that sizeable public or social benefits *do* exist in the form of increased taxes paid by college graduates. It is correct that these taxes represent real increments to production that students would not be likely to take into account when thinking about investing in college. But if one wishes to include these benefits in the benefit-cost calculation, then one must also include costs that the student may not take into consideration, such as the difference between full educational cost and the subsidized price he or she would face at either a public or private college.

Lee Hansen looked at this question in some detail in an April, 1963 article in the *Journal of Political Economy*, one of the earliest rate-of-return studies. He found, interestingly enough, that public subsidies make "the private rates of return net of tax considerably *more* attractive than the rate of return earned on total resource investment" (emphasis supplied). That is, relative to private benefits and costs, the incremental social benefits of college education are actually less than the incremental social costs.

Most studies over the years have supported Hansen's conclusion. Larry Leslie and Paul Brinkman, as part of their larger 1988 volume, *The Economic Value of Higher Education*, carried out a so-called meta-analysis of 15 studies that calculated social rates of return. Although Leslie and Brinkman warn of possible downward biases in these calculations, they nonetheless dutifully report that the social rates of return on undergraduate education "range between 11.6 and 12.1 percent—slightly less than the private rate of return values." Thus the taxes-as-benefits argument for providing additional public subsidies, once appropriately framed, has not generally been found compelling empirically.

All this is not to deny, of course, that there are many real non-financial benefits from higher education. One might mention, for example, the ancillary pleasures of life on a college campus, the aesthetic pleasure of learning, development of desirable personal qualities such as intellectual integrity and tolerance of change, general cognitive development, and so on. Note that these benefits are primarily private in nature.

It is probably appropriate to visualize a continuum of benefits along the scale of educational attainment, with the public-private mix of benefits changing as the education level changes. At the low end of general learning (elementary education), a substantial share of benefits is public; at the high end of specialized training (graduate education), virtually all benefits are private. Contention usually emerges about the precise mix during the last year or two of secondary schooling and the undergraduate years. I read the evidence to say that the benefits from undergraduate education are predominantly private in nature and that those of graduate education are almost entirely so.

Regardless of the degree to which one ascribes general benefits to society from postsecondary education, however, this argument does not, in itself, justify state policies that create low tuitions for the *non*-needy. The precise question to ask about the low-tuition state policy is: do students from well-off families *need* this subsidy to enroll in sufficient numbers, from society's perspective?

This question is raised and answered in the Hansen and Weisbrod article mentioned earlier:

> . . . the incentives seem adequate without subsidies—at least for those not near the bottom of the ability-to-pay ladder. Thus, even if social benefits are large, no public subsidy is likely to be necessary to encourage the vast majority of higher-income students to invest in college training.

Hansen and Weisbrod base their belief on evidence that the rate of return from college equals or exceeds that available from other investments. An additional consideration is that, *for well-off families*, the person realizing private benefits (the student) is not the person paying most of the costs (the parents). Presumably this leads such students to demand more postsecondary eduction than they otherwise would.

If private incentives are already sufficient to produce appropriate postsecondary enrollment levels, then, given the substantial subsidies that are currently provided to students in the public sector through the low-tuition approach, and in the private sector through tuition subsidies from endowment and contributions, and in both sectors through various federal programs, one would expect substantial *overinvestment* in higher eduction, at least from a labor market perspective. And, indeed, several investigators have found evidence of such overinvestment. For example, Russell Rumberger, in an article in the Winter, 1987 issue of the *Journal of Human Resources*, concludes that "a significant proportion of working Americans have completed more schooling than their jobs require."

- Postsecondary education as entitlement. Once one gets beyond the areas of basic Constitutional rights (e.g., free speech, suffrage), the question of what is a right or entitlement is a political one that is difficult to address on objective, analytical grounds.

As a factual matter, it is clear that higher education is not now an entitlement, unlike elementary and secondary education. That is, if my child were denied access to public elementary or secondary education in any state, I would have grounds for suing to get him or her admitted. But if my child were denied access to public higher education, I would not have such grounds (except in a few jurisdictions with totally open admissions policies). Further, even if my child were admitted, but could not attend because I could not afford the required tuition costs, I would still not have grounds for suing.

But the important question is not factual but normative: *should* higher education be an entitlement (for those who satisfy academic criteria for enrollment)? I believe very strongly, on equity grounds, that the answer to this question is no. Society always faces competing claims for available resources. Other things being equal, higher priority should be given to addressing the claims of those who are worst-off. An entitlement to higher education allocates resources to those who are, by definition, most likely to be the best-off as adults: the most intelligent (or at least the most educable). Although it is hard to make the allocation decision between helping an elementary school student to read and a college student to understand Hegel, our first duty is and always must be to the younger student.

Even if one were to assume for the sake of argument that postsecondary education should be an entitlement, however, that assumption does not imply the current low-tuition, direct-grants-to-colleges approach. One could as easily construct an entitlement program based on need-based subsidies to students from poor families, so that all students would be able to afford some decent level of public higher education. But more of this below.

- Subsidies to retain talent in-state. Reducing the price of in-state public postsecondary education, so that it is cheaper than the price of private education or of public education in other states (where the student would be from out of state and pay higher tuition), is similar economically to subsidizing a domestic industry to shelter it from foreign competition or, equivalently, imposing a tariff on foreign competition to induce the consumer to buy at home.

This subsidy-tariff is a very substantial one. In 1985-86, according to NCES, public tuition and fees (in-state) were only $1,044, compared with $5,778 at private colleges—private prices were *more than 5 times higher* than public prices. Worse, the disparity between the two has generally increased over the last 15 years. The private/public price ratio has moved from 4.5 in academic year 1973-74 to almost 6 in 1987-88. And although FTE-weighted figures for in-state versus out-of-state charges are hard to come by, it appears that the aggregate price differential between those two figures is in the same ballpark as the private-public differential.

Just like a tariff, the fact of these imposed price differentials produces baneful results. First, it shelters public institutions from competition from other institutions (private or out of state), allowing inefficient and more-costly-than-necessary provision of education services at any given quality level. Second, it distorts student choice, and can induce students for financial reasons to choose the wrong school for them. Third, although public institutions can generally count on their own state enrollments (as if, in international trade, the countries were dividing up the world market), the sum of their "tariffs" on private higher education puts private education at a distinct and unfair competitive disadvantage. The effect of this tariff is, at least, to distort private-sector pricing (as it struggles to maintain its enrollment share) and, at worst, to threaten its fundamental financial viability.

Interestingly, in the May, 1989 *American Economic Review*, Michael McPherson, Morton Schapiro, and Gordon Winston report just such a distortion for certain private institutions:

> . . . market segmentation is extremely important in understanding college . . . behavior. Poorly endowed private colleges have tuition rates that are within $1,000 or $2,000 of public college tuitions (that are heavily subsidized by state governments), and often compete for similar students. These pressures have probably contributed to keeping tuition increases relatively low at these schools.

There is an additional undesirable result of the public-private price disparity to note. Importing the tariff analogy from its normal realm of trading in private-sector goods and services is somewhat misleading because, for a variety of reasons, the ability of both the public and private higher education sectors to expand enrollment is more limited and certainly less rapid than is the ability of a private firm to expand production.

As the gap between public and private sector prices widens, more and more higher-income students may decide they don't want to pay private prices and will instead attend flagship state institutions. To the extent that flagship enrollments are limited, or capped, rationing crowds out disadvantaged students (who are, on average, less competitive in ability), who are then forced to attend proprietary schools or community colleges (which have much more elastic capacity), or to not attend at all. (Some may be induced to attend private schools with excellent aid packages, but the supply of such opportunities is limited.) A portion of the apparent decline in minority postsecondary enrollment in recent years may be due to such a phenomenon.

Finally, the institutionally tied or in-kind nature of the low-tuition may have the undesirable result of reducing the total amount of higher education provided, relative to use of an "untied" or portable money subsidy. Because the subsidy is not portable (unlike, for example, that of a Pell grant or a Guaranteed Student Loan (GSL)), a student wishing to go elsewhere must give up the tuition subsidy entirely to do so. In addition to distorting his choice, as noted above, if the price differential between a state school and, say, a private college is large enough, he may decide to go to the state school and accept the low-tuition subsidy *even though he would have been willing to spend more of his own money if an alternative eduction at some intermediate price had been available.*

In an intriguing study of this phenomenon in the January/February, 1973 issue of the *Journal of Political Economy*, Sam Peltzman estimated that "for each dollar now spent by government higher-education institutions, total [private] higher-education expenditures are reduced by at least seventeen cents more than they would be if government subsidies were rendered in money," indicating that "the expenditure-restriction effects of existing higher-education subsidies have been substantial."

- Promoting equal opportunity for students from low-income families. Of all the low-tuition arguments, this one is the most uniformly appealing but also, alas, the most seriously misleading and socially divisive.

Low tuition *does* help a student from a middle- or lower-middle-income family who could not afford an unsubsidized price but who can afford the low tuition plus non-tuition costs (books and supplies, transportation, room and board, etc.). But low tuition is *no* help to a poor student who cannot financially get over that remaining-cost threshold. As the Carnegie Commission report rather commonsensically noted, "A policy of low tuition by itself does no good for a student who cannot afford to go to college even at low tuition."

This is scarcely a theoretical curiosity; threshold costs are not trivial. Data for school year 1986-87 from the NCES National Postsecondary Student Aid Survey (NPSAS) indicate that full-time undergraduate students at public institutions, *including* those living at home with their parents, paid an average of about $2,700 in non-tuition, non-fee costs—a hefty sum, indeed, and the more so when added to tuition and fees that averaged about $1,300.

This threshold problem seems to have been ignored until the 1960s for two reasons. First, prior to then, there was no social consensus that significant numbers of poor—as opposed to lower-middle-income and middle-income—children wanted to go to college, were able to go to college, or should be expected to go to college. Thus the impact of any particular financing scheme on this group was of limited policy interest. Second, average real incomes were lower, and relatively wealthy families tended to send their children to private institutions, so that the amount of "untapped" family resources at public institutions was limited. This meant—given the assumption that few poor students were college-bound—that the low-tuition approach was a fairly efficient subsidy scheme: it relieved families of relatively small amounts of otherwise-expected family contributions. As the Carnegie Commission report put it:

> The policy of low tuition or no tuition in public higher education appealed strongly to the founders of state-supported institutions and their . . . legislatures in the nineteenth century. With populations that were predominantly agricultural, and containing relatively few wealthy families and far fewer members of the middle class than is true today, . . . low tuition seemed the most logical way of providing an opportunity for . . . higher education to the relatively small numbers of sons and daughters of farmers and shopkeepers who completed secondary school.

But rising real incomes, changing college attendance patterns among the well-off, and increasing aspirations of and lowered barriers for poor students, made the low-tuition approach obsolete. Rising real incomes and increased public sector attendance by wealthier students combined to make the state subsidy increasingly regressive, as parents escaped making more of the contribution to college costs that their wealth made possible. And, at the other end, more and more students found their college hopes thwarted by the non-tuition threshold.

A low-tuition policy *by itself* does not promote equal opportunity. *Just the opposite.* It provides a subsidy that increases as incomes rise, while providing insufficient assistance to provide the poor with real opportunity. It is manifestly and grossly inequitable.

- Avoiding "sticker shock"; low tuition as the best means politically of obtaining subsidies for poor students. "Sticker shock" is a real problem, particularly for students from low-income families. Indeed, it appears to happen well before the purchase is made: survey results consistently find that families facing college charges in the near future systematically and significantly overestimate the prices they will in fact encounter, leading many prospective college students in such families not even to consider application, or to apply only to lowest-sticker-price schools.

But this fact does not argue for distorting prices (hardly anything does) as much as it does for fuller, more effective publicity about the affordability of college and the availability of financial assistance for those who need it. If higher education did as good a job of publicity in this area as automobile companies or proprietary schools—and I see no particular reason why they can't, and every reason why they should—"sticker shock" would become a thing of the past.

As for arguments that a low-tuition approach is realistic politics, obtaining the greatest benefits possible for poor students (at an admitted price of subsidizing middle- and upper-income students), there are questions of both fact and value. As to facts, there are need-based grant programs in all states—many of them substantial—providing in total over $1.5 billion a year. What is the evidence that it is harder politically, for *each dollar of aid to the poor*, to expand these programs rather than state grants to institutions? (I add the "dollars to the poor" measure because it is important to remember that 100 percent of each need-based dollar goes to poor students, while much less than 100 percent of each untargeted tuition-subsidy dollar does.)

This caveat leads directly to questions of value. As we have seen, low tuition can provide needed and helpful subsidies to middle- and lower-middle-income students. But it does little, by itself, to help the poorest students because they cannot get over the substantial remaining-cost threshold. If this is the case, why is low tuition good politics for the poor? The answer is that it is not.

- Maintaining state control and accountability. Why should there be any significant level of public control, in the sense of detailed legislative or executive branch oversight, at all? The first answer given is to ensure the correct expenditure of state funds appropriated to state institutions. But the logic of the argument is circular: we finance public institutions primarily with state funds to ensure public accountability; the primary purpose of accountability is to ensure that state funds are well spent.

What is more important than the weakness of this argument for direct state financing of institutions are the unfortunate consequences it can have. (Note that these arguments would apply with equal force to similar federal involvement.) State oversight tends to reduce the authority that administrators and faculties of public higher education should have, and, in general, tends to reduce the autonomy that such institutions should enjoy from political intrusion in order to maintain their academic integrity and their responsiveness to changing markets. Further, by making the state rather than the student the primary purchaser of education services, student consumers have both less power to demand improvements in their education and less concern about doing so. In effect, the generosity of the state shelters public-sector institutions from efficiency-creating competition with private colleges and public institutions in other states.

Note, finally, that while I and others can argue that direct financing as a practical matter tends to lead to too-detailed state oversight, the need for *some* level of public control over these public entities does not in any way imply the specific approach of direct financing and low tuitions for all. The issues can and should be separated.

Many would argue, notwithstanding these various criticisms, that the wheel is not broken, and that any major "fix" to current state practice is therefore unnecessary and dangerous, possibly leading to serious disruption of public higher education. As I have tried to suggest above, the wheel *is* broken—analytically, if not yet politically. The current approach is bereft of compelling theoretical or practical rationales and has a large number of distressing consequences for taxpayers, for students (particularly poor students), for private higher education, and for public institutions themselves.

Why then, you may ask, do we not hear more about this matter? If this is such a big problem, why aren't people writing and talking about it more? A fair question, and one whose answer will help us see the "general plan" that is currently in operation.

## The Accidental Conspiracy of Silence

As we have seen, rationales for the low-tuition policy began to break down in the 1960s, as large numbers of poor students found the non-tuition threshold too great an obstacle to higher education. It is not too surprising, then, that significant levels of public discussion about the matter date from that period, with the greatest amount of interesting writing in the late 1960s and early 1970s. What is surprising is that this discussion lasted only a decade, culminating for all practical purposes in 1978 with chapters on state financing by Robert Berdahl and Colin Blaydon in *Public Policy and Private Higher Education*, edited by David Breneman and Chester Finn.

What happened? Why did all the voices fall silent? Why isn't anyone talking about state financing of higher education any more? There seem to be several explanations.

First, among academicians, all the analytic issues were fully explored. Not to put too fine a point on it, the several arguments against a low-tuition policy were so clear and powerful that there was quick academic consensus on what constituted both the problem and the solution. Empirical work that might have been undertaken in support of that consensus went largely undone due to a lack of funding and of good national data sets.

Second, beginning in the early 1980s, the executive branch began to oppose the efforts of Congress to liberalize further federal student-aid programs. The Reagan Administration attempted year after year to reduce student-aid subsidies, a combat that captured the attention of policymakers and unified all sectors of higher education in support of current federal policies. State policy received scant attention.

Third, there unexpectedly turned out to be more than enough students for everybody. Enrollment expanded sharply in the 1960s and 1970s and has held roughly steady since 1980. The forecast of sharp enrollment dips had led to predictions of tension between the public and private sectors over the low prices at publics; when the dip didn't materialize, private colleges found themselves with enough warm bodies to render an argument with the publics unnecessary. The private sector kept quiet (or, more accurately, went quietly in search of increased federal and state aid, and found it on several fronts).

Fourth, the enrollment growth benefitted the public sector greatly, and it expanded to accommodate it. Public colleges, to overstate a bit, were fat and happy. If they chafed at state controls, they were not sufficiently irritated to refuse big increases in aggregate levels of state support, primarily in the form of community college construction and financing. Public higher eduction was content to avoid competition and continue to rely on direct state financing.

Fifth, one by-product of enrollment growth in public colleges is that an increasing percentage of college-educated elites has gone to those colleges. Since these graduates tend to appreciate the subsidies they received as students (or simply, and understandably, believe that the way things were done at their schools is good because they got through successfully), the current system is becoming ever more self-perpetuating because this ever-growing pool of graduates finds it hard to question the traditional approach. It simply seems natural to them.

But these five reasons—even in combination—are not entirely convincing. None of them, after all, addresses the fundamental problem with the low-tuition approach that led to all the analytical fuss of twenty years ago: low tuitions do not help poor students who cannot get over the remaining-cost threshold. The question is: what, if anything, happened in this period to address the problem of providing access for poor students?

To ask the question is to answer it: the enactment of the Pell grant program in 1972. Congress recognized by the early 1970s that the higher education programs it enacted in 1965 (including predecessor programs like National Defense Student Loans incorporated into the act) were not working well enough in providing access for poor students. They intended to remedy this with the quasi-entitlement Pell program, *whose initial award maximum was consciously set at a level sufficient to pay non-tuition costs for a poor student at a public junior college, complementing low-tuition costs created by direct state appropriations.*

One might object that this oversimplifies, that Pell grant enactment had other, equally important objectives, such as achieving aid portability or establishing a program with national guidelines that applied equally to all. I suggest that these are properly viewed as means, not ends; the fundamental goal of Pell was to address the financing problem of low-income students that loan and campus-based programs had failed to address.

The Congress succeeded in this effort—I believe most people would agree—and some form of postsecondary education became affordable for virtually any poor student. To indulge in metaphor, Pell has, indeed, become the *linchpin* of student aid. But it is not, as it is so often incorrectly described, the *cornerstone* of student aid. *The cornerstone—the piece on which Pell rests, the policy to which Pell responds—is direct state aid to public institutions.*

Here we arrive at the great central irony of current student aid policy, of the current "general plan." The Pell program is explicitly (and correctly) intended, explained, and justified as providing needed subsidies to poor students. *Its implicit—but nonetheless real—function, however, is to protect and sustain the obsolete system of direct state aid to public institutions and the unnecessary subsidies to well-off students that that system delivers.* As we shall see below, that unnecessary implicit subsidy to well-off students is *more than twice* the size of direct Pell subsidies provided to poor students. The Pell program may help the poor, but it serves the well-off much more.

One could argue that other forms of title IV aid could just as easily be seen as supporting state low-tuition policies (money is money, after all), and that singling out Pell grants is thus unjustified. I am not persuaded. GSL was never intended as a primary source of aid for low-income students, and should not be thought of as a complement to low tuitions. As for campus-based programs, they were always intended primarily to ameliorate problems of low-income students at high-cost (i.e., private) schools. As annual award data show, a greater share of Pell than of all campus-based aid and of just Supplemental Educational Opportunity Grant (SEOG) aid has historically been channeled to public institutions, and these disparities have increased over time.

In any case, Pell was enacted after all these other programs were in place, presumably to remedy problems they hadn't solved. The key problem was the remaining-cost threshold. The Pell grant program, albeit unwittingly, *is* the villain of the piece.

## Possibilities for a New Debate

Although some of the conditions still exist that led a decade ago to an end of debate about state policies, most don't. National data sets are becoming available that allow simulation and quantitative analysis of the effects of different state and federal policies; one such simulation is described below. Reagan Administration-type challenges to student aid programs do not seem likely under the Bush Administration; analysts and policymakers are now likely to find it easier to look at student aid a bit more dispassionately and critically. Escalating private-sector prices are meeting with rising public resistance, increasing private-sector resentment at public-sector discount pricing.

Finally, Pell no longer, it is alleged, addresses the threshold problem. The claim is that too many poor students are having to borrow to finance their postsecondary educations, even at public colleges (the "grant vs. loans" debate, as it has uninstructively come to be called). The real problem is that Congress has liberalized Pell grant eligibility provisions so much in the last decade, thereby reducing the target efficiency of the program, that increasing the award maximum significantly has become too expensive to afford.

See, in this connection, Tom Mortenson's outraged article on the cost to poor students of Pell liberalizations in the Fall, 1988 issue of the *Journal of Student Financial Aid*. Mortenson documents the expansion of Pell eligibility for higher-income applicants in 1978 and 1986 amendments, consisting of reduced assessments against discretionary income, more liberal contribution offsets for number of children in college, and an exemption for state income taxes paid, *all* of which aid only families with discretionary (i.e., after offset for basic family maintenance costs) income. Poor families have little or no such discretionary income. He summarizes the analysis as follows: "Under the budgetary constraint of limited funding . . ., the additional costs of extended eligibility. . . have been financed by reduced growth in the maximum grant for Pell applicants from poverty backgrounds."

All of these relatively recent changes suggest that the time may be ripe for a reconsideration of the current "general plan."

# An Alternative to Current State Practice

I have hinted at this alternative "general plan" already. In general, the alternative would: 1) eliminate current-fund revenues from direct state aid to institutions (at least for operating costs); 2) allow tuitions to rise to the level needed to replace that lost revenue; and 3) provide sufficient need-based aid, in some appropriate, effective form(s), so that poor students are able to afford a decent postsecondary education. Such a change would respond to virtually all of the problems with current practice:

- By increasing tuition, unnecessary, regressive subsidies to well-off students are eliminated and equity is increased. In addition, substantial savings to state taxpayers are generated by the improved targeting.

- By increasing the price to public-college attenders to a level closer to real costs of their education and to prices at comparable institutions, economic efficiency is increased. Further, this price increase would likely lead to increased consumer pressure to hold down the real costs of providing higher education services, hopefully improving productivity in this sector of the economy.

- By placing more financing responsibility on the student-consumer, along with providing him or her with a greater share of student aid, student mobility and freedom of choice among schools and sectors is increased, increasing student welfare and enhancing competition among schools.

- By replacing direct payments to colleges with payments to students, the independence and autonomy of these colleges would likely increase; they become more sheltered from politics. Note, however, that states would still provide sizeable subsidies for public postsecondary education (in the form of need-based aid) and would retain their legal authority and oversight capability.

- By providing aid to low-income students more efficiently, these students are better able to afford a decent postsecondary education, since the "threshold problem" is addressed directly and explicitly. This is likely to increase low-income enrollment.

The question most often raised about this sort of large-scale change in higher education financing is: what is the net effect on who pays the bill? Unfortunately, until recently, no national data set existed that would allow simulation of such a change. The new National Postsecondary Student Aid Survey (NPSAS) mentioned above, first conducted by NCES in the 1986-87 academic year, does provide a source for answers.

NPSAS is a survey of both aided and unaided students that provides comprehensive data on how higher education is financed from the perspective of the student and his or her family. Since the NPSAS sampling unit is the institution, it is possible to link the student-finance data from it to data from another federal survey on institutional financing. With this integrated data set in hand, it is a relatively easy matter to simulate the costs of the alternative relative to current practice.

NCES has performed such simulations. Specifically, it simulated a situation in which all state and local direct appropriations to public institutions were withdrawn. Public tuition was then raised to a level designed to offset this revenue loss, in essence shifting all of these formerly public costs to students and their parents and producing significant taxpayer savings. (Interestingly, the resulting public tuition levels were still below those of private colleges.) However, using traditional approaches to calculating expected parent and student contributions to college costs, many of these families could not afford the higher tuition level. So, using the new, higher tuition figures in each state, unmet need was calculated for all students and assumed to be met *in entirety* from hypothesized new state grants, producing new taxpayer costs. (If the student had any unmet need before tuitions were increased, this need was met as well.)

Because some students and parents were able to pay some or all of the increased tuition costs, the taxpayer savings from withdrawal of the direct state and local appropriations exceeded the taxpayer costs from new state grants. The result is a *net taxpayer savings of about $8.6 billion*, representing costs shifted from taxpayers to better-off students and their parents who can afford to pay them.

Another way to interpret this result is to say that $8.6 billion was roughly the subsidy provided in 1986-87 to well-off families with dependents in state colleges, because of the current low-tuition approach as opposed to a need-based aid approach. To put this figure in perspective and to justify my assertion above that Pell's implicit subsidy to the wealthy—the $8.6 billion—is more than double its explicit subsidy to the poor, the relevant Pell appropriation figure (FY 1986)—the explicit subsidy—was only $3.6 billion.

It is important to understand what the results of this simulation mean. Assuming student and parent contributions as calculated under the need-analysis methodology then in effect (that is, no "extra" contributions are assumed), this alternative would in award year 1986-87 have generated sufficient savings to finance fully *all* student need at public institutions, finance the Pell grant program *in entirety* (at $3.6 billion), and still provide roughly $5 billion ($8.6 billion less $3.6 billion) left over—$5 billion that could be used to replace loans with grants, to improve remediation and support services to students, to improve instructional quality, and so on.

One caveat is in order. The simulation, unrealistically, assumed no change in total enrollment levels or in the sectoral distribution of enrollment as a result of the simulated finance changes. As noted above, the net effect of these changes on total enrollment is unclear. Because any need "created" by the assumed tuition increase is fully met with grant aid, however, I believe that the results are likely to be only minimally biased by holding enrollment constant.

## Reasons for Federal Involvement

Why hasn't this alternative or some close variant happened? Given the weaknesses shown in most of the arguments for the low-tuition, direct-grant-to-institutions approach and the availability of an alternative that would address the problem of the current approach and, we now see, produce as well multi-billion dollar savings that could be used for other purposes, what prevents change from occurring at the state level?

Besides a possible lack of understanding by policymakers of the issues discussed above, there seem to be three reasons, each of which suggests the need for intervention by an external actor if change is to occur.

First, there is simple inertia. Current practice has been in effect for over a century and is deeply entrenched both institutionally and, as importantly, in the hearts and minds of state residents. And it's the way things are done everywhere—from the perspective of any particular state, that's how *all* the other states do it, creating immense if unspoken pressure to conform. Current practice has become more than a policy; it is a virtually sacrosanct tradition.

Second, there are political difficulties in raising tuitions, even when raises are accompanied by increased need-based aid. Opposition will come from across the political spectrum, even from those who view the low-tuition-for-all approach as the surest way to secure subsidies for poor students. It may be too much politically to expect states to pursue alternatives that require large tuition increases. Especially after a full decade of college price hikes well in excess of inflation, parents and students will be hypersensitive to further price increases.

Third, there is a who-goes-first coordination problem that faces each state. If one state goes first with a large tuition increase, it raises its prices not only relative to the private sector but also relative to all other public colleges in other states—potential enrollment suicide.

The federal government could intervene to overcome this gridlock and inertia, take the heat for tuition increases, and solve the coordination problem by creating positive incentives for all the states to revise their policies at once. But the federal government in turn faces obstacles to action.

There is, most importantly, an appropriate, instinctive aversion to intruding in state prerogatives absent a compelling rationale. There is also no direct political incentive to get involved, since the immediate consequence of the alternative is likely to be screams about higher tuition. Not to mention screams for states to just stay out of their business.

A further obstacle is a broad if unfocused discontent with the need-based, direct aid to students approach. There is a feeling that this system has failed to live up to its promises, has failed to deliver. I do not agree with that assessment, nor do I believe that the facts support it, but the feeling is still real. The charge is that the need-based system has become too complex and administratively inefficient, and that failure of political will and competing resource requirements have reduced grant availability so that poor students are increasingly disadvantaged relative to better-off students. Further reliance on this financing approach would be difficult to sell in many quarters.

A final obstacle is the federal deficit. The overarching deficit problem severely restricts the field for policy initiatives, particularly for options that would solve a problem involving financing by other government levels by "buying it out." And, *under current program rules*, an increase in state tuition levels would lead to immediate increases in Pell and GSL costs. But against these obstacles there are two powerful reasons for federal involvement. First, the current low-tuition/Pell grant "general plan" is not adequate financially for many poor students, in the sense that they have had to borrow ever greater amounts to attend college. Since it has become terribly expensive to raise the Pell award maximum significantly, a new approach other than loans, which are already in disfavor, seems necessary if the government's commitment to the disadvantaged is to be met.

Second, it is the irrationality of current state practice that elicited the ever-more-costly Pell program in the first place—an expensive program whose primary function seems to be to prop up obsolete systems that deliver billions of dollars of unneeded subsidies to well-off students and their parents.

In the midst of current efforts to reduce the federal deficit—I won't dwell on the existence of sizeable state surpluses—it seems highly appropriate for the government to try to reduce its aid costs, or at least constrain their rate of growth, and to do so without reducing opportunities for low-income students. As the NCES simulation results indicate, the alternative plan more than meets that test. Indeed, rationalizing state policies would provide *billions of additional dollars* that could be used for additional need-based aid, increased services to students, and increased expenditures for instructional quality.

## A Policy Proposal

How could the federal government bring about a change in state practice? It does not, after all, control the states; the Secretary of Education is, thankfully, not a Minister of Education. There is little or no legal leverage in this area on state governments or on state colleges and universities.

One possibly would be simply to kick out the Pell prop, reintroducing the problem of low-income student access to higher education that led to Pell in the first place. Only this time, the government would leave the pressure on the states to remedy the problem. The unanswerable objection to this alternative is that many states might do nothing, leading to further injury to the disadvantaged.

A better response recognizes that, in this policy area, effective government leverage with the states, as exemplified in the State Student Incentive Grants (SSIG) program, is positive and financial. *The basic approach in trying to change current state practice must be to use the resource base of current title IV programs to create incentives for change.* The question is whether a program can be crafted that would help foster adoption of the alternative approach.

One strategy is to make the Pell program part of the solution instead of part of the problem: replace the current quasi-entitlement Pell structure of direct federal awards to students with a discretionary grant program to states, which would then, as in the SSIG program, make need-based grant or work-study awards to students at both public and private institutions. The basic proposal is to turn Pell into a very-much-expanded SSIG program, with a few additional bells and whistles.

The fundamental design problems, flowing from our discussion of current state practice, are 1) how to get states to increase tuitions at public colleges, and 2) how to get states to increase programs of need-based assistance that are targeted on those students most in need. As we have seen, increasing tuition while reducing direct state payments to colleges would generate more than enough revenue to finance more need-based aid, but there is no guarantee that states would use the money for this purpose.

Thus dual incentives—aimed at state tuitions and aid to students—appear to be necessary if the interests of low-income students are to be protected. Indeed, the more important incentive may be for expansion of need-based aid—this may be one of those rare cases in which it makes sense to put the cart before the horse.

Incentives for states to increase need-based aid could be created in several ways. One approach would be to make the new federal program a matching grant with a maintenance-of-effort (MOE) requirement, with allowable match limited to dollars above the MOE level. Since current state need-based aid to students is a little over $1.5 billion, compared with a Pell level of about $4.5 billion, even a generous 75/25 federal-state match accompanied by an MOE requirement would lead to a *doubling* in state need-based spending. (If $4.5 billion were 75 percent of the total, the 25 percent state match would be $1.5 billion—a 100 percent increase over the $1.5 billion state "base" subject to MOE requirements.) A 60/40 match—still more generous than the current 50/50 SSIG match—would yield a *tripling* of state need-based aid and equal federal and state efforts.

What if states refused to match? This seems highly unlikely because of the political popularity of aid to higher education (as opposed to AFDC or Medicaid, to mention two other state-match programs). It is hard to believe that states would resist constituent pressures to provide the necessary match here when the matching rate is favorable to the states and, most importantly, the match could be financed without new taxes, given appropriate increases in public tuitions.

If some states did in fact refuse, after due consideration, to provide matching funds, fine. They would forego funds that would be reallocated among participating states. The non-participating states would also experience, I would expect, a rather substantial enrollment decline as many needy students in those states sought lower net prices at schools in participating states. This might induce non-participating states to reconsider.

Another approach, which could be employed in addition to match and MOE requirements, would be to make some portion of the state allocation formula dependent on the relative mixture in each state of grants-to-schools and grants-to-students financing, with more funds going to states with higher amounts or shares of funds being delivered in the form of need-based grants to students. (Presumably, the core of the allocation formula would be to base each state's grant on its share of aggregate measured student need, similar to allocation of campus-based funds among schools.)

What about providing incentives to increase tuitions? This turns out to be the more difficult design question. On the one hand, to maximize the sensitivity of state grant eligibility to changes in tuition, one would like to limit allowable costs (i.e., costs the grant could pay for) to tuitions. This maximizes tuition sensitivity but fails to address the remaining-cost threshold problem. On the other hand, to address the remaining-cost problem, one would limit allowable costs to non-tuition items. This better ensures access for low-income students, but makes grant eligibility highly insensitive to tuition changes.

The trick here seems to be not to try to force one policy instrument (a single definition of allowable costs) to accomplish two objectives (ensure access by overcoming the threshold problem, create incentives for states to increase tuition). Instead, the definition of allowable costs or, equivalently, of the resulting student "need" (allowable cost minus expected family contribution) could be different for each objective. To create incentives for public tuition increases, define aggregate need *for the purpose of determining each state's grant allocation* using a definition of allowable costs limited to tuition and fees. However, to ensure access, define need *for the purpose of determining individual student grant awards* using a definition of allowable costs covering all costs of attendance, including such non-direct education costs as room and board and personal expenses.

Other key provisions of the proposed program:

- State eligibility. States would have to use these funds, along with any state match, in a way that did not discriminate between public and private sectors. Further, states could not discriminate in the pricing of state institutions between in-state and out-of-state students. No tariffs; free trade.

- Need analysis. Federal need analysis provisions would have to be used. Without such uniformity, a state could employ more liberal need analysis criteria to pump up "demonstrated" need and qualify for a larger grant.

- Student eligibility. Only undergraduates would be eligible. Because graduate students, as discussed above, derive almost entirely private benefits from their education, state subsidies to them should be replaced with self-help aid such as loans or work-study.

- Award rules. Some common-sense but non-trivial national award rules would apply. First, to ensure that expected family contributions are not supplanted, awards would not be able to exceed need, equal to the cost of attendance minus the expected family contribution. Second, to ensure horizontal equity, similar students at the same or equal-cost colleges within a state would be eligible for the same award. Third, to ensure vertical equity, at a given college students with more need would have to be eligible for higher awards, but no rule could result in one student, with greater pre-award need than a second student, ending up with less post-award need than the second student.

Other award rules (e.g., maximum and minimum grant, limits on financeable proportion of cost of attendance or of need) would be up to the states, as long as those rules didn't discriminate between the public and private sectors.

This is just the broad outline of a proposal, of course. It is not my intent here to detail a program so much as to illustrate how the current federal resource base could be redeployed to help bring a new "general plan" into being.

## Alternative Proposals

One of life's sad lessons is that the programmatically desirable is rarely the politically achievable. The prudent analyst, therefore, considers intermediate or incremental alternatives that may be more palatable to decisionmakers. Here are some alternative proposals that would at least help move state policy in the right direction. Note that each alternative, unlike the proposal outlined above, would by design require additional federal spending.

- Increase the Pell grant maximum award substantially. This proposal, in essence, says: if the federal government wants to help poor students, then the federal government should do so. Under this analysis, the Pell maximum award is now so low ($2,300) that it is essentially tuition-insensitive for a large number of students; the way to restore tuition sensitivity is to raise the award cap. With tuition sensitivity restored, states that refuse to increase tuitions in essence forego higher Pell awards to students at state colleges. Making this alternative affordable would probably require significant program reforms (e.g., higher contribution assessments on better-off families, tighter eligibility rules) that have been resisted by the Congress in the past.

- Increase the Pell grant maximum award substantially; make any award above the current maximum subject to a 50/50 state match. This proposal is a variant on the preceding one; it would retain Pell as a national program, oblivious of state boundaries, for grants up to the current $2,300 maximum. A higher maximum award would be authorized, however, subject in each state to the availability of a 50 percent state match of incremental award dollars. This alternative is less costly to the federal government but raises a number of unexplored administrative questions.

- Freeze the Pell maximum award where it is, and allocate any new student aid dollars to the SSIG program. This proposal, like the preceding one, would retain current Pell resources under the current Pell design to ensure the national availability of a base access grant for all needy students. Any available new resources, however, would be used to expand the SSIG program, thereby increasing state need-based aid spending and, hopefully, encouraging public tuition increases. An interesting variant would be to limit Pell-eligible costs only to non-tuition items while restricting SSIG-eligible costs only to tuition, thus ensuring both the financing of all or a great portion of threshold costs and the full tuition sensitivity of federal matching dollars at the SSIG margin.

## Conclusion

Complicated policy areas are complicated, and we shouldn't be surprised when simple solutions turn out to be inadequate. Policy arguments that appear convincing turn out on closer inspection to be misleading if not flat-out wrong; well-intentioned programs that appear well designed in fact have perverse consequences that dwarf intended benefits.

In the area of higher education finance, the venerable policy of charging low tuition at state colleges and universities was found to be obsolete, costly, ineffective, inefficient, and inequitable. An alternative plan of charging higher public-sector tuition, accompanied by an expanded program of need-based aid to students, addresses all of the serious problems of current state practice. Unfortunately, a number of obstacles stand in the way of moving to this new approach. Change appears unlikely without federal intervention of some sort. Redesigning and retargeting federal student-aid programs, particularly the Pell program, could create the positive incentives needed for states to move toward the alternative plan.

The important point here is the need to approach setting policy and designing programs, at both the federal and the state levels, in a context that takes into account both federal and state activities. The design of an efficient and effective intergovernmental "general plan" of higher education finance should always be the goal. One can hope that federal policymakers will approach the upcoming reauthorization of the Higher Education Act in such an Jeffersonian spirit.

# FEDERAL PROGRAMS AND POLICIES

# Guaranteed Student Loans:
## Great Success or Dismal Failure? (1991)

DAVID W. BRENEMAN

In 1991/92, Congress will reauthorize the Higher Education Act, extending and modifying programs that provide nearly $20 billion in student financial aid. By far the largest part of this aid is in the form of guaranteed student loans (GSL), which accounted for $12.3 billion in student credit in 1989/90.[1] Given the size of GSL[2] and its controversial history, we can safely predict that much time and energy will be devoted to rethinking the program in an effort to improve it. Already drafts are circulating within the policy community suggesting changes that range from minor tinkering to radical reform. Unlike such drafts, this paper espouses no particular reform package; instead, its purpose is to set a context for the debate by reviewing the history of GSL since its creation in 1965, together with the changes in the economy and in higher education that have occurred over that time. While many of those involved in the policy process are familiar with this history, others are not, and it is hoped that all may benefit from a review that links GSL to changes in the educational and economic context.

## A Vignette

GSL was created in 1965 at the height of Lyndon Johnson's Great Society, with its focus on Civil Rights and the War on Poverty, as well as the Higher Education Act. And yet, in one of the curious anomalies that mark this program, the motives for creating GSL had little to do with increasing educational opportunity or aiding the poor; instead, it was designed by the Treasury Department to head off legislation proposing a tuition tax credit.[3] GSL was established as a loan of convenience to middle class families facing cash-flow problems in meeting college costs. The original program was not meant to be subsidized, its purpose being to save the Treasury money. An ironic—and not particularly uplifting—beginning for a program that was to become the centerpiece of federal student aid!

Given this inauspicious debut, those present at the creation could hardly have imagined that 25 years later more than $102 billion dollars would have been loaned under GSL to 48 million students and their families.[4] It is always hard to know how to evaluate federal domestic programs, for the policy sciences are not immune to considerations of politics and ideology; nonetheless, on the face of it, GSL has played a powerful role in ensuring educational opportunity—both access and choice—for millions of citizens from all walks of life. Whatever its flaws, we should not lose sight of its enormous impact in providing the United States with a more educated populace.

Our vignette would not be complete, however, without an excerpt from Senator Sam Nunn's (D-Ga.) summary comments on the program, delivered in October 1990, following several days of hearings conducted by the Permanent Subcommittee on Investigations of the U.S. Senate:

> More specifically, what we have found is overwhelming evidence that federal student loan programs and, particularly, those involving trade and proprietary schools, are riddled with fraud, waste, abuse, and pervasive patterns of mismanagement. Our investigation was not confined to only one segment of these programs; to the contrary, we have examined every level of participation: schools, accrediting agencies, licensing agencies, lenders, guaranty agencies, secondary markets and, finally, the Department of Education. Unfortunately, over the span of all these hearings, we did not hear of even a single part of the guaranteed student loan program that is working efficiently or effectively.[5]

This sweeping statement is understandable given the focus of the subcommittee on fraud and abuse in GSL. When it is coupled with clear evidence that GSL has helped millions of students attend college, this statement poses the central dilemma for those who must undertake the forthcoming reauthorization: Is GSL the best of programs, or the worst of programs? Or is truth to be found somewhere in between? To gain perspective on these questions it seems wise to turn to history, not only of GSL, but also of the economy and higher education since 1965. We begin, however, with a prior question: Was the decision to finance higher education through student loans a mistake, regardless of the shape of the program?

## Do Student Loans Have a Sound Rationale?

Although there seems to be no evidence linking developments in theoretical economics in the late 1950s-early 1960s with the creation of GSL, nevertheless the work of Theodore Schultz, Gary Becker, and Jacob Mincer did establish the economic rationale for a loan program. These economists developed the theory of human capital, which argues that investment in people, primarily in the form of education but also in health care and related services, yields an economic return in the same way that investment in physical capital does. In a pathbreaking book published in 1964,[6] Gary Becker provided empirical data showing that investment in college produced a private rate of return in excess of 12 percent. However higher education had been viewed in the past, it would never be the same again. College is an investment, and a profitable one at that, for both the individual and society as a whole. Once this point is established, the case for borrowing to finance that investment is clear. The remaining problems are not of principle, but of practice; would-be students can offer no collateral, they have no credit record, they cannot make payments easily while enrolled, they have little current income, and many would simply be poor credit risks if standard measures were applied.

Many of the features of the current GSL program can be seem as responses to these imperfections in the capital market for investment in people. The loan guarantee was a first, and obvious, necessity, acknowledging the reality that default rates in this market would be higher than in conventional lending areas. Payments of interest by the federal government while the student was enrolled (the in-school interest subsidy) was a response to student cash flow problems while enrolled, adding a grant element to the loan.[7] Even the limits placed on borrowing levels reflect, in part, an unwillingness to allow loan finance to replace all other forms of financial support, an early fear of some loan critics.

Writing in the mid-1970s, Jack Morse, former Director of Governmental Relations at the American Council on Education, noted that the loan program ". . . was not devised, it just happened."[8] While not questioning that assessment, it is difficult to see how GSL could have grown as it did had it not successfully addressed the fundamental problems facing student borrowers noted above. Grand alternatives, such as an Educational Loan Bank, would have handled these issues differently, but a Loan Bank was not forthcoming. In any event, the economic logic for student debt was compelling and, in retrospect, it is clear that borrowing for college was bound to grow.

## The World of 1965

From the vantage point of 1991, it is all too easy to forget the enormous changes that have occurred in both higher education and the economy since the creation of GSL. The United States economy in 1965 was strong and not bedeviled by the numerous problems that the next two decades would bring. Inflation was not an issue, unemployment was low, and productivity was growing at an annual rate of 2-1/2–3 percent. Spurred by the coming-of-age of the baby boom generation, and by increased college-going rates, higher education was undergoing an unprecedented expansion in enrollments and in growth of new institutions. Between 1959/60 and 1969/70, total enrollment more than doubled from 3.6 million to 8.0 million, and the number of colleges and universities grew from 2,008 to 2,525.[9] Most of the increase in new institutions occurred in the public community college sector, the numbers rising from 328 in 1959/60 to 634 in 1969/70,[10] an average of one new community college opening every week and a half during that decade.

The student body in 1965 was also considerably different from what it is today. Most students were full-time, residential, and of "traditional" college-age—18 to 24. With only 39 percent of enrollment, women were not represented in proportion to their numbers in the population, nor were black and other minority students. The college-going rate for 18-24 year-olds, while increasing, was still below its level today (25.5 percent in 1967 vs. 30.3 percent in 1988).[11] More than one-third of all students were enrolled in private colleges and universities, the era of open enrollments and equal educational opportunity was only dawning, the War in Vietnam had not yet produced explosions of protest on the campuses, demand for relevance in the curriculum was still a few years away, and higher education was clearly on a cusp between the waning world of the 1950s and the madness of the late 1960s. It is perhaps easy to see how a federally-guaranteed loan of convenience for middle class families could arise at that moment. Events in the balance of the decade and in the early 1970s, however, would being dramatic change to the program.

The original plan for a simple program—unsubsidized, with no income test, and relying on states to guarantee the loans—fell apart almost immediately. While a few states, such as New York, Massachusetts, North Carolina, and Virginia had the necessary machinery in place, many states balked at starting their own guarantee agencies. In a time of rising money costs, banks soon rejected the 6 percent interest rate as unacceptable. Federal reinsurance of state-guaranteed loans was introduced to encourage more states to enter the program, the base interest rate was raised to 7 percent, and 1969 a special allowance of up to three percent was authorized to encourage more banks to lend.[12] A fallback provision for direct federal guarantees in states without a guarantee agency was included, and this program, known as Federally Insured Student Loans (FISL), was administered directly through the Department of Health, Education, and Welfare. Many of the key features of the program today were in place before the 1960s ended, as the initial hope for simplicity gave way to complications that remain to this day a source of confusion and criticism.

## The Troubled 1970s

The United States entered the 1970s a distraught country, increasingly torn over the War in Vietnam, with campuses in revolt, and an economy displaying the early signs of what would come to be called stagflation—high unemployment *and* high inflation. The idealism of the 1960s was still evident in the continued push to expand educational opportunity through open enrollments, more flexible scheduling for part-time and older students, and an emphasis on recruitment of minority students. Both the Carnegie Commission on Higher Education and the "Rivlin Report" called for a new federal program of need-based grants for undergraduate students to achieve these ends.[13] Leaders of higher education were pressing instead for direct federal support of colleges and universities, based in part on the number of needy students enrolled. The stage was set for the most significant of all reauthorizations, the Education Amendments of 1972.[14]

As noted above, the big battle concerned direct aid to students vs. direct aid to institutions, and aid to students won with creation of the Basic Educational Opportunity Grant program (now called Pell Grants). In addition, the older Educational Opportunity Grant program stemming from 1965 was retained as a campus-based program under the label Supplemental Educational Opportunity Grants. Another new program, State Student Incentive Grants, was authorized, designed to provide matching funds for states that started or expanded state scholarship programs. It is fair to describe the Educational Amendments of 1972 as the high-water mark for federal emphasis on grant as opposed to loan support for needy students.

At the same time, the 1972 Amendments did create the Student Loan Marketing Association (Sallie Mae), a government-sponsored private corporation, financed by private capital and designed to provide liquidity and a secondary market for student loans. The purpose in creating Sallie Mae was to ensure a steady flow of private loan capital, for that had been seen as a continuing problem for GSL. Automatic eligibility for loan subsidies based on income was changed to a requirement that financial need be demonstrated. Need-testing, which considers income, assets, and expenses, as opposed to a test of income alone, was introduced because a student from Minnesota had admitted to Congressman Al Quie that he had used proceeds from a GSL to buy a red Corvette.[15] Through these and other amendments, a complicated program was growing ever more complex. Although efforts were being made to expand access to GSL, the emphasis at this time was clearly on student grants for access, with loans occupying a subsidiary role, possibly helping students attend higher-priced colleges or serving as a source of funds for the self-help portion of an aid package.

Another decision with far-reaching consequences embodied in this legislation was the inclusion of proprietary (profit-making) schools in all federal student aid programs. A separate loan program for proprietary school students had originally been established under the National Vocational Student Loan Insurance Act of 1965, but this program was merged with GSL in 1968.[16] The all-inclusive policy of 1972—covering grant, loan, and work-study programs—was symbolized by the change in reference from "higher education" to "postsecondary education" throughout the legislation. With the benefit of hindsight, one can see this decision as among the most significant parts of the bill. By 1988, students attending these profit-making trade and technical schools received 24.4 percent of all Pell Grants and 34.9 percent of all GSLs,[17] an outcome unimaginable in 1972.

The first oil supply shock in 1973 signaled a new era in the economy, and coincided with an abrupt break in the pattern of productivity increases, an ominous sign for future living standards. For reasons not well understood, since 1973 the economy has generated little productivity gain, sharply slowing the growth in real incomes.[18] Not surprisingly, the economy did not function well in other respects, with an unusual combination of both high unemployment and high inflation plaguing it. Wage and price controls were implemented, with mixed results.

Nor were labor markets for the highly educated immune from economic difficulty. After decades of high rates of return to a college education, the economic pay-off fell in the 1970s, in part because of reduced demand for college-educated labor, in part because of large numbers of baby boom cohorts graduating and entering the labor force. A widely-read analysis of these trends bore the disturbing title, *The Over-Educated American*.[19] One result was a massive shift away from majors in the liberal arts and into professional fields; another was a drop in the college-going rate of high school graduates 18-24 years old from 33.2 percent in 1971 to 31.2 percent in 1979.[20] Professional schools of law, business, and medicine experienced heavy enrollment demand, while graduate programs in the Arts and Sciences suffered as the labor market for new Ph.D.s fell into deep decline. Colleges and universities tried to keep up with changing student demands, knowing that the era of dramatic growth was ending, and wanting to be favorably positioned for even tougher times ahead.

Despite this turbulence, total higher education enrollments grew by 45 percent during the decade, rising from 8.0 to 11.6 million.[21] Efforts to increase the number of minority students enrolled met with momentary success in 1976, when the college-going rate of black high school graduates (33.5 percent) slightly exceeded the level of white high school graduates (33.0 percent). Unfortunately, this success was short-lived, with college-going rates for blacks dropping to 28.1 percent in 1988 vs. 38.1 percent for whites.[22] Enrollment of students 30 years of age and older increased significantly between 1970 and 1980 (from 15 to 22 percent of total enrollment), as did that of part-time students (from 32 to 41 percent).[23] The student body was becoming more diverse than in the mid-1960s, with many students claiming financial independence from their families. The growth in number of independent students posed tricky new problems for a student aid system built around the assumption of dependence on family income.

The reauthorization of federal student aid programs in 1976 was largely uneventful, certainly in comparison with that of four years earlier. Most noteworthy from the standpoint of student loans was the decision to phase out the Federally Insured Student Loan program (FISL), run directly by HEW. The ability of HEW to manage a guarantee program directly had been tested and found wanting. As a result, the Education Amendments of 1976 added incentives to ensure that guarantee agencies were established or designated in every state, rendering FISL unnecessary. The system as we know it today was largely in place after the 1976 Amendments.

Normally, there would have been no further legislative changes in the 1970s, but these were far from normal times. Middle income families, feeling the pinch from a sluggish, inflationary economy lacking real income growth, rebelled at rising college costs and need-based student aid programs that excluded their offspring. Extraordinary pressure was brought to bear on Congress to produce some form of student financial aid for the middle class. The first response was that old standby, a tuition tax credit. Once again, the Treasury objected, as did the Office of Management and Budget, and the upshot was the Middle Income Student Assistance Act of 1978.[24] In addition to extending Basic Grants to higher income families, the Act removed the needs test for GSL eligibility. Students from a millionaire's family could now borrow under this subsidized loan program.

It does not take a financial genius to foresee the problem that this legislation would cause, particularly when interest rates soared in the years immediately following. Any family with a student in college would have been irrational not to have borrowed the full amount available, for the subsidy, already attractive, was irresistible in a world of 20 percent interest rates. Not surprisingly, annual loan volume jumped from roughly $1.7 billion in 1977 to nearly $7.2 billion in 1981.[25] With this growth came the surge in costs that has haunted the program ever since, for as currently structured, the federal government bears all of the interest rate risk. In the late 1970s, the special allowance to lenders was allowed to float at 3.5 percent over the 91-day Treasury bill rate, reduced now to 3.25 percent. A program not meant to have large on-budget costs grew suddenly from about $500 million in 1978 to $1.6 billion in 1980 and to over $3 billion in 1982.[26]

Congress acknowledged its mistake officially in 1981 when, under the Gramm-Latta bill, it repealed the open invitation to borrow under GSL. Students from families with incomes under $30,000 (and independent students with low income) remained automatically eligible, but those from families with incomes over $30,000 had to demonstrate financial need.[27] Two new programs—Parent Loans for Undergraduate Students (PLUS) and Supplemental Loans for Students (SLS)—were created to provide what the original 1965 legislation intended—unsubsidized loans to cover cash-flow problems.

# The 1980s: A Decade of Surprises

Higher education entered the 1980s accompanied by a set of studies bearing such titles as: *Surviving the Eighties; The Coming Enrollment Crisis; Challenges of Retrenchment;* and *The Three "Rs" of the Eighties: Reduction, Reallocation, and Retrenchment.* The beginning of a 15-year, 25 percent, decline in the number of 18 year-olds was one reason for a bearish outlook, as were continued problems in the economy—double-digit inflation, high unemployment, supply shocks, and low productivity increases. Furthermore, the mainline economics profession had few clear remedies to propose, for the economic situation defied the Keynesian logic that had guided policy in the post W.W. II years.

Rather than falling, total enrollment between 1980 and 1989 rose from 12.1 to a projected 13.4 million, a 10.7 percent gain.[28] The fact that the reality turned out to be so different from the forecasts has to be attributed primarily to the upsurge in the economy, and secondarily to responses and adaptations of colleges and universities. History's final judgment on the wisdom of Reagan economic policies is not yet in, but a sharp recession triggered by tight monetary policy begun in the waning days of the Carter administration and continued under Reagan broke the back of inflation, and expansionary fiscal policies and supply-side incentives helped to produce one of the longest periods of unbroken growth in modern times. Although federal budget deficits increased sharply, most state governments experienced significant revenue growth, a positive factor for higher education. A redistribution of income toward the wealthy[29] enhanced the fundraising potential of both private and public colleges and universities. In the final analysis, the well-being of higher education is so closely tied to the well-being of the economy that other factors pale by comparison; the only problem for educational planners is that no one can accurately forecast the economy.

Reagan administration domestic policies are well-known enough not to be belabored here. Suffice it to say that budget reduction became the prime focus, with annual proposals from the executive branch calling for draconian cuts in student grant and loan programs. In normal times, Congress would have brushed off such proposals without a glance, but the deepening economic and political problems of deficit budgets forced some accommodation to the administration's requests. Because all of the grant and loan programs except GSL are subject to annual budget action (GSL operates as an entitlement, not subject to direct control through appropriations), the result was predictable; GSL volume grew sharply relative to other forms of aid. In constant 1989 dollars, GSL grew 35 percent between 1980/81 and 1989/90; Pell Grants grew by 28 percent; and Supplemental Grants, State Incentive Grants, College Work-Study, and Direct (Perkins) Loans all declined by amounts ranging from 17 to 32 percent.[30] The budget environmental also led to a series of technical amendments to the Higher Education Act, which were designed to meet targeted savings. These changes resulted in the program becoming much more complex and thus more difficult for lenders, colleges, and guarantors to administer, and for borrowers to understand.

This shift from grants to loans as the main form of federal financial aid to students has been viewed in different ways. Many observers deplore the trend, arguing that we are overloading a general of students with debt, skewing their career, marriage, and child-bearing decisions as a result. Heavy reliance on debt is viewed by many as the wrong way to finance education for low-income students, particularly those who are first-generation college goers and unsure of their academic abilities. Others are incensed at the heavy use of GSL in proprietary schools, where it is alleged that those enrolling often do not realize that the papers they have signed are for a loan. In addition to these specific criticisms, it also seems clear that the shift toward heavier reliance on loans was not a policy that was explicitly debated or intended.

On the positive side, one can ask how much worse the situation would have been had GSL not been available as an entitlement form of aid when other programs (except Pell Grants) were being cut. The fact that the constant dollar value of borrowing increased from $8.9 billion in 1980-81 to $12 billion in 1989-90 meant that millions of students, many of whom would have been shut out without GSL, were able to enroll and pursue postsecondary programs during the decade. In an ideal world, it might have been better to have had some of those GSL costs picked up by grants or other forms of aid, but GSL was there and available. As the renowned philosopher, Woody Allen, has observed, 90 percent of success in life amounts to showing up!

The trend toward a more diverse student body continued in the 1980s, with growing numbers of older, minority, women, and part-time students.[31] Between 1976 and 1988, the proportion of students who were minorities grew from 15.7 to 18.9 percent of total enrollments, although the Black student enrollment share declined from 9.6 to 8.9 percent. Hispanic students increased from 3.6 to 5.4 percent of total, while Asian students increased from 1.8 to 3.9 percent.[32] The proportion of the student body over age 30 grew from 22 percent in 1980 to a projected 28 percent in 1989, while part-time students increased from 41 to a projected 43 percent. Women's share of total enrollment rose from 51 percent in 1980 to a projected 53 percent in 1989.[33]

The proprietary sector also continued to expand, attracting large percentage increases in first-time students. The contrast with traditional higher education is instructive; between 1980 and 1986, colleges and universities experienced a 14 percent drop in first-time freshman enrollments, while proprietary schools experienced a 37 percent gain in first-time students.[34] The explosive growth of proprietary school enrollments, their growing share of both Pell Grants and GSL loan volume, and the high default rates found in many of them, have brought this group of schools under increasing scrutiny during the 1980s. The hearings of the Senate Subcommittee on Investigations cited at the beginning of this paper focussed heavily on proprietary schools, where serious incidents of GSL fraud and abuse have occurred.

## The 1990s: Tension Between Costs and Purposes

Causes of the growing tensions that marked GSL during the past decade and up to the present should be reasonably clear by now. The program's rapid expansion increased the annual budgetary outlays to nearly $4 billion, with large cost exposure to interest rate increases. On-budget costs of the program are essentially made up of three components: the in-school interest subsidy, default payments, and the special allowance to lenders. Defaults and the in-school interest subsidy were running about $1.6 billion each in the late 1980s, while the special allowance was a relatively low $300 million; however, the federal government bears all of the interest rate risk, and special allowance payments would soar in an environment of rising interest rates. In 1982, for example, the special allowance on a much lower loan base totaled $1.5 billion.[35]

In an effort to reduce these costs, numerous proposals were advanced in the 1980s, including eliminating the in-school interest subsidy, raising interest rates to market levels, reducing the yield to lenders, and cutting back on federal payments to guarantee agencies.[36] A number of these proposals were partially adopted, including a five percent origination fee charged to borrowers, an increase in the borrower's interest rate, a reduction in the special allowance payments made to lenders, and the introduction of a "reinsurance fee" charged to guarantors, which effectively reduced the administrative cost allowance paid to guarantors by the federal government. The subsidy remains substantial, however, with estimates ranging between 30 and 44 percent of the face value of the loan.[37]

The educational side of the tension caused by greater reliance on GSL should also be evident from the data on enrollment trends. Loans are no longer being made primarily to middle and upper income young people from sophisticated families to ease the financing of a private college education; many of the borrowers today are high school dropouts from broken families in the ghetto enrolling in profit-making trade or technical schools. Changing populations of both students and schools within the program have inevitably led to increased costs in the form of higher default rates.

Because the issue of default rates has received so much attention in the press and in Congressional hearings, this facet of the program warrants brief discussion. Given that we have found little that is simple about this program, we should not be surprised to learn that complexity also surrounds the measurement of defaults. Currently, there are at least three difference default rates commonly reported: the cumulative rate, the net rate, and the cohort rate. The first two are dollar ratios, while the last is a borrower ratio. The cumulative rate is measured by dividing all claims paid to lenders by the dollar value of all loans that have ever entered repayment status. The net rate reduces the numerator by collections on defaulted loans; it is, therefore, a lower figure and a more meaningful measure of the actual cost of defaults. The cohort rate was established in the Budget Reconciliation Act of 1989 and applies to individual colleges, universities, and trade schools, It is a ratio calculated by dividing the number of students whose loans for attendance at a particular college entered repayment in a given year into the number of those students who defaulted in that or the subsequent year. When default rates by institution are reported in the press, it is this latter rate that is used.

The cumulative default rate nationally climbed from 12.5 percent in 1980 to 16 percent in 1990, although the net default rate has remained at 10 to 11 percent.[38] In a 1988 study of defaulted student loans, the General Accounting Office analyzed more than one million loans that were made in 1983 and were in repayment or default status in 1987. Their findings shed light on the nature of the educational and financial issues caught up in default:

> Overall, 35 percent of vocational students defaulted. This ranged from 13 percent for students dependent upon their families for financial support and whose families had incomes of $30,000 or more, to 53 percent for independent students—with family incomes of less than $10,000. In contrast, the overall default rate for students attending traditional 2- and 4-year schools averaged 12 percent, or about one-third the rate for vocational students. Default rates for students at 2- and 4-year schools ranged from 5 percent for dependent students from families with incomes of 30,000 or more, to 21 percent for independent students with family incomes of less than $10,000.
>
> Overall, almost 33 percent of those who attended school for one year or less defaulted on their loans, ranging from 23 percent for those who attended traditional 2- and 4-year schools to 39 percent for vocational school students. In contrast, 11 percent of borrowers who attended for more than one year defaulted, ranging from 10 percent for those who attended traditional 2- and 4-year schools to 22 percent for vocational school students.[39]

These data paint a clear picture of high default rates arising from high risk students in high risk programs, largely but not exclusively in the proprietary sector. There are two simple solutions to the problem, neither of which has had Congressional support to date: (1) Make grants rather than loans to high risk students, or (2) Eliminate such students and programs from GSL eligibility. The alternatives to such extreme measures are to accept high default rates as a fact of life for this population of students and schools, or to enforce much stronger regulation of those schools and colleges whose students default in large numbers. In the last year or two the hands-off approach of the administration and Congress has begun to change, allowing guarantee agencies to reject loans from schools with excessive default rates. Tighter eligibility standards for participation in GSL may be the most reasonable solution to the default problem.

The in-school interest subsidy and the special allowance are the other two components of cost likely to attract attention in the impending reauthorization. Over the years, many analysts have suggested that an unsubsidized loan program is not only feasible but desirable, with subsidies redirected to grants for the neediest students.[40] The PLUS and SLS programs within GSL already operate without interest subsidy, but in 1989/90 accounted for only 20 percent of loan recipients in GSL, with subsidized Stafford Loans making up the other 80 percent.[41] To move all borrowers onto an unsubsidized basis would require a significant change in repayment schedules if students are to remain in the program. In particular, many students would need to borrow their interest payments while in college, adding the accumulating interest to the principal of the loan. In the absence of subsidy, students would have larger loans upon graduation, and would require longer repayment periods.

The federal payment of in-school interest makes the loans much more valuable to lenders, however, because they can make a single quarterly billing for the loans in their portfolios, thus ensuring cash flow and avoiding the costs of capitalizing interest or billing the borrower for each loan. Any move to end the in-school interest subsidy is likely to unite students and lenders in opposition.

The third large cost of GSL, the special allowance to lenders, is not unrelated to the preceding discussion, for it is a key component of the total yield on loans (currently the 91-day Treasury bill rate, plus 3.25 percent) that makes such lending attractive. The special allowance is one of the costs of keeping private capital flowing into student loans. An appeal of GSL has been that it uses federal funds to leverage commercial capital, so that loan capital is not a federal expense. The outlays shown in each year's budget are the monies to be expended during the fiscal year; for GSL, these include the year's interest subsidy, special allowance, and default payments. By contrast, the costs of a direct loan program would have been the total capital expended on new loans during the fiscal year, along with administrative and support costs. Not surprisingly, under these accounting rules, large-scale direct federal lending to students has rarely been given serious consideration in recent years.

With the passage of credit reform provisions of the Budget Reconciliation Act of 1990, however, new accounting rules provide greater economic rationality in the computation of federal credit programs. The cost of a direct federal loan is no longer calculated to include the loan capital itself; instead, the cost is calculated as the present value of all subsidies, including default payments and administrative costs. For the GSL program, credit reform means that in each fiscal year the cash outlays shown in that year's budget will be the present value of total costs of the loans over their life for the cohort of loans made during the fiscal year, including interest subsidy, special allowance, and default payments.

Credit reform opens up a significant new issue for this reauthorization: Would a program of direct federal lending for student loans, with private lenders no longer supplying the capital, be less costly to the taxpayer than the current system? Could such a system be managed effectively, meeting the needs of students and educational institutions? Would default rates decline, increase, or remain unchanged under whatever new servicing arrangements develop? These and related questions arise now because credit reform places direct federal ending on a comparable budgetary footing with GSL, the difference between them being that Treasury would not have to pay the full 3.25 percent special allowance if it was doing the borrowing and lending directly—although it would have to bear the administrative and servicing costs now borne by lenders and guarantors. At this writing, it is not clear that the ramifications of credit reform for GSL have been thoroughly explored, including the details of how a program of direct federal lending would operate. A central issue is whether loans would continue to be available as an entitlement, or whether loan capital—even though not scored on the budget under credit reform—would be subject to annual appropriation in order to limit the program's volume. The guaranteed availability of loans is critically important to both students and colleges. Because of the claim of potential taxpayer savings from direct federal lending, however, one of the most important tasks of reauthorization will be to examine critically how such a program might work. Two programs that might be studied for lessons learned are the Perkins Loan Program (formerly National Direct Student Loans) and Federally Insured Student Loans (FISL). Their histories suggest Perkins Loans as a better model than FISL, with the caveat that Perkins has not operated as a guaranteed source of loan capital, being subject to annual appropriations.

# A Summing Up

Although no one intended it, GSL has become the largest and most important student aid program in America, providing access to higher education—and choice—for millions of undergraduate and graduate students each year. Borrowing for college and graduate school is increasingly the norm, with most students viewing loans as an investment in themselves and a more productive future. It is not an exaggeration to say that our system of higher education is fully dependent on the existence of credit for college, and few see that emphasis changing.

As our brief historical sketch has shown, GSL is a program that grew like Topsy, seemingly lacking any inner compass, but adapting to the changing needs of students, lenders, and institutions. As such, it is an easy program to criticize, and probably no one starting from scratch would intentionally design what we have today. Nevertheless, for all its flaws, it is now central to the financing of higher education in this country. The interesting question for the reauthorization, therefore, is not whether we can design yet another loan program with ideal characteristics, but whether an already successful program can be rendered even more effective and, at the same time, less costly.

# Notes

1. The College Board, "Trends in Student Aid: 1980 to 1990," (New York: College Entrance Examination Board, 1990), p. 6.

2. GSL currently has four components: Stafford Loans (the original program, renamed in 1988 for retiring Senator Robert T. Stafford (R-Vt.), Supplemental Loans for Students (SLS), PLUS loans to parents, and Consolidation Loans. Unless otherwise noted, in this paper the term GSL refers to all four components.

3. John F. Morse, in Lois D. Rice (ed.), *Student Loans: Problems and Policy Alternatives* (New York: College Entrance Examination Board, 1977), pp. 13-15.

4. U.S. Department of Education, "FY 1989 Guaranteed Student Loan Program Data Book," p. 14.

5. Opening Statement of Senator Sam Nunn, Permanent Subcommittee on Investigations, Hearings on Abuses in Federal Student Aid Programs, United States Senate, October 10, 1990, p. 1.

6. Gary S. Becker, *Human Capital,* (Chicago: the University of Chicago Press, 1964).

7. The in-school interest subsidy was established at the beginning of the program, but was limited to students with adjusted family income of $15,000 or less. Students not eligible for the subsidiary were required to pay accrued interest monthly or quarterly.

8. John F. Morse, in Lois D. Rice (ed.), p. 15.

9. National Center for Education Statistics, *Digest of Education Statistics 1990* (Washington, D.C.: U.S. Department of Education, 1991), p. 166. Subsequently referred to as *Digest.*

10. *Digest,* p. 228.

11. *Digest,* p. 181.

12. John F. Morse in Lois D. Rice (ed.), pp. 13-15, and Lawrence E. Gladieux and Thomas R. Wolanin, *Congress and the Colleges* (Lexington, MA: D.C. Heath and Co., 1976), pp. 58, 61.

13. Carnegie Commission on Higher Education, *Quality and Equality: New Levels of Federal Responsibility for Higher Education* (New York: McGraw-Hill, December 1968); *Revised Recommendations,* June 1970; and *Toward a Long-Range Plan for Federal Financial Support for Higher Education* (Washington, D.C.: U.S. Department of Health, Education, and Welfare, Office of the Assistant Secretary for Planning and Evaluation, 1969).

14. For an excellent study of that legislation, see Lawrence E. Gladieux and Thomas R. Wolanin, *Congress and the Colleges* (Lexington, MA.: D.C. Heath and Co., 1976).

15. Gladieux and Wolanin, p. 198.

16. Charlotte J. Fraas, "Proprietary Schools and Student Financial Aid Programs: Background and Policy Issues," (Washington, D.C.: Congressional Research Service, August 31, 1990), p. 51.

17. U.S. Department of Education, Office of Student Financial Assistance, 1988/89 Pell Grant End of Year Report; FY 1989 GSL Programs Data Book.

18. See Frank Levy, *Dollars and Dreams* (New York: Norton & Company, 1988).

19. Richard B. Freeman, *The Over-Educated American* (New York: Academic Press, 1976).

20. *Digest*, p. 181. These figures were also influenced by the end of the military draft.

21. *Digest*, p. 166.

22. *Digest*, p. 181.

23. *Digest*, p. 169.

24. For a discussion of this episode, see David W. Breneman, "Education," in Joseph A. Pechman (ed.), *Setting National Priorities, the 1979 Budget* (Washington: The Brookings Institution, 1978), pp. 117-125.

25. The College Board, "Trends in Student Aid: 1980 to 1990," pp. 6, 13.

26. David W. Breneman, in Joseph A. Pechman (ed.), p. 112, and The College Board, "Trends in Student Aid: 1980 to 1990," p. 8.

27. Legislation enacted in 1986 extended the requirement of demonstrated financial need to all borrowers regardless of income, with assets also included in the analysis.

28. *Digest*, p. 169

29. See Kevin Phillips, *The Politics of Rich and Poor* (New York: Random House, 1990).

30. The College Board, "Trends in Student Aid: 1980 to 1990," p. 7. It should be noted that the growth of Pell Grants was concentrated in the second half of the decade, and did not begin go make up for the elimination of Social Security Student Benefits and the sharp reduction of Veterans Educational Benefits that occurred in the early 1980s.

31. For a thorough treatment of these trends, see Arthur Levine (ed.), *Shaping Higher Education's Future* (San Francisco: Jossey-Bass, 1989).

32. *Digest*, p. 199.

33. *Digest*, p. 169.

34. *Digest*, p. 176, and *1989/90 Fact Book*, p. 113.

35. Lawrence E. Gladieux (ed.), *Radical Reform or Incremental Change*, p. 5.

36. Arthur Hauptman, "The National Student Loan Bank: Adapting an Old Idea for Future Needs," in Gladieux (ed), *Radical Reform or Incremental Change*, p. 79.

37. Congressional Budget Office, *Student Aid and the Cost of Postsecondary Education*, January 1991, p. 55, and Barry P. Bosworth, Andrew S. Carron, and Elisabeth H. Rhyne, *The Economics of Federal Credit Programs* (Washington: The Brookings Institution, 1987), p. 135.

38. *The Budget for Fiscal Year 1992*, Part Two-18.

39. United States General Accounting Office, "Defaulted Student Loans," GAO/HRD-88-112BR, June 1988, pp. 2-3.

40. For a recent argument of this type, see Barry P. Bosworth, Andrew S. Carron, and Elisabeth H. Rhyne, "Student Loans," in *The Economics of Federal Credit Programs* (Washington: The Brookings Institution, 1987).

41. The College Board, "Trends in Student Aid: 1980 to 1990," p. 10.

# New Ways of Paying for College:
## Should the Federal Government Help? (1991)

JANET S. HANSEN AND LAWRENCE E. GLADIEUX

The late 1980s found the American public deeply concerned about paying for higher education. In recent years, annual increases in college tuitions have exceeded inflation, growth in family and per capita incomes, and returns that savers can reasonably expect to receive on investments. Moreover, federal programs of student financial aid, after undergoing tremendous growth during the 1980s, leveled off just as tuition costs surged upward. Increases in state and institutional student aid could not compensate fully for rising college charges and the declining value of federal awards. Increasingly, student aid took the form of loans, with uncertain implications for young borrowers. Families who were unlikely to qualify on the basis of income for student aid also exhibited growing dismay about how to finance postsecondary education for their children.

What role should the federal government play in addressing these concerns and in fostering the development for new financing mechanisms? We approach these questions by first defining a framework for analyzing the federal responsibility for higher-education finance and then using that framework to describe how the federal government currently carries out its part in sharing the costs of higher education. We review evidence of shifts in financing patterns that have occurred in recent years. We look at the context in which decisions about the federal role will be made, particularly the financial and demographic issues, and conclude by discussing how the federal government should respond to recent concerns about college finance.

## Federal Roles and Responsibilities: A Framework for Analysis

In a recent study of the financing of higher education in five countries, D. Bruce Johnstone observed that the burden of educational costs must be shared by some combination of four partners or sources of revenue: parents, students, taxpayers, and institutions (that is, colleges or universities, which in turn obtain revenues from organized philanthropy and individual donors).[1]

The United States is unusually in the extent to which the burdens of college costs are shared relatively equally among these four sources. Parents are expected to contribute to the expenses of their children's higher education to the extent that they are financially able. Students, too, are expected to work or borrow to meet a share of college costs. These costs include not just living expenses, as in many other countries, but part of the instructional costs of higher education as well. Even public institutions, which receive large subsidies from state taxpayers, charge some tuition, and private institutions are heavily dependent on tuition income. (In other countries, there are often no tuition charges for higher education, or, if they exist, the government pays them for nearly

389

all students, especially citizens.) State and federal taxpayers support both colleges and students, with states taking the lead in institutional support and the federal government providing the lion's share of student financial assistance. Finally, philanthropists and individual donors (both current and past) pick up some of the burden by providing current operating support and by contributing to endowments.

This relatively equal sharing of the burden of paying for college has an important consequence. It helps explain why access to higher education is so much wider in the United States than in many other countries. Countries that do not expect contributions from all the partners educate a substantially smaller proportion of their population.

The burden-sharing model, by highlighting the role of the various partners, refines and amplifies our understanding of the federal government's responsibilities for financing education beyond high school. For the past quarter century, Washington's responsibilities have been seen as essentially twofold: providing financial assistance to students to promote equal educational opportunity and supporting researchers in universities (and the research capacities of universities). This shorthand description of the first responsibility, while accurate as far as it goes, is inadequate to describe the full extent of federal involvement in sharing and adjusting the burden of college costs. Thus, in this essay, we use Johnstone's burden-sharing model both to describe the range of current federal responsibilities and to assess whether Washington should sponsor new financing mechanisms.

Reexamining existing policies in this light, we see that the federal government carries out its part in sharing the costs of higher education by providing grants to students from families without adequate resources to pay for college on their own. Through these outright grants, federal taxpayers pick up part of the burden of paying for college. This need-based assistance is consonant with the widely recognized special responsibility of the federal government for equalizing educational opportunities for disadvantaged, underserved populations.

Washington also uses federal tax dollars to encourage the other partners to pick up their shares of the burden of college expenses. The federal government enables students to invest in their educations through student loans. It is generally agreed that private credit markets will not make loans available to young students with no work experience or credit histories. The federal government overcomes this "market imperfection" by providing loan capital to students through Perkins Loans and, more significantly, by creating access to private credit markets through the default guarantees and loan subsidies of the Stafford Loan (formerly Guaranteed Student Loan) program. It also enhances student employment through the College Work-Student program.

In addition to encouraging the private sector to open credit and employment markets to students, the federal government encourages parents to contribute to the higher education of their children, chiefly through provisions in the income tax code. Parents with a child who is a full-time student at an institution of higher education may continue to declare the child as a dependent for income tax purposes. Savings incentives such as Clifford Trusts were cut back in the 1986 tax return, but tax-advantaged methods of savings still exist, and a new savings incentive, college savings bonds, goes into effect in 1990 (see the discussion below). Parents can also borrow to meet educational expenses through a federally sponsored Parent Loan program that provides only minimal subsidies but carries a guarantee against default and for which there is no income limitation on eligibility.

Last among the federal encouragements, and again working through the tax code, Washington promotes philanthropic donations to colleges and universities by exempting charitable donations from taxable income.

In addition to sharing the burden of paying for college, the federal government provides counseling and academic support services to disadvantaged youth and adults, primarily through the so-called TRIO programs. These services take on added importance in the light of mounting evidence that early academic preparation and motivation are vital adjuncts to financial aid in helping at-risk students navigate successfully through high school and college.

These, in summary, are the ways in which the federal government acts to relieve the burden of postsecondary expenses and to encourage others to bear their share of the costs. Now we ask, Is the pattern of burden sharing among the partners changing in ways that might call for a federal response?

## Signs of Shifting Burdens

Data about who pays how much for higher education in the United States are frustratingly elusive. Nevertheless, a brief look at some basic statistical relationships indicates that the burdens of paying for college have shifted over time.[2] Sometimes these shifts have resulted from explicit policy decisions. Especially in recent years, however, the shifts have occurred more as a result of general economic and fiscal pressures that from a strong desire on the part of policymakers to alter the balance of responsibility for meeting college cost.

Figure 12.1 provides visual evidence of the increasing pressures felt by parents generally in meeting their share of college costs and suggest why rising tuition levels and the affordability of college have become major political issues in the last several years. The chart shows that college costs and median family incomes (both indexed with 1970 levels set equal to 100) rose at about the same rate until about 1980, when family income increases began to lag behind the growth in expenses in all sectors of higher education.

Figures 12.2 and 12.3 (again indexed with 1970 equal to 100) show the growing burden on parents and students—especially those who might consider applying for need-based financial aid. Figure 12.2 shows how college costs have changed relative to grant aid. The grant index was below the index for college costs in the 1960s but then rose noticeably above the cost index in the 1970s, suggesting that the cost burden was shifting from poorer families to the providers of grant assistance. Growth in federal grant programs was largely responsible for this change. In the 1980s, however, the burden of paying for college shifted back toward families, as the grant index fell relative to the costs of attendance. Here, as in the previous decade, changes in federal grant aid were responsible. Although state and institutional grants grew in the 1980s, as federal grants languished, they did not make up for the losses in aid from Washington.

Figure 12.3 provides another view of the shifting burden, focusing on student loans. Parallel growth in the indexes for loan availability and college costs in the early and middle 1970s suggests that the student share of college expenses was generally stable. Then, in the late 1970s, after passage of the Middle Income Student Assistance Act, the loan index started growing much faster than the cost index. Grant aid had not yet begun to slow, so the immediate effect of increased student borrowing may have been to reduce the burden on parents, at least for a few years. More recently, however, grant aid fell behind the growth in college costs, and new eligibility restrictions in the Stafford Student Loan program limited its use as a replacement for the parental contribution. Hence, the growing disparity between the loan and cost indexes indicates that students, particularly at lower income levels, are assuming more responsibility for paying college bills.

The graphic data, although oversimplified, support anecdotal evidence about the shifting burdens of college expenses over the past quarter century. Costs are outstripping income increases for virtually all families. Lower-income families who could qualify on the basis of financial need found their burdens lightened in the 1970s, as the federal government picked up a larger share. In the 1980s, however, the burden shifted back again toward parents and students, with the latter borrowing ever more heavily to make up for both slow-growing family incomes and grant aid that has failed to keep up with rising college costs. Given these changes, should the federal government respond, and how?

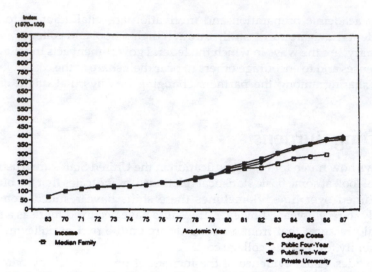

**Figure 12.1  Changes in Median Family Income and College Costs: 1963 to 1987**

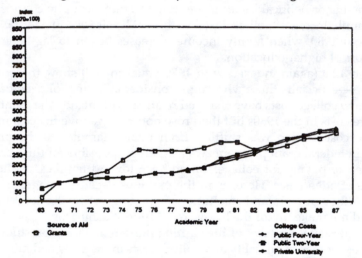

**Figure 12.2  Changes in Grants and College Costs: 1963 to 1987**

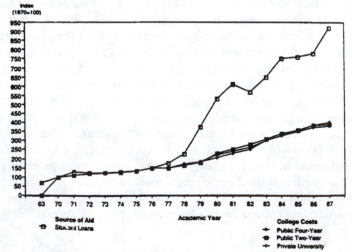

**Figure 12.3  Changes in Student Loans and College Costs: 1963 to 1987**

# A Context for Decision: Deficits and Demography

Decisions about the appropriate federal role in financing higher education will not be made in a vacuum. Our views about what Washington should and should not do are strongly influenced by two critical features of the current and foreseeable national landscape: the huge federal budget deficit and the changing characteristics of the American population.

The deficit will be the overwhelming fact of political life in the period ahead. Although largely ignored during the recent presidential campaign, it surfaced as a major concern as early as the interregnum between the Reagan and Bush administrations. President Bush vows to resist any tax increase or cuts in defense and social security programs and promises to reduce the deficit through a "flexible freeze" on most other federal spending and through growth in the economy at large. Legislators from both parties doubt that meaningful reductions in the deficit can be made in such relatively painless ways. Thus, the stage is set for a major confrontation on the nation's economic future.

Our own view is that however these issues are resolved, little or no new money is likely to be available for federal education programs any time soon, and it is possible that significant cutbacks could occur. To fulfill his promise of being an "education president," George Bush may try to increase spending in this area at the expense of other social programs. Congress has demonstrated over the past eight years its support for education in general and for student assistance programs in particular, as it resisted calls for massive cutbacks from the Reagan administration. But this executive and congressional goodwill will be increasingly difficult to translate into real growth in federal education programs.

Even if new monies become available, moreover, important trade-offs will have to be addressed. Should elementary and secondary education or preschool education programs be given a higher priority for additional funding than college programs? Will uncontrollable costs in the Stafford Loan program eat into the appropriations available for financial assistance in the form of grants? What will happen to need-based financial aid programs if eligibility for federal funds is broadened to families who do not now qualify for federal assistance on the basis of financial need?

This latter question takes on special urgency in light of the demographic changes under way in the United States. Families are increasingly headed by single parents, often women, whose economic prospects are limited. Even now, a fifth of American children live in poverty. Moreover, minority-group children, who will make up a third of the U.S. school-age population by the turn of the century, often are precisely those who need educational assistance most: they drop out of high school at higher rates and enroll in college at noticeably lower rates.

Arguments about equity aside, it is increasingly apparent that the nation can no longer afford to overlook these human resources. If labor market needs are to be met and economic growth encouraged, more of the children from traditionally underserved groups must graduate from high school and participate in postsecondary education. Adequate financial aid alone will not make this happen, but insufficient financial resources will constitute a serious barrier to equal participation by these groups. In an era of sharp fiscal constraint, this fact, too, greatly influences our judgments about how limited resources should be allocated.

# Old Roles and New Responsibilities

Having looked at the current federal role in postsecondary finance, at evidence of shifting financial burdens, and at the context in which decisions about future federal responsibilities must be made, we now come back to our initial questions: What should Washington's response to be current concerns about financing higher education? What responsibility should the federal government take for new financing mechanisms? We present our answers within the framework of the burden-sharing model, examining whether, and how, the federal government should pick up more of the burden directly from families, encourage and assist parents and students with their shares, or both.

The most widely discussed proposals for new financing options, savings plans and tuition futures, emphasize assisting parents with their responsibilities. Most propose some kind of subsidy, usually a tax benefit, to create an incentive for parents to plan ahead and save for college. Almost certainly, such plans would provide most of their benefits to middle- and upper-income families, who can afford to save for their children's educations.

On the assumption that new federal resources will be scarce, we give a higher priority to improving the buying power of direct grant assistance for the financially needy than to providing tax benefits for the middle class. Demographic changes suggest that programs such as Pell Grants will come under increasing pressure. The need for grant aid will certainly grow to the extent that the nation is successful in efforts to encourage more students from traditionally disadvantaged backgrounds to continue their educations. We suspect that it will be all Washington can do to keep the buying power of Pell Grants at current levels. Should new money unexpectedly be available, however, we think that providing more of a guarantee of assistance (for example, by making Pell Grants a true entitlement at some higher level than today) for students whose capacity to bear the burden of college costs is limited is more important than providing federal incentives to families who have the capacity, if not the will, to pay for college.

In other words, we do not favor a major federal investment in savings and tuition-futures plans. Congress's recent enactment of a limited college savings bond plan goes as far as we think Washington should go in this direction. This plan, scheduled to go into effect in 1990, will allow parents a tax exemption for the proceeds of U.S. savings bonds if the bonds are used to pay for tuition and required fees (net of financial aid). Tax benefits are to be phased out, beginning with families with adjusted gross incomes of $60,000 and disappearing entirely at $90,000 (with income limits each year adjusted for inflation). The rules about who can benefit from the tax exemption and what education expenses are eligible are carefully circumscribed to keep federal subsidies limited.

The availability of these education savings bonds, coupled with the college savings plans adopted in a number of states, should satisfy the need for explicit public policies aimed at encouraging family savings for college. The task now is to popularize the program and maximize its potential as a catalyst for precollege saving and investment. We do not, however, favor further expansion of such federal subsidies, either through wider eligibility for savings bonds or through a federal tuition-futures plan.

The concept of tuition futures pioneered in Michigan and under development in eight other states, has proven far more problematic that its sponsors originally indicated. The financial risks to government are uncertain and potentially high. The strongest argument for a federal plan, to avoid the balkanization of higher education that might result from multiple state plans, has lost force as states themselves have become warier of the concept and more inclined to enact savings plans instead.

Our comments to this point have reflected our preference for emphasizing current federal responsibilities for the financially needy rather than creating new financing mechanisms. In a similar vein, we think that attention should be paid to the way Washington encourages students to bear their share of the college cost burden, especially through student loans. The participation of students as partners in financing is crucial in maintaining access to higher education. Federal student loan programs (under which students now borrow $11 billion annually), together with the much smaller but important federal support for work-study, facilitate student "self-help" in the college financing equation. We have seen that the student-borne share of costs is growing, and we are concerned that the emphasis on loans versus grants has gone too far, especially for disadvantaged and low-income students. Yet there seems little likelihood that borrowing levels can be reduced in the foreseeable future; in fact, they are likely to grow.

We would therefore like to see some kind for insurance built into student loan programs to protect borrowers against the risk of low future earnings. The theory behind student loans is that education is in part an economic investment and that loans enable students to invest in themselves and the greater economic rewards that their education will bring. Although these assumptions undoubtedly hold true in general, there will always be individuals whose education does not pay off in the expected economic ways. Student repayment provisions could be adjusted to protect borrowers against this risk. This idea can only be suggested, not fully explored, here. But we suggest that this area would be a more appropriate target for federal subsidization if funds were available than some of the new financing tools under discussion.

Also important, but not possible to explore adequately here, is the larger issue of the structure and uncontrollable expense built into the federal student loan system. The government's cost exposure in Stafford Loans makes this program a shaky foundation for student assistance—and erodes support for grant programs. Rising default claims projected for the year ahead, combined with higher payments to lenders if interest rates rise, could generate another crisis-driven search for cost savings and could destabilize program operations, as students and institutions learned in the early 1980s. For the long haul, whether through restructuring or tightening of the current system, federal policymakers should consider reducing loan subsidies that are not directed toward needy students and stabilizing the long-term obligations that the government incurs when it guarantees loans to students and parents.

Having emphasized our judgment that the appropriate federal role in financing college should remain primarily the traditional one of lightening the burden to families of limited financial means, we turn now to proposals to reform dramatically the way in which grant subsidies to such families are given. Particularly, we refer to the proposals recently advanced by the Democratic Leadership Council and by Professor Charles Moskos in a report for the Twentieth-Century Fund to make federal student assistance contingent on participation in community or national service activities.[3] We cannot give our full analysis here, but we are wary of such proposals. Although advocates of national service may have worthy goals, a national service plan, in our view, cannot replace existing student aid programs. A critical roadblock is fiscal. Students who are not needy and those who are—who currently receive need-based financial assistance—cannot both be accommodated within the plans as currently described, yet the enlarged program that would be required by a "voluntary" plan open to all cannot be supported by the funds currently devoted to student aid. Moreover, some analysts have argued that educational opportunity would be restricted, rather than expanded, by a system that tied federal education benefits to mandatory national service.[4] There may be a role for the federal government in supporting some kind of smaller, more experimental undertaking, perhaps using education assistance as an incentive but not involving wholesale replacement of the existing student aid system. Here again, though, questions of budgetary trade-offs must be addressed head-on.

Finally, the federal government should look beyond narrow financing mechanisms as it assesses how best to carry out its responsibility to equalize educational opportunity in an era of limited resources and demographic change. So-called guaranteed-access programs, such as Eugene Lang's I Have a Dream Foundation model and the newly enacted New York State Liberty Scholarship program, include assurances of adequate financing for college as an incentive for young people to stay in school and acquire the proper academic preparation for higher education. But they also recognize the importance of individual guidance, tutoring, and encouragement in reaching at-risk youth. Perhaps the best and most equitable use of incremental federal funds in an era of fiscal constraint would be to support the federal TRIO programs, which bring such services to educationally and economically disadvantaged students.

# Notes

1. D. Bruce Johnstone, *Sharing the Costs of Higher Education: Student Financial Assistance in the United Kingdom, the Federal Republic of Germany, France, Sweden, and the United States* (New York: College Entrance Examination Board, 1986).

2. Data in all three charts are taken from College Board, *Trends in Student Aid,* various editions (New York: College Entrance Examination Board, 1983-1988).

3. Democratic Leadership Council, *Citizenship and National Service: A Blueprint for Civic Enterprise* (Washington, D.C.: DLC, 1988); Charles C. Moskos, *A Call to Service: National Service for Country and Community* (New York: Free Press, 1988).

4. See, for example, Richard Danzig and Peter Szanton, *National Service: What Would it Mean?* (Lexington, Mass.: Heath, 1986).

# A Budget Cure-All (1992)

## Robert B. Reich

At least credit Richard Darman for creative accounting in managing to squeeze the new White House budget into the spending categories and constraints of the 1990 budget agreement. But his efforts were doomed from the start; the agreement is obsolete, and everyone knows it. It was cobbled together before the cold war ended and before the recession started. The question is: What's to replace it?

The real scandal of the budget that President Bush sent to the Hill was not so much the expected deficit in 1993 ($351.9 billion), but the paltry sum that the White House expected to invest in the future ($133.1 billion). This isn't new, of course. For years federal borrowing has exceeded federal investment. To solve the problem, Democrats have talked about creating a "capital" budget or an "investment" budget, designed to make clear how much the nation is investing in the future. Bill Clinton has called for an investment budget. (I'm helping him in the campaign, but he shouldn't be burdened by the following musings.) Yet no one has ever provided a detailed blueprint. How might it look? A sane budget would be one whose spending categories and constraints, and whose sources of revenue, are logically connected to the generation of Americans that benefits from them. In particular: a budget that reveals how much we're borrowing from the future compared with how much we're investing in the future.

Begin with the basics. Ideally, any federal budget should be divided into three categories corresponding to different time-dimensions of government responsibility: 1. Past obligations to a previous generation of workers, to guarantee them a minimally decent standard of living. Included here would be most spending for Social Security and Medicare. 2. Present obligations to ourselves, to ensure that all Americans enjoy a safe, secure, and minimally decent standard of living. This category would include spending on welfare, criminal justice, and defense. 3. And future obligations to coming generations, to ensure they have the capacity to generate a good standard of living. This means spending on education, training, civilian research and development, and infrastructure.

Although the American population obviously doesn't divide neatly into separate generations, it's still useful to think about the needs of Americans ten or fifteen years from now as separate from their needs today and from the needs of people no longer able to support themselves. For example, revenues to support the retirement of the past generation of workers should come from workers' (and employers') contributions. People can debate about how progressive this system should be—what payments should be required of workers with differing incomes and what benefits should go to retirees of different wealth. And they can debate about whether (and to what extent) the system should be financed on a pay-as-you-go basis, with current workers picking up the tab for retirees. But the system should finance itself—and be separated from the rest of the federal budget. No dipping into the other categories. Likewise, neither of the other two categories should be able to raid *it* for funds.

The second budget category—to maintain the *current* safety, security, minimal living standard of Americans—is logically financed through taxes on current incomes (including investment income). Here again, we can debate how progressive this tax should be, but the principle is the same: revenues to pay for the current living expenses of Americans should come from the current incomes of Americans. There's no reason why one generation should be able to borrow from future generations to finance its own standard of living. Nor should they tap into their own retirement savings (by, say, using surpluses in the Social Security trust fund to offset current budget deficits).

Thus, so long as marginal tax rates don't change from year to year, spending in this second category cannot grow faster than improvements in the incomes of Americans. This seem logical. How can we expect to consume collectively, at a faster rate than we produce? (One small wrinkle: to enable the government to provide extra relief during troughs when incomes stagnate or dip, and to cool the economy during recoveries when incomes surge, the yearly spending cap might be based on a rolling average of national income gains during preceding years.)

The third and last category—investments in the *future* capacities of Americans to produce wealth—is appropriately financed through borrowing that must be repaid in the future, when the nation reaps the benefits of these investments. Such investments are subject to a different constraint than is spending in the other two categories. No self-respecting business executive fails to borrow money if the expected return is much higher than the borrowing costs. Similarly, so long as the likely returns to the nation's future productivity are high enough, borrowing in order to finance such investments makes sense regardless of the amount. In fact it would be irresponsible *not* to do so. Borrowing and investing shouldn't stop until the cost of additional borrowing is no longer worth it—given the expected return on such investments relative to what private investors could get on *their* borrowings.

So much for theory. This sort of budget is logical, and the public can readily understand it. But how would it work in practice? There are at least four big obstacles.

*What's an investment?* The first and most obvious problem is to decide what programs fit into which category. Since no one wants to have his favorite government program vulnerable to the spending constraints of either the first or the second categories, there's likely to be a stampede into Category Three. After all, the definition of an "investment" is hardly airtight. And when politics tangles with epistemology, politics almost always wins.

But this problem may not be insurmountable. Last Sunday afternoon, with nothing better to do now that football season is behind us, I took out a copy of the White House's new budget proposal and ticked off the items that seemed to me to be justly included within each of the three categories. Category One was fairly straightforward: Social Security and Medicare, including some additional retirement programs like veterans' benefits. But how to distinguish between Categories Two and Three—spending for today and investments for tomorrow? It wasn't nearly as difficult as I imagined. I simply asked myself whether there was any reason to believe that the program would pay off in the form of improved national productivity a decade from now.

Who's to say that my assumptions would be widely shared? Luckily, I had a test. Officials in the White House's Office of Management and Budget undertake a similar exercise each year (presumably with more thought and care than I gave to mine) as part of the budget presentation. The analysis is buried in the back of the budget document. I found their "investment" calculations for FY1993 and compared them with the ones I'd done.

The two sets of calculations were remarkably alike. For example, I put $13.1 billion of 1993s science, space and technology programs into my Category Three; OM dubs $10 billion of these programs "investments." I put $26.5 billion of 1993s transportation spending into the category; OMB puts $24.8 billion. I placed $31 billion of education, training, and social services into it; OMB's number is $37.6 billion. For a few programs, OMB is more generous: I didn't put a dime of federal spending on income security, justice, veteran's benefits, housing credits, or general government revenues into my Category Three; OMB tosses over $9 billion worth of these programs into it. There was one big difference. I nominated $20.3 billion worth of programs related to the health and nutrition of children; OMB includes just $10.1 billion of these. Would my number have been closer to theirs if I had more information about these programs? Would theirs be closer to mine if I had presented my arguments to them? Maybe.

The two sets of calculations totaled up about the same. Under my calculation, in 1993 the White House is planning to invest $124.2 billion in the nation's future—or about 8.2 percent of what it plans to spend that year. OMB's total is $133.1 billion—or 8.8 percent. Either way, a paltry portion of the federal budget.

My point is that there may not be *that* much disagreement over which programs fall into which budget category. Politicians will try to shoehorn their favorites into the investment category, of course. But the danger can be minimized (although not eliminated) by allowing into Category Three only programs that have been so designated by the White House with the concurrence of majorities of the House and Senate Budget Committees.

*How to measure the returns on public investment?* It's hard enough to predict the benefits of private investments, which at least show up on the bottom line. It's nearly impossible to predict how this or that program will affect the nation's capacity to generate wealth in the future. There are simply too many factors to take into account—and no clear-cut way to measure improvements in national productivity anyway. For year academics have been engaged in lively debates (lively, that is, for academics) over the value of public investments—and even livelier ones about the outcome of investments in education. Of course, some estimates are broadly agreed upon, such as those showing that children in Head Start are far more likely than other poor children to complete their educations and be self-supporting and law-abiding in later life. It's just that, by their very nature, attempts to measure the future productivity gains of public investments are imprecise and subject to debate.

And yet, these controversies notwithstanding, there's a remarkable degree of agreement on the rough *magnitudes* of the returns on such public investments. Almost every economist and policy wonk who has studied the subject has concluded that the United States has woefully underinvested in roads, bridges, sewer systems, worker training, child nutrition, child immunization, civilian research and development, and a host of other areas where the private sector can't be expected to do it all. Almost everyone recognizes that other nations, notably Japan and Germany, are investment far more, as a percentage of their national products, that we are.

Moreover, no one disputes the fact that federal spending on such investments has been declining as a percentage of GNP. Infrastructure spending dropped from 1.14 percent of GNP in 1980 to 0.75 in 1990. Spending on education dropped from 0.51 percent to 0.37 percent. Non-defense research and development, from 0.42 percent to 0.31 percent. So even though *exact* measures are impossible, it is possible to set broad goals for public investment over, say, the next decade.

*How to draw down the debt?* By 1994, according to Congressional Budget Office projections, the accumulated federal debt will total over two-thirds of the year's gross national product. So even if we raised taxes to cover current expenditures (Category Two), any additional borrowing to finance investments in future productivity (Category Three) would cause yearly interest charges to grow almost as large as those on my Visa bill.

That's why we also need a rule to draw down the accumulated debt as the national economy begins to grow faster—reaping the benefits of these new investments. Again, it's only logical that Americans in the future, who will enjoy a higher standard of living because of investments made today, should pay not only the interest on the debt but also bear some responsibility for reducing it. One possibility: an income tax surcharge that's triggered in any year when the economy grows faster than, say, 4 percent—the proceeds of which would be applied solely to debt reduction.

*How to get from here to there?* Even if we could agree on these categories and principles, we'd still have to face today's mess. Right now, Categories One and Three are being used to bail out Category

Two: that is, the Social Security surplus that's been created to help finance baby-boomer retirees is being used instead to offset the budget deficit, *and* most of the remaining deficit is being used to finance present living standards rather than to invest in the future. So we need a plan that over some period of years will raise tax revenues and reduce Category Two consumption until they become equal. Simultaneously, we have to reduce borrowing and increase Category Three investments until *they're* equal.

Can we do it? Seems awfully difficult. But remember that as public investment increases, we should expect the entire economy to grow faster. That means tax revenues will grow as well. I'm not suggesting a painless transition—only that one of the real objectives is to foster economic growth. And to the extent that we *invest* for the future, it will be that much easier to fulfill our current needs as they arise. But why should the public buy it? Why won't we (and our representatives in Washington) continue to prefer borrowing from the future to finance current consumption, without investing in the future? These are rhetorical questions, of course, to which most Washington-watchers have every right to give a cynical answer. I can offer only one small reason for hope. Most adult Americans *do* have children, and are at least a bit concerned about how their children will live. At best, a budget like the one I'm suggesting may handicap our efforts to deny that we're treating them far worse, collectively, than we would ever dream of treating them individually.

# CHANGING
# PUBLIC ATTITUDES

# Hostility, Maximization, and the Public Trust:
## Economics and Higher Education (1992)

GORDON C. WINSTON

There's a lot of hostility out there toward U.S. higher education. Although it appears to be spread around evenly, I want to concentrate on the hostility that's focused disproportionately on the private, "elite" part of higher education—like Stanford, Swarthmore, Harvard, and Wellesley—focused on tuition levels, research practices, problems with the government on indirect cost recovery, not to mention political correctness. There are lots of ways that public institutions share the problem, but—keeping in mind that we're all in this together—they're not what I'll concentrate on here. The elite schools have a special visibility and, therefore, responsibility that deserves special attention.

If there's hostility out there, there seems also to be an equal measure of bafflement within higher education about what it's all about. There's a strong sense that we're being misunderstood. In a panel at Williams back in October where the presidents of Amherst, Wesleyan, and Williams discussed the current state of higher education, they were asked, "Isn't it possible that there's some real *justification* for the anger and resentment we're collectively feeling?" Two out of three of their answers were clearly "No," while the third confessed to a worry that maybe humanities faculties have become so caught up in their own battles and have drifted so far into exotic private vocabularies of discourse theories and deconstruction—that surely sound arcane and very "academic," in the pejorative sense, to the workers and legislators and businessmen of the outside world—that what we're seeing is a sense of irritation at that sort of irrelevance. One or two members of the faculty — audience suggested other alternatives—that we've bowed to the pressures of the politically correct or we're eliminated the passion from our students—but it's fair to say that the session ended pretty much as it had started, with a recognition that those people out there seem pretty angry at us in here, but without any real sense of *why* they're angry.

## Economic Theory

I'd like to introduce some ideas into this discussion that come from what may seem an unlikely place: economic theory developed in the past two or three decades, ideas that can take us some distance toward understanding what's going on in higher education and the nation's attitudes toward it, and what we can do about it. The message, though it comes from the dismal science, has a good measure of optimism in it. However glum it might sound to say that—in part, at least—

we've brought this on ourselves, the implication is that we can likely do something about it. If we turned it on, maybe we can turn it off.

Let me begin with markets, as economists so often do. An apology is due those who find it aesthetically offensive to hear someone talk of a college as a "firm" and our students as the "customers who buy what we sell," but it might be useful to follow Coleridge's advice and willingly suspend disbelief until you see what insights can come from that sort of talk and set of analogies. I think you'll find that seeing higher education as an "industry" with a "market" takes us in useful directions you might not have expected. To those who are comfortable with the analogy—economists and their fellow travelers—an apology is also due because what follows may sometimes sound like a paean with a title like "In Praise of Inefficiency and Sloth." That's not, in fact, where it's going, so you, too, should be patient and see where it all comes out.

There's a market for higher education: colleges and universities produce educational services and sell them to students as our customers. Economists have spent a lot of time and energy on one question very central to understanding social behavior: "When do markets work and when do they fail to work?" If "they work," it means that markets organize transactions between people to give them what they want most, recognizing that they can't have it all. You might not guess that economists worry a lot about where markets work and where they fail, if you listen to the ideological lyricism about markets we're hearing from politicians and ex-Soviet experts on CNN. It sounds there like markets are the magic solution to all the world's problems because they work all the time in all circumstances and for all transactions. But, luckily, economics is very aware that markets are more complicated than that, that you can't analyze social behavior with an acoustic guitar or a public relations firm.

The relevant piece of economic theory is the theory of asymmetric information. It's pretty simple. It says that free, competitive markets can work very well if everybody knows what they're getting into—if everyone knows everything relevant about what they're buying and what they're selling; if buyers and sellers are both well informed about "the product." But when information is asymmetric, one side of the market knows what's being traded while the other side doesn't. The Berkeley economist who first articulated this, George Akerlof, illustrated it with used cars where the seller knows whether he's selling a lemon but the buyer doesn't—"the lemon principle." Akerlof showed that, under quite plausible circumstances, asymmetric information can cause a market to break down entirely: there will be buyers who want to buy a car at a price the seller's willing to accept, but nothing happens; there's no market transaction and neither party gets what he wants.

What screws things up is the combination of *maximization* of self-interest and *asymmetric information* that, together, make the potential buyer of that used car vulnerable. A profit-maximizing used car salesman—and we always assume he is—not only can be opportunistic when faced with a naive, uninformed buyer, *has to be* opportunistic, or he's not actually maximizing his own self-interest.

One solution is obvious. Akerlof showed that, if everybody were honest about the product's quality—if used car salesmen could always be counted on to tell you what's wrong with the car, whether it is a lemon, so they could always be trusted—then the market would work, even where asymmetric information is inherent. People who want to buy cars buy them, and people who want to sell cars can sell them—all at prices both find acceptable. In place of maximization, then, each party to the deal would instead be following a rule of honesty that justified trust.

Markets with asymmetric information can usefully be called "trust markets." They work best when the participants in those markets temper their desires for maximum personal gain with a measure of a self-denial that will justify the other guy's trust. They substitute a self-restraining ethic for a maximizing ethic. Maximization—self-serving behavior—and trust are in conflict in this sort of market. If you maximize, you exploit weakness; if you respect that weakness, you don't maximize.

Of course, honesty isn't the only way to address the problem. Legislators keep hoping that laws can be made stringent and specific enough to keep people from exploiting each others' vulnerability in these kinds of markets—i.e., laws on fraud and malpractice and insider trading. And certainly those laws do have an effect. But, to sound an economist theme again, that route is a good deal more cumbersome and expensive than honesty is—surveillance and enforcement are costly—even on that simple ground, we're better off if there's trust.

## Trust Markets

That's enough of abstraction. Are there lots of actual and important markets with asymmetric information? Obviously, there are. It's certainly the essence of the market for medical care. You go to the doctor because he knows more about the medical service he's selling you than you do—otherwise, you wouldn't be there. As an aside: what we're seeing in U.S. health care is a far a deeper revolution than is normally acknowledged, as we watch an important trust market be transformed into a market where maximization is the accepted ethic. Technology is driving that transformation and can't be wished away, but that is a reason to be more, not less, nervous about the change of market character in medicine. Other notable trust markets include nursery schools and day care, where the customers (children) aren't competent to understand what's actually being "sold" to them—done to and for them. For the same reasons, but at a very different stage of life, nursing homes operate in a trust market.

And, of course, higher education is sold in a trust market. Just like going to a doctor, our students come to colleges and universities in large part because they don't know what they'll get from us. If they knew what they'd learn, they wouldn't have to learn it. Sure, they can read college guides and the piles of literature we all send them, and they can talk to friends and parents and parents' friends, but ultimately there remains a whole lot of asymmetric information between buyer and seller inherent in the educational process. We know more than they do, so we operate in a market that has to rely on trust. (It's often described as "reputation," "status," "prestige"—what gives the customer assurance that she'll get what she pays for.) Kenneth Arrow, a Nobel in economics, recently said in a talk at Williams that "education is the supreme example of a product subject to asymmetric information."

## Nonprofit Firms

Before turning to why and how the recent behavior of colleges and universities fits into this, let me note another useful piece of economic theory, this from economists Henry Hansmann at the Yale Law School and Estelle James at SUNY-Stony Brook. It's no accident that when we look at trust markets, we usually see a whole lot of non-profit firms. The distinguishing feature of nonprofit firms is *not* that they can't make profits (which may surprise you as much as it did me when I first realized it); they often make large and handsome profits. But they can't distribute those profits to stockholders, the board, or any other outside owner, as a for-profit business firm would. They can only use those profits for the purposes of the institution, now and in the future. Hansmann called this "the non-distribution constraint" and argued that, because they can't distribute their profits, the managers of non-profit organizations are more trustworthy. When you send you $50 to WGBH or KPFA, you don't have to worry that it will simply be passed on to the owners of those stations as part of their yearly dividend; you have more reason to believe that it will be spent the way you want it to be spent, on public radio programming. So non-profits often dominate trust markets, as is the case with higher education.

## Colleges and Trust

This brings us back to our central question: what have U.S. colleges and universities been doing to provoke such unfriendliness from the nation? The general answer that follows is that we've let an unseemly interest in revenues—in income, making money—erode the public's trust in higher education. Other things may have contributed—like rising public expectations, opulent college building programs, and a competitive pursuit of "institutional excellence" that has bid star faculty salaries well into the six figures—but our collective attention to institutional income is surely central. (The major contribution of public universities to the erosion of trust has probably been—cold fusion aside—their promotion of a blatantly professional athletic-entertainment industry under the fig leaf of scholar athletics, with attendant self-promotion, big money scandals, and corruption.)

It would not be entirely inaccurate to call the past 20 years "The Age of Maximization" in elite higher education. Or, maybe, "The Age of Creeping Maximization." We've seen, over that period, the systematic introduction of "professional" and "rational" management in colleges and universities. While there is much about that to be applauded, to the extent that we've used our resources more carefully and more self-consciously, there is also something about it to be feared—as we may have so enthusiastically accepted the message of careful maximization that we've not noticed its erosion of trust.

## Maximization on Campus

"Maximization" means many things to economists in different contexts. It can simply mean getting the most out of your limited resources—using them efficiently—or it can mean getting the most out of your customers, your workers, or your suppliers. It's a portmanteau word. Being efficient is pretty unambiguously "a good thing." Getting the most out of your customers, in a trust market, is not so clearly "a good thing." With that distinction, let me briefly track the creep of maximization—the growth of hard, aggressive, rational behavior—in dealing with our customers.

Colleges like Williams, Amherst, and Wesleyan get their yearly income in roughly equal amounts from three sources. About a third comes from wealth, largely in the form of endowment income; about a third comes from student charges; and about a third comes from gifts. In an elite university, a fourth roughly equal source is added in the form of research grants and contracts. In a state four-year college or university, 55 to 65 percent of the support is from public funds—so 35 to 45 percent, even there, is from the same four sources as for private institutions.

The past 20 years have seen policies of maximization applied, one after the other, to each of these sources of income. It seems to have begun with the Ford Foundation's campaign in the '60s to persuade nonprofit institutions to loosen up a little and manage their wealth for "total return." At the time, endowment wealth was invested where it would provide the steadiest flow of interest and dividends so the college could plan on a predictable flow of income from endowment. But that policy denied colleges very lucrative, and safe, investment opportunities where the dividends were small but the long-run growth—capital gains—would be large. The Ford Foundation therefore decided that colleges should invest where the total returns—interest, dividends, and capital gains—were the greatest. They'd have to figure out a way to discipline themselves not to spend all that income (if they spent all interest and dividends, they weren't in trouble—but if they spent all the total return, their real wealth would be eroded). If self-discipline could be handled, schools would get more from their endowment wealth than they'd been getting. Indeed, they'd maximize. By the early '80s, most colleges and universities with significant endowments were trying to maximize total return.

Tuition income was next. Admissions offices have become masters of direct-mail merchandising techniques, using sophisticated searches of national student databases (buying mailing lists) to find and contact potential customers with an efficiency that would do Lands' End or J. Crew proud.

Our publications, tested by all the techniques of modern advertising psychology, have become more sophisticated, expensive, and, presumably, effective. We've maximized the impact of our admissions spending. And the larger pools of applicants that all the effort generated have let elite schools select measurably better classes of freshmen—with higher SATs, more diversity, and (for some of us) better football teams. Those applicant pools have also kept our tuition income growing with little fear of "pricing ourselves out of the market." With inflation now at about 3 percent, Stanford is increasing its tuition for next year by 7.5 percent, Williams by 5.7 percent, Harvard by 6.5 percent, and so on.

The transformation of college development offices—the institutional seekers after gift income—follows much the same pattern, using, in fact, some of the same aggressive marketing techniques and creating some more of their own. The criterion of efficiency in a development office is that they should push their activities until the last dollar of cost brings in just one last dollar of gifts. This warms the hearts of economics professors, since it represents one of the central lessons from Economics 101: a firm should expand any activity until its marginal cost just equals its marginal revenue. That is, significantly, the rule for a profit maximizing firm.

Finally, it was hard for any of us to avoid the news stories about the universities' maximization of overhead cost recovery from the government. A persuasive argument can be made that Stanford was unfairly singled out for nationally televised abuse—with repetitive references to yacht maintenance and a president's new brass bed—but, however much university administrations may have been encouraged in their practices (and there's a plausible case for a measure of entrapment), the fact is that they were pushing the outer limit with sharp accounting practices. Indeed, Stanford held seminars for accountants from less aggressive universities to teach them how to get the very last dollar in their indirect costs.

Clearly, this description of revenue maximization in four areas oversimplifies a range of complicated activities. It probably sounds sour about the devoted work of a lot of highly dedicated and imaginative people who have intended to serve their colleges well, and in important ways have succeeded in doing so. One obstacle to regarding this maximizing pattern as worrisome is that it's been done with the best of intentions by the most devoted of employees.

Too, my description of maximization risks leaving the impression that these things shouldn't have been done—that we should have stayed with the nice, comfy Mom-and-Pop management style dominating colleges and universities in the '50s and before, and that it was a mistake to be imaginative and aggressive in our more recent management practices. It would be an error to say that.

The mistake, I'm suggesting, came not in moving toward more professional management of higher education, but in paying too little attention to the cumulative effect these separate and individual steps were likely to have on how much people would trust us. Each move toward maximization made sense in itself, but each move toward maximization also sent a message to the world about how we viewed ourselves. And those messages were, increasingly, that we saw ourselves as pretty much the same as any other business, using the same techniques and taking advantage of the same opportunities. The more we're like other enterprises, the more easily trust is displaced by a familiar sense of "caveat emptor"—let the buyer beware.

It is no accident that the focus of the hostility toward higher education, from the Dingle Committee to Saturday Night Live, has been on our sharp dealing and maximization. The amount of money given back to the government by Stanford and MIT and Cornell—all with the implication that it had been gotten by shady practices—makes bold headlines. So do tales of scientific fraud, made more damaging by the aggressively outraged innocence of a Nobel scientist who turned out to be dead wrong. We can't trust scholars, it seems, to be scholars—such are the pressures on them for worldly and academic success. Even in scholarship, trust is eroded by money. And trust in higher education is not helped by the excesses—the personal maximization—in other non-profits: the $460,000 salary and Concord trips and free condos of United Way's former President Aramony seriously hurt us all.

It's worth noting here that there's not only an outside audience reading significance into our maximizing behavior. There's also an important internal audience—faculty, administration, workers—to whom our institutions have been speaking. And while evidence of sharp practices may leave the outsiders suspicious and less trusting, it seems destined to induce in many insiders more complex reactions. We will worry, too, about unseemly signals of institutional maximization. But we also don't want to miss out on the goodies being passed around, and the new message is that it's okay for all of us to hold out for a piece of the action. So, increasingly, we'll prepare new courses *if* we get extra money over the summer; we'll take on thesis students *if* we get partial course credit; we'll avoid committees because they take too much time from research, whence come our grants, mobility, and professional respect. Anyone over 50 is to be distrusted in such an observation as this—such is the nostalgic lure of when we were assistant professors—but it's easy to see a connection between our institutional maximization and a decline in the sense of community.

## More to Come?

I want to pose two final questions. First: "We've been through a lot of very public embarrassment—is more likely to come?" Second, let me ask the classic question, "So what?" If there's some truth in all this, what's the implication? What do we do about it?

First, the question of our continued vulnerability: Is there another shoe to drop, another place where colleges and universities, despite the fact that they've been playing it strictly according to the law, are close enough to the edge that a Dingle Committee can make us look really bad? Are we, in other words, vulnerable to yet another "expose" that will further erode the public's trust?

Unfortunately, there are, I suspect, *two* shoes that might yet drop. One has to do with how honest we're actually being; the other with the appearance of our honesty and loyalty to our own values. The first is the fact that the "budget deficits" we tell our communities and alumni and the press about—the deficits that are assumed to show how hard the times are getting to be, even for elite colleges and universities—are not at all what they seem to be. They *seem*, reasonably, to describe the economic fortunes of a college for the year: a deficit seems to show that the college spent more than it took in, and a surplus seems to show the opposite. That's what you, I, the press, and the public are led to believe. That's the way our family budgets and our checkbooks work. But, in fact, "the budget" for a college includes only a certain part—about two-thirds—of the total economic activity of the school. So whether that part shows a deficit or a surplus is arbitrary: money is regularly "transferred"—moved in or out of the budget, making it show red ink or black ink—at will, with no relation to how the college actually performed economically.

A college can, and often does, show a big budget deficit at the same time that a whole lot of savings are being generated to increase its wealth (or vice versa). Some colleges (like Swarthmore and Kalamazoo, and Harvard and MIT for a while) routinely move dollars around after the fact so that they'll always show they've operated with a balanced budget. Or a potentially embarrassing budget surplus of, say, three quarters of a million dollars that would seem to contradict an administration's protestations of hard times can, with the stroke of a pen or computer key, be turned into a politically comfortable deficit of $150,000. You want to $10,000 deficit instead? Or a $300,000 surplus to signal your prudent management? We'll give you one, even if the school actually lost money.

All of this is not even a dirty little secret: it is an openly acknowledged fact among those who work with college finances. They rarely even bother to wink or look conspiratorial when acknowledging it. But it appears to be a fact not always well understood by either the top administrators outside the financial area or by the boards that have ultimate responsibility for the college.

When the uninformative nature of those deficits and surpluses was first pointed out nearly 20 years ago by Harold Bierman and Thomas Hofstedt, a couple of Cornell accounting professors, it induced an Andy Rooney segment on CBS, a page-one feature in the *Wall Street Journal* with the title

"Ten Eastern Colleges Accused of Crying Wolf In Reporting Deficits," and a set of heated denials from comptrollers and a couple of Ivy League presidents. Bierman and Hofstedt showed that when MIT reported a $5 million deficit, they actually saved $100 million; Princeton's reported $1.5 million deficit went with $151 million in saving; and Harvard's $1.4 million deficit coincided with $314 million in saving. (These figures apparently weren't adjusted to reflect the erosion of wealth from the year's inflation. If that had been done, real saving would still have been $83 million at MIT, $132 million at Princeton, and $265 million at Harvard.) Yet the practice remains today, just as it was in 1973. It takes no vivid imagination to worry about what hay could be made if this deception were to be understood by Representative Dingle before it was eliminated by us. Those numbers are entirely legal—indeed, they're the result of long-established college accounting practices—but they're still deceptive and are used deceptively.

An article in *Forbes Magazine* (May 25, 1992) suggests that this particular cat may already be out of the bag. It describes the new Harvard accounting system with both hostility and the clear recognition that "a university has the ability to manage its own bottom line." Paradoxically, in this era of distrust, Harvard's effort to clean up its act and report more valid economic facts was interpreted by *Forbes* as an effort to inflate its costs in order to appear poor for purposes of appealing for more donations from hoodwinked alumni. Such is the environment of suspicion.

The other shoe that might fall tells less of deception that of our vulnerability, in elite and well-endowed schools, to charges of ripping off unsuspecting taxpayers to enhance our own already considerable wealth. It has to do with our widespread practice of *interest arbitrage*. It works like this: state and federal legislators, who apparently want to support elite higher education with taxpayers' dollars without making that fact too apparent to their constituents, have made it possible for colleges like ours to sell tax-exempt bonds, just as if we were the government. Because the people buying our bonds don't have to pay tax on the interest they earn, they're willing to let us pay them a lower interest rate. So the college pays less to borrow money. But the flip side of that arrangement is that the state takes in less in taxes. Or, putting it the right way around, the taxpayers are paying part of our interest bill on the money we borrow, the difference between the (taxable) market rate and what we actually have to pay. We borrow, say, at a 5 percent interest rate when the market rate is 10 percent, and the taxpayers of the U.S. and the Commonwealth pay the rest.

"Arbitrage" is a word that's been added to our general vocabulary in the '80s and made into a dirty word by the likes of Ivan Boesky, the ultimate "arb." It describes making money on price differences—simultaneously buying and selling the same thing and doing nothing else in the process. What makes us guilty of interest arbitrage is that wealthy colleges simultaneously loan money (our financial assets, the endowment, largely) to some people and borrow from others, dollar for dollar. But—and here's the magic of arbitrage—each dollar we lend pays us more interest than we pay out on the dollar we borrow. If we earn 10 percent on our assets and pay 5 percent on our borrowing, each dollar of simultaneous lending-and-borrowing earns us a nickel a year of arbitrage profits: $20 million of lending-and-borrowing earns us $1 million in arbitrage income each year. And that $1 million of profit is paid for by the taxpayers, available to us because we're allowed to borrow tax-free.

It's legal. The amounts aren't unlimited—the cap for any school is $150 million—and building projects must be nominally involved but, for wealthy schools, it's inescapably arbitrage. And, equally inescapably, it transfers money—resources, spending power—from the average taxpayer to Williams, Amherst, Harvard, and the rest.

The concern boils down, really, to whether wealthy colleges may not have so much to lose, from public accusation of being party to fast financial games played at the expense of the average citizen, that they should voluntarily withdraw from these arrangements—pay off their tax-exempt debts and eliminate their vulnerability to another erosion of public trust. For a school like Williams with $50 million in such debt, it would cost about $2.5 million a year to give up arbitrage income. One thing we'd get out of it is the ability to dissociate ourselves, clearly and as a matter of principle, from a practice that got a deservedly bad name in the '80s, to dissociate ourselves from Ivan Boesky's celebrated battlecry of the '80s, "Greed is good!" (A call, incidentally, that he issued in a speech at UC-Berkeley.) It's not clear that it is worth $2.5 million a year to avoid the taint of arbitrage and taxpayer exploitation, but it is clear that it's a question to be given serious thought on campuses before—not after—we're called to public account for it.

On matters of legality and moral purpose, as a final aside, it seems ironic that, where the elite colleges are being most explicitly charged with illegal behavior—the ongoing antitrust action on need-based student aid—we are in fact acting according to cherished egalitarian principles and being punished on the basis of a misreading of the analogy between a college and a private business firm.

## The Implications

Which brings me to the significance of all this. I should say, one last time, that the message is not that we should shun careful, thoughtful management of resources in wealth colleges and universities—either because we're so rich that we don't have to, or because we're so timid and fearful of looking like grungy businessmen. That would be a pretty silly conclusion. We're rich, but we're also trying to do a whole lot to protect some of our most cherished values, like need-blind admissions and need-based aid; we have to keep on—indeed, increase—our efforts to spend our money wisely. Our money is far more limited than our ambitions and will surely stay that way.

In fact, the first message I read in all this is that we need to increase and redirect our institutional attention toward *efficiency*, paying less of that attention to getting more income and more of it to how we spend the income we're already getting in ways that best serve our purposes. There's no doubt that it's politically and administratively more appealing to get more money than it is to be more careful and purposeful about how it's spent. It appears to be a basic American characteristic to feel, always, that the problem is that we don't have enough money to do what we have to do—and if we only had a little more. . . . The sentiment is as true for colleges as it is for individuals, and as true for income as it is for the length of your sailboat. But it's probably been a real mistake for colleges and universities to pay so much attention to getting. It's not at all clear that the hours and days and weeks of presidential time on our campuses spent in gift-getting might not be better devoted to leading the community in thinking about how the money should be used, about the purposes and objectives our spending supports.

My second message is that we need, as institutions, to be much more protective of the public's sense of trust in us. We need to hear what's being said to us now as a warning that our customers think we're drifting off course. It's far too early for us to be sure they're wrong, so we should fight the temptation to circle the wagons and dismiss their worries as wrongheaded. In a way, in the matter of trust, they can't be wrong—if they're telling us they don't trust us as much as they used to, we can't very well tell them they do. And it probably doesn't help to tell ourselves they should, that we're just being misunderstood.

Is there a practical implication in all of this? I think there is. If we recognize the central role that trust plays in a market like ours, we will be far more self-conscious in judging our own behavior in relation to it—more systematic about asking whether something that makes perfectly good, pragmatic sense might be seen by those outside of academe as a reason for lowered trust. On campus, we need to rebuild institutions and occasions that remind us—awkward and embarrassing though it may sometimes be—of our purposes. And we need ways to help new members of the community understand those purposes—their socialization isn't automatic. We need to pay less attention to what's legal and a good deal more attention to the appropriateness of what we do. We need, more often, to decide that some activities—especially when they are well-funded—simply aren't appropriate to our purposes.

We need, in short, to protect and rebuild the sense of public trust in a market where we must have our customers' trust—or we don't have much to sell.

# SECTION II
## FINANCIAL MANAGEMENT OF HIGHER EDUCATION

*This section contains articles on budgeting, resource allocation, and management of colleges and universities. Whereas articles in the first section concentrate on resource "acquisition" (who pays? who benefits? who should pay?), this section focuses on internal resource "allocation."*

# In Praise of Inefficiency (1978)

## KENNETH BOULDING

It is a pleasure to be here in a dual capacity, as a professor, to keep you honest, and as a trustee, to give you sympathy. I rather enjoy being a trustee after having been a university teacher for over 40 years; it is a bit like flying in a jet—you see a lot of the landscape, but you don't see it very clearly.

Now, I thought I ought to talk in praise of inefficiency, as long as you were all talking about cost effectiveness; perhaps a little sour note, or possibly a sweet note depending on your taste, would not sound amiss.

One of the things I have learned from the biologists (some of my best friends are biologists) is that inefficiency is an extremely important element in survival. I have taken great satisfaction in watching squirrels. I rarely see them doing any work. They run around trees, and they twitch their tails, and they play hide-and-seek, and they have an awfully good time. And they survive. Dolphins may be almost as bright as we are (their brains are apparently as large), but perhaps they have decided just to enjoy themselves.

## Efficiency Can Be Dangerous

On the other hand, a species which is highly efficient will expand to the limits of its environment, and then its environment worsens and its niche shrinks. There is a principle of the universe, that there is a very strong tendency for things to go from bad to worse. Then the efficient species may simply collapse into extinction. But an inefficient species has reserves in redundancy and irrelevance, which are the sort of things that universities have, and can draw on these reserves for survival.

This is a fairly comforting thought, that universities are repositories of redundancy in society, so that in a crisis they constitute an important reserve on which society may draw. The awful truth about the world is that the meek inherit the earth. In the long run it is the adaptable, which is another name for the meek, who survive, whereas the too-well-adapted get crowded out by changes in the environment.

Of course nobody wants to attack "efficiency." It is like "appropriate technology"—you can't come out against it. No one can defend the inefficient and the inappropriate. I always thought that the success of the school of logical positivism was the result of nobody wanting to be an illogical negativist.

But though nobody can come out against efficiency, it is not so easy to say what it is. All measures of efficiency are a measure of how much you get out of some system per unit of what you put in. But the critical question is, what is a significant output and what is a significant input? That is, in terms of human valuations. It is easy to conceive of a process in which we put more energy or materials in than we get out, but which is still worth doing because the energy or materials we get out is in a convenient and highly valued form and the energy we put in is crud. The peak of efficiency may be the gardener who literally puts crud in and gets potatoes out.

Engineering efficiency is usually defined as the amount of one kind of energy (for example, mechanical work) out per unit of all kinds of energy in. Beyond engineering efficiency, there is financial efficiency, the balance sheet and all that. Financial efficiency is better than engineering efficiency; at least you are putting crude human valuations on the inputs and outputs. On the other hand, we all recognize (even economists) that financial efficiency is only part of the story. There is something further, something you might call human efficiency. That, I believe, is what we really look for, efficiency in terms of some kind of well-considered human valuation. (One of the things we have to recognize is that of all the valuations we now possess, none are ultimate values. I believe some ultimate values must be lying around, just as I strongly suspect that there is a real world somewhere, in spite of all the evidence to the contrary. But even ultimate values have to be interpreted and approximated through human valuation.

## The Optimum in Waste?

Human efficiency involves getting as much in terms of human values out of any enterprise as we possibly can in proportion to whatever values we put in.

I am not, of course, advocating waste, which could be described as inefficiency beyond the optimum. Waste, however, is by no means easy to define. There may even be an optimum amount of it. Perhaps the principal pleasure of being rich is the ability to waste. The poor have to watch every penny; they have to be efficient or they will not survive. When the burden of poverty is lifted, there is room for experiment, for failures, even for extravagance and charm. I would hate to live in a world in which there was no rococo. The earth could support a much larger population if we all became vegetarians and worked 16 hours a day, but it would be hard to affirm that this was a better world, even though by some measures it might be regarded as more efficient.

Some of the redundancies and inefficiencies of universities are part of that ultimate product of human activity which is the reason for living at all. These redundancies are also an extremely important reserve of high-quality ability in time of crisis. To make universities narrowly efficient might well be the greatest disservice we offer society.

Again, there is a great deal of difference between short-run, narrowly measured efficiency and the long-run efficiency which leads to ultimate survival. We may have to have some of both kinds. Even in the short run, there are inefficiencies which are unnecessary, like administrative staff engaged mainly in keeping itself busy by collecting information that nobody really wants to know. But if short-run efficiency becomes the enemy of long-run efficiency, so much the worse for it.

## Numerical Measures of Efficiency

In this connection we have to be particularly careful not to be misled by numerical measures of efficiency, especially where numbers do not accurately represent the significant realty, as in general they do not. Thus, the concept of cost effectiveness is only valid when a product can be clearly defined, and equally clearly valued relative to other products. The production function by which inputs are transformed into products must also be well defined and *all* the relevant inputs and outputs must be known and capable of being measured. Perhaps the greatest superstition in the world today is numerology—the belief that somehow numerical information is always superior to qualitative, structural, and topological information. The plain truth is that numbers for the most part are a figment of the human imagination.

The real world gets along very well without them. Thus, they represent an abstraction from the real world. The real world does contain sets, structures, shapes, patterns and a few constant quantities like the velocity of light. (It is interesting to note that any number that we give to this is essentially arbitrary.) Numbers are essentially a human device that have the delightful property of being added, subtracted, multiplied and divided, and hence permit cheap and easy abstract descriptions of certain aspects of the real world.

Numerology easily leads into suboptimization, which I have been arguing is one of the most important names of the devil. This consists either in finding out the best way of doing something that should not be done at all, which is one of the main activities of engineers and management consultants, or it consists in the process of solving one problem by creating worse problems elsewhere.

Numbers can be extremely useful, however, as long as they are not believed. No businessman with any sense really believes his accountant, who is presenting only one small, numerical aspect of the vast reality that is a business, but the accountant's report is nevertheless important evidence in policy-making decisions. Everything indeed that is presented to the decision-maker in terms of numbers is evidence, not truth. There is nothing wrong with evidence as long as it is not mistaken for truth. To believe that evidence is truth is a sure recipe for making bad decisions. Decision results from an evaluation of the evidence and a very complex weighing of alternatives. It always transcends, though it does not necessarily reject, numerical information.

## In Higher Education, Inputs Look Like Outputs

The problem of decision-making, and evaluation, is particularly acute in higher education, where the product, which is presumably the educated person and the examined life, is extremely hard to measure and even to evaluate. It is even hard to tell the inputs from the outputs. To a certain extent the experience of the student as a consumer is itself a product quite apart from what it may produce in terms of higher incomes and the expanded life. Similarly, a faculty cannot teach without also learning, and the product of a university may be as much in the learning of the faculty as it is in the learning of the student. The university, furthermore, produces a sense of community and identity, a sense of the meaningfulness of life, even when this is expressed in football and alumni associations.

The problem is compounded by the fact that in any learning experience random elements are extremely important; the moment of imprinting, the awakening of the human spirit, the tide which has to be taken with the flood, the opportunity that is irretrievably lost. Aggregate measures of efficiency can never catch this vital random element, though over large numbers these random elements may even out in some degree. Even here a further question arises: Should we not judge a system by its peak rather than by its average? From the point of social evolution, one Newton may be worth a million teachers' certificates, though we also have to add that the quality of the teacher's certificate can have a considerable effect on the impact of the Newton.

## Preposterous But Delightful

I am not against measurement as such, or even cost effectiveness measures as such. We should by all means measure the measurable and we should have good feedback from unnecessary inefficiencies and eliminate them.

The danger of measurement, however, is that we will believe it and that we will regard it as the truth instead of as evidence. In universities this could be catastrophic. It is particularly important to remember that universities are institutions almost as preposterous and improbable as the human race itself, and this of course is what makes them so delightful. In university decision-making it is particularly important to take a very broad field of information into consideration. The great danger in all decision-making is in concentrating on the things that are easy to find out and neglecting the things that are hard to find out. The scientific community is by no means exempt from this temptation. It often concentrates its research on the things that are easy, which are not always the things that are important.

In looking at human efficiency, one sees that the things that are hard to find out are just as important, and often more important, than those that are easy. Trustees are asked to make extraordinarily difficult assessments. One of the most extraordinary things about the human mind is its capacity to go far beyond simple, numerical, linear information in its process of evaluation of large and complex systems.

How we make these assessments I do not know, and I doubt if anybody knows. It is an activity almost as mysterious as teaching itself. I have been teaching for forty years and I still do not really know how it is done. I believe I have occasionally taught somebody something, but I am also convinced that I have rarely taught anybody anything that he did not know in some sense already. The business of the outward teacher is to cooperate with and encourage that inward teacher that is present in all of us and is the essential intermediary in the growth of knowledge.

# Beware the Illusion of Certainty

I must confess that I worry a good deal about the rise of sophistication in decision-making, particularly when this is done with computers and flashing lights, wall charts and printouts, and neglects the delectable ambiguities of language. I have been involved recently with a committee of the National Academy of Sciences which has involved some contact with the world of Washington, which, as a dyed-in-the-wool provincial, I usually avoid. In Washington I am continually appalled at the influence of think tanks and the scenario writers, people who come up with projections, numbers and more numbers, in which the more dubious and the less dubious are hopelessly mixed.

We have to recognize that the overwhelming property of the future is irreducible uncertainty. Decisions under uncertainty are very different from those under certainty, if they ever existed. The worst possible decisions are those which are made under illusions of certainty. Sophisticated decision-making can easily produce these illusions. I wonder indeed when the history of the Vietnam War is written whether the development of political military gaming in the Pentagon will not be perceived as a major source of some very catastrophic decisions because it produced illusions of certainty.

In the university, illusions of certainty can be even more catastrophic. Here again, I am in favor of reducing uncertainty where we can. But it is the unfortunate property of a number, especially one produced by a numerological expert, that we all too rarely put plus or minus after it. I urge you, therefore, to respect the work of the numerologists, and even those who produce data and projections of the future, but for heaven's sake do not believe them. Treat them as evidence, and as evidence also which is much more dubious than it looks.

One of the most awful truths about the real world is that it is a muddle. Anybody who is clear about it is under an illusion. However carefully we refine our techniques, we must never desert the great tradition of muddling through. This is the only realistic way to approach the future of anything.

# The Economy and Higher Education (1990)

## RICHARD E. ANDERSON

According to some analysts the American economy is strong and the prospects for future growth are good. The most obvious and destructive problems, the budget and the trade deficits, have eased somewhat. The federal budget shortfall is still high by historical standards but it is not out of line with the budget deficits experienced by our major trading partners in the late 1970s and early 1980s. And, although the United States' widely publicized trade deficit is a major concern, the weak dollar has begun to energize our manufacturing sector.

Alarmists, on the other hand, point to the confluence of the trade and budget shortfalls and the long-term depressing effects of these deficits. They further observe that some of the reductions to the budget deficit are less significant than meet the eye and that a good part of the trade deficit is structural and will remain impervious to a weakened dollar. Finally, these pessimists point to the growing problem of unfunded pension liabilities and the general need to replace our infrastructure.

This chapter will consider the macroeconomic trends that shape our economy and the effects of those trends on higher education. Although the projections of the middle-of-the-road analysts will probably be more accurate than those of the extremists—things generally have a way of working out—the storm clouds are real and close enough that they bear serious attention. This chapter will, therefore, highlight the more pessimistic perspectives. If institutions are forewarned about these problems they will be in a better position to react should, or when, they need to.

## The Economic Environment

### Productivity

If the United States is to enjoy financial prosperity, it must be productive. The more goods and services produced, the more we can consume. The generally accepted gauge of the strength of our economy is the level and changes in the Gross National Product (GNP). GNP is a measure, albeit an imperfect one, of the total goods and services we produce. Among its four major components are measures of (1) *goods and services consumed by households* and (2) *those provided by governments*. It also includes (3) *capital investment* in manufacturing facilities and equipment and in other private and public infrastructure like houses, roads, airports, and offices. All this fixed investment is necessary for the country and the economy to continue to grow. In addition, the GNP gauges (4) *net export* of goods and services. It is important to keep these four components in mind. An increase in the consumption of goods and services by households and governments translates into an immediately improved standard of living. Increases in the creation of public and private infrastructure creates capacity for future growth and future increases in our standard of living. The shipment of products and services abroad results in the claims on the wealth of other nations, claims which can be redeemed for future consumption or to build productive capacity.

Over the last three decades GNP has grown at about 3 percent per year above inflation but this growth rate has been trending downward since the 1970s. (See Figure 2-1.) There has been a spurt of growth in the last few years, but most experts discount these increases because they were induced by disproportionately high deficit spending. As a *Business Week* article observed, "growth under Reagan was stimulated by deficits . . . nothing more than Keynesianism on steroids."

An acknowledged problem with the GNP measure is that all goods and services are not counted. Economics texts are quick to point out that the work of housewives is excluded from the GNP (as is that of househusbands). Should a woman enter the workforce and hire domestic help, an event which is much more common today that in the past, the GNP would increase by the wages of both the wife and the domestic. If GNP is corrected for number of workers (see Figure 2-2), the economic inertia of the last two decades is painfully obvious. Growth in GNP per worker has been practically non-existent since 1970. Again, only the deficit-induced growth of the last few years break this trend.

Our lagging standard of living was a cause for concern in the late 1970s and helped propel Ronald Reagan into the White House and generate the supply-side experiment. Unfortunately, we didn't work any harder during the last eight years. What has changed has been our spending pattern. We're no more productive but we're spending (i.e., consuming) as if we were. The most obvious transgressor is the federal government as it runs up huge federal deficits unprecedented in a peacetime economy. Families are also borrowing more and saving less. Consumer debt, for example, has grown from 60 percent of GNP in 1980 to almost 80 percent in 1988. Similarly, savings in the United States declined from about 7 percent of GNP in the 1970s to an all-time low of about 3 percent in 1987. It has since rebounded to the 4 to 5 percent range but our national savings rate is among the lowest of the developed economies. Japan, a model for personal thrift, saves at a rate of about 12 to 16 percent. Savings in the Western European countries is in the 7 to 10 percent range.

We have also propped up our standard of living by importing more goods than we export. Trade surpluses soak up GNP, requiring families or governments to consume less. Trade deficits have the opposite result. Collectively, the United States has lived better by importing what we do not manufacture and borrowing or selling assets to finance this consumption.

## The "Twin Deficits"

Both the trade and the federal budget deficits have received a good deal of attention in the popular press recently, concern that is very well deserved. Still, it is important to understand the magnitude of these deficits and the problems they create.

Some believe that the only proper status of the federal budget is balanced. This position is certainly too simple in a complex modern economy. It is expected that a government will spend more than it takes in during a war or other national emergency. Moreover, governments can reasonably use their spending authority to stimulate the economy during an economic slowdown. Ideally, budget deficits that spur the economy would be matched with budget surpluses created when the economy is strong. As Figure 2-3 shows, however, budget surpluses have been rare since 1960. Of greater concern is the uniformity and the magnitude of the budget deficits in recent years. Prior to 1980, the budget deficits, measured as a percent of GNP, swung from small positive balances to negative balances in the 2 to 3 percent range. (During many of these years we were financing the Vietnam conflict.) Only in 1975 did the deficit exceed 3 percent of GNP. Since 1982 the deficits have consistently exceeded 4 percent. In most of these years, the GNP has been growing so they cannot be characterized as "stimulative" deficits. The budget imbalance declined to just above 3 percent in 1987, but many economists are skeptical of this progress. They claim that some of the

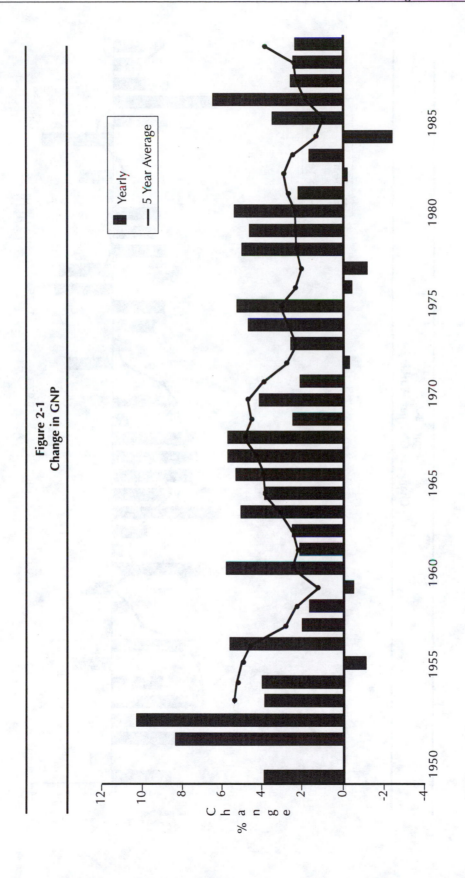

Figure 2-1
Change in GNP

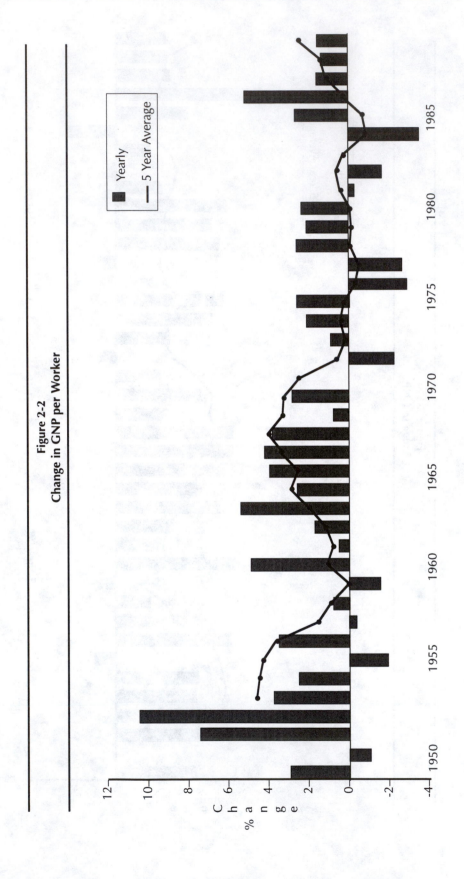

Figure 2-2
Change in GNP per Worker

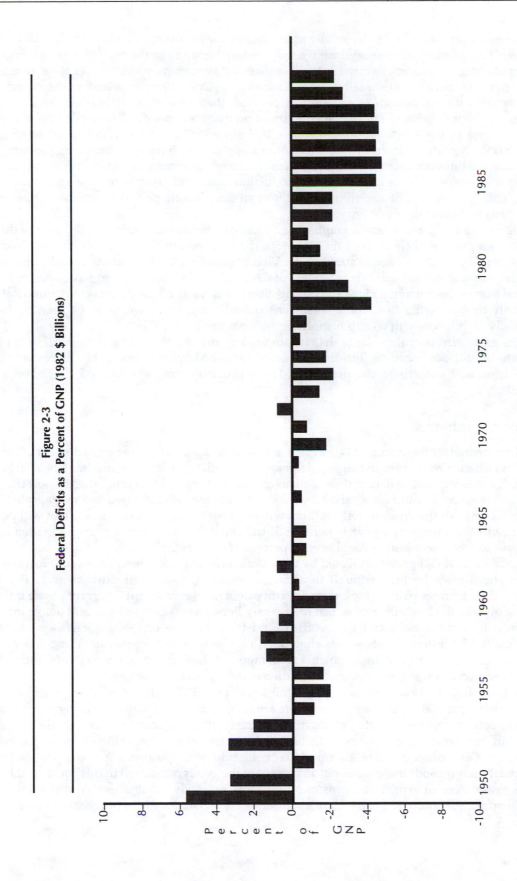

**Figure 2-3**
**Federal Deficits as a Percent of GNP (1982 $ Billions)**

deficit reduction was achieved by selling assets and by the inclusion of social security surpluses in the deficit calculation, surpluses which we will need in the future as the elderly population grows.

Apologists for the deficits observe that German and Japan have run large negative imbalances in government spending for equally long periods of time. One difference is that, while their deficits also occurred during periods of economic expansion, they were more than offset by large trade surpluses. Their deficits, in effect, helped to build productive capacity. The opposite is true in the United States in the 1980s. Figure 2-4 shows that since 1982 we have also had consistent, and extraordinarily high, trade deficits. In effect, our budget deficits have been financing consumption, not industrial buildup. During the last two decades American companies have shifted manufacturing capacity overseas. More and more U.S. production consists of assembling foreign-made components. This "hollowing" of our industry will take an equally long period to reverse and will slow any efforts to correct the trade imbalance.

Figure 2-5 offers a composite graph of our profligate behavior, displaying the sum of the two deficits as a percent of GNP. Until the late 1960s the trade and budget figures generally balanced each other. Under the economic strain of the Vietnam conflict, the total of the two deficits turned negative but was never more than 4 percent of GNP. Since 1983, both figures have been in the red and the sum is destructively high. The deficits have been financed partly by selling our assets but primarily by borrowing from foreigners. Consequently, real interest rates have been pushed to unusually high levels with wealth hemorrhaging from this country.

The exact effects of these large deficits are unknown, but one thing is certain; deficits of this magnitude will not continue into the indefinite future. Moreover, any delay in correcting the imbalances will exacerbate the problems. These problems can be classified as financial and structural.

## Financial Problems

The debt created by these deficits is the most obvious problem. In 1982 we were the world's largest creditor nation. Now we are the largest debtor nation, with net debt of approximately $700 billion. Moreover, it is impossible to turn these deficits around overnight. Most economists assert that *if* we sacrifice consumption and *if* we raise taxes, we can bring the deficits down to a manageable level. But to accomplish this in an orderly fashion without generating a recession, net debt will need to rise or some time, reaching a peak of perhaps $1 trillion dollars. As a result interest, dividends, and rent paid to foreigners could exceed several percent of GNP in the 1990s.

Another financial problem created by these deficits is that real interest rates (interest adjusted for inflation) must be high enough to attract a sufficient number of purchasers of our debt. Historically, the rates paid on long-term Treasury debt have been about 1 percent above inflation. During most of the 1980s the real return to Treasury Bonds has been 4 to 5 per cent above inflation. The recent record deficits and the need to fund them are one of the major reasons for these abnormally high interest costs—costs shared by all who wish to borrow, including colleges and universities. Unfortunately this problem can compound itself. If a country pays real interest at a rate which exceeds real growth, then the burden of debt grows ever larger.

A third financial consequence is that the value of the U.S. dollar is likely to remain low. Although the price at which foreign investors are willing to hold U.S. dollars is very complicated, the productivity and the expected productivity of the economy are major factors. To the extent that we drain our productive capacity with high debt to foreigners, the value of the dollar will be depressed. One consequence of a weak dollar is that domestic purchasing power will be further reduced. Foreign goods make up about 15 percent of the goods consumed in this country. If foreign goods rise 50 percent in price and consumption of foreign goods remains level (it will not but it has been surprisingly inelastic so far), families suffer a 7.5 percent decline in purchasing power.

## Structural Problems

During most of the 1980s, the U.S. economy grew at a satisfactory rate. The foundation of that growth, however, was consumption and not the creation of plant and equipment. Families and governments were spending at higher and higher levels and financing their purchases with debt. As a consequence the United States devoted fewer resources to plant and equipment. Entire industries developed offshore for which there is no domestic equivalent (e.g., consumer electronics). The lead in many other industries has shifted abroad (e.g., micro chips). In an effort to keep prices of domestically produced goods as low as possible. Many U.S. companies either moved production facilities abroad or imported major components for their products. A weaker dollar will tend to reverse this trend but it will take time to rebuild productive capacity.

It is important to note that most experts believe that a turnaround in trade is going to have to be led by manufacturing. It is a myth, according to these analysts, that we can prosper as a nation with a "service economy." One reason is that service that is exportable *and* that is not intricately tied to production is of too little consequence. Another reason is that there is no validity in the belief that this country can maintain a structural advantage in the production of services. The opposite, in fact, is likely to be true as many services in financial, legal, and other fields can be culture-specific.

The weak dollar lowers the price to foreigners not only of U.S. manufactured goods but of U.S. manufacturing facilities. As treasury debt matures, some foreign creditors are deciding not to repurchase debt but to buy U.S. companies instead. Stephen Roach, a Solomon Bros. economist, estimates that foreigners already own 10 percent of U.S. manufacturing facilities and this percentage is growing very rapidly. The profits of these companies will flow into foreign bank accounts with further depressing effects on our standard of living.

# Future Prospects

## Best-Case Scenario

Projections about the strength of our economy vary widely but recall that growth in GNP per worker has been virtually level since the 1970s. Therefore, barring a resurgence in productivity that violently breaks this pattern, a best-case scenario is for modest growth and the avoidance of a severe economic downturn. But this best-case scenario is not necessarily a rosy one. The basic foundation for this projected growth is that a weak dollar will make American-made goods cheap on the world markets and revitalize our manufacturing sector—a structural change that is going to require significant investment in plant and equipment and, consequently, diminished domestic consumption. The plan also calls for our major trading partners to reduce their exports and absorb ours. If our trading partners do not consume more, the world marketplace will be glutted with goods and a worldwide recession (some whisper depression) could occur.

Furthermore, this plan calls for some improbable changes in the domestic economy. We still need to service the mountain of debt that has accumulated as we shift from consumption to investment. The prospects for an improved standard of living under this "optimistic" forecast, therefore, are not at all bright. Debt payments, exports, and investment in plant and equipment will consume a larger share of economic output. Meanwhile, the weak dollar which is necessary to fuel manufactured exports, will make foreign imports more expensive. Former Commerce Secretary Peter Peterson estimates that to finance our debts and simultaneously to create the necessary productive capacity, consumption must decline by about $165 per worker per year over the next decade. To put this in perspective, consumption per worker rose by about $200 per year in the 1970s—a period many considered austere. It is far from clear that we can generate the political will in this country to make these necessary adjustments.

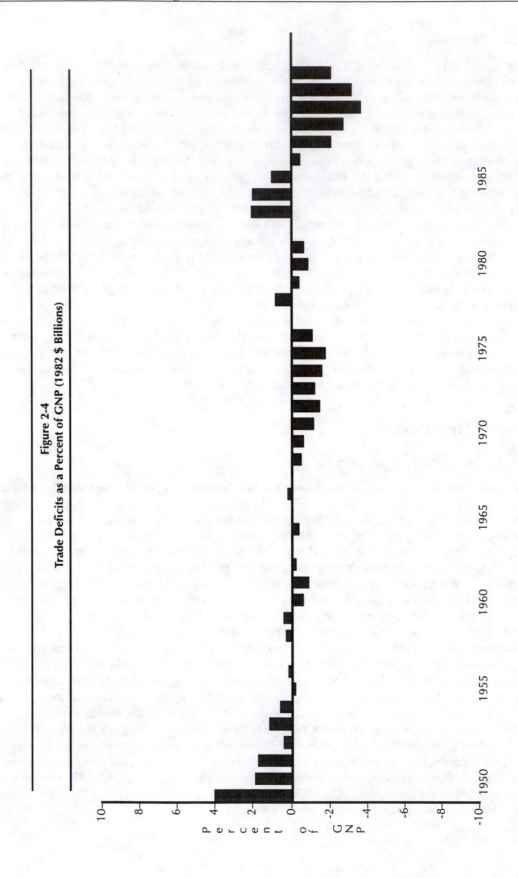

Figure 2-4
Trade Deficits as a Percent of GNP (1982 $ Billions)

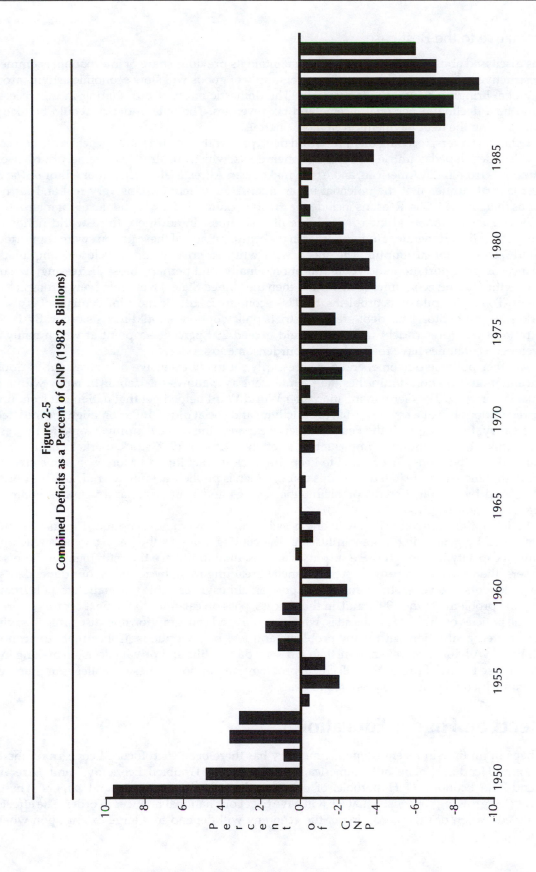

**Figure 2-5**
**Combined Deficits as a Percent of GNP (1982 $ Billions)**

## Alternative to the Best-case

If, as discussed above, each country tries to maintain its previous share of international commerce, a destructive trade war could result. The oversupply of goods will slow economic activity around the globe, bringing a worldwide recession. The domestic effect of our sharing in this recession would be a decline in personal income and tax revenues. The federal deficit would be likely to grow, making the debt payments even more onerous.

Other observers, focusing on third-world debt, proffer that even a mild cyclical recession could cause less developed countries to repudiate their debts, which are already extremely burdensome, as accounts from Latin American, and Africa make clear. Alfred Malabre, a senior editor of *The Wall Street Journal*, argues that the potential for an international debt crisis is very real and far more serious than in the 1930s. Reasons include the greater volume of debt, higher levels of international trade, and the commercial interdependence of economies. In addition, third-world nations are more politically independent today. Earlier in the century many of these nations were supported by a more stable colonial empire. The speed with which a crisis could develop is amplified by advances in transportation and communication. Finally, and perhaps most distressing, in earlier decades the leading economies (Britain, and then the United States) were relatively strong creditor nations. Today, in spite of its problems, the U.S. economy is still the most influential but is also the world's largest debtor. This debt greatly restricts policy options should a crisis occur. By 1992-93 the ratio of our foreign debt to exports could exceed 200 percent—a point at which many less developed economies have found debt too burdensome to service.

Another possible outcome, and not necessarily mutually exclusive of a recession, is double-digit inflation. Inflation diminishes the pain of debt as it allows the debtor to repay with a less valuable currency. The German inflation after World War I helped get that nation out from under war reparations but at a severe cost in productivity and social order. Inflation might be initiated in this country, for example, if the Federal Reserve expands the money supply in an effort to rescue failing financial institutions. (Immediately after the October 1987 stock market crash, the Fed promised "all the money necessary" to keep the stock market liquid.) Moreover, some observers believe that there is more bad debt in this country than is publicly acknowledged, an assertion that is bolstered by the farm credit problems, the savings and loan crisis, and veterans home loan program defaults.

Policy options are very slim, with one possible, and dangerous, exception. The social security system will be generating large surpluses in the coming years as the baby boomers reach peak earnings capacity. Although these surpluses are essential to finance the retirement of these same workers, the funds could provide some financial breathing room by reducing our dependence on foreign lenders. However, these funds also pose an almost irresistible temptation to politicians to postpone problems in the 1990s and, in the process, pass on calamity to the next century.

The policies of the last few decades, which encouraged consumption and discouraged savings, have created a situation with many problems and few policy options. Concern about economic well-being will dominate, even more than it does today, public and private decision making in the 1990s. These financial pressures will create problems and opportunities for colleges and universities with which they must be prepared to deal.

# Effects on Higher Education

Perhaps in no time in recent economic memory has there been such focused concern on the U.S. economy. Headlines blare out: "America, Wake Up!," "A Troubled Economy," and "Are We a Second-Rate Economy?" Hyperbole, of course, helps to sell magazines and papers. There is, however, a growing consensus that we will have to get our national finances in order. The effects on higher education of this reordering of the economy will depend to a large extent upon whether higher education is seen as part of the problem or part of the solution. Put another way, does higher education represent consumption or investment? The glib response is that expenditures on higher education are an investment—an investment in human capital. This may be true but the United States "invests" more in higher education than any other country and proportionately more than our major trading partners (3 percent of GNP compared to 1.7 percent in Japan, .7 percent in Germany, and .8 percent in France). In spite of these relatively high educational expenditures, our economy has grown at a far slower rate than most others in the industrial world. Moreover, even if higher education is part of the "solution," that will not insulate it from demands for efficiency (i.e., doing the same for less) as family and public budgets are strained.

This section is divided into two parts. The first considers the effects of the protracted economic strains on colleges and universities. The second looks at likely roles for higher education in resolving America's competitiveness problems.

## General Economic Strains

In the first part of this chapter it was argued that the coming decade is likely to be a financially spare one. As we repay our debts, build productive capacity, and export more goods, and as consumers pay a higher price for imports, the level of resources remaining to pay governmental and family expenses will be limited. This prospective austerity will affect all institutions including higher education.

### Effects at the Federal Level

As a consequence of these economic necessities, the resources available for higher education from the federal government are not likely to grow, and may even shrink in real terms. All new program initiatives and the refinancing of existing programs will bump up squarely against the financial constraints caused by the deficit. Similarly, favorable tax treatment of higher education will be weighed against the government's need for new revenues without breaking President Bush's campaign promises to hold the line on taxes. This pressure is already evident as colleges and universities are finding it increasingly necessary to defend the tax-exempt status of endowments and parts of auxiliary enterprises. It is important, therefore, that higher education constituents work collectively to maintain the advantages they now have. More important, all institutions must avoid abuses of their tax status that could trigger either a legislative or regulatory assault.

New tax incentives to support higher education are extremely unlikely. One possible exception is that there may be an opportunity for tax-advantaged savings that demonstrably increase family capital accumulation—but the savings would have to be clearly new and not displaced from other sources. The reason that special consideration might be given to savings incentives is that additional capital is needed to finance public and private infrastructure.

Inflation, should it reoccur, would put a special strain on the student aid budget that has been under attack for years. Between 1980-81 and 1987-88, federally-supported student aid declined about 4 percent after adjusting for inflation. Virtually all of the cuts were sustained by the social security educational benefits and by veterans benefits. Pell grants, on the other hand, increased 17 percent. Part of the relief for general student aid was achieved because of lower nominal interest rates (real interest charges remain high through the time of this printing, but inflation dropped from 15 to 5 percent). Consequently the special allowance interest payment to lenders declined from 52 percent of Guaranteed Student Loan (GSL) costs in 1982 to 7 percent in 1987 (Source: College Board). Should double-digit inflation return, interest costs will rise dramatically and the entire federal student aid budget is likely to be distressed.

A recession, of course, would expand the deficit as revenues decline and transfer payments increase. This clearly exacerbates all problems discussed above. Until the federal budget is in closer balance, new broad-based assistance for higher education is unlikely. Specially focused programs that have the potential to provide direct improvement of American economic competitiveness will undoubtedly be enacted.

## Effects at the State Level

The income and spending constraints of state governments will be similar to those at the federal level. Fortunately, states do not have as extensive a backlog of deficits as does the federal government. On the other hand, Steven Gold, director of fiscal studies for the National Conference of State Legislators, points out that state year-end general fund balances are precariously low. Since 1978, only 1983, a year at the tail end of a recession, showed lower year-end reserves. As a consequence, state budget options will be stretched by a laggard economy. A recession could cause a wave of state crises.

Although there are clear limits to states' abilities to finance education, including higher education, it has become a major policy issue. The reasons for increased state-level attention to education are complex and spring from a variety of public and private motivations, but clearly, desire to reinvigorate state economies is among the most prevalent causes. Linked to this is the concern that, although education is an important policy tool, the public is not getting its money's worth. Legislators and governors are demanding accountability in the form of evidence of educational achievement. If accountability is a manifestation of economic pressures, as I believe it is, the 1990s are unlikely to provide any relief to educational administrators. The opposite, in fact, should be expected. If economic strains grow—that is, if family incomes remain stagnant—the arguments may broaden from concerns about program and campus efficiency to basic questions about (1) sector roles (Should higher education be providing remedial instruction?); (2) access (How much higher education can we afford?); and (3) production technology (How important is tenure?). It is ominous that in Britain, a country whose economic weakness preceded ours, the protection afforded by faculty tenure has been significantly diminished.

## Effects on Institutions

Although financial stresses will affect public and independent institutions differentially, the general effects will be similar. Slow to no growth in family incomes will have a depressing effect on enrollments and, more specifically, on tuition income. A recession, however, could cause enrollments to spurt at public institutions. A weak dollar will reduce the cost of higher education to foreigners. Inflation will raise costs and high real interest rates. Finally, capital market volatility will generally increase the cost of financing and make investing more hazardous. In this environment independent colleges may be at special risk. Each of these eventualities will be considered briefly.

To paraphrase Mark Twain's famous telegram, past reports about the impending demise of private higher education have been greatly exaggerated. Is it possible, however, that these earlier concerns were well grounded and that only unanticipated intervention and events averted serious troubles. The rapid growth of federal student aid in the 1970s, for example, was just such a fortuitous intervention. Federal student aid, adjusted for inflation, doubled between 1970 and 1980. In addition, private higher education has undoubtedly benefited from the general, even if ill-founded, economic confidence of the 1980s. Some set of parents, the exact proportion is unknown, may have been willing to extend themselves financially to pay for expensive private education because the economy seemed strong, the market value of their home provided a sense of wealth, or because the wife was able to find a job and maintain the family's life style. More generally, the 1980s were not a decade for American self-denial. If this attitude turns, and I am arguing that this change is inevitable, families will review expenditures, including those for higher education, much more carefully. Some real-estate markets have already begun to decline and a number of economists asset that a recession is overdue. Should economic problems become especially severe, the long-heralded crisis in private higher education may arrive.

Perversely, a recession will magnify state financial problems but, as prior recessions have shown, an economic downturn is likely to result in increased demand for higher education as more young high school graduates cannot find a place in the workforce. This increased demand will, of course, be concentrated at the less expensive public institutions. In such an environment, public colleges may be asked to deliver more with less funding.

Any realistic projection of economic progress suggests that we will continue to need foreign capital for some time. As a consequence the dollar is predicted to stay depressed and real interest rates high. As noted earlier, the weak dollar will raise the cost of imports and reduce the purchasing power of domestic incomes. On the positive side, the sharp decline in the dollar should directly reduce the cost of American goods to foreigners. As it turns out, this generally hasn't occurred as manufacturers, wholesalers, shippers, and retailers all try to add on additional profit margins. But foreigners purchase higher education directly and these premiums are unlikely to appear—with the possible exception that state legislators may become restive about educating foreign competitors with public funds. Colleges that have strong programs for recruiting, assimilating, and educating foreign students should benefit immediately from the decline in the dollar.

Inflation, some analysts argue, is the only politically acceptable escape from our enormous public and private debt burdens. Double-digit inflation, *should it reoccur*, may affect institutions of higher education with special severity as it did in the 1970s. The generally accepted reasoning is that service industries, including higher education, are labor intensive. That is, their production process requires proportionately more labor that capital and, this conventional wisdom continues, it is inherently difficult to substitute capital (i.e., machines) for labor in service industries. Manufacturers, on the other hand, can tilt the production processes toward capital-intensive machinery. Partially as a consequence of this shifting, the price of manufactured goods did not rise as rapidly as wages in the 1970s. Clearly there is some truth in this notice, but higher education would serve itself poorly by hiding behind such a shibboleth. Phone companies are in a service business, moreover one that is also engaged information transmission, yet the real costs of telephone calls today are a fraction of what they were a few decades ago. This efficiency is a direct result of the effective use of technology. Higher education's apparent inability to use technology to reduce costs may have more to do with faculty values and the primacy of faculty  governance than higher education's immutable production process. Institutions that can adapt technology successfully will be better suited to survive in an economy with limited growth and soaring prices. More generally, the coming decades are likely to require that colleges and universities devote some considerable attention to improving efficiency. Former Secretary of Education William Bennett has decried the rapid tuition increases of the 1980s. Those exhortations, while irritable in tone, continue to reflect a broadly based concern and were premonitory, not a divergent opinion.

An inflationary environment, coupled with this country's continuing need to attract foreign capital, will obviously push up interest rates. High real interest rates will encourage parental savings but will raise the cost of borrowing to states institutions, and families. Once inflation has set in, parents and students will find debt a costly way to finance education. (During the process of inflation-acceleration, debt burdens diminish.) Similarly, institutions that need to borrow to replace and renew plant and equipment will also find debt more burdensome.

In this prospective environment, capital markets are especially volatile, as recessions drag down nominal interest rates and inflation pushes them up. Colleges should be especially cautious when borrowing; interest rate caps on variable rate debt may be well worth the added cost. Volatile capital markets also demand special vigilance for the management of endowment, and a more conservative approach to investment strategies should be considered. The emerging standard for the 1990s is likely to be capital preservation.

## Proactive Policies and Higher Education

William Baumol, a Princeton economist, observes that lagging productivity does not keep a nation from competing. Rather, it forces the country to compete in different ways—primarily through lower relative wages. In comparison to our major trading partners, wages in the United States have been declining for about two decades. Because of economic forces reviewed in this chapter, this trend may be irreversible for some time. In fact, wages may decline absolutely. Obviously, politicians and policy makers will not observe this trend passively. There will be positive, proactive responses. We have already suggested there will be increased scrutiny of public budgets. Efforts to improve the effectiveness of all public expenditures will be redoubled. Furthermore, budgets will be reorganized to target resources on areas that will have an immediate positive impact on our local, state, and national economies. All this is, of course, already occurring. The present analysis suggests that the problems will not pass quickly and that the coming environment is likely to be even more difficult.

### High Technology and Science

At the postsecondary level, funding of science and technology will continue, as will government efforts to galvanize corporate and university partnerships. So far most of the policy responses have been at the state level. Developmental corporations are being formed to smooth technology transfer from university laboratories to commercial production. In addition, states are encouraging, and sometimes financing, the development of research parks near universities. While anecdotal evidence suggests that these efforts can be successful, systematic reviews are just getting underway.

The federal government, relying primarily on macro-economic policy, has lagged behind the states in developing these more micro activities. One notable exception is Sematech, a federally funded project at the University of Texas at Austin. This venture will bring together researchers from the university and from the leading semiconductor producers in the United States. The goal of Sematech is to re-establish our lead in the production of state-of-the-art semiconductor chips. If Sematech is successful, and if the state ventures prove successful, more funds and energy will follow.

These initiatives are, of course, welcome. They probably cannot be halted. But higher education should be cautious. As Thomas Jefferson warned the nation against entangling alliances," these relationships are potentially constraining, even repressive. The University of Rochester stumbled when it briefly caved in to pressure from its benefactor, Eastman Kodak, and withdrew the acceptance of an applicant employed by Fuji Corporation. In this era of trade vulnerability, it is not difficult to imagine restrictions on foreign graduate students working in labs funded with federal money. Moreover, there will be a multitude of lively contests in the general arena of intellectual property rights as public funding authorities, corporations, universities, and faculty vie with one another for a "fair share" of generated gains.

### Mid-Level Technology and Industrial Extension

Scientific progress is obviously important to mankind in many ways, including economically. But national success at the scientific frontier does not necessarily translate into national economic success. High technology breakthroughs are expensive to achieve and difficult, as well as undesirable, to protect with parents. The success of America's trading partners was not built on expanding the frontiers of science but on adapting science to products and to the production process.

As we maintain our strength in basic science, we must also ensure that technological innovations find their way into the industrial process—this, of course, is the technology-transfer issue that has stimulated "incubator" programs, university-business cooperation, and science parks. There is, however, a more prosaic technology transfer that must occur: the transfer of mid-range technology to the design, manufacture, and distribution of goods. Certainly this is happening but not on the necessary scale. Moreover, too much of the innovation is limited to large, well-capitalized corporations within certain sectors. Higher education can plan an important role in bringing technological innovations to companies of all sizes and in all sectors of manufacturing.

Industrial extension, an analog to agricultural extension, has already been suggested and is being attempted at some large public universities. The idea needs to be further refined and expanded. For example, university-based research and development parks are typically built on high technology cores; the concept is that a concentration of scientists will form a synergy resulting in new ideas and new products. Their focus is on science and scientific products. Generally, covenants for these parks significantly restrict the type and amount of manufacturing in which tenants may engage.

As an alternative to science parks, states could create high technology production parks that invite companies involved in certain types of production to become tenants. The parks could be built near a university and some part of the lease payments would support process-development laboratories. It is conceivable that the state might match these funds. In addition to the university's role, community colleges could be enlisted to train students in the repair and service of related equipment.

Some years ago I was employed as a production engineer with General Electric. One plant at which I worked was developing a new process for manufacturing industrial capacitors. The developmental work was being done in a remote part of the facility, with those engineers being both socially and physically isolated. For most of us, our work day centered on production schedules, labor relations, cost containment, and similar concerns. The development engineers had no colleagues. A production park that had, for example, a commitment to metal shaping and joining could help to create the same synergy in production that we are trying to build in science. This type of corporate-higher education partnership does not have the glamor of recombinant genetic research or of super-conductivity, but it may have more immediate economic impact. Moreover, it probably provides a better fit with regional universities and certainly with area community colleges.

As higher education moves closer to industry, there are many academic and economic problems to be resolved, ranging from faculty compensation to site selection to efficient public subsidies. We must find answers to these problems if we are going to involve higher education effectively in national and local economic resurgence.

## Foreign Students and Modern Languages

One area of the liberal arts that is likely to prosper in the emerging global economy will be foreign studies and modern languages. For decades this country has charted its own scientific and economic course and the rest of the world has followed. As our technological and commercial hegemony wanes, traffic on these streets will increasingly flow in two directions. A number of the trade problems with Japan, for example, are attributed to cultural misunderstandings. There will be more demand for people who can communicate with and understand the cultures of our global partners—not just the major trading nations but lesser developed countries also where we will compete to place manufacturing facilities. Similarly, we can no longer assume that all major technological innovations will be immediately published in English, so demand for translators is likely to grow. Institutions that maintain effective foreign studies and language programs should benefit.

## Need for Balance

In this scenario of increasing attention to economic success, the tensions between the liberal arts and the sciences and other more directly commercial fields of study can only increase. As the goals of families and legislators bend even more toward preserving and improving their personal and public economies, college administrators and trustees will need to be watchful that an appropriate equilibrium is maintained. In addition, they must avoid short-term answers to long-term problems. Broadly educated, self-reflective, articulate graduates will be more valuable to the nation, economically and otherwise, than narrowly trained technicians.

Related to the question of balance of institutional mission is the danger that colleges and universities will promise more than they can truly deliver. In the 1960s and 1970s higher education was enlisted in the war on poverty. In fact, we were more than passive conscripts; we welcomed public funds and became active partners in promising an excellent education and upward socio-economic mobility to all who would spend four years. Subsequently we found public, especially federal, support to be inherently unstable, bringing attendant financial problems to our institutions. Real troubles, however, resulted from our inability to deliver on our promises. Simply stated, we failed to deliver upward socioeconomic mobility on the scale promised, and enrollments and public support waned. In retrospect the failure was inevitable. There wasn't enough room in the upper socioeconomic strata for the 60 percent of the age cohort who enrolled in our institutions.

The parallel concern today is that we may reorient our institutions to deliver economic growth that will halt the Japanese juggernaut. Having restructured our institutions, we could find that the ascendancy of our trading partners is not easily reversed or that we were fighting the wrong battle. Public policy, and funding, may turn elsewhere and leave colleges with the fixed costs of laboratories and business schools and a faculty too narrowly trained in the hard sciences and commerce.

## Summary

The real gross national product grew at an impressive 3.8 percent in 1988 and, as of this writing, there are few signs of the long-expected recession. Unemployment is still low and consumer spending remains strong. But current successes (or immediate problems) do not eliminate the pressing need to reduce the federal deficit, raise exports, and increase savings so that we can rebuild public and private infrastructure. The longer we wait, the more disruptive the reckoning.

Gross national product has four components: family consumption, government spending, capital investment, and net export of goods and services. As net exports rise, other components of the GNP must decline proportionately. To raise exports the United States must increase investment in plant and equipment, further diminishing the share going to family consumption and government spending. Moreover, much of government spending is unavoidable, ballooning debt payments being one inevitable expense. Unless this country's productivity is accelerated beyond its current lackluster standard, the prospects for a significantly improved standard of living are not bright.

The dependence of the United States on foreign capital will continue pushing interest rates upward and depressing the dollar. (A lower dollar will further diminish U.S. living standards.) We will, of course, learn to live within our means. But unless the transition to a more provident economy is coordinated with an increase in consumption by our trading partners, a major recession could occur. (Many economists argue that a cyclical recession is already overdue.) A recession, regardless of its cause, would exacerbate public and private budgetary problems. In addition, the threat of inflation remains as policy makers seek a politically acceptable escape from our debt problems.

Disruptions in capital markets will make debt financing, fund raising, and investment management more difficult. Although institutions will still try to achieve growth, attention to capital preservation will be important. High interest rates could severely disrupt Washington-based student aid as high GSL interest payments drain away federal support.

Voters will resist increased public spending as they try to minimize taxes and maintain personal living standards. Public funding for higher education will be most easily achieved when there are direct and measurable benefits—particularly economic ones. Similarly, personal incomes will be strained and family expenditures on higher education more closely examined. Moreover, our anemic savings rate and the growing number of two-income families are worrisome trends for private higher eduction. The typical family in the coming decade will have neither banked sufficient cash nor have a reserve worker (i.e., an educated housewife) for paying pricey tuition bills. Quality institutions will survive but glossy brochures and a "distinguished past" will be insufficient evidence of value. The current public and private call for productivity and accountability from colleges and universities could be only a murmur compared to the prospective clamor of the next decade.

---

An earlier version of this chapter appeared in 1988 as an edition of *Capital Ideas*, published by the Forum for College Financing.

# The Role of the Business Officer in Managing Educational Resources (1971)

## William G. Bowen

*Presented herewith is the text of the talk delivered by Dr. Bowen on November 22 during NACUBO's 1971 national meeting at The Waldorf-Astoria in New York City. Following it are excerpts from the remarks of his fellow panelists, Hans H. Jenny, of the College of Wooster; Clarence Scheps, of Tulane University; and Orie E. Myers, Jr., of Emory University.*

The question to which we have been asked to address ourselves this morning is: "How can the business officer best provide input to the academic world?" For reasons which I shall explain later I would like to propose a modest rephrasing of this question as follows: "How can the business manager contribute most effectively to the managing of educational resources under present (and prospective) conditions?"

In trying to answer this question more or less concretely, I find it convenient to think in terms of four different—but related—tasks. The first two are quite general and can be described briefly; the last two will require somewhat more elaboration.

## Assessing the General Financial Setting

Whatever may have been the case in times gone by, no college or university today can view itself as an island unaffected by the prevailing economic winds. The financial prospects facing any of our institutions are affected to some degree by the outlook for the economy in general as well as by quite specific actions of the Congress. Revisions of the tax laws and various parts of the new wage-price apparatus illustrate the important effects on colleges and universities of governmental measures designed for much broader purposes.

One of the functions of a business officer in an academic setting ought to be to provide some intelligence to his colleagues concerning developments of this kind. More specifically, I think that the business officer ought to assume a special responsibility for alerting his president and other appropriate officers to the likely effects on the university's financial condition of the general economic outlook as well as likely legislative or administrative actions. Right at the moment, for example, it appears to me as if earnings from endowments over the next year or two are likely to be disappointing—in part because of underlying economic factors and in part because of elements of Phase 2 of President Nixon's new economic program. Also, decisions regarding salary policies, rents (if there is college or university housing to be considered), student charges, and so on have to be viewed to some extent within the context of the national guidelines still being developed.

I hasten to add that only the bravest of you will speak with certainty about any of these matters. Indeed, contemplating the questions to which I have just alluded may make many of us look more favorably on the creation of Astrology Departments! Still, uncertainty is no excuse for saying nothing, and I think that business officers can be helpful to their colleagues by preventing them from foolish extrapolations if nothing else.

## Assessing and Describing the Economics of the University

The second task which I think most business officers ought to assume also involves the application of some general notions concerning the nature of our economy. Here, however, the task I have in mind is describing the economics of the educational institution itself in a lucid and helpful way. Increasingly, alumni, trustees, faculty, and students will be debating the financial policies of colleges and universities, and in the course of these debates assumptions will be made—explicitly or implicitly—about the basic economic characteristics of these institutions. Too often, however, these notions will be naive ones, bereft of any sense of fundamental economic concepts or, at the other end of the spectrum, representing a simplistic attempt to describe the college or university as if it were a producer of piston rings.

The business officer can perform an important function by helping all of the constituencies of the college or university to think intelligently about such concepts as "productivity" in an educational setting. In planning for the future, it is important to be realistic in recognizing the economic implications of being a handicraft industry—which is largely what we are. The opportunities for technological change, capital accumulation, and mass production are all less for educational institutions than they are for the economy at large, and this means that one ought to expect the *relative* costs of higher education to rise over time. And, it is important for the general public, in particular, to understand that in this respect education is a service industry, whose economic problems do not stem simply (or even mainly) from economy-wide increases in prices. Our costs would go up even if the general price level were steady, and this needs to be understood.

At the same time, the fact that it is harder to increase productivity in colleges or universities than in many industrial concerns is no excuse for failing to make any effort to become more efficient in the relevant sense of that important word. (Let me stress that by becoming "more efficient," I do not mean simply increasing class size. "Efficiency" and "productivity" in the relevant economic sense mean relating outputs to inputs, and increasing class size can mean sacrificing important qualitative aspects of education which in turn means less output, measured properly. This is not to say that class size should not rise—in many situations it probably should—but it is to argue that we ought to get our concepts straight and not define efficiency and productivity so as to make larger class size and greater efficiency equal by definition. That misuse of concepts serves only to beg the important and difficult question of the true relationship between class size and educational quality.) Questions of teaching methods and class size aside, there are things that can be done to increase productivity, and faculty members need to be encouraged to think about more efficient scheduling procedures for classes, sharing of scarce library and computer resources with other institutions, and so forth.

In describing the economic nature of the educational institution, the business officer also needs to help his associates understand such concepts as fixed costs versus variable costs. This simple dichotomy is important in analyzing the likely effects of changes in enrollment on teaching budgets and indirect costs. It is also important, as I have just had occasion to learn rather painfully, in studying the economics of food services. Furthermore, the concept of variable costs, and the need to relate incremental costs to incremental revenues, are also critically important in evaluating proposals for summer sessions, to cite but one more example.

It would be easy to list other basic economic concepts which have major implications for the managing of educational resources (for example, the need to impute capital costs when funds for a new dormitory are given by a donor.) However, you will think of other examples as quickly as I can, and the general point I want to make is simply that the business officer should not hesitate to point out the practical implications of these concepts for the operations of his own institution.

# Facilitating Decision Making and Control

Understanding the basic economic characteristics of a college or university is, unhappily, no substitute for making a great many hard decisions. The decisions to which I refer include both pricing decisions (what to do about tuition and room and board) and resource allocation decisions (how much should be spent for faculty positions, for the library, for supporting services, for student aid, and so on). Moreover, almost all of these decisions involve choices between the present and the future (how large a deficit can we afford to run now, what will be the long-run effects of a reduction in the library budget, what portion of endowment income can be spent in the current fiscal year without endangering the corpus of the fund, and so on).

All of these are "hard" decisions in two very different senses. First, they are hard because they involve genuinely difficult issues of choice which depend, among other things, on imperfect assessments of the effects of different courses of action on the educational program of the institution. Even if everyone were in agreement as to the relative importance of, say, graduate work versus undergraduate work, it might still be far from obvious how particular decisions concerning the Computer Center or the Library would affect either, especially in the long run. Second, these are hard decisions in the sense that they involve the well being of various groups and, indeed, of particular individuals. Under present budget constraints, there is pain aplenty to be borne (terminating appointments, allowing real standards of living to be reduced, increasing workloads), and whenever this is the case the decisions to be made are difficult ones for this reason alone. An enduring strength of many colleges and universities is that they are peculiarly human institutions, and thus the way in which these hard decisions are made and accepted becomes very important to the welfare of the institution as well as to the individuals most intimately concerned.

In the balance of my remarks this morning, I will try to spell out some specific things that I believe business officers can do to make the process of reaching hard decisions go as well as possible.

1. *The budgetary process should be structured from a timing standpoint so as to permit all competing claims on university resources to be evaluated more or less simultaneously.* Until recently, many of us were in the habit of making important budgetary decisions at different times during the year. For example, commitments concerning new faculty positions were often made well ahead of decisions regarding supporting staff or library appropriations. While it is easy to see the practical considerations that led to spreading out these decisions over a fairly long period, proceeding in this way simply is not conducive to making clear choices. If the decision making process is to be as rational as possible, it is necessary that expenditures on, say, athletics, be compared with expenditures on faculty positions and on supporting services *before any commitments are made.* In most instances, this will require an acceleration of the budget making process, with trial budgets prepared as early as late October or mid-November so that decisions regarding faculty positions can be made early enough to permit effective recruiting. Adjusting the timing of the budget process in this way will mean more work and will impose added strains on business officers and their staffs; this procedural adjustment, however, is a necessary first step to improved decision making.

Simultaneous consideration of competing requests to spend money also requires knowledge, fairly early on, of the total resources likely to be available in the next fiscal year. Hence, business officers need to project income from all sources soon enough to present a comprehensive picture of the financial condition of the institution before any decisions, even tentative ones, are made regarding expenditures. And, on the basis of some painful experience of my own, I would urge that this "comprehensive" picture be truly comprehensive—that it include all sources of income and all forms of expenditures, including sponsored research and charges to restricted accounts. It is tempting, in the interests of simplicity, to work only with "general funds" budgets. This kind of partial approach can lead, however, to serious errors of estimation and to wrong judgments concerning the needs of various departments and activities. The basic reason is that most colleges and universities are sufficiently integrated organizations that they simply cannot be split up into restricted and general funds portions without confusing rather than clarifying basic relationships. To repeat, I speak from painful experience.

2. *Financial data need to be organized according to the logic of decision making as well as according to the logic of control.* Different kinds of costs need to be grouped together under the program objective which they serve so that the college or university will know the full implications of pursuing, say, graduate work in Psychology. Thus, space costs, costs of supporting services, special library costs, and the costs of graduate student support need to be grouped with faculty salaries to provide a unified picture of expenditures for, say, graduate work in Psychology.

This is, if you will, a plea for program budgeting, but it is a plea for program budgeting with a small "p." I am not advocating grandiose systems which are costly to install and of marginal use, whatever their aesthetic appeal. Surely it would be wrong to apply cost-benefit analysis to everything but cost benefit analysis itself. What I am advocating is relatively simple rearrangements of budget entries to permit intelligent comparisons of alternative programs.

Let me give one example of what I am proposing. At my own university the ability of the Dean of Graduate School to evaluate the resource costs of graduate student support and to consider alternative modes of support has long suffered from the fragmented and decentralized nature of the entire process of providing funds to students. Some fellowships have been awarded at the departmental level from the restricted accounts, others have been obtained by individual students on the basis of national competitions, and still others have been awarded by the Dean of Graduate School himself from endowed accounts and from some appropriations of general funds. In addition, significant numbers of graduate students have received aid in the form of assistantships in research and in instruction, with the former determined largely by the leaders of sponsored research projects and the latter determined by department chairmen in consultation with the Dean of Faculty. Finally, many graduate students have been receiving support in the form of housing and dining subsidies, with the amounts here determined by the real estate department and the department of dormitories and food services.

As long as funds for graduate student support were relatively plentiful, this varigated structure, with budget entries related to graduate student support appearing under many headings in the chart of accounts, may have been satisfactory. Now, however, financial stringency requires a more comprehensive and coordinated set of data. Having worked for the last two years with overall estimates of support from every source, we believe that we are doing a better job of using the limited funds at our disposal—a better job both in terms of our ability to attract good students and in terms of our ability to allocate fairly what we have done.

One more word needs to be said concerning the treatment of graduate student housing, because it illustrates so well the general point I am trying to make. For many years Princeton has provided housing for some—but by no means all—married graduate students as well as single students. And, while this housing has carried rents well below market levels, there has often been controversy over proposed increases in rents. Needless to say, no one likes to see his or her rent increased, especially when the family is already hard pressed financially, as in the case of many graduate student couples. Under these circumstances, it was exceedingly difficult to have reasoned discussions of rental policies, and of attendant effects on equity among graduate students in and out of university housing, *so long as consideration of rents was separated from consideration of other forms of graduate student support.* As a result, there had been a steady increase for some time in the subsidies going to those graduate students fortunate enough to live in university housing.

With the advent of a budget for graduate student support constructed along more programmatic lines, however, it was possible to change the framework within which rental policies were set. We made it clear that subsidies on graduate student housing were viewed as a form of support just like fellowships, that there would have to be a set amount of funds available for graduate student support in all forms, and that therefore every additional dollar of subsidy for housing would mean one less dollar of fellowship money available. Once the situation was defined in these terms, it became easier to discuss the advantages and disadvantages of alternative modes of support. Housing subsidies came to be seen not as an end of policy, but as one among several methods of achieving an objective: namely, to use the limited funds available as effectively and as fairly as possible for the support of *all* students.

3. *It is important to include nonfinancial data along with financial data under various program headings.* All too often, decision-making in colleges and universities has been hindered by the lack of integration of data dealing with flows and data dealing with measures of educational activity (number of courses taught, number of students enrolled in different departments, and so on). In many institutions, the Controller's Office and the Registrar's Office have not always worked as closely as would have been desirable from the standpoint of managing educational programs. Fortunately, modern methods of data processing (and here again I do not mean to suggest overly elaborate approaches) make it possible to show on a single form, both the money costs of a program and the numbers of students served by it. This simple step in turn makes it much easier to compare various undertakings and to evaluate requests for additional funds.

4. *It is necessary to present data several years into the future.* We are past the point at which it is possible to make obeisance to forward planning and then to look seriously at the next year alone. Commitments made in the present almost always have financial implications into the future, and these implications need to be understood at the time the initial commitment is made. Also, the savings associated with a particular budgetary decision may seem very small if looked at only in the context of one year, but may look much larger when followed through the budget system for several years.

Increasingly, trustees, regents, alumni, legislators, and others from whom we seek support will want to know how well we are planning for the future. Business officers and others responsible for the overall planning of the university will have to be able to provide projections of costs and incomes under various assumptions. And, I want to emphasize that simple extrapolations will not suffice. What is needed is a coordinated set of multi-year plans for academic and non-academic departments which take account both of resources costs and associated levels of educational activity.

Again, perhaps an illustration will be useful. Providing adequate student aid has become one of the most difficult problems which all of us face. Rising tuition charges make it more and more difficult to achieve the diversity and equality of opportunity within the student body which are so important to the society as well as to each of our institutions. Faced with pressures to provide more scholarship funds, it is tempting to look at the financial aid budget on a one year basis. But, this is an exceedingly dangerous procedure if the institution feels a commitment to continue to provide aid to students initially admitted with support, as most of us do. In short, financial aid at the undergraduate level is, almost by definition, a four year commitment and it has to be viewed as such. In considering alternative student aid budgets at Princeton last year, we constructed detailed tables tracing through the effects four years into the future of each of the approaches under investigation.

This led us to be more realistic and also, I think, more honest with ourselves. As one result of this exercise, we separated the student aid appropriation between funds allocated to entering students and funds allocated to continuing students. While this distinction did not matter greatly from the standpoint of accounting for scholarship funds expended, it did matter greatly from the standpoint of future commitments. If the Bureau of Student Aid, on its own initiation, can shift $1,000 of scholarship aid from continuing students to entering students, it can, in effect, require a new $4,000 commitment in the future.

Presenting data several years ahead can also be very important from the standpoint of individual departments, as well as from the standpoint of the central university. In the absence of forward planning of some kind, an academic department may recommend Smith for a tenure position this year without realizing that what it is really doing is foreclosing a tenure appointment for Jones two years from now. Of course, all forward plans must permit modifications and must involve some degree of flexibility. However, if they at least make departments aware of the *probable* implications of a decision this year for a decision to be taken in the future, they will have served an important purpose.

5. *Planning, budgeting, and control functions must be closely integrated.* Now, let me add a word of caution. In recommending changes in methods of organizing, presenting, and analyzing data, I want also to recommend as strongly as I can *against* abandoning traditional methods of record keeping until the new system is fully established—and even then, it may well turn out that the older systems continue to be best for purposes of control. To speak again from painful personal experience, let me stress the importance of maintaining the closest possible relationship between whatever new forms of presentation are developed and established bookkeeping and accounting systems. Planning and budgeting decisions have to be translated into a controllable form if they are to mean anything, and the business officer plainly occupies a critical position in seeing that bridges are maintained between bookkeeping and accounting systems and presentations of data in a form more suitable for decision making.

I come now to my last heading: Facilitating understanding and acceptance of decisions which are bound to be unpleasant for many people. In hard times, in particular, there is simply no substitute for the understanding and cooperation of all those who share a commitment to the institution—students, faculty, research personnel, library staff, administrators, supporting staff, trustees, alumni, parents of students, and other friends. And, if we are to expect cooperation and goodwill from all of these groups—which, while sharing a common commitment to the university, often have particular interests which conflict sharply—we must provide information. We must explain frankly and fully the nature of our overall problem and what we believe can and should be done about it.

## Facilitating Understanding and Acceptance

The business officer can make major contributions to this important objective. In carrying out all of his tasks it is important that he do what he can to make the materials he presents comprehensible to a broad array of interested parties. For example, in projecting tuition income he should take pains to show how he arrived at his projection—what assumptions he made about enrollment, attrition, and so on. Thus, if someone has a different sense of likely attrition, it is possible to revise the projections accordingly. Business officers have a natural tendency to present materials in the form of tables and printouts. I yield to no one in stressing the value of material presented in this way. At the same time, I think it is essential that such tabular presentations be accompanied by footnotes and text. If we are going to include more people in the process of thrashing out answers to questions of resource allocation, as I think we must, we are going to have to help these people see the choices before them.

Perhaps it is clearer now why I chose at the outset of these remarks to rephrase slightly the question to be considered by this panel. More and more, I see the lines between various elements of the university community blurring, and I see the business officer as an increasingly active participant in many phases of the process of managing educational resources, not just as a producer of financial tables.

To sum up the theme of these last few remarks, one of my recurring worries about the financial crisis through which all of higher education is now passing is that it will increase divisiveness within the universities, and to an excessive degree. The age-old tensions between the student body, faculty, administration, and alumni are no doubt healthy, up to a point. I believe, however, that the kinds of stresses and strains we face now push well beyond this right degree of tension. We face a growing prospect of adversary relationships which will interfere significantly with the sense of community and with the climate for learning which are so important at educational institutions. Strict budget limits have a potential for exacerbating conflicts between races, and between the middle class and lower income groups, as well as between departments. As a result, contrary to the views of some other people, I do not believe that great economic adversity will prove conducive to reform. On the contrary, I think there will be a strong tendency to protect vested interests and that it will be more difficult, rather than less difficult to innovate.

Business officers can do much to avert this result. They can contribute importantly by reducing the mysteries surrounding educational finance, by making clear the need for choice—in short, by serving their colleges and universities as business officer who are themselves educators.

## Hans H. Jenny

### Vice President for Finance and Business
### The College of Wooster

Dr. Bowen has assigned the business officer quite a task. Of course, I am sure, he is aware of the fact that many of you have more or less successfully tried to fulfill the functions he has outlined for us. And if there are still people in the audience and in our association who either have not heard this message or whose professional counsel is not sought or is ignored by the chief administrators of their respective institutions, then let them read Dr. Bowen's message and pay it heed. Overall, I am sure, we should be flattered by the compliment he is paying the profession.

My first follow-up comment centers on the topic of "top college management organization for decision making." When we get past organization charts and beyond theory, we must realize that in the academic scheme of things the pecking order far too often places the financial and business management component in a subordinate position. Worse yet, until recently, and in to many of our private institutions questions of finance and business ranked among the last questions asked. . . .

· · ·

If I can make a recommendation it is this: that college and university presidents—particularly those from the private institutions—be given by their trustees some tough but meaningful financial constraints, such as that no major faculty, student services, development office, or other decision is taken without the full involvement of the finance and business office. Once this is accomplished, much of the rest may follow. I trust that many present here today would agree that appropriate organization and intelligent financial constraints are of the essence and seem to be lacking too frequently.

My second response is slightly different and addresses itself to the finance and business officer.

My own thesis runs something like this: *it is the chief function of the business officer to extend the life of the institution into the indefinite future. His main job is to manage the finances, the income, the expenditures, the people, so as to give his institution another chance, and then another, and another.*

He—the business officer—is the fiscal and operational guardian of the academic (in the broadest sense) enterprise. He must help the president so that the latter's promises and dreams can come true. Financial and business management are *enabling* activities and duties. Thus my second point: we are not obstructionists; we should not make academic policy; we are the men making possible the impossible.

From this stems one crucial opportunity which we as a profession have missed more often than we have taken it: *the opportunity to update our fiscal and management concepts and tools.* This is my third, and most important, response. . . .

There is all this talk abroad today concerning the financial crisis in higher education. Sack-cloth and ashes, no less. In our studies (Jenny-Wynn) of forty-eight private colleges, this seems indeed to be the case. Worsening deficits all over the place.*

I contend that the crisis is less financial than it is conceptual. The financial recession is to a large extent the result of stereotypes in financial management thinking. Not all stereotypes are bad, of course, but colleges and universities seem to cherish a surprisingly large number of dysfunctional and harmful management concepts.

I shall mention three problem areas where innovation is either imminent or long overdue, the first two merely in passing.

First, higher education is made up of several groups of institutions which are substantially different in their nature. Recognizing this, it would seem to be logical that policies (national and otherwise) and resource planning and management be designed to suit each type according to the requirements dictated by the special nature of each group. But instead, we organize our associations, committees, and concepts so as to reach an agreement across nationalities, so to speak. No wonder we move like one of those slow convoys during World War II, an easy target to lurking dangers; mostly we move not at all.

Second, at the other extreme, we act in such a decentralized manner that we have become perhaps the epitome of the self-centered, inner-directed set of institutions in existence in modern times. One aspect of this—which we all must have experienced at one time or another—is how each one of us is prone to reinvent the wheel, time and time again, and sometimes within a given college or university in several places at once! Division of labor, that old chestnut of production efficiency, is not very well known or found often in university and college management. The fetish of uniqueness, no less. Result: we all end up doing the same thing about the same way.

Third, since the problem of colleges and universities is resources—how much, what kind, and when—one would think that the financial managers had developed a well-reasoned set of theories of resources, of fixed plus variable costs, and of the long-range overall resources requirements.

The notion that current annual income must generate some capital formation has been repugnant to the industry for convoluted rationalization for the most part. Yet, the 1960s, for instance, could have been an appropriate time to implement as a general principle one of the soundest concepts available to us from industry: the user should make some small payment for using up capital.

. . .

Management concepts which are imaginative, which are tailored to changing times and changing needs are *our* responsibility. When you work with weak, dysfunctional, outdated concepts, you end up asking the wrong questions and may, among the bad answers, inherit a financial fiasco.

Maybe Dr. Bowen was too polite to say this; I am certain that he has thought of it; and we all must have the nagging thought that some of the blame for the present financial crisis in private colleges and universities must go to us.

Once we accept the responsibilities and the challenge, however, we shall find many new avenues for extending our institutions' respective life spans again and again.

# Clarence Scheps

## Executive Vice President
## Tulane University

I find myself in almost total agreement with Dr. Bowen on his definition of the role of the business officer in managing educational resources. In my judgment, Dr. Bowen thinks like a business officer—and this is the highest compliment that one can pay an academician.

As a frame of reference to my brief comments, I would like to focus on the role of the business officer in managing educational resources in the context of the seventies—a period characterized by financial distress, depression, uncertainty, eroding public confidence and change. As I see it, the role of all administrative officers will become more difficult, and more important, because of the multiplicity of the problems of higher education, especially the financial ones. The business officer has to develop new ways and new techniques, not only to provide meaningful input to the academic world but, of equal importance, to achieve a situation in which the academic world uses this input in making educational decision. In too many instances, in the past, the business officer has been a voice crying in e wilderness—information and analyses which he has prepared have gone unused.

Higher education in the seventies faces difficult times. There seems to be no question about the existence of a deep financial depression in higher education. . . . Until recently I was among those who contended that only through greatly increased revenues could the financial ills of higher education be cured. I no longer believe this. I am now convinced that both sides of the equation will have to be attended vigorously and imaginatively. That is, as we energetically pursue additional sources of revenue, we must at the same time strive to make our systems of higher education and our individual institutions more efficient. There is some evidence that these two goals are clearly interrelated, since our inability to produce sufficient additional revenues at this time may be due in part to the crisis of confidence on the part of those who would provide the funding—state legislatures, private donors, the Federal Government. Some of the erosion in confidence has resulted from the widespread belief that higher education has not managed itself as efficiently as it might. Progress, expansion, enrichment in higher education have been nothing short of miraculous in the past two decades. But our individual institutions as well as our statewide systems of higher education have been expanded with little thought of the costs of such expansion. In a real sense we were living in a dream world.

Now to turn specifically to the question posed by the panel: How can the business officer best provide input to the academic world—an input which will contribute to bringing about an improved coordination between revenues and expenditures? I can only underscore, and perhaps paraphrase, what Dr. Bowen has already stated in his excellent paper. I would mention four areas in which the business officer has much to contribute:

First, the business officer must do what he can to see to it that adequate academic planning and budgeting systems are developed and used in his institution. These systems should cover a time frame of more than one year and should provide the mechanism for intensive periodic review of past programs, activities, projects, and expenditure levels. Call this program budgeting if you will.

In the second place, the business officer must be responsible for developing ways of educating the president, the faculty, and the trustees on the advantages and benefits of sound financial administration. . . .

In the third place, the business officer must be available to all the constituencies of the institution on matters relative to the financial status of his institution. In my judgment, there is no valid basis for secrecy on a college campus. If we are to bring about change in our educational institutions, which will lead us away from the path of insolvency and bankruptcy, our faculty more and more must become responsive to the needs for change.

Finally, I am convinced that one important impediment to the task of increasing productivity in higher education is the nature of administration in the typical institution and the budgeting process traditionally employed. I am referring to the fact that in most institutions the development of programs, other than sponsored projects, is sharply separated from the administrative responsibility involved in securing support for these programs. . . . It seems to me that the budgeting process is going to have to be reformed so that the faculty member will feel a sense of responsibility for the entire budget process and will be in a position to help change the financial impact of programs and activities that he has advocated.

# Orie E. Myers, Jr.

## Vice President for Business
## Emory University

There are a couple of points that I would like to emphasize which I think are apropos today. My first point relates to a topic which has been alluded to by Dr. Bowen and touched earlier by Dr. McGill. I would like to suggest that if we are to be able to cope with these trying times in the field of higher education, which have been mentioned again and again, then one of the most effective manners in which we can handle these problems is to bring about an even closer working relationship, an even greater team relationship, between the chief business officer of the university and the chief academic officer. I think it is absolutely imperative that these two people develop an atmosphere of cooperation, an atmosphere or condition under which proper and effective decisions can be made, a cooperative atmosphere that is recognized throughout the campus. I must add my fear in this respect that perhaps all too often we are becoming alarmists; not that there is not plenty about which to be alarmed, but it is necessary that we approach these problems in a constructive rather than with an alarmist attitude.

· · ·

I think that we can be too much of an alarmist and too little of a team seeking to find answers to our problems. We must face these problems, using what Dr. Bowen referred to as a "decision-making process" which brings about effective decisions, understanding, and cooperation.

We must not let our decisions become spontaneous announcements of biases or proclamations based upon nothing. Rather, they must be decisions based upon a sound analysis of facts, a studying and a weighing of all of the possible alternatives, and then the arrival at a decision—a decision which is the decision of management, not just of the president, certainly not of the business officer or the chief academic officer, but a decision of the management team of the institution.

The second point that I would like to make is in reference to Dr. Bowen's statement concerning the simultaneous evaluation of all claims on financial resources of the university in its annual process of budgetary review. I certainly agree with that point as I agree generally with Dr. Bowen's excellent paper. But I would suggest that a great many of these "financial" decisions are not made in the strict budgetary process. Altogether too often we think that annually we sit down and decide how we are going to divide the budgetary pie, how we are going to allocate the financial resources of our university, when, in reality, most of those decisions have already been made on a day-to-day basis. Often when we think that we are making a minor operating decision, we do not realize that we are making a major budgetary decision. Often this is when the decisions are made that determine the slicing of the budgetary pie. Sometimes these decisions are made when we accept a gift or a grant, when we don't realize that we are allocating resources. But the implications of that gift involve the arriving at a decision on the allocation of financial resources. Often as we agree upon new policies for personnel, purchasing, auxiliary enterprises, and so on, not a budgetary decision *per se* but a policy or a procedural decision during the academic year, we have made a decision which has profound effects on the budget. The point here is that as we make day-to-day operating decisions, truly they are very often budgetary decisions. As you plant an acorn, you often become responsible for an oak tree—or even a forest.

---

*The Golden Years,* The Ford Foundation and The College of Wooster, 1970; *Turning Point,* The College of Wooster, 1971 (to be published).

# College and University Accounting:
## An Introduction (1992)

RICHARD E. ANDERSON

Financial accounting for colleges and universities has always been a complex topic. A primary cause of the complexity springs from a lack of clarity about the objectives of the number crunching exercise. Now the waters are murkier than ever as the organizations that set accounting rules are taking a much more pro-active role and it is uncertain what higher education financial reports will look like in a few years. Complexity and ambiguity notwithstanding, higher education administrators should have a rudimentary understanding of college and university accounting.

In editing this edition of the "Reader" it was impossible to find a comprehensive and up-to-date report on college and university accounting. Current articles and chapters tend to bog down in the technical changes that have just been approved or are being proposed. Because they are written for financial administrators, these articles do not explain basic accounting concepts. Consequently, we have retained the piece written in 1984 by Meisinger and Dubeck that was used in the 1986 edition of the ASHE Reader. It explains most of the important topics with which non-financial administrators should be familiar.

We are supplementing that chapter with a background discussion of college and university accounting in an attempt to explain the pressure for change. That discussion is followed with a very brief review of the regulatory environment and changes which have been approved or are being considered.

## Purposes of College and University Reporting

**Corporate Accounting:** Accounting serves three simultaneous purposes for corporations. These are listed below in roughly descending order of developmental effort:

1. managerial and investor decision making
2. determination of tax liability
3. control of funds.

The main goal of a firm is to earn a profit. Accounting is the mechanism by which the score is kept and decisions are made. Traditionally, corporate accounting policy makers have put enormous effort into developing accounting standards that will allow managers to evaluate and control the profitability of the firm and its various divisions. In addition the Securities and Exchange Commission has insisted on relevant and uniform reporting. Furthermore, there is an army of highly paid professionals on Wall Street that constantly examines accounting rules to be sure that they are fair and useful to investors. To the extent that reporting rules are inadequate for these purposes there is significant pressure to change them.

In maximizing shareholder return, the firm obviously wants to pay as little tax as possible. At the same time, the Internal Revenue Service has a vested interest in seeing that it gets its fair share of the profits. Again, as the stakes are high, the effort to refine the procedures has been commensurate. For example, in determining profit it would be unreasonable for a firm to deduct the full costs of buildings and equipment which will last many years. But the IRS recognizes that some annualized share of these capital items should be used to reduce the calculation of taxable revenue. As a result, complex depreciation rules have evolved over many decades to adjudicate this issue.

Finally, corporate accounting makes certain that the funds are" "accounted for" and that funds are not lost to theft and fraud. And while this custodial effort is a significant one, it has not been the driving force behind the structure of corporate accounting.

**Non-profit Accounting:** Profit is not a goal of non-profit organizations generally, and college and universities in particular. Although non-profit organizations want to use their resources wisely, finances are only a part of the decision equation—too often, only a minor part. Similarly, non-profit organizations do not pay taxes. Consequently, financial decision making and tax paying have taken a back seat in the development of non-profit accounting. In contrast to corporate accounting, the orientation of non-profit accounting has been a fiduciary one—with procedures being established to identify the sources of funds and track their use. This system is called *fund accounting*.

In fund accounting each gift that is restricted by a donor for a specific purpose must be accounted for separately. Consequently, colleges and universities may have hundreds or even thousands of funds. While the financial reports are aggregated into fund groups, the accounting system must track each of these entities individually. In corporate accounting the difference between assets and liabilities is called equity, reflecting ownership. In non-profit accounting that difference is more neutrally labeled fund balance. It has been this guardianship of fund use—making certain that the flows in and out of the funds are appropriate and that the fund balances are accurate—that has forged the development of non-profit accounting.

In recent years the fiduciary view of non-profit accounting has started to break down. With its heavy reliance on third party payers, hospital accounting has led the way. More evaluation- and decision-oriented rules, including depreciation, were introduced in the health-care field in the late 1970s. Now colleges and universities are being required to revise their accounting principals. Of course, it is impossible to draw precise connections, but the amount of resources higher education consumes and the strain that its appetite for funds places on both private and public budgets has undoubtedly hastened the reform process. The goal of the policy making bodies is to devise a set of rules that will permit outsiders to better understand a college's financial condition and how it got that way. Productive change is not going to come easily. Many college financial officials are aggrieved at these changes, but we should recognize the inevitable forces for reform.

# Accounting Reform

During the 1970s college and university accounting was guided by the American Institute of Certified Public Accountants (AICPA) with significant input from the National Association of College and University Business Officers (NACUBO) and other higher education organizations. Adherence to the new rules has been far from perfect, but considerable progress was achieved.

At the same time that higher education was attempting some reform, the accounting profession was reorganizing its regulatory mechanisms. In 1972 the non-profit Financial Accounting Foundation (FAF) was established and the Financial Accounting Standards Board (FASB—pronounced fazbee) became its rule setting body two years later. In the process of promulgating rules for nonprofit organizations, disputes between FASB and state and local governments arose. To accommodate state and local governments, FAF created the Government Accounting Standards Board (GASB) in 1984.

This bifurcation of rule setting causes problems for higher education which has feet firmly planted in both public and private camps. Uniform accounting across both sectors offers clear policy making advantages and higher education officials have worked hard to maintain uniformity. (It should be noted that while the rules were the same in the past, there were systematic differences in practice between the sectors.) The first major dispute between FASB and GASB erupted over depreciation. FASB was adamant that non-profit institutions should recognize capital usage in their accounting statements. GASB has so far demurred. How this will eventually be worked out is yet to be determined. But the fact is that there are now two rule making bodies for higher education—FASB for the private sector and GASB for the public sector.

**Current and Prospective Changes:** So far FASB has taken a more activist role. As mentioned above, independent colleges and universities are required to recognize depreciation in their financial statements. This recognition is limited to their balance sheets—institutions must reduce the value of their plant fund assets by an appropriate percentage each year. However, they need not show this reduction as an expense in their income and expense statements. Other prospective changes that FASB is considering include:

- unconditional pledges *must* be recognized as income in the year that the pledges are made;

- contributed services *must* be recognized as revenue with an offsetting expense;

- contributions of works of art and historical artifacts will be recognized as *revenue*;

- significant revisions to the presentation of financial information.

While FASB has been more proactive, GASB would bring the greatest change to higher education accounting if they should insist that public colleges and universities revise their reporting to coincide with other governmental agencies. So far GASB hasn't done that but anything is possible in this new environment.

# Summary

College and university accounting has a fiduciary tradition—making certain that funds are spent in the manner in which donors or other grant making organizations intended. While progress had been made in improving the display of information to outsiders, many leaders in the accounting profession considered the improvement inadequate. In recent years, new rule making bodies have been created and the pace of change has accelerated. It is uncertain exactly what college and university accounting will look like in just a few years, but the basic concepts are likely to remain. Therefore, the Meisinger and Dubeck chapter is recommended to the reader as a good introduction to the topic. Gordon Winston offers a forward looking paper on how higher education accounting can be significantly improved.

# Fund Accounting (1984)

## Richard J. Meisinger, Jr. and Leroy W. Dubeck

Designing an accounting system is an art form. The system can hide information or it can disclose various aspects of an institution's financial situation. Some accounting systems can do both simultaneously.

Most college and university accounting systems are designed in accordance with generally accepted accounting principles, especially those summarized in *College & University Business Administration*, 4th ed. (Washington, DC: National Association of College and University Business Officers, 1982), and *Audits of Colleges and Universities* (New York: American Institute of Certified Public Accountants, 1975). However, in accounting, as in most disciplines, there is disagreement over how to address certain situations. In those instances the accounting methodologies will differ from one campus to another. The design of the accounting system can also be determined in part by the nature of the institution (e.g., public versus independent, research-oriented versus instruction-oriented) and the institution's history.

An accounting system does not necessarily reflect all financial transactions that may influence the institution's financial status. Frequently these transactions are described in notes to the institution's financial statement. They might include such items as significant additions to plant and pledges of gifts. Items that do not appear in a financial statement might include a planned bequest by an alumnus to be made at an unnamed future date or the donation of rare books or works of art. The latter items increase the value of the institution's assets but would not be included in the financial statement. One must realize, therefore, that the institution's accounting system may not provide a complete financial picture.

What follows is a layman's guide to fund accounting, the basic framework for most college and university accounting systems. This is a brief overview of the most common types of accounts and funds and summarizes selected accounting principles. Attention is given to basic financial statements. The sample institution referred to throughout this chapter is examined in figures 1 through 5.

## Types of Accounts

### The Accounting Equation

The accounting equation involves the balanced relationship among three kinds of economic representations: assets, liabilities, and net worth. Assets are economic values that are owned by or are under the control of the institution. They are of two kinds. The first is cash and that which can be converted into cash, such as investments and accounts receivable. The other type of asset is represented by costs incurred at an earlier date that have not yet been attributed to a given fiscal period. Examples of this second type of asset are capital costs, depreciable equipment, buildings, inventories, prepaid expenses, and deferred charges.

There are also two kinds of liability accounts. The first represents amounts that are owed to organizations or individuals who are outside the institution itself. (An exception to this definition will be discussed later.) In general, liabilities represent amounts owed to others, including creditors, for a variety of reasons. Some liabilities may be amounts that are owed and must be paid in the near term or immediately. Other liabilities may be paid out over a period of many years. The second type of liability account is used to record deferred credits or deferred revenues. These liabilities represent amounts that have been collected in cash or whose collection is anticipated but for which an earnings process has not yet occurred. Until such a process begins, the institution carries these items as a liability.

The relationship between assets and liabilities or the difference between them produces the third kind of account, generally referred to as net worth, equity, or proprietorship. Net worth is also net assets, which represent the net difference between assets and related liabilities. In fund accounting the fund balance equals assets minus liabilities.

The accounting equation is the relationship among these three kinds of accounts and is expressed by the statement that assets minus liabilities equals net worth or by an algebraic transposition of that equation (i.e., assets equal liabilities plus net worth). Another way of interpreting the accounting equation is to state that equities are claims by an owner or creditor against assets.

## Real and Nominal Accounts

The accounts used in the accounting system to record asset values, liability values, and net worth or fund balance values are referred to as real accounts. These balances carry forward from the beginning of the organization until its end or until the particular type of asset, liability, or net worth no longer exists. Nominal accounts, on the other hand, expire at the end of a given fiscal period (e.g., the fiscal year) and are created anew at the beginning of the next period. Such accounts— called income and expenses—classify the increases and decreases in net worth and provide more detailed information about the sources and uses of net worth throughout the year. For example, increases in net worth may result from sales, gifts, endowment income, or contributions to capital; decreases may reflect expenses or losses in investments, among other possibilities.

In most cases financial statements deal exclusively with either real accounts or nominal accounts (special types of reports may deal with elements of both at the same time). In examining financial statements it is helpful to remember that net worth or fund balances are changed by increases or decreases in assets or liabilities (i.e., by income and expenses).

The concept of double-entry bookkeeping is built on the accounting equation. Thus, for each economic event that is recorded there is a balanced set of entries to record the event (i.e., a debit and a credit). At all times the system must balance so that debits equal credits. The total of assets must likewise equal the total of liabilities and net worth in the system.

The accounting equation and the principles of real and nominal accounts underlie all accounting and apply to fund accounting as well as to other forms of accounting. The next section examines fund accounting and explains why that methodology is used in college and university accounting systems.

# Types of Funds

## Restricted and Unrestricted Funds

Nonprofit organizations as a group often differ from profit-making enterprises in that they are the recipients of gifts, grants, contributions, and appropriations, which are restricted at the direction of the sources for particular purposes, functions, or activities. A donor, for example, may specify that a gift is to be used only for scholarships. This restriction is legally binding on the institution, which has no authority to use that money for any other purpose. That the institution may already have a scholarship program and that the gift would simply help to finance it are irrelevant. Another example of a restriction is a donor's specification that only the income from investing the donation may be used.

Restrictions imposed by a donor differ in two important respects from self-imposed limitations established by the governing board or from other kinds of conditions that characterize the relationship between the donor and the grantee (but which are not restrictions). First, the restriction must be set forth in writing or must be related to a representation made in writing. Second, the language used in the written instrument must be restrictive. Restrictive language is characterized by words that indicate a command or a demand or that establish an absolute limitation. The law distinguishes between restrictive language and precatory language, which represents only a wish, a desire, or an entreaty (but which is not restrictive).

If conditions are documented in writing and if the language is appropriately restrictive, the restrictions cannot be changed by the institution acting alone. In some jurisdictions even the institution and the donor together may not change the restriction once the gift has been accepted with the restrictions imposed. The removal of a restriction or the redirection of the resources into a related activity can be accomplished only through a formal or an informal application of the doctrine of *cy pres*. (This procedure requires formal court proceedings and involves the state attorney general.)

Occasionally, ambiguous language is used in the instruments conveying the donation, and sometimes the original documentation is missing. Legal review is almost always required in such situations. Institutions seeking relief through the courts would, if successful, receive a declaratory judgment.

In summary, it is important to distinguish between those resources that are truly restricted and those that are not. *Cy pres* relates only to externally restricted funds and not to internally designated funds (such as those designated in the budget process). The maintenance of the distinction between these two categories is a paramount responsibility of the fund accounting system.

Resources received by institutions are labeled in several ways to indicate the nature of any pertinent restrictions.

*Ownership vs. agency relationship.* When an institution receives new monies, the first question is whether the resources actually belong to the institution. Funds that do not belong to the institution are called agency funds and represent assets held by the institution on behalf of others. Alternatively, agency funds represent liabilities for amounts due to outside organizations, students, or faculty that will be paid out on their instructions for purposes other than normal operations. Institutions have on occasion used the agency fund classification inappropriately for funds that officials would like to use outside the constraints of the budget process.

*Restricted vs. unrestricted.* If the monies received by the institution are indeed owned by the institution, the next question is whether the monies are restricted or unrestricted. As noted earlier, the specific nature of the restrictions must be clearly stated.

*Expendable vs. nonexpendable.* If the monies received by the institution are restricted, it must be determined whether the monies are expendable or nonexpendable. If the monies are expendable (i.e., can be spent), one must ask for what specific purpose, function, activity, or object. If the purpose or character of the expenditure is such that it is a part of normal operations, it is classified in a category that relates it to current operations. If, on the other hand, the restriction is such that the monies must be spent to acquire land, buildings, equipment, or other types of capital assets, the expenditure is classified as a part of plant funds.

Nonexpendable funds can be distinguished by several types of restrictions. For example, endowment funds cannot be spent. Rather, they must be invested, and only the income can be used.

It should be noted that income from the endowment represents a new source of funds, and the nature of this money must be determined by the same series of questions outlined above. It is possible for a donor to restrict both the principal (i.e., the endowment monies) and the investment income.

Certain other funds cannot be spent but must be loaned to students or faculty. Under this arrangement the monies will be loaned, the borrowers will repay the loans, and the same resources will be reloaned to other borrowers.

A third nonexpendable fund is the annuity fund or life income fund. Here, the donor provides money to the institution with instructions to pay to an outside party for a period of time either a certain amount of money (in the case of an annuity fund) or the investment income (in the case of a life income fund).

All funds not restricted by the donor are by definition unrestricted. Generally, all unrestricted funds are to be used first as revenue for current operating purposes. A governing board may also designate unrestricted funds for long-term investments to produce income (in the manner of endowment funds), or for plant acquisition purposes (for which restricted funds are normally used).

Thus, certain unrestricted funds are intended for the same purpose as certain restricted funds. In the reporting of college and university financial matters, as evidenced in financial statements, funds that are either restricted or designated for similar types of activities are classified in a group that has a name indicating the purpose. However, within each one of these groups it is necessary to distinguish between those amounts that are in the group by reason of restrictions imposed by donors and those amounts that are in the group by reason of designation by a governing board.

## Selected Accounting Principles

Accounting principles are the standards that define how economic transactions are to be classified and reported. Recognition of proper accounting principles is important in establishing a college or university accounting system. Most institutions adhere to the accounting principles set forth by the American Institute of Certified Public Accountants (AICPA). These principles should be reflected in an institution's financial statement. When studying a financial statement that has been audited, one should see in the auditor's report a statement as to whether the financial statement has been prepared in accordance with generally accepted accounting principles. If the auditor notes an exception or denies that proper accounting principles have been followed, it will be difficult to evaluate the financial statement in a meaningful fashion.

### Funds and Fund Groups

A fund is an accounting entity with a self-balancing set of accounts consisting of assets, liabilities, and a fund balance account, in addition to nominal accounts that measure increases and decreases in the fund balance. Separate funds are established to account for financial activity related to a particular restricted donation, source of restricted funds, or designated amount established by the governing board. These accounting entries are set up to insure the observance of restrictions imposed by donors and of limitations on the use of unrestricted funds that have been established by the governing board. In many cases, however, funds of similar designation and restriction are grouped together for reporting purposes and for purposes of efficient management. Often the assets of like kinds of funds are placed in one set of asset accounts. Similarly, liability accounts related to those assets may be merged. Nevertheless, there would still be a series of individual fund balances for which a separate accounting would have to be performed. The total of all such assets would equal the total of all such liabilities and the total of the fund balances to which they relate. This grouping together for accounting and reporting purposes yields what is termed a fund group.

It is important to note that within each fund group it is necessary to continue to distinguish between the balance of funds that are unrestricted and those that are externally restricted. Within the restricted subgroup it is necessary to account for each separate restricted fund balance.

## Accrual Basis of Accounting

Accrual-basis accounting is often defined in comparison to cash-basis accounting. In the latter the only transactions recorded are those in which cash comes into the organization or goes out. Thus, an asset or an increase in the fund balance would be recognized only when cash is collected. Similarly, the assets and fund balance would be reduced only when a cash payment is made. Almost nothing else would be accounted for, making the cash basis of accounting rather unsatisfactory for most reporting and management purposes. Accrual-basis accounting was developed in response to this shortcoming in the cash-basis method. The accrual basis recognizes fund balance increments (i.e., revenue) when the amount is earned. Expenses and other types of deductions are recognized when the goods or services have been used up. An asset is recognized as an amount that has been received and has continuing value (i.e., unexpired costs), although a payment may not have been made for this amount. The measurement of revenues and expenses is called the accrual basis of accounting because accruals are used to convert cash receipts into revenue and cash disbursements into expenses.

The objective of accrual-basis accounting is to provide a more satisfactory matching of revenues and other fund balance additions with expenses and other fund balance deductions in the accounting period to which the financial statements relate. In other words, the accrual basis attempts to determine the real economic impact of what has occurred during a given period of time rather than simply determining how much cash was received or disbursed.

## Interfund Accounting

The concept of interfund accounting relates to maintaining the integrity and self-balancing characteristics of the individual funds. Problems arise, for example, when cash used for the benefit of one fund actually belongs to another fund. To illustrate, assume that an institution has a scholarship fund of $10,000 and has $10,000 in the bank for that fund. Also assume that in the institution's unrestricted current fund is another $10,000 that is available for any purpose. Assume that the institution makes a payment of $1,000 to a scholarship recipient out of the unrestricted current fund bank account, whereas the intent was to use the restricted scholarship fund. If the fund balance of the scholarship fund is reduced along with the amount of cash belonging to the unrestricted current fund, both funds would be unbalanced. That is, their assets (when examined separately) would not be equal to their liabilities and fund balances. In the fund that has made the disbursement (i.e., that has given up the cash), an asset account would be established representing the amount due from the fund that is ultimately to finance the activity. This arrangement puts the unrestricted current fund back in balance. In the restricted fund that is to be used for scholarships, a liability account would be established for the $1,000 paid on behalf of the restricted fund, and the fund balance would be charged the same amount. Again, the restricted fund would now be in balance and there would exist an interfund receivable and payable. The asset and liability would at some point be extinguished by a transfer of cash between the funds.

# Chart of Accounts

The chart of accounts in an accounting system is used to classify each transaction accounted for in the system, facilitating easy and accurate retrieval. It is based on (1) the accounting principles for proper classification of economic phenomena and (2) the reporting needs of management and external parties, calling for segregation of different kinds of transactions so that those transactions may later be aggregated and reported by type. . . .

Accounting systems in higher education usually involve both an alphabetical designation of the account name, which can be read, and a numerical or alpha-numeric designation of the account, which can be used for encoding purposes. This arrangement allows the system to work with a numerical or shortened reference rather than a long rational name.

It is important to remember that the purpose of the chart of accounts is to assist in the locating of discrete kinds of transactions. The only rules are those that make sense in terms of how much information and what kinds of categories should be reported. The information needs of many colleges and universities are the same in certain areas, particularly with regard to the production of basic financial statements.

## Types of Financial Statements

A college or university's financial statement is generally composed of four segments: (1) balance sheet; (2) statement of changes in fund balances; (3) statement of current fund revenues, expenditures, and other changes; and (4) footnotes to the above segments.

The balance sheet reflects the financial resources of the institution at a given time. The balance sheet contains the assets of the institution, the liabilities, and the fund balances. Thus, the status of the institution is generally expressed in terms of its real accounts. The assets can be viewed as the forms of the institution's financial resources, whereas the liabilities and fund balance are the sources.

The statement of changes in fund balances summarizes the activity within each group of funds during a specific fiscal period. This statement is comparable to the income statement and statement of changes in the stockholders' equity in the for-profit sector. For nonprofit organizations, however, the statement of changes in fund balances covers each set of funds.

The statement of current funds revenues, expenditures, and other changes is a detailed accounting of changes in the current funds column that are included in the statement of changes in fund balances. Sometimes this statement is referred to as the statement of changes in financial position. In fund accounting most useful information is already contained in the balance sheet and the statement of changes in fund balances, often making redundant the information contained in the statement of current funds revenues, expenditures, and other changes. On the other hand, there may be some activity that should be reported and has not been disclosed in any of the statements; this can often be taken care of by enhancing the statements with another presentation summarizing the changes in financial position or by adding footnotes to the financial statements. Footnotes summarize the significant accounting principles used to prepare the statements and provide other information essential to a full understanding of the institution's particular financial environment. No examination of an institution's financial statement is complete without a thorough perusal of the footnotes.

## Financial Statements: A Detailed Examination

### Interrelationships of the Three Basic Statements

The balance sheet—a report as of a particular time—states all the financial resources for which the institution's governing board is responsible. In figure 2 the balance sheet has columns for two dates (i.e., current year and prior year). The prior-year column is a point of reference and can be used as a standard to evaluate the current year's financial information. Note that for each category of funds, assets equal liabilities and fund balances for both the current year and the prior year.

The statement of changes in fund balances (figure 2) has a separate column for each fund group. The purpose of this statement is to show the gross additions to and gross deductions from each of the fund groups, to account for any amounts that may have been transferred from one fund group to another, to report the net change in fund balances for the year for each of the fund groups, and to show beginning balances (in order to account for ending balances).

It is worth examining the beginning and ending balances of the statement of changes in fund balances to trace their origins to the balance sheet. For example, at the bottom of the first column of figure 2, the beginning and ending fund balances of unrestricted current funds total $455,000 and $643,000, respectively. In the balance sheet (figure 1) these amounts appear on the liability side opposite the term "fund balance" under the heading "current unrestricted funds." The beginning balance on the statement of changes is the prior year's figure of $455,000. The ending figure is the current year's balance sheet figure of $643,000.

The balance sheet shows amounts for each of the fund balances for each of the fund groups. The statement of changes in fund balances reports all activity that resulted in changes in those fund balances during the year. For each different type of addition or deduction there is a separate line caption. Thus, within the accounting system there are separate classifications so that transactions may be reported separately in the statement. The statement of changes in fund balances addresses only the fund balances, not the assets or liabilities.

The statement of current funds, revenues, expenditures, and other changes covers the activity from the beginning to the end of the fiscal year and essentially expands on the information presented in summary fashion in the statement of changes in fund balances. It relates to current funds only and to transactions that have affected the fund balances of the current funds and has no relationship to assets or liabilities or to changes in funds other than current funds. In figure 3 the final numbers in each of the first two columns are the same as the net changes for the years that appear in the first two columns of the statement of changes, namely, $188,000 and $25,000, respectively.

The accrual basis of accounting can lead to confusion when one examines the statement of current funds, revenues, expenditures, and other changes. As mentioned earlier, certain kinds of funds are provided to the institution with earmarks categorizing them as current operating activity. Accordingly, these funds are classified in the group called current restricted funds. When the amounts are received, they are accounted for as additions to those funds, and such additions are reported in the statement of changes in fund balances. The difference between those two kinds of transactions and any transfers produce the net change in fund balance for the year.

An examination of the statement of current funds, revenues, expenditures, and other changes reveals something a bit unusual in terms of revenues. This statement attempts to match pure revenues with expenditures and other transactions in order to derive a more meaningful report that applies the accrual-basis concept to operations for the year. However, in the accrual basis of accounting one has not "earned" a current restricted fund until that fund has been expended for the purpose for which it was restricted (i.e., a revenue from current restricted funds does not exist until those funds have been expended). This is not unlike the deferred-credit concept in the for-profit sector, whereby a business may receive money from a customer in advance of having rendered the service. The receipt of such monies is treated as a deferred credit. As the services are rendered and the expenses incurred, these amounts are taken into revenue. This reporting convention gives the statement preparer a better basis for matching revenues and expenses, which is one of the objectives of the accrual basis of accounting. The potential confusion here, of course, is that these resources are treated as fund balances rather than as liabilities, as the for-profit sector would treat them. Thus, the two financial statements (figures 2 and 3) seem to conflict.

The differences are reconciled by an adjustment made to the statement of current funds, revenues, expenditures, and other changes. The adjustment represents the difference between the additions to current restricted funds for the current year and the amounts earned and therefore reflected in revenue. In the figures under consideration, the adjustment for the current year is the difference between $1,094,000 of additions (figure 2) and $1,014,000 recognized as revenue (figure 3), or $80,000. However, the adjustment is affected by another transaction (indirect costs recovered), which reduces current restricted fund balances but is not reported as a current restricted fund expenditure because it is an application of such funds to current unrestricted fund revenues. The amount for indirect costs is shown in figure 2 as $35,000. The difference between $80,000 and $35,000 accounts for the $45,000 adjustment, reported in figure 3 as excess of restricted receipts over transfers to revenues. As a result, figure 3 does reconcile with the same changes in fund balance amounts shown in figure 2 for current restricted funds.

The real purpose of the statement of current funds, revenues, expenditures, and other changes, then, is to provide greater detail about the sources of current revenues and the functions for which current funds are expended. One of the basic accounting principles involved in this statement is that at this level of aggregation revenues are to be reported by source and expenditures by function. This statement also enables the reader to identify the total financial activity for current funds during the year. The totaling function is accomplished through the columnar presentation, whereby current unrestricted funds and current restricted funds, revenues, expenditures, and other changes are combined in a column labeled "total." For comparison a total for the preceding year is provided.

It is interesting to note that the statement of current funds, revenues, expenditures, and other changes can be considered in an entirely different manner. If, for example, it is remembered that the purpose of the statement is to disclose certain types of information, the format of the statement is less mysterious than it might be otherwise. Thus, if details as to the sources of revenue are reported on separate lines in the statement of changes in fund balances (instead of being reported as a single amount as in figure 2), it would be possible to eliminate the section on revenues in figure 3, which in turn could be used to provide only the required itemization of expenditures by function for the unrestricted, restricted, and total current funds. Then it would be necessary to tell the reader only how the current restricted fund expenditures were financed. That information could be shown either as a tabulation at the bottom of figure 3 or in the notes to the financial statements. The discussion above is intended to highlight the importance of the information content rather than the specific format.

## The Balance Sheet—Current Funds

The balance sheet in figure 1 contains all of the assets, liabilities, and fund balances. They are arranged side-by-side in a horizontal fashion for each fund group throughout the statement. This format enables the reader to examine the assets and liabilities and fund balances of each fund group separately, and to see in juxtaposition with the current year's amounts the amounts that pertain to the previous year.

The first major fund group on the balance sheet is current funds. Within the current fund group a distinction is made between unrestricted current funds and restricted current funds. The current funds represent the results of operating inflows and outflows, or the "working capital" position of the institution. Assets and liabilities are the same as for a business if the account "due to other funds" is read as "due to other subsidiaries" and fund balances are understood as the working capital portion of the institution's total net worth, or equity. Assets represent the liquid resources or unexpired costs that pertain to day-to-day operations, and include such items as cash and investments.

The most frequently used basis for carrying assets is historical cost or, in the absence of cost, the fair value of the asset at date of donation. If the institution chooses, it may follow the market value method of accounting, whereby the carrying values for investments are changed from reporting date to reporting date to reflect changes in current market values. If this procedure is followed, all investments of all funds must be accounted for in that fashion.

Another asset listed is accounts receivable. Principles of accounting hold that such assets should be stated at their realizable amounts. Statements often show total accounts receivable less an allowance for doubtful accounts, with the net amount reflecting the difference.

Inventories are unexpired costs representing economic values that will have utility in the succeeding year. Inventories of consumable supplies and supplies for resale are included in this category. Some inventories are carried at the lower of cost or market value. Cost must be determined on some generally acceptable basis (e.g., first-in-first-out, average cost, or last-in-first-out).

Prepaid expenses and deferred charges include items such as prepaid insurance. Here, a policy premium covering more than one year has been paid in advance, with the premium portion that has expired during the year written off as an expense and the unexpired portion carried as the prepaid expense.

The liabilities of current funds are relatively straightforward. The accounts payable and accrued liabilities represent amounts that have to be paid to vendors and others who have provided goods and services to the institution and for which the institution has not yet made a cash disbursement. Student deposits represent amounts that may be applied against tuition at a later date or refunded, depending on the circumstances. Deferred credits represent amounts that have been received in advance by students during registration. After registration and the beginning of classes the credits would be treated as revenue, becoming an addition to the current unrestricted fund balance in that year. (This is another example of the accrual basis of accounting at work.)

The fund balance is shown separately on the statement (in figure 1 it appears as a single amount). If the governing board designates portions of unrestricted current funds for particular current operating purposes, it may be desirable or necessary to subdivide the fund balance between the designated and undesignated portions. It should be kept in mind that a designation is not a restriction.

The assets and liabilities of the current restricted fund group are similar in nature to the assets and liabilities of unrestricted current funds. The same rules and practices apply to the valuation of investments and to accounts receivable. Unbilled charges are usually related to contracts and grants and are amounts that become accounts receivable when billed. A difference between current restricted and current unrestricted funds is that the plural term "fund balances" is used in the restricted current fund, whereas the singular term "fund balance" is used in the unrestricted current fund. Fund balances are grouped in current restricted funds, but because each fund requires separate accountability, the accounts of the institution must maintain a fund balance account for each source and restriction. In the unrestricted current fund there is need for only one fund balance. Any others would simply be disaggregations of the larger fund balance. Such disaggregations reflect designations by the governing board.

The current fund balances, both unrestricted and restricted, are key reflections of the financial viability of the institution. In addition to acting as working capital, the current unrestricted fund balance ($643,000 in figure 1) represents an accumulated reserve from operations, or retained receipts comparable to retained earnings in a business. This most flexible reserve provides both a cushion against future operating deficits and a source of seed money for desirable new programs of instruction, research, and public service.

The current restricted fund balance ($446,000 in figure 1) can be thought of as representing a backlog of future business already committed. The extent of management control over the timing and use of these restricted funds determines the flexibility and importance of the funds in long-range planning. Just as the adequacy of and trends in the amount of working capital and operating reserves in a business must be continually evaluated in terms of sales volume, market risks, inflation, and possible future product needs, so should current fund balances be measured in an educational institution.

The quantity and quality of current fund assets should be routinely reviewed and the offsetting liabilities should be subject to governing board policies and oversight. Excess cash should be temporarily invested in accordance with sound cash management principles. As competition for students intensifies, colleges and universities—particularly the more expensive independent institutions—are under increasing pressure to provide more student assistance. Receivables, which should be compared with operating volumes and with the receivables of peer institutions, are growing. Designing sound collection policies is becoming one of management's more pressing responsibilities.

Inventories ordinarily do not represent very large commitments in service institutions; however, any investment in inventories is not available for other purposes and therefore should be justified by relevant economic considerations. The timing of payments should be in accordance with sound disbursement policies and procedures to avoid either uneconomic prepayments or reputation-damaging late payments. Current fund borrowings should be monitored closely. Techniques for managing and protecting current operating assets and working capital funds include appropriate cash-flow forecasts, reports on the aging of receivables, and reviews of significant changes in inventory levels.

Sometimes an institution's governing board or administration will transfer what might be considered excessive operating reserves, or accumulated current fund balances, to the long-term capital fund groups, with due consideration for any applicable external restrictions. Such transfers would convert the affected operating reserves to invested reserves, possibly increasing investment income but reducing operating flexibility. Likewise, the governing board or administration may "retransfer" any fund balances previously transferred to the long-term capital fund groups back to the current fund balances for needed current expenditures or to make up deficiencies, again with due consideration for any applicable external restrictions. Any retransfer would convert invested reserves to operating reserves, possibly decreasing investment income but increasing operating resources.

Examples of such transfers are shown in the statement of changes in fund balances (figure 2) and are discussed in more detail below. While the mandatory transfers are required by debt instruments or third-party providers, the category "unrestricted gifts allocated" ($650,000) represents management transfers of operating funds to loan, endowment, and plant funds, and the "portion of unrestricted quasi-endowment funds investment gains appropriated" ($40,000) represents a management decision to transfer or retransfer invested funds back to operating funds. Both these transfers should be done in fulfillment of current budgeting and long-range financial plans.

Finally, agency funds represent amounts that are received by the institution but that do not belong to it. Generally, the assets would be cash and investments (see illustration in figure 1). The accountability for these funds is to outside parties; thus the balance sheet shows a liability for the amounts held for others by the institution. This is the only fund group that does not have a fund balance. In this case, assets equal liabilities and there are no net assets that belong to the institution. For this reason the statement of changes in fund balances has no column for the agency fund. Clearly, the institution must account to the various parties for whom it is holding funds by showing receipts and disbursements, but such information is not required in these highly aggregated, general financial statements.

## Statement of Changes in Fund Balances

Long-term capital is required to finance assets that will not be recovered or converted to cash within the normal operating cycle. These assets include land, buildings, and equipment; student loans; and investments that provide an earnings base independent of current supporters. Long-term capital is provided directly by gifts and government appropriations, or indirectly through current operating funds.

Current operating funds may be expended for equipment and minor plant renovations directly from current accounts. Or, they may be transferred to the plant funds group, to be expended for debt service, major plant additions, and renewals and replacements, or to loan funds, or to endowment and similar funds, either as required by external agreements or benefactors (mandatory transfers) or as determined by the administration.

The statement of changes in fund balances (figure 2) shows these flows of long-term capital. Under "revenues and other additions," supporters with "private gifts, grants, and contracts—restricted" directly provided $100,000 to loan funds, $1,500,000 to endowment and similar funds, $800,000 to annuity and life income funds, $115,000 to funds for spending on plant, $65,000 for retirement of indebtedness, and $15,000 of "in kind" plant or equipment. An expired term endowment provided $50,000 directly for plant, and state appropriations provided another $50,000 for plant expenditures. Investment income (restricted), realized gains on investments, and accrued interest provided a total of $16,000 to loan funds, $169,000 to endowment and similar funds, and $38,000 to the various plant funds.

Transfers among funds include the long-term capital provided through current operations. Mandatory amounts of $340,000 for debt service (principal and interest) and $170,000 for renewals and replacements were transferred to plant funds as required, while $2,000 was transferred to loan funds for a matching grant. In addition, nonmandatory transfers of unrestricted gifts, which might be considered current operating surpluses, were made by the administration in the amount of $650,000, of which $50,000 was designated for loan funds, $550,000 for quasi-endowment (i.e., amounts set aside by the governing board from expendable funds), and $50,000 for plant. Offsetting this was $40,000 as the "portion of unrestricted quasi-endowment funds investment gains appropriated," or transferred from long-term invested funds to current use.

## Loan funds

The loan funds balance sheet reports the assets, liabilities, and fund balances of the institution's lending subsidiary, maintained principally to help students finance their education. This capital in recent years has been provided increasingly by the federal government and accounted for variously as refundable advances (liabilities) or restricted grants (fund balances). Loan funds specifically provided by interested private benefactors become restricted fund balances. The institution must often add matching funds, which then become restricted, or it may transfer unrestricted current funds to increase unrestricted loan resources. These inflows and certain outflows of loan funds, by refunds or write-offs, are illustrated in the statement of changes in fund balances.

Currently, the largest part of the loan fund group is represented by the National Defense Student Loan Program. The amount that has been received since inception, which has not been extinguished through the various kinds of write-off procedures available, must be shown as a separate amount owed to the federal government. This amount is ultimately a liability, but it is accounted for as a fund balance to provide an accounting of the increases and decreases in the amounts owed to the government that otherwise would not appear in the statement of changes in fund balances. It should be noted that when a loan is made, the asset classification changes but the fund balance is not affected.

In figure 1 the cash in the loan fund group is to be loaned to students in the future. The investments represent unloaned resources that will be liquidated when needed for loan purposes. The largest asset category is "loans to students, faculty, and staff, less allowance. ..." Because these loans are not always repaid, they should be reported at their net realizable value as of the reporting date. The high default rate has led most colleges and universities to make an allowance in their financial statements for doubtful loans receivable.

The fund balance, as illustrated, is divided between refundable federal government grants ($50,000) and university funds (of which $483,000 is restricted and $150,000 is unrestricted).

The statement of changes in fund balances shows the kinds of transactions that affect loan fund balances. Government monies are one source of change, as are private gifts and grants restricted to loan purposes. Investments of these funds yield income and gains that also produce changes in the fund balance. In the illustration (figure 2), there are no entries for the granting of loans or the repayment of loans because these result only in a change from one asset category to another (i.e., from cash to loans receivable). When the loans are collected, the repayments are deducted from loans receivable and are added back to cash.

Deductions from the loan funds on the statement of changes in fund balances include loan cancellations and write-offs, refunds to grantors, and charges for administrative and collection costs. Fund balances are also reduced by losses on investments of unloaned cash.

## Endowment and similar funds

The assets of endowment and similar funds are mostly long-term investments. Other assets are uninvested cash, some receivables, and instruments that are convertible to cash. The investments of this fund group are so important that extensive comments concerning them generally appear in the notes to the financial statements.

To understand fully the nature of the investments, two kinds of information must be in either the financial statements or the notes to the financial statements: (1) the basis of accounting (e.g., cost or current market value), and (2) the composition of the investment portfolio (e.g., stocks, bonds, mortgages). If accounting is done on a cost basis, information concerning the current market is required, as is information on the performance of the portfolio (e.g., income, gains, and losses in relation to cost and the market). In the example presented, note 1 to the financial statements illustrates the latter type of disclosure (figure 5).

1. Pooling of investments. The concept of investment pooling poses a special accounting problem with respect to investments of endowments and similar funds (and occasionally other fund groups). Though the ability to identify the assets belonging to each fund balance is important, as a practical matter totals are often recorded only for groups of funds. For example, in the current restricted fund group no attempt is normally made to keep separate cash balances for each current restricted fund. Instead, there is an amount that represents total cash for all current restricted funds. This total together with other assets equals the total amount of all fund balances in that group.

In a similar manner, the assets of the endowment and similar funds may be pooled to purchase investments for the benefit of all participating funds. This calls for a particular kind of accounting that treats the individual funds in the pool equitably in terms of the distribution of the income earned by the investments and the gains and losses from trading in investments.

The pooling concept involves the use of market values as the basis for calculating the distribution of participation units to each fund as it enters the pool. The procedure can be summarized as follows: the market value of all assets at the beginning of the pool is determined; units are given an arbitrary value and are then assigned to each fund depending on how much each has contributed to the pool. From that point on, the number of units held by each participating fund is used as a basis for distributing the income earned by the pooled assets and the gains and losses arising from the sale or exchange of investments held by the pool. When a new fund enters the pool, the current market value of the assets in the pool is recalculated, a new unit value (which may be higher or lower than the original value) is determined, and units are assigned to participants in the pool. This is also done when a fund is to be withdrawn from the pool. Note that the assignment of units to funds does not mean that the assets themselves are carried at market value. In fact, the assets may be carried at either market value or cost, depending on the accounting procedure adopted.

2. Types of funds. The fund balances in the endowment and similar funds group may represent several different conditions—for example, truly restricted funds such as endowment, or monies set aside by the governing board with the direction that they are not to be expended now (but may be in the future) and that only the income is to be used. Truly restricted funds are restricted in perpetuity, requiring the investment of the money contributed, and are referred to simply as endowment funds. The restriction on the second type of funds above has a terminal date or ends when a particular event takes place. This type of fund is known as term endowment. As of the balance sheet date, by law neither of these types of funds can be expended, and the governing board on its own cannot override that restriction.

By contrast, amounts set aside by the governing board from expendable funds can be expended and are therefore termed "quasi-endowment funds." Sometimes these funds are called "funds functioning as endowments." Both expressions are intended to indicate that the amounts so carried can be withdrawn from this category, restored to the current funds group from which they came, and expended for the purposes for which they were either restricted or designated. The fund group is labeled "endowment and similar funds" in recognition of the nature of quasi-endowment funds. If there are only endowment and term endowment monies, the fund group could be labeled "endowment funds."

3. Principal vs. income. An important consideration in accounting for endowments and similar funds is the need to distinguish between principal and income. Endowment funds are peculiar in that legally they are not trust funds but are viewed as such for certain purposes. However, accounting conventions that have been established for endowment funds are patterned after trust fund concepts, which distinguish between principal and income. These conventions dictate that the principal be preserved for the benefit of the remaindermen of the trust whereas the income is available for the life tenant or the income beneficiary. An institution with an endowment fund, however, is both the remaindermen and the life tenant or income beneficiary. One might ask why this concept is important in this situation. One reason for the need to define income is that the donor has stated that the institution can use only the income. Second, there is another party at issue (i.e., the future generation of students who will benefit from the income). Thus, the governing board has the obligation to balance its investment policies so as not to stress either current income or growth to the advantage of a particular generation of students.

The distinction between principal and income determines what monies are accounted for in the endowment and similar funds group. Principal includes the original contribution (or any additional contributions in the case of endowment or term endowment) or, in the case of quasi-endowment, the original transfers (or any subsequent transfers) made by the governing board. Additions to principal would be realized gains or, in accounting for investments at market, the increases in the carrying value of the investments. Deductions would be losses on investments of the endowment fund.

Income gets its definition from tax law, and includes items such as dividends, interest, rents, and royalties. In the case of real estate, income is the rental income less the expenses of operation and depreciation. The income arising from the investment of endowment and similar funds is accounted for in unrestricted current funds if the income is unrestricted, or in the appropriate restricted fund if the income is restricted. A donor occasionally specifies that the restricted income is to be added to the principal. It is important to note that the addition of income to principal by direction of the governing board does not create a true (new) principal in endowment funds.

Some clarification of terms is in order. Restricted endowment funds are actually endowment funds, the income of which is restricted. Quasi-endowment funds are usually classified as unrestricted and only at times as restricted. Unrestricted quasi-endowment funds are amounts that have been transferred from unrestricted current funds. Restricted quasi-endowment funds are established from restricted current funds set aside for investment (only the income is to be used). The accounting for gains, losses, and income of quasi-endowments follows the same rules as the accounting for true endowments; that is, gains and losses are accounted for as part of the principal of the quasi-endowment fund while the income is accounted for in unrestricted current funds (if the quasi-endowment is restricted).

4.  Total-return concept. The total-return concept—a relatively new development—eases restrictions on distinguishing between ordinary income and gains. Its intent is to encourage institutions to invest in growth stocks.

Many states have recently enacted laws patterned after a model law that prescribes how investments of institutions should be managed. Under this law it is legally permissible to use a portion of the gains of true endowment funds for the same purposes as ordinary income is used. (It was always possible for the gains of quasi-endowment funds to be so used.) In most states a portion of the gains may now be transferred from the endowment fund. Normally, there are requirements that such transfers can be made only in the face of gains (i.e., it is not possible to make a transfer that would reduce the fund balance below its historical contributed value).

The total-return concept is the means of determining how much of these gains will be used. First, the total earnings potential of the portfolio is estimated (total return is equal to the ordinary income or yield, plus net gains). A spending rate is then calculated that is sufficiently lower than the total-return earnings rate to ensure that the endowment portfolio is supplemented enough to allow for growth (or, at minimum, to compensate for the ravages of inflation). The spending rate is financed first from ordinary income. If the ordinary income is not sufficient to achieve the spending rate, the difference is financed by means of a transfer from gains. In figure 2 the transfer of $40,000, shown as "portion of unrestricted quasi-endowment funds investment gains appropriated," represents the amount necessary to cover the spending rate.

## Annuity and Life Income Funds

Annuity and life income funds, which are trust funds, are a special group of invested funds temporarily committed to supporting donor-designated beneficiaries (i.e., for the lifetime of the beneficiaries, or until specific time periods have expired, after which the remaining funds become institutional capital, operating or long-term, unrestricted or restricted, depending on the agreements with the donors).

This fund group is subdivided into annuity funds and life income funds. If the amounts of such funds are relatively insignificant, they may be reported as a subgroup within the endowment and similar funds group. The assets are cash and investments in other assets convertible to cash. The objective of these assets is to produce income.

The distinction between the two kinds of funds is as follows: in an annuity fund a fixed amount is established by the donor and must be paid out even if the ordinary income from investment of the fund is not adequate for the purpose. For this reason, in the payment of an annuity an institution may incur a liability greater than the amount of the income. In this case some of the original principal may have to be paid back. Thus, annuity funds are accounted for through a liability account that expresses the current value of all future payments that must be made, taking into consideration as well the future earnings. Any excess of the asset value over this liability is the fund balance. Periodically, the liability is reevaluated with regard to the estimated remaining life of the annuitant. The liability is then adjusted, with a corresponding adjustment made in the fund balance.

For a life income fund there is an obligation either to pay only the income earned by the specific investments of the fund or to pay a rate of return earned by a group of funds. Because only the income that has been earned is paid out, the obligation is limited and no liability exists as with the annuity fund.

Of the $2,505,000 shown as annuity and life income fund balances at the beginning of the year in the statement of changes in fund balances, only $10,000 matured and, as a restricted amount, moved to endowment for institutional use. A total of $800,000 was received under new agreements, and an additional obligation of $75,000 in actuarial liability was recorded, resulting in ending fund balances of $3,220,000.

The subject of annuity life income funds involves a number of rather complex tax, accounting, and legal issues. In many states annuity funds are regulated as forms of insurance and are subject to jurisdiction of the state insurance regulatory body (e.g., reserve deposits may be required).

## Plant Funds

Colleges and universities, as distinct from for-profit enterprises and some nonprofit-oriented ones such as hospitals, have traditionally segregated their plant funds accounting and have generally ignored depreciation. The reason is that most plant funds are originally given or appropriated as restricted or, if not, have been so irrevocably committed to fixed assets that they will never be available for any other purpose. If the resulting plant has been donated, the institution cannot very easily justify charging for depreciation or expecting customers to pay for something that was given in the first place to help those customers.

On the other hand, as shown earlier, some colleges and universities not only make capital expenditures out of current operating accounts but also transfer operating funds to plant for debt repayments and plant renewals and replacements, which could be considered a flow of depreciation-like expenses. The flow of funds into and out of plant accounts and the resulting plant assets and fund balances, or equity, are important in the management and protection of that part of the institution's long-term capital.

Direct external contributions to plant funds and amounts of current operating funds transferred to plant during the fiscal year are shown in the statement of changes in fund balances. At the top section of that statement (figure 2), $230,000 in new funds was added directly to unexpended plant funds from various sources. Under the transfers section at the bottom, $50,000 in unrestricted gifts was allocated by administrative decision from current to plant funds. Out of these receipts and the prior unexpended balance of $2,120,000, a total of $1,200,000 was expended for plant facilities (under "expenditures and other deductions" in the middle section of the statement), leaving an unexpended balance at the end of the year of $1,200,000 for future plant needs.

Similarly, $10,000 in new funds was received directly for renewals and replacements and $170,000 was transferred from current funds under third-party requirements (mandatory). Out of these receipts and the beginning fund balance of $380,000, a total of $300,000 was expended for plant facilities, leaving an ending balance of $260,000 for future renewals and replacements. Retirement of indebtedness received $78,000 in new funds from external sources and $340,000 in mandatory transfers from current operations for principal and interest. Out of those inflows and the $293,000 beginning balance, the institution's debt service obligations on its plant were fulfilled (under "expenditures and other deductions" in the middle of the statement), and $300,000 in debt service funds remained for the future.

The last column shows the changes in the institution's net investment, or equity, in its physical facilities (i.e., in its accumulated historical plant cost less associated liabilities). Of the year's additions to net investment in plant, $15,000 was from gifts in kind, $1,550,000 from expenditures by the other plant fund groups and from current funds, and $220,000 from retirement of indebtedness. During the period, $115,000 of plant facilities was disposed of, for a new addition of $1,670,000 and an ending balance of $38,210,000.

Beginning plant fund balances totaled $39,333,000. With all the above additions and deductions, the ending plant fund balances, or the equity in all plant funds, increased only $637,000, to a new total of $39,970,000. It should be noted that only $1,460,000 of the most flexible unexpended and renewal and replacement funds remained; there had been $2,500,000 at the beginning of the period. The difference was committed irrevocably to "bricks and mortar," or equipment.

Many donors, faculty members, students, and trustees do not realize that depreciation, or the cost of wear and tear on physical facilities, is not usually accounted for in tuition and fee charges or in the expenditures of colleges and universities.

In the statement of changes in fund balances (figure 2), the total of current operating funds made available for plant capital includes, under "revenues and other additions," $100,000 (as stated in the parenthetical note) and $220,000 for "retirement of indebtedness" (not interest), and, under "transfers among funds," $170,000 for renewals and replacements and $50,000 "allocated" to plant. Amounts funded from current operations, but really expended for plant, could be considered capital expenditures in lieu of depreciation. In the year illustrated, this would represent only 1.35 percent of the total investment in buildings and equipment, based on the balance sheet amount of $41,600,000 in figure 1.

The sample institution obviously depends heavily on funds from external sources for plant maintenance as well as plant additions. Unfortunately, externally restricted funds are more likely to be given for additions than for preservation of current physical facilities. Over time, this can result in buildings and equipment deterioration that is not recognized in operating statements or balance sheet valuations.

Several comments can be made about the four subgroups of the plant fund group.

1.  Unexpended. Unexpended plant funds arise from restricted grants, gifts, and appropriations that can be used only for the acquisition of plant. In the sample institution's statement of changes in fund balances (figure 2), unrestricted gifts were allocated by the governing board for this purpose. This $50,000 nonmandatory transfer will be accounted for in the unrestricted portion of the balances of unexpended plant funds.

When an expenditure of these funds is made, there is (1) a reduction in the fund balance and in cash, and (2) an equal increase in the plant funds subgroup labeled "investment in plant," where the cost of the asset acquired and the increase in net investment in plant are recorded.

Borrowings are an important source of funding for capital outlay. Monies borrowed for acquisition of new plant and equipment are accounted for in this unexpended plant funds subgroup. When the borrowed money is spent, the charge is against the liability account rather than the fund balance. In the investment in plant subgroup the credit is not to net investment in plant but to the reestablishment of a liability.

Construction in progress may be accounted for in unexpended plant funds until the project is complete. Accountability is then established in the investment in plant subgroup. The procedure most commonly followed is to remove the accountability for construction in progress from the unexpended subgroup as quickly as expenditures are made and to carry the construction in progress in the investment in plant subgroup.

2.  Renewals and replacements. This subgroup represents monies set aside to renew or replace plant assets presently in use. Here, too, the fund balances (figure 2) are subdivided between restricted and unrestricted. One of the sources of renewal and replacement funds is a portion of the mandatory transfer ($170,000 in figure 2); when mandatory transfers are received, they are classified as restricted funds. The assets (figure 1) consist of cash, investments, and amounts of money that have been turned over to a trustee in accordance

with an indenture. These assets ($100,000) are classified as deposits with trustees. Expenditure of these monies results in the reduction of assets and fund balances in this subgroup. Simultaneously, an equal amount is recorded as an increase in net investment in plant and in the investment in plant subgroup. These expenditures often do not result in the acquisition of a capitalizable asset. The amount of such expenditures not capitalized should be disclosed, as illustrated in the parenthetical note on the caption "expended for plant facilities" in the statement of changes in fund balances. (The note states "including noncapitalized expenditures of $50,000.")

3. Retirement of indebtedness. Funds for this subgroup may come from contributions or grants that are made for this explicit purpose and are restricted. (This is the case in the sample institution.) Most frequently, the monies for this subgroup come from a mandatory transfer (note the $340,000 shown in the transfer section of the statement of changes in fund balances). Amounts so received are classified as restricted fund balances. If the governing board sets aside excess funds for the retirement of indebtedness, such amounts in excess of what is required would be nonmandatory transfers and would be classified as unrestricted. Funds for retirement of indebtedness are used to meet two kinds of obligations: (1) interest expense, which should be shown separately (see the $190,000 deduction), and (2) amortization of the debt (see the $220,000 deduction). Amortization of the debt results in another set of entries in the investment in plant subgroup. In figure 1 there would be a reduction of the liability for bonds payable equal to the debt amortization payment made in the retirement of the indebtedness funds, and there would be a corresponding credit for increase to the net investment in plant of $220,000. Thus, as debt is reduced the equity in net assets is increased.

4. Investment in plant. The assets of this subgroup consist of the carrying values of land improvements, buildings, equipment, library books, museum collections, and other similar capital holdings with a long-term life. Some of these are depreciable.

These assets are to be carried at their historical cost until disposed of. In earlier years some institutions carried such assets at some other amount (e.g., periodic appraisal value), either out of preference or because the original cost records had been lost or destroyed. When historical cost information is not available, it is permissible for an institution to obtain a professional estimate of the *historical* costs and to use the estimate as the basis for reporting.

Rules must be established by the institution to determine when a particular expenditure results in the acquisition of a capital asset. For example, items of movable equipment should be capitalized, provided they have a significant value and that they have a useful life that extends beyond at least a year. (Otherwise the items do not have capital value.) The value thresholds vary widely from institution to institution. The Cost Accounting Standards Board established costing rules for all contractors employing federal funds and set certain limits beyond which an expenditure is classified as a capital addition. Another rule must be made to determine when a renovation becomes a capital asset. For example, a minor renovation probably has little value associated with it and would not be considered a capitalizable asset. On the other hand, a renovation that extended the life of the asset or permitted an entirely new use of an existing facility will probably be capitalized. Finally, new assets are added to the carrying values of the asset section of this subgroup, and assets that have been sold, destroyed, stolen, lost, or otherwise eliminated from the possession of the institution should be removed from the records (i.e., their carrying values should be removed).

If debt is incurred by the institution to finance working capital, it should not be carried in the plant fund but rather as a liability of current funds. This rule holds even though plant assets may be pledged as collateral against the loan. The reader of financial statements needs to know a great deal about the liabilities of plant funds and other liabilities of a long-term nature that may appear in other fund groups. Some disclosure requirements in this regard are therefore illustrated in the notes to the financial statements (see figure 5).

The fund balance of the investment in plant subgroup is referred to as net investment in plant. It is not classified as restricted or unrestricted because it is simply the accountability for the net asset values carried in this section. No further future use is intended. Thus, any restrictions that may have been imposed on the funds used to finance these assets generally have been met. There are, however, some instances of gifts that carry restrictions of a second-generation nature. For example, the initial restrictions may require that the funds be used for the acquisition of a building. An additional restriction might require that, in the event the building is later sold, the proceeds of the sale be used for a replacement building. This situation is rare, however.

In the statement of changes in fund balances (figure 2), increases in the net investment in plant arise from the expenditure of unexpended plant funds and renewal and replacement funds. Increases also arise from debt reductions (reflected in the decrease in funds for the retirement of indebtedness) and from contributions-in-kind such as a building, land, or equipment.

Decreases in the net investment in plant represent the elimination from the capital assets inventory of those assets that are retired, sold, disposed of, or destroyed. When such assets are eliminated, the total carrying value of the asset is deducted from the asset category and from the net investment in plant. Any cash proceeds received as a result of this retirement are taken in the unexpended plant fund, and, in the absence of any of the secondary types of restrictions mentioned earlier, are classified as an addition to the unrestricted portion of unexpended plant funds. Thus, the net gain or loss from the sale or disposal of the capital asset does not appear separately. Another major deduction would be the depreciation of capital assets (if such a practice is followed).

Net investment in plant can increase for a reason linked to the peculiar operations of colleges and universities. Many institutions include in the operating budgets of the various departments a provision for minor items of equipment. In some cases there is a policy of equipment replacement with respect to certain types of assets. For example, typewriters may be replaced on a scheduled basis. The amount that will be expended annually for this purpose is budgeted in that department. Therefore, the expenditure of current funds for this purpose becomes part of the functional expenditures set forth in the statement of current funds revenues, expenditures, and other changes and in the statement of changes in fund balances for unrestricted or restricted current funds. Another kind of capital outlay that might be financed in a similar manner from current funds expenditures is library books. These expenditures of current funds for the replacement of capital assets are reported first as expenditures of current funds, and are then picked up as assets and as additions to the fund balance of the investment in plant subgroup. In the sample institution $100,000 charged to current fund expenditures is also added to net investment in plant.

## Statement of Current Funds Revenues, Expenditures, and Other Changes

### Revenues

The sources of revenue include tuition and fee income; appropriations received from federal, state, and local government sources; grants and contracts from these same sources; private gifts, grants, and contracts; endowment income (i.e., income generated by the investments of endowment and similar funds); and sales and services of educational departments as well as sales and services of auxiliary enterprises (see figure 3). The sales and services of a hospital associated with the institution would be shown separately. They may be certain other institutional activities rendering unique services that would be separately accounted for, or accounted for as a separate source.

All unrestricted resources that are earned by the institution or come into the institution for the first time are accounted for initially as unrestricted current fund revenues. By contrast, all restricted amounts are accounted for initially in another fund group depending on the nature of the restriction.

## Expenditures

Expenditures are categorized according to the major functions of the institution (e.g., instruction, research, public service). Auxiliary enterprises and hospital expenditures are shown separately.

Mandatory transfers are shown on the statement of current funds, revenues, expenditures, and other changes, together with, but separate from, the current fund expenditures. The transfers are divided according to their relation to the educational and general programs of the institution, to auxiliary enterprises, or to a hospital. On the statement of changes in fund balances, mandatory transfers are shown in the transfers section.

## Mandatory Transfers

In the example (figure 3) a mandatory transfer represents an amount of cash to be transferred from the unrestricted current fund. It will go to that restricted fund for which the transfer is made. In most cases the transfer is mandated by a debt instrument (e.g., a bond indenture, which requires the periodic setting aside of funds to cover principal repayment), by interest expenses, and by the need to accumulate certain reserves for renewal and replacement. These required amounts are transferred to, accounted for in, and expended from the plant fund group. Through the transfer the amounts are deducted from current funds. In this example the amounts deducted are unrestricted, but when they are accounted for in the plant fund they are classified as restricted amounts because they are placed there by reason of the legally binding instrument.

Another mandatory transfer illustrated in the example is the matching requirement of the National Defense Student Loan program. The loan fund matching requirement in this example is being financed from the unrestricted current fund, and the mandatory transfer is to the loan fund group, where the amount transferred would have to be classified as a restricted balance.

## Nonmandatory Transfers

These transfers are discretionary in nature and are carried out by the governing board. Generally, they are amounts that are unrestricted and are shifted from one major fund group to another to reflect designations by the board. When unrestricted current funds are transferred on a nonmandatory basis to another fund group, it is imperative that the label "unrestricted" be carried along so that when it appears in the other group the reader knows that the amount transferred can be reversed. (Mandatory transfers, once made in accordance with the bond indenture, can never be reversed because they must be used exclusively to serve the debt.)

## Other Changes

One such change is the accounting for indirect cost recovery from funding sources. The primary source of this kind of cost recovery is federal funds that are used to finance various sponsored research, training, and other activities. The source of recovery becomes the revenue source used to account for the amount of indirect cost recovery. This accounting is difficult in that indirect costs are part of the total grant received by an institution. This total grant is first accounted for as an addition to a restricted current fund. The indirect cost recovery, however, is not viewed as an expenditure of a restricted fund but rather as an allocation of that amount into unrestricted current fund revenue for the purpose of reimbursing the institution. Two actions must be taken: (1) the amount must be deducted from the fund balance in restricted current funds (this can be seen as a separate line on the statement of changes), and (2) the amount must be recorded as revenue in unrestricted current funds. Although this amount is not separately labeled, it can be traced. In the federal, state, and local grants and contracts amounts in the unrestricted column of the revenue statement (figure 3), these three figures total $35,000, which is equal to the amount of indirect cost recovery deducted from the current restricted fund balances under expenditures and other deductions in figure 2. Another kind of deduction that is shown separately in both statements (in the amount of $20,000) is the refunding to a grantor of an unspent amount of a current restricted fund.

All revenues, additions, expenditures, and mandatory and nonmandatory transfers collectively yield the net change in fund balances for the year. These amounts must be shown at the bottom of the statement of current funds revenues, expenditures, and other changes, and also near the bottom of the statement of changes of fund balances (just before the fund balances themselves).

## Encumbrances

An encumbrance is a commitment to pay for goods or services when such are received. The encumbrance is accounted for as a reduction of available funds (i.e., as a commitment), but must at all times be distinguished from true liabilities. True liability exists once goods or services have been received. In many cases that liability may result in the incurrence of an expense (i.e., when a value is carried forward as unexpired costs, it becomes an asset). Therefore, neither encumbrances that are not true liabilities as of the reporting date nor outstanding unliquidated encumbrances are included in the statement. If the latter are reported at all, they are shown either as a segregation of the fund balance to which they relate or as amounts disclosed in the notes to the financial statements.

## Notes to Financial Statements

The purpose of these notes (see figure 5) is to provide further disclosure of key information that is considered necessary according to generally accepted accounting principles for colleges and universities. For example, some notes for the sample institution relate to such matters as the composition, market value, and performance of investments; outstanding commitments in the area of major items of construction; obligations under pension plans; and details concerning liabilities for short- and long-term debt.

The nature and the means of repayment of any significant interfund receivables must be disclosed in the notes to the financial statements. If the interfund receivable cannot be collected from the owing fund, consideration must be given to making a permanent transfer (thereby eliminating the interfund receivable and payable).

In their financial statements many nonprofit organizations, including a number of colleges and universities, record pledges receivable as assets and as accountabilities. However, many institutions document pledges or have relationships with potential donors such that it is not possible to determine the net realizable value of outstanding pledges. In those circumstances uncollected pledges are not included in the basic financial statements, though all significant pledges must be disclosed in the notes, as illustrated in the case of the sample institution.

## Figure 1
## Sample Educational Institution Balance Sheet June 30, 19_____ with comparative figures at June 30, 19_____

| Assets | | | Liabilities and Fund Balances | | |
|---|---|---|---|---|---|
| **Current Funds** | **Current Year** | **Prior Year** | **Current Funds** | **Current Year** | **Prior Year** |
| Unrestricted | | | Unrestricted | | |
| Cash | $ 210,000 | $ 110,000 | Accounts payable | $ 125,000 | $ 100,000 |
| Investments | 450,000 | 360,000 | Accrued liabilities | 20,000 | 15,000 |
| Accounts receivable, | | | Students' deposits | 30,000 | 35,000 |
| less allowance of | | | Due to other funds | 158,000 | 120,000 |
| $18,000 both years | 228,000 | 175,000 | Deferred credits | 30,000 | 20,000 |
| Inventories, at lower of | | | Fund Balance | 643,000 | 455,000 |
| cost (first-in, first-out basis) | | | Total unrestricted | 1,006,000 | 745,000 |
| or market | 90,000 | 80,000 | | | |
| Prepaid expenses and | | | | | |
| deferred charges | 28,000 | 20,000 | | | |
| Total unrestricted | 1,006,000 | 745,000 | | | |
| | | | | | |
| Restricted | | | Restricted | | |
| Cash | 145,000 | 101,000 | Accounts payable | 14,000 | 5,000 |
| Investments | 175,000 | 165,000 | Fund balances | 446,000 | 421,000 |
| Accounts receivable, less | | | | | |
| allowance of $8,000 | | | | | |
| both years | 68,000 | 160,000 | | | |
| Unbilled charges | 72,000 | — | | | |
| Total restricted | 460,000 | 426,000 | Total restricted | 460,000 | 426,000 |
| Total current funds | 1,466,000 | 1,171,000 | Total current funds | 1,466,000 | 1,171,000 |
| | | | | | |
| Loan Funds | | | Loan Funds | | |
| Cash | 30,000 | 20,000 | Fund balances | | |
| Investments | 100,000 | 100,000 | U.S. government grants | | |
| Loans to students, faculty, | | | refundable | 50,000 | 33,000 |
| and staff, less allowance of | | | University funds | | |
| $10,000 current year | | | Restricted | 483,000 | 369,000 |
| and $9,000 prior year | 550,000 | 382,000 | Unrestricted | 150,000 | 100,000 |
| Due from unrestricted funds | 3,000 | — | Total loan funds | 683,000 | 502,000 |
| Total loan funds | 683,000 | 502,000 | | | |
| | | | | | |
| Endowment and Similar Funds | | | Endowment and Similar Funds | | |
| Cash | 100,000 | 101,000 | Fund balances | | |
| Investments | 13,900,000 | 11,800,000 | Endowment | 7,800,000 | 6,740,000 |
| | | | Term endowment | 3,840,000 | 3,420,000 |
| | | | Quasi-endowment— | | |
| | | | unrestricted | 1,000,000 | 800,000 |
| | | | Quasi-endowment— | | |
| | | | restricted | 1,360,000 | 941,000 |
| Total endowment | | | Total endowment | | |
| and similar funds | 14,000,000 | 11,901,000 | and similar funds | 14,000,000 | 11,901,000 |
| | | | | | |
| Annuity and Life Income Funds | | | Annuity and Life Income Funds | | |
| Annuity funds | | | Annuity Funds | | |
| Cash | $ 55,000 | $ 45,000 | Annuities payable | $ 2,150,000 | $ 2,300,000 |
| Investments | 3,260,000 | 3,010,000 | Fund balances | 1,165,000 | 755,000 |
| Total annuity funds | 3,315,000 | 3,055,000 | Total annuity funds | 3,315,000 | 3,055,000 |
| | | | | | |
| Life income funds | | | Life income funds | | |
| Cash | 15,000 | 15,000 | Income payable | 5,000 | 5,000 |
| Investments | 2,045,000 | 1,740,000 | Fund balances | 2,055,000 | 1,750,000 |
| Total life | | | Total life | | |
| income funds | 2,060,000 | 1,755,000 | income funds | 2,060,000 | 1,755,000 |
| Total annuity and life | | | Total annuity and life | | |
| income funds | 5,375,000 | 4,810,000 | income funds | 5,375,000 | 4,810,000 |

(cont.)

| Plant Funds | | | | Plant Funds | | |
|---|---|---|---|---|---|---|
| Unexpended | | | | Unexpended | | |
| Cash | 275,000 | 410,000 | | Accounts payable | 10,000 | — |
| Investments | 1,285,000 | 1,590,000 | | Notes payable | 100,000 | — |
| Due from unrestricted | | | | Bonds payable | 400,000 | — |
| Current funds | 150,000 | 120,000 | | Fund balances | | |
| | | | | Restricted | 1,000,000 | 1,860,000 |
| | | | | Unrestricted | 200,000 | 260,000 |
| Total unexpended | 1,710,000 | 2,120,000 | | Total unexpended | 1,710,000 | 2,120,000 |
| | | | | | | |
| Renewals and replacements | | | | Renewals and replacements | | |
| Cash | 5,000 | 4,000 | | Fund balances | | |
| Investments | 150,000 | 286,000 | | Restricted | 25,000 | 180,000 |
| Deposits with trustees | 100,000 | 90,000 | | Unrestricted | 235,000 | 200,000 |
| Due from unrestricted | | | | | | |
| current funds | 5,000 | — | | | | |
| Total renewals and | | | | Total renewals and | | |
| replacements | 260,000 | 380,000 | | replacements | 260,000 | 380,000 |
| | | | | | | |
| Retirement of indebtedness | | | | Retirement of indebtedness | | |
| Cash | 50,000 | 40,000 | | Fund balances | | |
| Deposits with trustees | 250,000 | 253,000 | | Restricted | 185,000 | 125,000 |
| Total retirement of | | | | Unrestricted | 115,000 | 168,000 |
| indebtedness | 300,000 | 293,000 | | Total retirement of | | |
| | | | | indebtedness | 300,000 | 293,000 |
| | | | | | | |
| Investment in plant | | | | Investment in plant | | |
| Land | 500,000 | 500,000 | | Notes payable | 790,000 | 810,000 |
| Land improvements | 1,000,000 | 1,110,000 | | Bonds payable | 2,200,000 | 2,400,000 |
| Buildings | 25,000,000 | 24,060,000 | | Mortgages payable | 400,000 | 200,000 |
| Equipment | 15,000,000 | 14,200,000 | | Net investment in plant | 38,210,000 | 36,540,000 |
| Library books | 100,000 | 80,000 | | Total investment in | | |
| Total investment in | | | | plant | 41,600,000 | 39,950,000 |
| plant | 41,600,000 | 39,950,000 | | Total plant funds | 43,870,000 | 42,743,000 |
| Total plant funds | 43,870,000 | 42,743,000 | | | | |
| | | | | | | |
| Agency Funds | | | | Agency Funds | | |
| Cash | 50,000 | 70,000 | | Deposits held in custody | | |
| Investments | 60,000 | 20,000 | | for others | 110,000 | 90,000 |
| Total agency funds | 110,000 | 90,000 | | Total agency funds | 110,000 | 90,000 |

Source: College & University Business Administration, *4th ed. (Washington, DC: National Association of College and University Business Officers, 1982), pp. 456–457.*

## Figure 2
## Sample Educational Institution Statement of Changes in Fund Balances Year Ended June 30, 19____

| | Current Funds Unrestricted | Current Funds Restricted | Loan Funds | Endowment and Similar Funds | Annuity and Life Income Funds | Plant Funds Unexpended | Plant Funds Renewals and Replacements | Plant Funds Retirement of Indebtedness | Plant Funds Investment in Plant |
|---|---|---|---|---|---|---|---|---|---|
| **Revenues and other additions** | | | | | | | | | |
| Unrestricted current fund revenues | $7,540,000 | | | | | | | | |
| Expired term endowment—restricted | | | | | | 50,000 | | | |
| State appropriations—restricted | | | | | | 50,000 | | | |
| Federal grants and contracts—restricted | | 500,000 | | | | | | | |
| Private gifts, grants, and contracts—restricted | | 370,000 | 100,000 | 1,500,000 | 800,000 | 115,000 | | 65,000 | 15,000 |
| Investment income—restricted | | 224,000 | 12,000 | 10,000 | | 5,000 | 5,000 | 5,000 | |
| Realized gains on investments—unrestricted | | | | 109,000 | | | | | |
| Realized gains on investments—restricted | | | 4,000 | 50,000 | | 10,000 | 5,000 | 5,000 | |
| Interest on loans receivable | | | 7,000 | | | | | | |
| U.S. government advances | | | 18,000 | | | | | | |
| Expended for plant facilities (including $100,000 charged to current funds expenditures) | | | | | | | | | 1,550,000 |
| Retirement of indebtedness | | | | | | | | | 220,000 |
| Accrued interest on sale of bonds | | | | | | | | 3,000 | |
| Matured annuity and life income restricted to endowment | | | 10,000 | | | | | | |
| Total revenues and other additions | 7,540,000 | 1,094,000 | 141,000 | 1,679,000 | 800,000 | 230,000 | 10,000 | 78,000 | 1,785,000 |
| **Expenditures and other deductions** | | | | | | | | | |
| Educational and general expenditures | 4,400,000 | 1,014,000 | | | | | | | |
| Auxiliary enterprises expenditures | 1,830,000 | | | | | | | | |
| Indirect costs recovered | | 35,000 | | | | | | | |
| Refunded to grantors | | 20,000 | 10,000 | | | | | | |
| Loan cancellations and write-offs | | | 1,000 | | | | | | |
| Administrative and collection costs | | | 1,000 | | | | | | |
| Adjustment of actuarial liability for annuities payable | | | | | 75,000 | | | | |
| Expended for plant facilities (including noncapitalized expenditures of $50,000) | | | | | | 1,200,000 | 300,000 | | |
| Retirement of indebtedness | | | | | | | | 220,000 | |
| Interest on indebtedness | | | | | | | | 190,000 | |
| Disposal of plant facilities | | | | | | | | | 115,000 |
| Expired term endowments ($40,000 unrestricted, $50,000 restricted to plant) | | | | 90,000 | | | | | |
| Matured annuity and life income funds restricted to endowment | | | | | 10,000 | | | | |
| Total expenditures and other deductions | 6,230,000 | 1,069,000 | 12,000 | 90,000 | 85,000 | 1,200,000 | 300,000 | 411,000 | 115,000 |
| **Transfers among funds—additions/(deductions)** | | | | | | | | | |
| Mandatory: | | | | | | | | | |
| Principal and interest | (340,000) | | | | | | | 340,000 | |
| Renewals and replacements | (170,000) | | | | | | 170,000 | | |
| Loan fund matching grant | (2,000) | | 2,000 | | | | | | |
| Unrestricted gifts allocated | (650,000) | | 50,000 | 550,000 | | 50,000 | | | |
| Portion of unrestricted quasi-endowment funds investment gains appropriated | 40,000 | | | (40,000) | | | | | |
| Total transfers | (1,122,000) | | 52,000 | 510,000 | | 50,000 | 170,000 | 340,000 | |
| Net increase/(decrease) for the year | 188,000 | 25,000 | 181,000 | 2,099,000 | 715,000 | (920,000) | (120,000) | 7,000 | 1,670,000 |
| Fund balance at beginning of year | 455,000 | 421,000 | 502,000 | 11,901,000 | 2,505,000 | 2,120,000 | 380,000 | 293,000 | 36,540,000 |
| Fund balance at end of year | 643,000 | 446,000 | 683,000 | 14,000,000 | 3,220,000 | 1,200,000 | 260,000 | 300,000 | 38,210,000 |

Source: *College & University Business Administration,* 4th ed. (Washington, DC: National Association of College and University Business Officers, 1982), pp. 458-459.

**Figure 3**
**Sample Educational Institution Statement of Current Funds Revenues, Expenditures, and Other Changes Year Ended June 30, 19____**

| | Current Year | | | Prior-Year |
| | Unrestricted | Restricted | Total | Total |
|---|---|---|---|---|
| **Revenues** | | | | |
| Tuition and fees | $2,600,000 | | $2,600,000 | $2,300,000 |
| Federal appropriations' | 500,000 | | 500,000 | 500,000 |
| State appropriations | 700,000 | | 700,000 | 700,000 |
| Local appropriations | 100,000 | | 100,000 | 100,000 |
| Federal grants and contracts | 20,000 | $ 375,000 | 395,000 | 350,000 |
| State grants and contracts | 10,000 | 25,000 | 35,000 | 200,000 |
| Local grants and contracts | 5,000 | 25,000 | 30,000 | 45,000 |
| Private gifts, grants, and contracts | 850,000 | 380,000 | 1,230,000 | 1,190,000 |
| Endowment income | 325,000 | 209,000 | 534,000 | 500,000 |
| Sales and services of educational activities | 190,000 | | 190,000 | 195,000 |
| Sales and services of auxiliary enterprises | 2,200,000 | | 2,200,000 | 2,100,000 |
| Expired term endowment | 40,000 | | 40,000 | |
| Other sources (if any) | | | | |
| Total current revenues | 7,540,000 | 1,014,000 | 8,554,000 | 8,180,000 |
| | | | | |
| **Expenditures and mandatory transfers** | | | | |
| Education and general | | | | |
| Instruction | 2,960,000 | 489,000 | 3,449,000 | 3,300,000 |
| Research  100,000 | 400,000 | 500,000 | 650,000 | |
| Public service     130,000 | 25,000 | 155,000 | 175,000 | |
| Academic support | 250,000 | | 250,000 | 225,000 |
| Student services  200,000 | | 200,000 | 195,000 | |
| Institutional support | 450,000 | | 450,000 | 445,000 |
| Operation and maintenance of plant | 220,000 | | 220,000 | 200,000 |
| Scholarships and fellowships | 90,000 | 100,000 | 190,000 | 180,000 |
| Educational and general expenditures | 4,400,000 | 1,014,000 | 5,414,000 | 5,370,000 |
| Mandatory transfers for: | | | | |
| Principal and interest | 90,000 | | 90,000 | 50,000 |
| Renewals and replacements | 100,000 | | 100,000 | 80,000 |
| Loan fund matching grant | 2,000 | | 2,000 | |
| Total educational and general | 4,592,000 | 1,014,000 | 5,606,000 | 5,500,000 |
| Auxiliary enterprises | | | | |
| Expenditures | 1,830,000 | | 1,830,000 | 1,730,000 |
| Mandatory transfers for: | | | | |
| Principal and interest | 250,000 | | 250,000 | 250,000 |
| Renewals and replacements | 70,000 | | 70,000 | 70,000 |
| Total auxiliary enterprises | 2,150,000 | | 2,150,000 | 2,050,000 |
| Total expenditures and mandatory transfers | 6,742,000 | 1,014,000 | 7,756,000 | 7,550,000 |
| | | | | |
| **Other transfers and additions/(deductions)** | | | | |
| Excess of restricted receipts over transfers to revenues | | 45,000 | 45,000 | 40,000 |
| Refunded to grantors | | (20,000) | (20,000) | |
| Unrestricted gifts allocated to other funds | (650,000) | | (650,000) | (510,000) |
| Portion of quasi-endowment gains appropriated | 40,000 | | 40,000 | |
| Net increase in fund balances | 188,000 | 25,000 | 213,000 | 160,000 |

*Source: College & University Business Administration,* 4th ed. (Washington, DC: National Association of College and University Business Officers, 1982), pp. 460–461.

## Figure 4
## Sample Educational Institution Summary of Significant Accounting Policies  June 30, 19\_\_\_\_\_

The significant accounting policies followed by Sample Educational Institution are described below to enhance the usefulness of the financial statements to the reader.

### Accrual Basis

The financial statements of Sample Educational Institution have been prepared on the accrual basis except for depreciation accounting as explained in notes 1 and 2 to the financial statements. The statement of current funds revenues, expenditures, and other changes is a statement of financial activities of current funds related to the current reporting period. It does not purport to present the results of operations or the net income or loss for the period as would a statement of income or a statement of revenues and expenses.

To the extent that current funds are used to finance plant assets, the amounts so provided are accounted for as (1) expenditures, in the case of normal replacement of movable equipment and library books; (2) mandatory transfers, in the case of required provisions for debt amortization and interest and equipment renewal and replacement; and (3) transfers of a non-mandatory nature for all other cases.

### Fund Accounting

In order to ensure observance of limitations and restrictions placed on the use of the resources available to the Institution, the accounts of the Institution are maintained in accordance with the principles of "fund accounting." This is the procedure by which resources for various purposes are classified for accounting and reporting purposes into funds that are in accordance with activities or objectives specified. Separate accounts are maintained for each fund; however, in the accompanying financial statements, funds that have similar characteristics have been combined into fund groups. Accordingly, all financial transactions have been recorded and reported by fund group.

Within each fund group, fund balances restricted by outside sources are so indicated and are distinguished from unrestricted funds allocated to specific purposes by action of the governing board. Externally restricted funds may only be utilized in accordance with the purposes established by the source of such funds and are in contrast with unrestricted funds over which the governing board retains full control to use in achieving any of its institutional purposes.

Endowment funds are subject to the restrictions of gift instruments requiring a perpetuity that the principal be invested and the income only be utilized. Term endowment funds are similar to endowment funds except that upon the passage of a stated period of time or the occurrence of a particular event, all or part of the principal may be expended. While quasi-endowment funds have been established by the governing board for the same purposes as endowment funds, any portion of quasi-endowment funds may be expended.

All gains and losses arising from the sale, collection, or other disposition of investments and other noncash assets are accounted for in the fund which owned such assets. Ordinary income derived from investments, receivables, and the like is accounted for in the fund owning such assets, except for income derived from investments of endowment and similar funds, which income is accounted for in the fund to which it is restricted or, if unrestricted, as revenues in unrestricted current funds.

All other unrestricted revenue is accounted for in the unrestricted current fund. Restricted gifts, grants, appropriations, endowment income, and other restricted resources are accounted for in the appropriate restricted funds. Restricted current funds are reported as revenues and expenditures when expended for current operating purposes.

### Other Significant Accounting Policies

Other significant accounting policies are set forth in the financial statements and the notes thereto.·

Source: *College & University Business Administration*, 4th ed. (Washington, DC: National Association of College and University Business Officers, 1982), pp. 462–463.

## Figure 5
## Sample Educational Institution Notes to Financial Statements June 30, 19_____

1. Investments exclusive of physical plant are recorded at cost; investments received by gift are carried at market value at the date of acquisition. Quoted market values of investments (all marketable securities) of the funds indicated were as follows:

| | Current year | Prior year |
|---|---|---|
| Unrestricted current funds | $510,000 | $390,000 |
| Restricted current funds | 180,000 | 165,000 |
| Loan funds | 105,000 | 105,000 |
| Unexpended plant funds | 1,287,000 | 1,600,000 |
| Renewal and replacement funds | 145,000 | 285,000 |
| Agency funds | 60,000 | 20,000 |

Investments of endowment and similar funds and annuity and life income funds are composed of the following:

| | Carrying value | |
|---|---|---|
| | Current year | Prior year |
| Endowment and similar funds: | | |
| Corporate stocks and bonds (approximate market, current year $15,000,000, prior year $10,900,000) | $13,000,000 | $10,901,000 |
| Rental properties—less accumulated depreciation, current year $500,000, prior year $400,000 | 900,000 | 899,000 |
| | 13,900,000 | 11,800,000 |
| Annuity funds: | | |
| U.S. bonds (approximate market, current year $200,000, prior year $100,000) | 200,000 | 110,000 |
| Corporate stocks and bonds (approximate market, current year $3,070,000, prior year $2,905,000) | 3,060,000 | 2,900,000 |
| | 3,260,000 | 3,010,000 |
| Life income funds: | | |
| Municipal bonds (approximate market, current year $1,400,000, prior year $1,340,000) | 1,500,000 | 1,300,000 |
| Corporate stocks and bonds (approximate market, current year $650,000, prior year $400,000) | 545,000 | 440,000 |
| | 2,045,000 | 1,740,000 |

Assets of endowment funds, except nonmarketable investments of term endowment having a book value of $200,000 and quasi-endowment having a book value of $800,000, are pooled on a market value basis, with each individual fund subscribing to or disposing of units on the basis of the value per unit at market value at the beginning of the calendar quarter within which the transaction takes place. Of the total units each having a market value of $15,00, 600,000 units were owned by endowment, 280,000 units by term endowment, and 120,000 units by quasi-endowment at June 30, 19_____.

The following tabulation summarizes changes in relationships between cost and market values of the pooled assets:

| | Pooled Assets | | Net Gains (Losses) | Market Value per Unit |
|---|---|---|---|---|
| | Market | Cost | | |
| End of year | $15,000,000 | $13,000,000 | $2,000,000 | $15.00 |
| Beginning of year | 10,900,000 | 10,901,000 | (1,000) | 12.70 |
| Unrealized net gains for year | | | 2,001,000 | |
| Realized net gains for year | | | 159,000 | |
| Total net gains for year | | | $2,160,000 | $ 2.30 |

The average annual earnings per unit, exclusive of net gains, were $.56 for the year.

*cont.*

2. Physical plant and equipment are stated at cost at date of acquisition or fair value at date of donation in the case of gifts, except land acquired prior to 1940, which is valued at appraisal value in 1940 at $300,000. Depreciation on physical plant and equipment is not recorded.

3. Long-term debt includes: bonds payable due in annual installments varying from $45,000 to $55,000 with interest at 5-7/8%, the final installment being due in 19__, collateralized by trust indenture covering land, buildings, and equipment known as Smith dormitory carried in the accounts at $2,500,000, and pledged net revenue from the operations of said dormitory; and mortgages payable due in varying amounts to 19__ with interest at 6%, collateralized by property carried in the accounts at $800,000 and pledged revenue of the Student Union amounting to approximately $65,000 per year.

4. The Institution has certain contributory pension plans for academic and nonacademic personnel. Total pension expense for the year was $350,000, which includes amortization of prior service cost over a period of 20 years. The Institution's policy is to fund pension costs accrued, including periodic funding of prior years' accruals not previously funded. The actuarially computed value of vested benefits as of June 30, 19__ exceeded net assets of the pension fund by approximately $300,000.

5. Contracts have been let for the construction of additional classroom buildings in the amount of $3,000,000. Construction and equipment are estimated to total $5,000,000, which will be financed by available resources and an issue of bonds payable over a period of 40 years amounting to $4,000,000.

6. All interfund borrowings have been made from unrestricted funds. The amounts due to plant funds from current unrestricted funds are payable within one year without interest. The amount due to loan funds from current unrestricted funds is payable currently.

7. Pledges totaling $260,000, restricted to plant fund uses, are due to be collected over the next three fiscal years in the amounts of $120,000, $80,000, and $60,000 respectively. It is not practicable to estimate the net realizable value of such pledges.

Source: *College & University Business Administration*, 4th ed. (Washington, DC: National Association of College and University Business Officers, 1982), pp. 463–466.

# For Further Reading

Easy-to-understand pamphlets on the interpretation of financial statements are distributed by a number of stockbrokerages. One of the best is offered by Merrill Lynch. Although these documents address the for-profit sector, many of the principles of accounting are relevant to the nonprofit sector as well.

A good introduction to fund accounting is provided by Robert N. Anthony and Regina E. Herzlinger, *Management Control in Nonprofit Organizations*, rev. ed. (Homewood, IL: Richard D. Irwin, Inc., 1980). For those readers willing to tackle a technical discussion of accounting, a thorough text is Ray M. Powell, *Accounting Procedures for Institutions* (Notre Dame, IN: University of Notre Dame Press, 1978). A good overview of the technical aspects of institutional accounting is provided by *College & University Business Administration*, 4th ed. (Washington, DC: National Association of College and University Business Officers, 1982).

This chapter is a revision of material contained in *Financial Responsibilities of Governing Boards of Colleges and Universities* (Washington, DC: Association of Governing Boards of Universities and Colleges and National Association of College and University Business Officers, 1979), and *Conference for Women Administrators: Financial Management of Colleges and Universities* (Washington, DC: National Association of College and University Business Officers and Committee for the Concerns of Women in New England Colleges and Universities, n.d.). Permission to use this material has been granted.

# The Necessary Revolution in Financial Accounting (1992)

## GORDON C. WINSTON

The financial accounts of a college or university do not report economic information for the institution as a whole. Instead, the institution is divided into separate activities and a separate set of financial accounts—income statement and balance sheet—is reported for each of those activities. In effect, each activity at a college is treated as if it were a separate firm (Garner 1991). Often-complex loans and transfers between these "firms" are recorded in each set of accounts. Typically eight or nine separate fund accounts and their interwoven transfers make up the annual financial statement for even a small college. This peculiar system is called fund accounting.

Fund accounting has been a source of complaints among college and university trustees for decades, and among others who seek to determine the true financial condition of a college or university. Like the old saw about the weather, everyone complains but no one does anything about it.[1] I think a better way should and can be developed, especially since much of higher education is experiencing increasing difficulty in financing its operations. This article is an attempt to point the way.

My alternative to fund accounting is the result of a six-year effort to organize the vital economic information about a college's performance in a different and more useful way. I call the alternative *global* accounting because it presents an encompassing—all inclusive and integrated—view of a college's economic activities and its financial status. It is the kind of information that is essential to the management and governance of a college, the kind needed by the Board of Trustees, a faculty oversight committee, and top administrators. It describes the economic effects of each year's activities, and specifically the effects on the college's real wealth.[2]

The structure of global accounting is the antithesis of fund accounting. Instead of dividing the institution into a set of self-contained and balkanized accounting entities, global accounting brings economic information together about the whole college. The aim is to provide an annual picture of the financial condition of a college that is accurate, clear, and accessible.

## The Trouble with Fund Accounts

Fund accounting has an honorable history of service to government and nonprofit institutions; and there are still important questions that only fund accounts, or something like them, can answer. What is at issue is the inadequacy of fund accounts to provide the *sole* or *primary* way to frame economic information for colleges and universities. Here are some of the inadequacies:

1. Fund accounts obscure an overall, global understanding of an institutions economic performance.

2.  Fund accounts are very hard to read and understand. That is, they are inaccessible without a significant investment of time to grasp their mass of detailed information repeated for each fund and their often complex transfers and interactions among funds.

3.  They cause people to focus attention on understandable information that may be partial, misleading, or just marginally relevant. For example, people tend to focus on such items as the size of the operating budget, the budget surplus or deficit, or the market value of the endowment. But the operating budget leaves out a third or more of all current economic activity; budget surpluses or deficits are easily manipulated; and the endowment is only a fraction of the total wealth in even the best endowed universities (Winston 1988).

4.  There is an inherent temptation to present misleading information. Separate funds are potential shells that invite shell games. For instance, Williams College, in moving $5 million of current spending off the operating budget in the 1980s, markedly reduced the apparent (but not the actual) growth of its operating expenditures. Swarthmore boasted of 40 years of exactly balanced operating budgets (Swarthmore 1987, 17), a feat which was apparently achieved by transferring to the operating budget fund from other funds (after the fact) whatever dollars were needed to cover operating expenses. Harvard and MIT followed the same convention in the 1970s (Bierman and Hofstedt 1973).

5.  Fund accounting reduces higher education's ability to make economic comparisons among colleges and even to understand economic performance over time at a single school.

The rationale for fund accounts in colleges has been that the separate accounts make it easier to monitor performance in specific areas supported by outside agents, donors, and government agencies who give funds to the college for restricted purposes and need to know if those purposes are well served and managed (Harried, et al 1985, 722). That stewardship role remains. But it doesn't justify the use of fund accounts as the primary way of organizing economic information.

Some have tried to make fund accounting serve purposes of both stewardship and governance, for instance, by using ratio analysis (Chabotar 1989). Both these efforts have been only partially successful since they retain the shortcomings of fund accounting. On the other hand, global accounts that define the context and inform the governance and management of a college will always need to be complemented by sub-accounts fitted within the global reporting so that restrictions on the use of funds and other detailed information can be handled.

## What is Global Accounting?

The basic structure of global accounting is simple. For each year's economic activity, three elemental facts are reported:

1.  How much the college took in from all sources;

2.  What it did with that money; and

3.  The effect of these on the institution's real wealth.

That is the essential framework. (It is also the framework, often honored in the breach, of the familiar Income Statement and Balance Sheet.) What is centrally important is that the global accounts encompass the institution's complete activities. No flow or claim between the college and some outside agent—of income or expenditure or saving or liabilities—should be left out. And no financial flows or claims between funds should be included.

When we began constructing our system of global accounts, we intended only to reorganize the economic information already repeated in the fund accounts. Our global accounts were derived from the audited, published information, largely by combining fund activities and eliminating double counting among them (Winston 1988). And that worked, at first.

Indeed, a major question was whether the approach that generated global accounts from Williams College's fund accounts would work too for other colleges. We answered that question when Duncan Mann and I were able to create global accounts for Wellesley, Carleton, Swarthmore, and, for contrast, the 65-institution system of the State University of New York (Winston and Mann). The result was an accounting of the year's total income, total current spending, and total real financial saving or change in the institution's financial wealth.

But not all wealth. It has become increasingly clear that global accounts that merely reorganize existing information create a useful set of global *financial* records which monitor real financial wealth, but they share the shortcoming of fund accounts in being inadequate to the incorporation of *physical capital wealth*. Neither system could account for all of an institution's wealth. At Williams College, for example, they ignore more than half of the college's $645 million of net worth.

So the set of genuinely global accounts presented here, while still heavily dependent on a reorganization of published information, augments those data with a more realistic treatment of land, plant, and equipment, a treatment very much in the spirit of the current literature on capital planning in colleges (Dunn 1989; Probasco 1991). For some potential users, these full global accounts may go too far; not everyone is ready to monitor all of his or her institution's wealth. These users can retreat to the halfway house of global financial accounts, a system that is no worse than conventional accounting in its neglect of capital wealth and is a whole lot better in dealing with the other problems of fund accounting I have noted. So considerable improvement lies in using the global financial accounts, even if they are importantly incomplete. (Table 1 is repeated in the appendix as Table 1-A to show the same college in the abbreviated form of global *financial* accounts. But the rest of the text will deal with the fully global accounts that include all institutional wealth.)

In a significant and encouraging recent development, Harvard's new *Financial Report*, published in March of 1992, treats the physical capital stock much as described below, even though the increased realism raised Harvard's reported operating expenses by $77 million and gave the university a $42 million budget deficit (Harvard 1992). Harvard's decision not only reduces the risk to other schools of adopting these innovations in reporting economic information, but it indicates another way for an institution to move toward fully global accounts without embracing them all at once.

A caveat, before I describe the global accounts in detail. Their application is more immediately appropriate to private than to public institutions. The reason, of course, is the often-Byzantine arrangements of responsibility, ownership, and governance that have grown up between public colleges and state and local agencies, arrangements that can affect, *inter alia*, ownership of the school's capital stock, responsibility for tuition levels, and for salaries and fringe benefits, and even control over the use of any endowment wealth. So at public campuses the scope of responsibility and control may sometimes be different from that implied by these accounts. It remains, however, that global accounts, or something like them, are essential to public institutions if anyone is to know the real costs of public education and the effects of a state's policies on each institution's educational wealth.

How elements of global accounts work to form a coherent system of information will be clearer if they are embedded in a concrete example. Two years' data are presented in Table 1.[3] Consider the components in turn.

## College income

The income elements in Table 1 are fairly straightforward at a small school, but a few comments are useful nonetheless. The set of income sources is exhaustive: *all* income flowing into the college in the year is included, whether it comes from students,[4] donors, government, borrowers of the college's wealth, or purchasers of services from the college. Gift and Grant Income in Table 1 is separated according to the donor's wishes to recognize the fact that part of the gift income is

**Table 1**
**Global Accounts**

| | 1989–1990 $ | 1990–1991 $ |
|---|---|---|
| **1. COLLEGE INCOME** | | |
| Tuition and Fees | 29,262,691 | 32,543,540 |
| Gifts and Grants: | | |
| To Endowment | 7,066,669 | 8,744,806 |
| To Plant | 1,016,397 | 713,124 |
| All Other | 12,664,824 | 13,951,045 |
| Asset Income: | | |
| Interest and Dividends | 17,039,521 | 15,859,257 |
| Appreciation | 18,582,670 | 6,873,486 |
| Sales, Services and Other | 1,950,970 | 2,724,059 |
| Auxiliary Income | 11,599,559 | 11,862,813 |
| Total College Income | 99,183,301 | 93,272,130 |
| **2. CURRENT EXPENDITURES** | | |
| Operating Budget Expenditures | 62,425,303 | 66,924,329 |
| Other Current Expenditures | 6,304,914 | 5,634,728 |
| less Current Acct Maintenance | 703,276 | 642,167 |
| Total Current Expenditures | 68,026,941 | 71,916,890 |
| **3. ADDITIONS TO CAPITAL STOCK** | | |
| Investment in New Plant | 9,334,326 | 2,310,285 |
| less Deferred Maintenance | | |
| Real Depreciation | 7,500,000 | 8,097,195 |
| less Maintenance Spending: | | |
| In Current Account | 703,276 | 642,167 |
| In Plant Fund | 3,477,560 | 4,639,692 |
| Total Deferred Maintenance | 3,319,164 | 2,815,336 |
| Total Additions to Capital | 6,015,162 | (505,051) |
| **4. OPERATING COSTS** | | |
| Current Expenditures | 68,026,941 | 71,916,890 |
| Real Depreciation | 7,500,000 | 8,097,195 |
| Total Operating Costs | 75,526,941 | 80,014,085 |
| **5. WEALTH (EOY)** | | |
| Financial Wealth | | |
| Assets | 346,203,972 | 358,726,081 |
| less Liabilities | 50,596,648 | 49,355,661 |
| Net Financial Wealth | 295,607,324 | 309,370,420 |
| [Endowment Value] | [333,553,551] | [341,572,081] |
| Physical Capital Wealth: | | |
| Replacement Value | 323,887,799 | 341,438,861 |
| less Accumulated | | |
| Deferred Maintenance | 3,319,164 | 6,290,686 |
| Net Physical Wealth | 320,568,635 | 335,148,175 |
| Net Worth | 616,175,959 | 644,518,595 |

intended to expand the college's wealth and that that part is potentially different from gifts that donors intend should be used at the discretion of the college. Asset earnings include interest, dividends, and capital gains or losses (whether realized or not). Auxiliary income, in a small liberal arts college, consists largely of student charges for room and board. For a university, that line would be both larger and more complicated as would be "Sales, services and other," the catchall income line here.

## Current Expenditures

Current expenditures in the global accounts is both a more and a less inclusive category than "spending from the current fund" in fund accounting. It includes all current expenditures and it excludes maintenance spending. Current expenditures are included whether they appear within the operating budget, elsewhere in the current fund, the capital budget, the endowment fund, or somewhere else in the fund accounts. So in global accounting, there is no opportunity to reduce the apparent level or growth of current expenditures by shifting some of them from a closely monitored area like the operating budget to a less scrutinized part of the accounts, like off-budget current fund or endowment fund spending. Spending on maintenance of the plant and equipment is excluded because it is *not* a current expenditure; it is spending that buys a durable good, the restoration—"renovation and adaption"[5]—of the physical plant.[6]

## Additions to the Capital Stock

Predictably, the greatest departure from conventional reporting comes in the global accounts' treatment of the physical capital stock since that aspect of college management and college wealth is so effectively neglected in fund accounting. The purpose of global accounting of the capital stock is to report its real value and record the effects of the year's activities on that value. It serves, too, to inform a more accurate measure of the college's operating costs that recognizes both current spending and real depreciation of the college's physical wealth.

Additions to the capital stock are simply the year's gross investment in new plant less any value lost through deterioration of the capital stock—the year's "deferred maintenance." Investment in new plant is uncomplicated. It includes all additions, acquisitions of new land, plant, and equipment that will augment the capital stock. Deferred maintenance describes how much of the year's real depreciation of the capital stock was not repaired or renovated, how much the physical plant was allowed to deteriorate over the year.[7] Given depreciation, repairs and renovation reduce deferred maintenance. Deferred maintenance is not a money expenditure, *per se*, of course, but it is an expenditure of part of the capital stock—consequent on time and its use in production—and therefore a very real *cost* of the year's operations. Recognition of deferred maintenance is essential if the full effect of the year's activities on the value of the college's wealth are to be reported.

Real depreciation is an estimate of the potential amount of capital stock worn out or used up in the course of the year's operations, the amount it would have depreciated had there been no repairs, renovation, or adaption. The emphasis on "real" depreciation is intended to distinguish this estimate of *actual* decline in the value of a capital stock over the course of the year, due to time and its uses, from the more familiar but quite different matter of income tax liability in a for-profit firm. (For many, that's what "depreciation" has come to mean, both in accounting and the public mind.) In the global accounts it is pure economic depreciation.

Finally, maintenance spending, as noted above, is much the same as investment in new plant; it increases the value of durable capital through renovation and adaption. So it is treated the same in the global accounts. To the small amount of such spending found in the current account is added that portion of a conventional "investment in plant" entry that in fact pays for renovation and adaption.

In Table 1, real depreciation is estimated as 2.5% of the $324 million capital stock with which 1990–91 started, or $8.1 million.[8] But since that was offset in 1990–91 by an estimated $4.6 million of maintenance spending from the capital budget and another $64 million from the operating budget, deferred maintenance for the year is estimated, with rounding, at $2.8 million.[9] If current spending on maintenance had been $8.1 million for the year, deferred maintenance, of course, would have been zero.

Additions to the capital stock are the net result of all this: investment in new plant is augmented by maintenance spending and reduced by depreciation. Additions to the capital stock will be *positive* when new plant and maintenance, together, are larger than real depreciation, and *negative* when they are overwhelmed by the year's depreciation.

## Operating Costs

In the global accounts, the year's total real operating costs are reported directly. To total current expenditures is added the year's depreciation of physical plant. So both forms of current spending are recognized as operating costs: current expenditures of the usual sort (less maintenance spending) and current spending of the capital stock through depreciation. Together, these describe the costs of the year's operations.[10]

## Wealth: Assets and Liabilities

Assets and liabilities together describe the state of a college's wealth at the end of each fiscal year. They are the college's *stock* variables. Two aspects of the reporting of assets in global accounts should be noted. One is de-emphasis of the college's *endowment*. It shows up in Table 1 as a parenthetical notation sandwiched into the list of assets and liabilities that make up the college's wealth. The reason for this dismissive treatment is, simply, that the endowment has come erroneously to be seen as synonymous with "total financial wealth." While that was nearly true when colleges had very few non-endowment financial assets and, importantly, very little debt aside from some stray accounts payable, it is not true for many colleges now.

Again, Williams' numbers are instructive. In 1989, its endowment had a market value of some $307 million. But the college had another $22 million in non-endowment assets[11] for total financial assets of $329 million (Williams 1991). But those assets were encumbered by some $51 million in debt. So the global accounts report net financial wealth of $278 million—total financial assets less total liabilities—as the appropriate measure of the college's financial wealth. In 1990, the endowment was up to $334 million, but net financial wealth only to $296 million.

The other important differences in global accounts' wealth reporting are that physical capital assets—land, plant and equipment—are (a) accounted for in current replacement values rather than "book values" that the college originally paid for them, and (b) adjusted for accumulated deferred maintenance. At Williams, which is an old college, one major instructional building with seven large classrooms and 13,000 square feet has a book value of less than $50,000, and one faculty residence, not large but pleasant, is valued at only $850 (Williams 1991). Most other campuses would offer similar examples of the distortions inherent in using book values. So while the estimates of replacement values inevitably involve some guesswork, they are clearly a whole lot closer to the truth than are historical values. Accumulated deferred maintenance is treated as an offset against the replacement value of the physical assets, leaving net physical wealth as the measure of value of the capital stock. Table 1 assumes that there was no deferred maintenance before 1989–90, so there is little immediate difference between capital assets and net physical wealth. But Table 4 shows that over a long period, deferred maintenance will significantly reduce the college's net physical wealth. An example is Yale's current pressing problem (*New York Times*, February 3, 1992), with more than $1 billion of deferred maintenance.

Because financial and physical assets and liabilities are measured in the same current value terms, they can be added together to report the college's total wealth, its total net worth. We are adding apples and apples. For many purposes, it is essential to distinguish between these two forms of wealth (and saving); but for others it is useful to recognize total wealth, regardless of its form. In Table 1, reporting a total 1991 wealth of $645 million tells a very different and more complete story than either reporting an endowment of $342 million or financial wealth of $309 million.

## Saving and Wealth: Flow-stock Relationships

The usual tautological accounting relationship between economic flows and stocks apply to global accounts. Saving is the difference between income and spending over the period. Any change in wealth between two dates equals and must be due to saving over that period; net worth (wealth) at the beginning of a period plus income minus spending has to equal net worth at the end of the period. Of course, real depreciation must be added to current expenditures to account fully for the year's total spending. This done, the stock-flow identity holds for total saving and wealth (net worth) as well as for financial and physical saving and wealth, separately. It is just as relevant to global accounts as it is to one's checking account.[12]

## Operating and Capital Budgets

Operating and capital budgets are embedded in the global accounts, serving their managerial and planning functions, but firmly in the context of the college's overall activities. So total operating expenditures—the bottom line in an operating budget like that of Table 2—appears in the global accounts as a component of current spending (the largest). The effect, then, of operating budget performance on the college's wealth is incorporated immediately and directly. Though it is not made explicit here, the same is true for a capital budget which is mapped directly into the global accounts in the form of either new investment or as current spending on renovation and adaption.

Note that while operating *expenditures* are reported in a line in the global accounts, operating *revenues* do not appear. The reason is that a college's decision on how much of its total income to allocate to an operating budget as "revenue" is an internal and essentially arbitrary one. That decision may be influenced by some accumulated tradition: tuition and fees, for instance, may all go to the operating budget while only some gifts and a formulaic portion of asset income do. But a college can, by assignment and transfer of its income to and from the budget, make a budget deficit or surplus virtually anything it wants it to be, including, as Swarthmore and others have shown, always exactly zero.[13] Clarity is served, then, by focusing the global accounts on *spending* in the operating budget—or more broadly, on all current spending—as it encompasses an important set of activities in the college's educational enterprise. Attention to the arbitrary assignment of operating budget revenues—the result of shifting money between pockets—and the consequent budget "deficits" or "surpluses" can be replaced by attention to real current spending and to actual performance relative to an approved spending plan.[14]

# Using Global Accounts

The global accounts structure was first used to organize an historical review of Williams' economic behavior in order to provide a descriptive context for evaluating present and future performance (Winston 1988). It was done at the height of public criticism of cost growth in higher education when it was deemed wise to know how present performance compared with the past. We were able to generate long data series[15] on income levels and changes in its composition; on spending, its

**Table 2**
**Global Accounts: Current Expenditure Component**

|  | 1989–90<br>$ | 1990–91<br>$ |
|---|---|---|
| **OPERATING BUDGET** | | |
| Salary Pools: | | |
| Faculty | 10,194,014 | 11,415,331 |
| Administrative/Prof | 6,029,465 | 6,315,789 |
| Weekly | 11,568,273 | 12,101,430 |
| Total Salary Pools | 27,791,752 | 29,832,550 |
| Fringe Benefits | 7,258,226 | 7,816,225 |
| Financial Aid | 6,517,892 | 7,719,186 |
| Other Restricted Spending | 2,720,321 | 3,505,429 |
| Manager's Budgets | 18,137,112 | 18,050,939 |
| Total Operating Budget Expenses | 62,425,303 | 66,924,329 |
| Other Current Expenditures | 6,304,914 | 5,634,728 |
| less Maint. Spending | | |
| in Current Account | 703,276 | 642,167 |
| Total Current Expenditures | 68,026,941 | 71,916,890 |

composition and real rates of growth; and on real saving and its distribution between financial and physical capital wealth. The result provided a foundation for economic policies.

But the broader significance of global accounts appears to lie in their ability to describe, monitor, and evaluate a college's current economic performance and in the structure they give to economic planning. First, let's look to how they can help monitor and evaluate economic performance.

The global accounts don't force any specific criteria of performance evaluation on a college except implicitly in describing the totality of the school's economic activity. But they do make it especially easy to monitor the effects on its real wealth of the college's behavior and the economic circumstances it operates in: the difference between income and current spending is saving (or dissaving) and that, dollar for dollar, increases (or decreases) wealth. And global accounts make it easy to break that down to monitor, separately, the effects of college behavior on financial wealth and on physical capital wealth. There are many good reasons why a governing board might consider a dollar saved in a liquid financial asset to be very different from a dollar saved in constructing or renovating a building. Both are saving, but their different forms carry quite different implications for future flexibility, costs, returns, and performance. Even at the level of total saving, a board may think it wise to maintain real wealth or to increase it or to spend some of it down.[16] Or it may prefer only to monitor real wealth or income or spending or their components, rather than to define explicit policies in those respects. These are all decisions on which the structure of the global accounts is agnostic.

Using the data from Table 1, Table 3 illustrates one sort of evaluative summary that global accounts can produce to describe, in the broadest terms, a college's performance for a year.[17] Other summary data could be generated, but these I have listed are especially useful in informing broad questions of strategy and governance.

The first line of Table 3—saving, or the gain or loss of real wealth—is, in a sense, "the bottom line" of the global accounts. It describes the change in total real wealth that results from the college's activities for the year, recognizing all its sources of income, all its expenditures on current account and new capital and maintenance, all the depreciation of its physical capital stock, and the

**Table 3**
**Global Accounts: Summary**

| | 1989–90 $ | 1990–91 $ |
|---|---|---|
| **1. SAVING—GAIN (LOSS) OF** | | |
| **TOTAL REAL WEALTH:** | 10,171,785 | (651,974) |
| Gain (Loss) of Real Financial Wealth | 4,156,623 | (146,923) |
| Gain (Loss) of Real Physical Wealth | 6,015,162 | (505,051) |
| Gifts to Increase Real Wealth | 8,083,066 | 9,457,930 |
| Savings to Increase Real Wealth | 2,088,719 | (10,109,904) |
| **2. INCOME** | 99,183,301 | 93,272,130 |
| Real Growth Rate | –3.26% | –10.19% |
| **3. SPENDING** | | |
| Operating Costs | 75,526,941 | 80,014,085 |
| Deferred Maintenance | 3,319,164 | 2,815,336 |
| Investment in New Plant | 9,334,326 | 2,310,285 |
| Real Growth Rates | | |
| Operating Costs | 4.51% | 1.18% |
| Deferred Maintenance | 36.27% | –18.99% |
| Investment in New Plant | 4.35% | –76.36% |
| **4. SAVING: GAIN (LOSS) OF** | | |
| **TOTAL REAL WEALTH USING** | | |
| **SMOOTHED ASSET INCOME** | 7,276,151 | 8,600,747 |

contrary effects of inflation in eroding the real value of its financial wealth while increasing the nominal value of its physical wealth. In this fundamental measure, the fortunes of the college illustrated in Table 3 declined by some $11 million between 1989–90 and 1990–91, from real saving of $10.2 million to real dissaving of $.7 million.

The next four lines in Table 3 address two of the many questions that might be asked about the year's total real saving. The first two lines describe the distribution of total real savings between financial and physical wealth. Physical wealth fared better than did financial wealth in 1989–90 but had a slightly larger decline in 1990–91. The next two lines ask what would have happened to saving without the gifts that were targeted to increase wealth. Some of the increase in wealth on line 1 was the result of the explicit intentions of donors who gave the college money for the purpose of increasing its wealth, so that component might well be separated out from any change in wealth, or saving, that was due, instead to the college's decisions and external circumstances during the year. Without the gifts to wealth (to endowment and plant) of $8 and $9 million in the two years, the college would have saved in other ways some $2.1 million in the good year and lost a bit more than $10 million in the bad one. Again, governing boards would differ in their evaluation of these facts. Had the school's performance led to neither saving nor dissaving in those years, that might be considered good work by the board interested in real wealth maintenance, while it would be considered poor performance by a board that wanted, say, to catch up to Amherst or Swarthmore in wealth per student. So again, the global accounts are agnostic on policy aims.

College income is reported next in Table 3 in current dollars while its growth is reported in real terms, adjusted for inflation. Together they monitor the flow of total resources into the school over the year.

Direct monitoring of costs and spending levels and their real growth, as presented in the third section of Table 3, is a response to the criticisms of higher education in the 1980s and a conviction that real spending growth should be watched closely, both in detailed categories and broadly. Operating costs include both current expenditures and real depreciation as reported in Table 1. The year's deferred maintenance is reported as a separate line because of its usual neglect and its potential for causing serious long-term mischief. A board might adopt the policy that deferred maintenance should always be zero (giving top priority to protection of the physical plant, whatever the costs in other objectives). Or it might feel that deferred maintenance is simply one important aspect of performance that needs to be monitored attentively; that is, a board might conclude that deferring maintenance, like any other reduction in saving, can provide money to do other, more important, things. Again, global accounts inform policy by defining required maintenance spending and showing the cost of not doing it. Investment in new plant describes only spending for new physical capital.

The last section in Table 3 addresses an evaluation problem for well-endowed schools that report their financial assets at market values and thereby incur potentially large variations in reported income through capital gains and losses caused by market fluctuations. (Year-to-year comparisons of global performance will be hard to interpret if major changes in asset market value have dominated the numbers.) So in this last section of the table, the effect of the year's activities on the college's wealth are re-examined using a five-year moving average of asset income instead of actual asset income for each year. That smoothes out the volatile element while still reflecting its underlying changes in a subdued form.

These data for 1989–90 and 1990–91 illustrate the effect nicely. Between the two years, the college's capital gains income fell by almost $12 million, so much of the striking difference in the effects of performance on real wealth between the two years was due to that sharp (and uncontrollable) decline in income and not, as it might first appear, to the way the college was run in the latter year. Indeed, the effect of operations on real wealth was, with smoothed income, better in the second year. Without that abrupt decline in asset income, reductions in deferred maintenance and the growth of current spending would have increased saving by $1.3 million in 1990–91.

Now lets look at global accounting's ability to assist with economic planning.

Global accounts provide the framework for an economic planning model that has the scope and ability to integrate detailed management sub-plans while showing the global economic implications of the school's intended behavior and anticipated circumstances. Tables 4 to 6 illustrate such a model. Table 4 is a basic global economic plan; Table 5 is a sub-account giving more detail on planned current spending, "the operating budget;" and Table 6 gives the sort of evaluative summary data just described, here extended to include anticipated future performance over the period of the plan. All values are in current dollars with an assumed 5 percent inflation rate, and past accumulation of deferred maintenance is arbitrarily set at zero at the beginning of 1989–90. All planned and projected values are rounded.

Two years of historical performance data—1989–90 and 1990–91—are the starting point for projections of both anticipated circumstances (inflation, asset market conditions, etc.) and planned college behavior (staffing, salaries, tuition, resource allocation, etc.). The heart of a planning process is, of course, the thoughtful specification of these "planning parameters"—projections of future intentions, plans and expectations. But in terms of the plan structure that is at issue here, after the college has decided on those planning parameters—how it wants and expects the components of the accounts to change in the future—a global economic plan will show the effects of that behavior on the college's real wealth over the period of the plan.

It is, then, a "consistency-and-implications" model. The pieces have to fit together over any year and they have to fit together from one period to the next, satisfying the truism that wealth at the beginning of the period plus income less spending has to equal wealth at the end of the period. Each period's performance is anchored in the past year's, and the projections are anchored in the most recent history.

## Table 4
## Global Economic Plan
### (Current Dollars – Inflation Rate 5%)

| | 1989–90 $ | 1990–91 $ | Plan Parameters $ | Planned 1991–92 $ | Planned 1993–94 $ | Planned 1992–93 $ | ... | Projected 2001–02 $ |
|---|---|---|---|---|---|---|---|---|
| **1. COLLEGE INCOME** | | | | | | | | |
| Tuition and Fees | 29,262,691 | 32,543,540 | 6.0% | 34,500,000 | 36,600,000 | 38,800,000 | ... | 61,800,000 |
| Gifts and Grants: | | | | | | | | |
| To Endowment | 7,066,669 | 8,744,806 | $9 m | 9,000,000 | 9,000,000 | 9,000,000 | ... | 9,000,000 |
| To Plant | 1,016,397 | 713,124 | $1 m | 1,000,000 | 1,000,000 | 1,000,000 | ... | 1,000,000 |
| All Other | 12,664,824 | 13,951,045 | $14 m | 14,000,000 | 14,000,000 | 14,000,000 | ... | 14,000,000 |
| Asset Income: | | | | | | | | |
| Interest & Dividends | 17,039,521 | 15,859,257 | 6.0% | 16,800,000 | 17,800,000 | 18,900,000 | ... | 30,100,000 |
| Appreciation | 18,582,670 | 6,873,486 | 6.0% | 7,300,000 | 7,700,000 | 8,200,000 | ... | 13,000,000 |
| Sales, Services and Other | 1,950,970 | 2,724,059 | 6.0% | 2,900,000 | 3,100,000 | 3,200,000 | ... | 5,200,000 |
| Auxiliary Income | 11,599,559 | 11,862,813 | 6.0% | 12,600,000 | 13,300,000 | 14,100,000 | ... | 22,500,000 |
| Total College Income | 99,183,301 | 93,272,130 | | 98,100,000 | 102,500,000 | 107,200,000 | ... | 156,600,000 |
| **2. CURRENT EXPENDITURES** | | | | | | | | |
| Operating Budget Expenditures | 62,425,303 | 66,924,329 | On Table 5 | 70,900,000 | 75,200,000 | 79,700,000 | ... | 127,000,000 |
| Other Current Expenditures | 6,304,914 | 5,634,728 | On Table 5 | 6,000,000 | 6,300,000 | 6,700,000 | ... | 10,700,000 |
| less Current Acct Maintenance | 703,276 | 642,167 | $650,000 | 650,000 | 650,000 | 650,000 | ... | 650,000 |
| Total Current Expenditures | 68,026,941 | 71,916,890 | | 76,300,000 | 80,900,000 | 85,800,000 | ... | 137,100,000 |
| **3. ADDITIONS TO CAPITAL STOCK** | | | | | | | | |
| Investment in New Plant | 9,334,326 | 2,310,285 | $7m constant | 2,100,000 | 2,100,000 | 2,200,000 | ... | 2,600,000 |
| less Deferred Maintenance | | | | | | | | |
| Real Depreciation | 7,500,000 | 8,097,195 | 2.5% K-stock | 8,500,000 | 9,000,000 | 9,500,000 | ... | 14,600,000 |
| less Maintenance Spending | | | | | | | | |
| In Current Account | 703,276 | 642,167 | $650,000 | 650,000 | 650,000 | 650,000 | ... | 650,000 |
| In Plant Fund | 3,477,560 | 4,649,692 | 6.0% | 4,900,000 | 5,200,000 | 5,500,000 | ... | 8,800,000 |
| Total Deferred Maintenance | 3,319,164 | 2,815,336 | | 3,000,000 | 3,200,000 | 3,300,000 | ... | 5,200,000 |
| Total Additions to Capital | 6,015,162 | (505,051) | | (900,000) | (1,000,000) | (1,200,000) | ... | (2,600,000) |
| **4. OPERATING COSTS** | | | | | | | | |
| Current Expenditures | 68,026,941 | 71,916,890 | As Above | 76,300,000 | 80,900,000 | 85,800,000 | ... | 137,100,000 |
| Real Depreciation | 7,500,000 | 8,097,195 | As Above | 8,500,000 | 9,000,000 | 9,500,000 | ... | 14,600,000 |
| Total Operating Costs | 75,526,941 | 80,014,085 | | 84,800,000 | 89,900,000 | 95,300,000 | ... | 151,700,000 |
| **5. WEALTH (EOY)** | | | | | | | | |
| Financial Wealth | | | | | | | | |
| Assets | 346,203,972 | 358,726,081 | | 373,500,000 | 387,100,000 | 400,200,000 | ... | 481,100,000 |
| less Liabilities | 50,596,648 | 49,355,661 | $50 m | 50,000,000 | 50,000,000 | 50,000,000 | ... | 50,000,000 |
| Net Financial Wealth | 295,607,324 | 309,370,420 | | 323,500,000 | 337,100,000 | 350,200,000 | ... | 431,100,000 |
| [Endowment Value] | [333,553,551] | [341,572,081] | $350 m | [350,000,000] | [350,000,000] | [350,000,000] | ... | [350,000,000] |
| Physical Capital Wealth | | | | | | | | |
| Replacement Value | 323,887,799 | 341,438,861 | | 360,600,000 | 380,800,000 | 402,000,000 | ... | 617,000,000 |
| less Accumulated | | | | | | | | |
| Deferred Maintenance | 3,319,164 | 6,290,686 | | 9,600,000 | 13,200,000 | 17,200,000 | ... | 66,200,000 |
| Net Physical Wealth | 320,568,635 | 335,148,175 | | 351,000,000 | 367,600,000 | 384,800,000 | ... | 550,800,000 |
| Net Worth | 616,175,959 | 644,518,595 | | 674,500,000 | 704,700,000 | 735,000,000 | ... | 981,900,000 |

The result is neither an optimization model nor an equilibrium model. It can be made into a "long-run financial equilibrium model" if a constant rate of growth of wealth is imposed; but that remains an option and not a characteristic. It is hoped that its more modest logical structure may well be of greater practical value than the more abstract alternatives in actual planning, administration, and governance. The global plan takes the concrete form of a Lotus spreadsheet that is easy to use to ask, repeatedly, the question, "What will be the economic implications of the following behavior, now and in the future?"

The data in Tables 4 through 6 are based on Tables 1 through 3. But it is important that they carry no implication about future plans or projections for any actual school. They are illustrative only of the *structure* of the economic plan. To make very clear, planning parameter values in these tables have been entered as caricatures—most either as the constant rate of growth of the 6 percent (nominal) or as a constant nominal quantity[18]—with the hope that a high level of artificiality will make it starkly clear that these tables deal only with a model structure and that no privileged information is conveyed.

A cost of artificiality, though, is that the numbers in these tables are less revealing of an actual planning exercise than they would be with more realistic parameter values. Nonetheless, they show that if a college, starting with the historical performance described in the first two columns, were to plan its spending and anticipate income as described by these rates and levels, it would wind up as described in the last four columns. It would see increasing yearly dissaving, loss of more real financial wealth than physical wealth, real income growth hovering around zero with real operating costs that are increasing modestly, declining real new investment and declining but still positive real deferred maintenance.

If that pattern of behavior (and circumstances) continued until the academic year 2001–2, the college would find itself dissaving at an annual rate of $16 million, despite $10 million a year in gifts intended to increase wealth. Most of the dissaving would take the form of drawing down financial assets, but there would still be an accumulated deferred maintenance of some $66 million or a bit less than 10 percent of its equal capital stock (all in 2002 dollars). A governing board, looking at these results, would have to conclude that the projected behavior under the projected circumstances isn't sustainable. Elimination of asset income volatility makes a significant difference in the evaluation of short-run performance. But predictably, it has a declining effect on the evaluation of smoothly projected future performance. So the plan reveals that something more fundamental than asset income volatility is producing unsustainable results.

Given the artificiality of these numbers, the results of these plan projections probably don't deserve much more discussion. They should serve, however, to give a sense of the kind of strategic information that is generated by the global plan. It is, most generally, a description of the future resource implications of the behavior and circumstances envisioned by the college.

### Table 5
### Global Economic Plan: Current Expenditure Component

| | 1989–90 $ | 1990–91 $ | Plan Parameters $ | 1991–92 $ | 1992–93 $ | 1993–94 $ | ... | 2001–02 |
|---|---|---|---|---|---|---|---|---|
| OPERATING BUDGET | | | | | | | | |
| Salary Pools: | | | | | | | | |
| Faculty | 10,194,014 | 11,415,331 | 6.0% | 12,100,000 | 12,800,000 | 13,600,000 | ... | 21,700,000 |
| Administrative/Prof | 6,029,465 | 6,315,789 | 6.0% | 6,700,000 | 7,100,000 | 7,500,000 | ... | 12,000,000 |
| Weekly | 11,568,273 | 12,101,430 | 6.0% | 12,800,000 | 13,600,000 | 14,400,000 | ... | 23,000,000 |
| Total Salary Pools | 27,791,752 | 29,832,550 | | 31,600,000 | 33,500,000 | 35,500,000 | ... | 56,600,000 |
| Fringe Benefits | 7,258,226 | 7,816,225 | 6.0% | 8,300,000 | 8,800,000 | 9,300,000 | ... | 14,800,000 |
| Financial Aid | 6,517,892 | 7,719,186 | 6.0% | 8,200,000 | 8,700,000 | 9,200,000 | ... | 14,700,000 |
| Other Restricted Spending | 2,720,321 | 3,505,429 | 6.0% | 3,700,000 | 3,900,000 | 4,200,000 | ... | 6,700,000 |
| Manager's Budgets | 18,137,112 | 18,050,939 | 6.0% | 19,100,000 | 120,300,000 | 21,500,000 | ... | 34,300,000 |
| Total Operating Budget Exp. | 62,425,303 | 66,924,329 | | 70,900,000 | 75,200,000 | 79,700,000 | ... | 127,000,000 |
| Other Current Expenditures less Maintenance Spending | 6,304,914 | 5,634,728 | 6.0% | 6,000,000 | 6,300,000 | 6,700,000 | ... | 10,700,000 |
| in Current Account | 703,276 | 642,167 | $650,000 | 650,000 | 650,000 | 650,000 | ... | 650,000 |
| Total Current Expenditures | 68,026,941 | 71,916,890 | | 76,300,000 | 80,900,000 | 85,800,000 | ... | 137,100,000 |

# Premise and Promises

The premise of the global accounts has been that a college's administration or governing board wants to have meaningful and accessible economic information about the college's performance. But that may be naive. The fact that the operating budget can be a political document is often acknowledged and usually described as regrettable, but it is also of considerable value in avoiding questions and discussions that might be time-consuming, tedious, and challenging to administrative decisions.

That fund accounts can selectively hide or reveal transactions is often convenient. So is the emphasis on endowment wealth, as though there were no other kinds of financial assets and no offsetting debt. And so on. But the difficulty with the manipulation of economic information, or selective optimism in its reporting, is the old one that plagues any departure from scrupulous efforts to report the economic facts: the first victim of distorted economic information is often the author of those distortions.

It is hard to manage a place if you don't know what's going on. This is a lesson learned and relearned in the contexts ranging from the Soviet planned economy to the current gyrations of state and city budgets in New York and California. Unfortunately, as the government parallel suggests, governors and mayors change and so do college administrations, increasing the temptation those transients face to keep their economic numbers looking good and to let the sober facts show up later, "but not on my watch."

More positively, and more importantly, global accounts appear to represent a marked improvement over fund accounting both in informing the long-run policy issues that confront colleges and universities, and in monitoring their economic performance. The information these

### Table 6
### Global Economic Plan: Summary
(Current Dollars – Inflation Rate 5%)

| | 1989–90 $ | 1990–91 $ | Plan Parameters $ | 1991–92 $ | 1993–94 $ | 1992–93 | ... | 2001–02 |
|---|---|---|---|---|---|---|---|---|
| **1. SAVING – GAIN (LOSS)** | | | | | | | | |
| OF TOTAL REAL WEALTH: | 10,171,785 | (651,974) | | (2,200,000) | (3,600,000) | (4,900,000) | ... | (16,300,000) |
| Gain (Loss) of Real *Financial* Wealth | 4,156,623 | (146,923) | | (1,300,000) | (2,600,000) | (3,800,000) | ... | (13,700,000) |
| Gain (Loss) of Real *Physical* Wealth | 6,015,162 | (505,051) | | (900,000) | (1,000,000) | (1,200,000) | ... | (2,600,000) |
| Gifts to Increase Real Wealth | 8,083,066 | 9,457,930 | *Details* | 10,000,000 | 10,000,000 | 10,000,000 | ... | 10,000,000 |
| Savings to Increase Real Wealth | 2,088,719 | (10,109,904) | | (12,200,000) | (13,600,000) | (14,900,000) | ... | (26,300,000) |
| **2. INCOME** | 99,183,301 | 93,272,130 | *on* | 98,100,000 | 102,500,000 | 107,200,000 | ... | 156,600,000 |
| Real Growth Rate | –3.26% | –10.19% | | 0.12% | –0.45% | –0.39% | ... | 0.03% |
| **3. SPENDING:** | | | *Tables* | | | | | |
| Operating Costs | 75,526,941 | 80,014,085 | | 84,800,000 | 89,900,000 | 95,300,000 | ... | 151,700,000 |
| Deferred Maintenance | 3,319,164 | 2,815,336 | | 3,000,000 | 3,200,000 | 3,300,000 | ... | 5,200,000 |
| Investment in New Plant | 9,334,326 | 2,310,285 | 4 | 2,100,000 | 2,100,000 | 2,200,000 | ... | 2,600,000 |
| Real Growth Rates: | | | | | | | | |
| Operating Costs | 4.51% | 1.18% | *and* | 0.93% | 0.96% | 0.95% | ... | 0.93% |
| Deferred Maintenance | 36.27% | –18.99% | | 0.40% | 1.13% | 1.02% | ... | 0.26% |
| Investment in New Plant | 4.35% | –76.36% | | –14.18% | –2.25% | –2.32% | ... | –3.10% |
| **4. SAVINGS: GAIN (LOSS)** | | | 5 | | | | | |
| OF TOTAL REAL WEALTH | 7,276,151 | 8,600,747 | | 2,600,000 | 4,000,000 | (2,000,000) | ... | (17,100,000) |
| Using Smoothed Asset Income | | | | | | | | |
| **5. ACCUMULATED DEFERRED** | | | | | | | | |
| MAINTENANCE | 3,319,164 | 6,290,686 | | 9,600,000 | 13,200,000 | 17,200,000 | ... | 66,200,000 |

global accounts present has proven to be the sort that induces and encourages the discussion of strategic fundamentals, of issues that are basic to the governance of the institution, issues that take the form "If we keep on doing what we're doing, or what we're planning to do next year, what will happen to our economic wealth?" Such elemental questions are not readily induced or addressed by the kind of economic information now available with fund accounts to colleges and universities.

Global accounts describe the effect of a year's activities, actual or planned, on all of the college's real wealth, on the distribution of that wealth between financial and physical assets, on deferred maintenance, on levels and real growth of income from its various sources, and of spending on it various objectives. This it does, in an environment of inflation with its opposing effects on the values of financial and physical wealth. Global accounts describe the whole of an institution. Their data are designed to avoid omissions and partial truths, to be clear and accessible, and to direct attention to the most basic economic implications of a college's behavior.

# Endnotes

1. Actually, 20 years ago Cornell professors Harold Bierman, Jr. and Thomas Hofstedt showed how misleading conventional budget deficits can be, using an analysis similar in some ways to this article (1973). Their effort got them an Andy Rooney segment on CBS, a front-page *Wall Street Journal* article; and strenuous objections from campus controllers and presidents, but no changes.

2. The structure of global accounts was developed in 1986–88, given a shot of practicality during my stint as Williams' provost in 1988–90, and refined in 1991. I enjoyed support from the Andrew W. Mellon Foundation through its assistance for the Williams Project on the Economics of Higher Education. William Bowen, Shawn Buckler, Keith Finan, George Goethals, David Healy, Robinson Hollister, George Keller, Duncan Mann, Charles M. Mott, Saeed Mughal, Will Reed, Joseph Rice, Morton Schapiro, David Schultz, and Winthrop Wassener gave me valuable insights and helped improve the analysis. I am especially indebted to Harold Bierman, Roger Bolton, David Booth, Anne MacEachern, and Michael McPherson.

3. These are similar to historical data from Williams' published sources, so no legal issues are raised by their use here. In the description of an economic plan below, I present transparently unrealistic and uninformative planning parameters to illustrate only the structure of the plan and nothing of Williams' expectations or intentions.

4. Tuition and fee income in these accounts is gross. An alternative would leave institutional student aid out of both income and expenditures and report as income only net tuition and fees.

5. "Adaption" refers to action to offset depreciation due to obsolescence, in the trilogy described long ago by Terborg. The other sources are depreciation due to use and depreciation due to the elements; these would be addressed by "renovation" spending as used here.

6. Under present practice some of the renovation and adaption is embedded in current spending but the largest part of renovation and adaption spending typically appears as capital spending (labeled "investment in plant"). So usually only a relatively small adjustment to reported current spending is needed to purge total current expenditures of what is more accurately capital spending. At Williams, the maintenance part of current expenditures was only $703,000 in 1989–1990 and $642,000 in 1990–91.

7. "Deferred maintenance" is often used to describe the accumulated result of past failures to spend enough on maintenance to offset real depreciation. It reduces the value of a stock variable. Here we used the phrase, too, to describe a flow—the extent to which this year's maintenance spending failed to offset this year's depreciation. As usual, this year's flow is an increment to the previously accumulated stock. Note that there is nothing necessarily pejorative about "deferred maintenance." Often it will be advisable to let physical capital depreciate.

8. The 2.5% is a conservative estimate. Economists (Schultz 1960; O'Neill 1971) have put it at 2% of the replacement value of plant and equipment per year. But estimates more carefully done by university capital planners get 1.5–2.5% for renovation and another .5–1.5% for adaption (Dunn 1989). So the 2.5% used in the text and tables appears to be a conservative estimate of the total depreciation and therefore of the spending needed to eliminate all deferred maintenance.

9. An important departure from the facilities planning literature lies in the fact that the global accounts identify the year's deferred maintenance without implying that it must therefore be prevented. Recognition of the cost of real depreciation is not the same thing as funding it. (See Dunn 1989, or Probasco 1991).

10. An issue lurks under the surface here. It is the classic neglect of the opportunity cost of capital as a real cost of production in colleges and universities (and nonprofits in general). So it is inaccurate to call "total current costs" total when they leave out, in the case of Williams, roughly $30 million a year of real costs of production, half again as much as is typically reported (Winston 1991). Two facts might recommend that we continue to leave them out, however: (a) the global accounts are concerned with the total flows of income and spending by the institution from and to outside agents, so it may be permissible to neglect a real cost of production that is paid, by virtue of the college's ownership of its capital stock, back to itself as imputed income, even though the resulting accounts seriously distort the costs of production; and (b) strategically, it may be unwise to try to persuade people of the good sense of both the global accounts and an accounting of capital costs at the same time, though a courageous effort would take on both at once.

11. Though they may differ from endowment assets in other ways, the defining characteristic of these financial assets is that they are "owned" within the college, by a fund other than the endowment fund.

12. There is one awkwardness caused by the use of current market or replacement values for physical capital wealth in an inflationary environment. It lies in the need for an inflation adjustment to the value of the physical capital stock from year to year that doesn't appear here (as would be strictly appropriate) as nominal income. Strict adherence to the tautology would have to report the gain in physical asset value due to inflation as income (a physical capital gain) and then assign all of that income saving, thereby justifying the increase in the nominal value of the capital stock. But since that portion of "income" is always "saved" and serves only to keep the replacement value if the capital stock in current dollars, the better choice seems to be to introduce an apparent violation of the stock-flow tautology rather than insert a large piece of funny money income explicitly into the body of the accounts. So the replacement value of physical capital reflects inflation within each year as well as showing the effect of net investment. As presented in Table 1, then, the tautology applies directly to financial saving and wealth but not to physical capital or total saving and wealth, unless inflation-induced "physical capital gains income" is included. (For the reader who'd like to confirm this relationship: the replacement value of the capital stock was $300,000,000 in 1989 while the inflation rate was (rounded) 4.85% over 1989–90 and 4.71% over 1990–91, so the inflation adjustments in replacement value are $14,553,473 and $15,240,777 in 1989–90 and 1990–91, respectively. With these, net physical wealth and net worth at the beginning of each period, plus saving and inflation adjustment will equal net physical wealth and net worth at the end of the period.)

13. In addition to Bierman and Hofstedt's brief fame for showing that budgets are often highly misleading— when MIT reported a $5 million deficit, they actually saved $100 million; Princeton's reported $1.5 million deficit went with $151 million in saving; and Harvard's $1.4 million deficit coincided with $314 in saving, *inter alia*—a number of others have tried to sound the same warning. William Nordhaus, economist and provost at Yale from 1986 to 1988, for instance, recently cautioned against relying on operating budget deficits and surpluses because "actions are generally taken to produce a balanced budget" (Nordhaus 1989, p. 10).

14. Operating revenues are structurally a lot like a child's allowance, the part of the family income the parents assign for her to spend. Whether or not she can get by on, or even save from, her allowance is not an uninteresting question or one always viewed with dispassion. But it would be a mistake of some significance if the parents (or their creditors) were to represent the child's deficit or surplus on her allowance as a measure of the family's economic fortunes for the week. So in the context of higher education, a number of Princeton faculty members were unimpressed with the university's recent and much publicized operating budget deficits, convinced that there had to be more going on there than met the eye (Lyall 1989). Global accounts make it clear that there was.

15. Initially for the 30 years since Williams was a small, all-male college.

16. The four alternative objectives that Dunn described for endowment wealth are relevant in this broader context of total wealth: (1) protect its nominal value; (2) protect its purchasing power, its real value; (3) have wealth grow as fast as operating expenses; or (4) increase wealth per student as fast as that of competing or peer institutions (Dunn 1991, pp. 34–5).

17. The details of getting from Table 1 to Table 3 are included in an appendix table.

18. In practice, three kinds of parameter values might be used to describe plans and projections: (a) rates of growth (constant or changing from one year to the next), (b) levels (constant on real of nominal terms or changing over time), and (c) functionally dependent parameters reflecting things like the way institutional need-based financial aid expenses depend on tuition decisions.

# References

Bierman, Jr., H. and T. Hofstedt. 1973. University Accounting (Alternative Measures of Ivy League Deficits). *Non-Profit Report* (May): 14–23.

Chabotar, 1989. Financial Ratio Analysis Comes to Nonprofits. *Journal of Higher Education*, 60 (no. 2): 188–208.

Dunn, Jr., J. 1989. *Financial Planning Guidelines for Facilities Renewal and Adaption.* The Society for College and University Planning.

Dunn, Jr., J. 1991. How Colleges Should Handle Their Endowment. *Planning For Higher Education*, 19 (no. 3):32–37.

Garner, C. 1991. The Role of Funds. In *Accounting and Budgeting in Public and Nonprofit Organizations.* Jossey-Bass.

Harried A., L. Imdieke and R. Smith. 1985. *Advanced Accounting.* 3rd ed. John Wiley and Sons.

Harvard University. 1992. *Financial Report to the Board of Overseers of Harvard College.* Harvard University.

Lyall, S. 1989. Strife Over Style and Substance Tests Princeton's Leaders. *New York Times*, 4 December (B1).

Nordhaus, W. 1989. *Evaluating the Risk for Specific Institutions.* Yale University.

O'Neill, J. 1971. *Resource Use in Higher Education: Trends in Outputs and Inputs, 1930 to 1967.* The Carnegie Commission on Higher Education.

Probasco, J. 1991. Crumbling Campuses: What Are the Real Costs? *Business Officer*, 25 (no. 5): 48–51.

Schultz, T. 1960. Capital Formation by Education. *Journal of Political Economy* 68:6.

Swarthmore College. 1987. The Treasurer's Report. In *The President's Report, 1986–87.* Swarthmore College.

Williams College. 1991. *The Treasurer's Report, 1990–91.* Williams College.

Winston, G. and D. Mann. *Global Accounts: Reorganizing Economic Information for Colleges and Universities.* Forthcoming.

Winston, G. 1988. *Total College Income: An Economic Overview of Williams College, 1956–57 to 1986–87.* Williams College.

Winston, G. 1991. Why Are Capital Costs Ignored By Colleges and Universities and What Are The Prospects For Change? *Williams Project on the Economics of Higher Education, Discussion Paper No. 14.* Williams College.

## Appendix A
## Table 1-A
## Global Financial Accounts

| | 1989–90 $ | 1990–91 $ |
|---|---|---|
| **1. COLLEGE INCOME:** | | |
| Tuition and Fees | 29,262,691 | 32,543,540 |
| Gifts and Grants: | | |
| To Endowment | 7,066,669 | 8,744,806 |
| To Plant | 1,016,397 | 713,124 |
| All Other | 12,664,824 | 13,951,045 |
| Asset Income: | | |
| Interest & Dividends | 17,039,521 | 15,859,257 |
| Appreciation | 18,582,670 | 6,873,486 |
| Sales, Services and Other | 1,950,970 | 2,724,059 |
| Auxiliary Income | 11,599,559 | 11,862,813 |
| Total College Income | 99,183,301 | 93,272,130 |
| **2. CURRENT EXPENDITURES:** | | |
| Operating Budget Expenditures | 62,425,303 | 66,924,329 |
| Other Current Expenditures | 6,304,914 | 5,634,728 |
| less Current Acct Maintenance | 703,276 | 642,167 |
| Total Current Expenditures | 68,026,941 | 71,916,890 |
| **3. CAPITAL EXPENDITURES:** | | |
| Investment in New Plant | 9,334,326 | 2,310,285 |
| Maintenance in Current Account | 703,276 | 642,167 |
| Maintenance in Plant Fund | 3,477,560 | 4,639,692 |
| Total Additions to Capital | 13,515,162 | 7,592,144 |
| **4. FINANCIAL WEALTH (EOY)** | | |
| Assets | 346,203,972 | 358,726,081 |
| [Endowment Value] | [333,553,551] | [341,572,081] |
| less Liabilities | 50,596,648 | 49,355,661 |
| Net Financial Wealth | 295,607,324 | 309,370,420 |
| **5. FINANCIAL SAVING:** | | |
| Total Financial Saving | 17,641,198 | 13,763,096 |
| Breakeven Saving (Inflation Offset) | 13,484,575 | 13,910,019 |
| Real Financial Saving | 4,156,623 | (146,923) |
| Real Net of Gifts to Endowment | (2,910,046) | (8,891,729) |

## Appendix B
## Performance Calculations

|  |  | 1989–90 $ | 1990–91 $ |
|---|---|---|---|
| **Saving—Gain (Loss) of Real Wealth:** |  | 10,171,785 | (651,974) |
| Total Real Saving: | Y-X[hK*(t-1)-(mc+mk)]+iK*(t-1) | 38,209,833 | 28,498,822 |
| Breakeven Saving: | iNFW(t-1)+iK*(t-1) | 28,038,048 | 29,150,796 |
| **Gain (Loss) of Real Financial Wealth: Real Saving** |  | 4,156,623 | (146,923) |
| Total Financial Saving: | Y-X-K | 17,641,198 | 13,763,096 |
| Breakeven Saving (Inflation Offset): | i(NFW)(t-1) | 13,484,575 | 13,910,019 |
| **Gain (Loss) of Physical Wealth: Real Saving** |  | 6,015,162 | (505,051) |
| Total Physical Capital Saving | K-[hK*(t-1)-(mc+mk)]+iK*(t-1) | 20,568,635 | 14,735,726 |
| Breakeven Saving (Inflation Offset): | iK*(t-1) | 14,553,473 | 15,240,777 |
| **Composition of Saving:** |  |  |  |
| Financial Saving |  | 41% | 23% |
| Physical Saving |  | 59% | 77% |
| **With Smoothed Asset Income** |  |  |  |
| Saving–Gain (Loss) of Total Real Wealth: Smoothed |  | 7,276,151 | 8,600,747 |
| Total Saving |  | 35,314,199 | 37,751,543 |
| Gain (Loss) of Real Financial Wealth |  | 1,260,989 | 9,105,798 |
| Total Financial Saving: Smoothed |  | 14,745,564 | 23,015,817 |
| **Spending:** |  |  |  |
| Deferred Maintenance: | hK*(t-1)-(mc+mk) | 3,319,164 | 2,815,336 |
| Real Yearly Growth |  | 36.27% | –18.99% |
| Current Expenditures: | X-(mc+mk) | 68,026,941 | 71,916,890 |
| Real Yearly Growth |  | 4.72% | 0.97% |
| Operating Costs: | X-(mc+mk)+hK*(t-1) | 75,526,941 | 80,014,085 |
| Real Yearly Growth |  | 4.51% | 1.18% |
| Investment in New Plant |  | 9,334,326 | 2,310,285 |
| Real Yearly Growth |  | 4.35% | –76.36% |

K = new investment; K* = replacement value of capital stock; h = depreciation rate;
mc and mk = maintenance spending in Current and Capital-Budget, respectively (both included in X);
i = inflation rate; Y = income; X = (current expenditures + mc + mk).
(t-1) = end of previous period.

# The Other Side of the Mountain (1991)

## THE PEW HIGHER EDUCATION RESEARCH PROGRAM

Trustees like dark wood, round tables, and, on occasion, sessions devoted to "truth-telling." There is a story of one such session at which the board's chair informed his institution's senior officers almost cheerfully: "Friends, you cannot continue to tax the university's resources to finance new spending. Your job is to bring the institution's appetite into line with its financial means—and if you can't do it, we'll find others who can!"

A colleague of long standing was among those who "got the message" that afternoon. Having spent nearly two decades superintending the financial fortunes of the institution, he had learned more than a little about the interdependence of fiscal and academic management. As a member of the faculty, he could recite the justification for sustaining academic excellence at any cost; as an administrative manager, the voice of the board chair echoed a concern that had often sounded in his own mind. Still, it was troubling to have the matter put so bluntly by someone who was *of* but not *in* the institution. What came to mind, he reported later, were Robert Burns's lines:

> O wad some Power the giftie gie us
> To see oursel's as others see us!

What others see is one more American enterprise that is being put on a revenue diet. The public has run out of patience as well as pocket for tuition increases that exceed annual inflation by substantial margins. If Americans believed through most of the 1980s that those price hikes, along with substantial increases in state appropriations and in federal student aid, would purchase more—better teaching, more attention to the curriculum, and greater diversity within campus communities—they are no longer so sure that these promises are being kept. Many know now that colleges and universities themselves must change, drawing on the leadership and experience of their best faculty and administrators to develop strategic visions that are more purposeful, more focused, and more capable of encouraging targeted investments in specific programs rather than spreading out resources to preserve campus harmony.

## Prescribed Constraint

Whatever the intrinsic merits of the fairness of these judgments, they affect every college and university. It scarcely matters whether one accepts the view of those who described the sustained escalation of costs as a moral failure, or of those who understood that higher education was following the same course of economic "rational behavior" that accounted for most of the business excesses of the 1980s. Public and private, large and small, research and teaching institutions—all face the rigors of a revenue diet.

As our colleague Bruce Johnstone notes, the 1990s are shaping up to be a period of unprecedented austerity in the post-World War II history of the nation's public sector. No matter what the source of concern—the economy, declining tax revenues, or institutional inefficiencies—the message is the same: institutions need to live more effectively within reduced means. Colleges and universities will have to control the advance of what we have called the "administrative lattice" and "academic ratchet"—two mechanisms that, along with profusion of public regulation, have contributed to an institution's costs by increasing administrative staff and redirecting faculty energies away from institutional goals toward those of professional and career advancement (see *Policy Perspectives*, June 1990). Most of all, the message is that colleges and universities must learn to decrease or cut some, but clearly not all, expenditures in order to continue doing well—perhaps even better—what they have done well in the past.

This revenue diet will necessarily change the metric by which quality is measured, bringing about an adjustment of vocabularies and habits of mind to account for quality in increments of outcome rather than expenditure. A recent report by a task force at the University of Michigan, entitled "Enhancing Quality in an Era of Resource Constraints," illustrates the change:

> The natural reaction to the idea of managing or containing costs is a fear of reduction in quality. The University of Michigan has long tradition as a comprehensive research university of outstanding quality, and any potential threat to that quality is a legitimate cause for concern. We have become convinced, however, that in many areas of the University's operations there is an inverse relationship between cost and quality, so that cost containment (and even cost reduction) can go hand-in-hand with quality improvement.

Hardly music to an industry accustomed to equating quality enhancement with increases in funding.

## That and More

Any attempt to begin a successful regimen of cost reduction soon encounters matters simple enough on their surface, yet daunting in their sense of paradox. Discussions of cost reduction can easily invoke a Janus-like perspective that sees a current crisis in terms of cyclical patterns. There is, for example, never a "good" time to go on a revenue diet. Leaders of institutions that undertake cost containment during relatively good times are often heard to mutter, "What we need is a good recession to get everyone's attention and convince them that budget cuts are really necessary." Let those hard times appear, however, and leaders long for the stable conditions that might allow for a selective trimming based on a coherent vision and plan, rather than the wasteful across-the-board cuts a financial crisis too often brings.

Nearly every factor that contributes to the growth of administrative expenditure adds to the sense of paradox. With administrative status increasingly tied to the number of people who directly report to a given officer, personal advancement requires a constantly expanding empire of subordinates and an entrepreneurial base to extend one's own administrative lattice. Little wonder that so few managers, at any level, volunteer to reduce their ranks, even when staff functions have grown outmoded. The intuitive response to change is not to undertake "growth by substitution," but to argue for "that and more." By definition, any new responsibility must entail additional resources; to accept less is to acknowledge inefficiency in past performance and a diminution of stature within the organization.

"That and more" similarly describes the paradox inherent in the process by which state funds are appropriated for public higher education. The state appropriation derives from a compact of long standing between a state college or university and the state government, through the agency of its legislative and executive branches, or a state commission of higher education. In the main, this year's budget request is a function of last year's appropriation, which enshrined in legislative act the current understanding of the institution's mission and its means of fulfilling it. New budgetary lines—the legislative equivalent of cost-plus pricing—are justified through the authorization of expanded institutional mission. Success again requires institutional managers to request "that and more."

The dilemma of many state institutions is heightened by the fact that public funds are often appropriated on a "spend it lose it" basis, making it virtually impossible to save for future investment. To ask for a reassignment of budget lines in this environment runs counter to all instincts of institutional self-preservation, for such a request is tantamount to admitting that an existing line was not necessary in the first place. Equally important is the fact that these budget lines are usually perceived as entitlements by departments and administrative units within the institution. It is far safer for the public institution to express its ambition in terms of new budget lines, seeking to expand the whole, rather than shifting resources away from ineffective units toward activities that show greater promise in effectively realizing the educational mission. State colleges and universities collectively know that accepting less from their state government implicitly gives power to other claims on public resources with which higher education competes for funding, such as roads, prisons, and public assistance programs.

The academic ratchet, by which faculty become increasingly detached from the goals of their particular institution, contributes its own element of irony and paradox. Although tenured faculty effectively "own the enterprise," enjoying the greatest personal and professional security within an institution, they have come to have less attachment to its collective well-being. Those faculty whose credentials are in demand can shop institutions for the best deal, and those who become fixtures in a given institution often strike an attitude of high indifference toward efforts to realize educational goals in more effective ways. What the faculty say with fervent pride is all too true: "Deans and provosts come and go; we stay." In time, the academic ratchet causes deans and provosts to utter, "If you need something done, hire an administrator."

A final paradox derives from one of the least-understood facts about higher education—the substantial expenditure growth experienced by every sector and almost every institution for over a decade. Between 1975 and 1986, the last year for which data currently are available, the expenditures for core functions (academic and administrative, *excluding* financial aid) reported by colleges and universities grew, on average, 3 percent faster per year than the underlying rate of inflation, as measured by the GNP deflator; and almost all institutions grew by more than 2 percent per year. It was, the best-funded institutions—private research universities belonging to the Association of American Universities (AAU) and higher-priced liberal arts colleges—that grew the most, reporting, on the average, real growth in expenditures of more than 51 percent, or nearly 4 percent annually compounded over the 12 years. . . .

Probably the best way to gauge the magnitude of this expenditure growth is to ask of the average-sized institution in each sector. "How much did you add to our expense base in the last decade?" The answers, reported in Table 1 (page 4A), were calculated by subtracting from the 1986 average institutional expense for core functions the 1975 average institutional expense, expressed in 1986 dollars. The table also reports the percentage increase that change represents in terms of the institution's 1975 base (expressed in 1986 dollars).

The irony, of course, is that this expenditure growth was experienced by so many and celebrated by so few. Faced with a constant need to explain tuition increases and appropriation requests substantially in excess of inflation, the leadership of the nation's colleges and universities drifted into tough talk about the high cost of quality. Led by the most elite and costly institutions, colleges and universities talked almost incessantly, or so it seemed, about the need to remain competitive, to make up for past deprivations in terms of salaries, and ultimately to add administrative functions in order to manage better the modern academy in response to governmental and societal demands. Almost as a matter of necessity, there was an expanding litany of bad news and

### Table 1
### Mean Real Expense Growth in Constant 1986 Dollars: Core Functions 1975-1986

| Institutional Sector | Core Expense 1975 | Core Expense 1986 | Difference 1986-1975 | % Change |
|---|---|---|---|---|
| Lower-Priced (PR1) | 6,533,355 | 8,747,316 | 2,213,961 | 33.9% |
| Moderately Priced Private (PR2) | 7,560,196 | 9,887,900 | 2,327,704 | 30.8% |
| Higher-Priced Private (PR3) | 17,599,348 | 26,622,133 | 9,022,785 | 51.3% |
| Private Research Univ. (RPVR) | 193,623,829 | 286,790,636 | 93,166,808 | 48.1% |
| Public Research Univ. (RPUB) | 296,064,022 | 397,218,238 | 101,154,216 | 34.2% |
| Land Grant Coll. & Univ.l (LG) | 98,576,794 | 134,431,000 | 35,854,206 | 36.3% |
| State Coll. & Univ. (SCU) | 20,818,658 | 26,904,870 | 6,086,211 | 29.2% |

unexpected reversals as part of the annual justification of "that and more." Stanford's Don Kennedy captured much of that feeling when, in an oft-quoted speech, he asked of his university, "How Can We Look So Rich Yet Feel So Poor?"

Now, as colleges and universities begin yet another decade of tough choices and hard times, there is no one left to convince. Higher education becomes just another American industry left spent by the go-go '80s—another facet of the American experience that needs to see itself with other eyes before it can court new support. Indeed, more than any time in the last half century, American colleges and universities are likely to be on their own—left to their own best instincts and to draw upon their own talents and resources as they go about the business of adjusting their appetites to the provisions at hand.

## Lessons from the Trenches

What, then, in concrete terms, is being asked of higher education? How does an institution go about reducing its expenditures? Do all institutions face the same revenue diet?

In this issue of *Policy Perspectives*, we have developed a series of institutional "Cases" (pages 14B through 19B) that describes how two colleges, two universities, and one state system of colleges have brought about a reduction of their expenditure base—what in one institution is called "repositioning," in another, "strategic contraction," and in a third, "achieving financial equilibrium." These cases make clear that, along with their particular circumstances and distinguishing characteristics, there are remarkable similarities in the experiences of institutions that have gone on revenue diets. From these and other experiences, we have drawn eight broad lessons that have general applicability for most colleges and universities taking on the challenge of structural reform. None of them will be easy to put into practice. Collectively, they will test both the stamina and cohesion of the institution. We believe that they represent a strategy, however painful, for emerging from the revenue diet a strengthened institution.

1. *Plan now for reduced levels of employment.* Most institutions over the next decade will have to accomplish their missions with smaller staffs; in a personnel-intensive organization, cost containment cannot mean other than reduced employment. The first instinct will be to achieve that reduction through attrition, shrinking most those departments that have the highest turnover. Inevitably, managers and department chairs will seek to retain current staff, even if dissatisfied with their performance, for fear that every vacancy will be captured by the administration to balance the budget. These necessary reductions will be made all the more

painful by that habit of mind that celebrates employment as an end in itself: growth is good; increased staff and faculty billets are a sign of institutional vitality; reductions in faculty and staff bring about a loss of status, susceptibility to lawsuits, and financial stability.

The alternative is to begin planning now for lower employment levels, establishing realistic targets for each major function and division within the institution. With sufficient advance notice, most units will be able to reduce staffing levels through planned attrition—a judicious combination of early retirements, tough performance reviews, and, where necessary, layoffs that are both timely and fair. Given enough lead time, well-managed institutions will be able to hire key personnel even as their overall levels of employment decline. Poorly managed institutions, on the other hand, will delay too long in planning for employment reductions, with the result that their faculty and staff profiles will be shaped largely by the happenstance of death and resignation.

2. *Resist the temptation to make across-the-board cuts.* The instinct to take a little from everyone in order to minimize institutional discord seems eminently fair, though it almost never addresses the deeper symptoms of rising costs. The case against across-the-board cuts has been made often enough. No matter how well decisions to spread the austerity evenly might accord with the democratic notion of fairness, they remain no decisions at all—evasions, really, of the need to choose among competing versions of the institution's future. Democratic cutting represents not just a failure of will but, more significantly, a failure to understand that maintaining quality in some areas will require a reduction or elimination of others.

Across-the-board cuts also bring on a climate of rear-view planning, which transforms all initiatives into private strategies for reinstating what was severed. For any unit that suffers a loss of a position through even-handed cuts, the "agenda" becomes simply to restore that position, and this effort absorbs the energy and imagination that might have been directed to a redesign of operations to achieve better quality and efficiency with the resources at hand.

3. *Recognize that administration is not the business of the business.* Containing costs—reducing the administrative lattice and reversing the academic ratchet—will require that colleges and universities move to sustain educational quality in the most efficient ways. That process necessarily begins with an affirmation that an institution's primary goals are not to instill good morale or to ensure personal comfort, but to educate and add to the store of human understanding. Any costs a college or university incurs that do not contribute directly to these twin goals need to be reexamined in the hard light of mission and efficiency.

The keenest paradox of all may be that colleges and universities will be forced to become more businesslike than ever before, simply to preserve their special character as places where ideas can thrive in an atmosphere of freedom and independence from the flux of contemporary values. To maintain the intellectual sanctity of the academy will require a scrupulous application of the best of business practices.

4. *Engage faculty energy.* Because faculty norms are an inherent part of the problem, faculty have critical roles to play in making their institutions more cost-effective. The academic ratchet has not occurred from lack of industriousness on the part of faculty but from centrifugal movement of that energy away from institutional values and goals. It was the faculty's pursuit of professional, often extra-institutional, interests that led to much of the growth in higher education's costs, as we noted in "The Lattice and the Ratchet" (*Policy Perspectives*, June 1990). The expansion of administrative staff is, in part, a function of the disbursement of responsibilities once considered part of the faculty role.

The faculty's responsibility for helping to realize cost containment cannot rest with the Faculty Senate's traditional appetite for data that demonstrate administrative growth. That interest must be matched by a new willingness to confront the issue of the academic ratchet: to reconsider questions of workload, the requirements of tenure, and the commitment to institutionally defined norms—including the integrity of the curriculum—as opposed to norms arising from the confines of a single discipline.

Reform will come about only when faculty are full participants in the process of discovery and invention. They will know best how to get the job done—what kinds of intra-departmental reorganizations will yield the largest savings through increased efficiencies. They need to understand and subscribe to the vision of what the institution will look like in its meaner and leaner state. They need ample opportunity to question, to be heard, and finally, to join in the process of implementation. They too must understand that the nature of leaning out is such that including too much representation in the process is certain to undermine the result.

5. *Integrate top-down leadership with bottom-up management.* In sorting through the tangles of issues, personalities, and insecurities that are by-products of a planned program of cost reduction, an institution must demonstrate leadership and the capacity to develop a purposeful consensus. Regardless of mission, size, or governance, reform must begin with the intelligent coordination of top-down leadership and bottom-up management. This means, first of all, a clear designation of appropriate roles at each level. Even when an institution is strong on top-down vision and leadership, the result will be mere rhetoric unless there is an equally strong connection with the managerial skills and savvy of the "shop floor." Too much power residing in bottom-up processes makes executive officers, in effect, the employees of their employees, beholden to everyone who seeks involvement in the process of change. To the extent that top officials relinquish their leadership roles and regard themselves simply as players in a management team, the institution can expect to feel the effects of bad management decisions that proceed from fuzzy and contradictory images of the institution as a whole.

It is incumbent on chancellors, presidents, and provosts to articulate the broad goals, to empower the line managers and hold them accountable for the achievement of institutionally defined aims. Having established a responsible statement of the outcomes expected and the resources accorded to each unit, the chief executive or academic officer must be able to say to each of his or her principal administrative colleagues, "It's all yours from here." The CEO's obligation is to provide managers with, not a detailed plan of action, but a statement of expected outcomes. The manager's responsibility is to deliver those outcomes, using whatever resources and strategies are both effective and appropriate.

6. *Engage trustees as guides and goads, but not as micromanagers.* One of the more important leadership roles needs to be played by an institution's trustees. As the stewards of the institution and its resources, trustees have responsibility for determining, in broad outline, the course on which the institution embarks. The ideal board of trustees is one whose members possess an understanding and vision of the institution as a whole—even though their involvement may stem initially from an interest in particular parts. Effective trustees are those who evoke the confidence of the administration and faculty, and who keep informed of the key issues while resisting the temptation to micromanage.

Bringing expenditures into line with revenue is the one issue in which trustees have historically played a prominent role. Trustees tend to lead professional lives that are very much concerned with the bottom line and the long-range effects of current spending and investment habits. They are eminently qualified to prescribe a revenue diet to an institution in their keeping and to serve as partners, contributing valuable insight and experience during the process. In calling upon an administration to change the trajectory of spending in relation to investment, trustees empower the chief officers of a college or university to undertake real reform.

The caveat against micromanaging applies to trustees no less than to administrative officers in relation to their subordinate managers. Trustees who allow themselves to be buried in the minute details of an institution's operation, or who fail to rise above their constituent concerns to embody a larger vision of the institution and its future, are not likely to be effective leaders of cost reform—or of any other undertaking that involves the well-being of their college or university.

7. *Simplify the organization.* Probably the least-examined consequence of the growth of the administrative lattice is the organizational complexity it has contributed to most colleges and universities. Paralleling the numerical growth in administrative staff has been a growth in the number of separately organized functions, each with its own department or unit, often comprising fewer than four members.

Even if large universities wish to continue their investments in the administrative lattice and its concomitant organizational complexity, small colleges simply cannot. It is not a matter of fairness, but rather the workings of the competitive marketplace. Smaller institutions will have to become even more efficient if the industry's price leaders further up the competitive hierarchy limit their own tuition increases to inflation plus a point. With less new money to spend and more demands on their financial aid budgets, small colleges will have to make the same proportional reductions as their larger, often better-funded, competitors. The questions is, how? Bob Zemsky and Bill Massy suggest one approach, encouraging the combination of functions—particularly admissions/development and student service/human resources— with similar "back room organizations," even though they stand on opposite banks of the divide that separates traditionally academic and administrative units (see "Distillations," pages 7B and 8B). Another approach has been suggested by Dick Kneedler, the president of Franklin and Marshall College, who is exploring the possibility of creating more generalized service bureaus within his college and reducing the number of one- and two-person functions.

It will be much easier for larger institutions to make similar savings, principally by simplifying their transactional processes. The key lies in making the fundamental shift, already accomplished by most large firms, and moving from "pre-action clearance" to "post-action audit." Managers need to be freer to act, to make decisions, to initiate transactions without first getting permission. Forms, for example, should be processed for the most part automatically, without engaging large numbers of central staff who inspect the forms for accuracy and, when "errors" are detected, substitute their own judgments for those of the managers in the field. In return for greater autonomy, managers would have to know and enact clearly stated policies defining expected institutional behavior and goals. Managers who regularly fail to observe those norms or to achieve those goals would be replaced—as in fired!

The absence of such accountability has made administrative staff themselves a part of the problem. Too often, they encourage not so much the exercise of responsibility as the negotiation of differences—the striking of resolutions that satisfy everyone a little and achieve a common denominator of accord. Inevitably, the absence of accountability has diffused responsibility for decisions, imposing enormous costs on the institution both in the additional time needed to process transactions and in the quality of those decisions. The price everyone pays for feeling good is a net drop in efficiency, a dispersion of responsibility, an increase in costs, and, paradoxically, a decrease in the time and energy spent carrying out the educational mission of the institution.

8. *Last hired cannot mean first fired.* As higher education goes about the business of restructuring, a number of colleges and universities will face an additional dilemma. As an industry, higher education has substantially increased the diversity of its administrative staff. In many instances, diversity has been achieved by truly integrating the work force, bringing women and historically underrepresented ethnic groups into every facet and every level of the administrative structure. In other cases, however, diversity has been achieved largely by increasing the size of the administrative staff, often concentrating the new hires in human resources and student service positions. Institutions that have purchased only the appearance of diversity by

the creation of jobs not central to the educational mission will find themselves trying to strike an impossible balance between maintaining diversity and reducing employment levels. The standards to which all institutions must be held is simply stated: cost containment cannot be achieved at the expense of institutional diversity.

Sometime this decade, most colleges and universities will find themselves asking, "Are we really better off today than during the stagflation of the 1970s or the boom of the 1980s?" Then, as now, the question will invite speculation about higher education's peaks and valleys and the combination of forces that carries institutions up and down the scales of prosperity. Our colleagues Art Levine and Bruce Johnstone are right in reminding the Roundtable that, however distinctive higher education's current dilemmas may seem, there is always that sense that "we have been there before." When the bear climbs over the mountain, all that it can see is the other side of the mountain.

Higher education must now traverse the other side of the mountain along a path that leads downward in scale. Each college or university that travels this path is likely to recall its wounds as well as the anger that often accompanies staff and budget reductions. But each will have learned in the process to do better what it does best and to scale back or discontinue the costly things it does least well. Each will become an institution that has learned to articulate and act upon a clearer vision of itself—to see itself as others see it.

# If the Cut Is So Deep, Where Is the Blood?
## Problems in Research on
## the Effects of Financial Restraint (1986)

Michael L. Skolnik

Publicly funded universities in North America and numerous other areas (for the U.K., see Kogan with Kogan 1983; for Australia see Harman 1982) have been the target of financial austerity programs since the late 1970s or earlier. Expressions of concern about financial problems of universities in the United States date back to the early 1970s (Cheit 1971; Smith 1972). Leslie and Miller (1974) advised colleges and universities to prepare for the end of growth. Stadtman, in a national survey of college and university administrators (1980, 176), reported that 54 percent viewed finances as the most important issue facing higher education, far more than the percentage for any other issue; "quality," for example, was rated most important by only 15 percent. Magarrell (1982) reported that state appropriations for higher education were failing to keep up with the rate of inflation in half of the states. Leslie's (1983, 186) survey of finance officers indicated a weakening of funding-enrollment relationships for thirty-one states, and Slaughter and Silva (1985) reported that the financial situation was particularly adverse for institutions in the Northeastern states. A recent bibliographic handbook on the financing of American higher education identifies the late 1970s as a watershed between periods of "buoyant" and "bleak" funding, respectively (Quay and Olevnik 1984). In Canada, university systems in three provinces experienced declines in real operating income per FTE student between 1974 and 1981, with those in Ontario suffering the greatest decline—13 percent (Skolnik and Rowen 1984, 59). Universities in British Columbia had the second greatest increase in real operating income per FTE during that period but have since been subjected to a 15 percent cut, over three years, in the nominal value of provincial operating grants, which is their major source of income.

University spokespersons have voiced concern about the harmful effects of funding restraint upon universities' capability to educate students, advance knowledge, and serve communities. Various institutions, associations, and intermediary bodies have generated information intended to demonstrate the harmful consequences of these funding shortfalls on the resource needs of universities. Generally, these efforts have failed to reverse government funding policies (Hyatt 1983, 138). The relatively few studies on the topic of disinterested parties have been inconclusive (Anderson 1983) or paradoxical, that is, that "losing ground financially" often has been associated with "gaining ground academically" (Minter and Bowen 1980).

The general ineffectiveness of briefs from interested parties and the inconclusive, or paradoxical, findings of research studies on the impact of financial restraint upon universities raise some important questions, from the dual points of view of public policy development and research. If universities are being as badly damaged by funding limitations as they claim, why can't researchers uncover evidence of that damage? Why can't spokespersons for the universities communicate that damage effectively to governments? This paper will address these questions, drawing upon particular research studies of the impact of financial restraint upon universities, and referring to the Ontario experience as a well-documented illustration of a university system which has attempted to influence government funding policies by providing it with data.

The paper will describe and analyze the types of data and research which have been used to assess the impact of financial restraint upon universities and to estimate the financial needs of universities. It will identify important issues and problems relating to the methodology and credibility of this body of research, particularly emphasizing the central role of "academic quality" in the public debate over the adequacy of university funding. It will draw attention to the difficulties involved in producing persuasive information to back up claims that quality has been deteriorating as a consequence of financial constraint. Although the concept of academic quality remains as "elusive" to this author as to others who have pondered it (Scott 1981), the paper will conclude with suggested directions to emphasize in enhancing research on the impact of financial limitations on academic quality.

## The Public Debate on University Funding in Ontario

Unlike some jurisdictions which have experienced sudden drastic cuts in university funding, Ontario universities have been gradually reduced in operating income per student a few percent per year since the mid-1970s. The Ontario Council on University Affairs (OCUA), the body which advises the government on university funding and other matters, expressed alarm about the cumulative effects of such cuts in its 1979 White Paper, provocatively titled *System on the Brink*. The OCUA stated that as a result of inadequate funding, the Ontario university system "stands at the brink of serious trouble" and "faces a future of precipitous decline and turbulence." In 1981, a committee appointed by the government to consider the problem concluded that the government's only alternatives were to substantially increase its operating and capital grants to the universities or to drastically restructure the university system (Committee on the Future Role of Universities in Ontario 1981). Even after the OCUA and the Council of Ontario Universities (COU), an association which speaks on behalf of the universities, expanded and refined their claims about the harmful consequences of funding reductions in the aftermath of this report, the premier of the province told a delegation from the University of Toronto in February 1983 that "he did not believe that the university sector was underfunded" ("Premier Tells" 1983, 1).

Subsequently a high-profile, government-appointed commission reported that excellence in universities could be attained through a modest number of special (bridging) faculty appointments, a small reduction in enrollment, an increase in tuition, and a minor reallocation of resources from instruction to research (Commission on the Future Development of the Universities of Ontario 1984). This commission suggested further that the enrollment funding formula should be modified to provide financial incentives for excellence, using national research grants, fellowships, and provincial scholarships as evidence. Such use of performance funding is receiving attention in the United States (Peterson 1977) and may encourage greater efficiency, but it is not clear how this approach responds to universities' claim that they can no longer achieve high levels of performance because of inadequate basic funding. In short, the commission's advocacy of performance funding along with recommendations for modest increases and reallocations underscores a perception of the universities' situation that is very different from that of the universities themselves: that the problems are far too serious to respond to incremental funding adjustments.

From *System on the Brink* in 1979 to the 1984 commission report, public briefs have flowed steadily from the COU and the provincial confederation of university faculty associations. Editorials and articles abound in the public press. All parties claim to be open to evidence; and in June

1984, the chairperson of the OCUA begged members of the Canadian Society for the Study of Higher Education to find better ways of documenting the academic consequences of funding (Paikin 1984). To date, however, the evidence from both research studies and interested briefs or commission reports has been inconclusive—and certainly ineffective—in persuading the government to change its funding policies. In apparent frustration, the COU, in its 1982 operating grants belief, simply repackaged the same information provided previously and resorted to greater stridency and emotionalism, titling the brief, *Once More, With Feeling*.

To appreciate why research on the academic impact of financial restraint has had so little effect upon the public policy, it is necessary to consider the problems involved in such research. Our examination of those problems will describe the approaches taken in such research generally and will give examples of the main types of evidence Ontario universities and the OCUA have used in making their case for more money.

## Approaches to Research and Data Collection

Two classes of research data could conceivably provide evidence that universities require increased funding. One class involves establishing norms and constructing models to generate estimates of the amount of money which universities "need" or "should have," according to some standard. The other class consists of research documenting harmful consequences of current and recent funding levels, with the implication being that more money is needed to avoid or alleviate these consequences. Most of the studies by more disinterested researchers fall into the second class, while interested briefs follow both approaches. Taking these two classes of research data together, we can identify at least the following seven categories of data and/or analysis which could be or have been used in making the universities' case for more money:

1. Engineering production models

2. Comparisons between universities and other sectors

3. Comparisons of university funding across jurisdictions

4. Analysis of trends in inputs

5. Baseline analyses of funding needs

6. Surveys of perceptions of administrators, faculty, and students

7. Analyses of academic quality

## 1. Engineering Production Models

Thinking of education as a type of production activity suggests that the engineering production approach might be used for estimating what the costs of running a university, or a program, should be. This approach involves an *ex ante* study of a hypothetical production situation based upon the application of relevant scientific and engineering principles, controlled experiment, and the expertise and judgment of those who are familiar with managing the particular production process in question. This method has been widely used in the past for estimating costs in agriculture (Heady and Dillon 1962) and in industries which use highly centralized capital facilities, such as oil refineries (Chenery 1949). Using the engineering production approach to make normative estimates of the costs of higher education would require expert judgments about the way in which the educational process should be structured and organized and the amounts of different types of resources which should be employed in particular activities. The resulting estimates of resources required could then be compared with the actual levels provided. No doubt, something akin to the engineering approach is used in planning new institutions, colleges, or institutes.

However, given the variability of methods, the considerable possibilities for substitution among different types of resources, and the difficulties of specifying outputs, this approach is problematic when applied to higher education. While it would be interesting to see if consensus could be obtained in making such estimates, the author knows of no studies where this approach has been used in making normative estimates of costs in higher education.

## 2. Comparisons between Universities and Other Sectors

Comparisons between the funding of universities and the funding of other sectors obviously does not provide direct evidence related to the financial *needs* of universities. Nevertheless, such comparisons have been a recurring component of the annual briefs on operating grants submitted by the Council of Ontario Universities (e.g., 1982). The briefs have presented dramatic graphs showing a steady decline in real operating revenue per university student while other sectors, such as primary/secondary schools and hospitals, have been receiving increases in real operating revenue per client served. However, over the period of time covered by such graphs, school enrollment has declined substantially while university enrollment has increased. The author has calculated that over the past decade, the elementary and secondary school share of the Ontario budget has declined more rapidly than the university share (Skolnik and Rowen 1984, 125). The implication is that the schools have not been treated more favorably than the universities; but because of various institutional constraints, the government simply could not pull money out of the schools as fast as enrollment was declining. If there is any lesson from comparing the university funding with that of schools, it is that amelioration of decline in real expenditure per student can be purchased only by limiting enrollment, a strategy which most Ontario universities have been loathe to embrace.

Comparing expenditures on universities with expenditures on hospitals underscores the difference in the consequences of underfunding between the two sectors, or at least in the types of evidence which have been provided by each. When hospital administrators scream about underfunding (as they have in Ontario), they can point to cases where people have literally died while waiting for space on the operating table. When newspapers look for similarly tangible evidence of the effects of financial restraint in universities, frequently the best they can find is an instance of textbooks rotting because of inadequate storage facilities ("Textbooks Rot" 1983, 4).

Before comparisons between the funding of universities and the funding of other sectors can be useful, they need to be accompanied by evidence on the specific activities in question, the outcomes of those activities, and the consequences of various levels of funding. Failing that, such comparisons can at best indicate relative social priorities, and at worst be misleading and create schisms within the total educational community, as in the case of comparisons with school expenditures. But they do nothing to demonstrate the universities' funding needs.

## 3. Comparisons with Other Jurisdictions

Comparisons between universities, or university systems, across jurisdictions would seem to be more useful in establishing financial needs than comparisons between universities and other sectors within the same jurisdiction. However, interjurisdictional comparisons of university funding give rise to an almost intractable "identification" problem insofar as the "revenue theory of unit costs in higher education" is valid (Bowen 1980, 15-19). Do universities in Alberta spend 40 percent more per student than universities in Ontario because costs are that much higher in Alberta or because the government of Alberta is that much more generous to its universities than the government of Ontario? Since neither government has conducted or been given detailed cost studies and since the resource-led economy of Alberta has been so much more buoyant than that of Ontario, the latter answer seems more likely.

Slaughter and Silva (1985) have demonstrated a strong correlation between the growth of state budgets for higher education and the performance of state economies. This correlation, though, is by no means perfect in the United States and is a good deal weaker in Canada. For example, the province with the most rapid growth in provincial operating grants to universities during the past decade is Quebec. The rate of growth of Gross Provincial Product in Quebec during that period has been less than the national average, but Quebec has shown the highest propensity of any of the provinces to increase government expenditures through debt financing.

Variations in expenditure per student are much greater in the United States than in Canada. In the mid-1970s, educational expenditures per student in the highest ranking state (Montana) were 130 percent higher than in the lowest ranking state (Connecticut). The figure for New York was 60 percent higher than that in Massachusetts (Bowen 1980, 121). While such large differences in expenditure per student may lend themselves to rhetorical use on the part of the states and provinces with the lower indices, they call into question the plausibility of using expenditure per student as an indicator of cost. Within the range of the normal connotations of the word "cost," does it really cost twice as much to provide university education in Montana as in Connecticut? Or nearly 40 percent more in Alberta than in Ontario? There are no national quality ratings of universities in Canada, but there is certainly no widely held popular impression in the higher education community that the quality of universities in Alberta is substantially greater than that in Ontario (or the reverse either). No doubt universities on Ontario would like to be funded at the Alberta levels, and educators in Connecticut probably look as avariciously at Montana.

However, without more detailed comparison of the structural, staffing, and program characteristics of university systems in the different jurisdictions, it is difficult to persuade anyone (especially a state or provincial government) that a particular jurisdiction's university system is underfunded simply because the system in some other jurisdictions has more money. The government in the jurisdiction that is spending more on universities could just as easily ask its universities why they can't be as efficient as the universities in the jurisdiction that is less well funded. If one could establish some correlation between interjurisdictional differences in funding and differences in quality, effectiveness, or outcomes, then the interjurisdictional funding differences would take on more significance. Such an endeavor would necessitate more sustained and substantive research on quality, effectiveness, and outcomes than has been done to date. In the absence of such research, inter-jurisdictional comparison data provides little more than rhetoric, reflecting primarily differences among jurisdictions of prosperity, priorities, and politics.

## 4. Analysis of Trends in Inputs

Most of the research literature on the impacts of financial restraint and most of the data in financial briefs to governments consists of analysis of trends in various inputs, e.g., operating expenditures per student, student-faculty ratios, and expenditures on support staff, libraries, and equipment. While evidence on faculty workload seems to be the most persuasive type of data, this category of input data in Canadian studies has been the least developed and least used, primarily because of measurement difficulties. In Ontario, the ratio of FTE students to full time faculty has increased over the last decade from about 14.5 to about 15.5; but in the absence of data on part-time faculty, the trend in total student-faculty ratio is not clear. In the United States, Bowen estimated that during the 1970s the ratio of FTE students to FTE faculty increased from 13.3 to 14.5. However, when faculty numbers were adjusted to exclude faculty time devoted to research and public service and the number of students was adjusted for changes in their academic level, the ratio improved from 28.6 to 26.4.

Less ambiguous and more compelling evidence is contained in trend analyses of nonsalary expenditures. The steep declines in expenditures on library acquisitions and equipment for Ontario which have been reported by the COU are typical of those reported for numerous institutions in the United States (Minter and Bowen 1980). It is not clear, however, just what these figures mean. Clearly, they reflect decisions about institutional priorities. For example, at least until recently, median faculty salaries in Canada have kept pace with the rate of inflation (Skolnik and Rowen 1984). Arithmetically, Ontario universities could have maintained the constant dollar value of their library acquisitions over the past decade by allowing faculty salaries to slip only 3 percent. When operating income is failing to keep up with the rate of inflation, it is mathematically certain that constant dollar spending in *some* categories must decline and extremely probable that expenditures in some categories will decline more than in others. Most institutions have chosen to make nonsalary categories bear the brunt of cutbacks (Minter and Bowen 1980). To then chart dramatically the declines in these categories is merely to restate in other terms that overall funding has declined. It is also to run the risk of appearing to overemphasize the importance of these expenditure categories and to invite the question why universities have allowed these particular expenditures to decline so much if the items of expenditure are so important. This emphasis on expenditure categories such as facilities and equipment, which have borne the brunt of cutbacks, led the Ontario Confederation of University Faculty Associations to observe that the 1981 committee on university funding gave the impression that "universities are buildings . . . and that all the important contributions made by universities are performed by these buildings" (1981, 5).

The major problem of relying on input indices for tracking the effects of financial restraint is the lack of an established relationship between variation in inputs and variation in educational outcomes (Astin 1968; Rock, Centra, and Linn 1969; Bowen 1980). The recent national report, *Involvement in Learning*, observes that input indices are at best "proxies for educational excellence," and that "none of them tells us what students actually learn and how much they grow as a result of higher education," nor do they tell us "anything about educational outcomes" (1984, 15). Farmer (1979) warns of the danger of making financial indicators serve an evaluative function that is beyond their capability, and Kramer (1982) notes that as research tools, such indicators will be misleading unless accompanied by substantial amounts of additional data which explain how institutions have reached the state described by the indices.

While input indicators may be useful for institutional management, they do little to strengthen the case for more funding. The politicians who determine the funding know when real funding levels are declining. Presenting them with data on various inputs may tell them something about university spending priorities, but such statistics primarily repeat merely what is already known—namely, that funding has been declining.

## 5. Baseline Analyses of University Funding Needs

The most commonly used approach in estimating the financial needs of universities or university systems is to supply baseline analyses of university funding needs. This approach involves selecting, as a point of reference, a particular instance of what is deemed to be an at least minimally acceptable financial situation and then to extrapolate that financial situation, taking account of changes which may have occurred between the base year and the current or forecast year. For example, one may assume that the financial situation of the Ontario university system was acceptable in 1978 (as the OCUA does). Then one would determine what adjustments must be made to the 1985 budget to restore the 1978 conditions. Of the many possible target variables to choose from, the most widely favored is expenditure per FTE student.

One of the most instructive applications of this method is in Bowen's study of the costs of higher education. He found that between 1969-70 and 1979-80, instructional expenditures per student in the United States, in constant dollars, decreased by $118, or about 3.5 percent. The estimated amount of money necessary to restore the level of expenditure per student in 1979-80 to its 1969-70 level is given by multiplying the number of students in 1979-80 by $118 per student, resulting in a figure of $1.4 billion. However, for Bowen, that was not the end of the story, because he argued that the higher education system achieved this near stability of expenditure per student "only through substantial sacrifices that left the system weaker at the end of the 1970s than at the beginning." He then made numerous adjustments to restore what was lost through these sacrifices.

This approach to estimating the financial needs of a university system involves three major difficulties. First is the thorny problem of determining an appropriate base year. Bowen selected 1969-70 as "a kind of transitional year when public attitudes toward higher education were already becoming less enthusiastic but when unit costs had not yet peaked" (1980, 201). The selection of a base year is quite arbitrary, and it is extremely difficult to get consensus from relevant parties that a particular year is appropriate. Indeed, it would seem that without some evidence on the actual nature of the harmful consequences which have occurred since some earlier year, agreement on what constitutes an appropriate base year would be almost impossible.

A second problem is the nature of evidence used to support the adjustments made to the base year funding levels. The purpose of these adjustments is to freeze the system—analytically—in a kind of holding pattern corresponding to its internal and external characteristics in the base year. For example, Bowen observed that socially imposed regulations for the personal security of workers, work standards, equality of opportunity, increased participation in decisions, demands for public information and accountability, and environmental protection added to the costs of running universities between 1969-70 and 1979-80. These costs were not reflected in the expenditure figures for the base year. To take another example, Bowen saw a weakening of commitment to literacy, quantitative skills, and broad general education between 1969-70 and 1979-80, and felt that an adjustment should be made to reflect the additional funds needed in the later year to restore these commitments to their base-year level. The net adjustments (some negative, some positive) corresponded to about 20 percent of the total costs of higher education in 1979-80, of which about half was related to estimates of quality deterioration. In contrast, the mechanical part of the exercise, simply holding expenditures per student constant, corresponded to only about 3 percent of total expenditures. If Bowen's analysis is typical, it suggests that the more qualitative, subjective components will far outweigh the simple mathematical ones. What looks on the surface to be a simple process of quantitative modelling turns out to be a highly qualitative endeavor in which judgements about process, quality, effectiveness, and outcomes play the central role. That being the case, use of this technique is only as good as the evidence and arguments that are mustered to support judgments about changes in quality.

The alternative to introducing quality judgments is to limit baseline analyses of funding needs to straightforward mechanical exercises. This more pedestrian use of the technique gives rise to the other problem—damned if you do, damned if you don't! Used mechanically, baseline models convey a misleading objectivity and suffer from being insufficiently dynamic in nature. In such cases, the models assume implicitly that the objectives, methods, processes, and priorities of the earlier year are appropriate in the later year, irrespective of changes which may have occurred in composition of students or societal expectations and needs regarding higher education. The possibility that there may be more economical ways of running universities without incurring reductions in quality is ignored.

Essentially, the same limitations apply to the mechanical use of the baseline analysis technique as to the description of trends in input indicators discussed in the previous section. Without commensurate evidence on the decline in quality, or other harmful consequences, there is no compelling reason why the expenditure per student figure of an earlier year is more appropriate than that of a later year. The need for more direct evidence on quality and consequences would appear inevitable.

## 6. Surveys of Perceptions of Administrators and Others

One of the most direct ways to discover what is happening to quality as a result of financial restraint and to learn of other consequences of financial restraint is to ask people in the university system—administrators, faculty, and students. Unfortunately, there are a number of problems involved in surveys of perceptions which limit the validity and generalizability of the results. Some of these problems are inherent in survey methodology. Others are specific to the context in question. Of the latter, perhaps the most serious problem is that the university community has become highly politicized around funding issues, and it may be difficult for respondents to avoid thinking about the uses to which the survey results may be put when formulating their answers to specific items on a questionnaire. For example, faculty and students who wish to see more funding provided to the university system may be inclined, for that reason, to assert that, in their perception, quality has deteriorated, even if they would be unable to provide specific evidence, indicators, or examples of quality deterioration.

Administrators may be in an awkward Catch-22 situation when responding to questions about trends in academic quality during their tenure. On the one hand, they may want the survey results to show that quality declined to strengthen their case for more funding. On the other hand, they may not wish to acknowledge that they presided over programs of deteriorating quality—in spite of their financial obstacles. It is possible such mixed considerations are responsible for the paradoxical findings reported by Minter and Bowen. It is likely that the factors operating when administrators are confronted with such questions as "How has the academic health of your institution changed during your tenure?," involve more than simple egoism, i.e., the desire "to look good." Administrators who have made substantial personal investments of energy and commitment to maintaining or improving academic quality may be reporting what they expect to have occurred as a result of their efforts, or what they have selectively observed or been told by subordinates.

There is no completely satisfactory way in a survey to control for respondents' personal interest in the outcome of the study. However, the dimensions of this problem can be constrained somewhat by approaching the issues more indirectly. In the survey which my colleague, Norman Rowen, and I undertook of presidents and deans in Canadian universities, we first asked respondents to rate various potential indicators of academic quality and to amend our list with their own suggestions of possible indicators. We then asked them to indicate their perception of the changes in each of these indicators over the past five years. An advantage of this method is that it allows us to separate perceptions about what constitutes quality from perceptions of changes in a number of important facets of the university. It also helps to explicate what respondents actually mean when they use the term "quality."

Some of our results are illustrated in Table 1, which gives information on both respondents' ratings of various indicators and their perceptions regarding changes in those indicators. It will be noted that, generally speaking, input measures were not rated very highly as indicators of academic quality. For example, only 22 percent rated expenditure per student as a very good indicator. Instead, faculty morale and judgments of peers rated higher as good indicators of academic quality. Rated by peer judgment, college personnel reported very little perception of deterioration. Province-wide reviews of some programs have been conducted in Ontario, mostly at the graduate level. We would expect that if there had been a significant increase in the number of negative assessments in these reviews, this act would have been reflected, in responses to our survey. Earlier in our survey, we had asked respondents for their perceptions of changes in overall academic quality in their institutions over the past five years, and a substantial majority reported improvement, with only a quite small minority reporting any deterioration. The fact that, according to the second highest-rated indicator of quality, there had been no significant deterioration tends to further confirm overall perceptions that quality had not deteriorated.

## Table 1
## Ratings of Indicators of Academic Program Quality and Perceptions of Changes in These Indicators, 1983 (by Region)*

| Indicator | Western Provinces A | B | Ontario A | B | Quebec A | B | Atlantic Provinces A | B | Canada A | B |
|---|---|---|---|---|---|---|---|---|---|---|
| 1. Operating expenditure per student | 17.0 | 60.9 | 28.6 | 70.7 | 27.5 | 77.8 | 9.7 | 56.7 | 21.8 | 67.1 |
| 2. Value of library holdings | 46.8 | 51.1 | 51.5 | 62.1 | 61.0 | 65.9 | 53.3 | 67.7 | 53.1 | 61.1 |
| 3. Purchase of new equipment | 40.3 | 44.2 | 49.2 | 60.3 | 39.0 | 65.0 | 48.4 | 70.1 | 44.4 | 58.9 |
| 4. Condition of physical plant | 21.3 | 40.4 | 33.9 | 47.4 | 9.8 | 34.1 | 29.0 | 48.4 | 24.2 | 42.6 |
| 5. Average class size | 38.3 | 55.3 | 69.5 | 66.1 | 48.8 | 50.0 | 32.3 | 50.0 | 50.0 | 56.6 |
| 6. Number of courses offered | 23.4 | 21.3 | 50.8 | 30.4 | 32.5 | 38.5 | 29.0 | 30.0 | 35.6 | 29.7 |
| 7. Faculty teaching load | 68.1 | 57.4 | 81.4 | 62.5 | 39.5 | 53.8 | 45.2 | 48.4 | 62.3 | 56.6 |
| 8. Number of faculty publications | 57.4 | 10.6 | 66.1 | 22.4 | 73.2 | 10.0 | 51.6 | 26.7 | 62.9 | 17.1 |
| 9. Rate of program completion by students | 31.9 | 10.9 | 52.5 | 1.8 | 66.7 | 5.3 | 46.7 | 6.7 | 49.7 | 5.9 |
| 10. Amount of time spent by faculty on professional development | 34.0 | 17.0 | 44.1 | 21.1 | 42.1 | 25.0 | 35.5 | 13.3 | 39.4 | 19.4 |
| 11. Ratio of support staff to faculty on professional development | 27.7 | 53.2 | 37.3 | 66.7 | 15.0 | 67.5 | 35.5 | 45.2 | 29.4 | 59.3 |
| 12. The judgments of outstanding scholars in various academic fields regarding the quality of your programs in those fields | 72.3 | 4.3 | 74.6 | — | 90.0 | 5.3 | 63.3 | 6.9 | 75.6 | 3.6 |
| 13. Faculty motivation/morale for teaching, research, support to students, etc. | 85.1 | 34.0 | 89.7 | 37.5 | 87.8 | 32.5 | 77.4 | 33.3 | 85.9 | 34.7 |
| 14. Faculty-student ratio | 52.2 | 61.2 | 71.2 | 69.2 | 68.4 | 62.9 | 48.3 | 37.9 | 61.6 | 60.1 |

*Each Column A reports the proportions of respondents designating each item as 4 or 5 as indicators of academic program quality on a five-point scale (1 = no indicator at all; 2 = very limited indicator; 3 = moderately useful indicator; 4 = good indicator; 5 = primary indicator)

Column B reports the proportion of respondents who designated each item as 1 or 2 on a five-point scale, recording their perception of changes in the indicator during 1977–82 (1 = substantial deterioration; 2 = moderate deterioration; 3 = no change; 4 = moderate improvement; 5 = substantial improvement).

Source: Skolnik and Rowen, 1984.

However, evidence about the other leading indicator of quality is more equivocal. Respondents were divided almost equally among (a) deterioration in faculty morale, (b) no change, and (c) improvement. This category of evidence is more difficult to interpret because faculty morale is difficult to measure and its connection to quality is probably quite complicated.

Anderson (1983) has suggested that universities have been able to maintain quality with decreased resources primarily as a result of greater effort on the part of faculty. This finding is consistent with that of Peters and Waterman (1982), who note that commitment is one of the keys to productivity and effectiveness for most organizations. One might surmise that, as faculty morale declines, commitment and effort would wane, and *then* there would be a decline in academic quality. Thus, we have tended to interpret our survey results (only the highlights of which are summarized here) as suggesting that quality has not yet declined, but that it is likely to, given the continuation of those forces which have led to a decline in faculty morale. This conclusion, we think, provides for a tidy interpretation of our data which is consistent with Anderson, and Minter and Bowen's reports. However, our probes on the quality question are still limited to fairly generalized perceptions. Tidiness does not necessarily make for validity.

Primarily for logistical reasons we limited our survey to administrators, thinking that we might possibly do a subsequent survey of faculty, and possibly students as well. Anderson questioned faculty members about the impact of financial restraint upon their programs but concluded that most faculty did not have a broad enough vantage point to draw connections between the overall funding situation of their institution and their own particular experiences. Anderson's study is unique in the literature on the impact of financial restraint for a number of reasons, two of which are important to note here. First, he was not limited to the type of *ad hoc* questionnaire which we, and most others who have probed this area, have used. He used a validated instrument, developed in the late 1960s by the Educational Testing Service to assess institutional effectiveness, the Institutional Functioning Inventory (IFI). This instrument includes a number of scales pertaining to such aspects of universities as institutional esprit, concern for improvement of society, and concern for undergraduate education. The IFI is not a quality measurement instrument, but it certainly provides indirect evidence of many aspects of university operations which most would deem as reflecting quality. On balance, the use of a more systematic, validated instrument is probably beneficial, although the usefulness of the data collection exercise may in some ways be confined by the strictures of the instrument, e.g., there may be other important ways of demonstrating concern for the improvement of society than those referenced in the IFI.

Perhaps the greatest strength of Anderson's use of the IFI is that he was able to obtain independent sets of data from two periods, the beginning of the 1970s and the end of the 1970s. While we and most other researchers in this field asked respondents to speculate on how the quality and character of their institution has changed over time, Anderson compared observations about the quality and character of institutions made at one point in time with those made at another point in time. The advantage of his technique is that it helps to reduce further the potential bias arising from personal interest. Anderson collected substantial information on changes in the financial situation of the institutions to which the IFI was administered and did extensive multivariate analyses on financial indicators and responses to the IFI scale items. Over a period of time in which the financial health of institutions in this sample was generally declining, he found relatively little change in institutional effectiveness and found no correlations between changes in the various indicators of institutional effectiveness and changes in financial variables. Given the methodological advantages of Anderson's work over other studies (ours included), his findings reinforce the curious inability of other researchers to demonstrate significant harmful academic consequences of financial restraint. It is worth noting also that Anderson's "case studies" suggest that the ills of financial restraint often can be overcome through good leadership and planning, a point emphasized by Keller in his popular book on strategic planning (1983).

As consistent as the findings from surveys of perceptions may be with one another, it is well to keep in mind that they constitute only perceptual data and, for that reason, may be discounted sometimes by persons who do not agree with them. Concern over the credibility of perceptual data from surveys gives rise to an interest in more in-depth analyses of trends in academic quality, a subject which is examined in the next section.

# 7. Analyses of Academic Quality

Analyses of academic quality provide the greatest potential for assessing the impact of financial restraint upon academe. With suitable data from successive analyses of quality at different time points, it is conceivable that one could examine correlations over time between changes in quality and changes in financial conditions and draw inferences about the impact of the latter upon the former. While apparently promising, this approach suffers from a number of problems which limit its usefulness. A major problem is isolating the effect of financial changes from other internal and external changes which may influence quality, e.g., changes in leadership, in program goals, in student characteristics, in the interests of faculty members in a program, and so on. In addition, the state of the art of quality assessment imposes some limitations on this approach, as do conventional practices of academic program review.

Astin (1980) has observed that in general, there are four principal ways used to measure academic quality: reputational rankings, resources indices, outcome measures, and value-added measures. Reputational rankings are not particularly useful for assessing the impact of financial restraint, because they rely so heavily upon perceptions, with the consequent limitations discussed in the previous section.

A more serious shortcoming is that they are *relative* measures. If all institutions or programs are adversely affected to the same degree by declining finances, the reputational rankings will remain the same.

We commented earlier on the limitations of resource measures, namely, that they provide only tautological evidence of quality decline, unless they could be shown to be correlated with some other index of quality. Outcome measures seem to provide more independent evidence of quality, but they do not tell us anything about institutional impact or effectiveness. Astin reports that "a wealth of evidence from longitudinal research shows that most output measures depend more on the quality of students admitted to the institution than on the functioning of the institution or the quality of its program"; and thus reliance on them is "a kind of poor man's value-added approach that is methodologically suspect" (1980, 3). While the value-added approach is considered superior to the other three, Astin notes that this approach is extremely expensive (and difficult to obtain funding for), takes a long time, and that "the results are often so general that they are difficult for individual institutions to apply to their particular problems" (1980, 4). Time-series on value-added data likely would be ideal for assessing the impact of financial restraint; but in its absence, other sources of data must be considered.

The most extensive potential source of information on program quality is that of program reviews. Program reviews typically incorporate elements of the resources and outputs approaches, as well as subjective perceptions, and information on process, e.g., whether academic programs solicit student evaluations.

Available evidence suggests that the extent of program review in institutions of higher education is both substantial and growing. In a 1979 survey of 1082 institutions, Barak (1982) noted that 82 percent had a formal program review process and that 76 percent had initiated their policies on program review since 1970—more than half of these since 1975. He noted further that all fifty states have some sort of reviewing process at the state level. Marcus, Leone, and Goldberg (1983) reported that as of 1980 at least twenty states were conducting program audits and that a dozen states had full-time staff engaged in program evaluation. Peterson (1977) reported that six states were using outcome measures in higher education budgeting and that ten additional states were attempting to use indicators of performance as part of their budgeting process.

While reports on the volume of program review activity might suggest that such reviews constitute a readily available source of data for research on the academic impact of financial restraint, a number of issues must be addressed before one can make definitive conclusions about the suitability of this data source. Not the least of these is the remark, widely quoted in the literature on program review, that "quality has proven to be an elusive concept" (Scott 1981). One possible limitation on program review data is that of the confidentiality with which reviews frequently are treated, though proponents of confidentiality are on the defensive during a time of increased demands for accountability (Anderson and Ball 1978). Confidentiality should not be a serious barrier for accessibility of data to disinterested researchers who, depending upon the nature of their studies, may not need to identify institutions or programs. Another limitation might be inadequate timing or frequency of reviews for purposes of associating change in observed quality with changes in financial conditions.

More serious limitations may arise from the nature of the substantive contents of program reviews. Frequently, perhaps most frequently, program reviews do not provide overall quantitative indices of program quality. *The Encyclopedia of Educational Evaluation* notes that "the primary purpose of evaluating an education or training program is to provide information for decisions about the program" (Anderson, Ball, and Murphy 1975, 136). Although program reviews can be undertaken for a variety of reasons, usually program improvement is one of the primary reasons. Frequently, the principal outcomes of a program review are recommendations on specific strategies for improving a program. Thus, in comparing successive reviews of a program, it may be impossible (at least without very careful reading between the lines) to discern how overall quality has changed. Problems identified in a previous review may have been corrected, but new ones may have arisen. Where particular emphasis in a review is placed upon a few quantitative indicators, this may divert efforts from longer term or more intangible program goals (Sizer 1979), and, thus, improvements in these indices may mask deteriorations elsewhere. Conrad (1983) calls the narrowness of most program reviews a major flaw in the practice.

Although accountability demands and the increasing use of performance budgeting and performance auditing are resulting in more weight being given to standardized indices, the most frequently used models of program review have institutional or program goals at their core (Marcus, Leone, and Goldberg 1983, 43). If program goals change between one review and the next, identified quality changes may simply announce the differences between apples and oranges. Goals may also emphasize social need or accessibility to particular groups, and it may be politically difficult to disentangle the nature or volume of service which a program provides from the quality of that service.

Other political factors may intrude upon the review process: self-study and consultant appraisers may look upon the review as an opportunity to present a case for increased funding, or they may temper their assessment to take account of a program's limited or reduced resources. Inter-rater reliability has also been questioned (Conrad 1983).

In summary, a number of factors might make the growing body of program-review data less than ideally suitable for relating to financial data and assessing the academic impact of financial restraint. Yet program reviews constitute a large, potentially available source of information on the conditions of academe and frequently reflect quite intensive data collection efforts. They provide a focus and an opportunity for broader, more in-depth analyses than do the other approaches to study of the impact of financial restraint. In many places, they have achieved a reasonable measure of credibility, both internally and externally. Given the deficiencies of the other approaches to assessing the financial needs of higher education, a serious exploration of the potential of program review would seem to be worthwhile, recognizing, though, that the problems referred to in this section may not be easy to overcome.

## Conclusion: The Politics of Information

In spite of the reports on the volume and growth of program review noted in the previous section, it is still not clear just how extensive is meaningful, in-depth program review of the type that would be necessary to determine the academic consequences of financial restraint. Semrow contends that "self-studies that are evaluative in nature are the exception rather than the rule" (1977, 4). Numerous persons have questioned how genuinely critical accreditation reviews are (see Marcus, Leone, and Goldberg). It may well be that while large numbers of institutions have formal program review processes, not all programs are reviewed, reviews are quite infrequent, and many reviews lack something in depth and rigor.

While the growth of state review activity may reflect legislators' mistrust of self-regulated groups, state review, nonetheless, requires a great deal of institutional cooperation. It is easy to chide academics for their (at least sometimes) reluctance to place their activities under a public microscope and as easy to call naively for everyone to open their books to the public.

However, one should not, perhaps, dismiss too lightly the widespread adherence in academic circles to what Astin (1980) has termed the "mystical" view of quality. In this view, academic quality is something which can be appreciated only by those who have been inculcated into the academic priesthood, and the secrets of quality are closely guarded by the profession. One corollary of this view is that public debate over the quality of higher education is of limited value because the public cannot really appreciate what quality higher education is—and that the public should therefore accept the academic's judgment regarding quality and its financial requirements. While not exactly a corollary, it is perhaps only a minor leap from the mystical view of quality to the notion that the academic monopoly on detailed information related to program quality is justified to protect professional autonomy. Indeed, it is not unusual for members of a profession to guard professional knowledge of practice, technique, and standards; and a degree of monopoly over relevant information is almost inherent in the concept of a profession. While these arguments can be self-serving, they also can contain a measure of validity, depending upon one's beliefs about the role and implications of professional expertise and how it is best exercised in the public interest.

However, a profession which operates primarily through public financial subsidies is faced with a dilemma when information about the quality of its activities becomes central in the public debate about the level of public subsidies which are provided for those activities. Confronted by this dilemma, the profession can: (a) open up its books to public scrutiny in hopes that the evidence consequently made available will help it secure more funds, thus risking its autonomy; (b) continue to play its cards close to the chest, thus risking continued reductions in its level of financial support; of (c) continue to claim that it is not understood or appreciated by the public but without providing information that would contribute to such understanding or appreciation.

Publicly funded universities in Ontario (and most other North American jurisdictions, I believe) have opted for a mixture of (b) and (c). Some have probably made this choice from habit; others have weighed the virtues of autonomy against those of increased funding; and still others have perhaps doubted that information is a major determinant of funding levels anyway, believing the latter to be essentially a function of power and politics. There is no point in losing autonomy *and* continuing to be impoverished!

It is easy to second-guess those judgments, plump the glories of public information, and predict confidently that a fully informed government will always make the most (academically) virtuous decision. Yet, it is not inconceivable that the practice of giving wide publicity to detailed data from program reviews could have negative steering effects from both within and without the university community and that governments could continue to reduce funding but direct that limited funds be used to secure their particular objectives. There are obviously risks in detailed public reporting upon the consequences of financial restraint, risks of which university administrators who answer questionnaires on this subject are no doubt aware.

In the last analysis, how one assesses these risks is largely a matter of subjective judgment and of the value that one attaches to different outcomes. However, having made academic quality the primary rationale in its requests for increased funding, the academy has no choice but to provide far more detailed evidence of self-examination if it is to demonstrate the adverse consequences of financial restraint. If it chooses to provide this information, it should be wary of, and simultaneously warn against, possible misuses of such information. It should recognize also that much, if not most, of the data provided thus far on quality fails to meet the tests of either scholarship or persuasiveness. The best hope for both is through linking the substantial research on the finance of higher education with the growing corpus of academic program review, while continuing to strive for improvements in program review models and practices.

# Bibliography

Anderson, R.E. *Finance and Effectiveness: A Study of College Environments*. Princeton: Educational Testing Service, 1983.

Anderson, S.B., and S. Ball. *The Profession and Practice of Program Evaluation*. San Francisco: Jossey-Bass Publishers, 1978.

Anderson, S.B., S. Ball, R.T. Murphy, and Associates. *Encyclopedia of Educational Evaluation*. San Francisco: Jossey-Bass Publishers, 1975.

Astin, A.W. "Undergraduate Achievement and Institutional Excellence." *Science* 161 (Aug. 1968): 661-68.

_____. "When Does a College Deserve to be Called High Quality?" *Current Issues in Higher Education* 2, no. 1 (1980), pp. 1-9.

Barak, R.J. *Program Review for Higher Education: Within and Without*. Boulder: National Center for Higher Education Management Systems, 1982.

Bowen, H.R. *The Costs of Higher Education*. San Francisco: Jossey-Bass Publishers, 1980.

Cheit, E.F. *The New Depression in Higher Education*. New York: McGraw-Hill, 1971.

Chenery, H.B. "Engineering Production Functions." *Quarterly Journal of Economics* 63 (Nov. 1949): 507-31.

Commission on the Future Development of the Universities of Ontario. *Options and Futures*. Toronto: Ontario Government Bookstore, 1984.

Committee on the Future Role of Universities in Ontario. *Final Report*. Toronto: Ontario Ministry of Colleges of Universities, 1981.

Conrad, C.F. "Enhancing Institutional and Program Quality." In R.A. Wilson, ed. *Survival in the 1980s: Quality, Mission, and Financing Options*. Tucson: Center for the Study of Higher Education, University of Arizona, 1983, pp. 243-58.

Council of Ontario Universities. *Once More, With Feeling*. Brief to the Ontario Council on University Affairs. Toronto: Council of Ontario Universities, 1982.

Farmer, J. "Agenda for 1979." In American Council on Education, *Measuring the Financial Conditions of Colleges and Universities*. Washington, D.C.: ACE, 1979.

Harman, G. "The Razor Gang Moves, the 1981 Guidelines, and the Uncertain Future." In G. Harman and D. Smart, eds. *Federal Intervention in Australian Education*. Melbourne: Georgian House, 1982, pp. 163-80.

Heady, E.A., and J.L. Dillon. *Agricultural; Production Functions*. Ames: Iowa State University Press, 1962.

Hyatt, J.A. "Quality and Its Financing." In R.A. Wilson, ed. *Survival in the 1980s: Quality, Mission, and Financing Options*. Tucson: Center for the Study of Higher Education, University of Arizona, 1983, pp. 133-44.

*Involvement in Learning*. Final Report of the Study Group on the Conditions of Excellence in American Higher Education. Washington, D.C.: U.S. Government Printing Office, 1984.

Keller, G. *Academic Strategy*. Baltimore: Johns Hopkins University Press, 1983.

Kogan, M., with D. Kogan. *The Attack on Higher Education*. London: Kogan, Page, 1983.

Kramer, M. "What the New Indicators Cannot Tell Us." In Carol Frances, ed. *New Directions for Higher Education: Successful Responses to Financial Difficulty*, No. 38. San Francisco: Jossey-Bass Publishers, 1982, pp. 99-110.

Leslie, L.L. "Recent Financing Developments in the Fifty States." In R.A. Wilson, ed. *Survival in the 1980's: quality, Mission, and Financing Options*. Tucson: University of Arizona, Center for the Study of Higher Education, 1983, pp. 185-91.

_____, and H.F. Miller, Jr. *Higher Education and the Steady State*. Washington, D.C.: American Association for Higher Education, 1974.

Magarrell, J. "Recession Hits State Support for Colleges." *Chronicle of Higher Education* 25, no. 8 (20 Oct. 1982), p. 5.

Marcus, L., A. Leone, and E. Goldberg. *The Path to Excellence: Quality Assurance in Higher Education*. ASHE-ERIC Higher Education Research Report No. 1, 1983.

Minter, J.W., and H.R. Bowen. *Preserving America's Investment in Human Capital*. Washington, D.C.: American Association of State Colleges and Universities, 1980.

Ontario Confederation of University Faculty Associations. *Response to the Final Report of the Committee on the Future Role of Universities in Ontario*. Toronto, 1981.

Ontario Council on University Affairs. *System on the Brink: A Financial Analysis of the Ontario University System*. Toronto, 1979.

Paiken, M., Chairman, Ontario Council on University Affairs. Remarks in presence of author at plenary session of annual meeting of the Canadian Society for the Study of Higher Education. Unpublished. Guelph, Ontario, 4 June 1984.

Peters, T.J., and R.H. Waterman. *In Search of Excellence*. New York: Harper and Row, 1982.

Peterson, M.W. "State-level Performance Budgeting." In John K. Folger, ed. *New Directions for Institutional Research* 16. San Francisco: Jossey-Bass Publishers, 1977, pp. 1-35.

"Premier Tells GRAUT Delegation Universities Not Underfunded." *University of Toronto Bulletin* (21 Feb. 1983): p. 1.

Quay, R.H., and P.P. Olevnik. *The Financing of American Higher Education: A Bibliographic Handbook*. Phoenix: Oryx Press, 1984.

Rock, D.A., J.A. Centra, and R.L. Linn. *The Identification and Evaluation of College Effects on Student Achievement*. Princeton: Educational Testing Service, 1969.

Scott, R.A. "Program Review's Missing Number: A Consideration of Quality and its Assessment. A Position Paper." Indianapolis. ED 200 108, 1981.

Semrow, J.J. "Institutional Assessment and Evaluation for Accreditation." *Topical Paper No. 9.* Tucson: University of Arizona. ED 148 190, 1977.

Sizer, J. "Assessing Institutional Performance: An Overview." *International Journal of Institutional Management in Higher Education* 3 (May 1979): 79-89.

Skolnik, M.L., and N. S. Rowen. *'Please, Sir, I Want Some More': Canadian Universities and Financial Restraint.* Toronto: OISE Press, 1984.

Slaughter, S., and E. Silva. "Retrenchment: American Public Universities." *The Review of Higher Education* 8 (Summer 1985): 38-69.

Smith, V.B. "More for Less: Higher Education's New Priority." In L. Wilson with O. Mills, eds. *Universal Higher Education: Costs, Benefits, Options.* Washington, D.C.: American Council on Education, 1972.

Stadtman, V.A. *Academic Adaptations.* San Francisco: Jossey-Bass Publishers, 1980.

"Textbooks Rot at U of T for Lack of Funds." *The [Toronto] Globe and Mail* (22 Jan. 1983): 4.